MARKETING RESEARCH
Principles & Applications

PRELIMINARY

SECOND EDITION

Melvin Crask
Richard J. Fox
Roy G. Stout

CUSTOM SERVICES

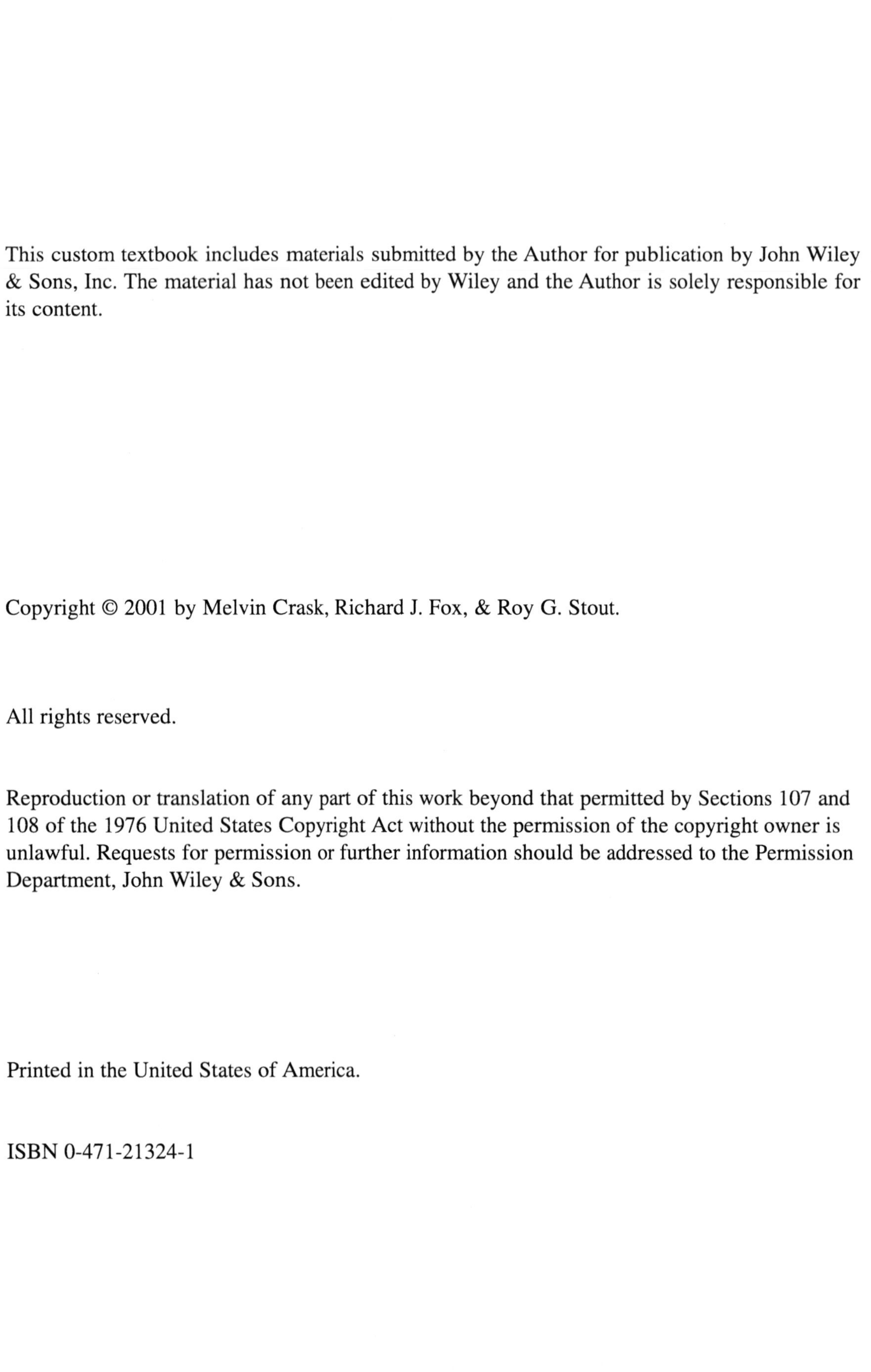

This custom textbook includes materials submitted by the Author for publication by John Wiley & Sons, Inc. The material has not been edited by Wiley and the Author is solely responsible for its content.

Printed in the United States of America.

ISBN 0-471-21324-1

PART I

The Nature and Scope of Marketing Research

Consumers in the United States typically have many brands to choose among in most product or service categories. The intense competition between these brands pressures marketing managers to make sure that their brands are available to consumers at prices they are willing to pay. As companies grow and expand into foreign markets, they are challenged by the peculiarities of the new customers and business practices. This problem is compounded by the fact that there is rarely a single consumer market for a product or service. Different types of consumers desire different attributes and benefits from the products and services the purchase.

The growing need for marketing information has led to the development of a multibillion dollar marketing research industry. Part I of this text, consisting of the first five chapters, serves as an introduction to this industry. Chapter 1 describes the evolution and structure of the research industry, provides an overview of the marketing research process, and presents ethical considerations involved in obtaining marketing research information. Research projects are often classified as exploratory, experimental, or descriptive in nature. Chapters 2 and 3 discuss in detail exploratory and experimental research respectively. Descriptive research, the third basic research type, is designed to answer fundamental questions about who, what, when, where, how, and why. Secondary and syndicated data, examined in Chapters 4 and 5 respectively, are often used to address such information needs. Descriptive research also frequently requires the collection of data using a survey or observational technique. The process of designing and executing such projects, as well as how the collected data are analyzed, will be discussed in Part II of the text.

CHAPTER 1

An Introduction to the Role of Marketing Research and the Research Process

Learning Objectives:

This chapter introduces the important role marketing research plays in today's complex marketing environment. After reading this chapter, you should be able to:

- discuss the impact of a market orientation on the evolution of marketing research,
- describe the marketing team,
- define the types of firms in the marketing research industry,
- list the steps in the research process, and
- discuss ethical issues in marketing research.

Within two years of its introduction, diet Coke became the diet soft drink sales leader and has held that position ever since. Marketing research provided invaluable assistance throughout the development of the diet Coke brand. One of the most critical decisions aided by marketing research information was whether to use the Coke brand name. Another was how to position the new brand relative to competing brands.

In the early 1960s, when the nonsugar or no-calorie soft drink category began, The Coca-Cola Company was very concerned about the impact of a brand called diet Coke on the company's flagship brand, Coca-Cola. At that time, the company decided not to leverage the Coke name and chose Tab for its first low-calorie cola. Tab was the leading diet soft drink in the market when the new diet Coke brand was later considered, so the company had to give serious consideration to the new brand's impact on Tab as well.

The graphic design chosen for the diet Coke can was red wording on a white background, a reversal of the colors used for the Coca-Cola brand. Several copies of this design were printed on paper, wrapped around 12-ounce soft drink cans, and secured with cellophane tape. These cans were then used in some of the early consumer studies designed to assess the impact that the Coke name might have on taste perceptions and on brand choice.

In one taste perception study, a group of consumers was asked to taste Tab and Diet Pepsi, identified as such by placing the corresponding cans beside the glasses containing the respective brands. Another group of consumers tasted the same two brands identified as diet Coke (actually Tab) and competing products. The percentage that preferred Tab to the competition was higher for the group that tasted Tab identified as diet Coke than for the group that tasted Tab correctly identified as Tab.

There was a need to test the impact of the Coke name on brand choice. Low-calorie soft drink consumers were asked to select their next ten purchases of soft drinks from a typical soft drink store display. The same consumers were then moved to a second room where they repeated the exercise with the exception that diet Coke was included in the display. The data from the first exercise provided benchmark data, which was used to gain insight regarding the degree to which existing brands would lose business to diet Coke. The number of simulated purchases of diet Coke convinced company management to leverage the power of the Coke name by using it for the new brand.

The results of the brand choice studies and the taste perception tests just mentioned are examples of how marketing research can help management assess the business opportunity. The next step was to assess the positioning of the brand. A study was conducted in which respondents were told: "Suppose a diet soft drink called diet Coke was on the market. When I read each of the following statements, I want you to tell me whether it best describes diet Coke or competing products." Factor analysis and perceptual mapping, two statistical techniques described in later chapters, were applied to the data to develop a positioning strategy for diet Coke which stressed taste. In April 1982, commercials representing four different executions of the positioning statement were tested. The results of this research led to choosing the slogan "diet Coke: you're going to drink it just for the taste of it," for the brand launch.

Stressing the taste of diet Coke was questioned because no manufacturer had yet made taste claims for a diet soft drink. The concern was whether a taste claim would generate a consumer expectation of a better taste than the product delivered. However, marketing research indicated that the product lived up to consumer taste expectations allaying fears associated with the brand's positioning.

The original "just for the taste of it" slogan remained the core of diet Coke advertising until 1992 when the company switched to a new slogan. Several years and several advertising slogans later, the company reinstated "just for the taste of it" for a second successful run as the brand's advertising slogan.

Exhibit 1.1 Diet Coke was one of the biggest new product successes of the 1980's

As the diet Coke example clearly illustrates, marketing research can provide invaluable insights during the development and marketing of a new brand. In today's complex world, success is not easy. Companies introduce thousands of new products and services each year but only a fraction survive the first year. In fact, approximately 90 percent of all new products are pulled from the market within two or three years.[1]

The high failure rate is even more astounding when you consider that companies examine many new product ideas before determining which few to introduce. A survey of managers reported that less than 10 percent of new product projects reach the market.[2] Furthermore, new product failures are not unique to small or fledgling companies. Industrial giant Ford Motor Company would like to forget the Edsel, introduced in the late 1950's and often cited as a classic new product failure. IBM introduced the PC jr. in 1983 to compete in the home computer market and heavily supported it with national television advertising. Unfortunately, the product failed to excite consumers and soon disappeared. Two more recent casualties include General Mills' cold breakfast cereal Benefit[3] and Kellogg's Heartwise cereal. Both contained psyllium, a soluble fiber grain which was purported to help reduce cholesterol. A number of "clear" products, distinguished by their lack of color, including Miller Clear Beer and Crystal Pepsi, failed to excite consumers.

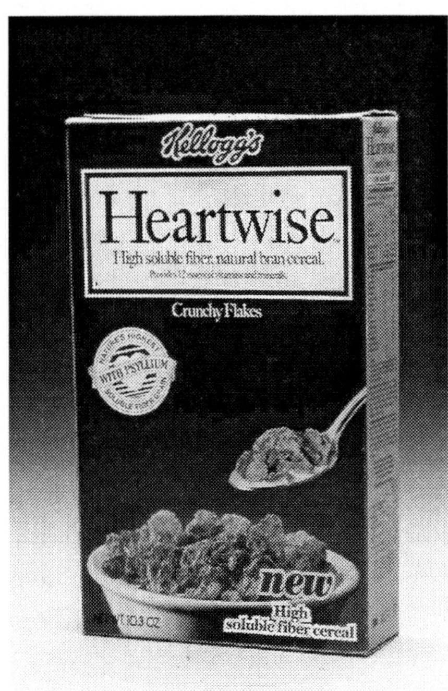

Exhibit 1.2 Kellog's Heartwise Cereal

Many classic product failures that line the shelves of the New Products Showcase and Learning Center were produced by giants in the packaged goods industry.[4] Product development engineers pay dearly to visit the center to learn from the past. Browsing thru the mistakes of the past will hopefully prevent history from repeating itself. However, new product introduction remains very risky business, but a vital activity.

The pressures new products and services face come from a number of directions. Consumers are becoming more and more sophisticated in their purchase decisions and in what they seek and expect in products and services. Companies also are facing increased competition, both from domestic and from foreign companies. Distributors are becoming increasingly powerful and are placing stronger demands upon the manufacturer. Existing products and services face the same factors that make it difficult for new products and services to succeed. The pressures existing brands face are compounded by the tremendous influx of new products. Thus, increasing an existing brand's share or even maintaining its current market position is a challenging task in today's complex markets. Companies can no longer rely on population growth and inflation to produce growth in sales volume and dollars. Future gains must come at the expense of competition.[5]

Companies have begun to realize that success in this increasingly complex and highly competitive marketplace is far from guaranteed. It is no longer enough simply to offer a product or service consumers need and want. Companies must actively market their brands. They must identify the target audience and effectively promote their brands to these consumers. They must see that their brands are available when and where the customer wants. They must price their brands appropriately and diligently monitor consumer perceptions and reactions to their brands. Companies must also coordinate their efforts with their distributors, understand their competition, and monitor progress toward their marketing objectives.

To succeed in today's complex markets requires information. Marketing research is the corporate function charged with obtaining much of this information, and marketing research is responding to the challenge. More and more information regarding the consumer, the effectiveness of individual advertising campaigns and sales promotions, and the market performance of brands is becoming available to the marketing manager. This information is also being provided at greater and greater levels of detail. Large computer information systems for organizing and summarizing the ever growing mountain of available relevant data are becoming commonplace marketing tools. In addition, decision support computer systems allowing the marketing manager to assess the impact of various alternative marketing activities are becoming available.

One outgrowth of modern information technology is database marketing. **Database marketing** involves the use of a computerized information system to monitor and record the activities of customers. Companies use this customer knowledge to develop programs and promotions to appeal to specific customer subgroups. The highly successful financial services company, USAA, markets insurance, banking services and mutual funds primarily to military officers and their families. The company's large customer database allows them to efficiently market their services. The database allows the company to identify and focus attention on those customers most likely to be interested in a particular service.

Tremendous database marketing potential exists in industries possessing large customer files. Telephone, power and video rental are examples of industries where extensive customer information is routinely collected in the process of doing business. Direct marketers, such as catalog sales companies, also have the opportunity to accumulate extensive information about customers. Applying Marketing Research 1.1 shows how one such company makes use of customer information.[6]

Applying Marketing Research 1.1

Spiegel sends women's clothing catalogs to millions of homes each year. The company determined customer preferences by studying purchase histories. Women who have shown a tendency to purchase romantic apparel are sent a small catalog containing items of this nature within a larger catalog. Women who prefer low price items receive a different small catalog, containing specially priced items, within the larger catalog. Hence, Spiegel tailors their marketing efforts to specific customer needs as determined from its database of sales activity.

Database marketing by definition speaks to an ongoing relationship between the marketer and the customer as opposed to a one-time sale. Relationship marketing refers in more general terms than database marketing to this ongoing process. **Relationship marketing** is the philosophy that focuses on building long-term relationships with customers to satisfy mutual needs.[7] Many companies are adopting this philosophy in their operation, and providing extensive training to their employees regarding the importance of pleasing and cultivating customers. Home Depot encourages its employees to spend whatever time is necessary to answer customers' questions and to educate them in the "how to" of home repairs.[8] Knowledge of customers, what they want and don't want, how they expect to be treated, changes they would appreciate in the process of buying goods and services, is, of course, vital to executing relationship marketing.

Market Orientation and the Evolution of Marketing Research

It is clear that success in today's marketplace is far from easy. Consumers are more knowledgeable, demand more than ever from the products and services they buy, yet are less brand loyal than in the past. Firms face increasing competition as markets become more and more international. Finally, the rate of change is increasing, so product life cycles are becoming shorter than before. Consequently, few of today's business decisions remain optimal tomorrow. More than ever, then, success requires a market orientation.

A **market orientation** requires an integrated organizational effort to gather information about consumers, competitors, and marketplace changes and to use this information to deliver superior solutions to customer needs. Market orientation is a natural evolution of the marketing concept that was touted as a management philosophy as early as the 1950s. The **marketing concept** emphasized the identification of consumer needs, and the development and production of products or services to meet those needs as well as the objectives of the firm.[9] However, the marketing concept implicitly ignored competition and market attractiveness factors, and did not explicitly incorporate the role of marketing research in identifying or serving consumer needs. On the other hand, the definition of market orientation explicitly mentions competitors and market changes, as well as consumers, and points out that information about all three must be collected. Marketing research is the corporate function responsible for these activities which include identifying consumer needs, aiding in the design of products and services to meet those needs, providing competitive and market intelligence, and gathering information on how satisfied consumers are with the company's products and services.

Although the notions underlying a market orientation may seem quite obvious, many companies have only recently discovered the idea. For example, it was only in the mid-1980s that the Chrysler Corporation took steps to integrate marketing input into the early stages of the new car development process. The new process replaced their old sequential system of planning, designing, engineering, purchasing, tooling, manufacturing, and <u>then</u> marketing.[10] Applying Marketing Research 1.2 describes how the Ford Motor Company adopted this same new market-driven approach in the development of the highly successful Taurus.[11]

Applying Marketing Research 1.2

The Ford Motor Company launched its largest consumer research program ever to provide consumer input into the design of the Ford Taurus (see Exhibit 1.3). This research led to such design features as a net in the trunk to hold grocery bags upright and bright yellow oil dipsticks for easy identification -- "little things that mean a lot to people."[12] They also extensively tested the ergonomics of the interior design by recruiting consumers to drive thousands of miles in the test cars.

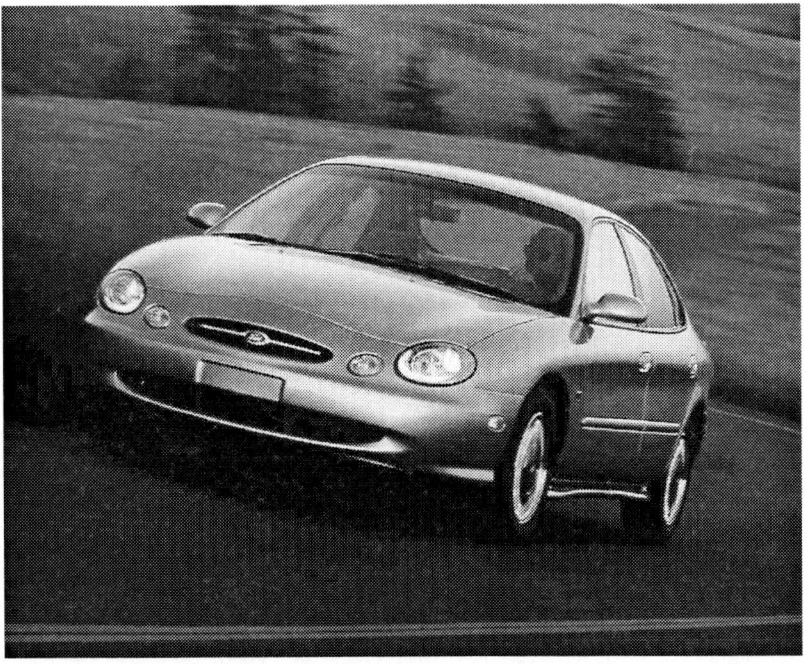

Exhibit 1.3 Marketing research findings played a major role in the design of the Ford Taurus

(Source: Courtesy of Ford Motor Company

The success of Ford's Taurus jolted Japanese car manufacturer Honda into action. The Honda Accord had been the best-selling car in America until it was displaced from this lofty position by the Ford Taurus. Honda immediately launched its most extensive consumer research project ever, the E. T. Phone Home Project. For several months, factory workers from the Accord assembly line phoned almost 50,000 Accord owners to find out whether customers were happy with their cars and to get ideas for improvements.[13] Many subsequent changes made to the Accord were initiated by the E. T. Phone Home Project.

Polaroid also benefitted from integrating marketing thinking and consumer input into the product development process for its Spectra instant camera as described in Applying Marketing Research 1.3.[14]

Applying Marketing Research 1.3

Polaroid, a company traditionally driven by technology, undertook the largest consumer research program in its history in conjunction with the Spectra project. For the first time, they let marketing, not research and development, drive the new product effort. One outcome of this approach was the incorporation of a simple side strap instead of the planned neck strap. The company learned through research that the side strap made it easier to steady and hold the camera.

In recent years, the value of marketing and a market orientation has spread to industries unfamiliar with these notions. Deregulation in the financial and airline industries has allowed banks and airlines to use marketing to differentiate themselves from their competitors. Marketing has spread to the health care industry as well. Mount Sinai Medical Center in Miami Beach sold its own brand of chicken soup in an effort to promote its reputation as a warm and soothing place.[15] Saint Joseph Medical Center in Burbank, California, touted its lithotripter, which disintegrates kidney stones using shock waves, with the slogan "Kidney Stones? Who Ya Gotta Call...Stonebusters!"[16] Even the Vatican is beginning to engage in marketing by entering mass licensing agreements that will put images from its art collection and architecture on T-shirts, glassware, candles and ornaments.[17]

Applying Marketing Research 1.4 is another example of an unexpected use of marketing research.

Applying Marketing Research 1.4

Before even opening its doors, the leaders of the Mecklenburg Church of Charlotte, NC hired a research firm to help them to understand what their "customers" want.[18] The church had already decided to attempt to attract the many people with no connection to a religious institution. The church sponsored a survey that revealed that non-churchgoers thought that church service was boring and not relevant to everyday life. The Mecklenburg Community Church adopted an unorthodox approach to services. The leaders included contemporary music in the services, loosened dress codes, and covered topics like parenting and money management in the sermons. The church sent out a direct mail piece with the tagline: "Church really can be different. Give us a shot." The results were impressive; 80% of the members of the church's congregation were previous non-churchgoers.

A by-product of having a market orientation is a focus on satisfying the customer. The groundswell of interest in serving and satisfying the customer has led some executives to refer to the 1990s as the "Decade of the Customer."[19] Some firms have linked pay raises and bonuses directly to customer satisfaction in order to focus employee attention on pleasing the customer. In order to implement such a policy, customer satisfaction must be monitored on an ongoing basis. This activity naturally becomes the responsibility of marketing research, and has been a major contributor to the industry's growth. Some marketing research firms position themselves as experts in the measurement of customer satisfaction, and there are annual conventions which provide a forum for discussion of problems related to this issue.

Today's marketing manager needs to understand and make use of the power of marketing research to succeed in today's environment. The increasing importance of marketing research has caused its role to evolve. Initially, consumer packaged goods companies used research to obtain market share and sales volume information for their brands. Service companies and retailers gathered information such as local population figures and traffic patterns to aid in the location of new branches or offices. Analyzing these data by separate markets led to this function being called market research. The American Marketing Association adopted this view when it defined **market research** as "the systematic gathering, recording, and analyzing of data about problems relating to the marketing of goods and services."[20]

Today's marketing managers want much more than a market description; they want research information that helps them make better decisions. They seek information to help them determine what products or services to offer to which consumers and how to differentiate their offerings. They want to know how to make these products or services most appealing to the target group of consumers, what price to charge, and how to promote the brand.

Examples of how marketing research input played a vital role in such decisions abound. Consumer research results showed Procter & Gamble that many users of liquid fabric softeners found them to be inconvenient because they had to be added during the machine wash cycle. P & G subsequently introduced Bounce, a dryer-added fabric softener. Consumer research helped AT&T develop and evaluate a successful advertising campaign designed to stimulate long-distance calling during low usage periods and among infrequent users of the service. Finally, extensive consumer research guided the development of cherry-flavored Rolaids antacid tablets and helped the Warner-Lambert Company pinpoint the target audience for the product.[21]

Applying Marketing Research 1.5 details how marketing research findings dramatically altered a company's strategy.

Applying Marketing Research 1.5

In late 1997, Levi Strauss & Company aborted the launch of a line of blue jeans called Special Reserve, likely to appeal to consumers 25 years old and up.[22] At a meeting held shortly before the decision not to launch Special Reserve, Levi managers learned the results of a year-long marketing research study designed to determine what kids of baby boomers— the Echo Boom generation – thought of Levi's. Teenagers generally viewed the blue-jeans king as a "has-been." They called Levi's jeans "uncool" and "more suitable for their parents than for fashion-conscious teens."

Levi management was shocked. Teenage indifference towards the brand was a scary proposition. Along with scrapping the Special Reserve line, the company increased its backing of the Silver Tab jeans line. Silver Tab apparel is baggy and uses more than just denim fabrics, and is considered "Levi's hippest clothes" by teens. The median age of Silver Tab buyers is 18. Levi is also spending considerable promotional dollars "jazzing up" its image among teens who are crucial to the company's success. These efforts include sponsoring rock concerts and outfitting characters in TV shows popular among teens with Levi apparel.

As the above examples illustrate, companies will no longer settle for research that simply provides information on markets. Today, they want marketing research, research dealing with marketing issues and marketing decisions. This expanded role of research is reflected in the American Marketing Association's most recent definition of marketing research:

> **Marketing research** is the function which links the consumer, customer, and public to the marketer through information--information used to identify and define marketing opportunities and problems; generate, refine, and evaluate marketing actions; monitor marketing performance; and improve understanding of marketing as a process. Marketing research specifies the information required to address these issues; designs the method for collecting information; manages and implements the data collection process; analyzes the results; and communicates the findings and their implications.[23]

The definition of marketing research differs significantly from that of market research. The marketing research function is expected not merely to provide *data*, but should ensure that the data provide *information* to management. Marketing research also expands the activities and the responsibilities of the marketing researcher. Although still involved in collecting and analyzing data, today's marketing researcher assumes a more active role. In fact, in many companies, the marketing research analyst has become a key participant in marketing decision making. The researcher assists in planning the marketing of the product or service and in determining what research should be conducted.

To accomplish these tasks, today's researcher must be knowledgeable about the marketing problem being faced. Today's researcher must be able to interpret the results and make inferences in light of this knowledge. He or she must also be able to communicate marketing research findings and their implications. Being able to discuss implications, rather than merely reporting results, implies that the marketing researcher understands marketing as well as the business issues facing the brand.

The Marketing Team

Marketing activities in most firms are a team effort. The team members team are shown in Exhibit 1.4.

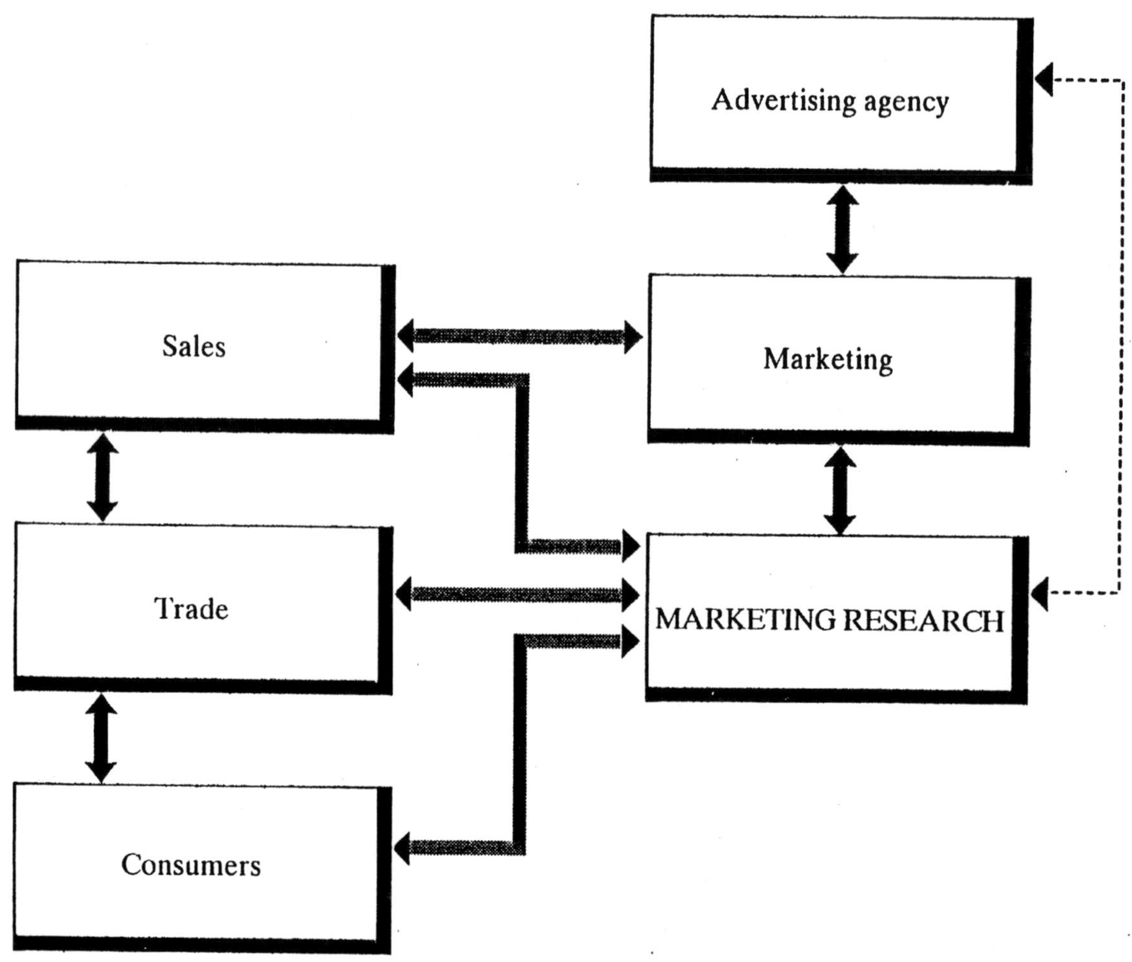

Exhibit 1.4 Marketing research supports marketing

The marketing function develops the strategy and tactics necessary to make the firm's goods and services available to the consumer. Marketing is also responsible for key decisions concerning the company's brands.

The sales function serves as an interface between the company and the market. To be effective, a sales person must understand the needs both of consumers and of the trade, as those involved in bringing the product to those consumers are called. This understanding is provided to the sales organization by marketing research information.

The firm's advertising agency is also an active member of the marketing team. An agency account executive heads a team of agency personnel organized to serve the needs of the brand. Furthermore, many agencies have their own marketing research departments that provide support to the agency team serving an account. In the optimal situation, these researchers have a solid working relationship with their counterparts in the client firm.

Marketing research, as the company's primary source of information, supports all of these key players. In most corporations, the marketing research department is a staff function designed to assist the key decision-making units of the firm, the line functions. In particular, the marketing research department assists the line function of marketing. Most of the interactions that the research department has within the firm are with marketing personnel. However, the marketing concept suggests that marketing must be integrated with other corporate functions such as engineering and research and development. Therefore, marketing research personnel also have contact with managers in these other areas.

Whether the marketing research department is line or staff may seem inconsequential, but it is important for understanding the role of marketing research within the firm. As a staff function, the marketing research department has minimal funds for gathering information. Marketing personnel must authorize and pay for such research, so decisions regarding what research to conduct are made by marketing managers. As part of the marketing team, researchers provide input to these decisions. They make suggestions to management, discuss implications of findings, and are consulted when key decisions concerning the marketing of the brands are being made. However, marketing managers make the final decisions.

Marketing research also provides critical support to the sales function. Scanner check-out technology, now commonly found in supermarkets and many mass-merchandisers, provides retailers with immediate feedback about the performance of all of the brands stocked and the impact of promotional efforts. The firm's sales staff must work closely with its marketing research department to become familiar with this information in order to operate on equal footing with their customers.

The Marketing Research Industry

As can be seen in Exhibit 1.5, a firm's marketing research group typically operates as an interface. On one side are marketing research firms which actually conduct research, called **research suppliers**. On the other side is the firm's marketing management. As an interface, the firm's marketing researchers work with both groups. They work with their marketing managers to design projects that meet the managers' information needs. They also choose suppliers for these projects, communicate with the supplier to ensure project objectives are met, and communicate the findings and implications to management.

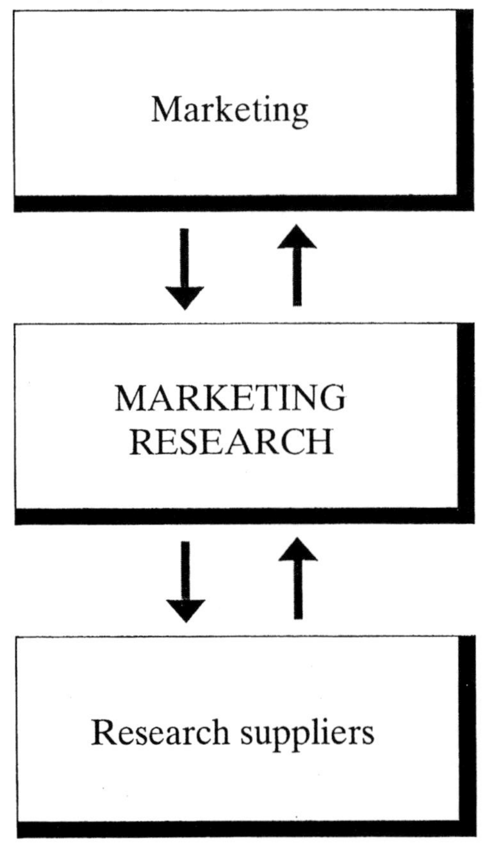

Exhibit 1.5 Marketing research as the middleman

The marketing research industry is made up of a wide variety of research suppliers, ranging in size from one-person operations to huge corporations that employ hundreds of people and generate millions of dollars in research revenues. As Exhibit 1.6 shows, the firms comprising the marketing research industry can be classified into three groups: those offering syndicated services, those offering custom services, and those offering standardized services.

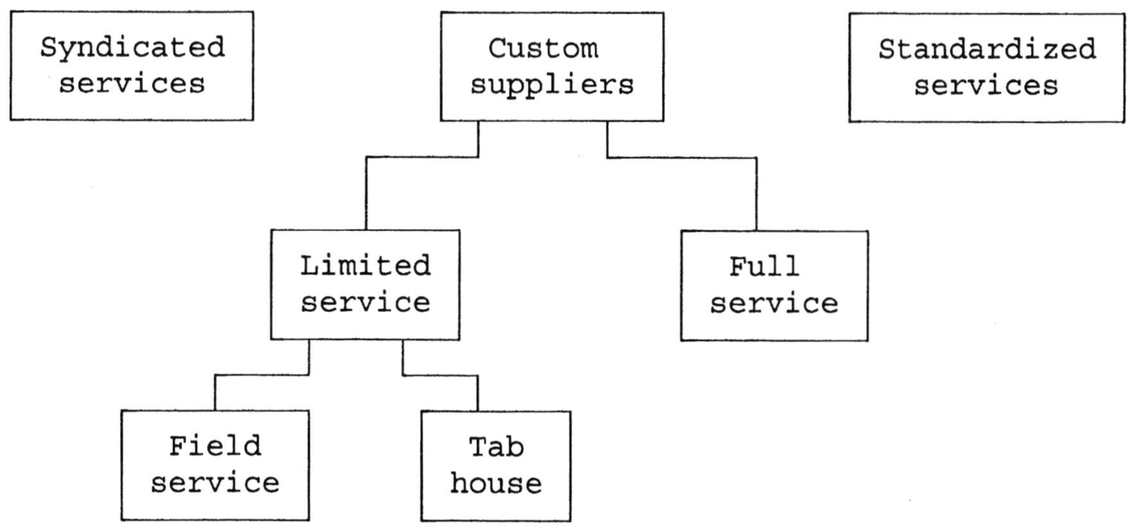

Exhibit 1.6 Types of research suppliers

Syndicated Services

Research suppliers who collect marketing information that is sold to multiple firms are called **syndicated services**. All or portions of the data collected by syndicated services are organized and reported to individual firms on a periodic basis. The price charged to each firm depends upon the amount of the data requested and the difficulty associated with using the reporting format the firm desires.

Companies purchase information from syndicated services instead of collecting the data themselves because of cost savings. Syndicated services can spend a great deal of money collecting the data because they can distribute the cost across all of the firms buying the service. For example, imagine a research project designed to obtain supermarket sales data on a regular basis for all brands in a product category from a nationally representative sample of stores. The cost, not to mention the logistics of organizing and maintaining such a system, would be prohibitively expensive for a single firm to bear. However, both the A.C. Nielsen Company and Information Resources, Inc., offer syndicated data of this type because they are able to spread the cost across the many companies who buy the data.

Custom Services

Suppliers who conduct projects designed specifically for a client are called **custom services,** since each project is customized to the needs of the client. Some custom service suppliers, known as **full-service suppliers**, are capable of completing an entire research project from design to analysis. A firm that has no marketing research staff of its own would choose a full-service supplier. Even firms that have a research staff increasingly use full-service suppliers due to tight budgets and downsizing of marketing research departments.

The concept of "partnershipping" with suppliers is gaining broad acceptance.[24] In the traditional client-supplier relationship, the client deals exclusively with an account executive and has little contact with other members of the research company's organization. In a partnership relationship, research firms become almost part of their respective clients' organizations. In some cases, research firm personnel actually have offices at the client firm and assume responsibilities formerly delegated to client staff.

A second group of custom service suppliers are limited-service suppliers. **Limited-service suppliers** specialize in one or more specific tasks associated with the research project. They complete only part of the research project and are able to perform their tasks at a low cost. These suppliers are either contracted by client firms or function as subcontractors for full-service suppliers. A full-service supplier can also be contracted to perform a limited-service role.

Limited-service suppliers can create cost savings in data collection. A supplier can conduct telephone or face-to-face interviews at a lower cost than can the firm's marketing research department, because they can generate enough business to keep their interviewers busy full-time. Client firms, on the other hand, would have to hire, train, and compensate the interviewers for only a limited number of studies per year. Limited-service suppliers that specialize in data collection are called **field services**.

Suppliers can also provide cost savings in data preparation and analysis. Many studies require that the data collected be transferred from a questionnaire onto a computer file or tape. The file must then be checked for accuracy before data analysis can begin. Costs associated with these tasks are lower if the data entry personnel can be used more frequently. **Tab houses** are limited-service suppliers specializing in initial data preparation and simple data analysis. Tab houses take advantage of economies of scale in data preparation and analysis.

Standardized Services

The last type of research supplier is the standardized service. **Standardized services** conduct projects for individual clients but always conduct the project in exactly the same manner for each client.

Firms do not use standardized services for cost savings. Standardized services are used because of their expertise in conducting a specialized form of research and because a company knows that the research will be conducted in precisely the same fashion each time. The standardized procedure allows results to be compared across projects without being concerned that the results are influenced by any peculiar aspects of a particular project.

Careers in Marketing Research

As you might surmise, a variety of different job opportunities exist in marketing research for college-educated individuals. Some jobs require training in sophisticated statistical procedures. Others demand general research, management, and people skills.

With a supplier you would normally begin your career as a research trainee. This position exposes the newly hired employee to the types of studies conducted by the firm and the procedures used. The next step in the career ladder would be account executive. The account executive is responsible for servicing the research needs of one or more of the firm's clients. Above the account executive level, various titles are found. Privately owned companies often offer partner and senior partner positions. Publicly held companies typically advance individuals through assistant, associate, and senior vice-president positions.

Research departments within client companies and advertising agencies are very similar in structure. A person with a college education usually enters at a junior analyst position. The junior analyst position allows a person to learn the company research policies and procedures in a closely supervised role. Junior analysts advance to the research analyst position. Research analysts design and implement the research activities for one or more of the company's brands or agency's clients. Most agency or client research departments are headed by a research director, although in some companies this would be a vice-presidential position.

Database marketing activities also often fall within the domain of marketing research. Growth in the area has fueled the need for researchers particularly skilled in the use of management information systems and statistical modeling. These individuals are needed to develop, organize, analyze and utilize customer databases. Surveys of various types are also conducted among samples of members of these large databases.

The area of competitive intelligence is also growing and, at the same time, is becoming much more formalized within companies. Many competitive intelligence activities are forms of marketing research. Hence, it is no surprise that these functions are often united, or at least closely allied, within a corporation. One medical products firm, Becten-Dickinson, hires individuals as opportunity analysts.[25] The job description for this position formally marries the duties of competitor monitoring and marketing research. Opportunity analysts monitor and evaluate competition in specific markets and identify opportunities in assigned markets. The latter involves conducting primary and secondary marketing research studies.

The majority of marketing students embark on careers in marketing, not marketing research. Nevertheless, marketing research often plays a prominent role throughout the careers of these individuals as well. Understanding of the value of marketing research is an important ingredient in a marketing manager's recipe for success.

As noted earlier in this chapter, today's marketing researchers must understand the many decision problems faced by marketing managers. Similarly, today's marketing managers must also understand enough about marketing research to know telecommunication companies, must continually monitor customer satisfaction and market needs.

The bottom line is that success in today's complex environment requires a close working relationship between the marketing researcher and the marketing manager. An understanding of each other's jobs is crucial to forge this close relationship. Only then will the full potential of marketing research be reaped.

The Steps in the Research Process

Designing and conducting a project can be very complicated because of the number of parties involved. Furthermore, a research project must be well-planned to ensure that money is well-spent. Organizing the project decisions into a series of steps simplifies the planning process.

Exhibit 1.7 lists the steps in the research process. In the remainder of this section, we will briefly describe the decisions that must be made at each step. Each decision will be covered in more detail in later chapters.

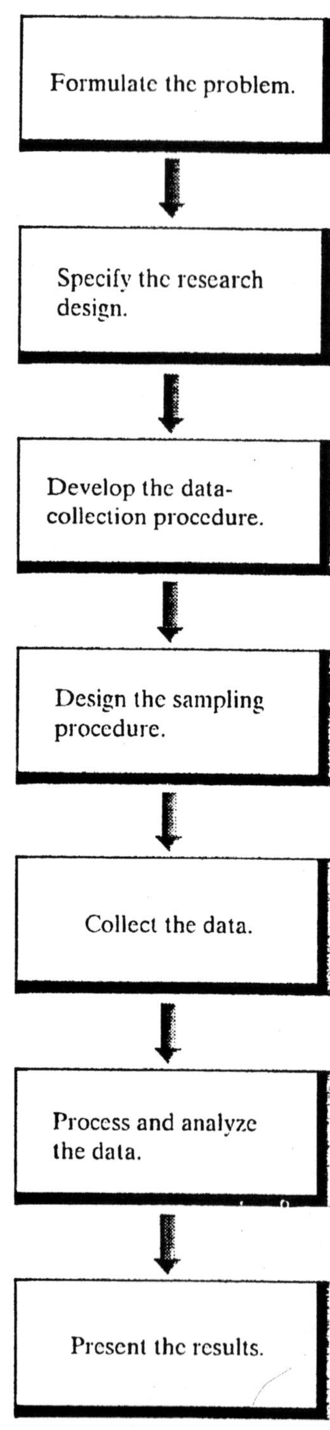
Formulate the problem.
Specify the research design.
Develop the data-collection procedure.
Design the sampling procedure.
Collect the data.
Process and analyze the data.
Present the results.

Exhibit 1.7 Steps in the research process

Formulate the Problem

A thorough understanding of the problem is essential when planning a research project. Otherwise, the data collected may not adequately address the problem. Unfortunately, problem definition can be difficult because not enough is known about the situation. If the problem is not properly defined, the data collected may be useless.

For instance, suppose that a manager observes that brand sales are below expectations. Why this is so may be a mystery. The lower sales could be caused by ineffective advertising, insufficient promotions, competitive activities, or a host of other factors. The manager might incorrectly assume that the advertising campaign is the problem when, in reality, the problem is competitive activity. No amount of money spent researching the advertising will solve the manager's problem.

Specify the Research Design

The second step in the research process is to specify the general design of the project. This step involves two decisions: the type of research to be conducted and the source of the data.

The research objectives determine which of the three general types of research shown in Table 1.1 is appropriate. If the objective of the research is to understand a problem or situation, **exploratory research** is required. If the objective is to identify cause and effect relationships, **experimental research** is conducted. If the research objective is to provide detailed data on who, what, when, where, how, why, and/or how often, **descriptive research** is used. Descriptive research typically takes the form of a survey such as the opinion polls that have become commonplace in our society.

Research type	Objective	Typical issues addressed
Exploratory research	Develop an understanding of an issue or identify alternatives.	What do consumers like or dislike about our advertising?
Experimental research	Determine and investigate cause and effect relationships.	Does an in-store display increase the sales of our brand and, if so, by how much?
Descriptive research	Describe phenomena or relationships by answering such questions as who, why, what, where, when, how, or how much.	What types of companies would be most likely to subscribe to a new business travel service?

Table 1.1 Types of research classified by the objectives of the research

After establishing the basic type of research to be conducted, the source, or sources, of the data to be collected must be determined. Marketing research data can be primary or secondary. **Secondary data** are data that have already been gathered for some other purpose but that also provide useful information for the current problem. The data provided by the U.S. Census of the Population is one valuable secondary data source. **Primary data** are gathered specifically for the project at hand. **Syndicated data** are primary data gathered by syndicated services and provided to all subscribers of the service. Hence, there are multiple sponsors of the research, all of whom share the expense. Syndication typically occurs because it is cost-prohibitive for subscribers to conduct the research on their own. The Nielsen Ratings, which indicate audience size for television shows, is a syndicated service.

Develop the Data Collection Procedure

When collecting primary data, whether for an exploratory, experimental, or descriptive study, the procedure to be used to collect the data must be developed. Typical decisions at this stage involve the selection of the method used to collect the data and the design of any necessary data-collection instruments.

A variety of methods exist to collect data. Either people can be questioned or their behavior can be observed. Questioning can occur in person or by phone or be self-administered. The appropriateness of each method varies across studies, and the researcher must determine which method is best for the study at hand.

The design of a data collection instrument can influence the accuracy of information collected in a study. Simple changes in wording or in the way the questionnaire looks can drastically influence the responses received. The researcher must ensure that questions are properly worded and that the instrument is properly designed.

Design the Sampling Procedure

For most studies, only a sample of all possible people or objects will be questioned or examined. Designing the sampling procedure to use is critical. Who is included as a potential sample member, how sample members are selected, and the size of the sample all affect what can be inferred from the results.

Collect the Data

As mentioned earlier in this chapter, companies typically hire field services to collect marketing research data. The data collected are only as good as the procedures used to collect them. Therefore, the researcher must institute procedures for selecting and supervising field services to ensure the integrity of the data.

Process and Analyze the Data

After the raw data have been collected, they must be prepared for analysis and analyzed. It is important that the researcher select appropriate data analysis procedures, given the information needs of the study and the type of data collected.

Present the Results

Marketing research findings are of little value unless their meaning can be clearly communicated to the manager requesting the study. Established formats exist for written and oral research presentations. The researcher must see to it that these formats are followed.

Ethical Conflicts in Marketing Research

A person's ethics provide the moral framework by which he or she judges what is fair and just in relationships with other people. Sometimes doing what is fair to one party involved in a relationship may not be in the best interest of another party. Such situations create ethical conflicts for the individual deciding what action to take.

Because of the number of different parties involved, ethical conflict situations abound in marketing research. Ethical conflicts can occur between corporate marketing researchers and their marketing counterparts within the company. Marketing researchers in supplier firms can find themselves in ethical conflicts with both their clients and the consumer. They must try to serve their clients' and their company's interests as well as protect the confidentiality of survey participants.

Ethical Conflicts Between the Marketing Manager and the Marketing Researcher

To maintain its credibility within the firm, the marketing research department must be viewed as an objective and unbiased source of information. Therefore, the marketing research department must conduct research in an appropriate manner and present the results objectively. Maintaining the integrity of their research given the pressures of the marketing manager is an ethical dilemma frequently mentioned by marketing researchers.[26]

Marketing researchers encounter several types of situations that could compromise the integrity of the research. A marketing manager might try to bias a study design so it yields the results that he or she desires. The marketing manager might fail to disclose certain findings to other managers, or might even misreport the findings in order to confirm a preexisting viewpoint. More accuracy might be attributed to findings than is warranted to sway a decision in favor of the alternative the manager prefers. Any such action creates an ethical dilemma for the marketing researcher. The marketing researcher wants to maintain a favorable relationship with the marketing manager, but is charged by the corporation to see that such abuses do not occur.

Ethical Conflicts Between the Client and the Supplier

A great deal of attention has been focused upon the ethical conflicts arising from the client/supplier relationship.[27] As with any business transaction, the goals of the two organizations often conflict. The research supplier wishes to reduce the costs of conducting the research in order to increase profit, while the client wants the highest possible quality research at the lowest cost. These differing goals lead to ethical conflicts for the supplier.

Suppliers can save money in many ways when conducting a project. Less expensive, but possibly less qualified, employees can be assigned to the project. Less time and effort can be spent preparing the project. Parts of the project can be assigned to less expensive suppliers who may not meet the standards expected by the client. A supplier could even ignore certain expensive project requirements specified by the client. Thus, ethical dilemmas often arise for suppliers trapped between the objectives of making money and providing high-quality service.

Suppliers can also face ethical dilemmas over the integrity of the research produced. For example, a supplier might discover a mistake in the execution of a project that could compromise the results obtained. Does the supplier alert the client to the potential problem or keep quiet and hope that the mistake goes unnoticed? Similarly, in competing with other suppliers for a research project, a supplier might misrepresent its skills or capabilities to win the project. If the supplier subsequently gets the job, it may not be able to deliver results of the quality expected by the client. What constitutes deception in this context may not be easy to define.

Client confidentiality can lead to another ethical dilemma for suppliers. Suppliers often possess a great deal of information about the problem a client wishes researched because of previous similar work done for other clients. How much of this knowledge must be kept confidential and how much can be considered background knowledge?

Clients also can face ethical conflicts in the supplier-client relationship. For example, a client might be tempted to solicit proposals from several suppliers with no intention of giving the contract to any of them. The client could use the accumulated information in all of the proposals to design a research project that is then awarded to a less-expensive supplier.

Ethical Conflicts Between the Researcher and the Respondent

Respondents are the most vulnerable party in the research process. They usually are not told who is sponsoring the research and very often do not know the purpose of the research. Respondents do have three commonly accepted, somewhat obvious rights.[28] They have the right to choose whether to participate. They have the right to be protected from physical, emotional, or psychological harm. They have the right to be informed about project details including the purpose of the study, what they are required to do, and how much of their time it will take.

Respondent rights can present an ethical dilemma for researchers because these rights can add to the cost of a project by reducing participation. Researchers can be tempted to violate respondents' rights to increase the participation rate for a study. For instance, a researcher might tell potential respondents that an interview will take less time than it actually does. Similarly, a researcher might fail to tell respondents that participation in the survey will expose them to follow-up surveys. A researcher might also deceive participants about the purpose of the research to increase participation.

Deception may also be used to get respondents to divulge sensitive information. For example, vacationers at a resort are sometimes contacted and questioned regarding demographics such as income, age, and family size. They are told that the information is being used to establish a profile of families who vacation in the particular area. The actual intent of the research is to develop a list of prospects for salespeople representing time-sharing or real- estate companies. This selling under the guise of research, called "sugging," is of great concern to the market research industry.[29]

Of equal concern is fund raising under the guise of research, or "frugging."[30] Each year, millions of Americans receive mail in oversized envelopes labeled "survey." The contents usually include a brief questionnaire from some advocacy group containing a few biased "YES" or "NO" questions. A solicitation, the main purpose for the mailing, is inevitably included. Telephone solicitations also can be initiated under the pretense of conducting a survey.

A blatant example of deceiving respondents about the purpose of a study was a survey conducted among a local television viewing audience. The survey asked participants to watch a particular local TV station as much as possible for one week. Respondents were told that the purpose of the study was to evaluate the station's programming.[31] The survey just happened to be mailed to thousands of local residents right before a period in which a syndicated service was estimating local TV station audience sizes. A competing TV station sued both the research firm and the local TV station sponsoring the "research" for attempting to manipulate the ratings. The relatively huge sample size for the research was cited as evidence. Clearly, respondents who took the time to complete the questionnaire were unhappy, and the industry's reputation was damaged.

Respondent anonymity is another area of potential conflict in the interface between supplier and respondent. In most studies, suppliers tell respondents that their identities will be kept confidential and will not be provided to the research sponsor. Furthermore, they are told that their responses will be combined with those of other respondents for analysis. The supplier faces an ethical dilemma if the research sponsor should request the identities of a specific group of respondents for follow-up inquiries, clarification, or solicitation. The supplier wants to please the client but at the same time has made promises to respondents.

The Need for A Code of Ethics

Ethical conflicts are reduced in any relationship with a well-defined set of rights and responsibilities for each party, a **code of ethics**, and trust. Each party must know, and agree to follow, the code of ethics governing the relationship. Each party must also trust that everyone will follow the code of ethics.

Most professional groups within the marketing research industry have their own individual codes of ethics and great similarity exists across these various codes. For example, each code stresses the importance of maintaining research integrity, the importance of fair treatment of all parties involved in the research, and the importance of maintaining confidentiality. However, the existence of several different codes creates confusion and reduces the effectiveness of each. A common code exists among professional marketing researchers in Western Europe, and representatives of the various U.S. groups have periodically discussed the benefits of a common code of ethics. However, they have not as yet been able to reach agreement on the tenets which would comprise a common code.

One major impetus behind the push for a common code of ethics is the industry's fear of restrictive governmental legislation due to the abuse of respondent rights. While marketing researchers no doubt are responsible for some respondent abuses, the research industry is often unfairly blamed for abuses committed by others. Consumers who have been approached by companies engaged in sugging or frugging often fail to distinguish these firms from marketing research firms when lodging their complaints. Such confusion reduces consumer willingness to participate in future legitimate research projects and might cause the marketing research industry to be unjustly included in legislation aimed at reducing or eliminating unethical practices.

International Issues

As the world rapidly moves to a global economy, many U.S.-based companies are now really international firms. For example, The Coca-Cola Company derives more of its profits from foreign operations than from the United States.

Marketing goods and services in other countries increases the need for marketing research because what a company knows about its domestic market may not be transferrable to another country. The firm faces not only a different economic environment, but cultural, religious, and political differences are also likely to impact upon the way business is conducted.

The same research process applies and the same parties are involved in the research process, regardless of the country being studied. However, obtaining marketing research information in other countries is far from easy. Secondary or syndicated data that a firm takes for granted in the United States may not be available in a foreign country. For instance, many countries do not conduct a census of their populations. The collection of primary data can be hindered by pitfalls not encountered in the United States. Muslim women are not encouraged to express an opinion; the Japanese are often unwilling to admit that they do not know an answer when asked a question.

We have included these "International Issues" sections at the end of selected chapters. In them, we address the subtleties involved in planning and conducting marketing research in other countries.

Summary

The widespread acceptance of the marketing concept and adoption of a market orientation by businesses has caused an evolution in the role of marketing research. The research information required to be successful in today's highly competitive environment go far beyond the somewhat crude market-level measures of the past. Also, today's marketing research department no longer merely collects data and makes results available to the marketing managers. Instead, they are a vital member of the firm's marketing team. As a team, the firm's research department, its marketing managers, sales force, and representatives of its advertising agency collectively develop, implement, and evaluate the marketing strategy of the firm's brands.

The research industry is comprised of three types general of research suppliers: syndicated services, standardized services, and custom suppliers. Syndicated services collect data and sell all or parts of it to multiple clients. Standardized services have expertise in one or more types of research projects and guarantee that the data are collected in precisely the same way each time. Custom suppliers design and implement research projects to an individual firm's specifications. Some custom suppliers, called full-service suppliers, can manage a research project from start to finish. Other custom suppliers, called limited-service suppliers, specialize in one or more of the tasks in a research project.

Designing and executing a research project involves the steps shown in Exhibit 1.7. The nuances and details of each step will be discussed in detail in Chapters 2 through 9.

An ethical conflict arises when doing what is fair to one party in a relationship will be unfair to another party. Ethical conflicts can arise between the marketing manager and the marketing researcher, between the marketing researcher and the research supplier, and between the supplier and respondents.

Key Terms

code of ethics

custom services

database marketing

descriptive research

experimental research

exploratory research

field services

full-service suppliers

limited-service suppliers

market orientation

market research

marketing concept

marketing research

primary data

relationship marketing

research suppliers

secondary data

standardized services

syndicated data

syndicated services

tab houses

The Nimslo Three-Dimensional Photography System

Among the photographic products available today is a disposable 3D camera marketed by ImageTech. The camera has 3 lenses and is designed to produce 16 photos which are three-dimensional to the naked eye. The camera, containing the exposed film is shipped in a mailer, which is included with the original camera, to a special photofinishing lab. The 3D photos, costing $1 each, are returned by mail. The 3D camera provides an interesting alternative to conventional photos for selected occasions. This technology is not new. The Nimslo Corporation introduced three-dimensional photography in 1982.

The Nimslo camera, the product of over ten years of intense research and development, was one component of an intricate system designed to produce photos that appear three-dimensional to

the naked eye. The camera was a simple "look and shoot" camera that used ordinary 35 mm color film. An electric light-sensing device built into the picture was taken, four negatives, each on a half frame of film, were created, and each negative captured from a slightly different perspective. A sophisticated printing process, also developed by the Nimslo Corporation, combined the four negatives. A special print material, manufactured exclusively for Nimslo, produced a picture that appeared three-dimensional to the naked eye.

The Nimslo Camera

Exhibit 1.8
The Nimslo camera is designed to create Photographs that appear three dimensional to the naked eye.

The introductory marketing plan called for the camera to retail for $225 to $275. Photofinishing, which could only be done by Nimslo, was designed to cost between 85 cents to $1.00 per picture, depending on the exposure length of the roll.

Nimslo obviously had high hopes for its new photographic system. They viewed their system as the fourth great innovation in photography: first came photographic imaging itself, then color photography, instant photography, and now three-dimensional photography. The Nimslo system had been anticipated anxiously by the photographic community. However, promise soon turned to frustration as sales were far from expectations and numerous executional problems were encountered by the company. By the end of 1982, the handwriting was on the wall. Camera, camera accessory, and photofinishing sales would not achieve the levels required to sustain the business. Only a scaled-down version of the company survived, providing photofinishing service for Nimslo camera owners.

In the late 1980's, Nishika Corporation, a U.S. subsidiary of the Nissei Corporation of Hong Kong, introduced the N8000 camera.[32] The company spent over one million dollars for the right to use Nimslo's patented system. Although priced significantly lower than Nimslo's original camera, the cost of prints was about the same as Nimslo prints. Nishika's N8000 camera was at best a very limited success. Perhaps ImageTech's idea of a disposable camera is the right approach.

What went wrong with Nimslo's introduction? Could the dramatic failure of the Nimslo system and the associated huge financial losses have been predicted from marketing research information collected by the firm?

We discuss the Nimslo system further at the end of chapters throughout the text. In particular, we use the Nimslo system (along with many additional examples) to demonstrate how various marketing research techniques can facilitate marketing decision making.

The Nimslo technology is fascinating and certainly qualifies the product for placement in the "hi-tech" category into which so many new products fall today. Further, we hope that using a relatively unfamiliar product as a continuing example will stimulate the reader's interest more than using a product with which the reader is already quite familiar. Finally, the use of Nimslo serves to demonstrate that carefully planned and executed research does not guarantee success. Research can provide guidance and facilitate decision making. However, decisions are made in an uncertain environment and failures will occur. A good decision-maker can only hope to minimize the number of failures.

Review Questions

1.1 What does market orientation mean? How does this differ from the marketing concept?

1.2 Compare and contrast the role of marketing research under the previous and current AMA definitions of marketing research.

1.3 What is meant by standardized versus custom marketing research? Give examples of each.

1.4 What is a syndicated marketing research service? Give an example of such a service.

1.5 Under what conditions would a firm opt to use a full-service supplier?

1.6 Why do opportunities exist for limited-service suppliers?

1.7 What are field services?

1.8 What are tab houses?

1.9 What is database marketing? Give an example.

1.10 What is meant by the research process? What purpose do the steps in the process serve?

1.11 How do the research objectives influence the design of a project? What alternative designs are available based upon the research objectives?

1.12 What is meant by ethics? Why are ethical considerations so prevalent in marketing research?

1.13 What is relationship marketing? Give an example of relationship marketing.

Discussion Questions

1.1 For each of the following situations, identify the ethical conflict(s) posed and explain why you feel the action is, or is not, appropriate.

a) Only a small percentage of individuals respond to a mail questionnaire the first time it is received. Some people never receive it, some forget to complete the survey, some forget to mail it, and some just ignore it. The total response to a survey can be increased by sending the survey to the same respondents several times. However, the cost of sending these follow-ups can be reduced if questionnaires are sent only to persons who have not yet responded. Suppose a company tells participants in a mail survey that their answers are anonymous. However, the company secretly codes each questionnaire so that it can be traced to an individual and conducts follow-up mailings only among individuals who have not yet responded to reduce cost.

b) A marketing research analyst is present at a meeting between the marketing manager for a laundry detergent and the brand's advertising agency team. The analyst had recently presented the marketing manager with research results which indicated that consumers were misusing the product by using more detergent than necessary. Using more detergent than necessary caused no increase in cleaning power; it merely wasted the product. The marketing manager has ignored these results in planning the new advertising campaign, but the analyst says nothing about this at the meeting.

c) French Marketing Research is a supplier that has been trying unsuccessfully for some time to solicit business from Acme Manufacturing. Acme conducts a substantial volume of marketing research, with most of the business going to Woodhaven Marketing Research. The French Marketing Research company hires the person who has been handling this account at Woodhaven and becomes the primary supplier for Acme.

1.2 Discuss the notion of market orientation and how it effects the role of marketing research in the corporation. What factors hinder a firm's efforts to adopt a market orientation?

1.3 List several new product or service failures. Discuss whether you think that marketing research could have prevented the failures. Can marketing research eliminate all market failures? Why or why not?

1.4 Discuss the notion of a "marketing team." What is the role of the company's marketing research staff on this team?

1.5 Discuss the impact of changing communications technology and the increasing use of direct marketing on the marketing research industry.

1.6 For each of the following situations, identify the objectives of the required research, the appropriate type of research based upon these objectives, and where or how you feel the data might be obtained.

A. Oscar Meyer wants to know the market share of its beef hot dogs and how this share varies by geographic area of the United States.

B. Oscar Meyer is concerned about the influence of hot dogs made from chicken or turkey on sales of its beef hot dogs.

C. Oscar Meyer wants to know what the impact of a twenty-cents-off coupon would be on the sales of its hot dogs.

D. Oscar Meyer wants to learn what consumers' perceptions of hot dogs are and how the decision is made concerning when to serve them.

Chapter 1 Endnotes

---

1. "Name of the Game: Brand Awareness," *Wall Street Journal*, February 14, 1991, p. B1.

2. "Survey: New Product Failure is Top Management's Fault," *Marketing News*, February 1, 1993, p.2.

4. "General Mills to Drop Benefit Cereal," *Marketing News*, February 5, 1990, p. 5.

3. "Where's Farrah Shampoo? Next to the Salsa Ketchup," *Marketing News*, May 6, 1996, p. 13.

5. Margaret Henderson Blair, Allan R. Kuse, David H. Furse, and David W. Stewart, "Advertising in a New Competitive Environment: Persuading Customers to Buy," *Business Horizons*, November-December (1987), pp. 20-26.

6. Paula A. Francese and Leo M. Renagban, "Finding the Customer," *American Demographics*, January (1991), pp. 48-51.

7. Michael R. Solomon and Elnora W. Stuart, *Marketing, Real People Real Choices* (Upper Saddle River, NJ: Prentice-Hall, 1997), p. 13.

8. *Ibid,* p. 23.

9. For example, William H. Cunningham, Isabella C. M. Cunningham, and Christopher M. Swift, Marketing: A Managerial Approach, 2nd ed. (Cincinnati, Ohio: South-Western Publishing Co., 1987), p. 16.

10. Raymond Serafin, "Marketing in Chrysler Product Mix," *Advertising Age*, October 6, 1986, p. 22.

11. Russell Mitchell, "How Ford Hit the Bull's-Eye with Taurus," *Business Week*, June 30, 1986, pp. 69-70.

12. *Ibid.*

13. Terence P. Pare, "How To Find Out What They Want," *Fortune*, 128-13 (Special Issue), 1993, pp. 39 - 41.

14. Lisa E. Phillips, "Spectra Unites Polaroid's `Family,'" *Advertising Age*, October 6, 1985, pp. 4, 100.

15. Stephen Koepp, "Hospitals Learn the Hard Sell," *Time*, January 12, 1987, p. 56, for a discussion of the use of marketing by hospitals.

16. *Ibid.*

17. Sylvia Sansoni, "Gucci, Armani, and . . .John Paul II?," *Business Week*, May 13, 1996, p. 61.

18. Cyndee Miller, "Churches Turn to Research For Help in Saving New Souls," *Marketing News*, April 11, 1994, pp. 1-2.

19. "King Customer," *Business Week*, March 12, 1990, pp. 88-94.

20. *Marketing Definitions: A Glossary of Marketing Terms* (Chicago: American Marketing Association, 1960), pp. 16-17.

21. John Pfeiffer, "Six Months and Half A Million Dollars, All for Fifteen Seconds," *Smithsonian*, October (1987), pp. 134-139.

22. Linda Himelstein, "Levis Is Hiking Up Its Pants," *Business Week*, December 1, 1997, pp. 70-71.

23. For example, *Marketing News*, January 2, 1987, p.1.

24. Peter Bogda, "`Partnershipping' Is Answer to More Competition

and Tighter Budgets," *Marketing News*, January 7, 1991, pp. 2, 10.

25. See Leonard M. Fuld, *Monitoring The Competition Find Out What's Really Going on Over There* (New York, NY: John Wiley & Sons, 1988), pp. 139-140.

26. Shelby D. Hunt, Lawrence B. Chonko, and James B. Wilcox, "Ethical Problems of Marketing Researchers," *Journal of Marketing Research*, 21-3 (1984), 309-24, for the results of a study of the frequency of mention of various ethical conflicts.

27. For example, Merle C. Crawford, "Attitudes of Marketing Executives towards Ethics in Marketing Research," *Journal of Marketing*, 34-2 (1970), pp. 46-52; Kenneth A. Coney and John H. Murphy, "Attitudes of Marketers toward Ethical and Professional Marketing Research Practices," in *Proceedings: Southern Marketing Association*, Henry W. Nash and Donald P. Robin, eds., (1976), pp. 172-4; K.L. McGowan, "Ethical Issues Involving the Protection of Marketing Research Practitioners and Respondents," in *Proceedings of the Institute of Decision Sciences*, J.F. Hair, ed., (1979), pp. 195-7; Patrick E. Murphy and Gene R. Laczniak, "Marketing Ethics: A Review with Implications for Managers, Educators and Researchers," in *Review of Marketing, 1981*, Ben M. Enis and Kenneth J. Roering, eds. (Chicago: American Marketing Association, 1981), pp. 251-66; Shelby D. Hunt, Larry B. Chonko, and James B. Wilcox, "Ethical Problems of Marketing Researchers," *Journal of Marketing Research*, 21-3 (1984), pp. 309-24; Ishmael P. Akaah and Edward A. Riordan, "Judgments of Marketing Professionals about Ethical Issues in Marketing Research: A Replication and Extension," *Journal of Marketing Research*, 26-1 (1989), pp. 112-20.

28. Alice M. Tybout and Gerald Zaltman, "Ethics in Marketing Research: Their Practical Relevance," *Journal of Marketing Research*, 11-4 (1974), pp. 357-68 for a complete description of these rights.

29. For example, "Research Group to Warn Violators," *Marketing News*, November 12, 1990, p. 5.

30. *Ibid.*

31. Gregg Cebrzynski, "TV Station Sues Over Alleged `Phony' Survey," *Marketing News*, August 28, 1987, pp. 1, 42.

32. Peter Kolonia, "A Born Again Nimslo," *Popular Photography*, November (1989), pp. 71-2.

Chapter 2

Exploratory Research

Learning Objectives:

In this chapter we will discuss the role of exploratory research. After reading this chapter you should be able to:

- o define exploratory research
- o explain the purpose of exploratory research
- o describe commonly used exploratory research techniques
- o discuss the situations where exploratory research is useful

Procter & Gamble conducted numerous large sample research studies before introducing a new Duncan Hines cake mix formula. They used nationwide surveys to gather information on baking habits, product likes and dislikes, and brand preferences. To insure that consumers preferred the new cake mix formula, hundreds of consumers tasted cakes made with alternative mixes. Yet, in spite of all of this research, the best way to communicate the moist, homemade taste of the final product remained a mystery.

The mystery was solved when, during in-depth individual discussions with only fifty packaged cake mix purchasers, one person mentioned that the crumbs from a moist cake stick to the fork. This single response became the focus of a very successful advertising campaign demonstrating the moistness of the Duncan Hines cake mix in just that manner.[1]

As Procter & Gamble discovered, the data provided by large-scale descriptive surveys or experimental research do not always yield the necessary information. Even if the required information could be gathered by such studies, the situation being studied may not be understood well enough to design such a study. The exploratory research techniques described in this chapter provide help in these situations.

What Is Exploratory Research?

Exploratory research is designed to further the understanding of a marketing problem or issue. Exploratory research can help clarify the real issues that need to be researched further. Exploratory research is useful for

exploring and explaining consumer motivations, attitudes, and behavior. It also can provide input to a future stage of research or development.

Commonly Used Exploratory Research Techniques

Some people mistakenly equate exploratory research techniques with qualitative research. While a great deal of similarity exists, the two are different.[2] **Qualitative research** refers to research in which the results cannot be statistically analyzed because of the limited amount of data or type of data collected. Hence, qualitative research is defined by the nature of the data produced by the research project. Exploratory research is defined by the purpose of the research.

Although many exploratory research techniques are qualitative in nature, exploratory research can be quantitative as well. Virtually any data collection technique can be employed for exploratory research. However, the techniques described in this section are especially suited for exploratory research.

Experience Surveys and Case Studies

One way to learn about a situation is to study other, similar situations. Ideally, what was learned in the other situations can be applied to the current situation. Experience surveys and case studies are two methods of exploring other situations.

An **experience survey** taps the expertise of people who have encountered a similar situation or who are knowledgeable about the situation being faced. When designing a marketing information system, a firm might seek the expertise of outside consultants who have designed other information systems. A manager whose brand faces severe price competition might question managers of other brands within the firm to determine how they had combated similar threats.

A **case study** attempts to apply what was learned in other situations to the situation at hand by developing a detailed, in-depth examination of the other situations.[3] A case study might entail following and observing one very effective and one very ineffective salesperson for a period of time. Differences in behavior noted become possible causes of success that can be subjected to further testing.

Experience survey data usually are obtained by talking to individuals. Case study data can come from a variety of sources besides interviews. Data from company records, published information, or simple observation might all help understand the case being studied.

Applying Marketing Research 2.1

In 1982, media across the United States broke the news story that people had died from cyanide poison found in some Tylenol pain-reliever capsules. Johnson & Johnson, the makers of the Tylenol brand, immediately pulled all Tylenol from retail shelves. It was later discovered that the fault did not lie with anyone at Johnson & Johnson; someone had tampered with the packages on store shelves.

Sales of Tylenol plummeted during this crisis. However, company executives immediately took costly and decisive steps to eliminate the risk of further poisonings. They were forthright and open in answering questions from the press, public, and the federal agencies involved. Within about a year, Tylenol regained almost all of its lost market share. Management's handling of the matter won the respect of consumers and competitors alike.[4]

The Tylenol situation was the first such product tampering, but not the last. Manufacturers later faced with similar product tamperings often used Johnson & Johnson as a case study to learn how to deal with such a crisis. For example, when cyanide-laced Sudafed capsules left two people dead in 1991, the Burroughs Wellcome Company closely followed the Johnson & Johnson model. They initiated a swift recall of all Sudafed capsules, suspended regular advertising, established a toll-free phone line, and offered a $100,000 reward for information leading to the capture of the person responsible.[5]

Focus Groups

Companies use focus groups more frequently than any other exploratory research technique. A **focus group** consists of eight to twelve persons who are led through an unstructured, one- to two-hour discussion of a topic by a moderator. The number of people in a focus group depends somewhat on the topic and the type of participants. Interesting topics usually require fewer people per group. The more articulate are the group members, the smaller is the size of the group necessary to keep the discussion moving.[6]

Focus group facilities are designed to make the respondents

feel comfortable and relaxed. Respondents often sit around a table, such as is shown in Exhibit 2.1. Soft drinks and coffee are usually provided. When discussing food or food preparation, the room may also be equipped with the necessary kitchen appliances.

Exhibit 2.1

Typical focus group setting (Courtesy of Elrick & Lavidge, Inc.

The moderator works with the research sponsor to prepare a moderator's guide. The moderator's guide provides a general framework for the discussion and includes the major topics to be discussed. Because of the unstructured nature of a focus group, the amount of time actually spent on each topic and the specific points discussed depend on the dynamics of the particular group.

Table 2.1 provides an example of a moderator's guide. This guide was used to lead a series of focus groups with college freshmen to explore their college selection decision. The general topics explored dealt with the timing of the decision, the importance of various formal and informal information sources, and how the final decision was made. The focus group results helped the university sponsoring this research improve its promotional materials and recruiting activities.

I. Warm-up

Interests. Activities. Self-description (shy, outgoing, etc.).

II. The Decision Process

A. When did it start? Why then? Were others/everyone/anyone also starting then? If not, why were you different?

B. What were your *official* sources of information? How did you learn about them? Which were most/least helpful? Why? Which were most/least believable? Why? Did you use the same sources as others? If not, why not? When did you use each source? In what sequence? (Have them rate each of the following sources on credibility, completeness, and timeliness: school counselors, college brochures, recruiters, on-campus visits.)

C. What *unofficial* sources did you use? Which were most/least useful/believable? How did you learn about them? (Have them rate each of the following on credibility, etc.: parents, graduates of certain colleges, current college students, rankings or college reputation, peers.)

D. Considering *all* of the sources you used, which were most/least useful/ believable? Why?

E. To how many schools did you apply? Why that number? Did you expect all of them to accept you? Did you select any "safe" schools? Did you visit all of the schools to which you applied? If not, why not?

III. The Selection Process

A. Were you accepted at more than one school? If yes, how did you decide between them?

B. To whom did you talk to help make up your mind? Who was most/least helpful?

C. What was the best/worst part of the whole process? Why?

D. If you were doing it over again, what would you do differently? What would make the process easier?

Table 2.1

Example of a focus group moderator's guide to leading a discussion of how college freshmen made their college decision

The moderator provides a written summary of the focus group findings to the marketing manager. Preparing the written summary is a time-consuming task. First, a written transcript of the audio- or videotape of each group is prepared. Then, the moderator studies the transcript carefully, looking for similarities and differences in the topics discussed across groups. Key similarities and differences and their interpretation are included in the report.

Focus Group Benefits

Table 2.2 lists several benefits accruing from the use of focus groups for exploratory research.[7] Two primary benefits are that focus groups can be conducted very quickly and are relatively inexpensive. Group dynamics create several additional benefits. Being in a group, individuals do not feel that they must respond to everything being discussed, so they respond more thoughtfully and seriously. Also, by listening to the comments of others, people quickly determine that they possess similar characteristics, behaviors, or attitudes. This common bond adds to their willingness to talk openly about issues. Focus groups also generate a lot of different comments, since what one person says can stimulate someone else to comment. A synergistic effect is often created, generating ideas that probably would not evolve from individual discussions.

Benefits	Limitations
Research can be conducted quickly.	Discussion can be dominated by a few people.
Groups are relatively inexpensive.	Little information can be obtained from each person.
Since people are not forced to answer, they tend to give thoughtful and serious answers.	There is uneven coverage of each topic.
People open up because they see that they are not any different from others.	Minority viewpoints can be stifled.
Group atmosphere stimulates people to talk.	
A "bandwagon effect" exists, where one comment generates another.	
Synergy is created by the group.	

Table 2.2 Benefits and limitations of focus groups

Limitations of Focus Groups

As Table 2.2 reveals, the group setting can also create limitations. Some people tend to talk very little in a group setting while others tend to dominate a group. Little information can be obtained from each person, even if everyone in the group talks the same amount. Only a few minutes is available for each respondent in a one- to two-hour block of time. Furthermore, within a particular group, certain topics may receive undue attention while some important topics get little mention. Finally, a few dominant individuals can easily stifle minority viewpoints in a group.

A good moderator can minimize many of the limitations inherent in a focus group setting. Techniques exist for ensuring that shy or reticent individuals and minority views get heard. With practice, a moderator can also keep the discussion flowing smoothly from topic to topic. In addition, having multiple groups discuss the same subject area helps ensure that important topics surface in at least one group. Multiple groups also reduce the chance of being misled by an aberrant set of comments made in only one group.

Uses of Focus Groups

Focus groups are appropriate for a wide variety of situations. Some of the more common marketing research uses are shown in Table 2.3.

To provide insights into a problem
To learn the language of the consumer market
To help structure later quantitative research
To bring statistical research findings to life
To generate ideas
To determine preliminary reactions to new ideas

Table 2.3

Common uses of focus groups for exploratory reserach

Focus groups can help managers more clearly define the problem they face. Their unstructured format provides the flexibility to probe an issue fully, to help define the boundaries of a problem, or to gain insights into a situation. Applying Marketing Research 2.2 demonstrates how focus groups help provide insights into a problem.

Applying Marketing Research 2.2

In 1989, Information Resources, Inc. (IRI), a Chicago-based marketing research supplier, began testing a supermarket shopping cart, called the Videocart, within three cities. The Videocart is equipped with a video screen that shows commercials from national advertisers and highlights store specials. Sensors in each supermarket aisle trigger appropriate advertising for the products displayed in that aisle. IRI hopes to introduce these carts nationally in the future and sell advertising space on them.

Early results indicated that, in spite of the novelty of the Videocart, many shoppers chose traditional carts. IRI commissioned focus groups with shoppers who had used the Videocart previously but had returned to traditional carts. What was learned from these focus groups played a big part in redesigning the Videocart.

IRI made the video screen brighter and its casing smaller. Entertainment programming and informational pieces on cooking were supplemented with tips on economical shopping. The new carts were also designed to allow the shopper to play back information from previous aisles.[8]

A second prominent use of focus groups is to help management learn consumer feelings and attitudes toward brands.[9] Most focus-group rooms are equipped with one-way glass, allowing viewers in an adjacent room to see and hear what is taking place in the session, while participants see only a mirrored surface. Thus, marketing managers can listen and watch real consumers discuss their likes and dislikes about various brands. For instance, Coca-Cola Foods developed and introduced Minute Maid Pulp Free orange juice after hearing some focus group participants say that they strained existing brands because they preferred pulp-free orange juice.[10]

A third use of focus groups is to uncover questions that need addressing in future descriptive or experimental research studies. Snackmaster, a division of M&M Mars, Inc., conducted several focus groups to gain insight into consumers' buying habits and consumption patterns for salty snacks. The findings helped them design later experimental research to evaluate the best product form for a new brand of snack they were developing called Combos.

Companies sometimes conduct focus groups after a large-scale descriptive or experimental study to gain a better understanding of the results obtained. For instance, Guinness Stout, an Irish brewery, sells a substantial amount of their beverage in the country of Sierra Leone. However, consumers rarely mentioned Guinness Stout when surveyed regarding beverage consumption. Subsequent focus groups revealed that Sierra Leone consumers did not mention Guinness Stout when surveyed about beverages because they considered it a medicinal tonic.[11]

The Guinness Stout situation illustrates another potential use of focus groups as well; they can aid in the design of questions to be asked to consumers by ensuring that the questions are understood correctly. Focus groups conducted prior to the Guinness Stout beverage consumption survey probably would have led to a different wording of the question on brands consumed.

Focus groups are also a useful idea-generation device. Group discussions can reveal new product ideas, new uses for existing products, or new ways to communicate a product benefit. For instance, focus groups presented a whole new market opportunity to managers of Arm & Hammer baking soda. One participant mentioned that she placed boxes of baking soda in her refrigerator to kill food odors. The concept of using baking soda as a deodorizer led to many new product opportunities. Similarly, Cascade's "virtually spotless glasses" demonstration in their advertising was the result of a respondent indicating that the effectiveness of an automatic dishwasher detergent could be measured by whether the washed glasses had water spots.[12]

Companies frequently use focus groups for quick, inexpensive reactions to a new idea. Advertising agencies often conduct focus groups as a "communication check" on new advertising. In this way the advertising agency can quickly determine what specific copy points are being communicated and can get creative guidance for new campaigns. Companies considering a change in their products often conduct focus groups to get an initial reaction to the proposed change. If the reaction is overwhelmingly negative, the idea is dropped. Such disaster checks can save research time and money.

Applying Marketing Research 2.3

In the early 1980s, American Express ran a "Do You Know Me?" advertising campaign. In the campaign, people with famous names but not well-known faces stated that they used the American Express card because they got treated like someone important. Consumers remembered and enjoyed the campaign. However, focus group research revealed that one important target market, career women aged twenty-five to forty, felt that the card was a male product.

American Express was puzzled over this finding because women had been featured in some of the commercials. Additional focus groups were conducted to try to understand this finding. These focus groups revealed that women in this target market did not equate success with achievement. To them, being successful led to an interesting life.

These findings led to the development of a new advertising campaign. The campaign consisted of thirty-second vignettes showing women in interesting situations using their American Express card. The number of women applying for American Express cards doubled when this new campaign was aired.[13]

Modified Focus Group Settings

Some firms have successfully employed variations of the traditional focus group setup. Sometimes companies run mini-groups. **Mini-groups** are focus groups held with four to six participants instead of the traditional eight to twelve people. Proponents of mini-groups argue that the smaller number of participants allows more information to be gained from each individual. Groups with three participants, called **triangle groups**, are occasionally conducted to bring people having different viewpoints together.[14] For instance, a triangle group might consist of a heavy user of a brand, a light user, and a nonuser.

Some researchers prefer sensitivity panels instead of focus groups. In a **sensitivity panel**, the same participants are brought together several times, possibly covering different topics each time. Proponents of sensitivity panels believe they provide more substantive comments due to the familiarity of the participants with each other and with the focus-group process.[15]

Depth Interviews

Depth interviews, often called "one-on-ones," are lengthy unstructured interviews conducted with one individual at a time. A depth interview often requires a highly skilled interviewer. Depth interviews can also be more expensive to conduct than focus groups. However, a depth interview can be a very valuable exploratory research tool, particularly in the situations listed in Table 2.4.[16]

A list of alternatives is desired.
A sensitive or embarrassing topic is to be discussed.
Hard-to-reach respondents are to be interviewed.
In-depth understanding of a process is desired.

Table 2.4 Situations favoring the use of depth interviews

Depth interviews are excellent for generating a list of ideas (*e.g.*, a list of product benefits or a list of competitive brands). Working alone, each respondent is not distracted by the comments of others. Therefore, a few people working individually usually come up with more different ideas than the same number of people working as a group.[17]

Depth interviews are very appropriate when discussing sensitive topics. Confidential topics, topics that may cause the respondent embarrassment, topics that are emotionally charged, or topics that may cause the respondent to give "socially acceptable" answers if asked in front of others are much easier to cover in a one-on-one format. For example, in the presence of others, individuals would be more reluctant to talk frankly about how they handle their financial matters than they would be in a one-on-one interview. Similarly, talking with people about their job in a one-on-one format should produce more frank and honest comments than if other coworkers are present.

For hard-to-reach individuals such as doctors, lawyers, or business executives, depth interviews might be the only available alternative. Attempting to survey hard-to-reach individuals by mail or phone generally yields a low response rate. The schedules of such individuals often prevent their attending a focus-group session.

Finally, depth interviews are particularly well-suited for probing decisions involving several people, outcomes comprised of a series of interrelated decisions, or decisions that tend to take a long time. Examples of such decisions include the choice of a car or home, selecting a college to attend, and when and where to vacation. Depth interviews allow for the development of a detailed step-by-step description of the process leading to the final decision.

Projective Techniques

Sometimes people are unwilling to answer truthfully. They may fear that a truthful answer will incriminate them, will make them seem socially deviant, or will appear rude to the interviewer.[18] At other times, people simply find it difficult to express themselves cogently about a topic when directly questioned.[19]

Projective techniques are a variety of exploratory procedures that ask the respondent to project his or her feelings, beliefs, or motivations onto another person, object, or situation.[20] Through this indirect approach, projective techniques tend to overcome the barriers of unwillingness and inability to answer that can prevent more direct approaches from getting at the truth.

One of the most well-known examples of the use of projective techniques in marketing research was conducted by Mason Haire in 1950.[21] Instant coffee had low consumer acceptance at that point in time, even though research revealed no differences between ground and instant coffee taste. Haire presented respondents with one of two shopping lists, identical except that one contained regular coffee and one contained instant coffee. Each respondent was asked to describe the characteristics of the woman shopping for the products on the list. Respondents frequently stated that the woman shopping for the products on the list containing instant coffee was lazy and uncaring about family members. The same comments were not observed for the other list. Thus, the intangible attributes surrounding the act of making coffee were inhibiting sales, not the product attributes. Directly asking the respondents why they did not buy instant coffee did not generate these responses. Only by projecting to a third party (the shopper) did these responses emerged.

Projective techniques are rooted in psychotherapy and psychiatry. The well-known Rorschach inkblot test, in which a respondent describes what each of a series of inkblots represents, is a projective technique once used in psychiatry. Projective techniques commonly applied in marketing research include association, completion, role playing, personalization, and psychodrawing.[22]

Association Techniques

Association techniques involve the presentation of a series of stimuli to a respondent and asking the respondent to indicate what comes to mind after experiencing each stimulus. Words or pictures are the most often used stimuli.

With the **word association technique**, respondents are shown a list of words, one at a time, and are asked to indicate what comes to mind after hearing each word. Sometimes only one response is requested for each word. At other times, the respondent is probed for more than one association. A common use of word association is to determine the image projected by a new or existing brand name.

With the **picture association technique** respondents are asked to indicate which pictures they are being shown are associated with a stimulus. The picture association technique is sometimes called a photo-sort technique. Each picture has been previously assessed to determine the particular personality traits, lifestyles, and respondent characteristics associated with it. Using picture association, the perceived user profile of a brand or the use occasions with which the brand might be associated can be determined. For example, one large U.S. hotel chain used the picture association technique to determine consumers' perceptions of the types of people who stayed at the hotel chain and whether or not their advertisements depicted the correct customer types.[23]

Completion Techniques

Completion techniques give the respondent an incomplete situation and the respondent provides the ending. The respondent might be given an incomplete sentence such as "The one thing I really don't like about banks is..." and be asked to complete the sentence. Similarly, the respondent might be provided with the background of a situation in the form of a story and be asked to complete the story. Another type of completion technique has respondents describe what is taking place in a cartoon, such as the one shown in Exhibit 2.2.

Exhibit 2.2

Cartoons are sometimes used in projective research

Completion techniques help uncover underlying motives or attitudes that the consumer might be unwilling or unable to verbalize if asked directly. Asking for the information indirectly, through the use of a sentence, story, or cartoon, allows respondents to project their true feelings into that situation. For example, the staff at Chicago's Lincoln Park Zoo learned through completion techniques that the emotional attachment people had to the animals in the zoo was more important than their attachment to the zoo as an institution. Thus, rather than asking for donations to the zoo, an "adopt an animal" campaign was developed.[24] The campaign was so successful that it several other zoos have copied it.

Role-Playing Techniques

Role-playing techniques require respondents to "play the role" of another person and react to a situation as they think the other person would react. For example, a respondent might be asked to pretend that he or she is chairman of the board of the company producing a particular brand and that the chairman is making a speech describing new improvements that will be incorporated into the brand. The respondent is then asked to tell what the chairman of the board says in the speech.

In role playing, a respondent must draw upon his or her own attitudes or experiences to answer. However, by projecting these responses to another person, the respondent is freed from any barriers that would inhibit an honest answer. For example, if asked directly, a person might indicate that automobile features such as gas mileage, safety, and price are important because these are the rational features to consider. When asked what features friends or neighbors seek in an automobile, however, the respondent may mention status, performance, and luxury.

Personalization

Personalization techniques require the respondent to create a personality for an inanimate object. Respondents are sometimes asked to pretend that they are the object of interest and to describe the object's personality. For example, respondents might be told to pretend that they are a particular fast-food restaurant chain and be asked to describe themselves by giving their age, sex, occupation, hobbies, and personality. Another version of the personalization technique asks respondents to identify the person or animal that would be the best spokesperson for the object. The characteristics of the spokesperson chosen reflect the perceptions respondents have of the object.

Personalization techniques are very useful for determining the image of a brand or a brand's users. While consumers could be asked to rate a brand on a series of predetermined dimensions or indicate the characteristics of the brand user in the same fashion, in many cases, personalization provides a richer description of a brand.

Psychodrawing

Psychodrawing forces respondents to attach abstract notions such as colors, shapes, or symbols to objects. Information on the perceived similarity of the objects is gained from what specific colors, shapes, or symbols are attached to each object. Respondents could be asked to name the color that they would associate with each of a series of brands. Brands would then be grouped according to the color associated with them to determine the degree of similarity among the brands. To gain more insight, respondents might also be questioned about why a specific color was attached to a brand or set of brands. Through the use of such an abstract task, respondents are less likely to consider items as similar because they feel that they are "supposed" to be similar.

Research Applications of Exploratory Research

As indicated at the beginning of this chapter, exploratory research develops insights and understanding about a marketing problem or issue. While exploratory research is applicable in numerous situations, it is extremely useful for understanding a problem, screening alternative solutions, and discovering new ideas. We will discuss these three applications in this section.

Exploratory Research for Understanding a Problem

Managers are often faced with situations that are so poorly understood that neither the real problem nor the available decision options are clear. For example, the marketing manager for Cheetos brand snacks may only know that sales are down. Not knowing the reason for the lower sales, the manager has no idea what to do to correct the situation. Sales could be down because of competitive activity, difficulties in the distribution of the product (perhaps stores have stopped carrying it or are out of stock), ineffective advertising, or any of a host of other reasons. A great deal of money can be wasted researching irrelevant issues if large-scale research projects are undertaken without a clear understanding of the nature of the problem. Furthermore, as Applying Marketing Research 2.4 points out, management can make the wrong decisions if they assume that they know the cause of the problem without any research guidance.

Applying Marketing Research 2.4

The Florida Citrus Commission is a trade association responsible for assisting in the marketing of Florida citrus products. They learned the hard way that the wrong assumption can result in money being wasted on ineffective remedies.

Faced with declining sales of Florida orange juice, the Florida Citrus Commission blamed their advertising. Their advertising stressed drinking orange juice at breakfast, a use occasion they assumed they already dominated. Thus, they initiated an $18.2 million advertising campaign designed to increase consumption of orange juice at times other than breakfast (see Exhibit 2.3). The campaign did little to increase orange juice sales.

Research later revealed that the source of problem was really a declining consumption of orange juice at breakfast. With changing lifestyles and more alternative breakfast drinks, orange juice no longer dominated as a breakfast drink. Fewer than one in four households were consuming orange juice at breakfast.[25]

FLORIDA DEPARTMENT OF CITRUS

ORANGE JUICE

"BACK TO NATURE"

COMM'L NO.: FCOJ 1330

LENGTH: 30 SECONDS

(MUSIC THROUGHOUT)
(SFX: WHISHHH)
GRANDDAUGHTER (VO): Grandma!

This back-to-nature stuff is work!

I'm gonna get some orange juice!

GRANDMOTHER: Mmmm... orange. One thing I don't grow myself--Don't have to--

Those Florida Orange Growers do it for me.

Orange Juice!

(MUSIC UP)

Can't beat natural things

for great taste!

GRANDDAUGHTER: Grandma, want some orange juice?

GRANDMOTHER: Thought you'd never ask!

ANNCR (VO): 100% pure orange juice

from Florida.

It isn't just for breakfast anymore.

Even if the problem is accurately diagnosed, the marketing manager may not know enough about its characteristics to develop decision alternatives. For example, even after the Florida Citrus Commission discovered the real problem, what should they have done to correct it? Would a new advertising strategy have increased breakfast consumption of orange juice? Did the price of orange juice need changing? Or, would it take something else entirely?

Many times, the manager can learn more about the characteristics of the problem being faced by conducting exploratory research. Knowing the characteristics can improve the manager's ability to make the right decision. For instance, exploratory research to learn why consumers drink, or do not drink, orange juice at breakfast would have put the Commission in a much better position to determine what strategy to follow.

Exploratory research can generate more questions than answers. That is, exploratory research often uncovers issues that need to be further researched using larger-scale descriptive or experimental research projects. Exploratory research might have helped the Florida Citrus Commission uncover reasons why people did, or did not, drink orange juice at breakfast. However, they still would have needed a larger descriptive study to determine the prevalence of each of these reasons.

Exploratory Research for Screening Alternatives

A manager faces a **decision problem** when two or more alternative courses of action exist and the manager is uncertain about which alternative to choose. Not all situations are decision problems. A situation in which only one course of action exists, even if its outcome will be bad, is not a decision problem because no choice, or decision, must be made. Likewise, even in the face of a multitude of options, a manager who is confident that one choice is best does not face a decision problem. However, most situations faced by a manager fit the requirements of a decision problem. These are the situations where research information is most valuable.

When faced with a decision problem, exploratory research can help the marketing manager remove some alternatives from further consideration. For example, exploratory research is often used to eliminate some of the possible names being considered for a new product or service. The intent is not to select the most appropriate name but to shorten the list quickly and inexpensively so that fewer options need to be researched in detail.

Applying Marketing Research 2.5

The management of American Express wanted to attract new cardmembers and increase the number of purchases that members made using their American Express card. They developed ten different strategic alternatives designed to reach this goal. They then conducted focus groups to reduce the number of alternatives to a few to be researched more carefully.

The results of the focus group research, as well as subsequent large-scale studies, confirmed that one alternative stood out from the rest. That alternative was a buyers' assurance program that extended manufacturer warranties on products purchased with an American Express card. When later implemented, the program increased both card usage and new memberships.[26] Since then, other credit card companies have copied this idea.

Exploratory Research for Discovering New Ideas

Sometimes managers are unable to come up with a solution to a problem situation. Perhaps the problem is that the brand dominates the sales in a category, such as Jello brand gelatin, and new uses need to be found for the brand to increase sales. Maybe the problem is finding the best way to communicate a product benefit, like the moistness of Duncan Hines cake mixes. Whatever the specific situation, managers often turn to exploratory research to generate new ideas that might solve the problem.

Applying Marketing Research 2.6

With rising admission prices and more consumers waiting until movies are released for home viewing on VCRs, attendance at movie theaters has declined. In addition, local competition among theaters is escalating. A box-office smash may be booked at more than one theater in a city at the same time. The combination of declining attendance and increased competition has theaters searching for ways to increase both theater patronage and loyalty. One theater chain, American Multi-Cinema, turned to exploratory research to seek solutions.

The results of focus groups commissioned by the management of American Multi-Cinema indicated that consumers were looking for additional value besides a movie when they attended a theater. Based upon one of the ideas uncovered in the focus groups, American Multi-Cinema management developed a promotion that awards points to customers for seeing movies at the theater in much the same way the airlines reward their customers through frequent flyer programs. The points are redeemable for admission to special screenings, for purchasing concession items, and for other prizes. American Multi-Cinema began testing this promotion in several cities in 1991 and, based on the test results, could expand it to all of their theaters.[27]

Exploratory research is ideally suited for discovering new ideas. Unlike descriptive or experimental studies, which tend to ask the same set of questions to each respondent, exploratory studies are more unstructured and flexible in nature. The unstructured format of a focus group or depth interview, for example, lends itself to the spontaneous generation of ideas. Specific comments and ideas generated can then be explored in depth.

International Issues

When a firm decides to market its products or services in another country, cultural differences can dictate a different marketing strategy than the one used in the domestic market. For instance, depending on the country, white, red, black, and purple are all colors used to signify mourning. Not realizing this, a brand's packaging or the dress of people used in advertising could send an improper message. Exploratory research can be critical for uncovering such cultural difference.

Very few, if any, differences exist in the way in which any exploratory research technique is conducted in other countries. However, cultural differences can impede the use of some techniques. In some Middle or Far Eastern countries, people are reluctant to express their true opinions in a group setting, making depth interviews preferable to focus groups. In Muslim cultures, women lead much more restricted lifestyles than do women in the United States. The idea of a Muslim female going alone to a research facility to be questioned about her attitudes and behavior would be totally unacceptable in that society. The appropriateness of projective techniques within a society should be carefully considered as well. People in some countries are much less adept at abstracting from verbal cues like those given in association techniques. In other societies, people have more difficulty with the visual cues often presented in completion techniques.

Summary

Exploratory research is designed to further understanding of a marketing problem or issue. Thus, it is defined by the purpose of the study, not the technique used to collect the data.

Five commonly used exploratory research techniques exist. These are experience studies, case studies, focus groups, depth interviews, and projective techniques. All of these techniques are designed to allow for an unstructured, uninhibited exploration of an issue.

Marketing researchers use exploratory research in three general research applications. They use exploratory research to help define a problem or situation; to eliminate alternatives quickly and inexpensively; and to discover new ideas that may deserve further research.

Key Terms

association technique

case study

completion technique

decision problem

depth interviews

experience survey

exploratory research

focus group

mini-group

personalization techniques

picture association technique

projective techniques

psychodrawing

qualitative research

role-playing techniques

sensitivity panels

triangle groups

word association technique

Nimslo's Use of Exploratory Research

Nimslo had high hopes for its new 3D photographic system, which had taken over ten years of intense research and development to perfect. After the prototype camera was developed, though, a lot of unanswered questions remained. How appealing would three-dimensional pictures be to consumers? Would these pictures appeal more to the serious photographer or to the person who takes but a few pictures a year? What problems might be encountered in getting trade acceptance for the product and the processing? Nimslo management turned to exploratory research to address these questions.

A series of focus groups were conducted with consumers. The focus groups explored how consumers would use the Nimslo camera, what quality they expected in 3D prints, and how much they thought the camera and photofinishing would cost. After these general discussions, participants' reactions to actual 3D prints were solicited, and participants were asked to handle the camera and comment on its ease of use.

The focus groups findings alerted Nimslo to two potential problems. Consumers expected to pay less for the camera than the price which Nimslo had been anticipating, suggesting the need for research to quantify the impact of various camera pricing strategies on sales. Also, consumers often held the camera vertically rather than horizontally when taking a picture. Held in this fashion, pictures would not be 3-D, so the company decided to include more warnings to this effect in the material packed with new cameras.

Depth interviews were conducted with camera shop owners to explore how the decision to stock various makes of cameras was made by these owners. Nimslo learned that the profits of camera specialty shop were being squeezed by price wars, and that these dealers would be receptive to new cameras that guaranteed a high margin. Such findings helped Nimslo develop a plan for encouraging dealers to carry their product. Additional depth interviews were conducted with photoprocessors to investigate incentives that might encourage prominent photofinishers to act as drop-off and pick-up sites for Nimslo photofinishing.

Review Questions

2.1 What is meant by exploratory research? How does exploratory research differ from qualitative research?

2.2 In what types of situations will exploratory research prove useful?

2.3 What is meant by a decision problem? How does exploratory research help a manager who is faced with a decision problem?

2.4 How might exploratory research help a manager screen alternatives? In what situations would exploratory research not be appropriate for screening alternatives?

2.5 What is meant by an experience survey? In what ways does an experience survey help a manager?

2.6 What is meant by a case study? How does a case study differ from an experience survey?

2.7 What is a focus group? What are some typical uses of focus group research? What advantages and disadvantages does focus group research have relative to other exploratory research techniques?

2.8 What are mini-groups? triangle groups? Why are mini-groups or triangle groups sometimes used instead of traditional focus groups?

2.9 What is a depth interview? What situations lend themselves to the use of depth interviews?

2.10 What is meant by a projective technique? Why are projective techniques used?

2.11 Explain association techniques, completion techniques, role playing, personalization, and psychodrawing.

Discussion Questions

2.1 Suppose, as a new manager of Ruffles brand potato chips, you wanted to find ways to increase consumption of your brand. How might exploratory research provide guidance? What type(s) of exploratory research might you use? Why?

2.2 What benefits does the focus-group setting provide? How does the group setting create drawbacks? How might these drawbacks be offset?

2.3 For each of the following situations, indicate the type(s) of exploratory research that might prove useful and why:

a. A company is considering the development of a new product that is unlike any that it now produces and that will be sold to a different target market than those for which its other products are manufactured.

b. A brand manager wishes get a better understanding of the image of his or her brand.

c. A company is searching for a name for a new product that it has developed.

d. A company selling computer hardware and software is interested in learning more about how firms select the vendor for new computer equipment purchases.

2.4 Why do the results from exploratory research usually provide insufficient information on which to make a decision?

2.5 *Ethical situation*: Advertising agencies routinely conduct focus groups with consumers in hopes of uncovering a catchy slogan or advertising theme that can be used for one of their clients' brands. Before allowing a person to participate, these agencies commonly require that a form be signed waiving all rights to anything said in the group. The waiver allows the agency to use any statement made in the focus group without fear of litigation from participants claiming that their ideas were stolen. Is it ethical to use ideas presented in a focus group without compensating the participants for them?

Chapter 2 Endnotes

---

1. Gerry Murphy, "Back to the Future in Consumer Research." *Advertising Age,* November 7, 1988, pp. 20, 24.

2. For further discussion of the distinctions between the two terms, see Rena Bartos, "Qualitative Research: What It Is and Where It Came From," *Journal of Advertising Research,* 26 (June/July 1986), RC3-RC6.

3. For a good discussion of the use of case studies for research, see Thomas V. Bonoma, "Case Research in Marketing: Opportunities, Problems, and a Process," *Journal of Marketing Research,* 22 (May 1985), pp. 199-208.

4. "Tylenol Restaging Was Made Possible by Firm's Solid Research and Consumer Trust," *Marketing News*, Oct. 28, 1983, pp. 1, 12.

5. Judann Dagnoli, "Brief Slump Expected for Sudafed," *Advertising Age*, March 18, 1991, p. 53.

6. Martin R. Lautman, "Focus Groups: Theory and Method," in Andrew A. Mitchell, ed., *Advances in Consumer Research,*Proceedings of the Association for Consumer Research, (1981), pp. 52-6.

the Association of Consumer Research, (1981), pp. 52-6.

7. For further discussion of the advantages of focus groups, see: John M. Hess, "Group Interviewing," in R.L. King, ed., *Marketing and the New Science of Planning*, Proceedings of the American Marketing Association, (1968),

pp. 193-6; William D. Wells, "Group Interviewing," in Robert Ferber, ed., *Handbook of Marketing Research*, New York: McGraw-Hill Book Co., (1974), pp. 2-133 -- 2-146; Lee Adler, "To Learn What's on the Consumer's Mind Try Some Focused

Group Interviews," *Sales & Marketing Management*, April 9, 1979, pp. 76-80; D.A. Miln, "Qualitative Research---A Summary of the Concepts Involved," *Journal of the Market Research Society*, 21, 2, (1979), pp. 107-24; and Martin R. Lautman, "Focus Groups: Theory and Method," in Andrew A. Mitchell, ed., *Advances in Consumer Research*, Proceedings of the Association of Consumer Research, (1981), pp. 52-6.

8. Cyndee Miller, "Videocart Spruces Up for New Tests," *Marketing News*, February 19, 1990, p. 19.

9. For a detailed discussion of focus groups, see William Co., (1974), pp. 2-133 -- 2-146.

10. Laurie Freeman, "Solve an Attitude Problem," *Advertising Age*, February 12, 1990, p. 45.

11. Mary Goodyear, "Qualitative Research in Developing Countries," *Journal of the Market Research Society*, 24 (April 1982), pp. 86-96.

12. These examples came from Gerry Murphy, "Back to the Future in Consumer Research," *Advertising Age*, November 7, 1988, pp. 20, 24.

13. Bernice Kanner, "Think Plastic: The Greening of

14. Peter Cooper, "The New Qualitative Technology," in Peter Sampson, ed., *Qualitative Research: The 'New', The 'Old' and A Question Mark*, E.S.O.M.A.R. Marketing Research Monograph Series, no. 2, (1987), pp. 7-25.

15. W. Schlakman, "A Discussion of the Use of Sensitivity Panels in Market Research," *Journal of the Market Research Society*, 26, 3, (1984), pp. 191-208.

16. For further discussion of the advantages of depth interviews, see D.A. Miln, "Qualitative Research---A Summary of the Concepts Involved," *Journal of the Market Research Society*, 21, 2, (1979), pp. 107-24.

17. Martin R. Lautman, "Focus Groups: Theory and Method," in Andrew A. Mitchell, ed., *Advances in Consumer Research*, Proceedings of the Association for Consumer Research, (1981), pp. 52-56; Edward F. Fern, "The Use of Focus Groups for Idea Generation: The Effects of Group Size, Acquaintanceship, and Moderator on Response Quantity and Quality," *Journal of Marketing Research*, 19 (February 1982), pp. 1-13; and Edward F. Fern, "Focus Groups: A Review of Some Contradictory Evidence, Implications, and Suggestions for Future Research," in Richard P. Bagozzi and Alice M. Tybout, eds., *Advances in Consumer Research*, Proceedings of the Association for Consumer Research, (1982) pp. 121-126.

18. A. M. Oppenheim, *Questionnaire Design and Attitude Measurement*, London: Heinemann, (1966).

19. Mason Haire, "Projective Techniques in Marketing Research," *Journal of Marketing*, 14 (April 1950), pp. 649-656.

20. See Harold H. Kassarjian, "Projective Methods," in Robert Ferber, ed., *Handbook of Marketing Research*, New York: McGraw-Hill Book Company, (1974), pp. 3-85 -- 3-100 for a detailed discussion of projective techniques.

21. Mason Haire, "Projective Techniques in Marketing Research," *Journal of Marketing*, 14 (April 1950), 649-56.

22. For further discussion of projective techniques, see

Elsevier Science Publishing Company, Inc., (1986), 29-56.

23. Edward J. Vatza, "Get Accurate Views from Consumers by Giving Them the VIP Treatment," *Marketing News*, January 2, 1989, 34.

24. Philip May, "Passing the Test: Don't Misdirect Your Research Efforts," *Marketing News*, April 16, 1990, p. 12.

25. Judann Dagnoli, "Breakfast Push Expected for OJ," *Advertising Age*, October 3, 1988, p. 32.

26. Jeffrey A. Trachtenberg, "Listening, the Old-Fashioned Way," *Forbes*, October 5, 1987, pp. 202-4.

27. March Magiera, "Movie Chains Test Brand-Building," *Advertising Age*, March 4, 1991, p. 43.

Chapter 3

Experimental Research

Learning Objectives:

After reading this chapter you will:

- understand the concept of cause and effect and how experimental research is used to identify such relationships in a marketing context.
- be able to define and discuss the various types of variables involved in an experiment.
- be aware of the different pitfalls associated with experimental research and ways to avoid them.
- understand the concepts of interaction and experimental validity.

In the late 1960s, much of the soft drink volume moved from bottles to the familiar cans of today. As cans gained in popularity, the need for a multi-can package emerged. The Coca-Cola Company considered three alternative forms: shrink-wrapping a six-pack with a plastic film, a cardboard wrapper, and a "hi-cone," a small plastic configuration containing six rings to fit around the tops of the cans. The costs of the three alternatives were quite different. The cardboard wrapper was by far the most costly. On a per case basis, this option was about 17¢ and 13¢ more expensive than the hi-cone and shrink-wrap options, respectively.

In order to assess the sales impact of the three options, an experiment was conducted in forty-eight supermarkets, sixteen in each of three cities. Within each city, four stores were randomly assigned to each of four conditions— the three secondary packaging options just discussed and a fourth, loose cans which was the status quo and thus, served as a control or benchmark in the study.

The stores assigned to each condition offered six-packs packaged in the prescribed manner. Soft drink sales in each store were expressed as sales per thousand store transactions over the test period. Thus, differences in total store sales was eliminated as a potential factor that might cause differences in the sales of Coca-Cola cans observed across the stores in the study. The test period lasted for six weeks. At the conclusion of the test, the numbers of cans of Coca-Cola sold per thousand transactions for the individual stores were then averaged across the twelve stores in each of the four groups. The average results for each group was then divided by the average for the loose can condition, and the result was then multiplied by 100 to produce an index relating sales in each group to sales in the status quo group. The index for the status quo or control condition was, of course, 100. The four resulting indices were:

Shrink wrap	131
Cardboard	134

Hi-cone	155
Loose cans	100

The results of the experiment showed, not unexpectedly, that offering six-packs as opposed to only loose cans increased sales. However, the results also indicated that the least expensive form of six-pack packaging, the hi-cone, produced the largest increase in sales relative to loose cans. This option raised sales about 50% versus the control, while the other two options raised sales 30% to 35%. The hi-cone was clearly the most profitable option.

The Coca-Cola Company adopted the hi-cone secondary packaging and the industry soon followed suit. Now, nearly 30 years later, the same hi-cone six-pack configuration is still widely used.

Cause and Effect

Exploratory research can help marketers define problems by putting boundaries on the problem and limiting the number of action alternatives. If a marketing manager whose brand of potato chips is not selling well learns from exploratory research that a taste problem exists, then he or she also knows that the solution to the problem will involve changing the product's ingredients and not its price, its packaging, or its advertising. Now, however, the marketing manager needs to determine *how* to improve the taste.

Experimental or causal research can help provide answers for the manager because the objective of experimental or causal research is to uncover cause-and-effect relationships. Events or factors have a **cause-and- effect relationship** if one (the effect) is the direct result of the other (the cause). For instance, in our potato chip example, the product development group might conduct an experiment by manufacturing different batches of potato chips varying only the type of cooking oil used. Separate groups of consumers could be asked to taste chips from the respective batches, including one batch made with the current oil, and rate the taste. Differences in the average ratings given to the tastes of the chips from the respective batches would be an effect caused by changing the cooking oil. In fact, one of the oils might result in a chip that is rated better on average than the current product, providing a way to improve the taste of the potato chip.

Most of us are very familiar with the use of experimental research to determine cause-and-effect relationships from our high school and college science courses. Laboratory sessions in which experiments are conducted typically accompany such courses. Often, the objective of these experiments is to demonstrate cause-and- effect relationships. For example, a piece of iron, nonmagnetic itself, can be converted into a powerful magnet by wrapping it with wire and passing electricity through the wire. The cause is the electrical current, and the effect is the magnetism produced.

Marketing managers can use experimental research to quantify the impact of various marketing activities on sales. In the opening vignette to this chapter, Coca-Cola management used a marketing experiment to assess how various types of six-pack packaging would affect sales. They quantified the impact of offering six-packs as opposed to just loose cans, and determined which form of packaging increased sales the most. As an added bonus, the option, hi-cone packing, which increased sales the most was also the least expensive option.

Correlations or associations should not be confused with cause-and-effect relationships. Applying Marketing Research 3.1 and 3.2 demonstrate that observed correlation or association may indeed not be indicative of cause and effect.[1]

Applying Marketing Research 3.1

In reviewing sales and attendance data, themanagement of a major-league baseball stadium notices that peanut sales and the number of fans requiring medical attention are positively related. On days when peanut sales are relatively high, the number of fans who visit first-aid centers in the stadium is also relatively high. On days when peanut sales are relatively low, the number of fans who require first aid is also relatively low. Should the stadium management remove peanuts from the concession stands? Of course not! The observed phenomenon is referred to as spurious correlation and is not a cause-and-effect relationship. Eating peanuts does not generally cause people to require medical attention. The two appear to be related because both are driven by a third factor -- attendance. Attendance is the real causal factor behind both peanut sales and the number of fans visiting first-aid centers.

Applying Marketing Research 3.2

A young marketing research analyst at a public utility supplying electrical power is part of a company team responsible for

organizing an appeal to the public utility commission for a residential rate increase. The analyst examines historical data pertaining to the company's residential rates and the federally mandated hourly

minimum wage requirement and notices a relationship -- both have increased steadily over time. The analyst thus argues that the company's residential rate increases over time have been caused by increases in the required hourly minimum wage. The analyst further argues that because the required minimum hourly wage has recently been increased, the company's proposed residential rate increase is justified.

Is such a conclusion valid? While the company's residential rate policy may indeed be driven by the minimum hourly wage, there are flaws in the argument presented by the marketing research analyst. Both the company's residential rate and the hourly minimum wage have risen because of inflation.

The observed relationship may again simply be a spurious correlation.

Because of spurious correlations, it is dangerous to look at historical data, observe an apparent relationship, and attempt to draw conclusions regarding cause and effect. The tendency for two factors to both be above or below average at the same time (positive correlation) or to move in opposite directions (negative correlation) may be due to a third, unobserved factor, which is driving both measured variables.[2] Only carefully designed experiments allow researchers truly to uncover cause-and-effect relationships.

Marketing research experiments are becoming commonplace. Confronted with a proposed experimental project or with the results of an experiment already conducted, the marketing manager must understand the terminology and principles underlying experimental research to be able to communicate effectively with marketing research personnel and to evaluate the adequacy of the experiment. The rest of this chapter introduces experimental principles and commonly used terms.

Experimental Variables

Any experiment, including a marketing experiment, involves a number of factors or variables that can affect the results (see Exhibit 3.1). **Independent variables** are those that the experimenter deliberately manipulates in attempting to establish cause-and-effect relationships. The **dependent variable** is the factor thought to be affected by the independent variable(s). Cause-and-effect relationships are indicated when changes (manipulations) in the independent variable(s) produce changes in the dependent variable.

In the Coca-Cola six-pack example discussed in the opening vignette to this chapter, the independent variable is the store condition in terms of six-pack packaging, and the dependent variable is sales of Coca-Cola cans. The increases in sales of Coca-Cola cans relative to the status quo condition are attributed to the various forms of six-pack offerings.

External variables are factors that are not manipulated in the experiment but that could affect the dependent variable. The researcher attempts to hold these external factors constant in the experiment to prevent them from causing changes in the dependent variable that would confuse the interpretation of the results. If the relevant external variables cannot be held constant, then they must be accounted for in the design of the experiment and the analysis of results. A control or control group, which we discuss later in this chapter, serves this purpose.

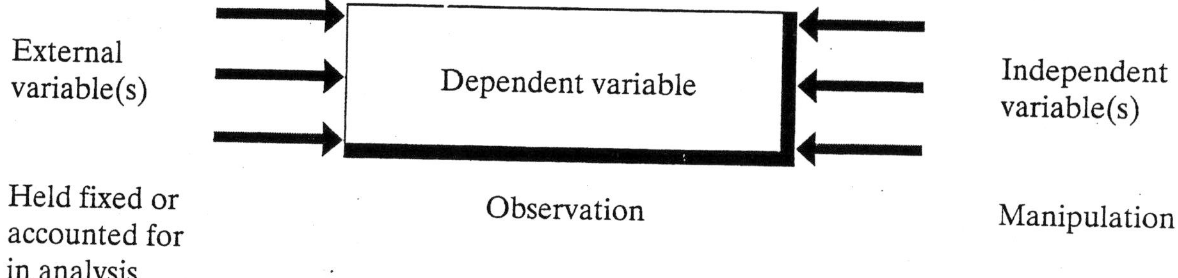

Exhibit 3.1 Experimental Variables

The following examples illustrate the independent, dependent, and external variables in an experiment.

Applying Marketing Research 3.3

In-store tests are frequently used by managers of brands like Pringles to determine how the display of the brand at the end of a supermarket aisle affects sales. Suppose that a set of twenty supermarkets in a large geographic region are randomly selected from among those that carry Pringles potato chips. The set of twenty stores is randomly divided into two groups of ten each. In one group, an in-store end-of-aisle display is set up for a three-week period. The other group is not changed at all, *i.e.*, it is business as usual.

In this experiment, the independent variable is the presence or absence of an end-of-aisle display, and the dependent variable is unit sales of Pringle's during the test period. The average sales of Pringle's in the two groups of stores are compared, and any statistically significant difference in average sales is attributed to the display. Furthermore, the results of this experiment allow marketing management to quantify any increase attributable to an end-of-aisle display. In the hypothetical results shown below, the use of an end-of-aisle display has increased average sales of Pringle's by 20 percent relative to typical store conditions.

Average Sales (in cases)	
End-of-Aisle Display	No Display
48.0	40.0

Competitive promotion is one external variable that can affect sales. However, any competitive potato chip promotions should affect all stores equally, thus preventing such activity from distorting the results.

Applying Marketing Research 3.4

Companies like Lever Bros., Inc., are continually introducing new products. Suppose that before introducing a new liquid detergent, Lever Bros. must decide among three options for the final package design. Three separate samples of two hundred target-market consumers each are recruited in a shopping mall, exposed to the product concept, and shown the product.

However, each sample sees one of the three alternative package designs. The participants are asked to describe their interest in the new product, using a number from 1 to 10, where 1 represents "not at all interested," and 10 represents "extremely interested." Any statistically significant differences in average interest across the three groups are attributed to the different package designs.

For the hypothetical results described below, package design B clearly generates more interest than either of the other two package designs.

Package Design	Average Purchase Interest
A	6.8
B	8.6
C	5.9

The independent variable in the experiment is the package design, and the dependent variable is interest. The manner in which the concept is presented is an external variable that could affect the level of interest. Hence, great care is taken to ensure that the concept descriptions are exactly the same except for package design, and the same procedures are followed for all three groups. The results of this experiment provide marketing management with a clear understanding of which package design generates the most consumer interest in the new liquid detergent.

In experimental research, different conditions created by varying the independent variable are often referred to as **experimental treatments**. Table 3.1 summarizes what constitutes the experimental treatments and the dependent variable, as well as potential external variables for Applying Marketing Research 3.3 and 3.4 just discussed.

	External Variables	Dependent Variable	Experimental Treatments
Example 3.3	Store size Store clientele Out-of-stocks Competitive promotional activity	Store sales of Pringles	End-of-aisle display No display (normal conditions)
Example 3.4	Consumer demographics such as age and income Manner in which new concept is presented Most recent similar product used	Interest in new liquid detergent	Package design A Package design B Package design C

Table 3.1 Summary of treatments, dependent variables, and potential external variables for Applying Marketing Research 3.3 and 3.4.

Avoiding Experimental Research Pitfalls

Experimental error introduces uncertainty regarding whether observed effects were really caused by the manipulation of the independent variable. Like all experiments, marketing experiments are subject to this possible problem. Decisions regarding when variables are measured, the measurement instruments used, the way the sample is selected, and the general nature of the experiment can be sources of such error. Before describing specific types of experimental errors that can occur and discussing associated means of their prevention in detail, we will briefly review techniques for avoiding experimental error in general.

Methods of Avoiding Experimental Error

Experiments are often conducted to assess the impact of a marketing action on sales, such as conducting a promotion for a brand. Such experiments are useless unless information is available regarding what would happen without the marketing action. For example, distributing discount coupons for Skippy Peanut Butter in selected stores and measuring sales of the brand for a short period of time after the coupon distribution is meaningless unless information exists regarding what Skippy sales would be in the same stores without the coupon. A reference point or benchmark with which to compare the value of the dependent variable obtained from manipulating the independent variables must be available. Only then can judgments be made regarding whether the independent variable had an impact on the dependent variable and if so, how much.

A **control** is an experimental treatment typically involving no manipulation of the independent variable, which is often included in an experiment to provide the necessary benchmark or point of comparison. In other words, normal conditions prevail for the control. In Applying Marketing Research 3.3, sales were monitored in ten stores in which no end-of-aisle display was used to provide a point of reference (control) for sales in the ten stores in which end-of-aisle displays were set up. The ten stores in which the display was used comprise the "test" group.

As the following example illustrates, the control can be an experimental treatment that involves a change from the normal conditions. However, the control treatment is structured in such a way that it still provides a point of reference or benchmark in the experiment.

Applying Marketing Research 3.5

Randomly selected shoppers entering a supermarket are given discount coupons for selected brands and are told that the coupons can only be redeemed during the current visit to the store. Two coupon books are used. These are identical, except that a coupon for one brand, for instance Skippy Peanut Butter, appears in one book and not in the other. Those shoppers whose telephone number ends in an even digit are given the coupon book containing a coupon for Skippy and comprise the test group. Those whose telephone number ends in an odd digit are given the other book, which does not contain a coupon for Skippy. These shoppers comprise a control group, comparable to and about equal in size to the test group. Purchases of Skippy for both groups are monitored at check-out. If sales of Skippy are higher in the test group than in the control group, the difference is attributed to the coupon.

Without the control group, the experimenter does not know whether or not Skippy's sales are above what they would have been without a coupon. Contrasting the results of the control group with those of a test group allows the experimenter to evaluate the Skippy coupon's impact on sales.

The use of a control serving as a reference point or benchmark is often crucial in experimental research.[3] As noted earlier, external factors can also affect the dependent variable in an experiment. Therefore the control must be chosen so that these external factors are operating in exactly the same manner for the control condition as for the test condition.[4] Otherwise, differences observed in the dependent variable could be the result of differences in these external factors, and incorrect conclusions regarding causal relationships could result. For instance, if shoppers in another store had been randomly selected for a control group in Applying Marketing Research 3.5, differences in the sizes of the two stores as well as differences in their customers could cause a difference in the observed sales of Skippy Peanut Butter between the two stores. Selecting both the test and control groups of shoppers from the same store eliminates these, as well as other, possible external factors from being the reason for an observed difference in sales because the external factors have the same impact on both groups. Hence, differences in the sales of Skippy between groups can be attributed to differences in the experimental treatments, *i.e.*, whether or not a Skippy coupon was included.

The objects or people comprising the groups in an experiment are known as **experimental units**. The experimental units in Applying Marketing Research 3.5 are individual shoppers, and in Applying Marketing Research 3.3 they are stores. If the composition of the experimental groups differs, these dissimilarities could be the reason for differences among treatment groups noted in the dependent variable.

Randomization involves using random chance to assign the individual experimental units to the groups. This prevents biasing the experiment due to differences in the composition of the experimental groups. In Applying Marketing Research 3.5, the shoppers who received the coupon books were randomly chosen from all the shoppers, and those receiving Skippy coupons were also randomly selected from the shoppers chosen to participate in the experiment. The random assignment to groups was accomplished by using the last digit of the telephone number (even or odd) to determine whether a coupon for Skippy was included in the coupon book. Assigning shoppers to groups in this way provides assurance that the groups are similar in composition.

Measurement timing refers to when measurements are taken in an experiment. This should be scheduled to avoid including temporary or superficial effects in the measurement of the dependent variable. For instance, an individual may drive more carefully immediately after participating in a safe-driving clinic. However, continued safe-driving behavior for an extended period of time would be required to establish the actual effectiveness of the clinic. Observed differences in the dependent variable can be the result of such short-term effects, and thus lead to incorrect conclusions about the impact of the manipulation of the independent variable. By carefully planning when to measure the dependent variable, the experimenter can avoid this error. We will discuss the inclusion of a control, randomization, and measurement timing further in the context of avoiding the specific types of experimental errors discussed in the next section.

Common Experimental Errors

We next define the common types of experimental errors, and discuss how each can be avoided. Table 3.2 provides a summary of this information.

Experimental Error	Problem	Solution
Premeasurement	Premeasurement itself induces changes	Control group
Instrumentation	Changes in measurement device	Control group
Maturation	Natural development or change occurring over the experimental period	Control group
History	Introduction of unexpected event or phenomenon that produces change	Control group
Sample Selection	Bias introduced by method of assigning participants to experimental groups	Randomization
Measurement Timing	Measurement distorted by short-term effects	Timing
Mortality	Differences in completion rates across experimental groups	Controlling for all external variables

Table 3.2 Methods of avoiding experimental error.

Premeasurement Error

Some experiments involve taking an initial measurement of the dependent variable prior to the manipulation of the independent variable. This initial measurement provides a benchmark to which a subsequent measurement of the same variable is compared to assess the impact of the experimental treatment. If the process of taking the first measurement affects the subsequent measurement, then the subsequent measure is affected by two things--the treatment and the premeasurement. **Premeasurement error** refers to confusion between the effect of the treatment and the effect of the premeasurement.

A control group permits the isolation of the effect due to manipulating the independent variable. For the control condition, the initial measurement and subsequent measurements are taken in a manner identical to the other experimental conditions. Therefore, any premeasurement effect is captured in the difference between initial and subsequent measurements in the control condition. Comparing the differences observed in the control condition to those observed in the other experimental conditions allows the experimenter to isolate the effect of the manipulated independent variable. Applying Marketing Research 3.6 demonstrates how premeasurement error can occur and how the use of a control group eliminates the problem.

Applying Marketing Research 3.6

A manufacturer of a relatively new candy bar conducts a survey among randomly selected high school students at several designated schools. The participants are shown print ads for various candy bars, including the relatively new one, and are asked questions regarding trial, repurchase and attitudes for the various brands. The survey itself generates interest in the new brand among participants, many of whom try the brand, like it, and become regular buyers.

The manufacturer launches a local radio and outdoor campaign to promote the new brand shortly after the survey is conducted. A second survey is conducted among the same high school students two months later when the promotional campaign ends. The second survey reveals increased trial and repurchasing of the new candy, as well as improved attitudes toward the brand.

This experiment is subject to premeasurement error. The initial survey stimulated interest in the new brand and one cannot separate the effect of the promotional campaign from the effect of the initial survey. A control group, similar in composition, who are not exposed to the campaign would be required to isolate one effect from the other. Increases in trial and repurchase rates, and attitudes toward the brand within the control group would be attributable to the survey itself. Increases above these levels observed within the group also exposed to the promotional campaign would be attributable to the campaign.

Even when there is no risk of premeasurement error, the use of a premeasure as a point of reference to evaluate experimental results can be risky. For instance, in Applying Marketing Research 3.5, a premeasurement of Skippy Peanut Butter sales in the same store for a comparable period of time in which no store coupons were distributed might serve as a benchmark instead of the control group of shoppers who receive all but the Skippy coupon.

No risk of premeasurement error exists, but we can't be sure that store conditions are exactly the same for the two periods of time for which sales of Skippy Peanut Butter are measured. A difference between the two sales measurements may not be due to the Skippy coupon but could be caused by another factor such as a competitive promotion run during one of the periods. Other potential errors, namely maturation, history, and instrumentation, which are discussed next, can also interfere with the use of a premeasurement as the point of reference.

Maturation

Maturation error occurs in experiments conducted over a period of time when there is gradual development or change in the dependent variable that is not caused by the independent variable. Differences in measurements obtained at the beginning and end of the study may be due to these developments and changes, *i.e.*, maturation, as well as to any manipulation of an independent variable. Once again, the use of a control, for which the same maturation is anticipated, eliminates the possibility of maturation error. Comparisons of the changes observed in the control group with those observed for other experimental treatments are

made at the end of the study and differences can be attributed to the variable manipulated.

Applying Marketing Research 3.7

Many companies use an internal sales training seminar for all new sales people. Suppose that the sales training consists of a two-week

program and is conducted after employees have spent six months with the company. Prior to the training, a measurement of sales effectiveness is made, and one year after having attended the sales training program, another measurement of sales effectiveness is made. Any increase in sales effectiveness is attributed to the two-week sales training seminar. It is reasonable to expect that the new salespeople will improve their sales skills naturally over a one-year period, so some of the increased effectiveness observed in the experiment is due to natural growth. The use of a control group, whose sales effectiveness is measured at the same times as the treatment group, but who do not have the benefit of the two-week sales training program, would provide the necessary reference point. The control group must of course be comparable in composition to the test group. Any increased effectiveness in the control group would be attributed to natural growth, and a difference between the changes in effectiveness observed in the test group and the control group would be attributed to the sales training program.

History Error

During the course of an experiment, an unexpected event can occur that affects the dependent variable being measured. **History error** refers to confusion between effects produced by unexpected events that occur during the experiment and the manipulation of the independent variable. History error differs from maturation error in that the latter refers to gradual change in the dependent variable over time rather than change due to a single event. Once again, the use of a control allows the experimenter to isolate the effect of the manipulation of the independent variable from effects produced by unexpected events.

Applying Marketing Research 3.8

Many companies use pre- and postmeasurements of consumer awareness to determine the impact of advertising campaigns. For example, suppose Mitsubishi Motors Corporation began testing the impact of a new advertising campaign in selected markets just before 29 female employees at the Normal, Illinois factory filed a sexual harassment lawsuit against the company. An initial measure of awareness was obtained by a telephone survey conducted among randomly selected consumers in the markets of interest prior to the initiation of the campaign. A similar survey was to be conducted one year after launching the new campaign. Any change in awareness of Mitsubishi was to be attributed to the new campaign.

The female plaintiffs charged that male co-workers routinely groped and grabbed at them.[5] Some of the women charged that they had to agree to sexual favors to win jobs. The case received great publicity and triggered an investigation by the U.S. Equal Opportunity Commission which eventually filed a second harassment suit on behalf of 280 female employees. The extensive negative publicity and media attention received by Mitsubishi raised consumer awareness of the company.

It would be impossible to determine how much the sexual harassment publicity affected awareness of Mitsubishi in the follow-up survey conducted to measure the impact of the new advertising campaign. Hence, the results would be basically uninterpretable. Increased awareness might easily be dismissed as being attributable to the publicity instead of the new advertising campaign, unless control markets, where no advertising change took place, were included in the experiment. For these control markets, awareness measures would be obtained in exactly the same manner and at the same time as the awareness measures obtained in the markets where the new advertising campaign was used. The impact of the new advertising campaign would be captured by any difference between the changes of awareness observed in the control and test markets.

Instrumentation Error

Instrumentation error can be introduced if the measurement devices or procedures are changed during the experiment. For example, in an experiment involving pre- and postmeasurements of the same variable, the people actually performing the two sets of measurements might not be the same, thus introducing a potential source of difference between the two sets of results. Once again, the use of a control allows for the isolation of the effect of the change in the independent variable from potential external effects such as instrumentation.

Applying Marketing Research 3.9

A company conducted an experiment to measure the effectiveness of an advertising campaign. The campaign was run in several markets. Effectiveness was measured by top-of-mind awareness obtained by telephone surveys conducted before and after the campaign, a span of six months. However, the market research firm that conducted the presurvey was unable to conduct the postsurvey, and another marketing research firm was hired to conduct the second phase of the research. Both the interviewers and some of the study procedures were different between the pre- and the postsurveys. These changes could, at least in part, cause a change in the top-of-mind awareness measure.

A control--market(s) in which no change in advertising takes place -- would normally be included in such an experiment to prevent external variables such as those associated with history error from confusing the results. The same control would also provide a means of protecting against unexpected instrumentation changes. Comparing changes in awareness observed in the control market(s) to those observed in the markets where the new advertising was used allows the experimenter to isolate the effect of the new advertising campaign from other potential effects.

We have discussed premeasurement, maturation, history, and instrumentation experimental errors. In each case, the use of a control group was noted as the preventative method. We next discuss some experimental errors that can occur even when a control group is used.

Sample Selection Error

Sample selection error occurs when bias is introduced into an experiment due to the way experimental units are assigned to experimental groups. A way to avoid this sample selection error is to assign experimental units randomly to the experimental groups. The random assignment reduces the potential for inequities in the group compositions.

Applying Marketing Research 3.10

In the hypothetical Skippy Peanut Butter experiment discussed in Applying Marketing Research 3.5, suppose coupon books containing a coupon for Skippy are distributed during the day, and books not containing a coupon for Skippy are distributed at night. A potential bias has been introduced in the experiment since daytime shoppers are more likely to be homemakers, and thus are more likely to have young children, than are night or evening shoppers. Therefore, the test group shoppers, those receiving the Skippy coupons, may be more prone to purchase peanut butter than their counterparts in the control group, those not receiving a Skippy coupon. The assignment of shoppers to groups has created a possible advantage (bias) for the test group. By randomly assigning shoppers to the two groups according to the last digit of each participant's telephone number as described earlier, this potential bias is eliminated.

Measurement Timing Error

Measurement timing error occurs if changes in the dependent variable are due to when measurements are taken rather than the manipulation of the independent variable. Applying Marketing Research 3.11 demonstrates this phenomenon.

Applying Marketing Research 3.11

A major Midwestern supermarket chain wants to determine whether proposed store renovations will increase sales. The changes include larger, more colorful, aisle directories, attaching store directories to the shopping carts, and changing the lighting in the store. Sales are measured for a two-week period in a sample of the chain's supermarkets, the changes are made, and sales are again measured in these same stores for the two-week period immediately following the alterations. A substantial increase in sales is observed.

Customers may see changes in the store environment as evidence that the company "cares" for its customers. This is likely to at least temporarily affect customers' shopping behavior regardless of whether the changes really make shopping more convenient and a more pleasant experience than before.[6] Further, the novelty of the store environment might attract new customers, at least for a while. The net result may be that the observed immediate sales increase is a short-term effect. More time should elapse before the second measurement of sales to allow the novelty effect to gradually disappear and warm customer feelings to possibly fade away. (In this revised experiment, a control group of supermarkets would also be included to control for possible maturation error and history error as discussed earlier.)

Mortality Error

Experiments conducted with the same subjects over an extended period of time, called longitudinal studies, are especially prone to mortality or attrition, *i.e.*, subjects dropping out of the study. If the completion rates among experimental treatment groups differ, there may be basic differences in the composition of the groups of participants completing the experiment. **Mortality error** occurs when differences in the compositions of the groups completing the study produce differences in the dependent variable across the experimental groups. If differences in attrition rates occur, the reason for these differences must be determined, and a decision must be made regarding whether the experimental results are confounded by mortality error.

Applying Marketing Research 3.12

A two-year study is conducted among children to determine the decay prevention ability of a chemical planned to be the basis for a new toothpaste product. The hope is to be able to market the product based on a claim of superiority in preventing tooth decay among children. A test group of children is asked to brush twice daily with toothpaste containing the chemical under examination. The control group is also given toothpaste, the current leading anticavity children's brand, and is also requested to brush twice daily. Both toothpastes are packaged identically using plain white tubes and cartons. Incidence of decay is measured for each group periodically over a two-year period. Comparison of the total number of cavities between the two groups is the basis for determining whether the toothpaste with the new chemical is more effective than the leading brand.

In any such study, there is mortality. Subjects are lost for various reasons--they move, they become ill, they lose interest, and so forth. Suppose in this experiment, an attrition rate of twenty percent is observed in the test group, and an attrition rate of only five percent is observed in the control group. Suppose the difference in completion rates is due to an unpleasant aftertaste produced by the new anticavity chemical, which causes more children to drop out of the test group; thus, those remaining in that group are generally more conscientious and dedicated than those remaining in the control group because test group subjects who complete the study had to tolerate the unpleasant aftertaste for an extended period of time. This more dedicated test group may have adhered to the test protocol, namely brushing their teeth twice a day, more than the control group. Hence, any difference in the number of cavities observed between the two groups can be due to factors other than the chemical itself.

Since differences in attrition rates cannot be observed until the end of the study, not much can be done to salvage the experiment if it is found that the compositions of the final groups differ. For example, if it is discovered after the study is completed that a taste problem exists for the test toothpaste, the damage has been done. The taste problem should have been detected and corrected before the study began.

Methods for Reducing Random Error

As is illustrated in Exhibit 3.2, an experiment is subject to two general types of error: experimental error and random error. Control groups, random assignment of experimental units to groups, and the appropriate timing of measurements are used to prevent experimental errors. In other words, these techniques allow the experimenter to isolate and measure the effect of the experimental manipulation. In many experiments, results are aggregated across the individuals comprising the experimental groups, and the resulting averages are compared. The calculated averages are sample means obtained from individual data points, which may vary considerably and are thus themselves subject to random error.

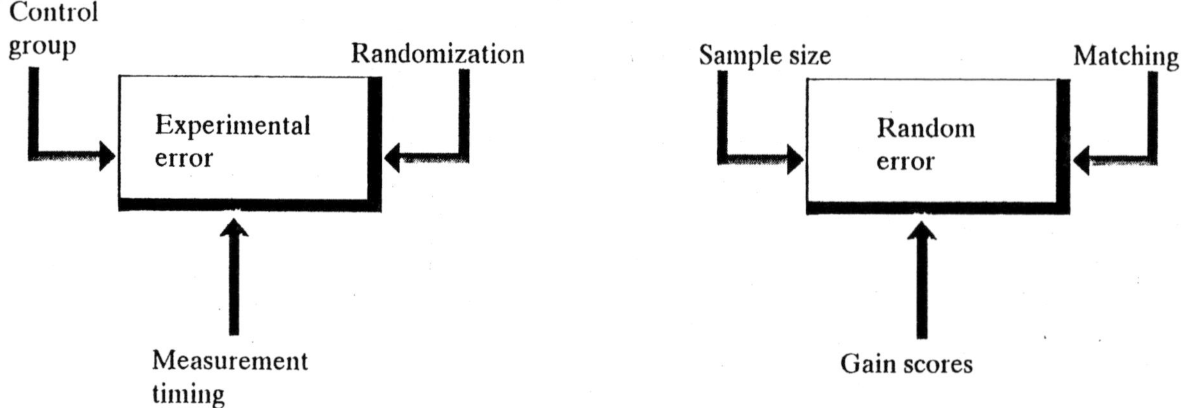

Exhibit 3.2

Designing the Experiment.

The amount of variation in the individual results (variance) and the size of the experimental groups (sample sizes) are key to determining the amount that two sample means must differ by to conclude that the difference is statistically significant (*i.e.*, larger than can be attributed to random error). This required difference is directly proportional to the amount of variance in the individual results and is inversely proportional to the sample sizes. The experimenter can choose sample sizes large enough to reduce the random errors associated with group sample means to desired levels and thereby guarantee that an observed difference in group means of a given magnitude will be statistically significant.

However, large sample sizes can be quite expensive and can make an experiment difficult to manage. The use of matching[7] and gain scores are alternative ways to reduce the amount of variance in experimental data. Used separately or in combination, these techniques can provide a substantial reduction in the amount of variation in the basic data, resulting in an increased sensitivity for detecting causal relationships. That is, the impact of the experimental manipulation does not need to be as great as would be required otherwise to be statistically significant.

Matching

Identical twins provide ideal pairs of matched subjects for many psychological experiments. One twin is randomly assigned to a test group while the other is assigned to a control group. An experimental manipulation is performed, and results are compared between the twins. Since, the twins are identical, any difference observed after the manipulation is attributed to the experiment. The average difference across pairs is usually calculated as the measure of the effect of the experimental manipulation. There could be dramatic differences across sets of twins, but these differences are neutralized by examining each pair of twins individually.

The rationale for using identical twins in psychology experiments applies to marketing experiments. **Matching** consists of organizing the experimental units into sets in such a way that there is consistency with respect to specified characteristics within each set. Then, one subject or experimental unit from each set is assigned to each experimental group (including the control). Differences within each set of experimental units are aggregated to measure the experimental effect(s). The following example demonstrates how large random error can be troublesome, and the subsequent discussion shows how matching can reduce this random error.

Applying Marketing Research 3.13

Suppose a company contracts a research supplier to test the effectiveness of a supermarket end-of-aisle display for its toothpaste. The supplier randomly selects ten supermarkets in a given area and randomly assigns five of the ten to a test group (stores that receive the end-of-aisle display), and the remaining five stores to a control group (stores for which no display is used). Unit sales (in cases) of the toothpaste are monitored for all ten stores during the two weeks in which the display appears. The results are shown below:

Unit Sales of Toothpaste (in cases)

Test Group (End-of-Aisle Display)	Control Group (No Display)
14	15
18	12
33	8

	12	10
	18	29
Average	19	15
Sample Variance	68	70

Note that the sample variances of store sales for the panels are 68 and 70. Because of this large variation in sales across stores, the conclusion is that observed difference in average sales between the two panels could very we well have been caused by chance alone. (The difference between the two means is not statistically significant at a reasonable risk level, as discussed in Chapter 9.) The large store-to-store differences (variance)in sales within the two groups makes it difficult to identify a significant experimental effect.

Suppose that, before the test, the random sample of ten stores in the above example was organized into five pairs based on all-commodity volume (ACV), an indicator of store size based on retail sales. That is, stores were matched on ACV so that the two stores comprising each pair were comparable in size. Next, one store from each pair was randomly chosen to receive the end-of-aisle display, while the other served as a control. Sales in the ten stores were then monitored during the two-week test period, as described

earlier. It is conceivable that the matching could have led to the results shown in Table 3.3.

By matching, the emphasis shifts to measuring the difference in sales within each pair instead of the difference in group averages. Note that the same sales occur in each group as was shown in Applying Marketing Research 3.13, but the sample variance of the differences is 6.0, which is much smaller than the sample variances obtained when no matching was performed. Matching has effectively eliminated store-to-store variance caused by differences in overall size or sales volume and results in a more sensitive test. The statistical question becomes whether or not the average difference is significantly greater than zero. The statistical test, based on the observed average difference and the corresponding sample variance, leads to the conclusion that the end-of-aisle display improves sales on average. (The average difference is statistically significant at a very low risk level, as discussed in Chapter 9.)

Pair	Display	No Display	Difference
1	14	12	2
2	18	15	2
3	18	10	8
4	33	29	4
5	12	8	4
		Average	4.0
		Sample Variance	6.0

Table 3.3 Unit Sales of Toothpaste (in cases)

Gain Scores

Using the difference between an initial and a posttreatment measurement, known as a **gain score,**[8] as the dependent variable is another way of eliminating the variance introduced by basic differences in the dependent variable among experimental units. Gain scores eliminate variance due to differences in starting conditions among the experimental units themselves. For example, in an experiment to measure the effectiveness of an appetite-suppressant diet product, initial weights would be obtained for subjects in the test group and the control group. Weights of the subjects at the end of the study would be obtained, and the amount of weight lost during the course of the experiment would be the actual measurement used for comparison of the test and control groups.

Applying Marketing Research 3.14

Suppose that a company has developed a one-day training seminar designed to improve scores on the Graduate Management Admissions Test (GMAT).

Research is conducted to test the effectiveness of the seminar before marketing it to college seniors. College seniors planning to pursue MBAs, but who have not yet taken the GMAT, are recruited and randomly divided into two groups--test and control. The test group attends the one-day training seminar and then takes the GMAT, while the control group only takes the GMAT (at the same time as the test group). For simplicity, suppose that there are only five participants in each group, and their corresponding GMAT results are:

	Test Group	Control
	523	460
	511	490
	481	530
	462	460
	528	480
Average	501	484
Sample Variance	808.5	830.0

Because of the large variance in test scores across the individuals within each group, the statistical test to compare the two sample averages concludes that the difference in average scores could well have been caused by chance alone. (The difference is not statistically significant.)

An alternate research design including an initial measure for each respondent could be used in Applying Marketing Research 3.14. That is, the test group students could take the GMAT, attend the one-day seminar, and then retake the GMAT. The control group students take and retake the GMAT at exactly the same times as the test group, but do not attend the one-day seminar. The experiment now focuses on the amount of improvement between the initial and subsequent GMAT scores--the gain scores. A difference in average gain scores between the two groups is attributed to the seminar. The results shown in Table 3.4 quite plausible for these same two groups of students.

Applying the statistical test to these improvement data leads to the conclusion that the training seminar improves scores on average. (The average gain is statistically significant.) Again, the reason for obtaining a significant result in this second approach, and not in the first, is the reduced variance and resulting enhanced sensitivity.

Test Group			Control Group		
Pre	Post	Improvement	Pre	Post	Improvement
510	530	20	460	470	10
500	520	20	490	505	15
480	504	24	530	535	5
460	486	26	460	470	10
520	530	10	480	500	20
Average		20.0			12.0
Sample Variance		38.0			32.5

Table 3.4

Given the obvious benefits of matching and the use of gain scores, you might wonder why these techniques aren't employed all the time. Unfortunately, potential biases can be introduced by both techniques.[9] Sometimes the initial measurement required to calculate a gain score and the treatment interact to produce an effect that biases the results.[10]

For instance, questioning individuals in a community regarding awareness of environmental issues and the use of recycling facilities prior to conducting a public-service campaign to encourage recycling could sensitize them to these issues, causing them to respond to the campaign by altering their behavior dramatically. A subsequent measure of the use of recycling facilities by these individuals would imply that the campaign was very successful even though the campaign might be totally ineffective in stimulating an unsensitized audience to use recycling facilities. The questioning necessary to establish the initial measurement and the publicity campaign interact to produce the end result, and this interaction interferes with the ability to measure the effect of the publicity campaign alone. A control group (not exposed to the campaign) would be of no help in isolating the effect of the campaign.

The initial measurement required for gain scores also takes time and money. In the GMAT seminar example just discussed, participants must take the GMAT twice, thus adding considerable time and expense, as well as additional executional considerations. It may be cheaper in the long run to increase the number of participants in the test and control groups substantially and not include an initial measurement. The increased sample sizes for the test and control groups will also increase the sensitivity of the experiment.

Matching also has its shortcomings--it is not always clear what the basis for matching should be, matching can become quite complicated when several variables are involved, and it may be necessary to obtain additional data on participants to perform the matching. Also, selection bias can be introduced because units that do not have respective matches are not included in the experiment. In the in-store test example above, it was implicitly assumed that there was an obvious matching of the sample of stores into pairs according to all commodity volume (ACV). These ACV numbers might have been quite different across the stores, making matching very difficult and perhaps more subjective than objective. Further, the ACV would need to be available for each store, and this number may not be easy to obtain. The bottom line is that matching may add more time, effort, and expense to a survey than it is worth. Increasing sample sizes may again be the preferred way to enhance sensitivity.

Measuring Interaction

Some marketing experiments, such as the ones described so far, involve only one independent variable. Others include several independent variables that the experimenter would like to investigate simultaneously. For example, researchers measuring the effects of the in-store display in Applying Marketing Research 3.3 might also want to test the effect of that same display in conjunction with price discounts of varying amounts. Research on the new liquid detergent in Applying Marketing Research 3.4 might involve alternative names as well as package designs. Determining cause-and-effect relationships in these cases becomes a much more difficult task.

Successive experiments can be designed to investigate one variable at a time. The other variables are held constant at some specified level while one variable is manipulated. However, the results of such experiments can be very misleading because of interaction. **Interaction** means that the effect of manipulating one variable can vary greatly depending upon the level at which the other variables are held constant. This phenomenon is illustrated in the following example.

Applying Marketing Research 3.15

Companies such as Procter & Gamble are constantly faced with making decisions regarding product specifics for new brands. Suppose Procter & Gamble is considering introducing a new hand and body lotion as a companion to its Wondra brand, and the project has evolved to the point of deciding between two perfumes and two colors for the final product. The two perfumes are a floral and a citrus scent; the two colors are white and pink. Successive experiments are conducted to determine separately the color and scent to use.

In the first experiment, a consumer test of the two perfumes (conducted in the white color) indicates that the citrus scent is preferred.

In the second experiment, the two colors are evaluated by consumers using the preferred citrus scent, and white is preferred. The conclusion would be to use the citrus perfume in the white color.

The conclusion seems completely reasonable on the surface. However, an extremely strong synergistic effect could exist between the floral scent and the pink color, which would make this combination the most preferred by far. This interaction would not be detected in the experiments conducted because the particular combination of floral perfume and pink color was never tested.

A single experiment, in which all variables are simultaneously manipulated, would be required to determine whether interactions truly exist. An experiment in which the dependent variable is observed for all possible combinations of levels of all independent variables is called a **factorial experiment**.[11] The results of such an experiment can be analyzed statistically to determine whether interactions exist and to measure separately the effects of the individual independent variables, as well as their interactions, on the dependent variable.

Table 3.5 describes a factorial experiment involving bank checking accounts and associated services. The independent variables being manipulated are minimum balance required to avoid a monthly service charge ($1000 or $2000), the amount of the monthly service charge ($6, $8, or $10), and the amount of overdraft protection ($500 or $1000). Therefore, a total of 12 (2 X 3 X 2) possible combinations are to be tested. Separate groups of consumers might each be asked to evaluate one of the services and to rate it on a scale from 1 to 10, where 1 represents "very poor" and 10 represents "excellent." The results are then statistically analyzed to determine how the three factors individually affect consumer acceptance and whether interactions exist.

Minimum balance required to avoid monthly service charge ($)	Monthly service charge ($)	Overdraft protection ($)
1000	6	500
		1000
	8	500
		1000
	10	500
		1000
2000	6	500
		1000
	8	500
		1000
	10	500
		1000

Table 3.5 Factorial experience for evaluating checking account services

The Importance of Experimental Validity

One of the most critical issues surrounding the use of experimental research techniques is the validity of the experimental results. **Internal validity** of an experiment concerns the degree to which changes observed in the dependent variable can be attributed to the manipulations performed on the independent variables. **External validity** concerns the degree to which results can be projected from what may be an artificial or highly controlled setting to a more natural environment.

An example in which internal validity is questionable is an "experiment" portrayed in one television commercial. The ad showed a dedicated user of one brand of razor blade being shaved by a barber using the major competition's brand of razor blade. The man receiving the shave claims that the shave is much closer than he typically experiences. The ad presents the brand of razor as the only variable changing in the experiment, so it must be the reason for the man's closer shave. However, there are really two variables changing in this "experiment": the person doing the shaving, an external variable, and the razor. Was it the barber or the razor blade that produced the closer shave?

Premeasurement, instrumentation, maturation, history, sample selection, measurement timing, and mortality all threaten internal validity. Each of these experimental errors impacts the ability to conclude that the observed differences or changes in the dependent variable are attributable to the experimental manipulation. Researchers strive to ensure internal validity in experiments by holding external factors that may have an impact on the dependent variable constant, using control groups to isolate the effects of the independent variable from those of changing external variables, randomly selecting and assigning experimental units to experimental groups and carefully timing measurements. However, controlling the experimental environment may decrease the experiment's external validity by raising questions about how generalizable the results are.

Television commercials portrayed as experiments also provide examples that illustrate when external validity is an issue. One such TV commercial, for the Sears DieHard automobile battery (see Exhibit 3.3), showed several identical cars, containing different brands of batteries, encased in ice for a long period of time. After chipping the ice away from the cars, an attempt was made to start the cars and only the car with the DieHard battery started. Does this mean that the DieHard battery will perform better than other batteries under the stress of ordinary driving conditions? That is, what happens if the effects of drastically changing temperatures; of using radios, lights, and other electrical accessories; or of changing from wet to dry weather conditions are introduced? The DieHard may indeed be a superior product, but this experiment has not established this fact for typical driving conditions.

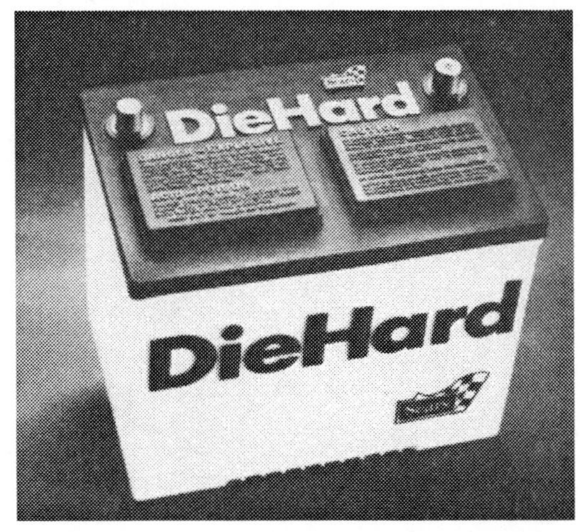

Exhibit 3.3 What is the external validity of the experiment described in the DieHard battery television commercial? (Picture courtesy of Sears.)

Issues of internal and external validity are particularly relevant to the sequence of steps associated with developing a new product or service. Exhibit 3.4 shows what happens to internal and external validity as the development process progresses. Early in the process, the research often entails **laboratory experiments**--experiments performed in a tightly controlled environment, such as is typical in a scientific laboratory. Laboratory experiments have high internal validity. The presence of a high degree of control over extraneous factors ensures that observed changes or differences can be attributed to the independent variables manipulated. However, external validity tends to be low in laboratory experiments because in order to achieve the control, an artificial environment is induced. Applying Marketing Research 3.16 illustrates a laboratory experiment.

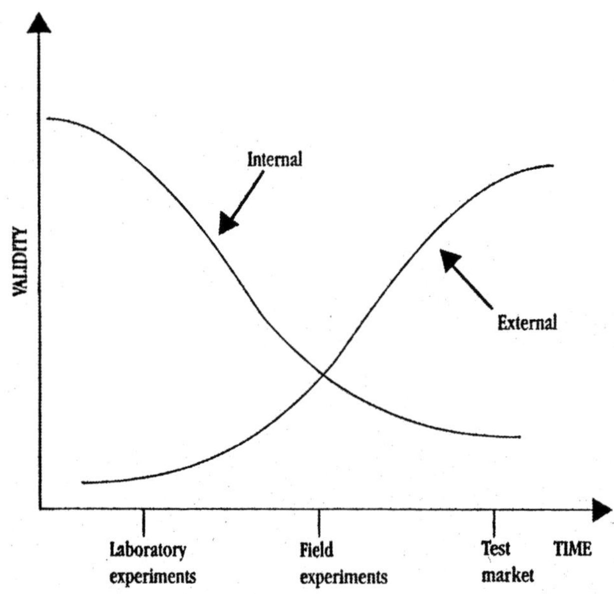

Exibit 3.4 The new product/service introduction process.

Applying Marketing Research 3.16

As part of an experiment to compare two germ-killing agents, a number of laboratory cultures are prepared containing comparable amounts of germ colonies. The cultures are randomly divided into two equal-sized groups. Each culture in one group is treated with a fixed amount of one agent, and each culture in the other group receives the same fixed amount of the other agent. The cultures are all stored in the same environment for the same length of time. Then, the two groups are compared on the basis of the number of remaining (live) germ colonies. An observed difference in this context is attributed to a difference in the germ-killing power of the two agents. Such a laboratory experiment could be the basis for an advertising claim of superiority for one deodorant bar soap versus another, for example.

As the new product development process continues, the research moves from the laboratory setting to the field. The term **field experiment** is used for an experiment conducted in a more natural and less controlled setting than a laboratory. Because field experiments involve a more realistic environment, they generally result in increased external validity. However, the realistic environment introduces uncontrolled extraneous factors that threaten internal validity.

Applying Marketing Research 3.17

Returning to Applying Marketing Research 3.16, suppose that the two germ-killing agents are tested among consumers. One group of deodorant bar soap users is given bars made with one of the agents, while another group, comparable in size, is given bars made with the other agent. The bars are identical except for the germ-killing agent used. At the end of a one-week usage period, test participants are asked to rate the deodorancy effectiveness of the product just used on a ten-point scale, where 1 denotes "very poor" and 10 denotes "excellent."

Suppose one of the agents is rated significantly

higher than the other on average. The implication is that one agent is superior to the other at killing odor-causing germs. However, we are not as sure about this conclusion as we were in the laboratory experiment of Applying Marketing Research 3.16. There is a chance that external factors, such as differences in group combination, the frequency and way the products were used by test participants, and the way the products were made could have produced the difference in perceived effectiveness observed in the experiment. Some internal validity has been sacrificed to increase external validity.

In the final stage of the development process, research is conducted in the actual market where many variables that affect the new brand's performance, such as trade and competitive reaction, are beyond the control of the company making the introduction. Thus, there are numerous serious threats to internal validity in the field experiments conducted at the last stage of the introduction process, but external validity is high.

Summary

A cause-and-effect relationship means that changes in one factor (the cause) directly product changes in another (the effect). Marketing managers obviously seek understanding of the effects of marketing efforts on measures of brand performance. Experimental research focuses on identifying cause-and-effect relationships, and hence is very important in marketing, just as it is in the physical sciences.

In an experiment, the independent variables are manipulated (potential cause), and a dependent variable is monitored for change (effect). However, changes in external variables that are not part of the experimental manipulation can affect the dependent variable during an experiment. The experimenter must control for these effects to separate them from the effect of the experimental manipulation. Failure to do so can result in experimental error that occurs when the changes in the dependent variable are not necessarily the result of the experimental manipulation. Control groups, randomization in the assignment of experimental units to groups, and carefully choosing the timing of measurements are used to avoid such error.

Experimenters are also concerned about the amount of random "noise" or variance in the measurements obtained in an experiment. Matching and gain scores are often used to reduce the amount of such noise.

Experiments involving more than one independent variable are subject to interaction. Two variables interact when the effect of one varies with the level of the other. Factorial experiments, in which the dependent variable is observed for all possible combinations of the experimental levels of the independent variables, are required to measure interaction effects.

Internal validity of an experiment refers to the ability to attribute the changes in the dependent variable to the manipulations of the independent variable(s). That is, internal validity refers to the degree to which the experiment is free from experimental error. External validity refers to the degree to which the conclusions of the experiment can be extended beyond the experimental environment to real-world situations.

Key Terms

- cause-and-effect relationship
- control
- dependent variable
- experimental error
- experimental treatments

experimental units
external variables
external validity
factorial experiment
field experiment
gain score
history error
independent variable
instrumentation error
interaction
internal validity
laboratory experiments
matching
maturation error
measurement timing
measurement timing error
mortality error
premeasurement error
randomization
sample selection error

Experimental Research at Nimslo

About one year before the introduction of the Nimslo camera into the Florida test market, a limited supply of camera prototypes was produced, and Nimslo's photofinishing operation had reached the point where it was able to handle a small demand. At this point in time, the company was faced with the strategic decision of how to structure the photofinishing system for the consumer. Ideally, Nimslo wanted to handle all photofinishing orders, both receipts and deliveries, by mail. To this end, they planned prepaid mailers to be sold at stores that carried the Nimslo camera. The company also planned to accept direct payment in the form of a check accompanying a photofinishing order. Nimslo's marketing management recognized that consumers might view having only these two options as a drawback. Many consumers use mail to send orders to photofinishing houses; however, consumers are also accustomed to being able to submit photofinishing orders at conveniently located kiosks, like those run by Photomat, as well as drugstores, camera specialty stores, and so drugstores, camera specialty stores, and so forth. Finished prints are then picked up at these same locations.

Another strategic issue facing Nimslo with respect to photofinishing was the printing policy. Some photofinishing operations printed all pictures and simply told the consumer they did not have to pay for those they did not want. Nimslo considered this policy inappropriate for their system primarily because of the potentially damaging publicity associated with having poor quality three-dimensional prints in circulation. Consequently, Nimslo decided subjectively to determine which prints were "quality" 3-D and only return these to the customer. Of course, if the customer demanded that a picture be printed, Nimslo would respect those wishes. Consumer data were needed to determine how consumers would react to such a policy.

Two separate experiments were conducted to investigate the two photofinishing issues just presented. For the issue of submission and

and receipt of photofinishing orders, the participants were all given a Nimslo camera and instructed in its use. The participants were randomly divided into two groups. For one group prepaid mailers were made available, and the other group had the option of using designated drop-off locations (camera stores, drug stores, and photofinishing kiosks) instead of mail. Monitoring usage of the camera, *i.e.*, the amount of picture-taking, and discussing the photofinishing options with panelists after several months of usage convinced Nimslo of the need to provide drop-off and pick-up locations. The company negotiated contracts with major photofinishers to accomplish this.

The issue of print policy was handled analogously. Participants were divided into two groups. The typical system of printing everything with liberal refund policy was used for one group. For the other group, Nimslo only printed quality 3-D pictures. Customer satisfaction was monitored, and Nimslo felt that the latter policy could be adopted based on the results of the experiment.

Review Questions

3.1 Are observed high correlations between variables always indicative of a causal relationship? Why or why not?

3.2 What is meant by a control or control group in an experiment? Why is it important to include control in an experiment?

3.3 Describe a marketing experiment, and label the independent and dependent variables.

3.4 What is meant by a factorial experiment? What is the primary value of factorial experiments?

3.5 What types of experimental errors can occur even if a control group is included?

3.6 Why is randomization in the assignment of experimental units to treatment groups important in an experiment? What particular experimental error is randomization guarding against?

3.7 What is meant by matching in designing an experiment? What is the value of matching?

3.8 What is the value of including an initial or premeasurement in an experimental design?

3.9 Why aren't matching and gain scores always used in experimental designs?

3.10 Define internal and external validity. Give an example of an experiment with high internal validity but low external validity. Give another example where the reverse is true.

Discussion Questions

3.1 Discuss the concept of a cause and effect relationship. What role does experimentation play in identifying such relationships? Give examples of relationships which appear to be cause and effect, but which are not.

3.2 Discuss the role of laboratory experiments in the process of developing a new product. What can be said about the internal and external validity of such experiments? Why? Are these experiments valuable? Why or why not?

3.3 Design an experiment to investigate the impact of the amount of the discount on the effectiveness of a coupon for Tropicana frozen orange juice concentrate. How would you define effectiveness, and how would you measure it?

3.4 Examine some television commercials that portray experiments to make points about product advantages. What variables are being manipulated? What are the respective dependent variables? Discuss the internal and external validity of each.

3.5 Describe the experimental errors potentially affecting the following experiments. How could these potential errors be avoided?

a) The Colgate-Palmolive Company introduces a new laundry detergent into several test markets and decides to measure consumer awareness of the test brand two months after introduction. A survey is conducted among households in the test markets and awareness is found to be only about 5 percent in all markets. The company decides to conduct an experiment to determine whether increased advertising spending can increase awareness. Colgate-Palmolive decides to use the results of the awareness survey as a premeasurement and will double advertising spending over the next three months. Another survey will be conducted in exactly the same manner to obtain a postmeasurement of awareness of the new brands at the end of this three-month period. Any increase in awareness will be attributed to the increased advertising spending.

b) A marketing research manager at H.J. Heinz, Inc., contacts a marketing research supplier to conduct a store test to compare the impact of an in-store end-of-aisle display promotion on sales of Heinz Ketchup. The marketing research firm recommends using a panel of twenty randomly selected Winn Dixie stores in a region as the test group, *i.e.*, the stores receiving the end-of-aisle display. Another panel consisting of twenty randomly selected Kroger stores will serve as the control group, *i.e.*, the stores receiving no in-store Heinz Ketchup display. The marketing research firm feels that using two separate chains, Winn Dixie and Kroger, will facilitate executing the test. A difference in average sales of Heinz Ketchup between the two panels will be attributed to the end-of-aisle display.

c) MCI, AT&T's major competitor for long-distance telephone business, decides to determine consumer awareness of and reaction to a promotion, which allows MCI customers to save 20 percent on phone calls to the twelve MCI customers they call most often. A survey is conducted among 400 randomly selected consumers in four geographically dispersed shopping malls (100 in each location). MCI discovers that awareness is far below expectations and decides to alter its advertising strategy, including an increase in advertising spending, to increase consumer awareness of the program. To measure the impact of the revised strategy, a second consumer survey will be conducted in three months, and the results of this future study will be compared to the results just obtained. MCI decides to use a nationally representative telephone survey for the future study so that the sample size can be substantially increased without much change in cost.

3.6 Ethical situation: Studies have repeatedly shown that products that do not contain an active ingredient can produce an effect. For instance, a person given a pill that, unbeknownst to him or her, contains no active pain killer may experience an actual reduction in pain. In an experiment, this psychological effect is an extraneous variable that cannot be eliminated by a traditional control group. Therefore, in some experiments, the control group receives a placebo--an experimental treatment that superficially resembles the other treatment(s) in the experiment but contains no active ingredients.

For example, to test the effectiveness of an over-the-counter appetite suppressant to aid dieters, the participants are first randomly divided into two groups. The test group is given the new appetite suppressant, and the control group is given a placebo product, which resembles the appetite suppressant but does not contain an active ingredient. Obviously, the control group is not told that the product they are using does not contain an active ingredient. Both groups use their respective products for the same period of time, and are periodically examined, weighed, and resupplied with product. The effectiveness of the appetite suppressant ingredient is measured by the difference in the average weight loss between the two groups.

Discuss the ethical considerations of using placebos in an experiment

Chapter 3 Endnotes

1. See, for example, N.R. Draper and H. Smith, *Applied Regression Analysis*. New York: John Wiley & Sons, Inc., 1966, p. 34.

2. See, for example, George W. Snedecor and William G. Cochran, *Statistical Methods*, 6th ed. Ames, Iowa: The Iowa State University Press, 1967, p. 189.

3. See Thomas D. Cook and Donald T. Campbell, *Quasi-Experimentation Design and Analysis Issues For Field Settings*. Boston: Houghton Mifflin Company, 1979, Chapter 3, for a discussion of the importance of control groups in experimental designs.

4. See, for example, Barry F. Anderson, *The Psychology Experiment*. Belmont, CA: Wadsworth Publishing Company, Inc., 1966, p. 31.

5. De'Ann Weimer and Emily Thornton, "Slow Healing at Mitsubishi," *Business Week*, September 22, 1997, p. 74.

6. This phenomenon is part of what is referred to in management as the "Hawthorne effect." See F.J. Roethlisberger, *Management and Morale*. Cambridge, MA: Harvard University Press, 1941, pp. 9-15.

7. Matching is a form of blocking that is discussed at length in statistical experimental design texts. See Thomas D. Cook and Donald T. Campbell, *Quasi-Experimentation in Design and Analysis Issues for Field Settings*. (Boston: Houghton Mifflin Company, 1979), pp. 175-182, for a good overview of matching and blocking.

8. *Ibid.*, pp. 182-185.

9. *Ibid.*, pp. 178-182, 184.

10. See, for example, A. Parasuraman, *Marketing Research*, (Reading, MA: Addison-Wesley Publishing Company, 1986), pp. 288-289.

11. See, for example, B.J. Winer, *Statistical Principals in Experimental Design*, 2nd ed., (New York: McGraw Hill Book Company, 1971), Chapter 5, for a discussion of factorial designs.

Chapter 4

Secondary Data Sources

Learning Objectives:

This chapter discusses one of the three general sources of marketing research data, secondary data. After reading this chapter you should be able to:

- o distinguish between internal and external secondary data.
- o describe the advantages and disadvantages of secondary data.
- o explain the role of secondary data in market monitoring.
- o list key secondary sources for market monitoring.
- o describe the procedure for efficiently locating secondary data sources.
- o discuss the impact of the trend toward the computerization of secondary data.

With annual sales of over five billion dollars, Frito-Lay is the world's largest salty snack manufacturer. In 1990 they began a national roll out the reduced-oil, "light," chips line shown in Exhibit 4.1. As the roll out began, Frito-Lay executives expressed confidence that this new product line would generate between $220 and $330 million in sales. This confidence existed even though Frito-Lay had scrapped a similar line, called Lightly's, just four years previously and Borden, Inc. had pulled their Lite-Line Snack Foods in 1984, after only a year in the market.[1]

Exhibit 4.1 Changes in the market led Frito-Lay to introduce a line of light snacks. (Courtesy of Frito-Lay Inc.)

By 1994, low-fat products accounted for ten percent of Frito-Lay's sales.[2] Finding that most of the sales of the low-fat products was incremental business and did not cannibalize existing brand sales, in 1995, they rolled out the baked line of salty-snack products shown in Exhibit 4.2. In 1996 they also began market testing salty snacks made with Olestra, the synthetic fat developed by Procter & Gamble that contains no calories.[3] The company expects one third of its total sales to come from low-fat/no-fat products by the year 2000.[4]

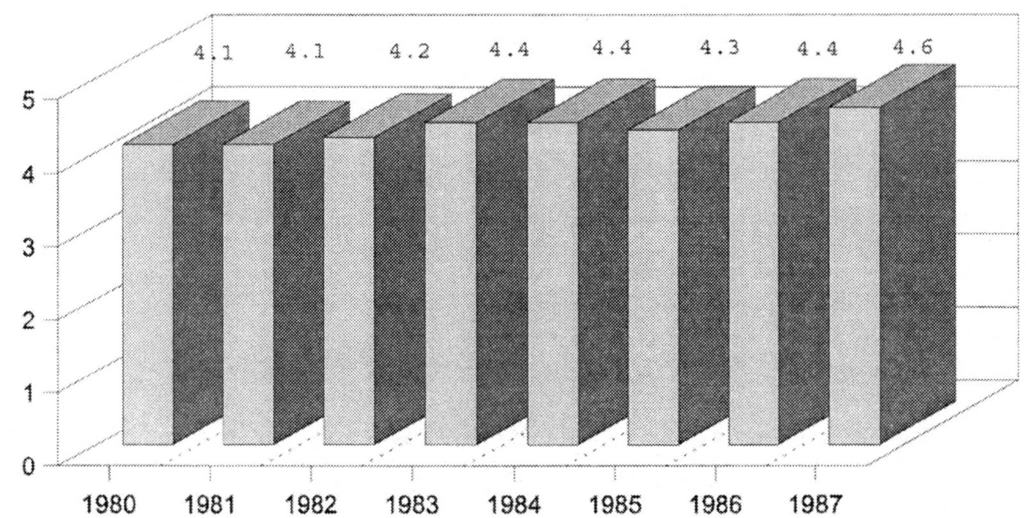

Exhibit 4.2 Per-capita consumption of potato chips in the United States, 1980-1987 (in lb/yr). (Source: Table 195: Fruit and Vegetable Consumption per Capita, *Statistical Abstract of the United States: 1989* [109th ed.], Washington D.C.: U.S. Bureau of the Census, 1989, p. 121.)

On what information did the executives at Frito-Lay base their confidence? What changes had they uncovered in the snack food environment that might bring success when similar ventures had recently failed?

A great deal of their confidence came from facts obtained from secondary data. For example, published reports indicated that most Americans planned to increase their consumption of reduced-fat foods.[5] Other secondary sources revealed a solid growth in snack food sales, with the average American in 1995 deriving 25 percent of his or her daily calories from snacks.[6] Furthermore, a large portion of the growth in snack food sales was expected to come in low-calorie, or light snacks.[7] In addition, numerous articles claimed that the fastest growing food segments in the 1990s were those addressing consumers' concerns over fat content and calories.[8] Finally, secondary data revealed that the target market for the light snack line---adults aged 35-54 who have annual incomes above $35,000---was growing in size.

For many people, marketing research conjures up images of people conducting surveys to gather information from consumers about products or services. The truth is, a great deal of valuable marketing information can be gained from a careful examination of **secondary data**---data already collected for other purposes. Many times, secondary data provide information necessary to evaluate the business environment in which a firm must operate. As was the case for Frito-Lay, these data often point to a new business opportunity.

Internal and External Secondary Data

A wealth of useful marketing information can be found in **internal secondary data**, data a company collects in the normal course of doing business. For example, accounting records dealing with shipments, sales invoices, and marketing expenditures provide information about customers, product movement, and costs. Likewise, the periodic reports that many companies receive from their sales force often contain information about competitive activities in the market and local market conditions. Information from previous marketing research studies conducted by the firm can also yield data that are pertinent to the present situation. Frito-Lay conducts thousands of consumer interviews every year. Even those not directly investigating the light snacks market probably contain information relevant to that market.

Already existing data that were not gathered by the firm are called **external secondary data**. Numerous organizations collect data that can prove useful for a firm's marketing intelligence. Federal, state, and local governments gather tremendous amounts of publicly available data. Likewise, trade associations often collect data from their members, compile these data, and produce summary reports for their members. Trade associations may even contract primary research and distribute the results to the membership. Finally, books, periodicals, and other published materials contain vast quantities of external secondary data.

Advantages of Secondary Data

Secondary data have three primary advantages over primary data: cost, completeness, and timeliness.

Cost

A company can often obtain secondary data at little or no cost. Much of these data are contained in company records or are freely available from public libraries. Even if a company subscribes to a variety of journals, periodicals, and magazines, the cost of having to collect the data contained in these sources would far exceed the subscription costs. For instance, the data included in the U.S. Census of the Population cost nearly one billion dollars to collect but can be purchased for a few thousand dollars.

Completeness

Respondents often have more incentive to provide the data to a secondary source so the data may be more complete and comprehensive than data generated from primary research. In some cases, such as the Census of the Population, respondents are required by law to participate. In other cases, respondents are willing to cooperate because they trust that the data will not be used inappropriately. Companies often provide proprietary data to their trade associations because they know these associations will not release any company-specific data. They also know that the association will not use the data in any way that might be detrimental to its members.

Timeliness

Perhaps the most important advantage of secondary data is the speed with which the data can be obtained. A search of secondary sources, if properly conducted, takes little time. Yet, these searches often uncover information that could take weeks, or even months, for a company to gather through primary data collection methods.

Potential Drawbacks of Secondary Data

Secondary data do have limitations. One obvious drawback is that the specific data needed by the firm may not be available from any secondary source. In addition, even if available, the firm must carefully evaluate the data before deciding to use them. Data bias, data accuracy, and data usefulness are three aspects that demand particular attention.

Data Bias

Never assume that secondary data are presented in an objective and impartial fashion. While you have probably heard that "the data speak for themselves," this statement is not really true. Data do not "speak"! People speak, and different people can interpret the same data in different ways. For example, a Chamber of Commerce will probably interpret demographic and economic data on its city somewhat differently than you might, since one of its roles is to attract new industry and new residents. Thus, while a 3 percent increase in disposable income may seem unimpressive to you, the Chamber may portray the city as a "high-growth" area in its publications.

Differing points of view also effect the kinds of data that are reported. Some of the demographic and economic information about our hypothetical city is likely to be positive, while other information will probably paint a more negative picture. The city may have experienced a large population growth in recent years, potentially a positive aspect. However, the negative aspects of this population growth could be an increase in the unemployment rate, a strain on the city's social services, and an increase in property taxes. The Chamber of Commerce, in keeping with its goals, is apt to gloss over, or even omit, the negative aspects of this growth in order to depict the city in the best possible light.

As this example illustrates, users of secondary data must carefully address the issue of data bias. Never assume that the data are objectively presented. Always pay attention to the source of the data and the purpose of the report, since both can influence the objectivity of the data.

Data Accuracy

Never assume that data are accurate just because they have been published. As you will learn when we discuss primary data collection procedures, a great many aspects of the collection process influence the accuracy of data obtained. Therefore, you need to determine whether the secondary source used sound methods to collect the data.

Usefulness of the Data

Another drawback of secondary data is that they may not be useful to the issue being examined. Many times, the broad scope of a study conducted by a secondary source make data analysis and reporting a complex and lengthy process. A study may be outdated by the time the data are published. Most of the data for the 1990 Census of the Population, for example, were collected during April 1990 and the first reports were not available until early 1991. While published much quicker than previous census reports had been, the earliest information was still almost one year old while the population examined was constantly changing.

Another reason that secondary data may not be useful is that the time periods covered or the categories of data reported differ from what is desired. A company may want monthly figures while the data are reported bimonthly. The population may be combined into five-year age groups when what is needed is the number of people aged twelve and under.

Sometimes, researchers attempt to adjust or extrapolate secondary data to approximate the desired information. A company may want to know the number of people aged twelve and under, and only five-year age groupings are available. They might add a percentage of those people in the 11- to 15-year-old age group to the two younger groups to estimate the desired figure. Any time such adjustments are made, they must be clearly communicated so readers are aware that the number is an approximation.

Using Secondary Data For Market Monitoring

Economic conditions, demographic shifts, social changes, legal or political forces, industry conditions, and competitive actions are all beyond the company's control. Yet each of these environmental forces has an impact on the results a company can obtain from any marketing strategy. Therefore, one key to making effective decisions is to know as much as possible about these environmental forces. Most large firms systematically compile secondary data dealing with environmental forces, a process known as **market monitoring**.

Some market monitoring systems take a traditional "hard copy" library form. Corporate librarians maintain updated secondary source materials and may even circulate relevant articles to various managers. More and more often, however, companies are improving access to this important information by computerizing these systems. With these computerized systems, managers can quickly access and scan current data on topics of interest.

Key Sources for Market Monitoring

Some secondary sources are particularly useful for market monitoring. To describe these key secondary sources, we have classified them according to whether they provide data on general economic conditions, industry trends, consumer markets, or competitors. Before proceeding, however, we need to mention one source that is so encompassing that no environmental scan would be complete without examining it. This source, the *Statistical Abstract of the United States*, contains over 1450 tables and charts of information on numerous aspects of all environmental factors.

Compiled from over 200 sources, the *Statistical Abstract* is a good starting point for finding facts or locating other secondary sources that might be useful for market monitoring.[9] For example, Exhibit 4.3 was developed from information found in the *Statistical Abstract*. As you can see, per-capita consumption of potatoes for chips in the United States has not changed in recent years, a fact no doubt of interest to a company like Frito-Lay. However, the data in Exhibit 4.3 also illustrate one of the weaknesses of secondary data. The most recent data included was three years old at the time the *Statistical Abstract* was published.

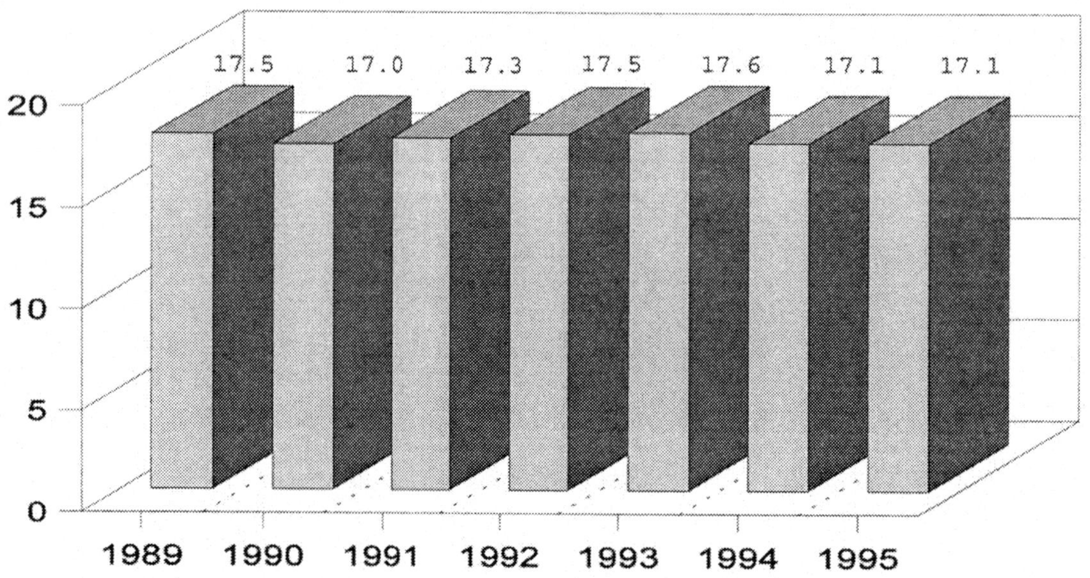

Exhibit 4.3 Per Capita Consumption of Potatoes for Chips in the United States, 1989-95 (in lbs./yr. Farm weight) (Source: Table 231: Per Capita Utilization of Selected Commercially Produced Fresh Fruits and Vegetables: 1980-1995, *Statistical Abstract of the United States*: 1996 (117th ed.), Washington, D.C.: U.S. Bureau of the Census, 1997, p. 150.)

Sources of Economic Conditions Data

The health of a nation's economy has a dramatic influence on the performance a company can expect from its products or services. Recessionary periods, high inflation, or high interest rates can all seriously reduce product demand, especially for expensive items like homes or for discretionary items like vacations. On the other hand, the same conditions can increase the consumption of some items, such as videotape movie rentals, as people opt for less expensive alternatives.

Because an understanding of the economic environment is so vital, companies gather as much information as possible about the economic outlook when developing plans. Of the several secondary sources of economic statistics available, one of the most widely used is the *Survey of Current Business*, a monthly publication of the U.S. government that provides a quick reference to the most current statistics on economic trends, GNP, income, and personal consumption levels.

Sources of Industry Data

Companies considering entry into a new industry need information on current industry sales and the sales trend of the industry. Even for those industries in which they currently operate, a company must monitor sales trends to decide how much investment is warranted.

Three secondary sources provide extremely valuable industry information. They are:

- o *U.S. Industrial Outlook*,
- o *Predicasts Basebook*, and
- o *Predicasts Forecasts*.

The *U.S. Industrial Outlook*, prepared from data gathered by the U.S. government, provides industry profiles and sales-trend estimates for over 350 United States industries. The two Predicast sources compile data and forecasts that have been published elsewhere and report these data in tabular form by industry.

A company can obtain a tremendous amount of information on an industry from these sources. As an example, the 1994 *U.S. Industrial Outlook* estimated that potato chip sales in the United States had risen from $4.99 billion in 1987 to $6.67 billion in 1991.[10] Frito-Lay would have found this fact extremely useful in their strategic planning.

The U.S. Bureau of the Census collects census data on industries as well as on the population. In fact, the population census is only one of the seven censuses the U.S. Bureau of the Census conducts. The other six, often referred to as the "business" censuses, are: Census of Retail Trade, Census of Service Industries, Census of Wholesale Trade, Census of Mineral Industries, Census of Construction Industries, and Census of Manufactures. These business censuses yield detailed information on each of those particular industries.

The business censuses organize firms into groups using Standard Industrial Classification (SIC) codes. A **Standard Industrial Classification (SIC) code** classifies a business entity based on what it produces or the functions it performs. Each business entity is categorized into a specific four-digit SIC category, and aggregate data for these firms are reported. However, if a four-digit category has fewer than three firms in it, similar four-digit categories are aggregated and are reported as three-digit, or even two-digit categories. Doing so prevents disclosing information that can be traced to a specific company. Obviously, the aggregated information is less useful than the information based on four-digit groups because less-similar companies are aggregated. For instance, Table 4.1 shows the various SIC categories that would include potato chip manufacturers. As you can see, the three-digit and two-digit categories contain many types of companies besides potato chip manufacturers. For some geographic areas, potato chip producers might be grouped together with "canned and cured fish and seafoods," "roasted coffee," or "manufactured ice" producers because all of these industries are classified in the same three-digit category, "Miscellaneous Food."

20 FOOD AND KINDRED PRODUCTS

209 MISCELLANEOUS FOOD PREPARATIONS AND KINDRED PRODUCTS

2096 POTATO CHIPS, CORN CHIPS, AND SIMILAR SNACKS

Table 4.1 Example of Standard industrial Classification (SIC) Codes (Source: *Standard Industrial Classification Manual*, National Technical Information Service, Springfield, Virginia, 1987.)

Sources of Consumer Market Data

Information on the size, demographic composition, and future trends in consumer markets is critical to marketers. Sales forecasts, resource allocation, and new product introductions are but a few of the decisions that rely heavily on consumer market data. Fortunately, numerous sources contain data on the characteristics of the U.S. population.

The *Census of Population and Housing* provides the most complete demographic and socioeconomic profile of the U.S. population. Conducted by the Bureau of the Census every ten years, the *Census of Population and Housing* contains detailed national, regional, state-level, metropolitan area, and ZIP code area descriptions of population characteristics. Furthermore, the Census Bureau has developed a system, called Tiger, that allows a person to gain access to census data by personal computer for any of about 7 million small geographic areas nationwide.[11] The level of geographic detail provided by the Tiger system allows marketers to pinpoint areas having consumers with specific characteristics.

Applying Marketing Research 4.1

When General Motors introduced the Buick Roadmaster station wagon, the company knew that only a small number of station wagons were sold each year. In fact, they anticipated selling no more than 40,000 Roadmasters per year. With such a small market, national advertising typical of most new car introductions would be very inefficient. Instead, GM attempted to focus its advertising only on those households felt to be most likely to purchase a station wagon.

Combining ZIP-code-level Census data with proprietary information on the characteristics of households most likely to be in the target market, General Motors selected slightly more than ten percent of the over 40,000 ZIP code areas as target markets. Roadmaster advertisements were run in seven national magazines only within the selected ZIP code areas. In addition, each of the seven magazines provided General Motors with a list of their subscribers living in the selected ZIP code areas. This allowed them to attach a personalized invitation to receive additional information to each subscriber's advertisement.

By focusing its advertising only on these

ZIP code areas, Buick was able to reach effectively the 20 percent of all U.S. households that represent 50 percent of the buyers of large station wagons. The procedure was not inexpensive, however, since General Motors had to purchase national advertising space in the magazines and insert either the Roadmaster ad or an ad for the broad-based Regal. Yet, the advertising efficiencies created by having detailed market data far outweighed the costs.

		Population
Ten Largest MSAs	New York, NY	8,546,846
	Los Angeles–Long Beach, CA	8,863,164
	Chicago, IL	6,069,974
	Philadelphia, PA–NJ	4,856,881
	Detroit, MI	4,382,299
	Washington, DC–MD–VA	3,923,299
	Houston, TX	3,301,937
	Atlanta, GA	2,833,511
	Boston, MA	2,870,669
	Nassau–Suffolk, NY	2,609,212
		Population
Ten Smallest MSAs	St. Joseph, MO	83,083
	Lawrence, KS	81,798
	Rapid City, SD	81,343
	Pittsfield, MA	79,250
	Jackson, TN	77,982
	Great Falls, MT	77,691
	Victoria, TX	74,361
	Cheyenne, WY	73,142
	Grand Forks, ND	70,683
	Casper, WY	61,226
	Enid, OK	56,735

Table 4.2 The ten largest and the ten smallest Metropolitan Statistical Areas.

One of the most widely used geographic breakdowns provided by the Bureau of the Census is the Metropolitan Statistical Area, or MSA. A **Metropolitan Statistical Area** is a population nucleus of 50,000 or more consisting of a city and its immediate suburbs, together with adjacent counties that have a high degree of economic and social integration with that nucleus.[12] Over 77 percent of the U.S. population lives within the 284 MSAs identified during the 1990 census. The ten largest and ten smallest of the MSAs are listed in Table 4.2

MSAs become critical components in the development of most marketing plans. Many companies have even begun developing regional marketing campaigns specifically tailored to particular geographic areas defined as one or more MSAs. In fact, Frito-Lay used this micro-marketing concept when they introduced their Light line of snacks.[13] The MSA breakdown is such an integral part of the development of marketing plans that many of the syndicated data sources we will discuss in the next chapter report their data by MSA to simplify integration with census data.[14]

Over the past few decades, vast metropolitan areas have begun to appear in parts of the United States. Two or more MSAs are often merged during the creation of the urban area. For instance, San Francisco, Oakland, and San Jose are all separate MSAs located in the San Francisco Bay area, but all are a part of a single metropolitan area.

The Bureau of the Census has created a classification, called a Consolidated Metropolitan Statistical Area, to address this urban sprawl. A **Consolidated Metropolitan Statistical Area**, or CMSA, is defined as two or more contiguous MSAs having a total population of one million or more. Currently, thirty-nine metropolitan areas, including both CMSAs and freestanding MSAs, have a population of over one million people. Table 4.3 lists the twenty largest of these metropolitan areas with their populations. The marketing importance of these large urban areas is evidenced by the fact that over 50 percent of the total U.S. population can be reached by marketing only to these thirty-nine metropolitan areas!

MSA/CMSA	Population
New York/Northern New Jersey/Long Island, NY–NJ–CT	18,087,251
Los Angeles/Anaheim/Riverside, CA	14,531;529
Chicago/Gary/Lake County, IL–IN–WI	8,065,633
San Francisco/Oakland/San Jose, CA	6,253,311
Philadelphia/Wilmington/Trenton, PA–NJ–DE–MD	5,899,345
Detroit/Ann Arbor, MI	4,665,236
Boston/Lawrence/Salem, MA–NH	4,171,643
Washington, DC–MD–VA	3,923,574
Dallas/Fort Worth, TX	3,885,415
Houston/Galveston/Brazoria, TX	3,711,043
Miami/Fort Lauderdale, FL	3,192,582
Atlanta, GA	2,833,511
Cleveland/Akron/Lorain, OH	2,759,823
Seattle/Tacoma, WA	2,559,164
San Diego, CA	2,498,016
Minneapolis/St. Paul, MN–WI	2,464,124
St. Louis, MO–IL	2,444,099
Baltimore, MD	2,382,172
Pittsburgh/Beaver Valley, PA	2,242,798
Phoenix, AZ	2,122,101

Table 4.3 Twenty Largest metropolitan areas in the United States

Between census years, one of the most widely used sources of population estimates is the *Survey of Buying Power* published annually by *Sales and Marketing Management* magazine. The *Survey of Buying Power* provides population, buying income, and retail sales estimates for states, counties, and metropolitan areas within the United States and Canada. The same data, plus maps and figures, are also published in a looseleaf form called the *Data Service*.

One attractive feature of the *Survey of Buying Power* is its Buying Power Index, or BPI. The BPI provides a quick assessment of the market potential of geographic markets for products, services, and retail establishments. The **Buying Power Index** is a weighted index computed as:

> [(5 X the effective buying income of the area) + (3 X the retail sales of the area) + (2 X the population of the area)]/10.

The weights attached to the three components of the BPI reflect the relative importance of income, retail sales and population on an area's buying power.

Sources for Competitive Intelligence

With a slowing in population growth, most product markets in the United States are experiencing little, if any, growth in sales. As market growth slows, increasing a brand's share of sales is more difficult, since the majority of new sales must come from competitors' customers. Therefore, a company must pay increasing attention to its competitors' actions and expected future actions and try to determine how these actions will influence its marketing strategies, a process known as **competitive intelligence**.

Competitive intelligence information can be gathered from numerous sources. A few of the most common sources are listed in Table 4.4. Articles in newspapers and magazines as well as published studies about competitors can provide a wealth of information about what they are doing or are considering. A source that might not be as obvious is help-wanted ads. Such ads not only highlight the size and nature of any expansion in competitors' labor forces, but can also reveal future plans, such as expanded production or new facilities coming on line where these persons would work.

1. Newsclippings
2. Published studies
3. Help-wanted ads
4. Specialty trade publications
5. Trade shows and product literature
6. Advertisements
7. Public filings requested by federal, state, and local government agencies
8. Wall Street reports (e.g., Moody's S&P's)
9. Commercial databases (e.g., Nexis, Dialog, etc.)
10. Personal contacts

Table 4.4 Ten Common Ways to Gather Competitve Intelligence Information (Adapted from Leonard M. Fuld, *Monitoring the Competition*, New York: John Wiley & Sons, 1988.

Trade publications, trade shows, company literature on product lines, and their current advertising, especially advertising done to the trade, are other sources that should not be overlooked. Many times a firm will mention future plans in its brochures or advertising, trying to get a positive trade reaction. Three specific secondary sources provide information about publicly-held U.S. competitors' advertising expenditures.

o *Standard Directory of Advertisers* lists, by company, the advertising budget and media used.

o *Ad $ Summary* lists, by brand, the advertising budget and media used.

o *Media Records* provides information about the amount of newspaper advertising for various companies in over 200 newspapers in eighty cities.

For instance, the 1995 edition of *Ad $ Summary* reveals that Procter & Gamble spent about $200 thousand advertising the Pringles Light line of chips in 1995. This knowledge could have helped Frito-Lay determine how much advertising would be necessary to effectively launch their baked line of chips that year.

A vast amount of data about U.S. businesses is available because of public filing requirement of federal, state, and local governments. For instance, a company's annual report is a Securities and Exchange Commission (SEC) reporting requirement. Other valuable sources of comparative corporate information are Wall Street reports such as:

o *Standard & Poor's Industry Surveys*, which provide continuous economic and investment analyses on sixty-five leading U.S. industries and approximately 1500 of their constituent companies; and

o *Moody's Investors Fact Sheets: Industry Review*, which lists the leading companies in approximately thirty-eight industry groups, ranked on financial categories such as revenue, net income, and return on capital.

The last two common sources of competitive intelligence are commercial databases and personal contacts. Commercial data bases, often computerized and on-line, can contain a wealth of competitive information and will be described further later in this chapter. Personal contacts, or experience surveys, can often yield data unobtainable anywhere else.

As with the other areas in market monitoring, we have barely scratched the surface as to the variety of sources that exist for competitive intelligence. Good compilations of such sources are available and provide excellent starting points for seeking such information. One such compilation is *The New Competitive Intelligence: The Complete Resource for Finding, Analyzing, and Using Information about Your Competitors*.

Secondary Data Search Procedure

Sometimes the desired information is not found in any of the sources just described. In such cases, a search must be conducted to see if the information is available elsewhere. This section describes how to conduct this search.

Searching for topical information within secondary data is a lot like a treasure hunt. Seldom are all of the clues immediately visible but, with some digging and detective work, information on most topics can be uncovered. Unfortunately, unless the search is conducted in an organized fashion, a lot of empty holes will be dug before the treasure is found. Exhibit 4.4 displays one method for conducting an organized search.

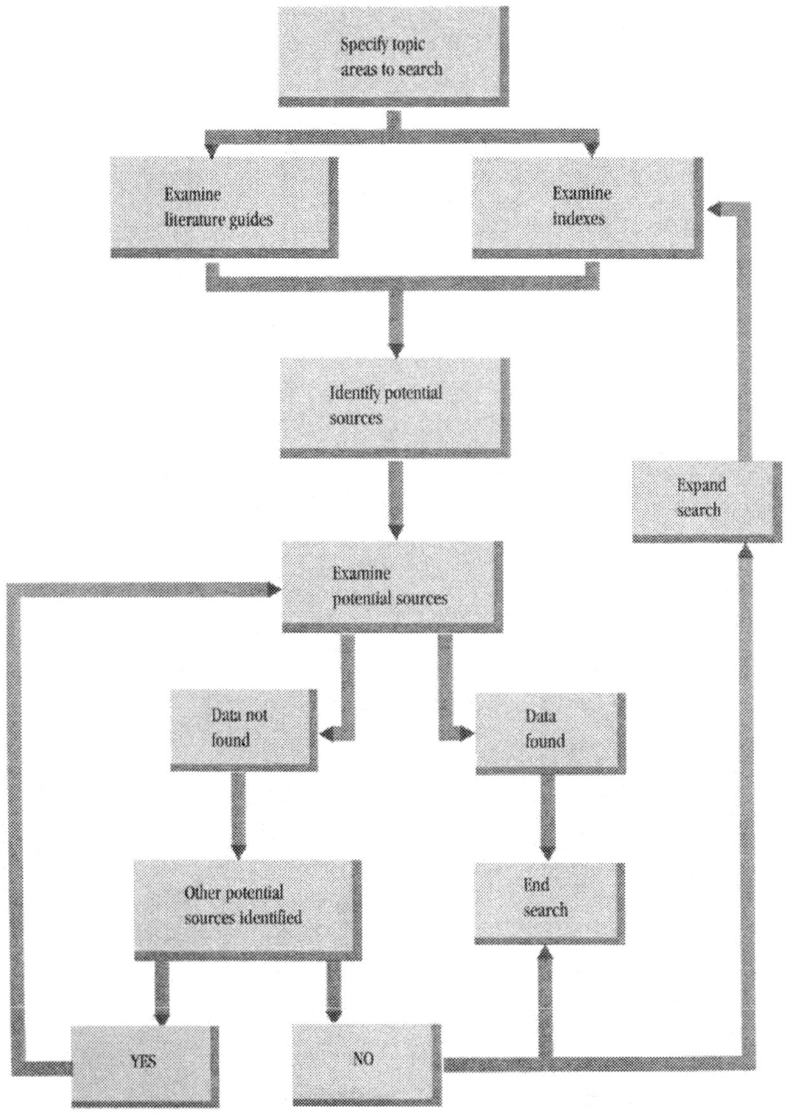

Exhibit 4.4 Secondary source search procedure.

The starting point in an organized search is to review guides to the literature and indexes, even though neither contains secondary data. A **literature guide** lists, by topic, books and periodicals that might contain relevant information. An index is more specific. A **literature index** lists articles and reports appearing in various periodicals that deal with particular topics.

Since literature guides and indexes arrange material by topic, you must determine what topic areas to explore. If the areas chosen are too specific, some relevant material will not be found. If the areas are too general, a large number of irrelevant sources will be searched. For example, thinking back to Frito-

Lay's introduction of a line of low-fat snacks, searching only "potato chips" as a topic area would probably miss some relevant material. "Food," on the other hand, would generate many sources that have nothing to do with salty snacks. Begin with the topic areas listed in the guides and indexes that appear most likely to provide the information and expand to more general topic areas as necessary.

Guides to the Literature

All literature guides do not include exactly the same sources. Thus, more than one guide should be examined to identify as many different potential sources as possible. Two useful literature guides covering business sources are:

o *Business Information Sources*, a guide to English-language sources in the business area, categorized by title, author, and subject; and

o *Encyclopedia of Business Information Sources*, a bibliography of business and commerce sources in English, arranged by subject.

Indexes

Several types of indexes are available. You may be familiar with one or more of the general indexes of business articles such as:

o *Business Periodicals Index*, a monthly publication covering approximately 300 business publications indexed by topic,

o *Public Affairs Information Service Bulletin*, a semimonthly index of articles, books, government documents, and reports issued by public and private organizations, or

o *Predicast's Funk & Scott's Index*, which covers a wide range of periodicals, trade reports, and the like.

Predicast's index is unique in that the information is compiled according to industry rather than topic, making a quicker search possible at times.

The best index to federal government publications is the *Monthly Catalog*, which lists all federal government documents and reports issued during that month.

Two useful indexes for statistical information are:

o *American Statistics Index*, which indexes and abstracts all U.S. federal agency publications that contain social, economic, demographic, or natural resources data, and

o *Statistical Reference Index*, which indexes and abstracts statistical publications from state government sources and some private organizations.

Two indexes even exist for published or commercially available market and business research studies. These indexes are:

o *Findex: The Directory of Market Research Reports, Studies and Surveys*, often referred to simply as *Findex*, and

o *Directory of Industry Sources, The United States And Canada*, also known as Harfax.

A wide array of topical information can be located in indexes. For example, in just one volume, the *Predicast Funk & Scott Index* alone referenced 144 articles dealing with snack foods. When considering its line of low-fat snacks, Frito-Lay could have learned the number and nature of new snack foods introduced, trends in the snack food industry, sales projections for different types of snacks, and demographic profiles of heavy and light snackers, just by scanning these articles. One article even mentioned an available 258-page market research report that had examined consumption patterns, trends, and purchasing behavior, as well as product development and marketing strategies within the salty snack market.[15]

Several research reports dealing with the snack food industry are listed in *Findex* and *Harfax*. One 335-page report, entitled Snack Food Market, provides information on the "size, growth, projected growth of markets and submarkets, company and brand share data, product mix, advertising trends, pricing, consumer demographics and buying patterns, company-related developments and financial news, and retail distribution channels."[16] All of the information in this report can be obtained for a purchase price of only $750. A second report, entitled *Potato Chips/Corn Chips*, costs only $395. This report summarizes the results of a nationwide mail survey of 2,000 randomly selected households. These reports cost only a fraction of what it would cost to collect the same data directly. However, as is common with secondary sources, the time period covered by these reports is several years earlier than the publication date of the index.

After identifying potential sources from relevant guides and indexes, the rest of the secondary search procedure shown in Exhibit 4.4 becomes iterative. Promising sources discovered in the guides and indexes are examined to see if they contain the desired data. These sources are also used to identify other potential sources. If the desired data are found, either the search will end or other sources will be examined to obtain additional information. If the data are not found, the other potential sources uncovered during the search are then examined for relevance. If all identified sources have been searched without finding the data, the topic areas can be expanded and the search procedure restarted. At some point, though, you may have to resign yourself to the fact that the data cannot be found and end the search.

Computerization of Secondary Data

While the number of secondary data sources just described may seem overwhelming, we have barely scratched the surface of all possible sources. In fact, one of the problems with using secondary data has been locating all potential sources, even when an organized search is conducted. Computerization is making it easier to do a more complete search.

Some secondary data sources are now available in computer-accessible form. For example, computer tapes or CD-Roms containing all of the Census of Population data can be purchased from the Bureau of the Census. The biggest impact of computerization, however, is the growth of online services.

Numerous computerized online services are now available that allow for a quick, systematic search of a host of databases and published sources. These services cross-reference all databases included in the service by key words to facilitate a more efficient search. By conducting a computerized search using several key words, all sources available in the online service can be quickly scanned for relevance. For example, some potential key words for our Frito-Lay example would be "snack foods," "potato chips," "salty snacks," and "light foods."

Some of these databases are like computerized indexes, providing bibliographical references to articles and reports. Others are like electronic directories, listing potential sources of relevant materials. The remainder provide access to complete documents. The *Gale Directory of Databases* published by Gale Research, Inc., provides a brief description of most of the databases existing at the time of its publication, but the growth of sources in this area makes any listing outdated as soon as it is published.

Several factors should be considered when selecting any online database. One obvious factor is the cost. Some online services charge a fixed amount per search; the cost of others depends on how long the search takes. A second important factor is the amount and types of information available in the online service's databases. Some online services provide instant access to hundreds of specific databases, for instance. A third factor is how powerful and easy to use are the search tools provided. Finally, some services are more user-friendly and have better user support.[17]

Traditionally, online services have been purchased and accessed through dedicated phone line connections. Now many of the same services can be accessed on the Internet as well. For instance, LEXIS-NEXIS, a full-text online service offering business news and legal information, and DIALOG, an online service containing over 450 business-oriented databases, both also have homepages on the World Wide Web. Furthermore, new online services are developing daily, many offering exciting new databases. For example, Profound, a recently-introduced Windows-based online service, provides news headlines, company financial reports, and research reports for each of over 190 countries.

Besides these professional search services, Internet users can conduct their own searches using the ARCHIE and VERONICA search programs as well as any of the numerous search engines that exist for the World Wide Web. Obviously, the more key words used in any online search, the less likely that a source will be missed. However, as the key word list is expanded, the length of time to complete the computer search increases, as does the cost. In addition, more irrelevant articles will be listed.

The impact of PC-scannable databases is evident from the growth of online searches. In 1974, fewer than one million online searches were conducted. By 1994, the number had grown to over 60 million searches.[18] This number will only continue to grow, as more and more information becomes available through the Internet.

International Issues

Until very recently, scant data were available when conducting an environmental analysis for most countries besides the United States. Now, however, a larger amount of data on most industrialized countries is available. The United Nations has established many international data collection projects that provide useful marketing information about foreign countries. Some sources are:

o *Demographic Yearbook*, which contains population characteristics for the countries of the world;

o *Industrial Statistics Yearbook*, which contains basic data on the industrial activities of each country of the world;

o *Yearbook of National Account Statistics*, which provides detailed information on the gross domestic product, income, and expenditures of 151 countries;

o *International Marketing Data and Statistics*, which includes marketing and consumer data on countries in the Americas, Asia, Africa, and Australia; and

o *European Marketing Data and Statistics*, which contains marketing and consumer data on countries in Europe.

Besides these sources, statistical yearbooks, much like the *Statistical Abstract of the United States*, are available for many countries. Furthermore, the governments of many countries now provide data similar to that provided by the U.S. Bureau of the Census. However, much of the data that are taken for granted when examining the U.S. market are still not available for other countries. For instance, many countries do not gather income data when conducting their censuses of the population.

The potential limitations of secondary data from other countries can be magnified as well. The data are more likely to be inaccurate or biased than are similar data collected in the United States. The data may not be collected frequently enough to be useful. Differing definitions used for various statistics also confounds the problem of comparing data across countries.

Summary

This chapter has introduced some of the key secondary sources for marketing research data. Internal secondary data are collected by the firm in the normal course of doing business.

Data that have already been collected by persons outside the firm are called external secondary data.

Secondary data have several advantages over primary data. They are often more complete, can be obtained more quickly, and are less expensive. However, not all data needed by the firm are available from secondary sources. In addition, secondary data can be biased, inaccurate, and not as useful as primary data.

A large number of factors outside the control of the firm, known as environmental forces, influence the firm's marketing strategies. A number of secondary sources exist that provide data on general economic conditions, industry trends, consumer markets, and competitors. Most large firms do market monitoring by systematically compiling such secondary data and making them readily available to their managers.

It is essential to seek information from secondary sources in an organized manner. Otherwise, relevant materials may never be located. One way of conducting an organized search is to begin with a search of relevant specific topics and to expand to broader topics if the information is not located.

Many secondary sources have now been computerized. In addition, the number of online services are proliferating as usage of the Internet grows. Online services speed up the search for secondary information and reduce the possibility that some sources will be overlooked.

Key Terms

Buying Power Index

competitive intelligence

Consolidated Metropolitan Statistical Area

external secondary data

internal secondary data

literature guide

literature index

market monitoring

Metropolitan Statistical Area

secondary data

Standard Industrial Classification (SIC) Codes

Nimslo's Use of Secondary Data

Many of the decisions that Nimslo made as it prepared for the national roll-out of its 3D camera were based on information gathered from secondary sources. The company conducted a thorough environmental scan of the photographic market and the information obtained helped the firm understand the economic, market, and competitive conditions it would face.

For example, information gathered from the *Survey of Current Business* and from other economic data sources revealed that Nimslo faced a difficult economic environment. Predictions for 1982 called for a slow growth in GNP, high unemployment, and for interest rates to hover above 17 percent. Not exactly the most opportune time to be introducing a new camera!

From the *Survey of Buying Power*, Nimslo developed a ranking of the top metropolitan markets based upon size, number of households with children, and household income. This ranking was used to prioritize cities for the roll-out, to develop sales territories, and to allocate the budget for spot television advertising. In advertising. In addition, Nimslo used *Census of Retail Trade* information to determine the availability of distributors within these metropolitan markets.

Finally, using *Ad $ Summary*, Nimslo was able to determine the amount of advertising spent by the major competitors. They found that in 1980, slightly more than $122 million had been spent on advertising for cameras, with Kodak and Polaroid accounting for nearly 60 percent of the spending. This information gave Nimslo insights into the amount of advertising money that would be required to compete in the camera market.

Review Questions

4.1 What are the potential advantages and drawbacks of secondary data as compared to primary data?

4.2 What is meant by market monitoring? Why do companies engage in market monitoring?

4.3 Briefly describe how to conduct a literature search efficiently.

4.4 What is a literature guide? an index? Why should multiple guides and indexes be used in a literature search?

4.5 For each of the following sources, indicate whether the source is: (1) a guide to business literature, (2) an index to business articles, (3) an index to government publications, (4) an index to statistical information, or (5) an index to published and commercially available marketing research reports.

a) *American Statistical Index*

b) *Findex: The Directory of Market Research Reports, Studies, and Surveys*

c) *Monthly Catalog*

d) *Statistical Reference Index*

e) *Business Periodicals Index*

f) *Public Affairs Information Index*

g) *Business Information Sources*

h) *Predicast's Funk & Scott's Index*

i) *Directory of Industry Data Sources, the United States and Canada*

j) *Encyclopedia of Business Information Sources*

4.6 What is meant by a Metropolitan Statistical Area? a Consolidated Metropolitan Statistical Area? Of what significance are these designations to marketers?

4.7 What three variables comprise the Buying Power Index? How and why are these three variables weighted?

4.8 Which of the following are sources of (1) economic data, (2) industry data, (3) consumer market data, and (4) competitive data?

a) *County Business Patterns*

b) *Survey of Current Business*

c) *Census of Population and Housing*

d) *Moody's Investors Fact Sheet: Industry Review*
e) *U.S. Industrial Outlook*

f) *Survey of Buying Power/Data Service*

g) *Ad $ Summary*

h) *Predicast's Basebook*

i) *Standard & Poor's Industry Surveys*

j) *Media Records*

k) *Standard Directory of Advertisers*

4.9 What are Standard Industrial Classification codes? What problems can be encountered when attempting to identify potential competitors using SIC codes?

4.10 What is meant by competitive intelligence? Briefly describe commonly-used sources for competitive intelligence.

4.11 What are the significant trends in secondary data? How are these trends effecting the usefulness of secondary data?

4.11 What kinds of secondary data are most likely to be available for countries other than the United States?

Discussion Questions

4.1 Several brands of nonalcoholic beers have recently been introduced. Discuss the environmental factors that you feel have led to the decision to introduce these products. What key words would you use to conduct a secondary search to find out more about these factors?

4.2 Many times when doing market monitoring, you will find different values for the same statistic depending upon what source is examined. For example, if you searched for the annual sales of potato chips, you might find several different estimates for the same year. Why is this likely to happen? What should you do if this occurs?

4.3 A great deal of information is available from secondary sources. However, not all of the types of information needed by a marketing manager can be found in these sources. Describe some of the kinds of information you feel would be useful to a marketing manager that probably cannot be found in secondary data.

4.4 General Foods introduced Maxwell House coffee in "filter packs," premeasured coffee enclosed in a coffee filter that can be placed in a coffee maker. Conduct a market monitoring and, on the basis of your findings, discuss whether you feel General Foods made the correct decision. Should Procter & Gamble introduce Folger's in a similar form?

Chapter Four Endnotes

---

1. Facts in this example are based on information found in "Frito-Lay Betting Any Health-Conscious Snacker Worth His Salt Will See the Light," *The Atlanta Journal and Constitution*, March 20, 1990, p. B-3.

2. Mark Edmond, "Salty Snack Foods, A C-store Pillar, Enjoy Dynamic Growth," *NPN: National Petroleum News*, 88(2), p. 74-5.

3. Shelly Garcia, "BBDO Chips Away At Fat With 'Max' Spot," Adweek, 37(18), p. 5.

4. Steve Dwyer, "While Dry Snacks Get 'Healthier,' Tradition Still Holds Some Chips," *NPN: National Petroleum News*, 87(8), p. 42-43.

5. Barbara White-Sax, "Salty Snacks Gain More Shelf Space With Low-Fat/Low-Salt Varieties," *Discount Store News*, 35(3), p. f14 and Jo-Ann Zbytniewski, "A Snack Food Free-for-All," *Progressive Grocer*, 71(9), p. 121-2.

6. Steve Dwyer, "While Dry Snacks Get 'Healthier,' Tradition Still Holds Some Chips," *NPN: National Petroleum News*, 87(8), p. 42-3.

7. Bob Messenger, "Prepared Foods 1986 Annual Trends Report: Consumers See the Light," *Prepared Foods*, November 1985, pp. 46-49.

8. IBID.

9. "You Can Look It Up: The Statistical Abstract Paints the U.S. by the Numbers," Time, May 22, 1989, p. 36.

10. *U.S. Industrial Outlook: Prospects for Over 359 Manufacturing and Service Industries*, Washington, D.C.: U.S. Department of

Commerce, January, 1990, p. 342.

11. Janet Myers, "Census To Give Marketers A Hand," *Advertising Age,* March 12, 1990, pg. 41.

12. *Patterns of Metropolitan Areas and County Population Growth: 1980 to 1984*, Current Population Reports, Series P-25, No. 976, Washington, D.C.: U.S. Bureau of the Census, 1985, p. 6.

13. Jennifer Lawrence, "Frito's Micro Move: How a Giant Found Neighborhood Niches," *Advertising Age*, February 12, 1990, p. 44.

14. IBID.

15. Carol Fischman, "Low Sodium Versions Help Salty Snack Sales," *Supermarket News*, January 15, 1990, p. 16.

16. *Findex: The Directory of Market Research Reports, Studies, and Surveys*, New York: FIND/SVP, 1989, p. 273.

17. For an excellent discussion of selecting online services, see John F. Lescher, *Online Market Research: Cost-Effective Searching of the Internet and Online Services*, Reading, MA: Addision-Wesley Publishing Company, 1995.

18. *Gale Directory of Databases*, New York: Gale Research, Inc., 1995, p. xxi.

Chapter 5

Syndicated Data

Learning Objectives

This chapter provides an overview of major syndicated data sources. After reading this chapter you will understand the importance of syndicated data sources to marketing managers in the context of:

- evaluating consumer attitudes,
- assessing the value of various media for reaching consumers, and
- understanding and monitoring household purchase behavior.

Borden, Inc., adopted a new marketing strategy to increase sales of its Classico pasta sauce, a premium product priced about 40 cents higher than the market leaders Ragu and Prego.[1] Borden identified the stores serving the highest concentrations of potential Classico customers and focused their marketing efforts exclusively on these retail outlets. Syndicated data figured prominently in Borden's ability to institute this strategy. Classico customers were identified through the Information Resources, Inc., household scanner panel system, a syndicated data service available to all packaged goods manufacturers. Borden provided this profile of the Classico target to another syndicated service, Market Metrics, which then generated a list of retail outlets that contained high concentrations of the target consumers among their respective customer bases.

Micromarketing, as just described, allowed Borden to advertise and promote the Classico pasta sauce in a far more efficient manner than the mass marketing approach previously used. The decision to use a micromarketing strategy was made possible by the availability of detailed information on shopping and buying habits of individual consumers, one of the many forms of syndicated marketing data routinely used by marketing managers.

As mentioned in Chapter 1, **syndicated data** result from multisponsored research. Typically, the reason for many sponsors is that the cost of the research is prohibitive for a single firm. While individual firms may request different analyses and report formats, the basic source data is the same. For example, A.C. Nielsen and IRI (Information Resources, Inc.) sell monthly retail sales figures to consumer packaged goods firms, who use the data to assess individual brand performance. Individual companies can request different levels of detail and different categories of goods as well as organizations of products within categories.

A large portion of annual marketing research expenditures goes to purchasing syndicated data. In fact, the four largest marketing research suppliers, in terms of revenues, all specialize in syndicated data services. Together these four firms account for more than one billion dollars of sales.[2] To remain profitable, a company collecting syndicated data must be able to provide information that is desired by a large number of firms and cannot be easily obtained otherwise. Data on consumers, media, and market performance meet both of these requirements and are commonly syndicated.

Exhibit 5.1 shows the spectrum of marketing activities and issues monitored by syndicated data. This exhibit provides the framework we will use for organizing and discussing syndicated services.

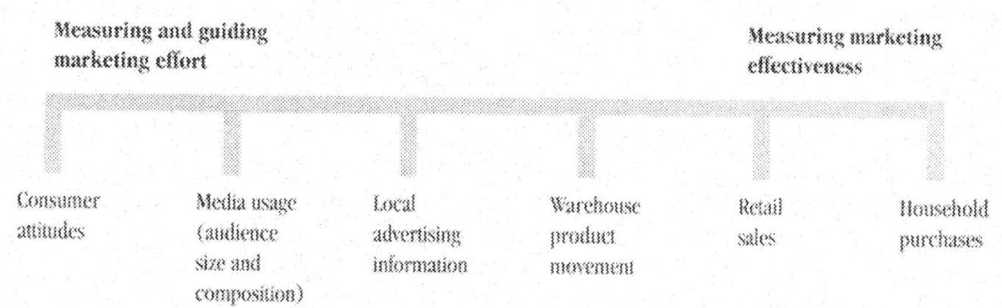

Exhibit 5.1 The scope of syndicated data services.

Consumer Attitudes

Understanding whether consumers are pessimistic or optimistic about the future, their buying plans, and their concerns about society, is obviously vital to companies. For example, manufacturers of durable goods can expect sales problems when consumers become concerned about deteriorating economic conditions and increasing unemployment. Likewise, companies in tune with consumers' growing concern over the environment and staying fit could have benefitted by adapting their products to these concerns.

Many companies subscribe to the Yankelovich *Monitor*, a monthly publication containing selected results from a nationally projectable telephone survey of U.S. households that Yankelovich conducts periodically. The survey is designed to determine social trends and consumer attitudes about economic conditions and the government.

The **Monitor** includes data on consumer confidence levels, buying intentions, and general consumer expectations about the future. However, since the *Monitor* deals primarily with general attitudes, companies use the data primarily as a barometer of current pertinent social issues and attitudes. In the late 90's, the *Monitor* signaled a change in Americans= attitude toward clothes. An increasing percentage (77% in 1997) of Americans was dressing to be comfortable, rather than Ato be seen.@[3] To these consumers, comfort was more important than appearance, which certainly has implications for apparel manufacturers. Changes in consumer confidence levels and buying intentions are also used to signal changes in the purchase of durable goods. Critics of the *Monitor* complain that it is too general and too difficult to apply to a specific situation.

Another barometer of consumer attitude is the *Confidence Index* published monthly by the Consumer Research Center of the Conference Board. This measure is based on a telephone survey of adults who are asked their opinions regarding both present and future conditions. The **Confidence Index** provides a vehicle for tracking consumers' feelings regarding the overall economic environment in the United States.

Exhibit 5.2 shows how consumer confidence continued to rise through '96 and '97, a period of steady economic growth.[4] The single largest jump in the index's twenty-two-year history, about 20 points, occurred in March '91, immediately following the United States' success in the Persian Gulf War.

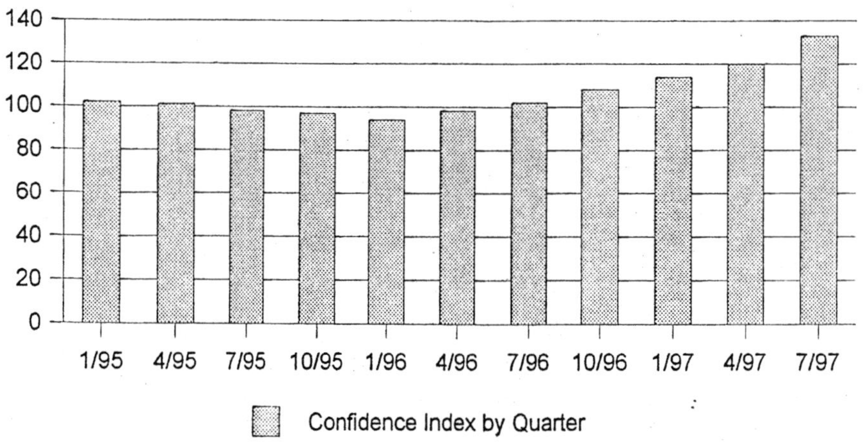

Exhibit 5.2 Consumer Confidence Index

The Consumer Confidence Index is also calculated separately for demographic subgroups. Interestingly, the large index noted in Exhibit 5.2 reflects two very different attitudes. The index for those respondents with annual household incomes in excess of $50,000 is about 150, while the index is only about 100 for those with household incomes less than $15,000[5]. This means that relatively poor people are no more confident about the future than they were in 1985.

Syndicated Media Usage Data

Marketing managers must make decisions regarding where, when, and how much to advertise. Once a target audience for a new product or service has been identified, the question of how effectively and efficiently to advertise to this audience must be addressed. Syndicated data can be of great assistance in this process as sources exist to gain insight into the sizes and compositions of the audiences of television and radio shows, as well as readerships of magazines. We discuss these issues briefly now and return to them in more detail in Chapter 15, which is dedicated to marketing research to support advertising decisions.

Audience Size

Media advertising tends to be priced according to the size of the audience delivered. For magazines and newspapers, audience size is usually equated with paid circulation, a relatively static and easily computed measure. For radio and television, however, the size of the delivered audience varies as people switch stations and tune in and out. This variability makes the measurement of radio and television audience size much more difficult to determine. Radio and television networks and independent stations rely on independent ratings services that measure audience size to determine advertising rates. A.C. Nielsen (television) and Arbitron (radio) are the prominent ratings services. These ratings are extremely important to the broadcasters themselves, and to those who advertise using these media, because the ratings are the measures of audience size, which in turn determines advertising rates.

Buying advertising time on network television can be very expensive due to the large audience generally delivered. The most expensive television show on which to buy advertising time is the Super Bowl because of the huge number of viewers. The cost of a thirty-second spot in the Super Bowl has grown continuously to now well over a million dollars. There is a bonus, however, to advertising during the Super Bowl, as the ads themselves have become a Aside show@ and are discussed and rated extensively in the media during the weeks following the game. In fact, new advertising campaigns are often introduced during the Super Bowl for this reason. We will discuss broadcast ratings services in more detail in Chapter 15 Advertising Research. For now, it suffices to say that much syndicated research is focused on measuring broadcast audience size.

Audience Composition

TV ratings data are supplemented by audience composition information--details on who watches what. For many years, the primary source of audience composition data was one-week or two-week TV viewing diaries kept by a sample of households. Exhibit 5.3 contains a sample page from a one-week diary. Technological developments, such as people meters, again discussed Chapter 15 Advertising Research, are rapidly changing how these data are collected. Analogous information is available for radio, magazines, and newspapers from a variety of research companies that have expertise in these areas.

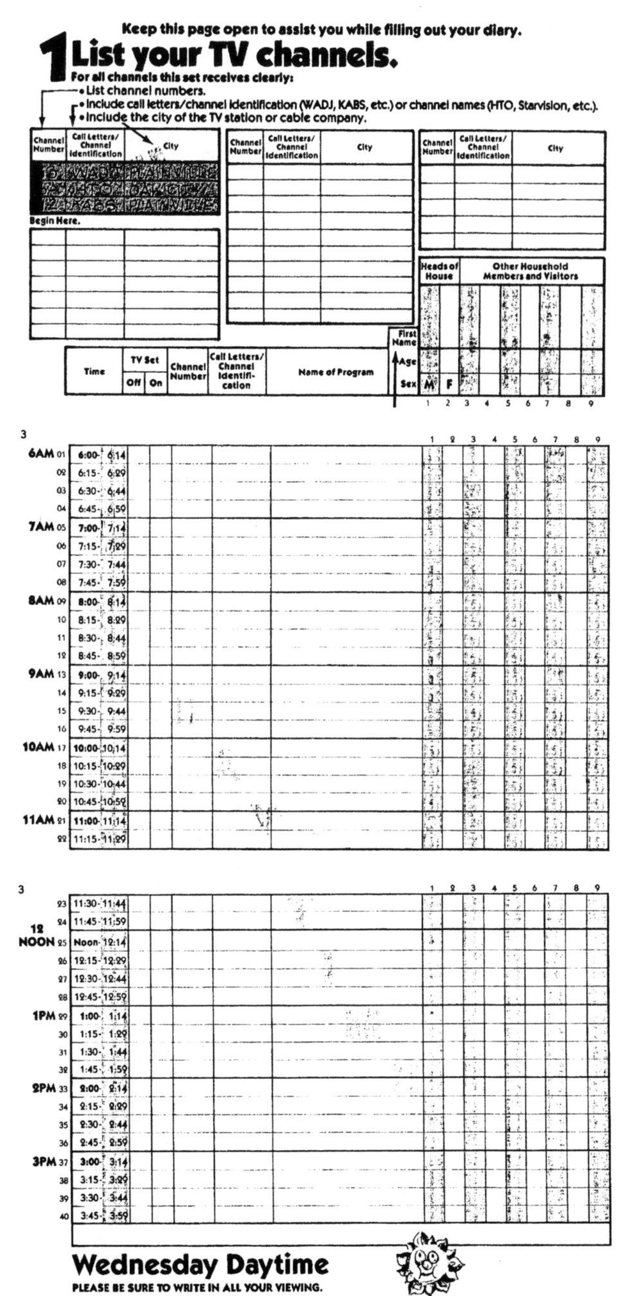

Keep this page open to assist you while filling out your diary.

1 List your TV channels.

For all channels this set receives clearly:

- List channel numbers.
- Include call letters/channel identification (WADJ, KABS, etc.) or channel names (HTO, Starvision, etc.).
- Include the city of the TV station or cable company.

Channel Number	Call Letters/ Channel Identification	City
6	WADJ	PLAINVILLE
[illegible]	HTO	OAK CITY
12	KABS	PLAINVILLE

Begin Here.

Channel Number	Call Letters/ Channel Identification	City

Heads of House		Other Household Members and Visitors						
First Name								
Age								
Sex: M	F							
1	2	3	4	5	6	7	8	9

3

		Time	TV Set Off	TV Set On	Channel Number	Call Letters/ Channel Identification	Name of Program	1	2	3	4	5	6	7	8	9
6AM	01	6:00-6:14														
	02	6:15-6:29														
	03	6:30-6:44														
	04	6:45-6:59														
7AM	05	7:00-7:14														
	06	7:15-7:29														
	07	7:30-7:44														
	08	7:45-7:59														
8AM	09	8:00-8:14														
	10	8:15-8:29														
	11	8:30-8:44														
	12	8:45-8:59														
9AM	13	9:00-9:14														
	14	9:15-9:29														
	15	9:30-9:44														
	16	9:45-9:59														
10AM	17	10:00-10:14														
	18	10:15-10:29														
	19	10:30-10:44														
	20	10:45-10:59														
11AM	21	11:00-11:14														
	22	11:15-11:29														

3

		Time						1	2	3	4	5	6	7	8	9
	23	11:30-11:44														
	24	11:45-11:59														
12 NOON	25	Noon-12:14														
	26	12:15-12:29														
	27	12:30-12:44														
	28	12:45-12:59														
1PM	29	1:00-1:14														
	30	1:15-1:29														
	31	1:30-1:44														
	32	1:45-1:59														
2PM	33	2:00-2:14														
	34	2:15-2:29														
	35	2:30-2:44														
	36	2:45-2:59														
3PM	37	3:00-3:14														
	38	3:15-3:29														
	39	3:30-3:44														
	40	3:45-3:59														

Wednesday Daytime

PLEASE BE SURE TO WRITE IN ALL YOUR VIEWING.

Exhibit 5.3 Sample page from Arbitron TV diary. (Copyright 1991 The Arbitron Company)

Exhibit 5.4 contains data from the ***Simmons Annual Survey of Media and Markets*** and demonstrates the kind of information pertaining to magazine readership that Simmons reports. The sample information pertains to adult (18 years and over)male readership of selected magazines by education level. The first column contains estimates of the number of adult males in the United States (in thousands) who read each magazine. The first entry in this column is the estimated number of adult males in the U.S.

The next set of four columns refers only to adult males who have graduated from college. The first entry in Column A is the projected number of total male college graduates. Subsequent entries in Column A are the projected numbers of adult male readers of each magazine who have graduated from college.

Column B is the percentage of all adult male college graduates who read each magazine. Thus, for *Esquire*, the percentage in Column B is calculated as 553/10257 = .0539. Column C is ratio of Column A to the first column expressed in percentage form. Hence, for each magazine, Column C contains the projected percentages of all adult male readers of the listed magazines who are college graduates. For *Esquire*, the entry in Column C is computed as 553/2890 = .1912.

Column D, the index, is the ratio of the Column C percentage to the percentage of total adult males who have graduated from college, that is the first entry in Column C, multiplied by 100. An index above (below) 100 indicates that a disproportionately high (low) percentage of a magazine's adult male readership has graduated from college. For *Esquire* the index is computed as (19.12/11.21)(100)= 171, indicating that a disproportionately high share of the magazine's adult male readers are college graduates. The entries in other two sets of four columns each are defined analogously.

The index can also be calculated as the ratio of the percentage of adult male college graduates who read *Esquire*, 5.39% (Column B), to the percentage of all adult males who read *Esquire*, 3.16% (2890/91482 = .0316). (The latter percentage is not provided in the table and must be calculated.) As you can see, this calculation produces the same index, (5.39/3.16)*100 = 171.

EDUCATION OF RESPONDENT
(MALES)

	TOTAL U.S. '000	GRADUATED COLLEGE A '000	B % DOWN	C % ACROSS	D INDX	ATTENDED COLLEGE (1-3 YRS.) A '000	B % DOWN	C % ACROSS	D INDX	GRADUATED HIGH SCHOOL A '000	B % DOWN	C % ACROSS	D INDX
TOTAL MALES	80052	16071	100.0	20.1	100	14142	100.0	17.7	100	29230	100.0	36.5	100
ATLANTIC MONTHLY	*371	264	1.6	71.2	354	40	0.3	10.8	61	61	0.2	16.4	45
BARRON'S	765	470	2.9	61.4	306	182	1.3	23.8	135	113	0.4	14.8	40
BETTER HOMES & GARDENS	4653	1037	6.5	22.3	111	915	6.5	19.7	111	1772	6.1	38.1	104
BON APPETIT	786	401	2.5	51.0	254	185	1.3	23.5	133	148	0.5	18.8	52
BUSINESS WEEK	3257	1560	9.7	47.9	239	715	5.1	22.0	124	557	1.9	17.1	47
CAR AND DRIVER	2930	526	3.3	18.0	89	733	5.2	25.0	142	1251	4.3	42.7	117
CBS MAG. NETWORK (GROSS)	15706	3212	20.0	20.5	102	3979	28.1	25.3	143	6371	21.8	40.6	111
CBS MAG. BLUE NTWK (GROSS)	9286	1925	12.0	20.7	103	2463	17.4	26.5	150	3721	12.7	40.1	110
CBS MAG. GOLD NTWK (GROSS)	6420	1286	8.0	20.0	100	1516	10.7	23.6	134	2651	9.1	41.3	113
COLONIAL HOMES	505	248	1.5	49.1	245	90	0.6	17.8	101	132	0.5	26.1	72
CONDE NAST LIMITED (GROSS)	4587	1418	8.8	30.9	154	1457	10.3	31.8	180	1198	4.1	26.1	72
CONDE NAST WOMEN (GROSS)	1590	462	2.9	29.1	145	411	2.9	25.8	146	457	1.6	28.7	79
CONSUMERS DIGEST	1462	451	2.8	30.8	154	351	2.5	24.0	136	487	1.7	33.3	91
COSMOPOLITAN	1700	453	2.8	26.6	133	379	2.7	22.3	126	546	1.9	32.1	88
COUNTRY LIVING	1263	400	2.5	31.7	158	367	2.6	29.1	164	380	1.3	30.1	82
DISCOVER	1286	519	3.2	40.4	201	302	2.1	23.5	133	357	1.2	27.8	76
EBONY	2729	434	2.7	15.9	79	510	3.6	18.7	106	1005	3.4	36.8	101
ESQUIRE	1235	500	3.1	40.5	202	284	2.0	23.0	130	319	1.1	25.8	71
ESSENCE	749	154	1.0	20.6	102	188	1.3	25.1	142	237	0.8	31.6	87
FAMILY CIRCLE	2376	435	2.7	18.3	91	486	3.4	20.5	116	992	3.4	41.8	114
THE FAMILY HANDYMAN	2662	533	3.3	20.0	100	454	3.2	17.1	97	1156	4.0	43.4	119
FIELD & STREAM	7693	789	4.9	10.3	51	1406	9.9	18.3	103	3732	12.8	48.5	133
FOOD & WINE	685	216	1.3	31.5	157	134	0.9	19.6	111	254	0.9	37.1	102
FORBES	1825	1182	7.4	64.8	323	338	2.4	18.5	105	234	0.8	12.8	35
FORTUNE	1719	1092	6.8	63.5	316	324	2.3	18.8	107	245	0.8	14.3	39
GQ/ GENTLEMEN'S QUARTERLY	2259	562	3.5	24.9	124	903	6.4	40.0	226	588	2.0	26.0	71
GLAMOUR	486	131	0.8	27.0	134	85	0.6	17.5	99	141	0.5	29.0	79
GOLF DIGEST	2082	837	5.2	40.2	200	507	3.6	24.4	138	599	2.0	28.8	79
GOLF DIGEST/TENNIS (GROSS)	2877	1134	7.1	39.4	196	769	5.4	26.7	151	814	2.8	28.3	77
GOLF MAGAZINE	1517	515	3.2	33.9	169	435	3.1	28.7	162	464	1.6	30.6	84
GOLF MAGAZINE/SKI (GROSS)	2550	854	5.3	33.5	167	789	5.6	30.9	175	710	2.4	27.8	76
GOOD HOUSEKEEPING	2717	646	4.0	23.8	118	515	3.6	19.0	107	986	3.4	36.3	99
GOURMET	728	360	2.2	49.5	246	177	1.3	24.3	138	139	0.5	19.1	52
HARPER'S BAZAAR	*469	164	1.0	35.0	174	50	0.4	10.7	60	180	0.6	38.4	105
HEALTH	770	229	1.4	29.7	148	132	0.9	17.1	97	222	0.8	28.8	79
HEARST GOLD BUY (GROSS)	2655	1000	6.2	37.7	188	570	4.0	21.5	122	790	2.7	29.8	81
HEARST HOME GROUP (GROSS)	2348	869	5.4	37.0	184	585	4.1	24.9	141	688	2.4	29.3	80
HEARST MAN POWER (GROSS)	8798	1545	9.6	17.6	87	1915	13.5	21.8	123	3716	12.7	42.2	116
HEARST WOMAN PWR PLUS(GROSS)	7149	1948	12.1	27.2	136	1549	11.0	21.7	123	2366	8.1	33.1	91
HOME MECHANIX	2833	482	3.0	17.0	85	704	5.0	24.8	141	1228	4.2	43.3	119
HOT ROD	3752	161	1.0	4.3	21	573	4.1	15.3	86	1990	6.8	53.0	145
HOUSE & GARDEN	1145	357	2.2	31.2	155	281	2.0	24.5	139	322	1.1	28.1	77
HOUSE BEAUTIFUL	579	221	1.4	38.2	190	128	0.9	22.1	125	177	0.6	30.6	84
INC.	963	535	3.3	55.6	277	201	1.4	20.9	118	191	0.7	19.8	54
JET	2745	254	1.6	9.3	46	509	3.6	18.5	105	1113	3.8	40.5	111
LADIES' HOME JOURNAL	1347	342	2.1	25.4	126	216	1.5	16.0	91	427	1.5	31.7	87
LHJ FAMILY GRP COMBO(GROSS)	3015	859	5.3	28.5	142	608	4.3	20.2	114	901	3.1	29.9	82
LIFE	4976	1319	8.2	26.5	132	1286	9.1	25.8	146	1594	5.5	32.0	88
LOS ANGELES TIMES MAGAZINE	1761	788	4.9	44.7	223	492	3.5	27.9	158	322	1.1	18.3	50
MADEMOISELLE	*309	59	0.4	19.1	95	100	0.7	32.4	183	102	0.3	33.0	90
MC CALL'S	2059	446	2.8	21.7	108	320	2.3	15.5	88	810	2.8	39.3	108
MC CALL'S/WRK MOTHER (GROSS)	2262	525	3.3	23.2	116	336	2.4	14.9	84	899	3.1	39.7	109
MODERN PHOTOGRAPHY	1531	341	2.1	22.3	111	579	4.1	37.8	214	559	1.9	36.5	100
MONEY	3086	1577	9.8	51.1	255	644	4.6	20.9	118	629	2.2	20.4	56
MOTHER EARTH NEWS	1099	212	1.3	19.3	96	300	2.1	27.3	155	507	1.7	46.1	126
MOTOR TREND	2154	421	2.6	19.5	97	503	3.6	23.4	132	884	3.0	41.0	112
MS.	**142	62	0.4	43.7	217	16	0.1	11.3	64	35	0.1	24.6	68
NATIONAL ENQUIRER	5914	563	3.5	9.5	47	1053	7.4	17.8	101	2552	8.7	43.2	118
NATIONAL GEOGRAPHIC	12480	4211	26.2	33.7	168	2780	19.7	22.3	126	4045	13.8	32.4	89
NATIONAL SUNDAY MAGAZINE PKG	49220	12157	75.6	24.7	123	9866	69.8	20.0	113	18315	62.7	37.2	102
NATURAL HISTORY	642	264	1.6	41.1	205	124	0.9	19.3	109	99	0.3	15.4	42
NEW WOMAN	*173	50	0.3	28.9	144	10	0.1	5.8	33	66	0.2	38.2	104
NEW YORK	418	245	1.5	58.6	292	69	0.5	16.5	93	78	0.3	18.7	51
THE NEW YORKER	1065	674	4.2	63.3	315	184	1.3	17.3	98	151	0.5	14.2	39
NEWSWEEK	9635	3575	22.2	37.1	185	2459	17.4	25.5	144	2610	8.9	27.1	74

Exhibit 5.4 Sample page from *Simmons Survey of Media and Markets*; adult male magazine readership by education. (Source: Simmons Market Research Bureau. Used with permission.)

Thus, if a marketer were seeking to reach adult males who are college graduates via magazine advertising, *Esquire*, *Bon Appetit*, *Golf Digest*, *Forbes*, and *Fortune* would be attractive choices because of their high indices. Analogously, *Essence* and *Guns and Ammo* would be avoided because of their low indices.

Applying Marketing Research 5.1.

Let's return to the new line of baked snack products from Frito-Lay, which was discussed at the beginning of the previous chapter. The first challenge confronting Frito-Lay was to make consumers aware of the line and its relative benefits. The company needed to communicate with consumers through advertising. Consider Lays Baked Potato Chips. What are effective and efficient ways to advertise this new brand? In which TV shows, radio stations, and magazines should the company buy time and space?

Once again the *Simmons Study of Media and Markets* can help. Exhibit 5.5 contains information similar to Exhibit 5.4, but this time for female homemakers who used potato chips in the last thirty days. The indices in the exhibit show *Hot Rod* and *Soap Opera Digest* to be particularly good magazines for reaching female homemakers who are heavy users, and *Inc.* and *The New York Times Magazine* to be particularly poor in this sense.

CORN & TORTILLA CHIPS & SNACKS - USAGE IN LAST 30 DAYS
(FEMALE HOMEMAKERS)

	TOTAL U.S. '000	ALL USERS A '000	ALL USERS B % DOWN	ALL USERS C % ACROSS	ALL USERS D INDX	HEAVY USERS FOUR OR MORE A '000	HEAVY USERS B % DOWN	HEAVY USERS C % ACROSS	HEAVY USERS D INDX	MEDIUM USERS TWO-THREE A '000	MEDIUM USERS B % DOWN	MEDIUM USERS C % ACROSS	MEDIUM USERS D INDX
TOTAL	82273	48308	100.0	58.7	100	9520	100.0	11.6	100	20365	100.0	24.8	100
ATLANTIC MONTHLY	*328	216	0.4	65.9	112	58	0.6	17.7	153	56	0.3	17.1	69
BARRON'S	*318	158	0.3	49.7	85	59	0.6	18.6	160	39	0.2	12.3	50
BETTER HOMES & GARDENS	16341	10575	21.9	64.7	110	1925	20.2	11.8	102	4526	22.2	27.7	112
BON APPETIT	2672	1857	3.8	69.5	118	429	4.5	16.1	139	602	3.0	22.5	91
BUSINESS WEEK	1378	802	1.7	58.2	99	179	1.9	13.0	112	269	1.3	19.5	79
CAR AND DRIVER	*336	244	0.5	72.6	124	24	0.3	7.1	62	97	0.5	28.9	117
CBS MAG. NETWORK (GROSS)	3658	2600	5.4	71.1	121	517	5.4	14.1	122	1173	5.8	32.1	130
CBS MAG. BLUE NTWK (GROSS)	2458	1703	3.5	69.3	118	315	3.3	12.8	111	731	3.6	29.7	120
CBS MAG. GOLD NTWK (GROSS)	1200	897	1.9	74.8	127	202	2.1	16.8	145	442	2.2	36.8	149
COLONIAL HOMES	1537	947	2.0	61.6	105	189	2.0	12.3	106	457	2.2	29.7	120
CONDE NAST LIMITED (GROSS)	9303	5741	11.9	61.7	105	1360	14.3	14.6	126	2200	10.8	23.6	96
CONDE NAST WOMEN (GROSS)	14524	9518	19.7	65.5	112	1987	20.9	13.7	118	4003	19.7	27.6	111
CONSUMERS DIGEST	1292	776	1.6	60.1	102	130	1.4	10.1	87	382	1.9	29.6	119
COSMOPOLITAN	6999	4683	9.7	66.9	114	905	9.5	12.9	112	2117	10.4	30.2	122
COUNTRY LIVING	3436	2251	4.7	65.5	112	368	3.9	10.7	93	1031	5.1	30.0	121
DISCOVER	726	492	1.0	67.8	115	98	1.0	13.5	117	155	0.8	21.3	86
EBONY	3727	1906	3.9	51.1	87	562	5.9	15.1	130	699	3.4	18.8	76
ESQUIRE	956	502	1.0	52.5	89	135	1.4	14.1	122	215	1.1	22.5	91
ESSENCE	1746	931	1.9	53.3	91	233	2.4	13.3	115	337	1.7	19.3	78
FAMILY CIRCLE	16548	10715	22.2	64.8	110	1973	20.7	11.9	103	4644	22.8	28.1	113
THE FAMILY HANDYMAN	1263	916	1.9	72.5	124	189	2.0	15.0	129	363	1.8	28.7	116
FIELD & STREAM	1859	1313	2.7	70.6	120	273	2.9	14.7	127	589	2.9	31.7	128
FOOD & WINE	675	424	0.9	62.8	107	87	0.9	12.9	111	240	1.2	35.6	144
FORBES	653	344	0.7	52.7	90	38	0.4	5.8	50	175	0.9	26.8	108
FORTUNE	798	552	1.1	69.2	118	112	1.2	14.0	121	209	1.0	26.2	106
GQ/GENTLEMEN'S QUARTERLY	765	551	1.1	72.0	123	127	1.3	16.6	143	191	0.9	25.0	101
GLAMOUR	5557	3712	7.7	66.8	114	771	8.1	13.9	120	1540	7.6	27.7	112
GOLF DIGEST	650	451	0.9	69.4	118	73	0.8	11.2	97	214	1.1	32.9	133
GOLF DIGEST/TENNIS (GROSS)	1063	714	1.5	67.2	114	133	1.4	12.5	108	349	1.7	32.8	133
GOLF MAGAZINE	484	374	0.8	77.3	132	58	0.6	12.0	104	207	1.0	42.8	173
GOLF MAGAZINE/SKI (GROSS)	968	752	1.6	77.7	132	165	1.7	17.0	147	372	1.8	38.4	155
GOOD HOUSEKEEPING	16160	10395	21.5	64.3	110	1986	20.9	12.3	106	4304	21.1	26.6	108
GOURMET	1531	956	2.0	62.4	106	185	1.9	12.1	104	392	1.9	25.6	103
HARPER'S BAZAAR	2506	1512	3.1	60.3	103	289	3.0	11.5	100	679	3.3	27.1	109
HEALTH	2061	1221	2.5	59.2	101	294	3.1	14.3	123	550	2.7	26.7	108
HEARST GOLD BUY (GROSS)	8457	5184	10.7	61.3	104	1109	11.6	13.1	113	2199	10.8	26.0	105
HEARST HOME GROUP (GROSS)	8293	5166	10.7	62.3	106	1071	11.3	12.9	112	2223	10.9	26.8	108
HEARST MAN POWER (GROSS)	1961	1273	2.6	64.9	111	270	2.8	13.8	119	583	2.9	29.7	120
HEARST WOMAN PWR PLUS(GROSS)	37328	24258	50.2	65.0	111	4613	48.5	12.4	107	10610	52.1	28.4	115
HOME MECHANIX	713	504	1.0	70.7	120	77	0.8	10.8	93	237	1.2	33.2	134
HOT ROD	*397	280	0.6	70.5	120	42	0.4	10.6	91	175	0.9	44.1	178
HOUSE & GARDEN	3589	2191	4.5	61.0	104	593	6.2	16.5	143	811	4.0	22.6	91
HOUSE BEAUTIFUL	3319	1969	4.1	59.3	101	514	5.4	15.5	134	735	3.6	22.1	89
INC.	*391	257	0.5	65.7	112	23	0.2	5.9	51	119	0.6	30.4	123
JET	2670	1404	2.9	52.6	90	419	4.4	15.7	136	504	2.5	18.9	76
LADIES' HOME JOURNAL	11615	7581	15.7	65.3	111	1519	16.0	13.1	113	3216	15.8	27.7	112
LHJ FAMILY GRP COMBO(GROSS)	16145	10565	21.9	65.4	111	2149	22.6	13.3	115	4539	22.3	28.1	114
LIFE	4258	2624	5.4	61.6	105	579	6.1	13.6	118	1147	5.6	26.9	109
LOS ANGELES TIMES MAGAZINE	1135	699	1.4	61.6	105	109	1.1	9.6	83	207	1.0	18.2	74
MADEMOISELLE	3184	2197	4.5	69.0	118	412	4.3	12.9	112	981	4.8	30.8	124
MC CALL'S	13488	8788	18.2	65.2	111	1641	17.2	12.2	105	3822	18.8	28.3	114
MC CALL'S/WRK MOTHER (GROSS)	14845	9802	20.3	66.0	112	1888	19.8	12.7	110	4278	21.0	28.8	116
MODERN PHOTOGRAPHY	644	411	0.9	63.8	109	96	1.0	14.9	129	175	0.9	27.2	110
MONEY	1577	974	2.0	61.8	105	171	1.8	10.8	94	449	2.2	28.5	115
MOTHER EARTH NEWS	1293	878	1.8	67.9	116	203	2.1	15.7	136	370	1.8	28.6	116
MOTOR TREND	*229	102	0.2	44.5	76	15	0.2	6.6	57	44	0.2	19.2	78
MS.	923	693	1.4	75.1	128	172	1.8	18.6	161	309	1.5	33.5	135
NATIONAL ENQUIRER	9196	5865	12.1	63.8	109	1332	14.0	14.5	125	2497	12.3	27.2	110
NATIONAL GEOGRAPHIC	10306	6523	13.5	63.3	108	1258	13.2	12.2	105	2500	12.3	24.3	98
NATIONAL SUNDAY MAGAZINE PKG	48210	28783	59.6	59.7	102	5669	59.5	11.8	102	11956	58.7	24.8	100
NATURAL HISTORY	481	274	0.6	57.0	97	35	0.4	7.3	63	129	0.6	26.8	108
NEW WOMAN	1734	1113	2.3	64.2	109	167	1.8	9.6	83	562	2.8	32.4	131
NEW YORK	487	297	0.6	61.0	104	39	0.4	8.0	69	94	0.5	19.3	78
THE NEW YORKER	1102	594	1.2	53.9	92	112	1.2	10.2	88	161	0.8	14.6	59
NEWSWEEK	6623	4443	9.2	67.1	114	942	9.9	14.2	123	1582	7.8	23.9	96
THE N.Y. TIMES DAILY EDITION	1205	497	1.0	41.2	70	79	0.8	6.6	57	146	0.7	12.1	49
THE N.Y. TIMES MAGAZINE	1907	811	1.7	42.5	72	154	1.6	8.1	70	263	1.3	13.8	56
OMNI	871	589	1.2	67.6	115	131	1.4	15.0	130	234	1.1	26.9	109
ON CABLE	1124	856	1.8	76.2	130	222	2.3	19.8	171	338	1.7	30.1	121
1001 HOME IDEAS	2469	1763	3.6	71.4	122	336	3.5	13.6	118	772	3.8	31.3	126

Exhibit 5.5 Sample page from *Simmons Survey of Media and Markets*; female adult magazine readership by corn and

tortilla usage. (Source: Simmons Market Research Bureau. Used with permissions.)

The Internet

The Internet is emerging as a major communications medium. A recent survey of over 1000 adults indicated that about sixty percent use a personal computer, and almost one-half of these computer users accessed the Internet or World Wide Web.[6] However, only about one-fifth of those who have gone online made a purchase throughout the Internet. Although Internet advertising currently only accounts for a minute percentage (considerably less than 1%[7]) of total U.S. advertising expenditures, this medium=s importance is expected to grow tremendously in the future.

The recent advertising experience of Bristol-Myers, who ran ads for Excedrin as Athe tax headache medicine@ on the Internet during tax season demonstrates the value of advertising on the Web. In just one month Bristol-Myers added 30,000 new names to its customer list, which tripled the company=s best-case expectation.[8] Further, the cost of adding these names was about one-half of the cost associated with traditional marketing methods.

Cost of Advertising on the Internet

The fee structure associated with Web advertising is still evolving. One method of charging for advertising is based on impressions or viewings. The cost per thousand (CPM) is the ad rate a Web site charges for every one thousand times the ad is displayed. The average cost per thousand impressions on the Web is about $17, which is considerably higher than $5 to $6 CPM associated with television audience.[9] A Web site might contain several ads, and a click through refers to whether a viewer actually responds to a particular ad by clicking onto it. The cost per click is the ad rate charged when a viewer clicks on the ad, that is, seeks additional information. Some advertisers pay only the basis of click throughs.

The cost per lead/sale refers to the fee charged to the advertiser only if the viewer provides personal information which can be used to contact the potential customer or actually makes a purchase. The amount charged using this basis would clearly be a function of customer potential value, or the cost of the good or service purchased.

Needless to say, much remains unsettled regarding Web advertising rates. Auditing companies can monitor traffic to Web sites thus providing data required to support specific advertising fees, but there is a crying need in the industry for objective third-party neutral information regarding Internet usage, i.e., syndicated data.

Syndicated Services Regarding Internet Usage

Both Web sites and advertisers seek information such as increases in the:

- o amount of published information
- o frequency of reports and analysis
- o ease of use of published data.[10]

They would also like standardization of reports to facilitate comparisons. Providers of syndicated data are responding to this need. Media Metrix provides Web usage and demographic data based on a panel of 10,000 U.S. households. This information allows advertisers to determine the most attractive Web sites for reaching a specific audience. Media Metrix also publishes Atop-line@ statistics, including the ten most visited sites and the top news and information sites. A similar service is @plan which provides data on a base of 40,000 Web users. Other companies offering similar services include Relevant Knowledge and National Family Opinion (NFO).

The high level of interest in who is using the Internet and how the Internet is used has prompted numerous surveys of the general population like the one mentioned at the start of this section. For instance, *Advertising Age* conducts an annual Interactive Media Study.[11] The 1997 survey indicated that the most frequent online activities were gathering news or information, sending/reading e-mail, conducting research and Asurfing@ (see Table 5.1). Although shopping remained a relatively infrequent online activity, there was about a twenty percent increase from the previous year in the percentage of Internet users who shopped online. Also, the survey indicated that slightly more than one-third of those who visited a company=s home page did so to shop (see Table 5.2).

Activity	1997* %	1996 %
Gather News/Information	87.8	82.0
E-Mail	83.2	80.5
Conduct Research	80.5	69.1
Surfing	75.3	66.9
Play Games	33.7	23.8
Chatting	30.8	25.3
Shop	17.8	14.9

Table 5.1 Online Activities. *Based on 584 U.S. residents who have been online in the past six months. (Source: *Advertising Age,* fifth annual Interactive Media Study).

Activity	%*
Seek Product Information	90.5
Seek Company Information	87.8
Shop	34.5
Obtain Discounts, Coupons, Etc.	31.7
Enter Contests	18.9

Table 5.2 Home Page Activities. *Based on 419 U.S. residents who have been online in the past six months and visited a company's home page. (Source: *Advertising Age,* fifth annual Interactive Media Study.

Market Performance Data

Measuring market performance is a fundamental issue for marketing managers since it is critical that these managers know the total sales in their brand's product category, what share of category sales respective brands are capturing, and how sales vary across regions and across channels of distribution. Only then can they set reasonable goals and establish strategies for achieving these goals. A company attempting to operate without this information is like a vessel attempting an ocean crossing with no navigational equipment.

Market performance can be monitored at various points of the distribution system. For example, by examining internal company records on how much was shipped and where these shipments went, a firm can get some feel for the performance of its brands. Unfortunately, such measures give no indication of how a brand's performance measures up against competitive brands. The brand's shipments to various outlets may be above, or below, what competitors shipped. Also, merchandise spends time in the "pipeline" and can accumulate in warehouses and retail outlets, so it may take considerable time for a retail sales problem to manifest itself at the shipment level.

Companies monitor sales of their brands and competitors at the retail level. These results provide a Ascorecard@ by which management assesses company performance versus competition. Weaknesses in sales of specific brands indicate problems that require attention in the form of marketing action. These data also provide invaluable insight regarding trends in category sales, as well as which specific competitors are gaining or losing sales in a category.

As we will discuss later in this chapter, monitoring purchasing at the individual consumer level provides vital information to the marketing manager. However, using such data to track market performance in the context of sales amounts to overkill. Individual household level data are far richer than is needed to monitor general sales performance, and, furthermore, the results for reasonably large samples have only recently been made available for selected local areas. Hence, marketing managers traditionally have relied on, and continue to rely on, retail sales data to monitor market performance of their brands. On the other hand, household level data provide information which is crucial to strategic planning.

ScanTrack

ScanTrack is a retail sales tracking service provided by the A.C. Nielsen Company. Data on brands sold through a carefully selected sample of about 3000 large geographically dispersed supermarkets are compiled, and monthly reports are provided to clients detailing the activity in the product category, or categories, of interest to each company. The data are collected using electronic check-out scanners linked to computers. As the scanner reads the UPC (Universal Product Code) for each item purchased to determine the price the consumer is charged, relevant brand information is also recorded and stored in the computer. Hence, the data collection process is essentially automated.

ScanTrack provides data on sales and market share, as well as information regarding factors affecting sales such as retail prices, store displays, local advertising features, and the use of coupons. The sample data are used to develop national projections of category sales and individual brand sales and share. Companies can also purchase market performance projections for fifty major markets.

Consumer packaged goods are of course also sold in drug stores and mass merchandisers. Nielsen=s Procision7 system uses scanner technology to measure sales in these distribution channels. Over 400 drug outlets and over 300 mass merchandisers are included in this system. Hence, the Nielsen services allow packaged goods companies to monitor sales of their brands, as well as competitors, in total, and within the three major distribution channels.

Applying Marketing Research 5.2

The Minute Maid Company based their claim that Minute Maid brand was the leader in the $3 billion orange juice market on syndicated data.[1] CEO Harry E. Teasley, Jr., cited Nielsen Marketing Research Group's ScanTrack system as providing data which showed that Minute Maid's retail volume and share were up nearly 19 percent and 1.3 share points respectively from the previous year. Teasley further stated that, based on these same data, that Minute Maid's share of the U.S. orange juice market was 23.4 percent, .3 share points higher than the nearest competitor.

Sales in small supermarkets or grocery stores, convenience stores, gas mini-marts and small drug stores are estimated using data obtained by physically auditing inventory and shipments received on a periodic basis for a sample of outlets for each category. Eventually, the need for these tedious, time-consuming, and costly physical audits will disappear as more and more retailers convert to scanner check-out technology.

For audited stores, the following equation is used to calculate sales for any outlet or group of outlets:

retail sales = beginning inventory + shipments received - ending inventory.

The information obtained from individual stores is aggregated to produce regional and national sales estimates. Naturally, the auditing yields other valuable information such as current inventory levels, incidence of out-of-stock (frequency of stores that carry a product having zero inventory), and distribution rate (percentage of stores carrying the product).

InfoScan

InfoScan is a syndicated data service offered by Information Resources, Inc. (IRI) and is the major competitor of A.C. Nielsen's ScanTrack. InfoScan provides subscribers weekly scanner data based on a national sample of supermarkets, yielding measurements of sales, market share, retail price, and distribution (measured as the percent of stores that stock the product and as the percent of total sales accounted for by stores stocking the product). In addition to providing market performance estimates for the national level, estimates are also available for sales regions, individual markets, and in many cases, key accounts. InfoScan also reports sales for the drug and mass merchandise channels based on large samples of scanner stores, for each channel.[12] IRI is also moving toward using scanner data to monitor the convenience store channel.

IRI recently introduced InfoScan Census for supermarket sales. This service basically expands the sample of stores used for the basic InfoScan service to roughly 11,000 supermarkets nationwide.[13] This huge number of stores represents about 70% of all chain supermarket sales in the U. S. The primary use of the service is to develop local campaigns, i.e., micromarketing, based on sales estimates for small local areas made possible by the breadth of the information provided.[14]

Services for Specialized Markets

The systems for monitoring market performance discussed so far focus on consumer packaged goods, but a critical need obviously exists for information of this type in all industries. Similar syndicated services are available in many of these industries. For instance, Audits and Surveys, Inc., provides retail sales inventory, distribution, and out-of-stock information to the photographic, sporting goods, jewelry, and household appliance industries. The data are obtained by conducting bimonthly physical audits in a national sample of retail outlets. Bimonthly reports of unit sales by brand and type of outlet are provided to all subscribers.

Household Purchases

Consumer Diary Panels

A **diary panel** typically consists of a sample of several thousand households chosen to be reflective of the country's household composition. Panel members are asked to maintain a diary providing information about all items purchased by the household. The diaries tend to cover weekly, biweekly, or monthly time periods.

Diary data provide insight into shopping and purchase behavior issues including specific product purchase cycles, brand loyalty, brand-switching tendencies, sizes of transactions, use of coupons, and price paid. Combining the diary information with the demographic characteristics of the individual panel members yields a wealth of information about the users of specific brands, who shops where, and demographic differences in the frequency of product or brand use. This is precisely the type of information used by Borden, Inc., to develop the profile of the Classico target customer mentioned at the beginning of this chapter.

Diary panel data are invaluable in determining the source of a brand's sales volume. For example, diary data allow the company to address the question of whether a brand has many customers, all of whom buy a little, or few customers, all of whom buy a lot, or some combination of these phenomena. Further, marketing managers may be able demographically to profile their important customers (frequent purchasers) and target efforts toward keeping them. The information derived from diary panels is crucial to developing brand strategies and tactics.

Panel data can be useful for designing promotions. For example, panel data revealed that a substantial portion of diet Coke purchasers also bought Diet 7Up. Coca-Cola brand management subsequently decided to place discount coupons for Diet Sprite, a Coca-Cola brand that is similar to Diet 7Up, on bottles of diet Coke. The promotion was obviously designed to encourage these customers who also buy Diet 7Up to buy Diet Sprite instead.

Electronic scanning of UPC codes has changed the way in which household purchases are monitored for consumer packaged goods. A combination of scanning and computer technology, which we discuss next, have eliminated the tedious recording of purchases in diaries by household members.

Until the late 1980s, the NPD Group of Marketing Research Companies national diary panel service covered about fifty product categories. However, the trend away from paper and pencil diaries to electronic scanning for recording household purchases led NPD to abandon its diary panel service for typical consumer packaged goods. The A.C. Nielsen Company acquired this service from NPD and used it as a basis to launch its electronic household scanning panel. The NPD diary panel service now focuses on products such as fresh meats, books, toys, and clothing, which do not lend themselves to UPC scanning.

Exhibit 5.6 contains a sample page from an NPD diary. This particular page focuses on beef and fresh fish and seafood. Panelists record all relevant purchases in the diary for one month and then return it to NPD. For each purchase, panelists record:

- o Purchase date
- o Type of beef or fish
- o Brand name
- o Weight (size)
- o Price paid
- o Name and type of store
- o Item location in the store

PAGE 11

BEEF: INCLUDE - Any Item Found In The Meat Case/Department, Fresh Frozen Beef (Such As: Burger Patties, Steaks), Prepared Beef In The Deli Case (Such As: Shish Kebab Or BBQ Beef) & Fresh Or Prepared Beef In A Gourmet Specialty Section (Such As: Aged, Branded, Etc.).
EXCLUDE - Frozen Prepared Dinners (Such As: TV Dinners, Gourmet Entrees), Deli Meat, Lunch Meat Or Other Processed Meat.

Note: Usually meat weight is listed in pounds & decimals. Please be careful to report weight in correct column.

Date Of Purchase | Is It?: Fresh, Fresh Frozen | Type of Beef/Veal From Label: If Ground – (✓) Kind: Ground Chuck, Ground Round, Ground Sirloin, Ground Veal, Ground Beef; Write In % Lean As Printed On Pkg. If Not Ground – (✓) Kind: Roast, Steak, Other Beef; Please Write In The TYPE OF BEEF/VEAL As Printed On Label. Such As Bottom Round Roast, T-Bone Steak, Corned Beef, Veal Cutlet, Liver, Cubed Beef, Etc. | Grade Of Beef (✓) One: Prime, Choice, Select, USDA Inspected, Do Not Know | Brand Name (If Available): Write In Such As: Certified Angus, Coleman, IBP, Etc. | Weight (Size) Enter Weight From Label In Appropriate Column Below: If Label Reads lbs. & Decimals Enter Below (For Ex: 2 .50); If Label Reads lbs. & ozs. Enter Below (For Ex: 2 lbs. 8 ozs.) | Price Paid: Amt. Paid (From Label If Given) Do Not Include Tax: $ ¢; (✓) Here If Special/Sale | Where Purchased?: Name Of Store Or Catalog Or Company Where Beef Was Purchased – Write In; Store Type (✓) One: Supermarket/Grocery, Warehouse Club/Store, Butcher/Meat Market, Neighborhood/Local Delicatessen, Convenience Store, Market Day/Other Co-ops, Other | Where In The Store Is This Item Found?: Fresh Meat Case, Deli Counter, Food/Salad Bar, Gourmet Specialty Section, Freezer Case, Other

FRESH FISH & SEAFOOD: INCLUDE - Any Item Found At The Fresh Fish Counter/Department, Fresh, Smoked Fish, Fresh Frozen, Cooked Seafood (Such As: Boiled Shrimp) & Frozen Breaded Products (Such As: Fish Sticks, Breaded Fillets, Etc.).
EXCLUDE - Canned Fish & Frozen Prepared Dinners (Such As: TV Dinners, Gourmet Entrees).

Put a (✓) in box(es) below if this month your household did NOT purchase any...
☐ Beef ☐ Fish/Seafood

Date Of Purchase | Is It?: Fresh/Raw, Fresh Frozen, Frozen Breaded, Cooked, Smoked | Type/Name From Label (✓) One Or Write In: Catfish, Clams, Cod/Pollock, Crab/Crabmeat, Flounder, Haddock, Perch, Roughy, Salmon, Scallops, Shrimp, Sole, Tuna (Not Canned); Other Write In | Brand Name (If Available): Write In Such As: Icelandic, Taste 'O Sea, Brilliant, Etc. | Weight (Size) Enter Weight From Label In Appropriate Column Below: If Label Reads lbs. & Decimals Enter Below (For Ex: 2 .50); If Label Reads lbs. & ozs. Enter Below (For Ex: 2 lbs. 8 ozs.) | Price Paid: Amt. Paid (From Label If Given) Do Not Include Tax: $ ¢; (✓) Here If Special/Sale | Where Purchased?: Name Of Store Or Catalog Or Company Where Fish Was Purchased – Write In; Store Type: Supermarket/Grocery, Warehouse Club/Store, Fish Market, Neighborhood/Local Delicatessen, Convenience Store, Market Day/Other Co-ops, Other | Where In The Store Is This Item Found?: Fresh Fish Case, Deli Counter, Food/Salad Bar, Gourmet Speciality Section, Freezer Case, Other

Exhibit 5.6 Sample page from Purchase Diary.

One of the concerns raised about diary panel data has always been its projectability. While the panels are designed to reflect the demographic characteristics of the population of the country, the purchase behavior of panel members still might be different from other consumers. The mere fact that they are willing to complete the diaries makes these panel members somewhat atypical, and hence their purchase behavior may not be representative of non-panel households. Another obvious concern with diary panels is accuracy. Panel members may forget to make entries. Relying on memory to complete diary entries rather than making the entries immediately after each shopping trip invites error so companies continually search for ways to improve the accuracy of such purchase data.

Scanner Panels

Check-out scanners, like those commonly used in supermarkets, provide great advantages to the retailer. The check-out process is faster and a source of error--manually entering the price in a cash register--is removed. Further, by connecting the electronic scanner to a computer that keeps track of all transactions, retailers can manage inventory and measure brand movement far more easily than in the past.

Retail scanners are also the basis for an alternative to paper and pencil diary panels. Instead of requiring individual household members to record purchases manually in diaries, **scanner panels** make use of UPC codes and store scanners to record panelists' purchases. IRI is one of the pioneers in the use of scanner technology to record household purchases as well as retail sales data. Their household scanner panel, part of the InfoScan system,

requires panelists to present a personalized identification card at the supermarket check-out. An electronic device reads the information from the card to the host computer, which then files the purchases for the occasion into the particular panelist's data base. Information pertaining to prices paid, use of discount coupons, and store data regarding advertising features and in-store promotions are also recorded. Demographic data for all panel households are collected when the household joins the panel and purchase data can be organized accordingly. The system provides periodic reports on the supermarket purchasing behavior of about 60,000 households. The households are grouped into Apods@ which are geographically dispersed across the United States. As noted at the beginning of this chapter, Borden, Inc., used this system to identify Classico customers and develop a micromarketing strategy for the brand.

Because of their size, household scanner panels provide information that can be analyzed at the local level. For example, the InfoScan household panel contains samples of over 1000 households for selected cities. The use of household sales data provided by a scanner panel to test a new advertising campaign, a new promotion, or a new brand locally provides much richer understanding than simply using retail sales data. Applying Marketing Research 5.3 demonstrates how scanner panel data can aid in understanding purchase behavior for a new brand.

Applying Marketing Research 5.3

Suppose a company develops a new toothpaste and decides to evaluate the new brand's potential by test marketing it in a city having a large household scanner panel. Exhibit 5.7a displays the sales volume data for the new brand obtained by monitoring retail sales. The sales volume has been increasing throughout the first months and has reached a level that is higher than the company had expected. Things look very promising!

However, the high sales volume may be primarily due to consumer trial. In other words, brand sales are primarily to first-time customers. In order to be a successful entry, the new brand must generate repeat buying. Purchases among scanner panel households can be identified as trial or repeat so that the new brand's sales volume among panel households can be decomposed as shown in Exhibit 5.7b.

The picture painted in Exhibit 5.7b is not so bright. In fact, projecting these results yields the future sales volume depicted in Exhibit 5.7c. The new brand is really not a viable market entry.

In this case, the household scanner panel data raise a red flag for the new brand long before the retail sales results do. The household panel data might even prevent the company from misinterpreting sales results and proceeding to a costly roll-out of a new brand that will ultimately fail.

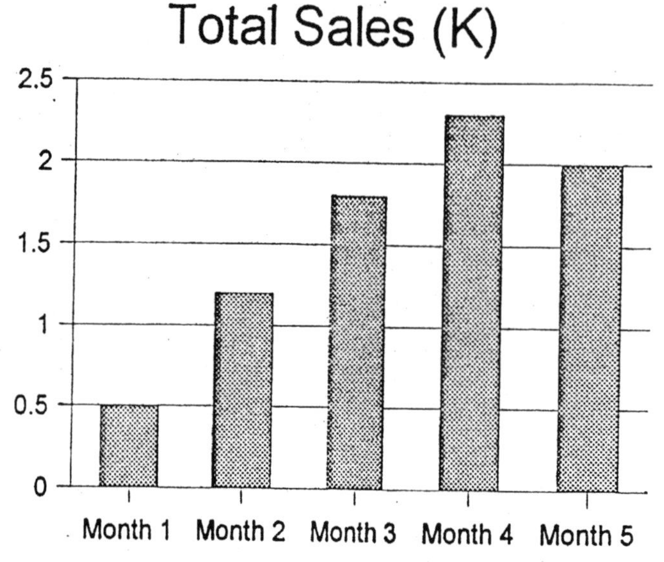
Total Sales (K)
2.5
2
1.5
1
0.5
0
Month 1
Month 2
Month 3
Month 4
Month 5

(A)

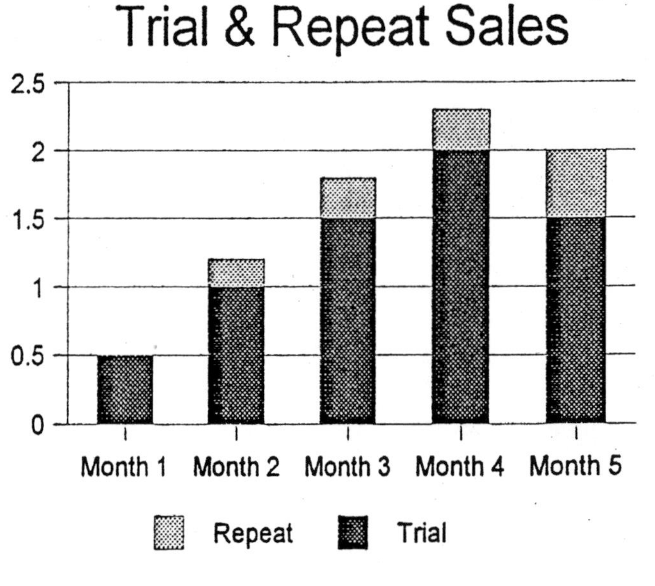
Trial & Repeat Sales
2.5
2
1.5
1
0.5
0
Month 1
Month 2
Month 3
Month 4
Month 5
Repeat
Trial

(B)

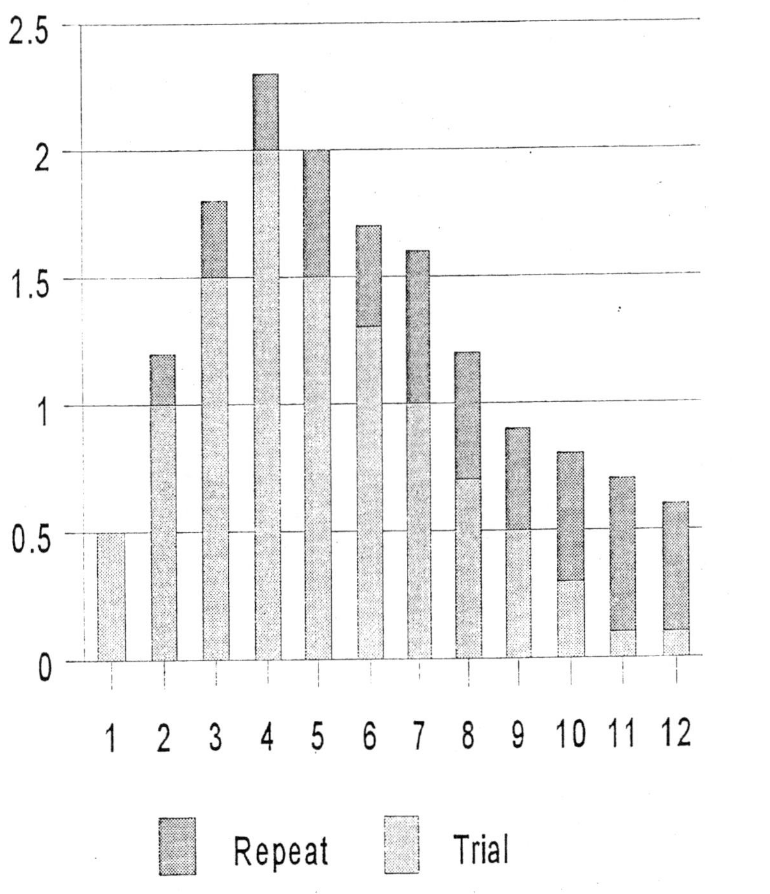

Exhibit 5.7 Test Market Sales of new toothpaste: (a) brand's retail sales; (b) trial and repeat components of sales based on household panel data; and (c) projected sales volume based on household panel data.

The major problem with the system just described revolves around the percentage of purchases made in supermarkets where scanner data are collected. In some product categories, such as breakfast cereal, this percentage is very high. However, for other categories, such as soft drinks and snack foods, the percentage is much lower since many purchases for these items are made in convenience stores or mass merchandisers.

Nielsen=s ScanTrack National Electronic Household Panel is designed to capture household purchases of all packaged goods consumed in the home, not just those scanned in the supermarket as is the case for the IRI system described above. The Nielsen system relies on panelists to use computerized wands to record purchases. When passed over a product's UPC code, the hand-held wand records and stores the code in a small computer contained in the wand. The purchase data are periodically transmitted to a large computer using standard telecommunications systems. The Nielsen household panel is comprised of over 50,000 households spread across 19 markets.

IRI has augmented its household panel by adding about 20,000 households equipped with Ascan keys.@ The additional households provide data on purchases from outlets other than supermarkets. The lack of information for channels other than supermarkets had been a disadvantage for IRI=s household panel as compared to Nielsen=s.

From a data collection standpoint, the main advantage of scanner panels over diary panels is the relatively passive nature in which purchases are recorded. Scanner panelists are not required to record purchases in a diary, so a more accurate purchase history is anticipated than that provided by diary panels. However, concerns regarding panel representivity and accuracy remain.

International Issues

The information readily available to U.S. marketing managers through syndicated services is not always available for foreign countries. This is not meant to imply that marketing information is primitive in the rest of the world. For example, syndicated household purchase data from over 1000 households in the London area were used to establish the existence of two soup-buying segments--year-round and peak-season-only buyers.[15]

Nevertheless, scanner technology has yet to be extensively used in many countries, so retail sales information and household level purchasing data are collected in relatively unsophisticated ways, if at all. Further, in some countries the typical channels of distribution make collecting retail sales data extremely difficult. In South America, supermarkets are not nearly as commonplace as in the United States and products such as soft drinks are sold primarily in small Mom-and-Pop establishments.

Scanning wands used by panelists to record household purchases require telecommunications systems to download the data. However, telephone household penetration levels are quite low in many foreign countries. Further, many countries have yet to adopt the equivalent of a UPC system, hence eliminating any scanner-based system from consideration as a means of obtaining household level purchasing data.

As pointed out earlier, great effort is spent in the United States to measure television audience size and composition. However, this issue is relatively unimportant or even irrelevant in some foreign countries. The ban on television advertising in the Scandinavian countries was finally lifted in the late 80s, but consumers in these countries have not responded positively to this method of advertising.[16] There appears to be a latent distrust of TV advertising in the Scandinavian countries, and as a consequence, advertisers rely relatively heavily on print. Many other countries have strict government controls over what can be advertised on television and when commercials can be scheduled.[17]

Summary

Syndicated data sources provide marketing managers with information ranging from what consumers are generally thinking to the last brand of toothpaste purchased. The Monitor and Consumer Confidence Index measure optimism regarding the future. Syndicated services also provide information regarding what consumers are watching on television and listening to on the radio, and what periodicals they are reading. Further, the Internet is emerging as a major advertising medium and syndicated services are beginning to profile visitors to specific Internet sites. A.C. Nielsen and Information Resources, Inc., sell data to manufacturers regarding retail sales of packaged goods brands. Similar services sell retail sales information for other consumer goods and services. Finally, scanner technology has facilitated the development of large panels for monitoring individual household purchase behavior and routinely providing this information to marketing managers.

The world of syndicated data continues to change. Many of the new technologies and data collection procedures, only in existence for a few years, can be expected to have a short life span because of rapid innovation. For instance, sensing devices, which provide passive audience measures for television, may soon be worn as jewelry. Likewise, electronic point-of-sale systems, frequently scanner-based, to collect and organize sales data for catalog showrooms, hardware stores, and fast-food restaurants are emerging. These systems promise much richer, more organized, and more accurate information about sales in these types of outlets than before.

Key Terms

Confidence Index

diary panel

InfoScan

Monitor

ScanTrack

scanner panels

Simmons Annual Survey of Media and Markets

syndicated data

Syndicated Data for the Nimslo Camera

Nimslo management was obviously very interested in retail camera sales. In particular, they needed information pertaining to sales volume for various types of cameras, such as instant, disc, instamatic, and 35 mm, by the major channels of distribution--camera specialty stores, mass merchandisers, and catalog showrooms. These data were needed to develop sales volume forecasts, which were vital to estimating revenue under various scenarios.

Nimslo subscribed to Audits and Surveys, the syndicated service for manufacturers of photographic equipment mentioned in the chapter. On a bimonthly basis, Nimslo received estimates of total unit sales of different types of cameras and unit sales by channel of distribution. The estimates were based on physical inventory and shipment audits of a nationally representative sample of retail outlets for photographic equipment. Nimslo received a bimonthly presentation and report which was organized as follows:

Unit Sales

(November - December '82)

	Total	Camera Specialty Stores	Mass Merchandisers	Catalog Showrooms
35mm SLR				
33mm Non-SLR				
Instant				
Instamatic/Pocket				
Disc				
Nimslo				

The national reports gave Nimslo management important insight into what was taking in the photographic market but initially contained no information regarding Nimslo sales. Nimslo contracted with Audits and Surveys to expand their sample in Florida, Nimslo's test market, and to provide a separate report for the state of Florida. Hence, Nimslo received vital information on camera sales during the test market period. Audits and Surveys also supplied Nimslo with information pertaining to out-of-stocks, inventory levels, and distribution (percent of outlets in a category carrying an item). This information allowed Nimslo to anticipate problems arising from accumulating inventory and to assess the sales force's effectiveness at convincing vendors to carry the Nimslo camera and at keeping vendors supplied.

Review Questions

5.1 What kinds of data are included in the Yankelovich Monitor? Why is it important for companies to subscribe to services such as the Yankelovich Monitor? What criticisms have been raised about the use of Monitor data?

5.2 What is the Consumer Confidence Index? Why is it important?

5.3 Why is household level purchase data important? What information can be obtained through such a service?

5.4 Who are some of the companies supplying household purchase panel data? How do these services differ? How has electronic scanning changed the way household purchase data is collected.

5.5 What are the Nielsen Ratings? Why are they important?

5.6 In what ways can a company track product movement? What are the advantages and disadvantages of the use of each method?

5.7 How has scanner data changed the way retail sales are measured? Without scanner data, how are retail sales measured?

Discussion Questions

5.1 Discuss the role of syndicated services in the marketing research industry. Why do such services exist? Give examples of the more prominent syndicated data services.

5.2 Discuss the importance of TV ratings data. Why is so much attention paid to these measures? Discuss the problems VCRs create for measuring audience size. How is technology changing how TV audience measurement is conducted?

5.3 Discuss the impact of UPC codes and electronic scanning on measuring product movement in supermarkets. How has this technology changed the way supermarket chains and individual stores operate? What does this mean to manufacturers and their sales forces?

5.4 Given all the concerns over measuring household purchasing, how can the information such systems provide be valuable?

5.5 Discuss the Internet as an advertising medium. What makes the Internet different from other media? What syndicated services are emerging for understanding Internet usage?

Chapter 5 Endnotes

1. See Michael J. McCarthy, "Marketers Zero In On Their Customers," *Wall Street Journal*, March 18, 1991, pp. B1, B8.

2. See "Top Research Companies by U.S. Research Revenues," *Advertising Age*, June 3, 1991, p. 32.

3. See AClothes Call,@ *American Demographics*, May, 1997, p. 32

4. Gene Koretz, AThe Upbeat Mood Trickles Down,@ *Business Week*, October 20, 1997, p. 30.

5. Paul Magnusson, AIt Just Won=t Stop Humming,@ *Business Week*, September 15, 1997, pp. 34-36.

6. See ABusiness Week/Harris Poll A lot of Looking, Not Much BuyingCYet,@ *Business Week*, October 6, 1997, p. 140.

7. Linda Himelstein, Ellen Neuborne and Paul M. Eng, AWeb Ads Start to Click,@ *Business Week*, October 6, 1997, pp. 128-139.

8. *Ibid.*

9. *Ibid.*

10. See Kate Maddox and Patricia Riedman, AResearch Firms Respond to Need for More Data,@ *Advertising Age*, September 8, 1997, pp. 34, 38 for a discussion of emerging syndicated data services providing internet usage and user data.

11. Kate Maddox, AInformation Still Kills APP on the Internet,@ *Advertising Age*, October 6, 1997, pp. 42,48.

12. See *Product Directory*, Information Resources, Inc., 1994, for a description of the various IRI services.

13. Judann Pollack, AP&G Taps InfoScan=s Census Data,@ *Advertising Age*, September 15, 1997, p. 72.

14. *Ibid.*

15. Dee M. Wellan and Andrew S.C. Ehrenberg, "A Case of Seasonal Segmentation," *Marketing Research*, 2-2 (June 1990), pp. 11-13.

16. John Shannon, ATV Ads Struggle in Scandanavia,@ *Marketing Week*, 19 (26), September 20, 1996, p. 26.

17. See, for example, William F. Arens and Courtland L. Bovée, *Contemporary*

Case I.1

Expansion of Major League Baseball

Expansion is a major issue in every professional sport. The establishment of franchises in new cities generates enthusiasm for the sport by keeping it in the headlines and adding to the base of core fans. The new cities benefit from increased tax revenues generated by the events and visiting fans. Expansion also provides large infusions of revenue for existing franchises as new owners are charged huge fees to join the league.

The success of the Carolina Panthers in the National Football League, the Florida Panthers in the National Hockey League, and the Colorado Rockies in major league baseball has led many cities to bid for future franchises to be awarded by the various professional sports. Competing cities present their cases to a review board comprised of league officials, and this board eventually awards the new franchise(s) to those cities that have the most to offer from the league's perspective. Many factors, including population size, local interest in the sport, an existing or planned arena or stadium, anticipated growth in the area, local business support, proximity to other existing franchises, size of local TV market, and so on, enter into the decision.

Imagine yourself as the owner of a small marketing research firm. Suppose that you have been invited to make a presentation to a group seeking a major league baseball franchise for Jacksonville, Florida. The purpose of your presentation is to demonstrate how your firm can help this group prepare its petition to the league representatives. Describe how marketing research can provide information relevant to the petition. What secondary data would provide valuable insight? What primary data would you collect? What would you stress in your presentation to the local group?

Case I.3[1]

Tone Soap

Tone soap is marketed by the Dial Corporation in the complexion bar soap category. The primary competitors are Procter & Gamble's Camay, Ivory Moisture Care and Oil of O=Lay, and two Lever Brothers' brands, Dove and Caress. Tone is positioned as containing cocoa butter, which makes it exceptionally mild to the skin, and is available in bright yellow and cream colors. In response to a commonly held perception that cocoa butter is brown, Dial at one point considered changing Tone from yellow to an almond color. The brand management team used marketing research to explore the impact of changing the color of Tone from yellow to almond and at the same time to evaluate the consumer appeal of a new package design.

The following experiment was conducted to assess the impact of the new package and the switch to an almond color. Three separate groups of females, age 25 to 54 (the primary target audience for this product category), who use complexion bars were recruited in geographically dispersed shopping malls to participate in the experiment. Each group consisted of about 300 women, 100 of whom were users of Tone. The women were asked to view a display of the major complexion bars (brands and colors) all shown outside their respective packages. A poster containing the brand's basic strategy was placed next to each brand. The three groups differed in the Tone display, but the Tone strategy statement was not changed. For one group (Cell 1), the current colors and package were used; for another group (Cell 2), the new package was used; and for the third group (Cell 3), the new package was used and the one bar color was changed from yellow to almond.

---

[1] The data and situation for this case are contrived and are in no way meant to reflect current thinking of Tone management.

The participants were asked to distribute five poker chips among the various brand-color combinations to represent their likely next five purchases in the category. A person who was totally loyal to a single brand would place all five chips next to that brand, and so forth. The average percentage of chips awarded each brand was calculated, and the results are reported in Table I.3.1. Participants who gave no chips to Tone were asked why they did not, and those who gave chips to Tone were asked why they did. These results are reported in Tables I.3.2 and I.3.3 respectively.

Discuss the experimental design and the internal and external validity of the experiment. Analyze the findings of this experiment, and decide what you would recommend if you were the Tone brand team.

TABLE I.3.1

CHIP ALLOCATION

	Total cell			Tone users			"Other" users		
	Cell 1 Control	Cell 2 New package	Cell 3 New package and Almond color	Cell 1	Cell 2	Cell 3	Cell 1	Cell 2	Cell 3
	(319) %	(336) %	(328) %	(99) %	(97) %	(102) %	(238) %	(247) %	(241) %
Tone	28.6	31.3	32.0	55.2	55.0	52.6	15.6	18.8	20.4
Dove	27.6	23.9	22.8	13.8	8.0	13.5	32.2	28.2	27.1
Caress	22.5	21.8	24.5	16.8	21.0	19.5	27.2	27.8	28.0
Camay	8.0	7.5	7.3	5.0	4.4	4.8	8.6	7.5	8.2
Oil of O=Lay	7.7	7.2	7.0	4.0	7.4	4.7	8.1	8.5	9.1
Ivory Moisture Care	6.6	8.3	6.4	5.2	4.2	4.9	8.3	9.2	7.2

TABLE I.3.2

REASONS FOR NOT ASSIGNING CHIPS TO TONE

(Table 3.5 of 1st Edition)

	Total cell			Tone users			"Other" users		
	Cell 1 Control	Cell 2 New package	Cell 3 New package and Almond color	Cell 1	Cell 2	Cell 3	Cell 1	Cell 2	Cell 3
	(138) %	(134) %	(128) %	(0) %	(4) %	(16) %	(138) %	(130) %	(115) %
Prefer own brand	42	40	44	-	-	-	41	40	44
Never use it	27	29	24	-	-	-	27	30	25
Don't like cocoa butter/oil	26	21	21	-	-	-	26	20	22
Don't like color	13	21	9	-	-	50	13	20	8
Don't like fragrance	16	12	12	-	-	-	16	13	13
Makes skin breakout	9	5	17	-	-	50	9	5	17
Leaves skin dry	5	6	15	-	-	25	12	6	9
Doesn't leave skin soft/smooth	2	2	17	-	-	25	2	3	6
Too expensive	2	1	9	-	-	25	2	1	9
Don't like packaging	6	4	-	-	100	25	5	4	-
Don't like shape	3	5	2	-	-	-	3	5	2

TABLE I.3.3

REASONS FOR ASSIGNING CHIPS TO TONE

(Table 3.6 of 1st Edition)

	Total cell			Tone users			"Other" users		
	Cell 1 Control	Cell 2 New package	Cell 3 New package and Almond color	Cell 1	Cell 2	Cell 3	Cell 1	Cell 2	Cell 3
	(181) %	(202) %	(220) %	(99) %	(93) %	(86) %	(100) %	(117) %	(125) %
Has cocoa butter	42	38	36	33	25	29	53	43	47
Keeps skin soft/not dry	45	43	33	53	48	35	37	38	28
Smells fresh/ clean/good	25	25	22	31	31	28	16	20	16
Has moisturizers oils/creamy	23	19	22	19	21	20	28	25	29
Like shape of bar	8	8	10	6	9	11	7	7	8
Use regularly	13	11	9	20	20	12	3	1	1
Leaves skin feeling good	12	101	8	15	14	9	9	6	7
Like colors	5	7	10	5	6	6	4	8	14
Mild/doesn't irritate skin	4	6	5	4	7	2	7	6	7
Lathers good	2	7	4	3	10	6	-	6	2
Cleans well	4	2	5	5	3	8	6	3	3
Like packaging	1	10	8	-	8	8	1	12	8

Case I.4

Frito-Lay Baked Lays

Representatives of Market Metrics, located in Lancaster, Pennsylvania, made a pitch to the marketing managers of Frito-Lay for their new Supermarket Solutions computer system. The system consists of two large data bases containing information for over 30,000 supermarkets. One of the data bases uses U.S. Census information to establish the demographic profile of the shoppers in the trade area of each supermarket as well as each respective chain. The other data base contains physical information about each of the supermarkets, such as size and number of checkouts. Market Metrics was attempting to convince Frito-Lay to make use of the system to market its products efficiently.

When Frito-Lay was rolling out its Baked Lays potato chips, mentioned in Chapter 4 and in Applying Marketing Research 5.1., Frito-Lay's marketing managers were convinced that the appeal of the brand would vary considerably by type of consumer. It was clear to the marketing managers that shopper demographics were related to the tendency to purchase the brand. The Baked Lays marketing team decided that they could make good use of Market Metrics to develop a micro-marketing plan for the brand.

Describe how Supermarket Solutions could be used by Frito-Lay's Baked Lays marketing team to develop a micro-marketing plan. What other information would be needed, and where might that information be obtained? Further, how could this information be used in developing advertising and promotion plans, as well as setting priorities with respect to stores and/or chains?

Case I.5

Lucky Pet Foods

Mae Dell Rosenthal was the owner of Lucky Pet Foods, located in Boise, Idaho. She had started the company 15 years ago, based on the premise of providing high quality pet foods containing essential vitamins and minerals for various stages of a pet's life. Since that time, the company had grown into a multi-million dollar business employing over 150 employees.

A key to the success of Lucky Pet Foods had been the personalized mail order distribution developed for their products. A new customer provided background information about pets, such as their breeds, ages, weights, and so forth. From this information, a specialized food blend was created for each pet and the food was packaged in airtight bags, each containing exactly one serving. The composition of the product was altered over the life of the pet as its nutrition needs changed, as was the serving size. The company kept track of each customer's past order dates and a new food supply was automatically mailed when the past inventory was nearly depleted.

Mae Dell was thinking about expanding the company's product line to include pet treats for dogs. Before embarking on this venture, she needed to estimate the market potential. She felt that published information must exist on the size of the market for pet treats such as chewy snacks, dog biscuits, and other food items that are not substitutes for regular feeding, but she was unclear about how to find such information. She also wanted to learn more about how consumers who own dogs decide whether or not to buy their pets treats. Some of the issues of interest to Mae Dell were: when the decision is made to purchase (before entering the store or in the pet food aisle); why the purchase/no purchase decision is made; how the choice of snack type is made; and when and why snacks are given.

Conduct a secondary search to find information on pet snacks. In addition, design a research project (that may consist of several studies) to try to answer Mae Dell's questions.

Case I.6

Ben and Jerry's[i]

Ben Cohen and Jerry Greenfield met in a 7th grade gym class in Merrick, NY (Long Island) in 1963. In 1977, they moved to Vermont, and with an initial investment of $12,000 opened their first ice cream store in a renovated gas station in Burlington, VT. From these humble beginnings, Ben and Jerry's Homemade, Inc., has blossomed into a public company, with annual sales of about $170 million - - not bad for two hippies-turned-ice-cream-moguls who reached the heights of American business prominence by rejecting corporate America. Today, the company boasts over 700 employees and more than 80 franchise shops.

Ben Cohen and Jerry Greenfield are the brainpower behind what is often referred to as "yuppie porn," an upscale product that sells for about twice the price of most brands of ice cream. In 1980, they began packing their ice cream in pints to distribute to neighboring groceries and Mom & Pop stores. In 1983, independent ice cream distributors began selling the ice cream in Boston. In 1984, they took the company public, and since then, have expanded their business throughout the U.S. The company makes ice cream flavors with unique names like Cherry Garcia®, named after the now deceased guitarist Jerry Garcia of the Grateful Dead, and Chunkey Monkey®. Their Burlington, VT headquarters is reputed to be the state's second most popular tourist attraction, with a typical tour featuring the clown-like antics of the two head honchos.

From its inception, Ben & Jerry's has displayed a strong sense of civic pride and "social consciousness." Company stores in Vermont have been used as voter registration centers. In 1985, the Ben & Jerry's Foundation, which funds community-oriented projects using 7.5% of the company's annual pretax profits, was founded. In 1989, the company introduced Rainforest Crunch® ice cream. The nuts in the ice cream are from rainforest trees, and sales of this flavor benefit rainforest preservation. The company has also helped promote solar energy, "farm aid" and the development of future community leaders.

Ben & Jerry's success and expansion have created a new set of problems for the company. To compete at the national level with large corporations, the company must have information regarding such issues as the market share of Ben and Jerry's as well as that of competitors, consumer buying habits and practices, and customer profiles.

Suppose that Ben and Jerry hired you as Director of Marketing Information and Research and, as your first assignment, asked you to develop a list of syndicated data services to which the company should subscribe. Develop a presentation to management describing your recommendations. For each syndicated service recommended, give a description of the information provided and a discussion of why the company needs this information.

[i] [a]The information provided in this case was obtained from Hoover's on-line Internet company profile service.

PART II

The Process of Collecting Primary Data

Marketers frequently encounter situations where the needed information cannot be obtained from secondary or syndicated data sources. The company must then initiate a project to collect the data themselves, i.e., commission a primary data-collection project. Regardless of whether the purpose of the study is exploratory, descriptive, or experimental, the decision to conduct primary research cannot be made lightly, because of the expensive and time-consuming nature of such projects. Furthermore, if the project is not well-conceived, properly designed, and appropriately executed, the resulting data may not provide the desired information or may cost more than the information is worth.

The steps in the research process were shown in Exhibit 1.7. To recapitulate, these are:

1. Formulate the problem.
2. Specify the research design.
3. **Develop the data collection procedure.**
4. **Design the sampling procedure.**
5. **Collect the data.**
6. **Process and analyze the data.**
7. **Present the results.**

Steps 3 through 7, the ones shown in bold type, are unique to designing and executing a primary data-collection project. The chapters in Part II of this text discuss each of these steps.

When developing the data-collection procedure, decisions must be made on how the data will be collected and how the data-collection instrument will be designed. In reality, only two methods exist to collect information from individuals: questioning and observing. Decisions pertaining to the selection and design of an observation or questioning procedure are addressed in Chapter 6. We address issues surrounding the design of the data-collection instrument in Chapter 8.

In designing the sampling procedure, a series of decisions must be made about the number of participants to be included in the study and how these participants are to be selected. An entire chapter (Chapter 7) is devoted to these critical sampling decisions.

Procedures to ensure the proper execution of the project when collecting the data are described in Chapter 9, alond with analysis of the data collected. Only a few basic forms of data analysis that are typically applied to large data-collection projects are discussed in Chapter 9. Other, more sophisticated data-analysis techniques are introduced in later chapters in specific research contexts.

Once the data have been collected and analyzed, the results must be presented to the person or persons requesting the research. Chapter 9 describes how such results are typically organized and presented, either in written form or orally.

Chapter 6

Primary Data-Collection Alternatives and Data-Quality Issues

Learning Objectives:

This is the first of four chapters that address the process of collecting primary data. Specifically, after reading this chapter you should be able to:

o explain how the decision is reached to collect primary data.

o list the issues involved in designing a primary research project.

o explain the two primary data-collection alternatives available.

o discuss the potential errors that can have an impact on the quality of the data collected.

Blocks and Marbles Brand Toys, Inc., developed a unique set of building blocks containing grooves and holes. The blocks allow children to create structures that can then be knocked down with the set's marbles. Prior to committing resources for the production of this toy, the company had to determine whether children would like the toy and parents would buy it. They conducted primary research to find the answers.

First, they produced a small number of toy and had researchers observe children playing with the toy. These observations provided insights as to whether children enjoyed the toy and how quickly they tired of playing with it. Encouraged by the results, Blocks and Marbles instituted additional research to identify the types of families most likely to purchase the toy. This additional research also provided a more realistic assessment of how long children would continue to enjoy the toy.

Blocks and Marbles contracted with a company to manufacture a limited number of toy sets and obtained distribution in fifty retail stores. Purchasers of the toy were asked to leave their names and phone numbers. Over 1000 purchasers were contacted by telephone within a few months of purchase. The results of the interviews revealed that parents liked the educational nature of the of purchase. The results of the interviews revealed that parents liked the educational nature of the toy and that children continued to enjoy it long after purchase. Based on purchaser demographics, the market see <BI>med broad-based.

Blocks and Marbles began full-scale production and distribution of the product based on the results of their research. By the second full year of operation, the toy grossed over $1,000,000 in sales.[1]

The management of Blocks and Marbles needed information that was not available from secondary or syndicated sources. Managers often find themselves in this situation. In such instances, the only way to obtain the needed information is to gather data specifically for the problem at hand. This entails designing and implementing a primary data-collection project. However, before embarking upon any primary research project, management must decide whether the project is justifiable.

Deciding If Primary Research Is Warranted

A lack of information is not sufficient reason to conduct a primary data-collection project. A primary research project is warranted only if the information is actionable and worth the collection costs.

Is the Information Actionable?

Actionable results have an impact on the manager's decision. To decide if a research project will yield actionable information, the manager should continually ask such questions as:

- Why is the information important to me?
- What might I do differently if I had the information?
- How might my actions or decisions vary depending upon the specific results obtained?

Is the Information Worth the Cost?

Even if a primary data collection project will provide actionable results, research may still not be warranted. The worth, or value, of the information to be obtained must also exceed the cost of collecting it. Put simply: the more severe the consequences of making a wrong decision, the greater the value of actionable research information. For example, suppose that two managers face decisions. One manager has to decide whether to spend an additional five thousand dollars for a brand promotion. The second manager has to decide whether to commit five million dollars to introduce a new product. Obviously, the first manager has much less to lose if wrong than does the second manager, so research information that reduces the chance of making a wrong decision has much more value to the second manager.

The value of the information to be provided by a research project sets the upper bounds on how much money should be spent to gather the information. The cost of a primary research project is influenced by the way the project is designed and executed, so information value also has a direct impact on these aspects of the research. Indeed, management may find that the information is not worth what the project will cost, regardless of how the project is designed or executed.

Sophisticated statistical procedures exist that provide estimates of the value of research information.[2] However, such procedures are rarely used in practice. More subjective assessments of research value based on the input of the members of the marketing team are commonly used instead.

Issues in Designing a Primary Research Project

Upon concluding that a primary research project is warranted, four major issues must be resolved to design the project. These issues are:

1. choosing the data collection method;

2. designing the data collection instrument;

3. defining from whom the information will be gathered; and 4. determining the appropriate data-analysis procedures. The rest of this chapter will describe the first of these issues and will also introduce you to factors that, if not controlled, can cause the data obtained to be inaccurate. The remaining three issues will be addressed in the other three chapters comprising Part II of the text.

Primary Data Collection Alternatives

Basically, two techniques exist for gathering information from people: direct questioning and observation. Direct questioning is the most commonly used technique but, for some situations, observation is preferred.

Observation Techniques

Observation involves recording information without relying on respondent answers or memory. Using mechanical devices attached to television sets to determine the size of television audiences, as described in Chapter 5, is an example of an observation technique. Having someone pose as a customer with a complaint to observe the salesperson's reactions is another example.

Why Use Them?

Observation is useful if many respondents would refuse to answer direct questions. People may refuse to answer questions that they feel are personal or embarrassing, for example. Observation is also useful if respondents are not likely to tell the truth if directly questioned. Asking people how often they watch public television or how much money they give to charities will often lead to an overstatement of the real amount. As an example of how direct questioning can produce different answers than an observation, one observation study found that almost one-third of U.S. citizens do not wash their hands after using the restroom although 94 percent in a telephone survey claimed to do so.[3]

Accurate responses are also unlikely when respondents are directly questioned about topics that are of little importance to them. In these cases, respondents do not intentionally give incorrect answers. Rather, they do so because they never knew, or simply have forgotten, the correct answer. For example, can you remember what price you paid the last time you bought gasoline or how many gallons you bought? When see <BI>king information about topics of little importance to the respondent, observation can lead to more accurate information.[4]

Applying Marketing Research 6.1

When Procter & Gamble filmed women washing dishes, they discovered that the procedure was different from the one described by the women. One key difference was that a greater amount of dishwashing detergent was actually used than the women said they used. This finding led P&G to develop less-concentrated formulas that they could sell at a lower price per ounce, reducing the cost per use.[5]

Some groups are difficult to question, making observation imperative. Small children, for instance, have short attention spans and have a difficult time understanding and answering questions. The use of observation such as described in the Blocks and Marbles example that introduced this chapter can overcome these barriers.

Requirements for Use

By their very nature, observation techniques require that the data be observable. Thus, factors such as the attitudes that people hold or the reasons behind their behavior cannot be measured by observation. In addition, to be practical and cost-efficient, observation must meet two other requirements. First, either the situation to be observed must occur frequently or the time of the next occurrence must be predictable. Second, the time needed for the observation must be relatively short. Not meeting these requirements increases observation costs dramatically. For example, observing a person involved in the decision to purchase a new automobile would not be feasible. The observation not only would require identifying the point in time that the decision process began but also could entail a long period of observation before the purchase is made.

Types of Observation

The notion of observation tends to conjure up an image of a person surreptitiously watching something occur. In reality, observations take many forms. In general, observation techniques can vary according to each of the four factors listed in Table 6.1.

Human* vs. *mechanical	Will the observation be made by a person or a machine?
Natural* vs. *contrived environment	Will the behavior be observed as it naturally occurs, or will it be forced to occur?
Open* vs. *disguised procedure	Will the individuals know they are being observed?
Direct observation* vs. *historical evidence	Will the observation take place while the behavior occurs, or will the behavior be estimated from records?

Table 6.1 Factors along which an observation technique varies.

Human vs. Mechanical Observations. Observations do not have to be conducted by people. In fact, mechanical observation, if feasible, is often preferable. Mechanical observation eliminates human error and is less costly, especially as the number of observations increases. Mechanical observation is also useful if the presence of a human observer might alter the behavior being observed. In addition, a human observer may not adequately be able to see <BI> and record all that takes place. For example, a human observer would have a difficult time determining how a shopper visually scanned a shelf display or what aspects of a print advertisement first catch a reader's eye. This behavior can be readily observed by having the shopper or reader wear specially designed eyeglasses that track eye movement.

Mechanical observations are best suited for situations where simple tallies are sought (such as using a turnstile to measure attendance at a ball game). We are exposed to a variety of such mechanical devices daily such as the checkout scanners shown in Exhibit 6.1. On the other hand, complex behaviors often require human observers to adequately identify and record what takes place.

Exhibit 6.1 The supermarket scanner, with which we are all familiar, is a mechanical observation device.

Natural vs Contrived Situation. If at all possible, observations should occur in a natural environment. Creating an artificial, or contrived, environment in which to observe the behavior can jeopardize the validity of what is observed if it causes people to change what they would normally do. However, situations not occurring frequently enough or predictably enough to allow natural observation may require a contrived situation. For example, observing a consumer after the purchase of a lawnmower to determine the clarity of the assembly instructions would be difficult in a natural environment. A contrived alternative would be to recruit people for the purpose of observing them assembling the lawnmower.

Applying Marketing Research 6.2

Designers at NEC conducted natural field observations of people using notebook computers to assist them in the final configuration of their Ultralite Versa notebook computer. One of the most striking things they noticed was that people often double-tasked while starting up notebook computers. That is, they were often doing something else, such as talking on the telephone or writing a note, when they opened the computer. Therefore, an opening device requiring two hands, like most notebook computers used, was not practical. Thus, the NEC machine was designed with a single center-mounted latch that opened easily with one hand. The use of snap-in components that allowed the user to customize the machine's configuration and a swiveling screen were other design features added from the consumer input. It is doubtful that some of these findings would have been uncovered if the observation had taken place in an artificial environment.[6]

Disguised vs Open Observations. In a disguised observation, respondents are unaware that they are being observed. A disguised observation is useful when respondents might change their behavior if they know that they are being observed. In an open observation, respondents know that they are being observed. When using open observations, a warm-up period is often included to acquaint respondents with the procedure. The warm-up period also allows the respondents to return to more typical behavior patterns after the novelty of being observed wears off. The data collected during the warm-up period are usually discarded.

Applying Marketing Research 6.3

Foote Cone Belding advertising agency once used an interesting disguised observation project to learn how events were influencing consumers' attitudes and behaviors. The agency's marketing planning unit initiated periodic visits to a small Illinois town the agency code-named "Laskerville." While there, the researchers attended town functions, read local newspapers, eavesdropped, and engaged in casual conversations with residents to gather information about trends and values.

The true identify of the town was a closely

guarded secret; even the CEO of the firm did not know. The true name of the town was not mentioned in any report and mileage figures were altered on expense reports so its location could not be determined. The agency hoped that, by keeping its research activities disguised and the town's identity a secret, the data would be more valid.[7]

Direct vs Historical Observations. Sometimes it is impossible to observe the situation of interest directly. What occurred has to be reconstructed using historical evidence or physical traces left behind. Using historical evidence in marketing research is directly analogous to what an archaeologist does to determine what occurred in ancient civilizations.

Estimates of previous traffic levels across store areas could be obtained by studying the wear patterns in the floor of a store. Packages, bottles, and cans discarded in garbage can be used to estimate purchase or consumption behavior. For instance, United Airlines stopped serving butter on many of its short-range flights after examination of the garbage from these flights revealed that few passengers were eating the butter provided.[8]

Direct Questioning Techniques

As the name implies, **direct questioning techniques** gather the required information by asking questions of persons who are thought to have the information. When deciding to use a direct questioning technique instead of observation, three options exist: personal interviews, telephone interviews, or self-administered surveys. Table 6.2 compares each of these questioning techniques on several important factors and, as you can see <BI>, no one technique is best on all factors. The method to use depends on the purpose of the study, the types of questions necessary, and available resources (such as time, money, and staff).

Personal Interviews

	In-home	Central Location	Telephone	Mail
Data collection costs	High	Medium	Low	Low
Speed of data collection	Low	Medium/High	High	Low
Interviewer influence	High	High	Medium	None
Quantity of data collected	High	Medium/High	Medium	Low
Ability to use a complex survey	Good	Good	Fair	Poor
Severity of refusal rates	Medium/High	Medium/High	Medium	High
Sample control afforded	Excellent	Fair	Good	Poor

Table 6.2 Comparison of direct questioning methods.

Personal Interviews

Personal interviewing involves conducting interviews in a face-to-face setting. A trained interviewer asks the questions and records the responses. Because the interviewer does most of the work of completing the survey, such as writing down the responses, one advantage of personal interviews is that response rates are relatively high.[9] Another advantage is that displays, product demonstrations, or other visual cues can be included easily. Finally, a rapport can develop between the interviewer and respondent that discourages respondents from abruptly terminating an interview before it is completed.

One drawback of personal interviews is that mistakes can be introduced by the interviewer. The presence of the interviewer can also cause respondents to give untruthful answers. Respondents may be embarrassed, or unwilling, to tell the interviewer the truth or may give answers they think will please the interviewer.

In-home Interviewing. Historically, most personal interviews in the United States were conducted in people's homes. However, in-home interviewing now has become impractical for most projects. With people being home less and less, it is becoming increasing difficult to contact chosen respondents. In addition, refusal rates have become extremely high because people are more reluctant to let strangers into their homes. Furthermore, because of high crime rates, interviewers are unwilling to enter some geographic areas to conduct interviews.

Central-Location Interviewing. Because of the difficulties associated with in-home interviewing, central-location interviewing is normally used in the United States instead. As the name implies, with **central-location interviewing**, face-to-face interviews are conducted at one or more specified locations. For example, respondents might be recruited to come to a school auditorium to participate in a research project.

The most common form of central-location interviewing is to interview respondents at a mall shopping center, known as **mall-intercept interviewing**. Mall intercept interviews are widely used in marketing research. Data can be collected quickly and respondent reactions to product ideas, product tastes, advertising, or other stimuli can readily be obtained. In fact, the major share of the market research budget for large consumer goods companies goes for mall-intercept interviews.[10]

The major concern about central-location interviewing, particularly mall-intercept interviewing, is sample representativeness. Since only those persons shopping at the selected mall while interviews are being conducted have a chance of being chosen, the respondent sample may not reflect the population of interest. In fact, research has shown that mall-intercept samples typically do not match the demographic characteristics of the population of the surrounding area.[11] The methods used to select respondents tend to reduce the representativeness of mall-intercept studies as well.

Telephone Interviews

Within the United States, most companies have turned to telephone interviews for marketing research projects requiring a representative sample of the target population. Telephone surveys are quickly completed and cost less than personal interviews. It is also relatively easy to implement techniques that increase the representativeness of the sample of respondents.

One reason that a survey can be completed quickly is the way telephone interviewing facilities are designed. The telephone interviewing facilities of most field services can accommodate a large number of interviewers so several interviews can be conducted simultaneously (see <BI> Exhibit 6.2). Completion time can be reduced even further through the use of Computer-Assisted Telephone Interviewing, or CATI.[12] In a **CATI** system, the logic of the interview and the questions to be asked are programmed into a computer. The interviewer reads the questions from a computer screen and answers are recorded directly into the computer. Direct computer entry eliminates the time necessary to transfer data from paper to computer. CATI also reduces interviewer error because the computer will not allow incorrect input and handles any necessary adjustments to the questionnaire, such as questions that should be skipped or added for a particular respondent.

Exhibit 6.2

A typical CATI telephone interviewing facility.

(Courtesy of Elrick & Lavidge, Inc.)

Applying Marketing Research 6.4

The use of telephone polling of American attitudes by politicians is skyrocketing. In the three years he was in office, President Kennedy conducted only 16 polls. Two presidents later, Richard Nixon commissioned 233. By the time Ronald Reagan sought the Presidency, political polling was big business.

During President Reagan's successful campaign for the 1984 presidency, consumer attitudes and key issues were monitored closely through research. A major portion of this research involved a massive telephone survey research program, costing over $2 million to execute. Five telephone interviewing centers having a total of about 250 CATI stations were networked by phone lines to a master computer. With this system, up to 7800 interviews could be conducted in an evening, if necessary. Each morning after the interviews, about 300 tables of data were made available to Reagan's campaign strategists.[13]

This reliance on consumer polls has continued with successive presidents. During just his first two years in office, nearly 150 polls were conducted for President Clinton.[14]

Because most U.S. households have telephones, telephone surveys can include a much broader representation of the population than can central-location interviewing. In addition, long distance services, such as WATS lines, keep the telephone charges incurred for geographically spread samples to a minimum. However, the representativeness of the sample is an issue if existing lists, such as telephone directories, are used to select the sample for a telephone survey.[15] For this reason, many companies have turned to some form of random-digit dialing.

With **random-digit dialing** a computer generates telephone numbers at random to be dialed instead of using numbers located in a telephone directory or published list. Random-digit dialing allows any possible telephone number to have an equal chance of being selected. Households with unlisted telephone numbers can be reached as easily as can households with listed numbers. One drawback of random-digit dialing is that a large percentage of the numbers the computer generates are likely to be nonworking numbers since all possible telephone numbers are not in service at any point in time. Fortunately, several methods have been developed that increase the efficiency of random-digit dialing by raising the percentage of working numbers generated in any sample.[16]

While telephone interviews might see <BI>m to be the perfect direct questioning technique, they do have shortcomings. Respondents usually are not willing to spend as much time answering questions by telephone as they are with personal interviews. Another shortcoming of telephone interviews is that respondents cannot be shown materials to evaluate like they can in a personal interview, unless these materials are mailed beforehand. Refusals to cooperate or premature termination of the interview become potential problems as well, since the respondent can easily take these actions over the telephone. In spite of these limitations, telephone interviewing is used extensively, especially when a geographically-dispersed sample is desired.

Recently, companies have begun experimenting with Totally Automated Telephone Interviewing, or **TATI**. With TATI systems, individuals are mailed a card inviting them to call a toll-free number to participate in the survey. Upon calling the number, participants are led through the survey by computer, much like a voice-mail system. If TATI systems prove to be successful, their use would dramatically reduce interviewing costs.[17]

Self-Administered Surveys

Self-administered surveys are usually the least expensive direct questioning technique, since interviewer costs are eliminated. In addition, because no interviewers are present, they can have no an influence on the answers given. Self-administered surveys are normally conducted by mail or in a central location. Both methods have some serious disadvantages, however.

One disadvantage of mail surveys is that complex questionnaires must be avoided because no interviewer is present to assure that the respondent correctly completes the questionnaire. It is also impossible to ensure that the right person completes the questionnaire. For example, in one study, a major U.S. firm discovered that 42 percent of the questionnaires it had addressed to the male head of the household were actually completed by the female. Another disadvantage of mail survey projects is that they take more time to complete than do mall intercepts or telephone studies.

The biggest disadvantage of a mail survey, though, is a low response rate. Mail surveys suffer from low response rates for several reasons. First, mail surveys require more effort from the respondent than do telephone surveys or personal interviews. No interviewer is present to help the respondent read and complete the questionnaire. Second, mail questionnaires are often set aside to be completed later, forgotten, and eventually discarded. Third, mail surveys are often mistaken for junk mail or sales brochures and are discarded without ever being opened.

Because a low response rate threatens the validity of a study's results, researchers have developed elaborate procedures for the preparation and handling of mail surveys.[18] In general, these procedures incorporate five guidelines that have been shown consistently to improve response rates.[19] First, create a questionnaire that does not appear crowded or difficult. Second, provide a stamped, self-addressed return envelope. Third, develop a good cover letter to accompany the survey. Fourth, make several follow-up contacts. Fifth, provide a monetary incentive along with the survey.

The many limitations of mail surveys have led researchers to see <BI>k better methods of delivering self-administered surveys. Sending surveys by FAX instead of mail has been used with some success, for instance. Other researchers have mailed a computer disk containing the survey to respondents who are asked to boot up the disk, record answers on it, and mail it back.[20] Recently, Internet surveys have gained popularity as well, as illustrated in Applying Marketing Research 6.5. While these new delivery methods currently generate higher response rates than traditional mail surveys, one must wonder if these higher rates will continue as the novelty of these approaches wears off.

Applying Marketing Research 6.5

Research and polling organizations have begun making collaborative arrangements with Internet access companies such as America Online Inc. In some cases, subscribers take part in polls online in return for a reduction in their monthly bill. In others, users are recruited to take part in specific research projects in return for prizes such as prepaid phone cards.

J.C. Penney used an online survey with 417 women to evaluate 60 swimsuits being considered for inclusion in their stores. The women viewed each suit on the screen and indicated their likes and dislikes. The management of Avon Products claims that an online test accurately predicted the one million sales orders for a Santa wind chime when conventional testing predicted only 300,000 orders. Another aspect of online testing that appeals to these companies is the cost. Such projects currently run only about two-thirds the cost of conventional surveys.[21]

Self-administered surveys are sometimes conducted in a central location instead of using mail. For example, hotels and restaurants typically provide customers with patron satisfaction cards that are completed and returned on the premises. Advances in computer technology now provide the opportunity to have consumers self-complete surveys at free-standing kiosks, often located in areas where large numbers of potential respondents can be found. These Computer-Assisted-Self-Administered Surveys, or **CASI**, are commonly conducted in central locations such as airports, convention facilities, and malls. Besides using the Internet as indicated in Applying Marketing Research 6.5, the J.C. Penney Company also uses CASI in conjunction with direct broadcast technology to have consumers view merchandise items on a television monitor and indicate on a CASI system how likely they are to purchase each item. The information Penney's collects aids their merchandise buyers in determining what products target consumers are most likely to buy.[22]

Central location self-administered projects tend to be completed faster than mail surveys. CASI systems also allow for more complexity in the questionnaire as well, since the computer simplifies the flow of the questions relative to a traditional paper-and-pencil format. The novelty of direct computer interaction also has created fewer refusals than for mail surveys. However, the representativeness of the sample obtained may be questionable since the researcher has little control over who completes the survey.

The limitations of the self-administered format cause marketing researchers to use them primarily for short, simple-to-answer questionnaires where the information is not needed quickly. For example, automobile manufacturers often obtain information on how satisfied new car purchasers are with their car dealers from mail surveys. Similarly, warranty registration cards that are packaged with the product and mailed to the company by the purchaser provide durable goods manufacturers with basic information on a brand's customers.

Mixed Mode Techniques

Companies are continually searching for ways to obtain direct questioning data with smaller nonresponse and less cost. Such searches not only have led to the use of FAX and Internet surveys as mentioned earlier, they also have led to **mixed mode techniques**, that is, more than one direct questioning technique being used in the same study. The most common mixed mode techniques are phone/mail, phone/disk, and phone/fax. In these studies, participants are recruited by telephone, taking advantage of the higher response rates of this questioning mode. The survey is then sent by mail (on paper or on disk) or by FAX, taking advantage of the lower cost of this method. Use of such mixed mode methods is likely to increase in the future.[23]

Data Quality Issues

Anytime that data are collected, the possibility exists that they are inaccurate. Two distinct factors cause inaccuracies: sampling error and nonsampling error. In designing a research project, the impact of both factors must be understood and controlled.

Controlling Sampling Error

Sampling error is the statistical imprecision caused when a sample is used to estimate a target population value. For example, a sample mean will rarely be *exactly* the same as the target population mean. However, if the right sampling techniques are used, sampling error can be statistically estimated to determine how close the sample mean is to the population mean.

Sampling error does not lead to any bias in the sample estimate. That is, sampling error is just as likely to lead to an underestimation of the target population value as to an overestimation. Furthermore, sampling error can be systematically reduced by increasing the size of the sample. Indeed, for a census, no sampling error is present. Therefore, sampling error tends to be much less of a problem than is nonsampling error.

Controlling Nonsampling Error

A **nonsampling error** is an inaccuracy caused by anything other than sampling error. Unlike sampling error, nonsampling error is difficult to measure. Nonsampling error can also lead to a biased estimate of the target population value. The possibility of obtaining biased estimates is a key reason that controlling nonsampling error is so crucial.

Nonsampling error comprises the largest proportion of total error in the data collected from most studies.[24] But, unlike sampling error, the imprecision caused by nonsampling error usually cannot be measured in a completed study. Therefore, efforts must be undertaken during the design and execution of the project to reduce the potential impact of nonsampling error. These efforts must be directed toward each of the components of nonsampling error that are shown in Table 6.3.

1. Sample quality error	Error caused by the sample not reflecting characteristics of the target population
2. Nonresponse error	Error caused by some sample members not being contacted or by contacted members refusing to cooperate
3. Respondent error	Error caused by respondents not providing accurate answers
4. Interviewer error	Error caused by intentional or unintentional interviewer mistakes
5. Instrument error	Error caused by the design of the survey instrument
6. Processing error	Error caused by mistakes in data recording, analysis, and the like

Table 6.3

Factors causing nonsampling error

Sample Quality Error

Sample quality error is the inability of the sample to produce accurate estimates of the population values because the sample does not reflect the characteristics of the population of interest. How well the group from which the sample is drawn mirrors the population of interest impacts the amount of sample quality error. So does the sampling procedure used. Sample quality error will be addressed further in the next chapter when we discuss sampling procedures.

Nonresponse Error

Nonresponse error exists when all members of a chosen sample are not contacted or when a contacted member refuses to participate. Nonresponse error leads to biased estimates if the sample statistics would have been different had the nonrespondents been included.[25] As the number of nonrespondents increases, so does the potential for significant bias in the data.

Data collected from members of the Council of American Survey Research Organizations (CASRO) illustrate the magnitude of the nonresponse problem in marketing research.[26] For the 1,387,000 consumer survey contacts CASRO examined, overall refusal rates averaged 38 percent. Because nonrespondents tend to differ demographically from respondents, estimates based on less than the full sample are likely to be biased.[27] Therefore, everything possible must be done to achieve the best possible response rate, and even small costs to potential respondents (in time, money, or effort) must be minimized.[28]

One of the most common reasons for refusal is that the survey occurs at an inconvenient time. Thus, rescheduling the interview to a more convenient time can capture many of the initial nonrespondents. However, more and more people are refusing to cooperate with surveys, especially telephone surveys, because they fear that it will result in a sales pitch. The research industry lobbied Congress for a long time to prohibit companies from selling under the guise of research, or sugging. In 1995, the Telemarketing and Consumer Fraud and Abuse Prevention Act was passed which mandated that companies indicate "promptly" disclose that they are selling something when a household is called.[29] The research industry hopes that, with sugging banned, consumers will be more willing to respond to legitimate surveys.

It is unlikely that *any* survey has ever been completed with a 100 percent response rate. Therefore, nonresponse is a problem in all studies. Nevertheless, the seriousness of nonresponse depends not only on the nonresponse rate, but also on the potential for the nonrespondents' answers to change the sample estimate. Applying Marketing Research 6.6 illustrates how the impact of nonresponse error might be estimated.

Applying Marketing Research 6.6

Suppose that a random sample of 1000 purchasers of a particular CD system were surveyed by mail regarding their satisfaction with the system. If 400 respond and 200 of those indicated that they were satisfied, our best estimate of the population satisfaction rate is 200/400, or 50 percent. However, that estimate assumes that the same ratio of satisfied to dissatisfied consumers is found in the 600 people who did not respond. In the most pessimistic case, all 600 of those consumers would be dissatisfied, yielding a population estimate of 200/1000, or a 20 percent satisfaction rate. In the most optimistic case, all 600 would be satisfied, yielding 800/1000, or an 80 percent satisfaction rate.

Now suppose that we send a second mailing to the 600 people who did not respond the first time, that 200 of them respond, and that 80 of those are satisfied. Now what is our satisfaction estimate? We now have 280 satisfied consumers out of the 600 who have responded, or a 47 percent satisfaction rate. By increasing our response rate from 40 to 60 percent, we have also reduced the range of our optimistic and pessimistic estimates. The pessimistic estimate would now be 280/1000, or a 28 percent satisfaction rate and our optimistic estimate would be 68 percent [(280 + 400)/1000]. Thus, you can see <BI> how increasing the response rate reduces the impact of nonrespondents on the population estimates.

Respondent Error

Even when a person agrees to complete a survey, answers may be given that are unintentionally or intentionally inaccurate, creating what is known as **respondent error**. Unintentional respondent error can occur because the respondent accidentally marks the wrong response category, misunderstands the question, or is simply mistaken about the issue in question.

Respondents may intentionally give incorrect answers. People do not like to admit that they engage in behaviors or possess attitudes that are not generally accepted in their society. For this reason, a respondent might provide what he or she believes to be a socially acceptable answer instead of telling the truth. People also like others to view them favorably, so they may understate their ages, add a few dollars to their stated salaries, or embellish their job descriptions. The story of the man who listed his occupation as "subterranean sanitation engineer" instead of sewer worker is a case in point.

Sometimes respondents will intentionally give incorrect answers because they feel that it is more helpful to provide answers that they think the interviewer or company conducting the study wants to hear. Also, some respondents may follow the "if you can't say something nice about someone, don't say anything" approach and be overly positive in all of the responses. Other respondents may be overly critical of everything.

As we have indicated earlier in this chapter, the method used to collect the data, especially the presence of an interviewer, can influence the amount of unintentional and intentional respondent error. Respondent error can also be influenced by the way in which questions are asked. Chapter 8 will discuss the impact of questionnaire design on respondent error more thoroughly.

Interviewer Error

For projects requiring that an interviewer collect the data, mistakes made by the interviewer, known as **interviewer error**, are likely. Like respondent error, interviewer error can also be intentional or unintentional. An unintentional error is created if the interviewer marks an incorrect response to a question by accident. Similarly, the interviewer may unintentionally deviate from the desired survey procedure. Some questions are asked that should not have been, some get asked in the wrong order, or some do not get asked at all. A simple thing like not reading the questions exactly as written or changing one's voice intonation can create an unintentional interviewer error.[30] For instance, notice the differences in the inference of the question "Why did you buy that product?" if you stress the various words in the sentence.

Intentional interviewer error is created if the interviewer cheats or provides fraudulent data. For example, an interviewer might not conduct an interview, but merely fill out the survey instrument as though an interview had been conducted. An interviewer might intentionally mark an incorrect answer for a certain question because the incorrect answer allows a large portion of the remainder of the questionnaire to be skipped.

Both unintentional and intentional interviewer errors can be controlled through proper training and supervision.[31] In addition, companies discourage interviewer cheating by validating the accuracy of completed surveys. Interviewers know that some of the respondents will be recontacted and the answers to particular questions checked for accuracy.

Instrument Error

The survey instrument, or questionnaire, used to collect the data can create nonsampling error. Errors caused by the questionnaire are known as **instrument error**. Instrument error can be created by see <BI>king information that the respondent does not know or does not remember. Question wording or question sequencing can also cause instrument error. Instrument error can also occur because the questions that are being asked do not accurately measure what is intended. Chapter 8 will describe how to minimize instrument error through proper questionnaire design.

Processing Error

Responses to survey questions are usually assigned numeric values and filed in a computer data base. Incorrect assignment of values and mistakes in data entry or data analysis create **processing error**. Good processing procedures, such as those discussed in Chapter 9, help minimize processing errors.

The Importance of Controlling Total Survey Error

Nonsampling errors are likely to increase as the sample size is expanded. Larger samples have more opportunities for one or more of the causes of nonsampling error to occur. Thus, attempting to reduce sampling error by enlarging the sample size may contribute to an increase in nonsampling error. Conversely, a reduction in sample size to provide greater control over nonsampling error will increase sampling error. Therefore, the researcher must be concerned with reducing the *total* error present in the data instead of focusing solely on either sampling or nonsampling error. Exhibit 6.3 visually illustrates how total error is impacted by by sampling and nonsampling error. This tradeoff of errors can make a well-designed sample preferable to a census. Even though no sampling error is present when using a census, the total error may be less for some samples than for the census.

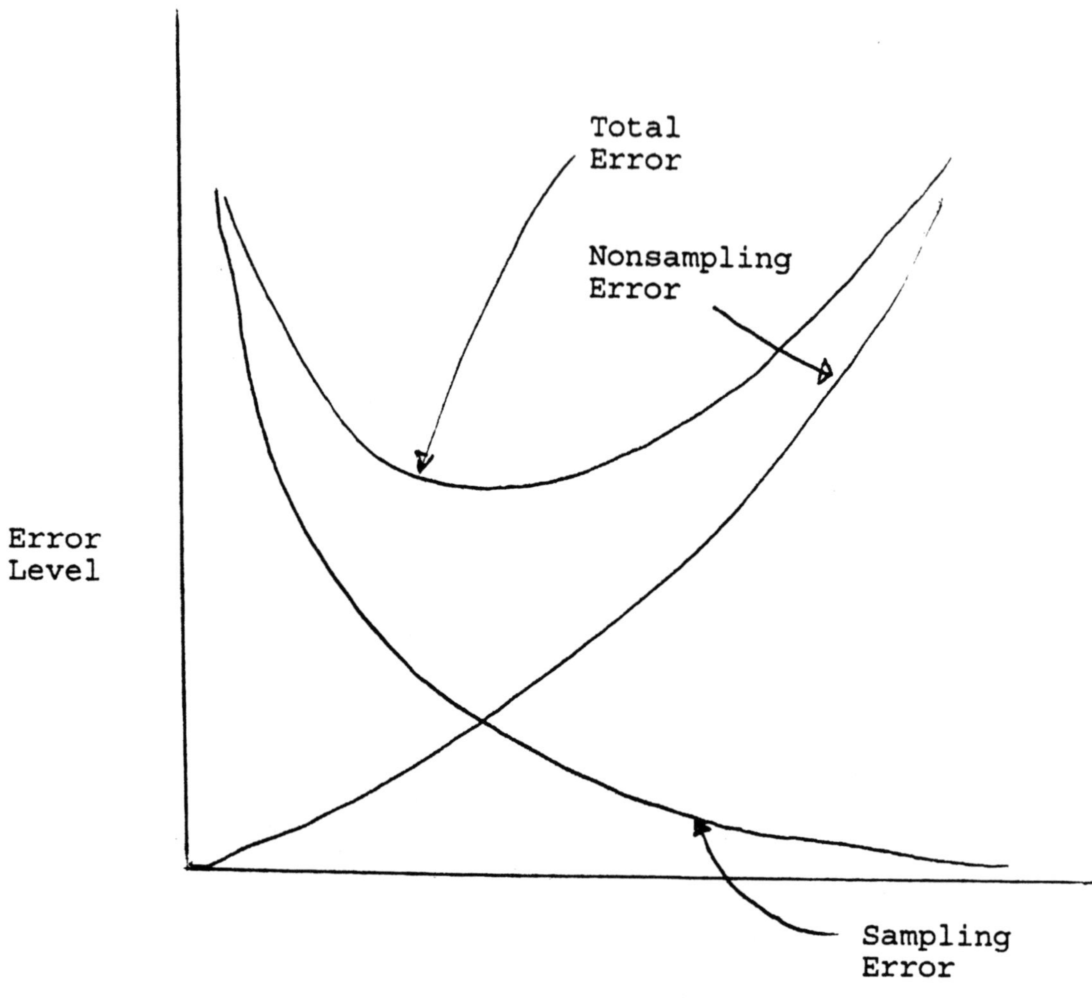

Exhibit 6.3

The tradeoff between sampling and nonsampling errors influences total error.

International Issues

Although in-home interviews are rarely conducted in the United States, they are still the dominant direct questioning method in many countries.[32] Lower labor costs and higher participation rates in these countries make in-home interviewing an attractive alternative. Furthermore, low levels of telephone ownership and low literacy rates often hamper the use of telephone or mail surveys.

In many countries, the number of households having telephones is too small to use telephone interviewing effectively. Even in some European countries, only about one-third of the households have telephones. In developing countries, telephones may be available in only one or two percent of the households. Literacy rates in many developing countries are too low to make self-administered questionnaires practical. Even the types of questions that can be asked in a personal interview may be limited by the respondent's ability to comprehend.

The infrastructure of many countries also impedes the use of some data-collection procedures. Mall-intercept interviewing may not be feasible because a country has few, if any, shopping malls. Observational data collected by scanner check-out systems can rarely be obtained due to the limited number of stores outside of the U.S. that have scanner systems. Postal systems in many countries are often inadequate for using mail surveys.

Cultural differences can impact nonsampling errors as well. In some countries, such as Japan, the desire not to contradict another person makes yea-saying and upward scale bias more prevalent than in the United States.[33] Even the type of incentive selected to increase participation can influence nonsampling errors. For instance, giving a travel clock for participation would be a poor choice in China since the timepiece would denote death to the Chinese.[34]

In spite of what may appear to be insurmountable problems, companies are able to collect data within other countries. The key is recognizing that what works in one country may not work in another. On the positive side companies often find that response rates in foreign countries are much higher than in the United States. As an example, one research company interviewing shoppers at three department stores within the former Soviet Union found that shoppers were so excited about the honor of being interviewed that they stood in line to wait their turn!

Summary

Sometimes, the only way to obtain necessary information is to conduct primary research. Before collecting primary data, however, the manager must be sure that the project will generate actionable results. In addition, the value of the results must be worth the cost of obtaining them.

Four issues must be resolved in designing a primary research project. The data-collection method must be chosen; the population from which the data will be collected must be defined; the instrument used to collect the data must be developed; and the appropriate data-analysis procedure must be determined.

A primary data-collection project can entail observation or direct questioning. Observation techniques gather information without relying on respondents' memory or answers. They are useful when inaccurate information is likely to be obtained if a person is questioned about the topic. To use an observation, the behavior in question must be observable, must occur in a short period of time, and must occur frequently, repetitively, or predictably. Direct questioning techniques involve surveys conducted in person, over the telephone, or by self-administration. No one direct questioning technique is perfect. Each has its own advantages and disadvantages.

The quality of data collected is impacted by sampling and nonsampling error. Sampling error can be controlled through by proper sampling procedures and by the size of the sample. Nonsampling errors are numerous and difficult to measure. Each of the factors shown in Table 6.3 contribute to nonsampling error.

Key Word List:

CASI

CATI

central-location interviewing

direct questioning techniques

instrument error

interviewer error

mall-intercept interviewing

mixed mode techniques

nonresponse error

nonsampling error

observation

personal interviewing

processing error

random-digit dialing

respondent error

sample quality error

sampling error

TATI

Nimslo's Use of the Observation Technique

The Nimslo Company used the observational technique in a very interesting fashion after the

3D camera was introduced. The company monitored photofinishing orders and kept records of the types of pictures taken with the Nimslo camera as well as the most common mistakes that consumers made in taking 3D pictures. Information on picture-taking helped the Nimslo Company learn if the 3D camera was being used in the same fashion as other 35mm cameras.

The company used the information regarding mistakes to develop informational flyers designed to help consumers avoid common picture-taking errors. These flyers were packaged with new cameras and returned photofinishing orders in which these mistakes were observed. This information was also used to determine priorities for camera design changes that would reduce consumer errors. For example, future cameras were redesigned to contain devices that would prevent the shutter from opening unless the camera was held properly for taking 3D pictures.

Review Questions

6.1 What factors must be considered in deciding if a primary research project is warranted?

6.2 What is meant by actionable results? What causes some results to be actionable while others are not?

6.3 What are the reasons observations might be preferred to a direct questioning technique?

6.4 What conditions are necessary for the use of observation techniques?

6.5 What decisions must be made when designing an observation project?

6.6 When might mechanical devices be preferred to human observers?

6.7 What are the advantages and disadvantages of a natural observational environment *vs* a contrived environment?

6.8 What are the ethical ramifications of a disguised observation? What are the potential problems with using an open observation?

6.9 What are the advantages and disadvantages of in-home interviews? central-location interviews? telephone interviews? mail surveys?

6.10 What is random-digit dialing? What is the purpose of using random-digit dialing?

6.11 What is a CATI system? a TATI system?

6.12 What new technologies are being used in self-administered surveys? Why are companies turning to them?

6.13 What is sampling error? How is sampling error controlled?

6.14 Define each of the following types of nonsampling error and indicate how each is controlled:

a. sample quality error

b. respondent error

c. nonresponse error

d. instrument error

e. interviewer error

f. processing error

6.15 Why can't one minimize total survey error simply by minimizing both sampling error and nonsampling error?

Discussion Questions

6.1 What factors do you feel are making it more and more difficult to interview consumers by telephone? What might the research industry do to try to overcome these barriers?

6.2 Give examples of some of the types of research issues that might be adequately studied using mall-intercept interviewing and some types of issues that might not be adequately studied there. Explain your reasoning.

6.3 With two fellow students, observe behavior for one hour at the vending machines in a snack bar or break area on your campus. Each of you should individually record what is observed. How much similarity exists in what each of you recorded? What differences are noted? How important do you feel the lack of similarity between the three observations would be in obtaining accurate data? Why?

6.4 For years, the A.C. Nielsen Company measured television audience size and composition using two different techniques. Audience size was estimated with a mechanical observation device and audience composition was measured with weekly viewing diaries mailed to a random sample of households. In 1987, Nielsen moved to a mechanical device where people pushed keypad buttons to indicate which household members were watching. This device, the people meter, measured both audience size and composition. Preliminary results from the people meter revealed dramatically smaller network audience size estimates than previous methods and provoked the networks to challenge the validity of the new methodology. Why do you think the networks were expressing so much concern over this new technology? In what ways do you think the people-meter system improves the accuracy of the diary system? How might the people-meter system cause inaccuracies not found in the diary system? What type of system would be required to eliminate the inaccuracies found in both systems?

6.5 *Ethical Situation:* Suppose a retail firm that was interested in knowing what made some of their retail clerks better salespeople than others secretly videotaped (with sound) the various salespeople as they interacted with customers. The interactions were separated into two types: those that resulted in a sale and those that did not. The two types of interactions were examined to determine whether any differences were apparent. Discuss the ethics of this research situation.

Chapter 6 Endnotes

1. This example is based upon information in Mary Guterson, "Block By Block," *Venture*, December 1988, p. 54.

2. Good descriptions of these Bayesian analysis techniques can be found in Joseph W. Newman, *Management Applications of Decision Theory*, New York: Harper & Row, 1971 and in Robert Schlaifer, *Analysis of Decisions Under Uncertainty*, New York: McGraw-Hill, 1989.

3. Michael Wilke, "Germs Star for Bayer, Lysol: Hand-washing, Antibiotics Concerns Prompts Moves," *Advertising_Age*, September 23, 1996, p. 12.

4. See Yoram Wind and David Lerner, "On the Measurement of Purchase Data: Surveys Versus Purchase Diaries," *Journal of Marketing Research*, 16 (February 1979), pp. 39-47; and J.H. Parfitt, "A Comparison of Purchase Recall with Diary Panel Records," *Journal of Advertising Research*, 7 (September 1967), pp. 16-31 for discussions of this issue.

5. Gayle D. Moberg, "The Recall Process: Moving Beyond Superficial Response," *Journal of Data Collection*, 27 (Fall 1987), pp. 16-18.

6. Gary McWilliams, "A Notebook That Puts Users Ahead of Gimmicks," *Business Week*, September 27, 1993, pp. 92 & 96.

7. Information for this example came from Carrie Goerne, "Researchers go undercover to learn about `Laskerville,' *Marketing News*, May 11, 1992, p. 11.

8. "Business Bulletin," *Wall Street Journal*, August 11, 1983, p. 1.

9. L.M. Sharp and J. Frankel, "Respondent Burden," *Public Opinion Quarterly*, 47 (Spring 1983), pp. 36-53.

10. Katherine T. Smith, "Most Research Firms Use Mall Intercepts," *Marketing News*, September 11, 1989, p. 16.

11. John P. Murry, Jr., John L. Lastovicka, and Gaurav Bhalla, "Demographic and Lifestyle Selection Error in Mall-Intercept Data," *Journal of Advertising Research*, 29 (February 1989), pp. 46-52.

12. See R.M. Groves and N.A. Mathiowetz, "Computer Assisted Telephone Interviewing," *Public Opinion Quarterly*, 48 (Spring 1984), pp. 356-69.

13. Jack J. Honomichl, *Honomichl on Marketing Research*, (Lincolnwood: Ill., NTC Business Books, 1975), pp. 53-55.

14. "Consulting the Oracle - Everyone Loves Polls. But Can You Trust Them?" *U.S. News & World Report*

15. See Gerald J. Glasser and Gale D. Metzger, "National Estimates of Nonlisted Telephone Households and Their Characteristics," *Journal of Marketing Research*, 12 (August 1975), pp. 359-61; and Clyde L. Rich, "Is Random Digit Dialing Really Necessary?", *Journal of Marketing Research*, 14 (August 1975), pp. 300-5 for findings on listed versus non-listed household characteristics.

16. Martin R. Frankel and Lester R. Frankel, "Some Recent Developments in Sample Survey Design," *Journal of Marketing Research*, 14 (August 1977), pp. 280-93, provides a good description of several methods of random digit dialing.

17. Triplett, Tim, "Survey System Has Human Touch Without the Human, *Marketing News*, October 24, 1994, p.16.

18. A good description of one of these methods can be found in Donald Dillman, *Mail and Telephone Surveys: The Total Design Method*, (New York: John Wiley & Sons, 1978).

19. See Richard J. Fox, Melvin R. Crask, and Jonghoon Kim, "Mail Survey Response Rate: A Meta-Analysis of Selected Techniques for Inducing Response," *Public Opinion Quarterly*, 50 (Winter 1989), pp. 467-91; Leslie Kanuk and Conrad Berenson, "Mail Surveys and Response Rates: A Review," *Journal of Marketing Research*, 39 (Spring 1975), pp. 82-101; and Julie Yu and Harris Cooper, "A Quantitative Review of Research Design Effects on Response Rates to Questionnaires," *Journal of Marketing Research*, 20 (February 1983), pp. 36-44 for reviews of these findings.

20. Neal, William D., "New Technologies in Marketing Research, 1995-2000, *Alert*, 35(3), p.1,3,6,7.

21. Furchgott, Roy, "If You Like the Suit, Click Here," *Business Week*, November 17, 1997, p.8.

22. Information for this example was obtained from Jeff Wiss, "Meet MAX: Computerized Survey Taker," *Marketing News*, May 22, 1989, p.16 and from Christy Fisher, "To Buy, Or Not To Buy: Retailers Focus On Compterized Sessions," *Advertising Age*, May 13, 1991, p.27.

23.Neal, William D., op cit.

24. See, for example, Henry Assael and John Keon, "Nonsampling vs Sampling Errors in Survey Research," *Journal of Marketing*, 46 (Spring 1982), pp. 114-123.

25. See R.M. Durand, H.J. Guffey, Jr., and J.M. Planchon, "An Examination of the Random versus Nonrandom Nature of Item Omissions," *Journal of Marketing Research*, 20 (August 1983), pp. 305-13; G.S. Omura, "Correlates of Item Nonresponse," *Journal of the Market Research Society*, 25 (October 1983), pp. 321-30; and J.R. Dickinson and E. Kirzner, "Questionnaire Item Omission as a Function of Within-Group Question Position," *Journal of Business Research*, 15 (February 1985), pp. 71-5.

26. *Your Opinion Counts: 1986 Refusal Rate Study* Chicago: Your Opinion Counts Steering Committee of the Council of American Survey Research Organizations.

27. See, for example, James R. Chromy and Daniel G. Horowitz, "The Use of Monetary Incentives in National Assessment Household Surveys," *Journal of the American Statistical Association*, 73 (September 1978), pp. 473-78; J. Duncan, "Mail Questionnaires in Survey Research: A Review of Response Inducement Techniques," *Journal of Management*, 5 (September 1979), pp. 39-55; T.J. DeMaio, "Refusals: Who, Where, and Why," *Public Opinion Quarterly*, 44 (Summer 1980), pp. 223-33 and A.L. Stinchcombe, C. Jones, and P. Sheatsley, "Nonresponse Bias for Attitude Questions," *Public Opinion_Quarterly*, 45 (Fall 1981), pp. 359-75.

28. Alison Fahey, "Survey Researchers Study Unity Options," *Advertising Age*, October 8, 1990, p. 61.

29. Diane K. Bowers, "Sugging Banned, At Last," *Marketing Research*, 7 (4), p. 40.

30. For further discussion of this issue, see W.A. Collins (1970), "Interviewers' Verbal Idiosyncracies as a Source of Bias," *Public Opinion Quarterly*, 30 (Fall 1970), pp. 416-22; A. Barath and C.F. Cannell, "Effect of Interviewer's Voice Intonation," *Public Opinion Quarterly*, 36 (Fall 1976), pp. 370-3; M. Collins, "Interviewer Variability," *Journal of the Market Research Society*, 2 (1980), pp. 77-95; and C. Tucker, "Interviewer Effects in Telephone Surveys," *Public Opinion Quarterly*, 47 (Spring 1983), pp. 84-95.

31. D.S. Tull and L.E. Richards, "What Can Be Done About Interviewer Bias?", in J. Sheth, *Research in Marketing*, 3rd ed. (Greenwich: JAI Press, 1980), 143-62 and L. Andrews, "Interviewers: Recruiting, Selecting, Training, and Supervising," in Robert Ferber, *Handbook of Marketing Research* (New York: McGraw Hill, Inc., 1974), 2.124-2.132.

32. Jack J. Honomichl, "British, U.S. Researchers Ponder Their Differences," *Advertising Age*, August 28, 1989, pp. 42 & 49.

33. Sabra E. Brock, "Marketing Research in Asia: Problems, Opportunites, and Lessons," *Marketing Research: A Magazine of Management & Applications*, 1, 3 (September 1989), pp. 44-51.

34. *Ibid.*

Chapter 7

Sampling Issues

Learning Objectives:

This chapter will introduce you to the issues involved in determining from whom the data will be collected in a primary data-collection project. Specifically, in this chapter you will learn:

- o how the population of interest is defined.
- o why a sample may be preferred over a census.
- o various probability and nonprobability sampling methods that can be applied.
- o how the appropriate sample size is determined.

When Ross Perot ran for President of the United States in 1992, one of his major platforms was a proposal to govern the country through an "electronic town hall." He suggested that major issues facing the country be explained on television. Viewers would then call an 800 number to vote on how Congress should act on these matters. Votes could easily be tabulated by Congressional district so individual representatives would know how their constituents voted.

The problem with the notion of electronic town halls, or other call-in voting methods, is that viewers who call in are not representative of the total U.S. public. The mere fact that these people take the time and trouble to call in indicates that they have stronger feelings on the issues discussed. Therefore, they are likely to give a distorted picture of overall public opinion.

Such distortion was evident when CBS tried to implement a nationwide call-in poll based on the President's State of the Union address.

Responses for nearly 300,000 call-ins were tabulated, but the answers turned out to be much different from those obtained from a random sample of U.S. the public. For example, 53 percent of the callers said they were "worse off" than a year ago, while only 32 percent of the representative sample said so. Similarly, 44 percent of the representative sample said economic conditions were about the same as a year ago, while only 19 percent of the callers said so.

Using proper sampling procedures, a small sample of the U.S. population can provide an accurate estimate of the opinion of the total population. Such scientific sampling methods are used to predict election winners, for instance, and the accuracy of their forecasts can be astounding. However, self-selected public opinion polls are not likely to produce accurate estimates.[1]

When would it be appropriate to take a sample of the population instead of a census? If a call-in sample is not representative, what is the appropriate sampling method and how would the sample size be determined? These are the types of sampling issues that will be addressed in detail in this chapter.

Defining the Target Population

The population of interest is called the **target population**. Data should only be gathered from objects in the population of interest. Properly defining the target population is a crucial step in the design of the research project.

Deciding whether to include a particular object in the target population depends on the characteristics required of target population objects. For example, a Kroger store in Indiana *would* be included in the target population of all chain supermarkets, but the same store would *not* be included in the target population of all supermarkets west of the Mississippi. While we commonly think of a population as being comprised of people, this example illustrates that a target population can be other objects as well. Households, companies, or stores often comprise the target population.

If the target population is not properly defined, the information collected may not be relevant for the research question. Improperly defining the target population is known as **population specification error**. For instance, in a study concerned with how the choice of a particular brand of women's perfume is made, the appropriate target population may not be women. Depending upon the specific research question, the target population might be *both* men and women, since men often purchase perfumes as gifts. Likewise, suppose a supermarket chain wants to learn the attitude of customers towards changes that have been made in the layout of their stores. Defining the target population as only female heads-of-households would create a population specification error. A large percentage of their customers are likely to be male-heads-of-households and their attitudes may be completely different from those of the female heads-of-households.

After defining the appropriate target population, the next step is to determine the **sampling frame**, the "list" of target population members from which data actually can be collected. The sampling frame ideally should coincide perfectly with the target population but, in practice, it often excludes some population members. The accuracy of inferences made about the population based on a sample drawn from a sampling frame depends on how well the characteristics of frame members mirror those of the target population. That is why selecting the sampling frame is such an important decision.

Besides not including some members of the target population, sampling frames tend to suffer from two other limitations. First, the frame may include the same members more than once. Second, the frame may include members that are not part of the target population. **Sampling frame error** refers to discrepancies between elements comprising the sampling frame and those comprising the target population. The greater the sampling frame error, the more erroneous can be conclusions drawn about the target population. Applying Marketing Research 7.1 illustrates this problem.

Applying Marketing Research 7.1

Suppose that the manager of Golden State Banks in San Diego, California, asked for your help in estimating the average household income for the bank's trading area. The manager had defined the bank's trading area as the geographic area within the city limits of San Diego. The target population, comprised of all households within the city limits, is illustrated by the lefthand circle in Exhibit 7.1. Now, let's assume that you decide to use the San Diego telephone directory as the sampling frame. The right hand circle in Exhibit 7.1 represents the names listed in the telephone directory.

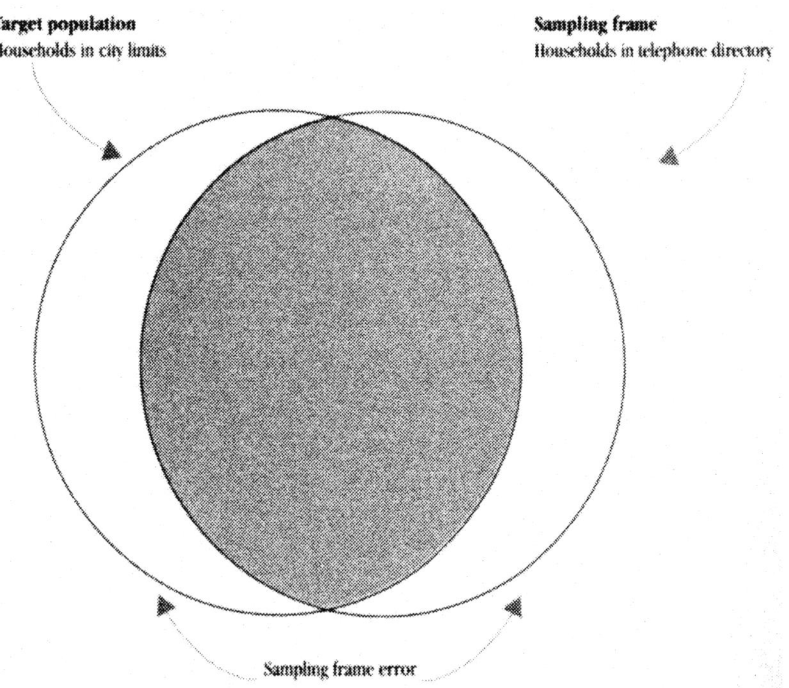

Exhibit 7.1

Illustration of sampling frame error.

Some households in the city limits will not be included in the telephone directory because they have no telephone. Others will not be included because they had a telephone installed after the telephone directory was published, or because they have unlisted numbers. These households, in total, create the unshaded area of the lefthand circle.

Some numbers in the telephone directory will not correspond to target population members because the numbers belong to households outside of the city limits. These numbers comprise the majority of the unshaded area on the right. Those households in the target population with more than one family member listed in the phone book or having more than one phone number will be included more than once in the sampling frame. These extra listing are also included in the unshaded area on the right.

The two unshaded segments of these circles (where the circles do not overlap) comprise

> sampling frame error, which can lead to an inaccurate estimate of the average household income for the bank's trading area. For example, households with unlisted numbers maytend to have relatively high incomes. If so, the average income of households estimated from the names listed in the directory would likely understate the true average household income of the trading area. If households in the directory but outside the San Diego city limits tend to have low incomes, the problem would be compounded.

Once the sampling frame has been chosen, the researcher must make a series of decisions concerning the selection of the sampling frame members from whom data will be collected. The first of these decisions is whether or not to collect data from all members. If the data will only be collected from a sample of the members, a second decision concerns the method to be used to select the sample members. Finally, the decision of how large to make the sample must be made. These three decisions will be discussed in detail in the following sections.

A Census or a Sample?

To obtain the required information, data could be collected from all members of the sampling frame, *i.e.*, a **census** could be conducted. The alternative would be to sample only some of the members and use the sample data to make inferences about the frame. A census is feasible if the project involves a small target population and an accurate sampling frame. For example, if Dupont wished to gather information about customer satisfaction with a specialized polymer used in the production of paper, a census would be appropriate since the number of paper-producing companies using the polymer is relatively small, and these companies are easily identified. Normally, though, the limitations of a census make a sample of the target population the preferred option.

Limitations of a Census

Cost

The most obvious potential drawback to conducting a census is its cost. As an example, the final cost for the last Census of Population conducted by the U.S. Bureau of the Census was nearly three billion dollars.[2] Thus, for most projects, the cost of a census is feasible only when the target population is small.

Time

Even if a company is willing to accept the cost of a census, the length of time necessary to complete a census often makes it impractical. Management usually needs the information more quickly than a census can be conducted. Furthermore, information from a census may be outdated by the time it is collected and analyzed.

Inaccuracy

As you learned in the previous chapter, errors can occur whenever data are collected. A question can be misinterpreted, an answer can be recorded incorrectly, or any number of other mistakes can be made. Close supervision of the data-collection process reduces the number of such mistakes, but supervision is costly. In most cases, not enough money is available to provide the same level of supervision in a census that can be instituted in a sample. Therefore, census data can have more inaccuracies than sample data.

Applying Marketing Research 7.2

Even with all of the money spent designing and executing the U.S. Census of the Population, errors occur. For example, the number of people over 100 years of age was severely over-estimated in one census because many people checked the wrong box when specifying the decade of birth for members of their households. This mistake resulted in many people being classified as having been born in the 1860s when they were actually born in the 1960s.[3] Such mistakes help fuel the controversy over whether more accurate estimates of the characteristics of the U.S. population would be provided by a well-designed sample involving extensive supervision.

Limitations of Sampling

Even though the limitations of a census typically lead to the use of a sample, sampling has its own limitations that need to be considered.

Cost

Many times, no accurate sampling frame for the target population is readily available. For example, where would one find a sampling frame containing only people who had eaten bran muffins within the past two weeks or one that contained only left-handed males in Seattle? In such cases, a sampling frame for a larger population that contains the target population as a subset must be used to locate target population members.

When using the sampling frame for a larger population, the typical procedure is to select members of the larger sampling frame, screen them to see if they meet target population characteristics, and sample only those who do. Therefore, the **incidence level**---the number of target population members in the larger sampling frame relative to the total number of members in that sampling frame---has an impact on the cost of sampling. The cost of obtaining a sample of the target population members increases as the incidence level decreases, because the time and effort required to screen for people who meet target population characteristics increases. Applying Marketing Research 7.3 illustrates this situation.

Applying Marketing Research 7.3

Suppose that the marketing manager for the Wheaties brand of breakfast cereal wanted to

gather information from U.S. females, aged 18-55, who had purchased cold cereal within the past two weeks. Obviously, no sampling frame exists that contains only members of this specific target population. A sampling frame for a larger group that contains this target population must be used to locate target population members. If the manager assumes that most of the target population members have telephones, a sample can be obtained by contacting telephone households in the United States. These households can then be screened to see if they have the target population characteristics.

Table 7.1 illustrates the ramifications of using this approach to reach target population respondents. First of all, only about three-fourths of the telephone households contacted would have a female member. In addition, only about 90 percent of the females reached will meet the age requirements of the target population. About half will meet the purchase requirements. The net result is that the incidence of targetpopulation members is 34 percent. That is, only about one household in three will be a member of the target population.

Households Where Female Is Contacted		Age 18–55		Purchased Cold Cereal in Past Two Weeks		Net Incidence
75%	×	90%	×	50%	=	.34

Table 7.1

Example of the impact of sample restrictions on net incidence.

Inaccuracy

As was mentioned earlier in this chapter, sample data may not accurately reflect the target population due to sampling frame error. You will learn in the next section that some sampling procedures, even when applied to a representative sampling frame, may not yield data that accurately reflect the sampling frame, and hence, the target population. A manager can easily make incorrect decisions if such sampling procedures are used and the data are assumed to reflect target population characteristics accurately.

What Sampling Method Will Be Used?

A wide variety of methods can be used to select sample members. Those used most often in marketing research are listed in Table 7.2. As you can see, some are known as probability sampling methods, while others are called nonprobability sampling methods.

Probability Methods	Nonprobability Methods
Simple random sampling	Convenience sampling
Systematic sampling	Judgment sampling
Stratified sampling	Quota sampling
Cluster sampling	

Table 7.2

Most commonly used methods of sample selection.

Probability Sampling Methods

A **probability sample** involves some form of random selection so that every member of the sampling frame has a nonzero chance of being included in the sample. A probability sampling procedure has the advantage that sample data used to estimate population values have a known level of statistical precision. **Statistical precision** is the ability to determine how closely the sample estimate approximates the sampling frame value (and hence the target population value) that is being estimated. That is, the manager knows, with a given level of statistical confidence, that the quantity of interest lies within a particular range of values.

Each of the probability sampling techniques listed in Table 7.2 has its own advantages and disadvantages. The best particular technique depends on the nature of the sampling problem.[4] We will now examine each of these sampling methods in more detail.

Simple Random Sampling

In **simple random sampling**, all possible subsets of the sampling frame that have a size equal to the sample size are equally likely to become the sample. Hence, each sampling frame member has an equal chance of being chosen and sample members can be selected in a variety of ways. For instance, a simple random sample of 10 companies from a sampling frame containing 50 companies could be selected by randomly drawing 10 names out of a hat containing the names of all 50 companies. Alternatively, members could be assigned identifying numbers from 1 to 50 and the sample of 10 selected by choosing ten random numbers from 1 to 50 using a random number table.

Most people are familiar with the notion of a simple random sample. Yet, simple random sampling is seldom used in practice. Drawing a probability sample using simple random sampling can be very cumbersome and time-consuming if a large sampling frame is being sampled. Imagine trying to select a simple random sample of 50 students from your school. A great deal of time would be spent writing student names on slips of paper to be placed in a large "hat" from which 50 names would be drawn. Even if you assigned each name a unique number, such as their social security number, and used a table of random numbers to select the sample members, the task still would be quite time-consuming.

Simple random sampling is usually reserved for projects having a small sampling frame or for situations in which the sample can be drawn using computer technology. For example, telephone interviews with a simple random sample of households having telephones can be conducted quickly and easily using the random-digit dialing procedure discussed in the last chapter.

Alternative, easier-to-implement procedures that mimic simple random sampling are sometimes used when simple random sampling would be difficult to implement. The results obtained from these alternative procedures are usually treated as if they had been generated by simple random sampling. Doing so, even though technically incorrect, allows for the calculation of statistical precision. Systematic sampling, which we discuss next, is one such alternative method.

Systematic Sampling

If a list of the sampling frame members is available, a probability sample can be generated quickly by choosing members located at selected positions on the list, a procedure known as **systematic sampling**. The first step when using systematic sampling is to divide the total number of members in the sampling frame by the desired sample size to produce a sampling interval. For instance, if there were 1000 members in the list, and a sample of size 100 was desired, the sampling interval would be 1000/100, or 10. The next step is to select the first member to be included in the sample at random. However, the first member's position on the list must be less than or equal to the sampling interval. In our example, then, any member from the first to the tenth on the list is eligible. Finally, the remaining sample members are those whose position on the list is a multiple of the sampling interval from the first member selected. Therefore, if the first member selected in our example was third on the list, the other sample members would be the thirteenth, twenty-third, thirty-third, and so on. Our sample would include a total of 100 members.

By selecting the first sample member at random, systematic sampling produces a probability sample. In fact, each member has the same chance (1/10 in the above example) of being included in the sample. Yet, all possible subsets of 100 members are not equally likely to be sampled. Due to the requirement that each sample member be a sampling interval away from another sample member, it is impossible for most subsets containing 100 members to actually become the sample. In fact, in our example, only 10 possible samples exist, since the first sample member is one of the first ten on the list. Hence, systematic sampling is not the same as simple random sampling. Nevertheless, it is often used because sample member selection is much simpler and faster.

Stratified Sampling

Researchers often want information about particular subgroups in the target population as well as about the entire target population. **Stratified sampling** techniques are probability sampling methods that are used to ensure that subgroups of interest within the target population are adequately represented in the sample. Another advantage is that, for a given sample size, stratified samples almost always produce estimates of population values that are more precise than the comparable estimates obtained by simple random sampling.[5]

If each subgroup of interest is represented in the stratified sample in the same proportion as in the sampling frame, the procedure is called **proportionate stratified sampling**. If some subgroups in the stratified sample are over- or under-represented relative to their sampling frame proportions, the procedure is known as **disproportionate stratified sampling**.

Disproportionate stratified sampling is often used to ensure that small subgroups of interest are adequately represented in the sample. It is also used to concentrate sampling power in those subgroups where the quantity being measured varies greatly across elements within the subgroup. Applying Marketing Research 7.4 clarifies the distinction between proportionate and disproportionate stratified sampling.

Applying Marketing Research 7.4

Supermarkets account for the majority of the sales of many brands. Therefore, an accurate estimate of market share within supermarkets is a vital piece of information for managers of these brands. Let's examine why a disporportionate stratified sampling technique might be preferable to a proportionate one in this instance.

If we examine the characteristics of the population of supermarkets in the United States, we find the following:

Type of Store	% of Pop.	% of Sales	Ave. Store Sales
Chain stores	10	60	$4,000,000
Large Independents	10	25	$2,000,000
Medium Independents	40	10	$300,000
Small Independents	40	5	$150,000

Therefore, if we stratify by type of supermarket, a proportionate stratified sample of 1,000 stores would have 100 Chain stores (10%), 100 Large Independents (10%), 400 Medium Independents (40%), and 400 Small Independents. However, the data in the second two columns suggest that a disproportionate stratified sampling approach might increase sampling power.

Only small percentages of total supermarket sales occur in Medium and Small Independent supermarkets, but these store comprise 80 percent of the proportionate stratified sample. Furthermore, average store sales for Large Independents and Chain stores are much greater than for Medium and Small Independent stores. Thus, much greater variations in a brand's sales might be expected within the two large store groups than within the two other groups of stores. That is, if the average Chain store has sales some 40 times larger than the average Small independent store, it stands to reason that sales of the brands sold in these chain stores will vary more in Chain stores than in Small Independent stores. For this reason, it will be advantageous to increase the number of

Chain and Large Independent stores in the sample and decrease the number of sample stores for the other two categories. If the decision is made to use a disproportionate stratified sample, any sample for which the share of each strata in the sample does not equal the strata's share of the population is a possibility. Sometimes, the number of sample members to include from each strata is determined to maximize the statistical precision of the estimate for the total population. At other times, the optimal sample compositions are modified to ensure that a sufficient number of sample members are available in all strata to allow for analysis of results for each individual strata by itself.

Cluster Sampling

Cluster sampling is a probability sampling method where the population is divided into mutually exclusive and exhaustive subsets, called clusters, and a sample of clusters is taken. If each cluster possesses all of the heterogeneity of the target population, sampling of only one cluster would suffice. A random sample of one cluster would be drawn and all members of that cluster become sample members, called **single-stage cluster sampling**. If it is felt that each cluster is not a perfect representation of the target population, a random sample of more than one cluster can be taken and only a sample of the members of each selected cluster used, called **multi-stage cluster sampling**. For instance, if the target population was divided into 100 clusters of equal size, a single-stage cluster sample of one cluster would create a sample size equal to one percent of the population. A multi-stage cluster sample selecting two clusters and randomly sampling one-half of the members of each of these two clusters would also generate a sample size equal to one percent of the population. The less heterogeneous each cluster is felt to be, the greater the number of clusters that should be selected and a smaller sampling rate applied to each.

By concentrating sampling within a few clusters, sampling costs can be reduced when the population is geographically spread and personal interviews are required. In such cases, persons within a specific geographic area become members of a unique cluster and travel costs are reduced since sampling takes place within smaller geographic areas. Cluster sampling is also used when sampling frames are non-existent. For instance, if a company producing air hammers wanted to talk to a random sample of industrial users of their product, they may not have a sampling frame of users. However, they may have a list of the companies that have purchased their air hammers. By designating each company as a cluster, a few companies could be randomly selected and a list of employers in each selected company who are users of the air hammers could be developed and sampled. Having to generate this sampling frame for only a subset of the total companies reduces costs dramatically.

Nonprobability Sampling Methods

In a **nonprobability sample**, the probability of selecting a member of the sampling frame is unknown. As a consequence, it cannot be said that every member of the sampling frame has a nonzero chance of being selected. Furthermore, statistical precision cannot be calculated when using nonprobability samples, so the researcher is unable to determine how closely the sample results reflect the true population values. In fact, a nonprobability sample is not guaranteed to be at all representative of the sampling frame. Yet, the use of a nonprobability sampling technique is justifiable if the sample is not being used to estimate a population value. For instance, nonprobability sampling techniques are often used in exploratory research, since the purpose is to uncover issues that might be worthy of further investigation, not to yield a precise estimate of a population value.

Convenience Sampling

Convenience samples are nonprobability samples in which the sampled members are chosen because they are easily accessible. No attempt is made to insure that the sample is representative of the sampling frame. Asking some of your friends or classmates whether a particular professor was a good teacher would be an example of a convenience sample. The answer you obtained would not be projectable to all students and might be a biased view of how all students feel about the professor. The professor might actually be a much better, or much worse, teacher than your friends or classmates think.

Judgment Sampling

In **judgment sampling** the researcher subjectively chooses sample members on the basis of some criterion, such as being particularly knowledgeable about the topic being studied. For instance, a manufacturer of sophisticated hi-tech instruments might elect to seek feedback about a new product idea from a few firms which make extensive se of this equipment because of their special expertise in the area. Because the researcher has a purpose in mind for selecting sample members, judgment samples are often called purposive samples.

Judgment sampling might be used to obtain a crude sales forecast. For instance, H.J. Heinz might ask McDonald's, Wendy's, Burger King, and a few other major fast-food chains how much Heinz ketchup they anticipate purchasing in the coming year. A large proportion of the total institutional sales of Heinz ketchup would go to these chains. Therefore, projecting any change in sales anticipated by these firms to the total institutional sales volume would yield a rough estimate of next year's institutional sales.

Judgment sampling can also be used to select cities in which to test market a new brand. Test market results help a company decide whether or not to introduce a brand into the national marketplace. Thus, judgment sampling is used to select test-market cities whose characteristics particularly reflect the United States as a whole to test the new brand's viability in the market. The company hopes that, by choosing test-market cities in this manner, the test-market results will be indicative of what will happen if the brand is marketed nationally.

Quota Sampling

When using **quota sampling**, the researcher specifies the number of respondents with particular characteristics to be included in the sample and selects sample members in a nonrandom manner. No other respondents with the same characteristics are sampled once the specified number of particular respondents, known as a quota, is reached. Quota sampling can be viewed as the nonprobability equivalent of stratified sampling.

As you have learned, in a proportionate stratified sample, the percentage of the sample devoted to each subgroup is equal to that subgroup's percentage of the population. With a quota sample, the researcher can mimic a proportionate stratified sample by setting quotas so that each group's percentage of the sample equals its population percentage. Similarly, quotas can be set disproportionately large for small subgroups to guarantee a sufficient number of these subgroup members in the sample.

Although quota and stratified sampling techniques look similar, they differ in the way that sample members are chosen. Sample members are selected using probability sampling techniques, such as simple random sampling, in stratified sampling. Nonprobability techniques, such as convenience sampling, are used in quota sampling. Because nonprobability methods are used to select sample respondents, quota samples may not be representative of the target population and the statistical precision of the results cannot be calculated.

How Large Does the Sample Need to Be?

Determining the size of the sample is not a decision that should be made lightly, because of the impact sample size has on the cost of a research project. A variety of methods, some sophisticated and some rather simple, can be used to decide upon sample size. Four of the most common methods, listed in Table 7.3, will be described briefly here.

Method	Question
Precision requirements	What sample size will give the desired accuracy?
Company tradition	What sample size is suggested by company guidelines?
Subsample requirements	What sample size will allow subsample analysis?
Cost limitations	What sample size can be afforded?

Table 7.3

Methods of determining sample size.

Determined by Precision Requirements

As mentioned earlier, a major advantage of probability sampling techniques is that the statistical precision of the results can be calculated. Sometimes the sample size for a project is predicated on the precision required in the answer. Fortunately, the sample size needed to guarantee a specified level of precision can often be determined in advance when using probability sampling procedures. We discuss how this is done in Chapter 9.

Determined by Company Tradition

Many companies stipulate a specific sample size they always use for similar projects. For example, Nabisco might dictate that all taste tests be run with 200 respondents. This procedure has the advantage that statistical considerations are constant across similar studies. A statistically significant result in one study is also likely to be significant in other similar studies.

Determined by Subsample Requirements

Managers often want to uncover any differences that exist among the answers of various groups of respondents. For instance, do women answer differently than men? Do users of the product category respond differently than nonusers? In such cases, a target number of respondents for each subgroup may be specified to guarantee a sufficient number of respondents for subsample analysis. The total sample size is determined as the sum of the subsample sizes.

Determined by Cost Limitations

Obviously, cost enters into the sample size decision for all projects. Sometimes, though, management is willing to make a tradeoff between precision and data collection costs. Such a tradeoff is reasonable as long as management understands the ramifications. Unfortunately, in some instances, managers let cost drive the sample size decision without considering the consequences.

Managers unfamiliar with research may set an unreasonably low budget for a project. After costing out all of the other components of the project, sample size is determined simply by the amount of money remaining for data collection. The resulting sample size can easily turn out to be too small for the manager to be comfortable with the precision of the estimates derived from the sample data, much less for any important subgroups.

International Issues

In many countries, obtaining a representative national sample is not practical because no complete sampling frame is available. The number of households having telephones is often too low for telephone interviews to yield a representative sample. Detailed geographic maps of residential locations are frequently not available, making the selection of a random sample a problem for door-to-door interviewing. Postal systems are commonly too inefficient to provide adequate coverage for a mail survey.

Even in countries having a good postal system, companies often find that lists of eligible respondents are not available. For instance, only in the United States can car manufacturers obtain a list of recent automobile purchasers.[6]

Because of the difficulties encountered in finding a good sampling frame, probability sampling methods are rarely used in many countries. Instead, companies turn to quota samples or judgment samples instead. These nonprobability sampling techniques make it impossible to generalize the results or to calculate statistical precision. Therefore, it is difficult to compare results across studies or across countries.

Summary

One of the most critical sampling decisions is the proper definition of the population of interest, known as the target population. An improperly defined target population can generate data that can lead to invalid conclusions. It is also essential that the sampling frame used to select target population members be accurate.

Research projects rarely conduct a census of the target population. A census tends to be expensive, takes a long time to complete, and is subject to greater nonsampling error than a sample. A census is feasible only when the population is small and members are easily located. However, sampling some populations can also be expensive and, unless properly designed, a sample can also generate inaccurate data.

The researcher must decide whether to use a probability or a nonprobability sampling technique. With a probability sample the researcher can determine how closely sample estimates approximate the value that would be achieved from a census of the population. With a nonprobability sample, no such approximation can be made. A variety of probability and nonprobability sampling methods exist. Four commonly used probability sampling methods are simple random sampling, systematic sampling, stratified sampling, and cluster sampling. Convenience sampling, judgment sampling, and quota sampling are the typical nonprobability sampling procedures used in practice. The particular probability or nonprobability method used depends on the nature of the sampling problem.

Sample size has an impact on the cost of the project, so the size of the sample is not a decision to make lightly. However, it is imperative that the sample size be large enough to yield sufficient information. For probability samples, sample size can be determined based on the required statistical precision of the results. We will discuss this issue in Chapter 9 where basis statistical analysis methods are covered. Other, more subjective, methods can also be used for both probability and nonprobability samples. These methods determine sample size based upon company tradition, subsample requirements, or project budget.

Exhibit 7.2 contains a diagram of the sampling process indicating where various types of sampling errors can occur and how inferences are made.

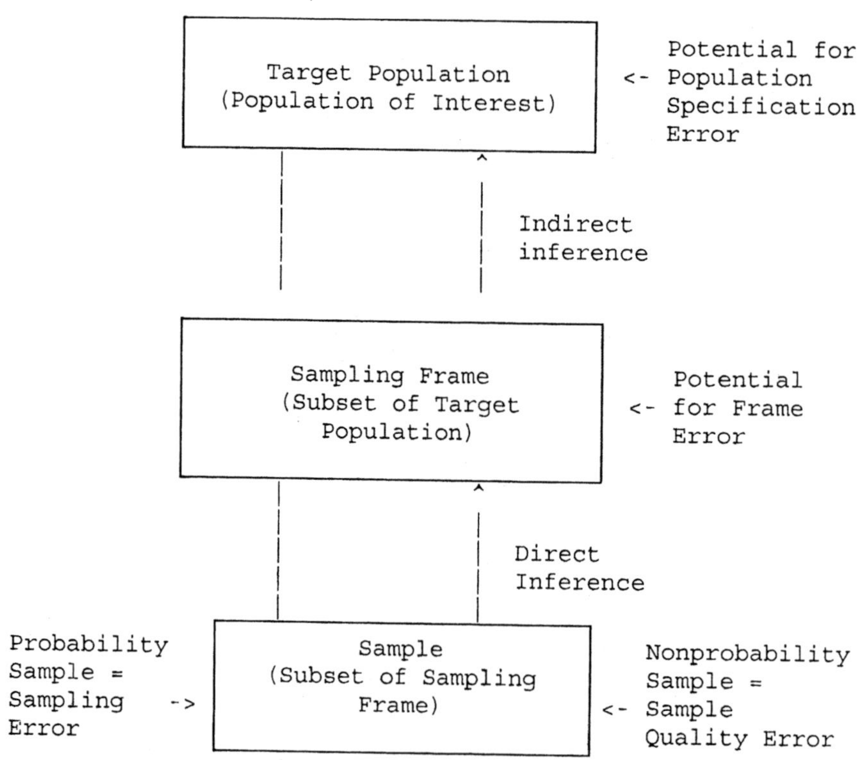

Exhibit 7.2

Sampling Paradigm

Key Terms

census

cluster sampling

convenience sample

disproportionate stratified sampling

incidence level

judgment sample

multi-stage cluster sampling

nonprobability sample

population specification error

probability sample

proportionate stratified sampling

quota sampling

sampling frame

sampling frame error

simple random sampling

single-stage cluster sampling

statistical precision

stratified sampling

systematic sampling

target population

Sampling Issues for Nimslo

The Nimslo Company conducted several surveys prior to and during the introduction of their Nimslo 3D Camera. Before any of this survey work was begun, however, the company had to specify the target population. One option was to define the target population as any adult, since the 3D camera would be purchased primarily by adults. Alternatively, the company could define the target population as only those adults most likely to be interested in purchasing the camera. Nimslo decided to use the latter definition for their survey work.

The company decided that the primary target market for the 3D Camera would be upscale families who already owned a 35mm camera and who had children. The company used this target market for much of their survey research. Because no sampling frame existed that contained only these target market consumers, Nimslo was forced to sample from the general population and screen potential respondents based on income, children, and 35mm camera ownership. This led to a low incidence of qualified respondents and substantially increased the cost of their survey work.

Review questions

7.1 What is meant by a target population? Why is proper definition of the target population so important?

7.2 What causes sampling frame error? What are the consequences of having sampling frame error?

7.3 Why do most marketing research projects rely on a sample instead of a census of the target population?

7.4 What is meant by incidence? How does incidence impact the cost of sampling?

7.5 What is the difference between a probability sample and a nonprobability sample? In what situations would a nonprobability sample be adequate?

7.6 What is statistical precision?

7.7 What are the advantages of using stratified sampling as compared to simple random sampling?

7.8 Why would a researcher choose a disproportionate stratified sample instead of a proportionate stratified sample?

7.9 How would a systematic sample be drawn?

7.10 What is meant by cluster sampling? Why is cluster sampling used? What is the difference between single-stage and multi-stage cluster sampling?

7.11 What is a convenience sample? Give an example.

7.12 How are sample members selected for a judgment sample? Why are judgment samples used? Give two situations where judgment samples are useful.

7.13 What is the purpose of using quota samples? How are they distinguished from stratified samples?

7.14 What methods are used to determine sample size?

Discussion Questions

7.1 Is the sample being drawn in each of the following situations a probability or nonprobability sample? What specific sampling technique is being used in each situation? What is the target population and sampling frame in each case? For each situation, do you feel that sampling frame error is a serious problem? Why or why not?

a. A marketing professor is responsible for scheduling performers for the university concert series. He surveys two of his marketing classes to determine which performers would be most popular with university students.

b. A reporter for the local newspaper interviews 100 persons of voting age as they pass her on the street to determine what voters think about an upcoming bond referendum.

c. A telephone survey using random-digit dialing is conducted with 100 single women, 100 married women, 100 single men, and 100 married men to determine music preferences by sex and marital status. The population contains about equal numbers of men and women, but about twice as many married as single adults.

d. Two hundred patients were randomly chosen from a physician's patient files and interviewed to determine the percentage of the doctor's patients who would use a Saturday clinic if it was available.

e. A company's twenty-five largest sales accounts were interviewed to ascertain the level of satisfaction among the company's customers with the services provided.

7.2 Each time that the United States prepares to undergo another census of the population, a debate ensues over whether a sample of the population should be conducted instead of a census. Do you feel that a sample or a census of the population should be conducted? Why?

7.3 A company needing mall-intercept interviews contracts with a field service to have the interviews conducted. The company specifies the total number of interviews to be completed and the characteristics of the target population. Because mall management only allows interviews to occur within specified mall areas, interviewers stand at given locations and wait until shoppers walk by who might fit the target population description. These shoppers are then approached and asked a series of screening questions to determine if they meet target population criteria. Qualified shoppers are then taken to the interview rooms. What type of sampling procedure do you feel is being followed? What is the sampling frame? How much impact do you feel sampling frame error would have? What other types of nonsampling errors might be particularly prevalent? How might these be reduced?

7.5 Design a sampling plan that would allow you to survey a sample of students at your college to determine the percentage of students at your school who have checking accounts at each local bank.

7.6 *Ethical Situation*: Discuss the ethical implications of a company overestimating the incidence of the target population to the field service when commissioning a research project.

Chapter 7 Endnotes

1. Fishkin, James. "Point of View," *The Chronicle of Higher Education*, July 1, 1992, p. A10.

2. Stephen Barlas, "Marketing Strategy Developed to Ensure Accurate '90 Census," *Marketing News*, March 27, 1989, pp. 1, 2.

3. U.S. Bureau of the Census (1980), *Census '80: Continuing the Factfinder Tradition* Washington, D.C.: U.S. Government Printing Office, p. 182.

4. See, for example, L.J. Kish, *Survey Sampling* New York: John Wiley & Sons, Inc., 1965; or Seymour Sudman, *Applied Sampling* New York: Academic Press, 1976, for discussion of various sampling alternatives.

5. See W.G. Cochran, *Sampling Techniques*, 2nd ed. New York: John Wiley & Sons, Inc., 1963, for the formula to compute the standard error of a stratified sample and for a discussion of the increased efficiency of stratified samples.

6. Herschel H. Bowyer, "Multi-Country Marketing Research: Apples to Apples?" presented at the American Marketing Association Consortium on Marketing Research, Michigan State University, June 26, 1989.

Chapter 8

Questionnaire Design

Learning Objectives:

Continuing our discussion of the issues involved in designing and executing a primary data collection project, this chapter describes the steps involved in writing a questionnaire. After reading this chapter you should be able to:

- explain the value of flowcharting a questionnaire,
- discuss the advantages and disadvantages of open-ended and closed-ended questions,
- describe the pitfalls surrounding the writing of survey questions,
- discuss alternative measurement scales, and
- explain good questionnaire construction principles.

When Burger King ran an advertising campaign stating a consumer preference for their "flame-broiled" Whopper over McDonald's "fried" hamburgers, the claim was substantiated using results from a survey conducted for them. As part of the survey, respondents were asked:"Do you prefer your hamburgers flame-broiled or fried?" The results showed a three-to-one preference for flame-broiled.

When another marketing research firm repeated the study at McDonald's request, they got completely different results. In this study, respondents were asked: "Do you prefer a hamburger that is grilled on a hot stainless-steel grill or cooked by passing the raw meat through an open gas flame?" Over half the respondents indicated that they preferred hamburgers grilled on a hot stainless-steel grill---McDonald's frying method. When the question was further modified to indicate also that the gas-flame hamburgers were warmed in a microwave oven prior to serving, respondents favored the grilled hamburgers by almost a six-to-one margin!

Which survey results were correct? Neither probably provided a completely accurate measure of consumer preference because of the way the questions were asked. The point is, completely different conclusions are reached, depending upon the way the question is worded.[11]

questions were asked. The point is, completely different conclusions were reached, depending upon the way the question is worded.[2]

As the Burger King example illustrates, answers to questions can vary greatly depending upon the way they are written. Additional instrument error can be created by the order in which questions are asked, the types of questions asked, the physical appearance of the survey instrument, and a host of other factors.

Therefore, to assess the quality of collected data, a manager must be able to determine whether the instrument has been properly designed.

Designing the Survey Instrument

Proper design of the data-collection instrument helps to minimize error. It also ensures that the data collected will provide the required information. The six steps shown in Table 8.1 apply to the design of data-collection instruments for both observation and direct questioning techniques. However, these steps are usually much more critical when using direct questioning due to the amount and nature of the information to be collected.[3] Because of this, our discussion will focus upon developing instruments for direct questioning techniques.

1. Determining the necessary information
2. Deciding upon the question sequence
3. Writing the individual questions
4. Developing required scales
5. Constructing the instrument
6. Pretesting the questionnaire

Table 8.1

Steps in questionnaire construction.

Determining the Necessary Information

The researcher must know exactly what information is required before beginning to design the questionnaire. Careful coordination between the person designing the instrument and the person requesting the information is essential to determine the objectives of the study and the exact information needed. Failure to specify the information needs accurately can lead to questions being asked that are not relevant or, worse yet, can lead to a study that fails to ask for information that is vital. As discussed in Chapter 2, exploratory research is frequently used to help define the study objectives.

Deciding On the Question Sequence

Determining the order in which the questions are to be asked should be based upon two considerations. The first consideration is to make the task of responding to the survey as simple as possible. A survey in which the questions follow a logical order reduces both interviewer error and respondent frustration, resulting in fewer interview terminations and more accurate information.

The second consideration is to make sure that questions appearing early do not bias the answers to subsequent questions. Obviously, questions about Perrier brand botteled water followed by questions designed to determine the awareness of various brands would result in an overstatement of the awareness of the Perrier brand. In a similar vein, personal or embarrassing questions can lead to termination of the survey if asked early in the survey or can create respondent error by influencing the respondent's mood. Therefore, these types of questions should be asked toward the end of the questionnaire, after respondents have become more involved in the survey and are less likely to be unduly influenced by them.

Flowcharts are useful for deciding the appropriate sequencing of questions. Exhibit 8.1 shows a flowchart for a study investigating why consumers buy a particular brand of pet food and their reactions when that brand is not in stock. As you can see, a flowchart does not show the specific wording of each question. It merely indicates the question sequence.

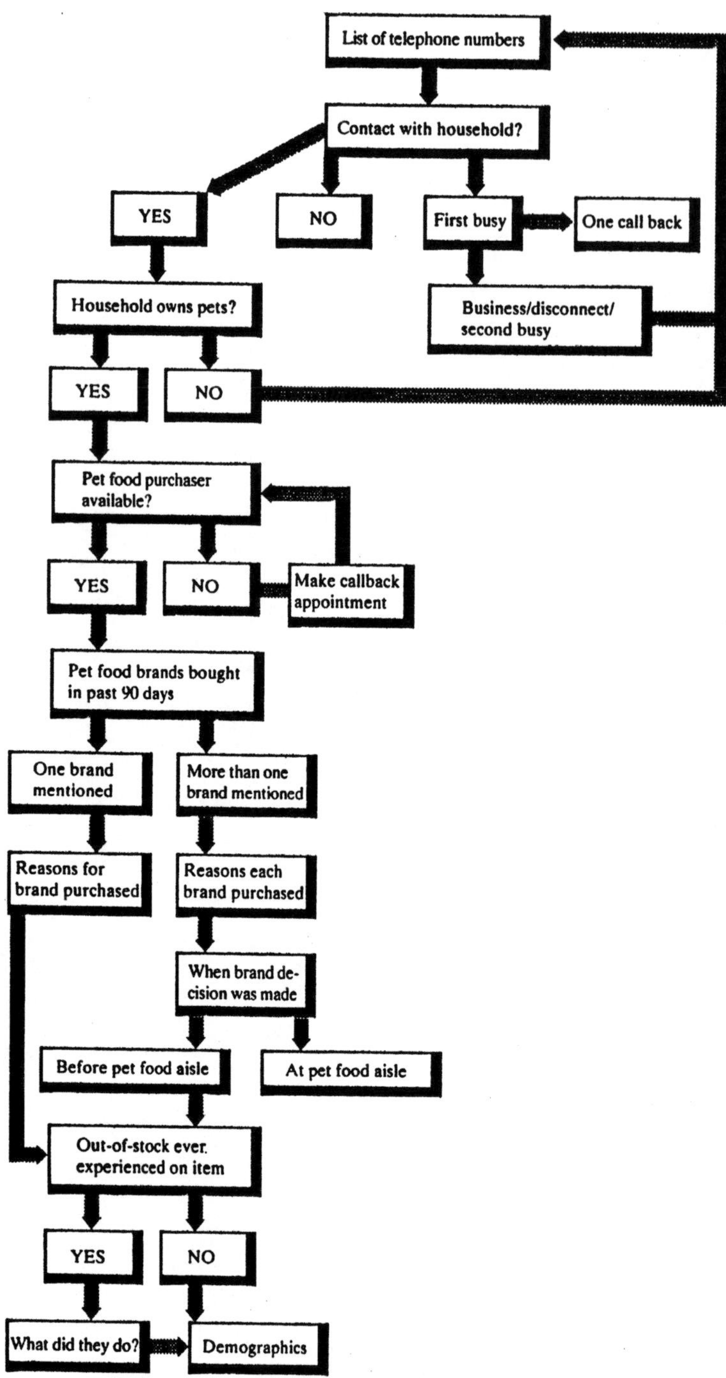

Exhibit 8.1

An example of a questionnaire flowchart.

One aspect of question sequence is the skip pattern. A **skip pattern** indicates when a respondent is not supposed to answer a particular question. An example of a skip pattern is shown in the flowchart in Exhibit 8.1. Persons who have not experienced an out-of-stock on the brand they intended to purchase skip the question asking what was done when an out-of-stock was experienced. Flowcharts help uncover any flaws in the logic of the survey design, especially flaws related to skip patterns.

By forcing the researcher to specify a logical order for the questions, a flowchart prevents the researcher from building a questionnaire where the respondent answers irrelevant questions or skips relevant ones. Flowcharts are also a good tool to use when discussing the information to be collected with the person requesting the study. Since the wording of specific questions is not provided, the discussion can focus upon the information to be produced instead of upon the nuances of how the questions are to be asked.

Writing the Individual Questions

Developing the questions to be asked is not an easy task. Answers received can vary depending upon the form of the question or the way the question is constructed. Even the specific words that are used have an impact.

Choosing the Form of the Question

Written questions can take one of two forms. A **closed-ended question** provides respondents with a list of the possible answers. An **open-ended question** does not provide the possible answers to the respondent. Table 8.2 illustrates how the same information might be obtained using closed-ended or open-ended questions.

Open-ended Alternative	Closed-ended Alternative
What is your age?	Which of the following categories contains your age? a. under 21 ___ b. 21-34 ___ c. 35-44 ___ d. 45-54 ___ e. 55 or older ___
How satisfied were you with the service you received?	Thinking about the service you received, would you say you were... completely satisfied ___ somewhat satisfied ___ neither satisfied nor dissatisfied ___ somewhat dissatisfied ___ completely dissatisfied ___
If this product was available, how much would you be willing to pay for it?	If this product was available, would you be willing to pay... less than .49 ___ .50 to 1.00 ___ more than 1.00 ___

Table 8.2
Open-ended and closed-ended question options.

Because open-ended questions allow respondents to answer in their own words, respondents are not biased by the presence of a list of possible answers. However, open-ended questions take more time to answer than do closed-ended questions so they increase the cost of conducting the survey. Open-ended questions are also harder to analyze than closed-ended questions because individual responses must be examined and organized into groups according to similarity. These disadvantages tend to restrict the use of open-ended questions to gathering facts that the respondent can provide without elaboration or for probing or clarifying an earlier answer.

Not only do responses to closed-ended questions cost less to collect and analyze, they are also easier for the respondent to answer than open-ended questions. However, closed-ended questions are more difficult to create since a list of all possible answers must be provided. To ensure an exhaustive list of responses, respondents are often provided with an "other" response category, which is designed to allow them to mention anything not listed. Closed-ended questions not only require an exhaustive answer list but also exclusive categories that allow any response to fit only into one category. Otherwise, respondents would be unsure which category to select because two or more categories could be chosen.

Avoiding Common Pitfalls in Question Wording

Instrument error is easily introduced when writing survey questions. The questions on the survey should seem conversational and not make respondents feel that they are being interrogated. Every question should be clearly understood by each respondent and should lead to accurate answers. While these admonitions may appear to be common sense, writing questions without introducing instrument error is not as easy as it might seem. What may seem to be minor wording differences can have a dramatic impact on the results obtained. For instance, one poll found that, by a 67-to-27 percent margin, the American public would rather prevent cuts to Medicare than balance the federal budget. At about the same time, another poll that referred to limits to Medicare spending instead of cuts found only a 51-to-41 percent preference for sparing Medicare instead of balancing the budget.[4] Following four simple rules will help avoid many common wording pitfalls.

1. **Don't use unfamiliar or ambiguous words.** A questionnaire is not the place for the person developing the survey to demonstrate his or her command of the English language. Simple, familiar words should be used so that their meanings will be clear to all respondents. In addition, all words used in a questionnaire should have a single meaning or an intended meaning that is clear in the question context. However, even simple, commonly-used words, such as those shown in Table 8.3, can create problems because their meanings are ambiguous. A perfect example is the word "you," which is the same in both singular and plural contexts. Therefore, some respondents will answer a question about products purchased assuming that "you" refers to their households, while others will answer the same question considering only their individual purchases. Because of this problem, the phrase "you, yourself" is often used in surveys to identify the singular context.

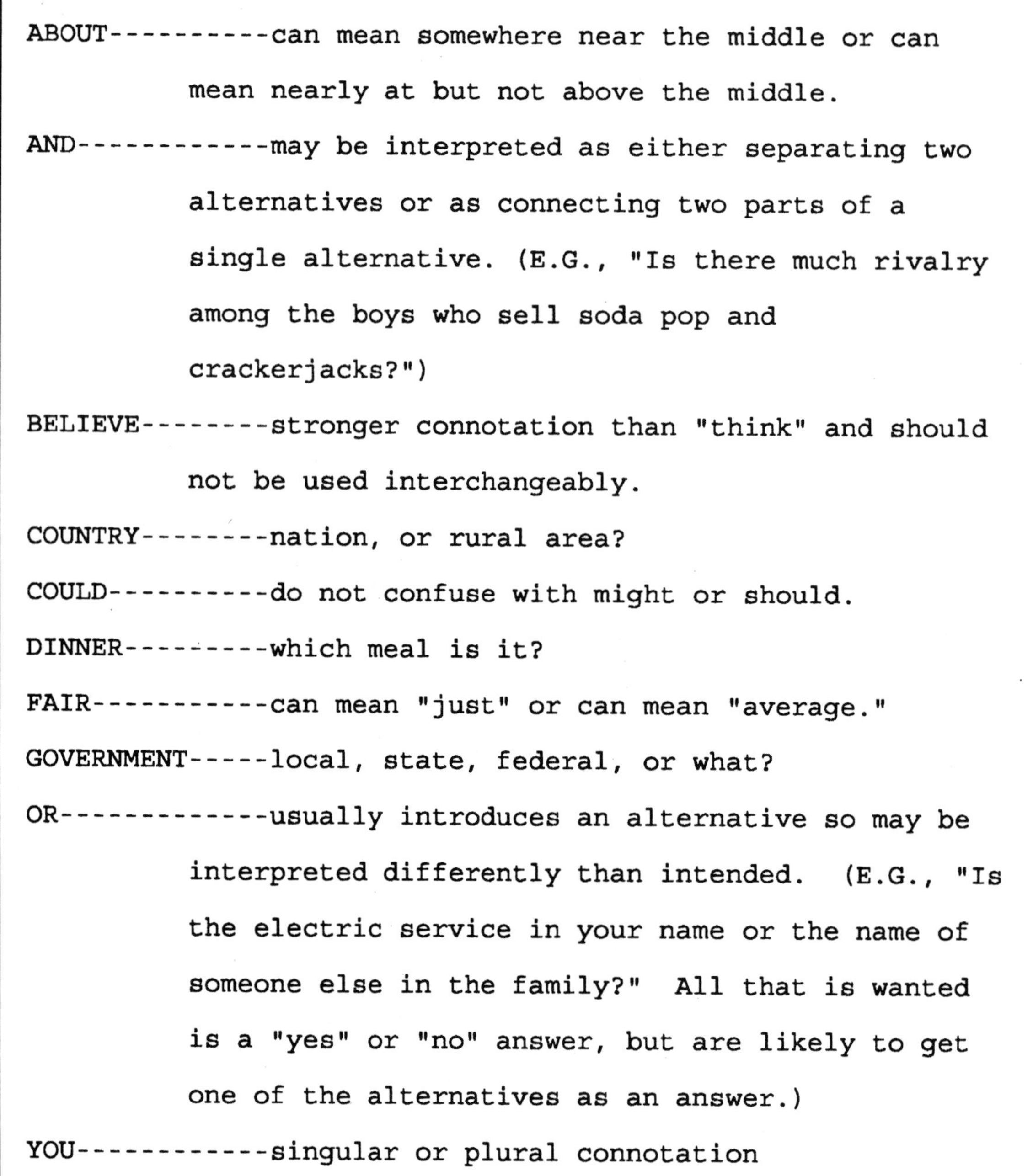

ABOUT----------can mean somewhere near the middle or can mean nearly at but not above the middle.

AND------------may be interpreted as either separating two alternatives or as connecting two parts of a single alternative. (E.G., "Is there much rivalry among the boys who sell soda pop and crackerjacks?")

BELIEVE--------stronger connotation than "think" and should not be used interchangeably.

COUNTRY--------nation, or rural area?

COULD----------do not confuse with might or should.

DINNER---------which meal is it?

FAIR-----------can mean "just" or can mean "average."

GOVERNMENT-----local, state, federal, or what?

OR-------------usually introduces an alternative so may be interpreted differently than intended. (E.G., "Is the electric service in your name or the name of someone else in the family?" All that is wanted is a "yes" or "no" answer, but are likely to get one of the alternatives as an answer.)

YOU------------singular or plural connotation

Table 8.3

Some examples of "problem" words for questionnaire design.

Special care must be used when children are to be interviewed to ensure that they understand the meaning of all words used. For instance, young kids do not have the same concept of time that adults do. Thus, they cannot accurately answer how often something has occurred in a paticular week or a month because they do not know what those time periods are. Similarly, what words mean to them may be entirely different from what the same words mean to adults. To young kids, a crunchy product is one you can hear when it is bitten, for example.[5]

2. **Don't use slang or colloquial expressions.** Intentional use of slang words or phrases should be avoided in a questionnaire because their meanings and usage are ever-changing. Furthermore, care must be exercised when using words or phrases that have slang counterparts since respondents may be offended if they assume that the slang meaning of the word was intended. In a similar vein, colloquial expressions, those used by only a segment of the population to refer to something totally different than what the rest of the population would read into the expression, must be avoided. For instance, in some parts of the United States, it is not uncommon for people to say that they went to "see" a doctor instead of saying that they visited a doctor's office. In spite of this, respondents to a survey should not be asked when they last "saw" a doctor because all sorts of unwanted answers would occur.

3. **Don't talk down to respondents.** Saying that one should not talk down to respondents may seem at odds with using only simple, easily understood words. Yet, talking down to a respondent is seldom caused by using simple words. Instead, the most common cause is when a word, phrase, or abbreviation in a question must be defined so that all respondents understand exactly what is meant. For instance, most college students know what "SAT" stands for. However, to make sure that no one is confused, we may also wish to define SAT in the question. Writing the question as "What score did you make on the SAT, that is, the Scholastic Aptitude Test?" appears to talk down to the respondent more than "What score did you make on the Scholastic Aptitude Test, that is, the SAT?" As a general rule, it is better to follow the less familiar with the more familiar instead of the other way around.

4. **Don't let question wording influence the respondent's choice.** Some words, such as "Capitalism," "Communism," and "American-made," can bias answers to a question due to their emotion-laden nature. At other times, the way that the question is stated creates bias. For example, "Shouldn't federal control of water quality be increased?" would generate a different set of responses than would "Should federal control of water quality be increased?" Finally, "dead giveaway" questions bias responses because only one possible answer to the question is feasible. For instance, who would answer "no" to the question "Do you think there are any people in business who would cheat you?" Words like "any" and "ever," are dead giveaway words in a question because respondents will answer assuming that at least one instance exists

where the statement is false while the opposite is assumed for words like "always," "never," and "every".

Avoiding Question Construction Problems

Evaluating the individual questions that have been written goes beyond examining the words used. Even if the principles discussed above are followed, instrument error can still occur due to the nature of the questions asked or the way they are constructed. Thus, the marketing manager should examine each question with the following seven principles in mind.

1. **Ask only one question at a time. Double-barreled questions** ask about more than a single issue within a single question, making the responses uninterpretable. For instance, consider the question: "Do you like potato chips and dip?". A "no" answer could mean that the respondent does not like either potato chips or dip. However, it could also mean that the respondent likes dip and does not like potato chips, likes potato chips but not dip, or does not like potato chips with dip!

2. **Make sure all response alternatives are mentioned in the question.** An **implied alternative** is one that is not explicitly stated in a question. Responses to questions containing implied alternatives are biased towards the stated alternatives. For instance, the question "Did you think that the second product you tasted was better than the first product you tasted?" is biased in favor of the second product because only the "better" alternative is explicitly stated. This question should be re-written as "Did you think that the second product you tasted was better, not as good, or about the same as the first product you tasted?" so that all possible responses are given.

3. **Make sure to rotate the order of alternatives listed.** When a list of alternatives is read or shown to a respondent, the position of an alternative on the list influences how often it is chosen. Items near the beginning of a list shown to respondents tend to be selected more often while the same holds for items toward the end of a list read to respondents. Thus, ask people which is more exciting, tennis or soccer and 65 percent will say soccer, but only 23 percent will say soccer if it is listed first.[6]

4. **Watch out for double negatives.** From the time we begin to learn the English language, we are cautioned against using two negatives in the same sentence because their meaning will be reversed. Thus, "don't use no negatives," translates to "use negatives." Even with all of these admonitions, however, double negatives sometimes slip into a question. As Applying Marketing Research 8.1 illustrates, the ramifications on the resulting answers can be dramatic.

Applying Marketing Research 8.1

In October and November 1992, the Roper Organization, a well-respected polling firm, conducted a national survey of 506 high school students and 992 adults. The results stunned the Jewish community. Nearly one-third of the respondents had doubts that the Holocaust, Nazi Germany's extermination of 6 million Jews, ever occurred. The finding was carried by news wire services and was given prominent coverage by most major newsmagazines, newspapers, and television news shows.

Soon after, the firm announced that the results were not accurate due to a poorly-worded survey question. That question was, "Does it seem possible or does it seem impossible to you that the Nazi extermination of the Jews never happened?" A respondent believing that the Holocaust occurred had to agree with a double negative (that it was impossible that it never happened).

To confirm that the results were biased by the wording, a Gallup Poll was conducted where half of the respondents were asked the Roper question. The other half were asked, "Do you doubt that the Holocaust actually happened, or not?" The Roper question again got high denial while only 9 percent of the respondents to the second question doubted that the Holocaust occurred.[7]

5. **Make sure the respondent can answer the question**

The person writing a survey assumes that the respondent can answer the questions being asked. All too often, however, respondents never knew the answer to the question or, if they did at one time, they have forgotten it now. Can you remember the amount of gasoline you put in your car the last time you got gas? How about the amount you last spent at the grocery, or what time it was the last time you took a pain reliever? Asking for the recall of events that are not important to the respondent or of events that occurred a long time ago will lead to answers containing a great deal of inaccuracy because respondents cannot answer accurately.

6. **Make sure the respondent will answer truthfully.** People are hesitant to admit to behaviors or attitudes that are not socially acceptable. The tendency of respondents to give socially acceptable, but untrue, answers can be reduced by counterbiasing the question. **Counterbiasing** is an attempt to write a question so that respondents feel that the behavior or attitude in question is more common than may be thought. For instance, most men who wear pantyhose for functional reasons would be reluctant to admit to this behavior when questioned. A counterbiasing effect could be achieved by mentioning in the question that professional football players and construction workers sometimes wear pantyhose to keep warm, that lifeguards sometimes wear pantyhose to prevent jellyfish stings, and men unaccustomed to horseback riding are encouraged to wear pantyhose on long rides to prevent chafing.[1]

7. **Make sure the context of the question is clear.** "How important is it for a store to carry a wide assortment of brands within a product category?" The answer one gets will depend upon whether the respondent answered from the store's viewpoint or from the consumer's viewpoint. Unless the context of the question is made clear ("How important to you is it that a store..." or "How important to a store is it for them to carry..."), different people may give different answers even if their true feelings are the same because they are viewing the question from different contexts. Similarly, if a respondent must make some assumptions in order to properly answer a question, these assumptions must be explicitly stated so that all respondents use the same assumptions. For instance, respondents cannot accurately answer how important it is that a personal computer have a built-in CD player until they know what the impact would be on the cost of the unit. If they make individual cost assumptions, different answers can be obtained because of different assumptions. It is much better to specify the cost assumption so that everyone answers from the same context.

---

[1]Another technique, called the randomized response technique, has been proposed as a way to get at sensitive information. However, research has not conclusively shown that this technique is any better than asking about the topic directly. Furthermore, only limited data analysis can be performed and the number of marketing applications of this technique is limited. For a simple description of the randomized response technique, interested readers should see Cathy Campbell and Brian L. Joiner, "How to Get the Answer Without Being Sure You've Asked the Question," *American Statistician*, 26 (December 1973), pp. 229-231.

Applying Marketing Research 8.2

The importance of the context in which a respondent answers was made very clear to one insurance company. The company had conducted a large survey to determine what led to customer satisfaction. One characteristic that respondents were asked to rate was "the agent responds quickly." Respondents consistently rated this characteristic as important.

When the company probed customers about what they meant when they said the agent should respond quickly, they found that the definition varied. A response within 24 hours was felt to be quick for routine matters but, in an emergency, the agent should respond as quickly as was humanly possible. Thus, an agent could respond at the same speed in each situation, but be rated much differently by two respondents.[8]

Developing Measurement Scales

Marketing research is often designed to gather information about particular characteristics of objects, events, or people. The characteristics of interest can be tangible, such as the amount of income spent weekly on gasoline, or intangible, such as attitudes toward a particular brand. Measurement scales are used to gather such information. A **measurement scale** assigns numbers to objects, events, or people according to a set of rules. While this term may be new to you, the general notion of a measurement scale is not. You use measurement scales all of the time to measure such things as temperature, weight, height, or attendance at a football game. A measurement scale is not used to measure the object itself, but rather is used to measure the amount of the characteristic of interest present in the object being measured. How warm is an oven? How much does an individual weigh? How tall is someone? How long is a particular movie?

Different measurement scales can be developed to measure the same characteristic, depending upon the rules used for assigning the numbers on the scale. For example, temperature can be measured by Fahrenheit, Celsius, or Kelvin scales. Many common variables measured in marketing, such as consumer attitudes, preferences, satisfaction, and brand image, are also measured by a variety of different scales.

The wide use of measurement scales in marketing research requires that the marketing manager understand how the type of measurement scale influences data interpretation, the issues involved in choosing the particular form of the measurement scale developed, and the importance of assessing the accuracy and reproducibility of the data collected. The next three sections address these areas.

Types of Measurement Scales

Four types of measurement scales--called nominal, ordinal, interval, and ratio--can be developed. Both the interpretation of the assigned numbers and the types of analysis that can be performed on the data vary according to the scale type. Therefore, the marketing manager must understand the differences between these scale types.

The properties of each scale type are shown in Table 8.4. Each scale in Table 8.4 has all of the properties of the scales that appear above it plus the additional property shown for it.

Markets: (5)

Birmingham.....1
Charlotte......2
Dallas/
Ft. Worth....3

Job#1-828

DO NOT WRITE IN THIS BOX

Ref. #________
(1-4)

CHICKEN VIENNA SAUSAGE STUDY
- Screening Questionnaire -

Hello, I'm from____________________representing______________Opinion Research. We are talking to people today about meat products they might use in their homes and would like to ask you a few questions.

1. Do you or does any member of your household work for a marketing research firm, an advertising agency, or a manufacturer or distributor of meat or poultry products?

(6)
Yes...........1 → THANK, TALLY & TERMINATE
No............2 → CONTINUE

2. Have you purchased any Vienna Sausage in the past 3 months?

(7)
Yes...........1 → CONTINUE
No............2 → THANK, TERMINATE & TALLY

3. What brand or brands of Vienna Sausage have you purchased in the past 3 months? (DO NOT READ LIST)

(8-12)
Armour Star..................1
Libby's......................2
Hormel.......................3
Julia's......................4
Swift........................5
Don't know...................6
Other:
__________________7
(SPECIFY)

4. Have you ever heard of Chicken Vienna Sausages?

(13)
Yes...........1 → CONTINUE
No............2 → THANK, TERMINATE & TALLY

5. Have you purchased any Chicken Vienna Sausage in the past 3 months?

(14)
Yes...........1 → SKIP TO Q.7
No............2 → ASK Q.6 AND THEN THANK, TERMINATE & TALLY

6. Why have you not purchased any Chicken Vienna Sausage?

____ (15-17)
____
____

Table 8.4
Scales of Measurement

Nominal Scales. A **nominal scale** assigns numbers to objects in order to classify the objects according to the characteristic of interest. For example, a number could be assigned to each respondent based upon their gender. All men would be assigned the same number. All women would be assigned the same number, but their number would differ from that given to men.

With a nominal scale, the relative sizes of the numbers have no meaning. They only provide a classification code. Thus, analysis of nominal data is basically restricted to determining how frequently each classification code occurs.

Ordinal Scales. An **ordinal scale** assigns numbers to specify relative amounts on the characteristic being measured. An ordinal scale makes it possible to determine whether an object has more or less of the characteristic than another object by examining the relative sizes of the numbers assigned. A ranking of objects based upon the characteristic being measured is an example of an ordinal scale. Thus, the third column in Table 8.5 is an ordinal scale; the five oriental food brands have been ranked based upon the sales volumes shown in the second column.

Brand	Actual Case Sales	Ranking Based on Sales Volume
Garfield	362,000	4
Masterpiece	297,000	5
Dragon Fly	631,000	2
Tiger Lily	1,640,000	1
Gold Pagoda	395,000	3

The averages of the rankings are equal:

Garfield and Dragon Fly brands = (4 + 2)/2 = 3.

Masterpiece, Tiger Lily, and Gold Pagoda brands = (5 + 1 + 3)/3 = 3.

But, the averages of the sales are not:

Garfield and Dragon Fly brands = (362,000 + 631,000)/2 = 496,500

Masterpiece, Tiger Lily, and Gold Pagoda brands = (297,000 + 1,640,000 + 395,000) = 777,333

Table 8.5

Illustration of the danger of computing an average for ordinal data

An ordinal scale makes it possible to determine that one

object has more or less of the characteristic than another object. However, you cannot determine *how much* difference exists. For example, in Table 8.5, the difference in sales volume between the Dragon Fly and Gold Pagoda brands is much larger than the difference between the Gold Pagoda and Garfield brands. Nevertheless, the differences between their rankings are equal.

Because equal differences between scale values do not correspond to equal changes in the characteristic being measured, it is improper to calculate an average for data obtained from an ordinal scale. The danger associated with computing a mean for ordinal data can be easily verified using the data presented in Table 8.5. The average rank for the Garfield and Dragon Fly brands is the same as the average rank of the remaining three brands. However, to conclude that the average sales for these two groups of brands is about the same would be incorrect. In fact, there is a huge difference between the average sales of the two sets of brands.

Because it is inappropriate to compute a mean, analysis of ordinal data typically involves reporting how frequently an object is ranked at or above a certain level.[2] For example, the percentage of respondents who ranked each brand first, or the percentage who ranked each brand as one of the top two, might be reported.

Interval Scales. For many research projects, it is important to be able to measure how much difference exists between objects. This requirement demands an interval scale. With an **interval scale**, equal differences between scale values correspond to equal differences in the quantity being measured. Both the Celsius and Fahrenheit temperature scales are examples of interval scales. The difference in the amount of heat represented by 100 degrees compared to 80 degrees is the same as the difference in the amount of heat represented by any other two temperatures which differ by 20 degrees on the same scale.

The mean values of measurements obtained using an interval scale do not have the same shortcomings as do means obtained using ordinal scales. Hence, a wide range of statistical techniques can be applied to interval data. For this reason, interval scales are developed whenever possible for most marketing research projects.

---

[2] Nominal and ordinal scales are often called nonparametric scales because the parameters of the distribution, e.g., the mean and variance, cannot be computed. Therefore, a body of statistics have been created to analyze nonparametric distributions. See Sidney Siegel *Nonparametric Statistics for the Behavioral Sciences*, (New York: McGraw-Hill Book Company, 1956) for examples of these statistics.

Ratio Scales. A **ratio scale** is an interval scale containing a zero point signifying the absence of the property being measured. The presence of a natural zero allows one to meaningfully talk about ratios of the numbers assigned. One can say that one scale value is "twice as large" or "half as large" as another, for example. Variables such as brand share or sales volume can easily be measured by ratio scales, but many other marketing variables cannot. Nominal, ordinal, or interval scales must be developed for these variables instead.

Unfortunately, people often mistakenly compute ratios of interval, or even ordinal, scale values. You have probably heard someone remark that it will be "twice as hot tomorrow as today," for instance. Because the Celsius and Fahrenheit temperature scales are only interval, this statement is not true. Ratios of scale numbers are only appropriate if measured by a ratio scale.

Selecting the Form of the Scale

Measurement scales can be either categorical or continuous. Each of these scale forms has its own particular advantages and disadvantages.

Continuous Scales. **Continuous scales** present the respondent with some form of continuum, such as an unmarked line, on which to provide a rating. An advantage of the continuous scale is that it is easy to design. It also gives the respondent a great deal of flexibility in providing a rating and works well when measuring a continuous variable. An example of a continuous scale is:

> On the line below, please mark your overall rating of the flavor of the cracker you just tasted.
>
> Very poor______________________________Excellent

The researcher would measure from the left side of the line to the point marked, and this length would be the score, or scale value, given to the respondent.

The major drawback of a continuous scale is that the scale values must be calculated. Translating points on a continuum to actual ratings can be a time-consuming process, adding considerable cost to data processing. Furthermore, far more precision may be attributed to such scale values than is warranted because what is being measured cannot always be evaluated that precisely by the respondents.

Category Scales. **Category scales** provide the respondent with a limited number of response categories that have been predetermined by the researcher. For instance, one possible category scale might be:

> Please mark the category which indicates your overall rating of the flavor of the cracker you just tasted.
>
> | ____ | ____ | ____ | ____ | ____ |
> |---|---|---|---|---|
> | Poor | Fair | Good | Very Good | Excellent |

Numerical values (e.g., 5, 4, 3, 2, and 1) would be assigned to each of the categories in the above scale. The assigned numbers also can be used to designate the response categories:

> Please circle the number which indicates your overall rating of the flavor of the cracker you just tasted.
>
> | 5 | 4 | 3 | 2 | 1 |
> |---|---|---|---|---|
> | Poor | | | | Excellent |

Category scales are frequently used in marketing research instead of continuous scales. These scales can be nominal, ordinal, interval, or ratio, depending upon how they are designed. Category scales are far more practical and processing the information is much less expensive than for continuous scales. However, designing a category scale to measure a continuous variable presents its own set of problems. The issues which must be addressed in designing a category scale are highlighted in Table 8.6.

1. How many response categories will be provided?
2. Will the respondent be given an equal number of response categories on either side of the issue?
3. Will the respondent be given a "neutral/no opinion" choice?
4. Will each category have a verbal descriptor? If so, what descriptors will be used?

Table 8.6
Issues to be resolved in designing a categorical scale.

One issue that must be resolved is the appropriate number of response categories to use. Too few categories limits the sensitivity of the scale. For instance, if a respondent was asked to rate five items the respondent felt were unique, a scale would have to have at least five categories to capture this uniqueness. On the other hand, too many categories increases respondent frustration due to an inability to distinguish between the categories. Researchers tend to use between five and nine response categories[9], but the best number of categories to use is a hotly-debated issue.[10]

A second issue is whether or not the scale will be balanced. A balanced scale provides an equal number of rating categories on both sides of the issue. An unbalanced scale provides more categories on one side of the issue. In most instances, scales should be balanced because unbalanced scales tend to bias the answers toward the side of the scale with the larger number of categories. Unbalanced category scales are useful, though, when the researcher is interested in more detailed information about one side of the issue than the other. For instance, a firm might only be interested in determining how positively a new product concept was rated since any concept rated negatively, no matter how slightly, would not be considered further. Thus, the firm might choose the unbalanced scale shown earlier: excellent, very good, good, fair, and poor.[11]

Another issue is whether to include a "neutral" response category. The scale is said to be "forced " if a neutral category is not included, since respondents have to make a choice. Advocates of forced scales argue that many respondents will choose a neutral response, if available, instead of revealing their true feelings. If, on the other hand, a large number of people are believed actually to have no opinion on the issue, a neutral category is recommended. Applying Marketing Research 8.3 illustrates how different the responses can be with and without a neutral point.

Applying Marketing Research 8.3

Market Facts, Inc., maintains a large consumer mail panel that many companies access to gather information about a variety of topics instead of conducting random mail surveys. Periodically, Market Facts will sample some of its panel members to assess the impact of varying the way a question is worded, the ordering of response categories, or any number of other issues related to primary data collection. Reports on the findings are made available to clients as a service.

In one such study, 1,000 panel members were asked to evaluate the U.S. Postal Service on a five-point scale containing the labelled categories: 1-very satisfied, 2-somewhat satisfied, 3-neither satisfied nor dissatisfied, 4-somewhat dissatisfied, and 5-very dissatisfied. Another 1,000 panel members were asked to write in a number between 1 and 5 to indicate their evaluation, where 1 would signify very satisfied and 5 would signify very dissatisfied. One of the most striking findings of this study was that 34% of the first group selected the neutral category, while only 11% of the second group wrote in a 3 when not explicitly given the neutral response.[12]

A fourth issue is whether to place a verbal descriptor on each response category and, if so, what descriptors to use. If verbal descriptors are placed on each category, research has shown that the ratings given will depend upon the descriptors chosen and that some descriptors may cause a scale to become ordinal instead of interval.[13] For example, the difference in purchase intention conveyed by categories labelled "definitely will buy" and "probably will buy" is not the same as the difference conveyed by the categories "definitely will not buy" and "probably will not buy."[14] Instead of being interval, the purchase intention scale looks more like what is shown in Exhibit 8.2. Athough verbal descriptors placed only on the endpoints yield an interval scale, other problems are then created. For instance, respondents may be reluctant to select the unlabelled categories because they are unsure what they indicate. Furthermore, two respondents selecting the same unlabelled category may actually be giving different ratings to the object because they attach different labels to the category. The lack of verbal descriptors makes it more difficult to interpret or explain the results as well.

ASSUMED:

Definitely Would Buy	Probably Would Buy	Might or Might not Buy	Probably Would not Buy	Definitely Would not Buy

ACTUAL:

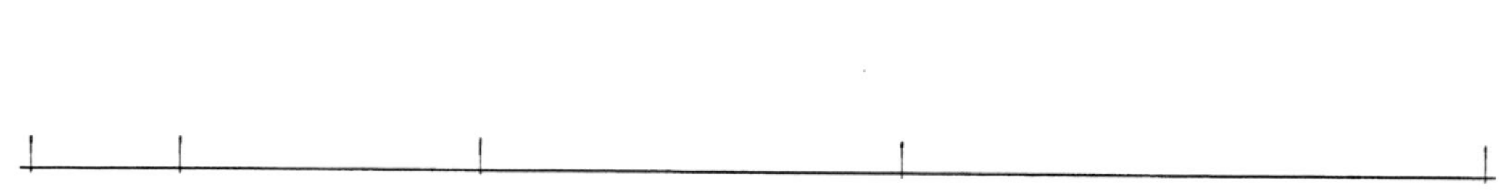

Exhibit 8.2

What the purchase intention scale is assumed to look like and what it really looks like.

Three Commonly Used Category Scale Formats

Three particular category scale formats, the semantic differential scale, the Stapel scale and the Likert scale, are widely-used used in marketing research to measure attitudes and opinions.[15] These three formats will be briefly described in this section.

Semantic differential scales present respondents with a

sequence of unlabelled categories anchored at the ends by two bipolar adjectives. The closer a rating is to one of the adjectives, the more that particular adjective applies. Semantic differential scales provide a useful way of visually displaying the profiles of several brands according to their average rating on each of a series of characteristics, as is shown in Exhibit 8.3. One can easily see that the ratings for Store 1 and Store 2 are dramatically different on dimensions like "good service" and "good return policy" and very similar on dimensions such as "prices too high" and "carries a good selection of merchandise."

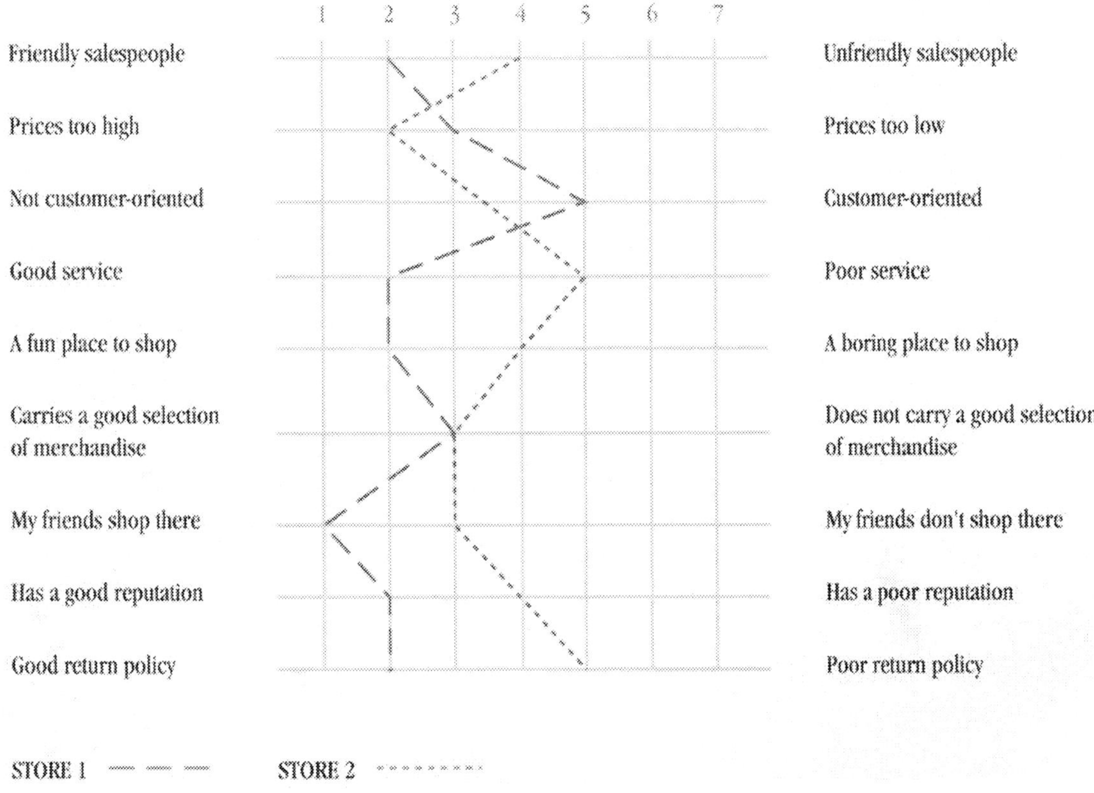

Exhibit 8.3

Example of the use of a semantic differential scale to profile two retail stores.

The **Stapel scale** is used in an identical fashion to a semantic differential scale, but respondents are given only a single adjective for each characteristic.[16] As shown in Table 8.7, scale values for each characteristic typically range from +5 to -5. Respondents choose a numeric category to indicate how well each adjective applies to what is being evaluated. The larger the rating, the better the adjective fits. One advantage of a Stapel scale over a semantic differential scale is that the researcher does not have to develop bipolar alternatives for each dimension. Another advantage is that Stapel scales are easy to use in telephone interviews.

	+5
	+4
	+3
	+2
	+1
Low priced	
	−1
	−2
	−3
	−4
	−5

Table 8.7

Example of a Stapel scale

With the **Likert scale**, a number of statements are developed to measure different aspects that might influence the respondent's overall attitude toward the object being evaluated. Like the semantic differential and Stapel scale formats, a profile based on individual statement responses can be created. The respondent's attitude can also be measured as the sum of the scale ratings across all of the statements. Table 8.8 illustrates some of the statements that might be used to create a Likert scale to measure respondents' attitudes toward retail stores.

	Strongly Disagree	Disagree	Neither Agree Nor Disagree	Agree	Strongly Agree
The store has convenient hours.	___	___	___	___	___
The store has a courteous sales staff.	___	___	___	___	___
The store is easy to get to.	___	___	___	___	___
The store carries the brands I like.	___	___	___	___	___
The store provides adequate parking.	___	___	___	___	___

Table 8.8

Example of Likert scale questions.

Assessing Scale Validity And Reliability

Two important characteristics of any measurement scale are reliability and validity but a complete discussion of these topics goes beyond the objectives of this text. Thus, we will provide definitions of these terms, briefly describe how each is assessed, and how they influence the accuracy of any scaled results. The reader interested in learning more is referred to any of the good pyschometric texts available on this subject.[17]

Scale reliability. **Scale reliability** refers to the

reproducibility of the scale results. Most measurements contain some random error or statistical "noise." Because there is not a tendency to consistently overstate or understate the quantity being measured, these random errors do not introduce any bias into the answers. However, random error makes it less likely that the result obtained will be reproducible. For instance, the amount of money an individual spends at the supermarket probably varies greatly from shopping trip to shopping trip. Using the amount spent on one visit to measure the average amount spent per visit by the individual would therefore be an unreliable measure because of the presence of a large amount of random error.

Test-retest reliability compares the respondent's answers to the same scale given at two points in time. The correlation between the two sets of answers is assumed to measure the reliability. Unfortunately, the correlations obtained are influenced by the length of time between measures. Retesting too quickly will inflate the correlations since respondents are able to reproduce the first set of answers from memory. Waiting too long to retest can create low correlations because true changes may have occurred in the way a person intends to answer.

Alternate form reliabiity compares the results of two versions of the same scale given to the same people at two points in time. Slightly different versions of a scale are used in alternate form reliability to overcome problems caused by giving identical scales to the same people twice in the test-retest method. Unfortunately, the use of two versions of the scale means that low correlations may be caused by non-equivalence of the two forms instead of low reliability.

Many scales are comprised of multiple statements because it is impossible to find a single statement that adequately captures all of the nuances of the concept being measured. **Internal consistency** measures split the statements on a multiple-item scale into two groups and correlate the group responses. If all statements are indeed measuring the same concept, the correlation should be high. However, the obtained correlation will vary depending on the way the statements are split. The most popular internal consistency measure, **Cronbach's alpha**, overcomes this problem since it is equivalent to the mean correlation of all possible splits of the statements.[18]

Scale validity. **Scale validity** assesses whether the scale measures what it is intended to measure. For instance, one might assume that the brand of beer a consumer ranks first in a preference ranking of an exhaustive list of brands of beer would be a valid measure of the brand the consumer buys most often. Unfortunately, this assumption may not be correct; factors such as price and availability can influence actual purchases so that the most preferred beer is not purchased. Likewise, using the response categories "way below average," "below average," "average," "above average," and "way above average" to measure household income is likely to overstate actual household income. This scale is biased upward because people will not want to admit that their income is below average. A valid scale is free of such bias.

Assessing the validity of a measure is more subjective than assessing its reliability. Several forms of validity are typically examined to lend credence to the claim that the scale is measuring what is intended. One form, called **content validity**, examines whether the measure appears to adequate measure the concept of interest. **Convergent validity** examines how well the scale correlates with other scales intended to measure the same concept. **Discriminant validity** looks for low correlations with scales that measure concepts unrelated to the one supposedly being measured, while **predictive validity** hopes to find high correlations with concepts that are related to it theoretically.

Scale accuracy. A scale can be reliable, but not valid; the results are very reproducible but the scale is not measuring what is intended. Similarly, a scale may be valid, but not reliable because the results contain a lot of random variations. An accurate measurement scale must be both reliable and valid. Hence, **scale accuracy** refers to the degree to which a measurement scale is free of both bias and random error. If a scale is lacking either validity or reliability, the scale is inaccurate, so neither can be ignored.

Constructing the Survey Instrument

As was shown in Table 8.1, the fifth step in designing a questionnaire is the development of the overall survey instrument. Constructing a survey instrument requires more than merely accumulating all of the questions that have been written. The final instrument must also include all of the necessary instructions to ensure that the survey is properly completed. In addition, unless the survey is conducted by CATI, information is normally included that will assist the data-entry personnel in entering the data into the computer. In mail surveys, care must also be taken to ensure that the overall questionnaire is constructed in such a manner as to maximize the response rate.

One of the key elements in maximizing the response rate in mail surveys is the preparation of the cover letter. A second key element is the overall appearance of the survey instrument. A questionnaire that appears crowded or difficult is likely to generate a low response rate.

The questionnaire shown in Exhibit 8.4 illustrates many of the important points of instrument construction. Because this particular survey was conducted by telephone, the appearance of the instrument is of less importance than if it was to be self-administered. However, you can see that interviewers are given clear instructions, typed in all capital letters to distinguish them from questions and response categories, to ensure that the proper procedure is followed. Similarly, the numbers in parentheses above each question's response categories aid the data-entry people by indicating the data column where the answers will appear in the data set. Skip patterns are clearly indicated by lines and arrows. One last thing you should note about this survey is that the first nine questions are designed to determine if individuals meet the necessary conditions to be considered a qualified respondent according to target population parameters.

Markets: (5)

Birmingham.....1
Charlotte......2
Dallas/
Ft. Worth....3

Job#1-828

DO NOT WRITE IN THIS BOX

Ref. #________ (1-4)

CHICKEN VIENNA SAUSAGE STUDY
- Screening Questionnaire -

Hello, I'm from____________________representing______________Opinion Research.
We are talking to people today about meat products they might use in their homes and would like to ask you a few questions.

1. Do you or does any member of your household work for a marketing research firm, an advertising agency, or a manufacturer or distributor of meat or poultry products?

(6)
Yes...........1 → THANK, TALLY & TERMINATE
No............2 → CONTINUE

2. Have you purchased any Vienna Sausage in the past 3 months?

(7)
Yes...........1 → CONTINUE
No............2 → THANK, TERMINATE & TALLY

3. What brand or brands of Vienna Sausage have you purchased in the past 3 months?
(DO NOT READ LIST)

(8-12)
Armour Star..................1
Libby's......................2
Hormel.......................3
Julia's......................4
Swift........................5
Don't know...................6
Other:
____________________7
(SPECIFY)

4. Have you ever heard of Chicken Vienna Sausages?

(13)
Yes...........1 → CONTINUE
No............2 → THANK, TERMINATE & TALLY

5. Have you purchased any Chicken Vienna Sausage in the past 3 months?

(14)
Yes...........1 → SKIP TO Q.7
No............2 → ASK Q.6 AND THEN THANK, TERMINATE & TALLY

6. Why have you not purchased any Chicken Vienna Sausage?

______________________________ (15-17)
____
____

Exhibit 8.4
Sample Questionnaire

Pretesting the Survey

The final step in questionnaire construction is to pretest the survey. **Survey pretesting** involves administering the questionnaire to a small sample of respondents to determine if the questions are understood and if the survey procedures work. Regardless of the experience of the researcher in designing surveys, mistakes can occur. It is incumbent upon the researcher to identify any problems by pretesting the instrument before the study begins. Ideally, the survey instrument should be pretested both with persons knowledgeable about survey design and with subjects similar to the intended respondents, since different types of mistakes are uncovered using the two different groups.[19]

The importance of pretesting can be demonstrated by what was discovered during a study designed to measure the frequency of in-home banking. People who use in-home banking access their bank account files electronically via in-home computers. When the pretest revealed much higher levels of in-home banking than was anticipated, the researchers looked for reasons to explain these results. They learned that respondents were interpreting in-home banking to include paying bills from checking accounts by telephone. Fortunately, the researchers were able to change the wording of the questionnaire to correct this misinterpretation before the study was conducted.

International Issues

Developing a questionnaire to be used in another country is an extremely difficult undertaking. Even if the questionnaire does not have to be translated to another language, the people in the foreign country may use a different word to signify an object. For example, an elevator is a called a "lift" in England. Thus a survey conducted in Australia or England may have to be written differently than one used in the United States. Furthermore, within some countries, languages may vary, requiring different versions of a questionnaire *within* the same country. For instance, India has fourteen official languages and a French and English version of survey may be necessary in Canada.

To ensure that the results of a multicountry survey can be compared across countries, the wording used in the questionnaire must have the same meaning in each country. Backtranslation is often used to assess the meaning of words used. With **backtranslation**, the English version of the survey is translated into the foreign language by one group of people, and then a second group translates the survey back into English. The goal is for the backtranslated version to be identical to the original. However, even a survey which backtranslates well may not convey the same meaning in a foreign country. McCann-Erickson, a United States advertising company, learned this lesson from some research they conducted in Czechoslovakia.

McCann-Erickson had been hired to determine if the Czechoslovakian market for portable telephones was large enough to warrant the introduction of the Eurotel brand of portable telephones. A questionnaire was designed, backtranslated, and the survey conducted. However, the survey results were not very useful because, as was later discovered, Czechs thought that portable phones were walkie-talkies or CB radios.[20]

Some information routinely gathered in U.S. surveys may not be obtainable in other countries. For example, respondent age may be difficult to get in Vietnam because birthdays are not a significant event in the Vietnamese culture.[21] Also, abstract scales commonly used in U.S. research, such as an unlabeled category scale, may not be readily understood in some cultures.

Summary

The survey instrument used to collect the data in a primary data collection project can introduce inaccuracies to the data in numerous ways. Slight differences in wording or in the way the survey is designed can lead to huge differences in the responses obtained. Each of the steps involved in designing the questionnaire must be carefully monitored to minimize these errors. Of utmost importance is the first step---deciding what information must be collected. Without a clear understanding of the information needs, the project will not be successful, no matter how well the remaining steps are implemented. Then, individual questions have to be written, and any required measurement scales have to be developed. Next, the instrument has to be constructed, including any required instructions. The final step is to pretest the instrument before the study begins, searching for any errors that have gone undetected.

Key Word List:

alternate forms reliability
backtranslation
category scale
closed-ended question
content validity
continuous scale
convergent validity
counterbiasing
Cronbach's alpha
discriminant validity
double-barrelled question
implied alternative
internal consistency
interval scale
Likert scale
measurement scale
nominal scale
open-ended question
ordinal scale
predictive validity
ratio scale

scale accuracy
scale reliability
scale validity
semantic differential scale
skip pattern
Stapel scale
survey pretesting
test-retest reliability

Nimslo's Use of Survey Data

The Nimslo Company conducted a number of surveys during the development of the Nimslo camera. Not only did the company encounter the typical problems associated with developing a survey instrument, but they also faced two problems that were particularly troublesome.

First, the company found that consumers had a difficult time identifying or categorizing the type of camera that they presently owned. Nimslo was particularly concerned with gathering information about consumers who owned single lens reflex (SLR) 35 mm cameras. However, compact, non-SLR 35 mm cameras were being introduced at about the same time as the Nimslo camera, and many people mistakenly assumed that their cameras were SLRs because they required 35 mm film. Survey questions inquiring about camera ownership had to be carefully worded to identify respondents who actually owned 35 mm SLR cameras.

A second problem the company encountered was the interpretation of intention to purchase measures. Companies often use results obtained from research studies of similar concepts to adjust purchase intention scores so that they more accurately reflect actual future purchase behavior. Since Nimslo had no previous research experience, no such adjustments were possible. Therefore, the company used purchase intention scores to compare purchase interest across groups of respondents instead of using them to project buying behavior. For example, purchase intention results were compared across similar groups of respondents exposed to the Nimslo camera concept at different price levels to determine price sensitivity.

Review Questions

Chapter 8

8.1 What are the six steps in designing data-collection instrments?

8.2 How can improper question sequencing create errors in the data obtained?

8.3 What is a questionnaire flowchart? What purposes are served by developing a questionnaire flowchart?

8.4 What is a skip pattern?

8.5 What are the advantages and disadvantages of open-ended questions? closed-ended questions?

8.6 What are four rules of question wording?

8.7 What are seven principles of question construction?

8.8 What is meant by a dead giveaway question? A double barrelled question? An implied alternative?

8.9 What is counterbiasing? Why would you counterbias a question?

8.10 What is meant by a measurement scale?

8.11 What are the four types of measurement scales? How does each differ?

8.12 What are the advantages and disadvantages of continuous measurement scales?

8.13 What issues must be considered when developing a category scale?

8.14 What is meant by a balanced measurement scale? What are the advantages of a balanced scale? When, if ever, would you wish to you an unbalanced scale?

8.15 What is a semantic differential scale? a Stapel scale? a Likert scale?

8.16 What is meant by scale reliability? How is scale reliability assessed?

8.17 What is meant by scale validity? How is it assessed?

8.18 What is meant by scale accuracy? How does accuracy differ from reliability and validity?

8.19 What is meant by questionnaire pretesting? Why is pretesting important?

8.20 What special problems are creating when creating questionnaires that will be used in other countries?

Discussion Questions

Chapter 8

8.1 What, if anything, is wrong with the way each of the following questions is written?

a) When did you last see a doctor?

b) Do you think that the product tastes good and is a good value for the money?

c) Is your home heated by gas or electricity?

d) Into which of the following categories does your income fall?

1. Under $20,000
2. $21,000-$25,000
3. $26,000-$30,000
4. $31,000-$35,000
5. $36,000-$40,000
6. Over $40,000

e) Do you plan to purchase a new automobile in the near future?

f) Which of the following categories includes your age?

1. Under 20
2. Between 20-25
3. Between 25-30

4. Between 30-35

5. Over 35

g) How many times in the past week have you eaten breakfast?

8.2 What is meant by counterbiasing? What is its purpose? Do you see any potential problems with its use? Give three examples of situations where counterbiasing might be useful.

8.3 Explain why measurement scales are forms of closed-ended questions but not all closed-ended questions are measurement scales.

8.4 Why is the choice of scale type an important issue? Why isn't an interval scale chosen for the measurement of all variables?

8.5 Select any four words not shown in Exhibit 8.3 and discuss why you feel that their usage in a question would create problems.

8.6 Explain how a measurement scale can be reliable but not valid.

8.7 Several books have been written about mistakes companies have made when attempting to market products in other countries. Many times, these mistakes are caused by a failure to completely understand differences in how words will be translated. Using one of these books as a reference, describe one example of such a mistake.

8.8 *Ethical Situation*: Suppose that Ford Motor Company wished to conduct worldwide studies to measure consumer satisfaction with their automobiles. One question which had been used on the survey in all countries where interviews had already been initiated asked respondents to indicate how frequently their automobile was used "for driving on hilly or mountainous roads." When initiating the survey in Venezuela, the research company that had been contacted to collect the worldwide data was informed by the local field service that the above question should be translated into Spanish so that the English translation was "for driving on roads with steep inclines." The survey had already been initiated in several Spanish-speaking countries, and no one else had mentioned this fact. The research company decided not to tell the Ford Motor Company about this suggestion, since they did not think that the change was that significant and they were afraid that the company would force them to re-institute the process in the other countries with no additional compensation.

Endnotes Chapter 8

1. Christy Marshall, "Have It Your Way With Research," *Advertising Age,* April 4, 1983, p.16.

2. Christy Marshall, "Have It Your Way With Research," *Advertising Age*, April 4, 1983, p.16

3. A number of books have been written discussing the pitfalls inherent in designing questionnaires for direct questioning. See, for example, Stanley Payne, *The Art of Asking Questions*, (Princeton: Princeton University Press, 1951), Patricia Labaw, *Advanced Questionnaire Design*, Cambridge: Abt Books, 1981), H. Schuman and S. Presser, *Questions & Answers in Attitude Surveys*, (Orlando: Academic Press, 1981), and S. Sudman and N.M. Bradburn, *Asking Questions*, (San Francisco: Jossey-Bass Publishers, 1983).

4. "The Management Brief," *Alert*, (Marketing Research Asociation), February 1996, p. 4

5. Betsy Spethmann, "Focus Groups Key to Reaching Kids," *Advertising Age*, February 10, 1992, pp. S-1 and S-24.

6. "The Management Brief," *Alert*, (Marketing Research Association), February 1996, p. 4.

7. This example is based on information found in "Poll Finds Some Doubt Holocaust," *Boston Globe*, National/Foreign section, April 20, 1993, p.5, "Pollster Repudiates His Finding of Some Doubt on Holocaust," *Boston Globe*, National/Foreign section, May 19, 1994, p.7, and "Poll Finds Most Believe Holocaust," *Boston Globe*, Metro section, July 2, 1994, p.20.

8. Michael L. Garee and Thomas R. Schori, Focus Groups Illuminate Quantitative Research, *Marketing News*, September 23, 1996, p. 41.

9. Fred D. Reynolds and John Neter, "How Many Categories for Respondent Classification," *Journal of the Market Research Society*, (October 1982), pp. 345-6.

10. Eli P. Cox III, "The Optimal Number of Response Alternatives for a Scale: A Review," *Journal of Marketing Research*, 17 (November 1980), pp. 407-422 provides an excellent summary of this debate.

11. G. Brown, T. Copeland, and M. Millward, "Monadic Testing of New Products---An Old Problem and Some Partial Solutions," *Journal of the Market Research Society*, (April 1973), pp. 112-131.

12. "Variations in Semantic Differential Scales," *Research on Research*, no. 3, Market Facts, Inc., Chicago, IL.

13. See, for example, Albert R. Wildt and Michael B. Mazis, "Determinants of Scale Response: Label versus Positioning," *Journal of Marketing Research*, 15 (May 1978), pp. 261-7; H.H. Friedman and J.R. Leefer, "Label Versus Position in Rating Scales," *Journal of the Academy of Marketing Science* (Spring 1981), pp. 88-92; and Melvin R. Crask and Richard J. Fox, "An Exploration of the Interval Properties of Three Commonly Used Marketing Research Scales: A Magnitude Estimation Approach," *Journal of the Marketing Research Society*, 29 (July 1989), pp. 317-39.

14. For a discussion of this, see Melvin R. Crask and Richard J. Fox, "An Exploration of the Interval Properties of Three Commonly Used Marketing Research Scales: A Magnitude Estimation Approach," *Journal of the Market Research Society*, 29 (July 1989), pp. 317-39.

15. Barnett A. Greenberg, Jac L. Goldstucker, and Danny N. Bellenger, "What Techniques are Used by Marketing Researchers in Business?" *Journal of Marketing*, 41 (April 1977), pp. 62-8.

16. See Irving Crespi, "Use of a Scaling Technique in Surveys," *Journal of Marketing*, 25 (July 1961), pp. 69-72; and Del I. Hawkins, Gerald Albaum, and Roger Best, "Stapel Scale or Semantic Differential in Marketing Research?", *Journal of Marketing Research*, 11 (August 1974), pp. 318-22.

17. See, for example, Jum C. Nunnally, *Psychometric Theory*, 2nd ed. (New York: McGraw-Hill, 1978), Fred N. Kerlinger, *Behavioral Research: A Conceptual Approach* 4th ed. (New York: Holt, Rinehart and Winston, 1978), and J.P. Guilford, *Psychometric Methods* (New York: McGraw-Hill, 1954).

18. For more on this measure, see L.J. Cronbach, "Coefficient Alpha and the Internal Structure of Tests," *Psychometrika*, September 16, 1951, pp. 297-334.

19. Shelby D. Hunt, Richard D. Sparkman, Jr., and James B. Wilcox, "The Pretest in Survey Research: Issues and Preliminary Findings," *Journal of Marketing Research*, 19 (May 1982), pp. 269-73.

20. Ann Marsh and Ken Kasriel, "Road to E. Europe Paved with Marketing Mistakes," *Advertising Age*, October 25, 1992, pp. I-3 & I-21.

21. Catherine M. Coffey, "Multi-lingual, Multi-cultural Interviewing," *CATI News*, vol.5, no.2 (Fall 1992), pp. 1-4.

Chapter 9

Project Execution, Data Analysis

And Reporting The Findings

Learning Objectives:

Chapter 9 concludes the discussion of primary data collection. The steps involved in actually collecting the data and preparing the data for analysis, as well as basic methods of data analysis are discussed. Chapter 9 ends with an overview of a typical research report. After reading this chapter, you should be able to:

- describe the details surrounding the execution of a primary data collection procedure.
- explain editing, coding, data entry, tabulation, and cross-tabulation.
- conduct basic types of data analysis, including computing measures of central tendency and dispersion, computing confidence intervals, testing hypotheses related to population values using sample statistics, and quantifying relationships among variables.
- describe how results are reported to management.

Collecting the data for the United States Census of the Population takes nearly a year, costs billions of dollars, and requires the services of hundreds of thousands of temporary employees. Without a doubt, this continues to be the largest, costliest, and most complicated primary data collection project ever executed. However, the time spent collecting the data pales in comparison to the time required to process and analyze the data. After issuing preliminary summaries, the Census Bureau continues to publish hundreds of reports detailing small geographic areas and profiling various segments of the population throughout the subsequent decade.[1]

Counting the population in total, and by geographic region, is a very difficult task. The sizes of some population subgroups cannot be calculated by counting, but rather must be estimated. For instance, the 1990 census was the first to attempt to estimate the number of homeless people. Enumerators were placed in areas known to be refuges for the homeless. However, how does one determine if a vagrant is really a homeless person? Obviously, direct questioning cannot be used. Rules were developed for classifying people as street people. One such rule was as to count all those remaining on a subway platform after a train departs as homeless.

Some homeowners, particularly in large urban areas, illegally use their basements as rental units. Enumerators working for the Census Bureau must essentially operate as undercover agents to obtain information about the number of people living in such units.

Crucial decisions are based on census results. A state's number of congressional representatives may be changed on the basis of census figures. Census data are also the basis for projections of regional populations and demographic group sizes, which often dictate government policy and research funding priorities. For instance, the forecast of a rapidly increasing number of retirees and aged Americans prompted the U.S. government to consider raising the age eligibility for social security benefits.

Given the magnitude of the decisions based on census data, it is no wonder that great care is taken to make sure that proper data collection, preparation, and analysis procedures, and, when required, appropriate sampling and projection methods are used to produce census results.

Although the scope of the Census of the Population and the magnitude of many of the associated decisions dwarf the scope and decisions of the typical data collection project, the same concerns apply. Care must be taken to ensure that errors are not introduced by how the data are collected. After the raw data are obtained, they must be carefully prepared for analysis and properly analyzed so that an accurate report of the findings can be written. Marketing managers, who make crucial decisions based on research results, must understand how improper data collection, preparation, and analysis can jeopardize the accuracy of the findings.

Executing the Research Project

Once the research project has been designed, a series of steps must be taken to execute the project, *i.e.*, collect the data. First, an estimate of the project cost is necessary to determine whether the project should be funded. Then, a research proposal specifying all project details and authorizing the project must be prepared. Finally, the data must be collected. We next examine these steps in more detail.

Estimating the Cost of the Project

As you learned in Chapter 6, data collection costs vary depending on whether the data are collected by telephone, by mail, or in person. The incidence level also influences the cost of data collection, as does the length and complexity of the data collection instrument.

The Impact of Incidence on Cost

As was discussed in the Chapter 7, the greater the number of restrictions placed upon respondent characteristics, the lower the incidence of qualified respondents. As the incidence level declines, the total cost of the study increases because more time and effort is required to locate a potential respondent. In fact, as you can see in Exhibit 9.1, the cost of a typical ten-minute telephone interview escalates rapidly as incidence levels get smaller. Completing a single interview costs nearly $300 at a one percent incidence level but only slightly more than $30 at incidence levels above fifty percent.

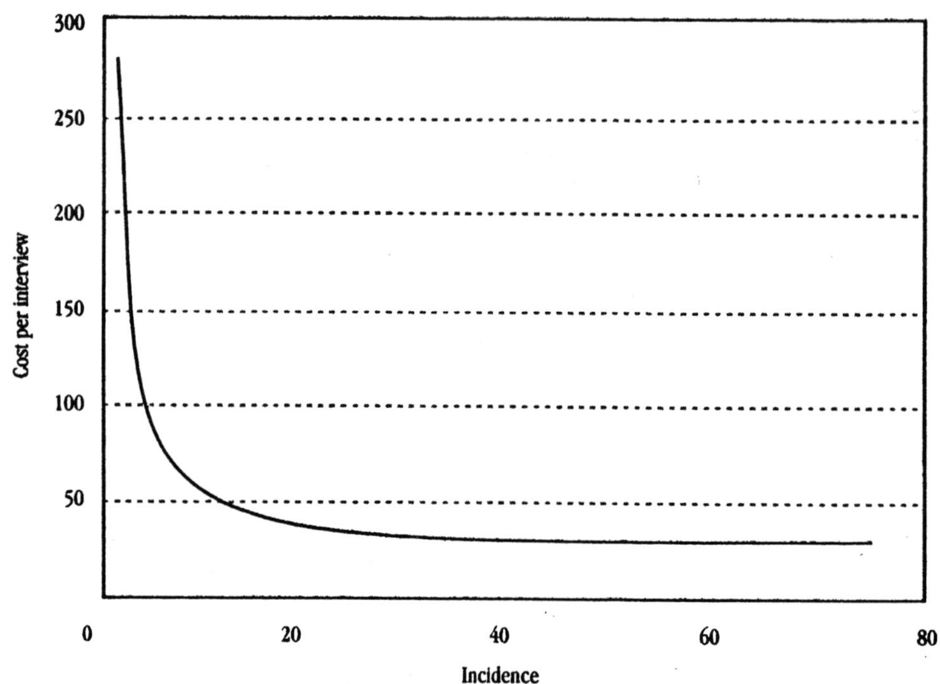

Exhibit 9.1
The relationship of incidence and per-interview cost.

The Impact of Survey Length And Complexity on Cost

Long, complex data collection procedures increase the cost of a study in two ways. First, if an interviewer is used, such studies become costly because of the increased amount of interviewer time required. Second, long studies and those that are difficult for the respondent to complete tend to have high refusal and termination rates. High refusal and termination rates mean that a large number of individuals will have to be contacted to obtain the desired sample size. The time necessary for these additional contacts adds to the cost of the project.

Determining Project Costs

With accurate estimates of incidence, study length, and study complexity, obtaining cost estimates for a project is relatively straightforward. In fact, most suppliers use computerized pricing models which incorporate these project design factors. The cost estimate helps determine whether the information is worth collecting.

Preparing the Project Proposal

Most companies require that a project proposal be written and approved before a project is executed. The project proposal specifies the purpose of the study, how it is to be conducted, who will collect the data, who will analyze the data, when the project is to be completed, and the expected cost of the project. As such, the project proposal serves as a schedule of research expenditures and is a very important control function. Furthermore, because the signature of the individual authorizing the expenditure is required, there are no misunderstandings about what the project is expected to provide and whose budget will be billed. Exhibit 9.2 illustrates a typical project proposal form.

PROJECT TITLE ON-AIR LAB TEST

PROJECT NUMBER PP-2976-RMH

PROJECT START DATE February 27, 1993

CURRENT DATE February 11, 1993

SUPPLIER(S) NAME(S) West Research

PROJECT SPECIFICATIONS

OBJECTIVES

To measure the communications effectiveness of a new animatic execution in terms of its:

1 - Memorability
2 - Registration of specific copy points
3 - registration of specific executional elements

METHOD

Airing: The test commercial aired live on a one-half hour daytime sitcom. Commercial scheduling controlled by research supplier.

Sample: Composed of female household heads age 18+. Recruited day before air date and asked to watch the one-half hour sitcom. No mention is made of commercial. Pre-recruited audience called back day after air date for interview. Past experience indicates final sample size of 125-150 composed of respondents who watched the program.

Evaluation: Interviews produce scores for memorability and registration of specific copy points and executional elements which are comparable to established "all commercial" norms.

Timing:	Air Date	Interview Date	Verbal Topline	Verbatims Available	MRD Final Report
	3/4	3/5	3/6	3/7	3/26

Location: St. Louis

Cost: $2,100 +/- 10%

Exhibit 9.2
Marketing Research Project.

Fielding the Project

As mentioned in Chapter 1, the actual data collection, known as "fielding" the project, is often performed by a research supplier or field service instead of by the company requesting the data. As the proposal is being prepared, potential suppliers must be alerted to the upcoming job so that they can schedule adequate time and resources to complete the job by the deadline. While alerting suppliers and scheduling the project may seem like minor details, you must remember that other companies are likely to be conducting research at the same time and with the same set of suppliers. With insufficient lead time, the preferred supplier may not be able to schedule the project and a less-desirable alternative may have to be found.

Companies are rightly concerned about the quality of the procedures used to collect the data. After all, quality decisions cannot be made without quality data. Therefore, specific safeguards should be instituted during fieldwork to assure data quality.

Field Instructions

Well thought out, explicit field instructions should be given to the field service. Field instructions outline such things as how the sample is to be obtained, who is a qualified respondent, and the preparation and presentation of materials to the respondent. Good field instructions remove much of the ambiguity surrounding the data-collection procedure and reduce the possibility of interviewer error. A briefing session held by the field service and attended by the client helps ensure that all interviewers understand the field instructions.

Monitoring Data Collection

The client should confirm that the field service assigns field supervisors to monitor the individual interviewers so that proper field procedures are followed. For example, in a telephone study, a field supervisor will periodically listen to interviews without the interviewers being aware. If the interviews are conducted using CATI, the supervisor will monitor not only the interview, but also the answers being input into the computer to see that no errors are made. Clients can also monitor interviewers to satisfy their own concerns.

Validation

After the data have been collected, validation procedures should be implemented to ensure that the data have been collected properly. **Validation** involves re-contacting 10 to 20 percent of the interviewed respondents to determine whether they are qualified respondents and whether interviews actually took place. The answers to certain questions may also be validated.

Validation reduces the chance that an interviewer merely fills out questionnaires without conducting the interviews. In addition, validation helps guarantee that proper procedures are being followed by the interviewer when screening for qualified respondents. If an interviewer's work is found to be suspect during validation, it is common practice to validate all of that interviewer's work.

Depending upon the severity of the errors found, the data from that interviewer might be excluded from the project.

Data Preparation

Once data have been collected, several steps typically precede data analysis. These steps include editing, coding, data entry, tabulation, and cross-tabulation.

Editing

Editing involves examining each completed questionnaire to determine whether the proper sequence of questions was asked and answers given to closed-ended questions were correctly marked. Typical mistakes discovered during editing are: recording more than one answer when only one answer is allowed; recording an answer that is out of the range of acceptable answers (e.g., recording a "5" when the only possible answers are "1" through "4"); and incorrectly skipping a question. Mistakes found during editing can lead to some or all of the data collected in an individual interview or observation being deleted from the data.

Most computer-assisted interviewing systems are self-editing. Because answers are keyed directly into a computer as the interview proceeds, the computer can be programmed to reject unacceptable answers to closed-ended questions. Likewise, the sequence in which the questions are to be answered, including any skip patterns, is also programmed into the computer, preventing any errors of this nature. Also, the computer can perform logic checks to determine the feasibility of an answer. For example, the reported total number of household members should equal the sum of the reported numbers of household members in each age category. Discrepancies would be resolved before the interview proceeded. Requiring the interviewer to check such logic is difficult, but is a simple computer programming task.

Coding

Open-ended questions not only are expensive because they lengthen the interview, but also because the responses to such questions require a great deal of preparation prior to analysis. Responses have to be organized into categories, a process called **coding**. Coding each response into general categories allows the researcher to determine how often each general response category was mentioned. However, coding open-ended responses is not a simple task. Deciding on the specific categories depends on the purposes of the study, the types of responses given, and the level of detail desired. Furthermore, rules for coding specific verbatim comments must be developed and consistently applied.

Interviewers often probe respondents for clarification of open-ended responses to reduce ambiguity at the coding stage. For example, a respondent using the word "tank" to describe a particular automobile could mean that the car was sturdy, box-like in appearance, or something else entirely. Unless the interviewer probed for the meaning of the word during the interview, the appropriate code would be impossible to determine.

Data Entry

When computer-assisted interviewing is not used, data from each interview must be typed into a computer data file before analysis begins. Even when using computer-assisted interviews, the original data base must be modified to include coded results for open-ended questions. Since data entry is another opportunity for errors to occur, validation procedures are used to monitor accuracy. Sometimes data from questionnaires are input twice and checked for any differences by computer. If no differences are noted, one file is deleted and the remaining file is subjected to analysis. If differences are noted, they are reconciled and a single correct data file is obtained.

Tabulation

Once the data file has been created, a tabulation of the data is usually the next step. A **tabulation** is merely a frequency count of each question's answers. Table 9.1 contains an example of a tabulation that indicates that 150 of the 400 people questioned had purchased a cassette tape or compact disc within the past thirty days (answered "yes" to the question), and 250 had not (answered "no" to the question).

Question: "Have you purchased a cassette tape or compact disc within the past 30 days?"		
YES	150	(37.5%)
NO	250	(62.5%)
TOTAL	400	(100.0%)

Table 9.1

Example of a question tabulation

A tabulation of the data provides a quick check data to see if all sample requirements are met. For instance, tabulation of the results of the question pertaining to the brand of window cleaner used would indicate whether a study included two hundred users of Windex as requested.

Tabulation also provides an additional editing check. Impossible responses which were missed in the original editing or mistakenly entered are identified. The original questionnaires are then examined to determine what the input should have been, and corresponding changes are made.

Finally, a tabulation of the results helps to define specific respondent subgroups among which results are to be compared. Subgroups can be created based on responses to specific questions. Examination of the tabulated results reveals the number of respondents comprising various subgroups and thus identifies subgroups that are too small to provide meaningful results.

Cross-Tabulation

A **cross-tabulation** is the simultaneous tabulation of responses to two questions. A cross-tabulation makes it possible to determine how many respondents gave a particular pair of answers to the two questions. Table 9.2 contains separate tabulations of responses to two questions from a survey -- Question 17, pertaining to coffee shopping behavior when faced with an out-of-stock, and Question 8, pertaining to type of coffee purchased most often. The cross-tabulation of the responses for these two questions also appears at the bottom of Table 9.2. This table shows, for example, that fifty-four of the respondents buy instant coffee most often <u>and</u> buy the same brand in a different size when the size of the brand they want is not available. More importantly, the results of the cross-tabulation for Questions 17 and 8 provide insight into how each group of coffee users (instant, ground, and bean) behaves in an out-of-stock situation. For instance, about 26 percent (37/145) of instant vs. 48 percent of ground coffee users do not buy when faced with an out-of-stock.

Question 17: "The last time you went to the supermarket to buy coffee and the particular brand and size you wanted was not on the shelf, what did you do? Did you . . . "

Buy same brand/different size?	135 (45%)
Buy different brand/same size?	15 (5%)
Buy different brand/different size?	45 (15%)
Not buy coffee at that store?	105 (35%)
Total	300 (100%)

Question 8: "What type of coffee do you tend to purchase most frequently? Is it . . . "

Instant?	145 (48%)
Ground?	120 (40%)
Bean?	35 (12%)
Total	300 (100%)

Cross-tabulation of Question 17 by Question 8:

	Instant	Ground	Bean	Total
Same brand/different size	54	57	24	135
Different brand/same size	9	6	0	15
Different brand/different size	45	0	0	45
Not buy	37	57	11	105
Total	145	120	35	300

Table 9.2

Example of the cross-tabulation of two questions

Cross-tabulation results presented in raw frequencies, like those provided in Table 9.2, are not easy to interpret because the user groups differ in size. Converting the raw frequencies to percentages makes for easier interpretation.

Three different percentages can be computed from a cross-tabulation. The *total percentages* (dividing the number in each cell by the total number of respondents) reveal the proportion of the time that a particular pair of responses occurred *for all respondents*. The *row percentages* (dividing the number in each cell by the corresponding row total) indicate the percentages of *each subgroup defined by responses to the row question* who gave each of the responses to the column question. Finally, *column percentages* (dividing the number in each cell by the corresponding column total) reveal the percentages of *each subgroup defined by responses to the column question* who gave each of the responses to the row question. Each type of percentage conveys a different meaning, and the appropriate one to use depends upon whether you wish to compare responses across all respondents, across rows, or across columns.

Cross-tabulations as shown in Table 9.2 are rarely used in the marketing research industry. Instead, a banner format is typically used. Using a **banner format**, each question on the survey is tabulated for the entire sample and for each of a set of subgroups selected to comprise the "banner," or column headings. Each column on the banner is known as a **banner point** and corresponds to a particular respondent subgroup. For example, if the question concerning coffee user type was included in the banner, each coffee user type would be a banner point and all of the questions on the survey, would be tabulated for each of the three types of users.

The number of banner points that can be included in a banner is restricted by the width of the computer paper on which the results are printed. Since suppliers charge extra for additional banners, the banner points should be carefully selected. Demographic, socio-economic, and geographic questions are frequently chosen as banner points to determine whether results vary by factors such as age, income, or region of the country. In addition, awareness or usage of products and brands is commonly used to define banner points.

Table 9.3 provides an illustration of a banner in the context of a study involving two versions of a snack food. As you can see, the banner points are defined by: cell (whether the new or standard version of the snack food was tasted), rating of purchase interest in the top two boxes based only on a concept description, sex, age, and markets (Los Angeles versus the other three locations where the test was conducted). Thus, the banner has eighteen banner points -- nine per cell. Table 9.3 presents the tabulations for the purchase intention rating based on taste. A separate table is usually provided for each question on the survey.

	CELL 1 - NEW									CELL 2 - STANDARD								
	*****	TOP 2	****SEX****		*******AGE*******			**MARKETS**		*****	TOP 2	****SEX****		*******AGE*******			**MARKETS**	
	TOTAL	CONCEPT	MALE	FEMALE	9-11	12-17	18-54	LA	OTHER 3	TOTAL	CONCEPT	MALE	FEMALE	9-11	12-17	18-54	LA	OTHER 3
TOTAL	198	98	100	98	67	63	68	50	148	202	108	102	100	65	71	66	50	152
	100.0	100.0	100.0	100.0	100.0	100.0	100.0	100.0	100.0	100.0	100.0	100.0	100.0	100.0	100.0	100.0	100.0	100.0
DEFINITELY WOULD	76	56	40	36	28	25	23	24	52	80	58	39	41	30	28	22	23	57
BUY IT = 5	38.4	57.1	40.0	36.7	41.8	39.7	33.8	48.0	35.1	39.6	53.7	38.2	41.0	46.2	39.4	33.3	46.0	37.5
PROBABLY WOULD	78	28	40	38	23	29	26	17	61	82	40	42	40	28	27	27	14	68
BUY IT = 4	39.4	28.6	40.0	38.8	34.3	46.0	38.2	34.0	41.2	40.6	37.0	41.2	40.0	43.1	38.0	40.9	28.0	44.7
MIGHT OR MIGHT	27	6	12	15	12	7	8	4	23	20	6	11	9	3	10	7	6	14
NOT BUY IT = 3	13.6	6.1	12.0	15.3	17.9	11.1	11.8	8.0	15.5	9.9	5.6	10.8	9.0	4.6	14.1	10.6	12.0	9.2
PROBABLY WOULD	8	3	5	3	2	1	5	2	6	14	3	6	8	4	5	5	5	9
NOT BUY IT = 2	4.0	3.1	5.0	3.1	3.0	1.6	7.4	4.0	4.1	6.9	2.8	5.9	8.0	6.2	7.0	7.6	10.0	5.9
DEFINITELY WOULD	9	5	3	6	2	1	6	3	6	6	1	4	2	-	1	5	2	4
NOT BUY IT = 1	4.5	5.1	3.0	6.1	3.0	1.6	8.8	6.0	4.1	3.0	.9	3.9	2.0		1.4	7.6	4.0	2.6
TOP 2 BOXES	154	84	80	74	51	54	49	41	113	162	98	81	81	58	55	49	37	125
	77.8	85.7	80.0	75.5	76.1	85.7	72.1	82.0	76.4	80.2	90.7	79.4	81.0	89.2	77.5	74.2	74.0	82.2
TOP 3 BOXES	181	90	92	89	63	61	57	45	136	182	104	92	90	61	65	56	43	139
	91.4	91.8	92.0	90.8	94.0	96.8	83.8	90.0	91.9	90.1	96.3	90.2	90.0	93.8	91.5	84.8	86.0	91.4
BOTTOM 3 BOXES	44	14	20	24	16	9	19	9	35	40	10	21	19	7	16	17	13	27
	22.2	14.3	20.0	24.5	23.9	14.3	27.9	18.0	23.6	19.8	9.3	20.6	19.0	10.8	22.5	25.8	26.0	17.8
BOTTOM 2 BOXES	17	8	8	9	4	2	11	5	12	20	4	10	10	4	6	10	7	13
	8.6	8.2	8.0	9.2	6.0	3.2	16.2	10.0	8.1	9.9	3.7	9.8	10.0	6.2	8.5	15.2	14.0	8.6
NO ANSWER	-	-	-	-	-	-	-	-	-	-	-	-	-	-	-	-	-	-
MEAN	4.03	4.30	4.09	3.97	4.09	4.21	3.81	4.14	3.99	4.07	4.40	4.04	4.10	4.29	4.07	3.85	4.02	4.09
STD. DEV.	1.04	1.06	.99	1.09	.99	.82	1.23	1.11	1.02	1.02	.79	1.04	.99	.82	.97	1.18	1.16	.97
STD ERROR-MEAN	.07	.11	.10	.11	.12	.10	.15	.16	.08	.07	.08	.10	.10	.10	.11	.15	.16	.08

Table 9.3

Example of banner tabulations—"Based on how this snack tastes, how interested would you be in buying it?"

Table 9.3 is a typical format of a banner presentation. Not only are the actual numbers of responses presented in each entry of the table, column percentages are also provided so comparisons can be made across groups defined by the banner points. For example, the percentage giving a "definitely would buy" rating decreases with respondent age for both versions of the snack food.

A **tab plan** specifies the particular banner point groups that provide the information required to answer the research questions. Developing a tab plan before constructing a questionnaire helps ensure that the questionnaire actually used in the study will provide the necessary information. After the data are collected, though, this initial tab plan may need to be modified because some banner points may have an insufficient number of respondents.

Data Analysis

Very seldom is the marketing manager interested in the individual responses obtained in a study. Instead, the manager is interested in ways to summarize the data to make the information easier to understand. While a tabulation provides one method of summarizing the responses to a question, the marketing manager often wants even more simplification. The manager might only wish to know which response to a particular question was selected most often, which response was in the middle of the frequency distribution, or what the average response was. Answers to

these questions require computing measures of central tendency.

Measures of Central Tendency

Three measures of central tendency, the mode, the median, and the mean are commonly computed. The **mode** is the value or values that occur most frequently. For the data presented in Table 9.4, you can see that 3 is the mode. The **median**, the value at or below which fifty percent of the responses fall, is 4. The **mean**, the arithmetic average, is 3.98 (199/50).

Numeric Value	Frequency of Occurrence
7	5
6	5
5	9
4	10
3	11
2	6
1	4
Mode = 6 and 7	
Median = 4	
Mean = 3.98	

Table 9.4

Data to illustrate measures of central tendancy

Which measure of central tendency is appropriate often depends upon the nature of the data. As you learned in Chapter 8, data may be nominal, ordinal, interval, or ratio. A mode can be computed for any of these data types, but at least ordinal data is required before a median can be computed. Interval or ratio data is necessary when computing a mean.

Measures of Dispersion

Data sets can have the same mode, median, or mean, but can have tremendously different frequency distributions. Measures of dispersion, which show the spread or variation existing in the data, are typically computed to complement the measures of central tendency. The **range** of the data---the difference between the smallest and largest values found in the data---is a simple measure of dispersion. However, the most commonly used measure of dispersion is the variance. The **variance** of the population from which the data were collected is the average squared deviation of the individual population values about the mean and is normally denoted by __. The population variance is computed as:

Install Equation Editor and double-click here to view equation.

where μ is the population mean, Install Equation Editor and double-click here to view equation. are the individual population values, and N is the size of the population.

The square root of the variance, _, is known as the **standard deviation.**

The larger the variance, the greater the dispersion in the data. The following example illustrates this point.

Applying Marketing Research 9.1

Two frequency distributions are shown in Table 9.5. You can easily prove for yourself that both distributions have the same mean, but, in examining these two frequency distributions, you can also see that the first distribution is more spread out (has more dispersion) than the second. The variances for the frequency distributions are 3.63 and 1.26 respectively. This difference in dispersion is apparent when the data are graphically displayed as in Exhibit 9.3.

Distribution 1		Distribution 2	
Value	Frequency	Value	Frequency
1	4	1	0
2	7	2	0
3	9	3	7
4	16	4	21
5	27	5	38
6	14	6	21
7	11	7	12
8	8	8	0
9	4	9	0
$s^2 = 3.67$		$s^2 = 1.23$	

Table 9.5

Two frequency distributions with the same mean but different dispersions.

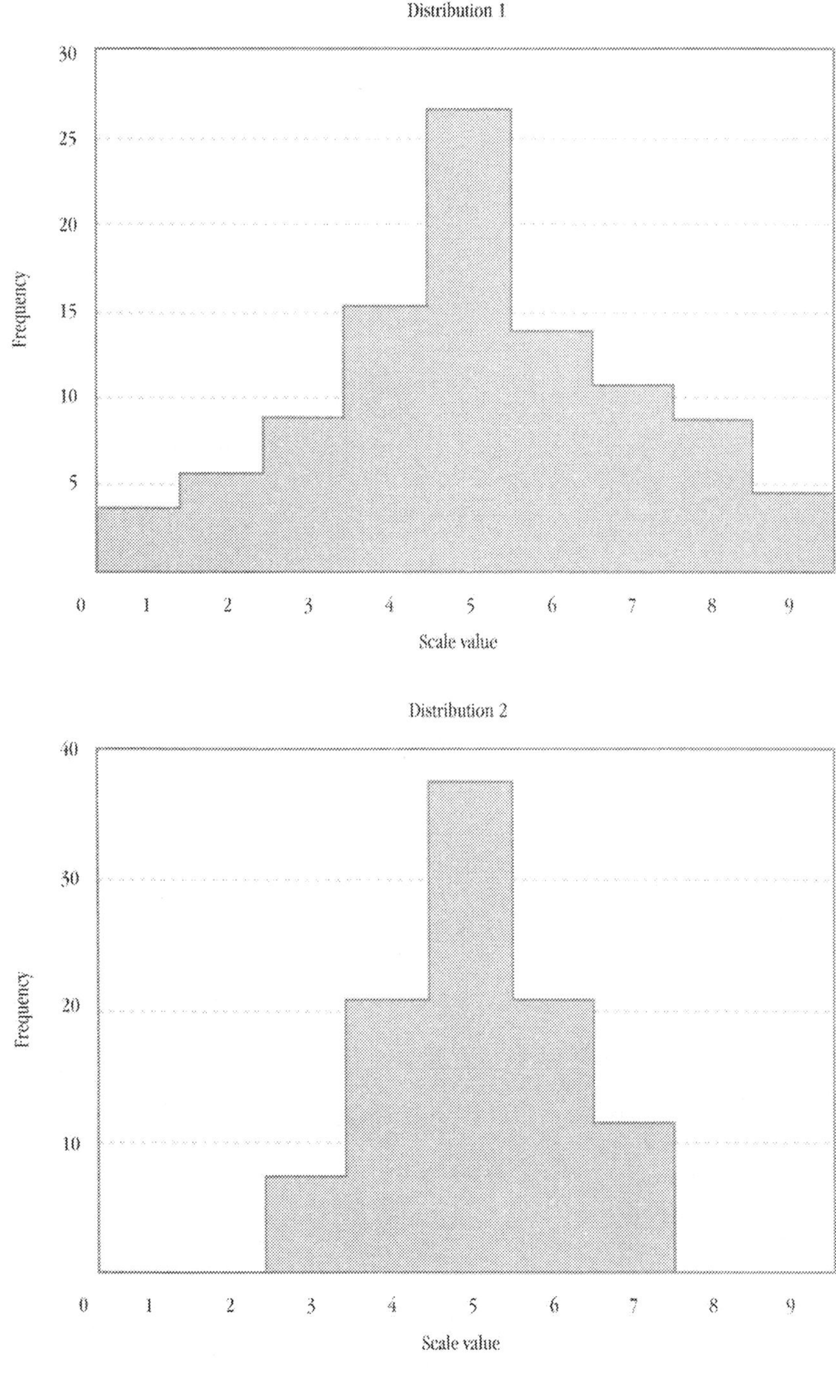

Exhibit 9.3

Graphs of the two distribution shown in Table 9.5

Sample Estimates versus Population Values

As discussed in Chapter 7, in the typical situation, information about a population of interest (target population) is inferred from a sample or subset of the population. In particular, the population average or mean, μ, and the population variance (or standard deviation) are estimated from the sample values. The sample mean, denoted by Install Equation Editor and double-click here to view equation. is an estimate of the population mean, μ, and the sample variance, denoted by s^2, is an estimate of the population variance, σ^2. The sample variance, s^2, is computed as the variance of the sample data, substituting the sample mean Install Equation Editor and double-click here to view equation. for the population mean μ and (n-1) for N, where n is the sample size. That is:

Install Equation Editor and double-click here to view equation.

Analysis of the data generated by the research project may consist of nothing more than tabulations and cross-tabulations of the data, along with the appropriate measures of central tendency and dispersion. Many times, however, additional analysis is necessary to provide answers to questions such as:

- What range of values are we reasonably certain contains the target population mean?
- Based upon the sample mean, can we say with confidence that the mean for the target population differs from a specified value?
- Are two sample means different enough to say that the respective population means are different?
- Is there a relationship between the answers respondents gave for two questions?

Computing Confidence Intervals

The answer to the first question posed above involves the calculation of a confidence interval. A sample estimate of a population value will almost never be exactly equal to the population value. However, most estimates obtained from probability samples are accurate in the sense that there is no bias present. In other words, there is no tendency for the estimate to consistently understate or overstate the quantity being estimated. In the absence of bias, an estimate's precision, which concerns the size of the difference between the estimate and its target, becomes a primary consideration.

Precision is normally described using a **confidence interval**, which is a range of values, centered at the sample estimate, known to contain the value being estimated with a given degree of certainty. Naturally, the more certainty (confidence) desired, the wider the confidence interval must be.

For example, if a market share estimate of 10 percent was obtained using a probability sample, it is highly unlikely that the brand's actual market share is exactly 10 percent. However, depending on the sample characteristics, we might be able to state that we are 90 percent confident that the actual market share is within one percent of the estimate obtained from the sample. That is, there is only a one-in-ten chance that the actual market share is not between 9 percent and 11 percent. The plus-or-minus error refers to the statistical precision and 90 percent is the **confidence coefficient**.

Confidence Interval for the Population Mean

The theoretical basin for the calculation of a confidence interval for the population mean is the Central Limit Theorem studied in Statistics. This theorem states that, regardless of how the values of the population being sampled are distributed, the distribution of possible sample means associated with a simple random sample of size n, approaches a bell-shaped curve called the normal distribution as the sample size n increases. This bell-shaped distribution has the same mean as the population being sampled, _, and a variance which is the population variance divided by the sample size, that is, _^{2}/n. Analogously, the hypothetical distribution of all possible standardized sample means, that is, Install Equation Editor and double-click here to view equation. , based on a sample of size n, approaches a standard normal distribution which has a mean of 0 and a standard deviation of 1. Percentage points for this particular normal distribution, the standard normal distribution, are given in Appendix Table I. This distribution becomes the reference point for confidence intervals.

From the discussion immediately above, it follows that a value of _ can be obtained from Table I, such that for any fraction, say 1-_ (0 < _ < 1), the probability that Install Equation Editor and double-click here to view equation. falls between Install Equation Editor and double-click here to view equation. and Install Equation Editor and double-click here to view equation. is 1 - _. The value of _ is typically small, e.g., .05, so that 1 - _ is close to one, e.g., .95. The percentage of the standard normal distribution to the right of Install Equation Editor and double-click here to view equation. is _/2. Equivalently, the probability that the interval Install Equation Editor and double-click here to view equation. contains _, the population mean, is 1 - _.

Hence, a confidence interval for a population mean is computed using the formula:

Install Equation Editor and double-click here to view equation. ,

where Install Equation Editor and double-click here to view equation. is the sample mean, _ is the standard deviation of the population, Install Equation Editor and double-click here to view equation. is the determined from Appendix Table I and depends on the confidence coefficient, and n is the sample size, which is implicitly assumed to be large.[2]

In practice, the actual population standard deviation, _, is rarely known, so the sample standard deviation, s, is used instead of _ in the above equation.

The two computed endpoints of the interval are called the **confidence limits**. As shown in Exhibit 9.4, the width of the confidence interval is determined by three factors: the standard deviation of the target population or sampling frame, the sample size, and the confidence coefficient. As one would expect, increasing the sample size reduces the width of the confidence interval, and the larger the variance (standard) deviation of the population being sampled, the wider the confidence interval. Also, the more confidence desired, the wider the confidence interval. For example, from Appendix Table I, ninety-five percent of the standard normal distribution falls between the symmetric limits of -1.96 and +1.96, so Install Equation Editor and double-click here to view equation. for a 95 percent confidence interval is 1.96; for a 90 percent confidence interval, Install Equation Editor and double-click here to view equation. is 1.645.

Factors	Impact
Population Standard Deviation (σ)	The larger the variance (or standard deviation of the population), the wider the confidence interval.
Sample Size (n)	The larger the sample size, the narrower the confidence interval.
Confidence Coefficient (100*(1 - α) percent)	The more confidence required (the smaller the α or equivalently, the larger 1-α) the larger $Z_{\alpha/2}$ and hence, the wider the confidence interval.

Exhibit 9.4
Factors determining width of confidence interval

The following example demonstrates the use of confidence intervals to determine the range of values that can be reasonably certain to contain the population mean.

Applying Marketing Research 9.2

Suppose that a manufacturer was contemplating the introduction of a new model of lawn and garden tractor. To estimate potential sales, 100 randomly-selected dealers (n = 100) were sent a description of the new model and were asked to indicate what first year sales of the model they would anticipate. The average of the annual sales estimates from these 100 dealers Install Equation Editor and double-click here to view equation. was $60,000 per dealer, and the standard deviation (s) was $35,000. What is the 90 percent confidence interval (1 - _ = .90 so _ = .10 and _/2= .05)for the mean sales for all dealers?

Using Appendix Table I in the back of this textbook, we find that the Install Equation Editor and double-click here to view equation. is 1.645. Substituting s = $35,000 for _, and using Install Equation Editor and double-click here to view equation. = $60,000, Install Equation Editor and double-click here to view equation. = 1.645 and n = 100 in the equation, the 90 percent confidence limits are $60,000 ± $5,757.50, so the 90 percent confidence interval is $54,242.50 to $65,757.50. Thus, company management can be 90 percent sure that the projected average sales volume for the entire population of dealers is between $54,242.50 per dealer and $65,757.50 per dealer.

If the sample size is small (n < 30 is typically considered small), two assumptions must be made in order to construct a confidence interval using the calculation just described. First, the actual population (or sampling frame) from which the sample is being selected must be approximately normally distributed. That is, if a frequency plot or histogram of the population values were constructed, it would be bell-shaped, centered at the mean _. Second, _ must be known because, with the small sample size, it cannot be safely assumed that s, the sample standard deviation, closely approximates _. If these two assumptions can be made, then the confidence interval would be calculated as described above, using the actual _ of course.

If the first condition - the population values are normally distributed - is satisfied, but the second is not, a confidence interval can still be constructed but the calculation of the confidence limits must be modified. Instead of using a value of Z, a value of t, obtained from a table or percentiles of Student's t-distribution (Appendix Table II), is used. The t replaces the Z, and s replaces _ in the calculation of the confidence limits. Like Z, t depends on the confidence coefficient. However, one other factor, the degrees of freedom (d.f.) must be considered in determining the value of t. The number of degrees of freedom is equal to the sample size minus 1, that is, d.f.=n-1. For a given confidence coefficient, the t decreases as the degrees of freedom increases.

The number of degrees of freedom reflects the confidence in *s* as an estimator of _. The larger the degrees of freedom, the larger the sample size and the more likely that *s* is close to _. Hence, it is no surprise that, in Appendix Table II, the value of t approaches the corresponding value of z as the sample size, and thus the degrees of freedom, increases. Applying Marketing Research 9.3 demonstrates the use of t in the calculation of confidence limits.

Applying Marketing Research 9.3

A survey is conducted among a random sample of ten customers of a manufacturer of industrial chemicals. The client companies are each asked to provide the dollars (in $000's) spent annually testing the quality of purchased bulk chemicals for use in manufacturing. The chemical supplier is considering offering such a service to its clients and wants an estimate of the amount of money companies spend on such testing. The survey results in a sample mean of $480 Install Equation Editor and double-click here to view equation. and a sample standard deviation of $20 (s = 20).

Assuming that the population of values of annual dollars spent on quality testing is normally distributed, a 90 percent confidence interval for the population mean is

Install Equation Editor and double-click here to view equation.

.

The t corresponding to a 90 percent confidence coefficient (_ = .10 and 1 - _ = .90)and 9 (10-1) degrees of freedom obtained from Appendix Table II is 1.833 (the corresponding value of z is 1.645). The resulting confidence limits are

Install Equation Editor and double-click here to view equation.

or

Install Equation Editor and double-click here to view equation.

Therefore, the manufacturer is 90 percent confident that, on average, its customers spend between $468,400 and $491,600 on quality testing of bulk chemicals.

Determining Required Sample Size When Estimating a Population Mean

The formula for confidence limits can be used to determine the sample size required to obtain a specified level of statistical precision at a given level of confidence. If we specify the allowable error (the maximum allowable distance between the sample mean and the upper or lower confidence limits) as _, then _ = Install Equation Editor and double-click here to view equation. . Solving for the sample size, n, yields the following equation:

$$n = (Z_{\_/2} * \_/\_)\_.$$

(It is implicitly assumed that the sample size will be sufficiently large to justify the use of the normal distribution.) To use this equation, _ must be known before the study begins, which is not the case in most applications. However, estimates of the standard deviation might be available from past studies, or the largest anticipated value of _ can be used to derive a conservative sample size. The actual interval reported after taking the sample and computing the sample mean would involve using the sample standard deviation (s) in place of _ as noted earlier. Applying Marketing Research 9.4 shows how this equation can be used.

Applying Marketing Research 9.4

Trade associations like the United Dairy Farmers Association frequently conduct surveys to provide useful information to their membership. Suppose that the United Dairy Farmers Association conducts a survey to estimate the annual per capita consumption of milk and wishes to be 95% confident that the estimate is no more than .5 gallons away from the actual population average. What sample size is needed?

From a table of values of Z, we find that the value of Z associated with a 95 percent confidence level is 1.96 ($Z_{.025}$ = 1.96). The allowable error, _, is .5 gallons. All that is needed, then, is an estimate of the standard deviation. If the United Dairy Farmers Association has reason to believe that the standard deviation is approximately four gallons, all of the necessary components are available.

The required sample size can then be computed as follows:

n = [1.96 *4/.5]_ = 246.

Therefore, if 246 people are sampled (and if the resulting sample standard deviation computed is actually about 4 gallons), The United Dairy Farmers Association can be 95 percent sure that the sample mean is no more than .5 gallons away from the true average annual per-capita consumption of milk.

Exhibit 9.5 summarizes how to calculate confidence intervals for the population mean under various conditions.

Situation	Confidence Limits
n > 30	
σ Known	$\pm Z_{\alpha/2}\ \sigma/\sqrt{n}$
σ Unknown	$\pm Z_{\alpha/2}\ s/\sqrt{n}$
n ≤ 30 + Population Normal	
σ Known	$\pm Z_{\alpha/2}\ \sigma/\sqrt{n}$
σ Unknown	$\pm t_{\alpha/2}\ s/\sqrt{n}$ (n - 1 degrees of freedom)

Exhibit 9.5
Summary for calculating confidence interval for population mean

Confidence Interval for a Population Proportion

Management often desires an estimate of a proportion, such as the fraction of the population aware of a new brand or the proportion of people who prefer one brand to another. In this case, the population standard deviation, _, depends upon the actual population proportion, which we call *P*, and is given by the following equation:

Install Equation Editor and double-click here to view equation.

The sample proportion, called Install Equation Editor and double-click here to view equation. , observed in a simple random sample, is typically used to estimate a population proportion. Again, assuming the sample size, n, is large, the confidence interval for a proportion is obtained in

exactly the same way as in the case of a mean:[3]

Install Equation Editor and double-click here to view equation.

In practice, Install Equation Editor and double-click here to view equation. replaces *P* in the calculation of the upper and lower confidence limits just as *s* replaces _ in the case of estimating a sample mean. Applying Marketing Research 9.5

demonstrates the use of confidence intervals in this context.

Applying Marketing Research 9.5

Suppose that a manufacturer conducted a survey among 400 randomly selected target market households in the test market for its new disposable diapers. The objective of the survey was to determine the trial rate for its new brand.

If the sample trial rate was 20%, that is Install Equation Editor and double-click here to view equation. , then the 95 percent confidence limits would be

Install Equation Editor and double-click here to view equation. ,

or Install Equation Editor and double-click here to view equation. ,

or Install Equation Editor and double-click here to view equation. .

Hence, the company can be 95percent certain that the actual test market trial rate is between 16.1% and 23.9%.

Determining Required Sample Size When Estimating a Proportion

Again, prior information, in this case information regarding the value of *P*, is needed to determine the sample size required to obtain desired precision at a given level of confidence. However, if no such information is available, a worst-case scenario can be assumed. It is easily shown that Install Equation Editor and double-click here to view equation. is largest when *P* is equal to .5. Therefore, assuming that *P* is equal to .5 produces a conservative sample size estimate since, for a sample of that size, the actual limits calculated using the observed sample proportion cannot be any larger than the specified allowable error. The following example illustrates how to compute the required sample size using this approach.

Applying Marketing Research 9.6

Returning to Applying Marketing Research

9.5, suppose that the manufacturer wanted to be 95 percent confident that the difference between the sample estimate and the actual trial rate of

the new brand of disposable diapers was no more than 4 percentage points. What sample size is required to give this level of precision at the desired confidence?

The formula to compute the sample size is basically the same as is used when estimating a

Mean:

Install Equation Editor and double-click here to view equation.

The Value of Z corresponding to a 95 percent confidence level is 1.96, and the allowable error, _, is .04. Assuming the population proportion, *P*, to be .5, using $Z_{.025}$ = 1.96 and _ = .04, the required sample size can be computed as:

Install Equation Editor and double-click here to view equation.

Therefore, if a sample size of 600 is used, the company can be sure that the computed 95 percent confidence limits will be no larger than

Install Equation Editor and double-click here to view equation.

.

The required sample size for any level of confidence and desired precision can be computed in exactly the same way as demonstrated in Applying Marketing Research 9.6. Table 9.6 demonstrates the impact of precision and confidence on the required sample size, assuming that .5 is the actual proportion.

Precision	Confidence		
	90%	95%	99%
± 1%	6,972	9,603	16,640
± 2%	1,743	2,401	4,160
± 3%	774	1,067	1,848
± 4%	435	600	1,040
± 5%	278	384	665

Table 9.6
Sample sizes required for various levels of precision and confidence (using .5 as the proportion value)

As discussed earlier, P(1-P) or equivalently
Install Equation Editor and double-click here to view equation.
, is largest when P = .5. Also, P(1-P) increases from 0 to its maximum value of .25 as P increases from 0 to .5, and decreases from .25 to 0 as P increases from .5 to 0. Noting this, prior information about P might be useful in determining the required sample size to produce a desired precision at a specified level of confidence. If in Applying Marketing Research 9.6, it was known that trial could not exceed .30 (30%), that is P ≤ .30, then P = .30, instead of P = .50, would be used to calculate a conservative sample size. Proceeding in this way yields n = Install Equation Editor and double-click here to view equation. or n = 504. Hence, the sample size required is reduced by about 100, which could result in a considerable cost savings.

Comparisons Involving Sample Mean(s)

As you have learned, rarely will a sample mean exactly equal the population mean. Yet, based upon the sample mean, a manager often wishes to know, with some degree of statistical confidence, that the population mean is different from a specified value. Suppose, for example, that a new product concept, tested with a random sample of potential buyers, received an average rating of 3.3 on a five-point scale (where 5 = excellent and 1 = poor). If the average rating on this 5-point scale for all similar concept tests is 3.8, the manager might like to know, with some level of confidence, whether the value of 3.3 obtained from this sample is sufficiently small to conclude that the corresponding population mean is actually different from 3.8.

Sample means are not just compared to specified values. Managers also often need to know whether two population means are different, based on the two corresponding sample means. For instance, the manager conducting the concept test just described might want to compare the mean ratings for males and females in the sample to see if it can be said with reasonable confidence that the average appeal of the concept varies by sex.

Hypothesis testing is the statistical procedure used to compare a sample mean to a specified value or to compare a pair of sample means. Statistical confidence intervals, which we have already discussed, can be used to perform these tests of hypotheses.

Comparing a Sample Mean to a Specified Value

To determine whether it can be concluded, at a prescribed level of confidence, that a population mean is not equal to a specified value, the corresponding confidence interval around the sample mean is first computed. If the specified value falls within the confidence interval, it cannot be said that the population mean differs from the specified value at the prescribed risk or confidence level. That is, the hypothesis that the population mean is equal to the specified value is not rejected. If the specified value falls outside the confidence interval, it can be said that the population mean is not equal to the specified value, at the given risk level. That is, the hypothesis that the population mean is equal to the specified value is rejected. Furthermore, depending on whether the specified value is above the upper limit or below the lower limit of the confidence interval, the population mean can be said to be smaller or larger respectively than the specified value. The following example illustrates how to perform this statistical test.

Applying Marketing Research 9.7

Suppose in Applying Marketing Research 9.2 that the management is interested in knowing whether the average sales volume anticipated by the dealers is different from $50,000 per dealer,

which is the average sales last year for the old model tractor. The 90 percent confidence interval that was computed in Applying Marketing Research 9.2 was $54,242.50 to $65,757.50 per dealer. Hence, management can reject the hypothesis that average sales per dealer is $50,000 and can conclude that the average sales per dealer is greater than $50,000 because $50,000 is below the lower limit for the 90 percent confidence interval. The corresponding

risk level associated with this conclusion is 10 percent since the calculated confidence interval contains the actual population mean 90 percent of the time.

On the other hand, management could not conclude that the average sales per dealer is different from $55,000 at the 10 percent risk level because this value lies within the computed 90 percent confidence interval.

Comparisons Between Two Sample Means

A slightly different formula is applied when computing a confidence interval for the difference between two population means from two independent samples. The formula is:

Install Equation Editor and double-click here to view equation.

where Install Equation Editor and double-click here to view equation. and Install Equation Editor and double-click here to view equation. are the respective sample means, $Z_{\_/2}$ is the value obtained from a table of the standard normal

distribution needed to achieve the desired statistical confidence, Install Equation Editor and double-click here to view equation. and Install Equation Editor and double-click here to view equation. are the respective population variances, and n_1 and n_2 are the respective sample sizes.

Since both sample means are subject to sampling error, both variances must be included. As before, Install Equation Editor and double-click here to view equation. and Install Equation Editor and double-click here to view equation., the respective variances, are typically not known, so Install Equation Editor and double-click here to view equation. and Install Equation Editor and double-click here to view equation. replace

Install Equation Editor and double-click here to view equation. and Install Equation Editor and double-click here to view equation. in the calculation of the confidence limits.

Using the above formula, the hypothesis that the two population means are equal is rejected at the given risk level if the corresponding confidence interval does not contain zero. The mean for the first population, estimated by , is inferred to be larger (smaller) than the mean for the second population, estimated by Install Equation Editor and double-click here to view equation. , if the confidence interval contains only positive (negative) values.

Applying Marketing Research 9.8

Manufacturers continually search for ways to improve their products. Suppose that a taste test among 100 potato chip eaters yielded an average score for "overall taste" of 4.9 for a new Lay's chip. Suppose a similar test using the current chip yielded an average overall taste

rating of 4.3 (where larger values imply better taste). Suppose the sample variances in the scores for the current and new chip were 1.7 and 1.8 respectively. The 95 percent confidence interval for the difference between the mean scores would be:

Install Equation Editor and double-click here to view equation.

or

Install Equation Editor and double-click here to view equation.

The 95 percent confidence interval contains only negative values, ranging from -.97 to -.23. Therefore, we reject the null hypothesis that the two population means are equal at the 5 percent risk level, and conclude that potato chip eaters are more favorably disposed to the taste of the new chip than to the taste of the old one.

Comparisons Involving Sample Proportion(s)

Statistical tests of hypotheses pertaining to proportions can be performed using confidence intervals in the same manner just described for population means.

Comparing A Sample Proportion to a Specified Value

If the confidence interval for a population proportion contains a specified value, then the hypothesis that the population value is equal to the specified value cannot be rejected at the risk level corresponding to the calculated confidence interval. Applying Marketing Research 9.9 demonstrates how to test such a hypothesis using confidence intervals.

Applying Marketing Research 9.9

Suppose in Applying Marketing Research 9.5 that the hypothesis to be tested is that *P*, the test market trial rate, is .25, that is, 25%. The value of 25% corresponds to the goal of the introductory marketing plan. This hypothesis would be rejected at the 5 percent risk level because the 95 percent confidence interval, .161 to .239, does not contain .25. In fact, it would be concluded that the test market trial rate is less than the goal of 25 percent.

Comparing Two Sample Proportions

Following is the formula for the confidence interval for the difference between two population proportions:

Install Equation Editor and double-click here to view equation.

where Install Equation Editor and double-click here to view equation. and Install Equation Editor and double-click here to view equation. are the population proportions, $Z_{/2}$ is determined by the desired confidence and obtained from Appendix Table I, and n_1 and n_2 are the respective sample sizes. In practice Install Equation Editor and double-click here to view equation. and Install Equation Editor and double-click here to view equation. replace the unknown values Install Equation Editor and double-click here to view equation. and Install Equation Editor and double-click here to view equation. in the calculation of the confidence limits.

The above formula is generally used to calculate a range of possible values for the difference between two population proportions. However, in the context of testing the hypothesis that the two population proportions are equal Install Equation Editor and double-click here to view equation. , a slight adjustment is made. Because the hypothesis being tested is the equality of Install Equation Editor and double-click here to view equation. and Install Equation Editor and double-click here to view equation. , it is assumed that Install Equation Editor and double-click here to view equation. and Install Equation Editor and double-click here to view equation. are equal to conduct the test. Hence, a common or "pooled" estimate,

Install Equation Editor and double-click here to view equation.

replaces Install Equation Editor and double-click here to view equation. and Install Equation Editor and double-click here to view equation. in the calculation of the confidence limits. This estimate, Install Equation Editor and double-click here to view equation. , is simply the result of treating the two samples as if they came from the same population.

Applying Marketing Research 9.10

A total of 180, or 90 percent, of a random sample of 200 owners of automobile brand A responded in a survey that they were satisfied with the way their cars performed. Similarly, 160, or 80 percent, of a random sample of 200 owners of automobile brand B responded that they were satisfied. For 95 percent confidence (_ = .05), $Z_{\_/2}$ is 1.96, and the 95 percent confidence interval for the difference between the population satisfaction rates is:

Install Equation Editor and double-click here to view equation.

or

Install Equation Editor and double-click here to view equation.

Can the management of brand A draw the conclusion that the percentage of satisfied owners is higher for their brand than for brand B at the 5 percent risk level? To address this, we first calculate Install Equation Editor and double-click here to view equation. . Adjusting the 95 percent confidence limits to test the hypothesis of equality of the two population owner satisfaction rates, we obtain Install Equation Editor and double-click here to view equation. or Install Equation Editor and double-click here to view equation. .

Because the 95 percent confidence interval does not include zero, the management of brand A can reject the hypothesis of equality of proportions at the 5 percent risk level. A statistically significant difference favoring brand A does exist at the 5 percent risk level.

Relationships Among Measurements

How much would sales of my brand increase if its advertising expenditures were doubled? Are people with relatively high incomes more likely to purchase my brand than other people? Do purchasers of my brand watch more television than nonpurchasers? These are examples of marketing questions that require determining whether a relationship exists. Two statistics, the Chi-square statistic and the correlation coefficient, are commonly used to explore relationships between variables.

The Chi-square Statistic

For variables that have been cross-tabulated, it is often of interest to know whether the relative frequencies of occurrence of the categories of one variable are consistent across the categories of another. If this is the case, the two categorical variables are said to be independent. If not, the variables are said to be dependent or related.

For instance, Table 9.7 contains the cross-tabulation we discussed earlier in this chapter, which pertains to behavior when faced with an out-of-stock situation and the type of coffee purchased. As you can see, behavior appears to vary substantially by type of coffee used. Within each row the percentages tend to vary across the columns of the table. What we would like to know is whether these differences are statistically significant or whether they can be attributed to random chance. For this test, the chi-square statistic Install Equation Editor and double-click here to view equation., which is computed as follows, is used:

Install Equation Editor and double-click here to view equation.

where O_{ij} is the observed frequency in the *i*th row of the *j*th column, E_{ij} is the expected frequency in the *i*th row of the *j*th column if no relationship is assumed, *R* is the number of rows in the table, and *C* is the number of columns.

Behavior	Coffee Type Used			
	Instant	Ground	Bean	Total
Bought:				
Same brand/different size	54 (37%)	57 (48%)	24 (69%)	135 (45%)
Different brand/same size	9 (6%)	6 (5%)	0 (0%)	15 (5%)
Different brand/different size	45 (31%)	0 (0%)	0 (0%)	45 (15%)
Did not buy coffee	37 (26%)	57 (47%)	11 (31%)	105 (35%)
Total	145 (100%)	120 (100%)	35 (100%)	300 (100%)

Table 9.7
Cross-tabulation of coffee type used and behavior when faced with

an out-of-stock situation

The expected frequency in any cell, E_{ij}, is the frequency that should occur in the absence of a relationship between the two variables. For example, since 45 percent of the total sample (135/300) in Table 9.7 purchased the same brand in a different size, about 45 percent of each coffee-type group would be expected to behave this way if no relationship exists between coffee-type and out-of-stock purchase behavior. Hence, the expected frequency for the first cell in the table is .45 * 145 = 65.25, and so on.

Equivalently, the expected frequency for each cell can be computed as the product of the number of observations in that row and the number of observations in that column divided by the total number of observations. Thus, the expected frequency in the lower right-hand cell of the table is (105 * 35)/300, or 12.25.

The greater the amount of difference between what is observed and what is expected across the cells, the larger the chi-square value and the less likely it is that no relationship exists. To determine whether the pattern observed in the data is consistent with the assumption of independence, i.e., to test the hypothesis of no relationship between the two variables, we simply compare the computed value of the chi-square statistic to a value obtained from a table of chi-square values (Appendix Table III at the end of this book). The table value to use depends on the risk level associated with the test and on the degrees of freedom associated with the chi-square statistic. Degrees of freedom, calculated as ® - 1)*(C - 1), adjust for the fact that cross-tabulations contain different numbers of cells.

Applying Marketing Research 9.11

For the example in Table 9.7, substituting the expected and observed frequencies into the above formula yields:

Install Equation Editor and double-click here to view equation.

Install Equation Editor and double-click here to view equation.

Install Equation Editor and double-click here to view equation.

Install Equation Editor and double-click here to view equation.

Install Equation Editor and double-click here to view equation.

Install Equation Editor and double-click here to view equation.

The degrees of freedom are (4-1)*(3-1) = 6. Testing at the 5 percent risk level, the ninety-fifth percentile for 6 degrees of freedom found in Appendix Table III in the back of the book is 12.592. Thus, in the case of 6 degrees of freedom, a chi-square statistic at least as large as 12.592 only occurs 5 percent of the time. Since 65.92 is greater than 12.592, we reject the hypothesis that the two variables are independent at the 5 percent risk level, and we conclude that a relationship between the type of coffee used and out-of-stock purchase behavior does exist.

Examination of the cells that contribute most to the calculated chi-square, that is, those cells for which Install Equation Editor and double-click here to view equation. is relatively large, either positively or negatively, provides insight into how out-of-stock behavior differs across groups. In Applying Marketing Research 9.11, ground and bean coffee users appear to be much more brand loyal than instant users are.

The Correlation Coefficient

For interval or ratio-scaled data, the strength of the relationship between two variables is commonly measured by the **product moment correlation**, often simply called the **correlation coefficient.** The value of the correlation coefficient ranges from -1.0 to +1.0 and is estimated from sample data using the following equation:

Install Equation Editor and double-click here to view equation.

where Install Equation Editor and double-click here to view equation. and Install Equation Editor and double-click here to view equation. are the pairs of sample values for the two variables of interest, and Install Equation Editor and double-click here to view equation. are the sample means and sample standard deviations respectively.

A positive correlation signifies that the values of the two variables move together, that is, as the value of one variable increases or decreases, so does the values of the other. A negative correlation indicates that the values of the two variables move in opposite directions, while a correlation coefficient of zero indicates no relationship between the two variables. Correlation coefficients that in absolute value are close to 1 indicate strong (positive or negative) relationships between two variables. In other words, knowledge of one variable is quite useful in predicting the other. (A correlation of +1.0 or -1.0 means that a perfect straight-line relationship exists between

the two quantities.) Exhibit 9.6 provides graphic illustrations of various correlations.

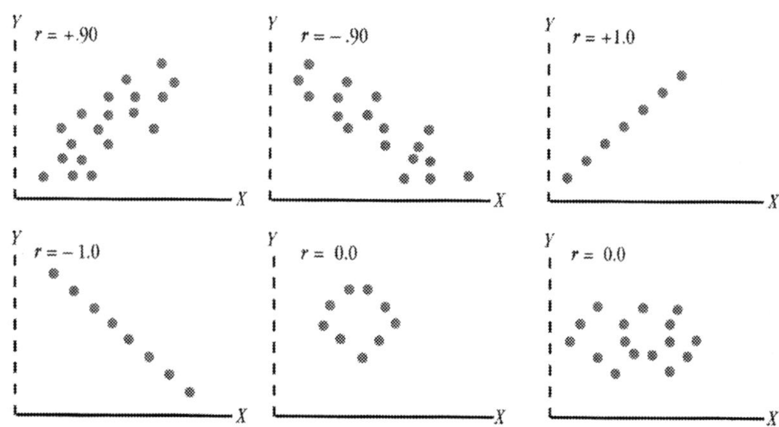

Exhibit 9.6
Correlation coefficients associated with various data plots.

A statistical test for correlation between two variables can be conducted based on *r*. Under the assumption that sample values are normally distributed and that the population correlation coefficient representing the relationship between these two variables is zero, then Install Equation Editor and double-click here to view equation. follows a Student's t-distribution with n-2 degrees of freedom.[4] Hence, sample values are used to calculate *t* and the result is compared to tables of the t-distribution (Appendix Table II), using n-2 degrees of freedom, to determine whether or not the sample correlation coefficient r is significantly different from zero at the given risk level.

It is important to recognize that correlation does not imply causation. As noted earlier in Chapter 3 (Experimental Research), examination of historical data might indicate a correlation between two phenomena, but this association may not be a cause-

and-effect relationship at all. Such correlations are often referred to as spurious correlations. Again as noted in Chapter 3, a spurious correlation occurs when the two seemingly related variables each have a cause and effect relationship with a third variable.

Regression Analysis

In **linear regression** analysis the correlation between two variables is used to develop a predictive equation. The dependent variable, *y*, is represented by a simple straight line function of the independent variable, *x*. A random sample of pairs of observations of y and x is used to develop a predictive equation:

Install Equation Editor and double-click here to view equation.

where Install Equation Editor and double-click here to view equation. stands for the predicted value of *y* for a given value of *x*, *a* is the estimate of the y-intercept and *b* is the estimate of the slope of the straight-line relationship.

The **coefficient of determination,** Install Equation Editor and double-click here to view equation. **,** measures how well the independent variable, *x*, predicts *y*. Install Equation Editor and double-click here to view equation. is equivalent to the square of the sample correlation coefficient (*r*). Hence, Install Equation Editor and double-click here to view equation. , and the larger the value of R^2, the greater the predictive power of the independent variable. If Install Equation Editor and double-click here to view equation. , then a perfect straight line relationship (positive or negative) exists between *y* and *x*. If Install Equation Editor and double-click here to view equation. , then the independent variable *x* is of basically no value in predicting *y*.

The sample estimates of the y-intercept, *a*, and the slope, *b*, of the straight line are used to test hypotheses regarding the population y-intercept and slope. Computer programs that perform regression analysis routinely include tests of significance of the hypotheses that the y-intercept is zero and that the slope is zero. Other information routinely reported is the value of R^2 and the estimate, s^2, of the unexplained or remaining variance about the straight line relationship. This variance represents how much individual observations of *y* vary for a given value of *x*. (If R^2 = 1, then s^2 = 0, because a perfect straight line relationship exists in the sample data.)

The estimate s^2 is calculated as follows:

Install Equation Editor and double-click here to view equation.

where n is the sample size and Install Equation Editor and double-click here to view equation., are the predicted values. Large values of s^2 indicate that considerable variance remains unexplained. In other words, knowing x and predicting y accordingly, there is still substantial noise that can cause an individual observation to deviate considerably from the line. The combination of R^2 and s^2 should be used to evaluate the predictive value of a simple linear regression model as demonstrated in Applying Marketing Research 9.13.

Applying Marketing Research 9.13

A real estate company hires a small marketing research firm to develop a model to calculate the approximate price of a home, using only its square footage. The real estate company feels that such a model will be useful in helping customers set the list prices of their homes. The marketing research firm decides to use a linear regression approach to predict list price (y) as a straight line function of square footage (x).

List Price ($000's)	Square Footage
75.9	1750
61.0	1590
110.0	2100
83.5	1800
94.6	1890
54.5	1360
96.0	2050
70.7	1760

50.8	1500
69.4	1650
87.5	1700
105.0	1920
76.5	1800
103.2	2150
59.0	1600

The estimates of the y-intercept, *a*, and the slope, *b*, are respectively -61.07 and .08, both of which are highly statistically significant (i.e., the hypothesis that these population values are zero are both rejected at very low risk levels). The predictive equation is therefore:

Install Equation Editor and double-click here to view equation.

For example, the regression model yields $98,930 as the predicted value for the list price of a 2000 square foot home. According to the model, an increase of 100 square foot in living space results in an $8,000 (.08 x 100) increases in list price on average.

The value of R^2 is .85, meaning that 85 percent of the variance in list price is explained by the regression model. The unexplained variance is estimated by s^2 = 59.2, or s = 7.7 (measured in 000's). Hence, for any value of square footage, a range of roughly Install Equation Editor and double-click here to view equation. (two standard deviations) contains the list price 95 percent of the time (assuming a normal distribution about the line). Although R^2 is quite large, there remains substantial unexplained variance.

The discussion of regression analysis so far has focused on using a single independent variable, *x*, to predict a dependent variable *y*. One can envision situations where several independent variables might be used in concert to predict a dependent variable. In the situation described in Applying Marketing Research 9.13, variables other than the square footage of a home, such as lot size, age of the home, and real estate tax rate also play a role in determining the list price. **Multiple regression** analysis is used to develop a predictive equation involving more than one independent variable. If there are *k* independent variables, x_1, x_2, ...x_K, then the predictive equation obtained by multiple regression takes the form

Install Equation Editor and double-click here to view equation.

Values of R^2 and s^2, as well as the predictive equation, are obtained in multiple regression and are interpreted the same way as in linear regression. That is, R^2 represents the percent of variance in the dependent variable explained by the variables $x_1, x_2, \ldots, x_K$ and s^2 is the estimate of unexplained or remaining variance.

As would be expected, R^2 increases and s^2 generally decreases, as additional independent variables are included in a multiple regression model. However, when developing a predictive equation using multiple regression, the goal is often to obtain a model with a high value of R^2, using relatively few variables and variables that make intuitive sense. For example, suppose the inclusion of lot size, age of the home, and real estate tax rate into the model described in Applying Marketing Research 9.13 yielded a predictive equation in which the coefficient for square footage of the home was negative. This equation lacks credibility because the it implies that predicted list price decreases as the square footage of the home increases. In this situation, the researcher might accept the lower R^2 associated with a model which does not use all four variables, but has more credible coefficients. (In Chapter 17, Applying Marketing Research 17.1 provides an example of the use of multiple regression for forecasting sales.)

Analysis of Variance

Earlier in this chapter, the statistical procedure for comparing two sample means representing two different populations was presented. **Analysis of Variance (ANOVA)** is a statistical technique for simultaneously comparing the means of more than two populations. First, based on sample data from several populations, a test of the hypothesis that the means from all the populations are the same is conducted at a prescribed risk level. If the result of the test is statically significant, that is, the hypothesis of equality of population means is rejected, then one of several multiple comparisons procedures is used to identify specific differences among the population means.

The assumptions for the statistical test are that the population variances are the same and the underlying populations all have normal distributions. The calculated test statistic is the ratio of two separate estimates of the common population variance and follows the F-distribution under the assumption that the population means are all the same. If this hypothesis is not true, that is, there are differences among the population means, then the calculated test statistic is inflated because differences among the means cause the numerator to overstate the population variance.

Statistical tables of the F-distribution for determining when to reject the equality of means hypothesis, that is, when the test statistic is "too large," are given in Appendix Table IV. These tables have two separate degrees of freedom values. The degrees of freedom for the numerator of the test statistic is one less than the number of populations or groups being compared. The degrees of freedom for the denominator is equal to the sum of the degrees of freedom available within the groups, where the degrees of freedom for each group is one less than the sample size for the group. Applying Marketing Research 9.14 demonstrates the use of ANOVA.[1]

Applying Marketing Research 9.14

Packaged goods manufacturers frequently test supermarket promotions prior to using them in the market. Suppose Lever Bros., Inc. is planning an in-store end-of-isle display to promote its Lever 2000 bar soap. The marketing team has narrowed the choices of display to three alternatives,

say *A*, *B* and *C*, and contracts with a marketing research firm to conduct an in-store evaluation of the options. Twenty supermarkets in the northeast are

[1]More specifically, this example illustrates a one-way ANOVA since the different populations are defined by a single categorical, or classification, variable.

randomly selected for the study, and five of the stores are randomly assigned to each of four experimental conditions: end-of-aisle display A, B, or C, and control (no display).

The respective sales volumes are shown in Table 9.8. Also shown in Table 9.8 is the corresponding one-way ANOVA table for testing the hypothesis that average store volume is the same for all four experimental conditions. Note that the test statistic is calculated to be 31.1 and has (4-1), or 3, and (4*(5-1)), or 16, degrees of freedom, and thus is highly statistically significant ($F_{.01;\ 3,\ 16} = 5.29$) indicating that there are significant differences in means among the experimental conditions.

Table 9.8 also contains the four group means and identifies how these means differ using the Duncan Multiple-Range Test[5] -- one of several multiple comparison procedures which can be applied.

The conclusion is that display *C* is superior to the other three experimental conditions, and display *A* is superior to both display *B* and the control condition.

Sales Volume Results

Display *A*	Display *B*	Display *C*	Control
15	12	28	10
18	13	26	11
21	10	25	15
16	16	30	17
20	14	35	12

ANOVA Results

Source	Degrees of Freedom	Sum of Squares	Mean Square	*F*-value
Groups (display)	3	832.4	277.5	31.1
Error	16	142.8	8.9	
Corrected total	19	975.2		

Group Means

Condition	Mean
C	28.8
A	18.8
B	13.0
Control	13.0

Note: Two groups comprising a pair of means not connected by a vertical line are significantly different at 5 percent risk level using the Duncan Multiple-Range Test.

Table 9.8
Analysis of variance (ANOVA) table and comparison of group means for Applying Marketing Research 9.14.

Presentation of Results

At the conclusion of a study, a complete written report summarizing the study and its findings is presented to the manager who requested the study. Often, a **topline report**, a brief one- or two-page summary of the major findings, is distributed prior to the completion of the full report. The information in the topline report gives the manager the option of acting upon the findings before the complete report is received. For many studies, an oral presentation describing the research project and what was learned is also made to management.

The Research Report

All research reports should be easy to read and comprehend. Managers receiving research reports are not concerned about the nuances of a particular research design. Also, they do not want to be overwhelmed with an elaborate discussion of the statistical analyses. Instead, they want to know why the study was conducted, the findings, and what the results mean.

Each company tends to have its own specific report style. Nevertheless, each style tends to include the same basic material. One typical research report format, shown in Exhibit 9.7, will be discussed here.

I. Executive Summary

II. Introduction

III. Method

IV. Findings

V. Conclusions and Recommendations

VI. Appendices

Exhibit 9.7
Typical Research Report Outline

Executive Summary

The executive summary is a short, one- to three-page, nontechnical synopsis of the study. The executive summary is designed to give managers who have not been closely involved with the project a quick description of the project and the key findings. It may be the only portion of the report read by these managers and should be written accordingly.

Introduction

The introduction to the report describes the background of the situation that led to the study and states the purpose of the study. The introduction sets the stage for what follows in the report.

Method

The method section indicates how the study was conducted. It should incorporate information about who was surveyed and how the survey was conducted. The method section should be complete enough to allow a replication of the study at a later date. A manager reading this section should also be able to assess the adequacy of the study design. Any limitations to the study that influence the interpretation of the results should also be stated here.

Unfortunately, researchers sometimes have a tendency to become enamored with the study design and provide unnecessary detail. The method section should not dwell on nuances of the design that would only be of interest to other researchers.

Findings

The findings section of the report presents the results obtained from the study. Findings should be presented in a manner that makes them easy for nonresearchers to understand. The use of charts and graphs greatly enhances the readability of this section.

Conclusions and Recommendations

The conclusions and recommendations section of the report indicates how the findings relate to the overall purpose of the study. Aside from the executive summary, the conclusions and recommendations section is the most important section of the report for managers. While the manager will be the person who actually makes a decision as to what action to take, it should be remembered that the research was conducted to help make that decision. Therefore, this section should not be a mere summary of the findings, but should indicate what alternatives under consideration appear to be most attractive given the findings.

Appendix

The appendix of the report usually contains supplementary tables, perhaps a copy of the survey instrument, and other materials which are of interest to some readers, but are not essential components of the report.

The Oral Presentation

For major research projects, the manager who requested the research and the research analyst who was involved in the project often present the results to upper management personnel. Sometimes these presentations are merely informational, serving to keep upper management apprized of various activities. At other times, the purpose of the presentation is to convince management to commit additional resources, based on the findings. Regardless of the purpose of the presentation, the credibility of the findings and the persons presenting them are strongly influenced by the quality of the presentation.

Effective oral presentations require good planning. All equipment to be used should be checked beforehand to ensure that it is in working order. Contingency plans should be in place in case of any equipment failures during the presentation. The size of the room and the seating arrangements should be considered in preparing visual materials. Finally, the presentation should be thoroughly rehearsed to make sure that it fits within the allotted time and is delivered professionally.

International Issues

One might assume that the types of analysis that can be conducted are independent of the country or countries where the data are collected. In one sense, data analysis is independent of the source of the data. However, when analyzing data, particularly data obtained in surveys conducted in foreign countries, care must be exercised to ensure that required data assumptions are met before applying a particular method of analysis.

Most of the analysis techniques described in this chapter, as well as those discussed later in this text, require interval- or ratio-scaled data. As mentioned in the previous chapter, respondents in some countries have difficulty answering questions taken for granted in the United States. For example, consumers in some countries are not used to providing semantic differential and Stapel scale responses. Therefore, data obtained from such questions may not be interval-scaled as is typically assumed in U.S. data, making some analysis techniques inappropriate.

A problem that must be confronted in multi-country studies is the comparability of the data. Idiosyncracies inherent in the data collected in each country can make comparisons meaningless. For instance, respondents in one country may be less likely to say anything bad about a person or brand than are respondents in another country. Thus, comparing the average ratings of a brand between two countries could reveal differences that are merely a function of the different response tendencies. The observed difference is not necessarily indicative of a difference in attitude toward the brand.

Summary

To execute, or field, a primary data collection project, several issues have to be resolved. First, an estimate of the total cost of the project must be obtained. This cost estimate, along with other details of the project, is included in the research proposal. Upon management's agreement with the research proposal, the suppliers to be used must be selected and procedures developed to ensure that the project is conducted according to specifications.

Prior to the development of computer-assisted interviewing systems, data collected in a marketing research project were recorded on paper questionnaires. The questionnaires from a single study frequently filled several moderately-sized cardboard cartons. Besides the storage and handling problems created by these large amounts of paper, each questionnaire required editing and typically coding before data entry. Until recently, data were entered directly onto a data tape or computer file from a computer terminal. However, in a computer-assisted interviewing environment, data are recorded directly to a computer file when collected. Further, the data-collection process in self-editing as the computer does not accept invalid entries. Coding of open-ended responses is also often performed as part of the interviewing process.

Data tabulation produces frequency counts and relative frequencies of the responses to each question. Cross-tabulation refers to tabulating results for specified subgroups, called banner points. These tables allow the researcher to determine whether key subgroups differ in their responses. Examination of tabulations and cross-tabulations provides basic but crucial understanding.

Marketing research data are also frequently subjected to various statistical analyses. Measures of central tendency including means, medians, and modes, and measures of dispersion, including the range and standard deviation, are usually calculated. Confidence intervals, which provide insight regarding the precision of estimates of target population values, are often reported. Tests of hypotheses are used to make decisions that depend on these unknown target population values.

The Chi-square statistic is used to test for association between two categorical variables such as gender and brand most preferred. The correlation coefficient quantifies the association between interval- or ratio-scaled variables such as age and annual income. Regression analysis is used to develop predictive equations that capitalize on correlation.

The statistical review presented in this chapter is not designed to be a substitute for a basic statistics course. For a more in-depth discussion of the concepts discussed, you should read the appropriate sections in one of the many good statistics texts that are available. Also, a wide variety of statistical procedures that are more advanced than those we have covered in this chapter are available to analyze interval- or ratio-scaled data. Rather than review these additional procedures in this chapter, we will introduce many of them in the contexts of the marketing research applications where they are frequently applied. Exhibit 9.8 is a guide to where these advanced statistical procedures are discussed in the text.

	Chapter 10	Chapter 12	Chapter 13	Chapter 16	Chapter 17
Analysis of variance				XX	
Cluster analysis		XX			
Conjoint analysis		XX	XX	XX	
Correspondence analysis		XX			
Discriminant analysis		XX			
Factor analysis		XX			
Multidimensional scaling		XX			
Perceptual mapping (general)	XX	XX			
Multiple regression analysis					XX

Chapter 10, Generating Ideas and Testing Concepts; Chapter 11, Product Testing; Chapter 12, Positioning and Segmentation; Chapter 13, Name/Package/Price Research; Chapter 16, Promotion Research; Chapter 17, Sales Analysis and Sales Forecasting.

Exhibit 9.8
Chapters in which advanced statistical procedures are discussed

The results of a research project are presented to management in a written report. Along with the written report, management may also receive a topline report that highlights the major findings. In some cases, details of the study and its findings are also presented to management orally.

Nimslo's Use of Linear Regression Analysis

to Forecast Sales Volume

Estimating camera sales volume obviously was crucial to Nimslo's management. Not only would camera sales provide the vast majority of initial revenues for the company, the number of cameras sold was the prime factor in determining future photofinishing revenues. The first step in developing an estimate of Nimslo camera sales for the introductory year was to forecast the total volume of sales for 35 mm SLR (single lens reflex) cameras, which typically were priced comparably to the Nimslo camera. Trade information regarding annual unit sales of 35 mm SLR cameras was available for previous years. The first year of this historical data was arbitrarily assigned the value zero, and subsequent years were sequentially numbered one to seven. A regression analysis was conducted using sales volume of 35 mm SLR cameras as the dependent variable (y), and the number of years from the base year (x) as the independent variable. The input data are shown in Table 9.9.

The regression analysis indicated a significant relationship between x and y. The correlation was .96, yielding an R^2 of .92. Hence 92 percent of the variance in unit sales of 35 mm SLRs was explained by time. The linear relationship is given by the equation.

$$y = .66 + .35x.$$

Nimslo used the above equation to estimate unit sales volume of 35 mm SLRs for the introductory year (eight years from the base year) by setting x equal to 8 in the above equation. Sales of SLR cameras were estimated to be 3.46 million units. Nimslo then applied their estimate of a 15 percent market share in this price category for Nimslo cameras, producing a sales estimate of 519,000 potential total Nimslo units. Next, this estimate was reduced to account for the fact that the Nimslo camera would be rolled-out gradually and would only be available for varying portions of the introductory year in each region of the country. The resulting figure of 250,000 cameras provided an estimate of Nimslo camera sales for the introductory year. These sales were distributed across the months of the first year of operations according to the roll-out plan and seasonality of camera sales and became the basis for a model for forecasting photofinishing volume.

Estimated Unit Sales Volume of 35 mm SLR Cameras (in millions) (y)	Years from Base Year (z)
.75	0
.9	1
1.1	2
1.6	3
2.5	4
2.7	5
2.6	6
2.9	7
3.46[1]	8

[1]Projected value

Table 9.9
Annual unit sales of 35 mm SLR cameras

Key Word List:

Analysis of Variance

banner format

banner point

Chi-square statistic

coding

coefficient of determination

confidence coefficient

confidence interval

confidence limits

correlation coefficient

cross-tabulation

editing

hypothesis testing

linear regression

mean

median

mode

multiple regression

product moment correlation

R^2

range

standard deviation

tab plan

tabulation

topline report

validation

variance

End of Chapter Review Questions

Chapter 9

9.1 How does incidence affect the cost of a study?

9.2 How does study length and complexity affect a study's cost?

9.3 What purposes does a project proposal serve?

9.4 Why is validation of fieldwork necessary?

9.5 What is the function of data editing?

9.6 How is data coding conducted?

9.7 What are the reasons that data tabulations are run?

9.8 What is meant by a cross-tabulation? Why are cross-tabulations useful?

9.9 What is meant by a banner? What is meant by a banner point?

9.10 Why might categories of responses be combined to create banner points for cross-tabulations?

9.11 What is a tab plan? Why is a tab plan useful in designing a primary research project?

9.12 What is meant by a measure of central tendency? Do measures of central tendency provide sufficient information about the distribution of data?

9.13 Frito-Lay's marketing management wants to conduct a survey in the test market for its new salty snack product to measure household trial. How big should the sample size be in order to guarantee that the 95 percent confidence limits for the trial rate are no more than ± .05 (i.e., ± 5%)? If this sample size were used for the survey and the observed trial rate for the sample was .25 (25%), what would be the 95 percent confidence limits? What would be the 90 percent confidence limits?

9.14 A survey of n = 100 households having personal computers and subscribing to an online service indicated that the service was used for an average of 6.0 hours per week. The sample standard deviation for the sample was calculated to be 4.0 (s = 4.0). What are the 90 percent confidence limits for the average connect time to an online service for all households having personal computers and subscribing to such a service? If the sample size were n = 400, what would be the 90 percent confidence limits?

9.15 Returning to the previous problem, suppose that the same survey is to be repeated again. Assuming that the same standard deviation applies (i.e., assuming _ = 4.0), what sample size is required to guarantee that the 95 percent confidence limits are ± .5? Suppose the confidence coefficient is relaxed to 90 percent, what would be the required sample size?

9.16 Hidden observers followed 9 randomly selected municipal waste removal trucks for one typical work day. The average amount of time taken for rest breaks, lunch, and so forth was 2.2 hours Install Equation Editor and double-click here to view equation. . The sample standard deviation was .75 (s = .75). Assuming that non-working time follows a normal distribution, what are the 95 percent confidence limits for the mean non-working time per day across all trucks and typical work days? What would be the 80 percent confidence limits based on these sample results?

9.17 A clothing retailer is unsure of the percentage of the adult population (> 18 years of age) aware of a long-term promotion the store is running. However, the retailer knows from past studies that it is highly likely that no more than 20% of the adult population is aware of the promotion. If a survey were conducted to measure awareness among adults, what sample size would you recommend to guarantee that the 90 percent confidence limits are at most 3% (i.e., .03)?

9.18 Interpret a correlation of .80? For a correlation of .80, what is the R^2? What does this value of R^2 mean?

9.19 Suppose a Chi-square test of a cross-tabulation of 300 survey respondents according to their response to two questions yields $\_^2$ = 25.6 with 6 degrees of freedom. Is this result statistically significant for testing the hypothesis of independence of the answers to these two questions at the 10 percent risk level.

9.20 What is meant by a topline report?

9.21 What is the purpose of an executive summary?

Discussion Questions

Chapter 9

9.1 How is computer technology used to assist in the preparation of data for analysis?

9.2 Interpret the following cross-tabulation which shows the number of users and nonusers of a brand in different age groups. Can you say, at the 5 percent risk level, that a relationship exists between respondent age and use of the brand?

	Bran User	Bran Nonuse	Tota
Under 30	59	31	90
30 - 39	61	49	110
40 - 49	61	59	120

50 - 59	43	57	100
60 or older	26	54	80
Total	250	250	500

9.3 Suppose that *Consumer Reports* magazine road-tested one brand of steel-belted radial tires. On average, the 200 tires tested had a 47,514 mile tread life, and the sample standard deviation was 9000 miles. Is there sufficient evidence to question the advertising claim that this brand of steel-belted tire lasts 50,000 miles on average at the 10 percent risk level? Why, or why not?

9.4 A baking company found a correlation of .70 between the number of persons in a household and the consumption of bread. They also found a correlation of -.35 between household income and bread consumption. How would you interpret these findings? How much of the variance in household bread consumption is explained by a linear regression model using the number of persons in the household as the predictor variable?

9.5 The correlation coefficient between a company's annual sales and advertising expenditures based on the last 20 years of data is .54. Test the hypothesis of no correlation between annual sales and advertising expenditures at the 5 percent risk level. Does a statistically significant correlation between sales and advertising imply a causal relationship? Why, or why not? If these data were used to develop a linear regression model to predict annual sales from annual advertising expenditures, what would be the value of R^2?

9.6 Concept testing is used to explore the impact of price on the appeal of a new product concept. Four samples of 100 consumers each are exposed to a version of the concept and are asked to rate its appeal on a ten-point scale (1 = extremely unappealing and 10 = extremely appealing). The versions of the concept are the same except for price. Fill in the blanks in the following one-way ANOVA table corresponding to these data:

ANOVA Table

Source	Degrees of Freedom	Sum of Squares	Mean Square	F-value
Groups (Concept)	3	20	6.67	________
Error	________	800	________	
Corrected Total	399	820		

Is the hypothesis of equality of means for each of the four price levels rejected at the 5 percent risk level? What is the next step? Discuss.

Chapter 9 Endnotes

---

1. Based upon information contained in David Wessel, "Counting the Homeless Will Tax the Ingenuity of 1990 Census Takers, "*Wall Street Journal*, November 14, 1989, pp. A1 and A6, and in Stephen Barlas, "Census Data Will Be Available Sooner," *Marketing News*, March 27, 1989, p. 2.

2. In order for the equation given for confidence limits to apply, the sampling distribution of the sample mean must be assumed to be normal. The Central Limit Theorem assures this for "large" examples. See, for example, Leonard J. Kazmier and Norval F. Pohl, *Basic Statistics for Business and Economic Decision, second edition*, (New York: McGraw-Hill, 1984), pp. 160-164.

3. Ibid, pp. 387-389.

4. See for example, Amir D. Aczel, *Complete Business Statistics*, (Homewood, IL.: Irwin, 1989, pp. 442-447.

5. See, for example, Rupert G. Miller, Jr., *Simultaneous Statistical Inference*, (New York: McGraw-Hill, 1966), pp. 81-102, or Allen L. Edwards, *Experimental Design In Psychological Research Fifth Edition*, (New York: Harper and Row, 1985), pp. 120-133, for a discussion of multiple comparison procedures including the Duncan Multiple-Range Method.

Case II.1

XYZ Supermarket Experiment

The XYZ supermarket chain was planning to run an in-store sales promotion in all of its stores. Three options were under consideration -- free coffee and donuts for all shoppers each morning for a week (A), a free _ gallon of milk for every purchase of $25 or more for a week (B), and daily in-store demonstrations of "healthy cooking" methods lasting for one week. The company decided to conduct a test to evaluate these three alternatives. A random sample of 20 stores was chosen for the test. Five of the stores were to be assigned to each promotional condition and five were to comprise a control group (D). Sales were to be recorded for the same one week period under the specified store environment.

Suppose that the random sample of 20 supermarkets was divided into five groups of four supermarkets each, and that within each of these five groups sales volume was fairly consistent. One store from each of these five groups was then randomly assigned to each of the four in-store conditions. This experimental design, called a randomized block design, eliminates one source of variance, namely store size, from the data. Hence, this approach provides a more sensitive test for differences among the promotional conditions than a one-way ANOVA (see the discussion of matching in Chapter 3).

The results and associated analysis of the experiment, are presented in Table II.1.1. Notice now that the ANOVA table contains a line associated with block as well as a line associated with type of promotion and finally a line associated with error. The test statistic for comparing the group means associated with the different display conditions is now based on the mean square for type of promotion versus the mean square error

Table II.1.1.

Results of randomized block design to compare in-store promotions

Sales Volume Results					
	Block				
Promotion	1	2	3	4	5

A	33	34	29	27	23
B	21	21	18	20	13
C	19	17	13	11	8
D (Control)	18	16	13	14	6

Analysis of Variance (ANOVA) Table

Source	Degrees of Freedom	Sum of Squares	Mean Square	F-value
Promotion	3	821.8	273.93	144.8
Blocks	4	265.7	66.43	35.1
Error	12	22.7	1.89	
Corrected total	19	1110.2		

Table II.1.2 contains the mean sales for the four store conditions. The LSD (least significant difference) i.e., the amount by which two means corresponding to different promotional conditions must differ to be statistically significant at the 5% risk level, is 1.88. Interpret the results of this experiment.

Table II.1.2 Mean sales for different store conditions

Store Condition	Average Sales
A	29.2
B	18.6
C	13.6
D	13.4

Case II.3

Bigtop Supermarket

Fran Berkovitz was puzzled as she returned to her desk at Clifton Research and found a phone message to call Bob Bonacci, the manager of the Bigtop supermarket. Had she left something in the shopping cart when she went to the store last evening? Worse yet, had her check bounced? Somewhat apprehensively, Fran dialed the number.

As she hung up the phone from talking to Bob Bonacci, Fran laughed at herself for being so paranoid. Bob had explained that he had gotten Fran's number from another of her clients, who had recommended her for some research that Bob wanted conducted. Bob had gone on to explain that he was going to embark upon a large remodeling project and wanted information about the in-store shopping habits of his customers to help in redesigning the store. Bob felt that if he knew more about such things as which areas of the store were visited most frequently, which types of products tended to be purchased together, how long it took people to shop at his store, and how people shopped while in his store, he could design a store tat would be both easier for his customers to shop and more profitable for him.

As she pondered what she knew about the store from shopping there, Fran could think of nothing atypical about the store. Bigtop was equipped with scanner check-outs and had all of the departments and sections normally found in a large supermarket.

Even though the final details of the data-collection project could not be defined without a longer discussion with Bob to determine exactly what information was desired, Fran had promised Bob that she would develop a tentative data-collection procedure to discuss with him in the morning. Bob had also indicated that he was going to contact a couple of other research suppliers besides Clifton Research and would make the decision on which company got the contract after hearing the proposals of each, so Fran was aware that her presentation needed to be topnotch. Fran was glad that she had just eaten lunch because she knew that she would be working late into the evening getting ready for her meeting with Bob.

Develop a proposal for a data-collection project to gather the information that Bob wants. Be sure to justify the decisions that you make in your proposal.

Case II.4

Public Opinion Polls

Public opinion polls, covering topics ranging from political issues to favorite flavors of ice cream, are commonplace today. During the White House sex scandal involving Monica Lewinsky, opinion polls were conducted overnight to determine whether President Clinton's approval rating had been damaged. ESPN, the nation's number one sport's network, annually presents the ESPY Awards. Presentations of these awards are made at a banquet attended by many celebrities from the world of sports and entertainment. Winners in the various categories, including most exciting sports play of the year, most exciting college basketball player, and so forth, are determined by public polling. Individuals vote by accessing either ESPN's website on the Internet and casting a ballot, or by calling a "900" number. Each telephone call costs about $1.

It is quite common for local news stations to poll the public about controversial current events as part of the evening news programming. A running tally is kept during the show and the final results reported at the conclusion of the show. These polls generally involve individuals using the telephone to call one 800 number to register a vote of "yes," and another 800 number to register a vote of "no." Many people attribute a high degree of validity to polls of this nature because the final tallies reflect so many voters.

The opening vignette to this chapter speaks of Ross Perot's proposal to conduct "electronic town hall" meetings as part of his political platform for election during his presidential campaign.[i] Again, individuals would vote on political issues by calling selected 800 telephone numbers, to represent their opinions.

The Internet is quickly becoming a vast communication medium. Some companies are conducting "marketing research" by questioning individuals who visit their websites. Further, research suppliers have engaged panels with access to the Internet to participate in surveys conducted over the Internet. As this medium expands and accumulates more and more users, it is likely again to become a major source of polling and survey research.

Develop a position paper regarding the validity of polling conducted by Internet or by television via 800 or 900 telephone numbers. Apply the sampling paradigm discussed in Chapter 7 to such polls. Where are the potential problems? Discuss the impact of the large base sizes of these polls on validity.

---

[i] [a]See James Fishkin, "Point of View," *The Chronicle of Higher Education*, July 1, 1992, p. A.40.

Case II.5

Triumph Cigarettes

At one time, the Lorillard Company ran an advertising campaign based upon what they called a "National Taste Test." The campaign claimed consumer preference for Lorillard's Triumph brand cigarettes over the Marlboro Lights and Merit cigarette brands produced by the Philip Morris Company and over the Winston Lights, Salem Lights, and Vantage brands produced by the R.J. Reynolds Company. Both the Philip Morris Company and the R.J. Reynolds Company filed suit claiming false and misleading advertising.

The Lorillard National Taste Test was conducted in 25 shopping centers across the country. Blind taste tests were conducted between Triumph and one or more of the competing brands using a paired comparison format. The taste tests were called blind because the cigarettes each consumer smoked were identified only by number to prevent any bias caused by the consumer knowing the brand name.

After smoking one or more of both of the cigarette brands in the paired comparison test (one cigarette was the Triumph brand while the other cigarette was one of the other brands mentioned above), respondents were told the tar content of each numbered cigarette and were then asked which cigarette they would prefer to smoke (The Triumph brand had lower tar than any of the other brands tested.). Still referring to the cigarettes identified only by number and tar content, respondents were then asked to compare the taste of the cigarette which was actually the Triumph brand against each of the other brands smoked.

The results of this test revealed, for example, that 53% of the respondents would prefer to smoke Triumph over Merit and 60% of the respondents felt that the taste of Triumph was equal to or better than Merit. Consumers also indicated higher preference for Triumph than for each of the other brands smoked. These results formed the basis for the claim made in the Triumph advertising.

Evaluate this research design, commenting on any aspects that you feel could form a good basis for the competitor's lawsuits.

Case II.6

Georgia Vidalia Onions[1]

Vidalia onions are grown only in a small section of central Georgia. The combination of soil, climate, and growing conditions makes the Vidalia onion extremely mild and flavorful. Although other areas of the country, such as Texas, boast of their mild onions, the Vidalia onion is unique.

The Vidalia Growers Association, a voluntary group of onion growers, instituted a program to ensure that no other onions could use the Vidalia name. An authentication seal was placed on each Vidalia onion sold so consumers would know that an onion claiming to be a Vidalia onion must have the certification seal. At the same time a television advertising campaign was developed to educate consumers about this authentication and to stimulate demand for Vidalia onions. This campaign was to be run for three months in local markets within the Southeastern part of the United States. Meetings were also held with key supermarket accounts to inform them of the change and of an upcoming advertising campaign, in hopes of encouraging them to better merchandise the produce.

To assess the effectiveness of the advertising at meeting its objectives, the Vidalia Growers Association hired Pendergrass Research to evaluate the effectiveness of the advertising campaign in meeting its goals. The research design used by Pendergrass is described in the following paragraphs.

Mall intercept interviews were used to evaluate the effectiveness of the advertising campaign at generating awareness of the new certification seal. Fifty interviews were conducted with women aged 18-65 in each of six metropolitan areas in the Southeastern part of the United States. A total of 300 interviews were conducted. Interviewers were instructed to screen potential respondents to ensure that they met the age requirement and, if they did, to ask them a series of questions designed to determine their level of knowledge about Vidalia onions in general, and the certification seal in particular. The percentage of women who knew of the certification seal was to serve as an indicator of the effectiveness of the campaign at generating consumer awareness.

To evaluate the effectiveness of the advertising campaign at stimulating store merchandising efforts, two groups of supermarkets were selected. A control group of 10 supermarkets were chosen. Control group stores carried Vidalia onions, but were not within the chains that the Vidalia Growers Association had met with to discuss their plans. Another group of 10 stores, that were affiliated with those chains, formed the test group. Each Wednesday, observers visited each of the 20 stores and completed a survey form that indicated the amount and types of merchandising support the store was giving

---

1 While Vidalia Onions are real, the rest of this case is hypothetical and in no way is meant to show what has been done to market these onions or to evaluate any past marketing.

to Vidalia onions. Differences noted between the two groups formed the basis for evaluating the advertising's effect on merchandising.

Discuss this research design. What additional information would be helpful to you in assessing the adequacy of the design? What, if anything, could have been done to improve the design?

PART III

Using Research to Bring a New Brand to Market

The same basic process is followed to varying degrees for bringing either a new consumer packaged good, durable good, or services to market. Ideas are generated and converted into concepts to be tested among consumers. For those concepts receiving strong consumer support, product prototypes are developed and tested. This product testing is iterative in that feedback from each round of tests is used to refine the product. In addition, the testing is evolutionary, moving from artificial environments such as laboratory or mall settings to more realistic in-home use tests.

While product testing is being conducted, research is also undertaken to determine how the market is segmented and to select the positioning strategy, brand name, price, package characteristics, and advertising strategy. If the product meets the product testing objectives, the other elements of the marketing mix are incorporated to obtain a sales or market share estimate for the new product. The first sales estimate is often obtained from a model that simulates the impact of the new brand on the market place. If the results of the simulated test market are good enough, a test market is conducted to verify the simulated test market results and to refine the marketing strategy. A successful test market leads to a roll-out of the product to additional parts of the country.

In Part III of the text, we discuss how marketing research assists decision making in the new-product introduction process. Many of the marketing research techniques discussed in these chapters also apply to existing brands. However, the new-product introduction process provides a natural ordering for the discussion of these applications and is also the exclusive context in which some of the techniques are used.

In Chapter 10 we describe how marketing research assists in the generation and testing of new product or service ideas. Chapter 11 introduces the various product testing techniques used to gain insights regarding the acceptability of prototypes developed from the product concepts. In Chapter 12 we discuss how marketing research aids in identifying market segments and in positioning a new product or service to reach a particular market segment. We examine the use of research to determine the name, package design, and price for a new product in Chapter 13. Finally, in Chapter 14, we discuss simulated test markets and test marketing.

Chapter 10

Using Marketing Research to Help Generate Ideas and Evaluate Concepts

Learning Objectives:

Few people would argue that innovation, in the form of new products and services, plays a critical part in the profitability and growth of most companies. But how do new products come about? In Chapter 10 you will learn:

- approaches to stimulating creativity and generating ideas for new products and services.
- steps involved in the process of turning ideas into concepts.
- methods for testing concepts among consumers.

Advances in computer and telecommunications technologies have dramatically changed the way that people conduct business, communicate, and go about their daily lives. Banking activities are no exceptions. People can now conduct financial transactions and other banking business in the comfort of their own homes using personal computers, or can use automatic teller machines to eliminate the need to visit a teller's window. These advances have greatly reduced the space requirements for bank branch offices. As a consequence, one major bank's management explored the possibility of renting space in their branches to small businesses. Such a strategy would generate incremental revenue, maintain the size of the bank's network by space requirements for their branches. avoiding branch consolidation as the means to eliminate wasted space, bring in potential customers, and perhaps enhance the bank's image because of an expanded service offering.

The concept appeared to have merit, but a number of concerns existed. Branches were open from 9:00 AM to 5:00 PM, but would off-hour access be required to attract businesses? During business hours, would the bank lobby become overcrowded, and would parking for bank customers become a problem? What physical modifications to existing facilities would be required? Would an administrative staff be required at each branch to provide tenant management? Finally, and most importantly, how would customers react to such a concept, and what types of businesses would be most attractive to them?

Consumer input and managerial insight were incorporated to refine the concept. Brainstorming sessions were used to generate lists of options and factors to consider. Focus groups were conducted with customers to identify potential problems, as well as to screen and perhaps enhance the options. Alternative viable business options that were well-received in the focus groups were then concept-tested with customers to determine which configurations were most appealing.

The bank's management learned that renting space to some types of businesses could downgrade the bank's image and cause safety concerns. Customers felt that some retail businesses might attract thieves or muggers to the bank lobby and provide a convenient place for undesirables to loiter. Among the businesses consumers reacted most positively toward were: a floral shop, a post office or privately run postal service, a travel agency, a ticket agent, and a newsstand, although differences in preferences existed between small towns and urban/suburban areas. In addition, more possibilities appeared to exist for small town branches than for urban/suburban branches because of the limited number of retail outlets available to small-town residents.

Although consumers expressed considerable enthusiasm toward the refined retail configuration in concept testing, concern over security and logistical problems associated with reconfiguring space and finding appropriate tenants have made management disinterested. However, the issue of excess space must ultimately be addressed, and the bank may yet resort to renting bank space to retailers.

Nabisco Brands, a past winner of the American Marketing Association's "New Product Marketer of the Year" award, derived more than 12 percent of its revenues from products introduced within the two years preceding the award.[1] Nabisco simultaneously introduced eighteen new products in the year they received the award, and launched another seven new lines of cookies and crackers the year following the award.[2] These examples come from only one company, but the message is clear: new products and services are vital to the long-term success of today's corporations.

The changing marketing environment often drives new product and service introductions. Economic, social, demographic, and lifestyle changes create new needs and desires, and hence, provide opportunities. Consumers' concerns about their health, for instance, triggered waves of new products boasting low cholesterol, high fiber, soluble fiber, fewer calories, low fat, and other health-related claims. Similarly, changes in social values regarding alcohol consumption led to the introduction of several nonalcoholic beers (see Exhibit 10.1). Technological innovation led to many new products and services, such as the ubiquitous automatic bank teller machine (see Exhibit 10.2). The American Marketing Association's "Edison Awards," given annually to recognize excellence in new product or service introductions, offer other examples. In a recent year, one-third of the 36 winners were food products having either reduced fat or no fat, such as Oscar Meyer's FREE fat-free hot dogs.[3]

Exhibit 10.1
Non-alcoholic beers introduced due to changing social values

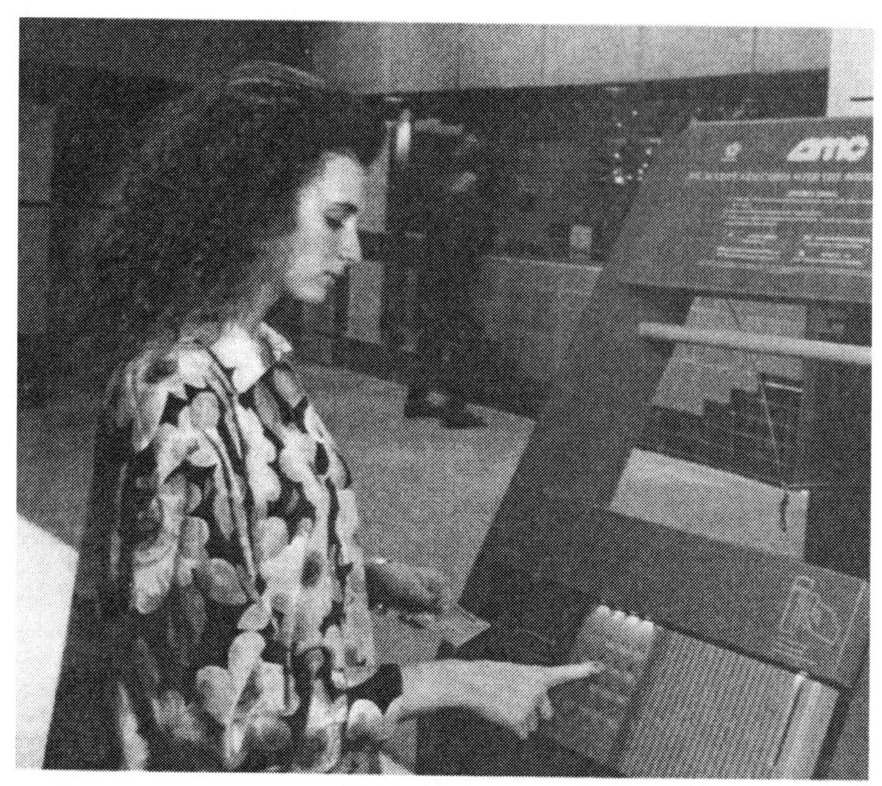

Exhibit 10.2
Some new products and services are driven by technological innovation.

Outside forces such as government regulation and material shortages can spawn new products or services. The government's ban of the use of cyclamates as artificial sweeteners sent manufacturers scurrying to find and develop alternatives. Many saccharin-based products emerged.[4] When the FDA announced its intention to ban the use of saccharin the search for low-calorie artificial sweeteners heated up again.[5] Turmoil and anti-American sentiment in the Middle East have periodically created havoc with gasoline supplies in the United States. Prices accelerated rapidly, and gas rationing and long lines at service station pumps became commonplace for a period of time. Consequently, considerable attention was given to developing gasohol, a mixture of gasoline and grain alcohol, as a fuel alternative.[6]

Successful new products and services are seldom accidental. They frequently result from a long process that involves generating ideas, turning those ideas into concepts, refining the concepts based on consumer input, and then testing refined concepts among consumers before the tedious process of developing the actual product even begins. We will explore how marketing research can aid this process in the rest of this chapter.

Stimulating Creativity and Generating Ideas

Creativity plays an important role in the new-product development process. Although some people are more creative than others by their nature, anyone can benefit from a systematic approach to idea generation. Approaches for stimulating creativity or facilitating the generation of new ideas can be organized into five general categories:

1. approaches that examine available products, called attribute-analysis techniques;

2. approaches that focus on the wants and needs of users, called needs-assessment techniques;

3. approaches that encourage one to see new relationships between things not normally related, called relationships-analysis techniques;

4. approaches that attempt to forecast future environments to uncover new product ideas, called scenario-analysis techniques; and

5. approaches that attempt to use group synergy to generate ideas, called group-creativity techniques.[7]

Attribute Analysis

Attribute analysis refers to techniques designed to develop lists of characteristics pertaining to a particular product category. Two common attribute- analysis procedures are dimensional analysis and checklists.

Dimensional analysis lists all of the physical characteristics of a product type.[8] Having obtained such a list, creativity can be triggered by asking questions such as: "Why is the product this way?" "How could the product be changed?" or "What would happen if one or more of the characteristics were removed?" For instance, applying dimensional analysis to a supermarket, one might challenge the way items are typically organized in the store. Why not place picnic items such as mustard, relish, catsup and pickles together? Why not place salsas, dips and chips together? How about placing the various items that go into preparing a pasta dinner, i.e., pasta, prepared sauces and Parmesan cheese, near each other? Such reorganization of supermarket aisles may not only result in an added convenience for shoppers, but may increase sales by reminding consumers of an item they may otherwise overlook.

A **checklist** is a list of relevant questions whose answers may provide insight into new product possibilities. For example, questions regarding whether an existing product could be adapted to other markets, how the product might be modified, whether it could be combined with something else, and so forth might be addressed. Several different sets of questions that might be asked have been developed and successfully applied by various researchers.[9]

A useful qualitative consumer research tool for developing a list of relevant product dimensions is the **Kelly repertory grid.**[10] Respondents first review stimuli (perhaps in the form of index cards) that represent individual items or brands in a broad product category, and completely unfamiliar items are eliminated. Familiar stimuli are then presented to each respondent three at a time, and the respondent then identifies two of the three items as similar and different from the third. The basis for separating the items is recorded, and another three items are presented, and so on. Bases for the similarity judgments are recorded until respondents fail to generate new ones. The final list of characteristics (dimensions) is obtained by merging the lists of differentiating bases obtained from the respondents. The following example shows how this procedure works.

Applying Marketing Research 10.1

Respondents are given index cards (stimuli), each containing a bakery item such as a cinnamon bun, glazed donut, jelly donut, or croissant. Each respondent identifies and removes any items with which he or she is totally unfamiliar, and the remaining items are then sequentially presented to the respondent three at a time. Respondents identify one item as being different from the other two in each triplet, the rationales used to determine similarity or difference are recorded, and the lists from different respondents are merged. The final list of relevant product category dimensions, in this case, would include such things as fruit *vs.* nonfruit flavor; sweetness; degree of messiness; dry *vs.* moist texture; type of filling, if any; and type of coating, if any.

By examining its current offerings in the context of these dimensions, a bakery could generate ideas for new products. For example, why not offer a doughnut filled with a choice of soft ice creams when purchased, or a cream-filled croissant?

Need Assessment

The primary cause of new product failure is that the product or service does not address a specific consumer need or problem.[11] Consequently, many marketers look toward consumer need as the basic source of new product or service ideas. **Need-assessment techniques** attempt to identify unsatisfied consumer needs or reveal problems that are not solved by existing products or services.

Problem Analysis

Problem analysis is a need-assessment technique designed to develop an inventory of consumer problems in a particular product or service category and to serve as a basis for new product or service ideas.[12] Consumer input using focus groups, user panels, panels of experts, or complaint records might be used to develop such an inventory.

Some problem-analysis techniques ask users to verbalize the problems they encounter with current products. For instance, asking consumers about problems with adhesive bandages, managers at the Johnson & Johnson Company learned that consumers did not like the fact that the bandages were so apparent when worn. This finding led to the development of Band-Aid Sheer Strips, a product made of a sheer plastic film that blended more readily with various skin tones.[13]

Other problem-analysis techniques, sometimes referred to as **problem inventory analysis,**[14] approach the question of consumer needs at a general level. Rather than asking consumers to identify problems associated with a particular product, problem inventory analysis provides consumers with a list of problems that may be present in many product categories and asks consumers to specify particular products that they associate with the problem. Problem inventory analysis is based on the assumption that consumers find it easier to relate known products to suggested problems than to generate problems for a given product.

Sentence completion techniques, as described in Chapter 2, are often used to elicit responses. Thus, participants might be asked to fill in the blank in the following sentence:

> My children would love to be able to take ____ to school for lunch, but it is too difficult to do.

Answers to this question would be items that consumers felt would be good for school lunches, but for one reason or another could not easily used or included. Having identified such items, management would decide if they could change the items in some way to eliminate the problem.

Results of all problem-analysis studies must be interpreted cautiously. The problems identified must be important. Furthermore, the solution must have consumer acceptance. A watery catsup, for example, would pour easily, solving a frequently mentioned problem, but would likely have little appeal.

Benefit Structure Analysis

Benefit structure analysis[15] (BSA) determines what specific benefits and characteristics are desired by consumers within a particular product or service category and identifies perceived deficiencies in what is currently provided. Focus groups, depth interviews, or other forms of qualitative research are used to develop a complete list of characteristics and benefits of the product or service category being investigated. Large-scale research is then conducted to uncover the desirability of each characteristic and benefit as well as perceived deficiencies of current offerings in the category. This quantitative phase also provides relatively complete information as to the conditions surrounding the use of the product or service, such as the time of day when usage occurs, other persons present during usage, and the task for which the product or service was applied. Applying Marketing Research 10.2 describes how Black & Decker used this approach to develop their Quantum line of power tools.

Applying Marketing Research 10.2

Black & Decker learned through research that a lot of non-professional do-it-yourselfers were price sensitive. They were unwilling to pay the price necessary to buy the DeWalt line offered by Black & Decker, but did not want to trade down to the Black & Decker line. Not wanting to lose these potential customers, the company embarked on research to determine what they needed to offer in a mid-priced line.

Using an independent research supplier, Black & Decker located 50 male homeowners, ages 25 to 50, who owned more than six power tools, and who would be willing to provide data to Black & Decker. For three months, these men were questioned about the tools they used and why they bought them and were observed in their workshops. Researchers even tagged along on shopping trips. The findings were substantiated by interviewing hundreds of Black & Decker customers who had mailed in warranty cards.

Black & Decker learned a great deal about the benefits these consumers were seeking in their power tools. For instance, they wanted a cordless drill that did not run out of power before the job was completed. These men also did not like the mess created from sawing or sanding wood nor the safety hazard of an electric saw blade that continued to spin after being shut off.

Armed with these findings, Black & Decker designed a new line of tools known as the Quantum line. The cordless drill has a more powerful battery that recharges in only an hour, instead of overnight. The sanders and electric saws have small vacuums and attached bags to suck up sawdust before it becomes a mess. An auto braking system was designed into the electric saws that stops the blade from spinning within two seconds of being shut off. Free maintenance checks and a toll-free hotline for service questions are also provided. Much of the success of this line can be attributed to carefully researching the benefits the target consumers desire in these tools.[16]

BSA was specifically designed to determine new product opportunities in broad product or service categories. For a broad category of goods, BSA provides information pertaining to:

- the number of general types of products that could be on the market, based on benefits delivered;
- potential additional uses for existing brands;
- insight into new products that could deliver a specific combination of benefits for a particular use or group of uses; and

- how to reposition an existing brand by stressing additional benefits provided.

Gap Analysis

Gap analysis focuses on determining how various brands are perceived relative to each other. An opportunity for a new brand exists when gap analysis indicates that no brand occupies a particular niche for which there is a consumer demand. Perceptual mapping is a technique that yields graphic displays showing how consumers perceive various brands. Areas in the map that contain no brands are potential gaps. Although perceptual mapping will be discussed in detail in Chapter 12 ("Segmentation and Positioning"), its usefulness for gap analysis is demonstrated in Applying Marketing Research 10.3.

Applying Marketing Research 10.3

Suppose that the Procter & Gamble Company, a leading manufacturer of laundry products, conducts a survey among female heads-of-household to determine their perceptions of existing brands of liquid laundry detergent. Exhibit 10.3 shows a hypothetical perceptual map depicting how consumers view the brands included in the study. Two major dimensions, mildness and effectiveness as a cleaner, appear to be used by consumers to differentiate among the brands. Further, no existing brand of liquid detergents is perceived as being both mild and effective, possibly creating an opportunity for a cleaner that provides both benefits.

Before proceeding, however, Procter & Gamble would need to determine whether a market exists for such a product. In other words, is there a segment of the market who place a high degree of importance on both of these benefits? On the surface, it would appear that many consumers would find such a product very appealing. However, mildness and effectiveness are somewhat contradictory, and consumers may not believe that a laundry detergent can provide both benefits. Hence, it could be a very difficult uphill struggle for a brand to achieve this niche in consumers' minds.

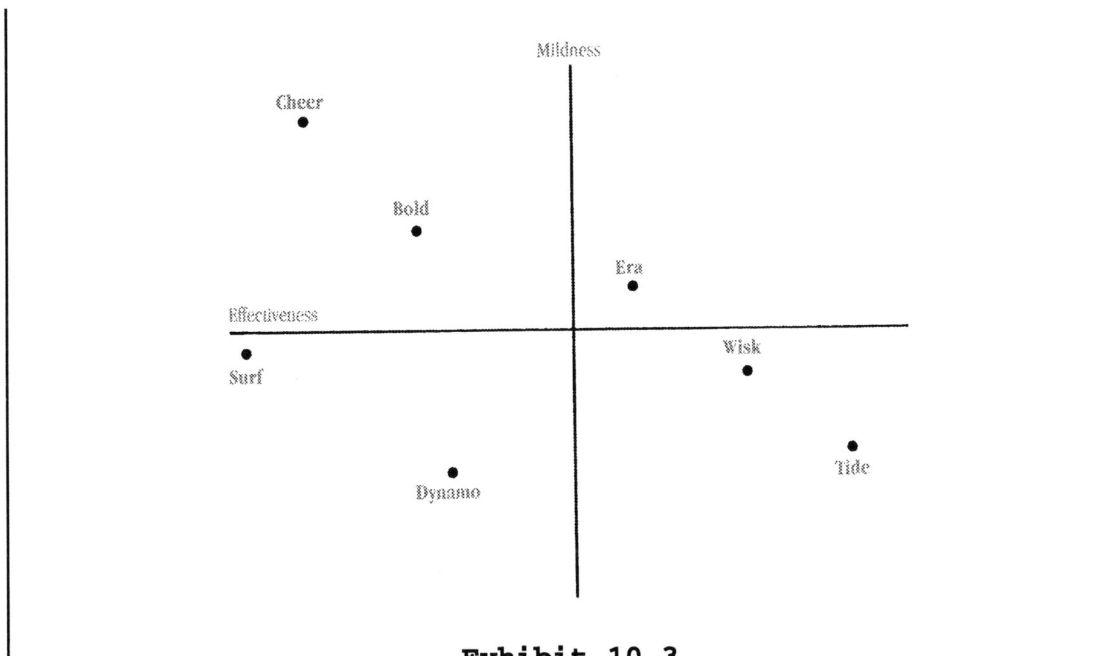

Exhibit 10.3
Hypothetical perceptual map of the liquid detergent market.

Relationships Analysis

Relationships-analysis techniques for stimulating creativity entail examining relationships that are normally not considered. In its simplest form, the researcher using relationships analysis creates a two-dimensional matrix, where the rows represent the possible values or levels of one physical dimension of the product, and the columns represent the values or levels of another physical characteristic of the product. For example, the rows of the matrix for household cleaners might be possible cleanser forms, and the columns might be particular cleansing ingredients, such as pine oil and ammonia (see Exhibit 10.4).[17] The cells of the matrix would define possible cleanser forms/cleanser ingredients products. Cells containing no existing brands are potential product opportunities. While relatively easy to use if two dimensions are examined, the number of possibilities explodes rapidly when more dimensions are considered.

Form	Special Cleaning Ingredient				
	Pine oil	Ammonia	Pumice	Bleach	. . .
Liquid					
Powder					
Gel					
Solid					
Disposable pad					
Spray					
. . .					

Exhibit 10.4
Relationship analysis matrix for household cleaners.

Another form of relationships analysis is analogy. **Analogy** is indirect, in that one seeks new product ideas for one context by examining a different but related phenomenon. Examining how fruits are naturally protected in their native environment can provide ideas for new packaging systems. One manufacturer developed a list of ideas for new kitchen furniture by examining how meals are served on airplanes.[18]

Scenario Analysis

The goal of a **scenario analysis** is to identify opportunities by capitalizing on projected future environments and associated consumer needs. Scenarios are constructed by forecasting the environment at some future date and potential product or service opportunities are identified by visualizing how consumers will perform tasks that current products are designed to help them do. Changes required in a particular product category to adapt to the future environment are identified, and products are redesigned or new ones created. Obviously, careful monitoring of consumer trends with respect to demographics, psychographics, lifestyle, and technology are very important in this context. Projections based on such trends play a vital role in the construction of future scenarios.

As an example of how scenario analysis may be applied, diminishing available liveable space has forced the Japanese to consider developing underground communities.[19] Artificial light will be used exclusively in such environments, making many current types of house plants impractical. A product opportunity exists for developing plants that can survive exclusively in artificial light, thus allowing consumers to enjoy the pleasures of house plants while living underground. This environment might also create the opportunity for a product, perhaps used in a clothes dryer, that freshens laundry just like leaving it out in the fresh air.

Scenario forecasting is not only useful for generating new product ideas. Companies use this approach to generally plan for the future. Companies first develop possible future scenarios by identifying major changes that could take place in the world. Next, they engage in planning exercises assuming these different future scenarios. These "practice" experiences helped Royal Dutch/Shell react quickly to major shocks to the petroleum industry including the OPEC boycott of 1973, the plunge in oil prices in the early 1980s and the collapse of the Soviet Union.[20]

One reason for the growth in popularity of scenario forecasting is the fact that changes occur so rapidly in today's business environment. In the early 1980s, California used steady standard demographic projection methods, based on birth and death rates, to forecast a gradual decrease in the number of children statewide. At the time, the state's population had apparently stabilized and the demand for primary schools was expected to decline. State education planners had not foreseen the huge wave of immigrants arriving from Asia and Latin America beginning in the mid-1980s. These immigrants included many young women with high fertility rates. Further, baby boom women delayed childbearing until later in life which altered the birth rates for various age groups. Today, contrary to predictions, new classrooms open regularly in California.

It is inappropriate to accuse the California education planners of failing to do their jobs. The planners had used standard, accepted methods for projecting the sizes of subgroup populations. What is important is to recognize that unexpected events do occur, and developing contingency plans is a valuable exercise. Marketing research, being the firm's primary source of external information, will likely play a critical role in the identification and analysis of possible future scenarios.

Group Creativity

Brainstorming involves assembling a group of knowledgeable participants and soliciting as many ideas as possible about a product or problem.[21] This technique is perhaps the most familiar group-creativity approach. Two basic principles of the brainstorming approach are: affirmative judgment, *i.e.*, avoiding negative reactions to ideas; and quantity breeds quality. However, brainstorming does not always work.[22] When sessions fail, disappointed participants generally find out that they have not followed the guidelines. Also, the group of participants should be chosen to include differing perspectives to maximize interaction.

Synectics, another popular group-creativity approach, is a more structured extension of brainstorming.[23] The word synectics comes from Greek and means "joining together of different and apparently irrelevant elements." Individuals with different backgrounds are integrated into problem-stating and problem-solving task groups.[24] Analogy is the key idea-generating vehicle, and various techniques are used to encourage speculation and deferral of judgment. The process involves making the strange familiar by drawing on known things to view problems in a different way. Also, new perspectives are developed by making the familiar strange, *i.e.*, changing the everyday way of looking at things. Synectics, Inc., specializes in the use of this approach and conducts new-product idea-generation sessions over several days, involving company personnel and heavy category users in the process.[25]

From Ideas to Concepts

Not all the ideas generated by the techniques described above will lead to successful products. It is necessary, therefore, to establish a method for eliminating losers and fine-tuning the winners. Some ideas are eliminated from further consideration without any primary consumer research -- **internal screening**. Others are found to have fatal flaws when tested among consumers.

Internal Screening

Internal screening has two stages. The informal stage involves management's initial reaction to the idea in terms of compatibility with existing products, capital requirements, or other factors. Ideas passing this initial stage are subjected to more formal market analyses and corresponding financial calculations in the second stage.

Table 10.1 contains a list of factors to be considered when a corporation is judging a new product idea. Market research aids in the initial screening by providing analyses that help to clarify some of these issues. For example, secondary data sources might be used to define the size of the market, projected growth, the competitive environment, and typical distribution channels.

Capital Investment Requirements

Distribution Channels

Product Development Time

Competitive Environment

Match with Corporate Culture/Personality

Corporate Resource Requirements

Market Size and Growth Projections

Potential Return on Investment

Projected Potential Share and Annual Sales Volume

Technological Challenge

Table 10.1
Internal Screening factors

Financial projections, based on market size and anticipated growth, weigh heavily in the decision to continue exploring an idea. By combining different projected market share or volume levels for a new product with capital investment requirements, anticipated product-development time, corporate-resource requirements, and roll-out strategy, managers can calculate expected return on investment. The return can be calculated for different scenarios, *e.g.*, various roll-out strategies and sales volumes.

Factors other than financial projections can be equally important. The technological challenge might be perceived to be too great, the amount of capital investment or resource requirements might be viewed as placing too much of a financial strain on the corporation, or the distribution channels might be foreign to the corporation. A new idea might also be rejected because the proposed product does not fit the corporation's culture or personality. Ben & Jerry's, which takes pride in its culture of social responsibility, would likely not attach its name to a product containing alcohol because of the social controversy surrounding such products.

Concepts

Before any attempt is made to collect primary consumer data, promising ideas must be turned into product concepts. A **concept** is a description of the proposed product or service consisting of attributes and benefits. The attributes describe the product or service while the benefits define what the consumer will gain from purchasing it. The concept statement positions the product idea relative to alternative products and provides a basis for obtaining consumer reaction. Applying Marketing Research 10.4 demonstrates statements that are concepts and statements that are not.

Applying Marketing Research 10.4

Consider the following statement:

A new detergent containing iodine. This statement is not a product concept because no consumer benefit is presented. Only a particular attribute is mentioned in the statement. No reason is given for the consumer to purchase the detergent. On the other hand, the following statement is a product concept:

A new powder detergent with iodine provides the cleaning power you expect from a powder detergent with the safe germ-killing power of iodine to make sure that your laundry is germ-free.

Iodine is the ingredient (product attribute) that provides the germ-killing benefit.

Developing a concept statement from an idea is not a trivial task. Care must be exercised to ensure that the concept communicates the intended message to the consumer before any consumer research to assess the concept's potential is initiated. Technical jargonese must be avoided; familiar wording must be used. The somewhat far-fetched example in Applying Marketing Research 10.5 helps dramatize this point.

Applying Marketing Research 10.5

A new spray cleaner has been developed that contains powerful emulsifiers to provide more vertical hangup than you imagined possible.

The term emulsifiers is very familiar to product development engineers, as is the phenomenon of vertical hangup, which refers to how the liquid clings to a surface when applied. However, most consumers would have a hard time understanding this proposed concept statement.

It would be a waste of money to conduct formal research among several hundred potential users to determine the appeal of a product concept only to discover that the concept has basic fatal flaws or that consumers misunderstood a key feature. For this reason, focus groups or depth interviews play a valuable role in investigating the message delivered by a concept statement. Several alternative ways of expressing a concept can be explored among potential users of the product or service to determine how best to both structure and phrase the concept. Refining complex concept statements is often an iterative process involving several waves of qualitative research, sometimes referred to as **concept optimization.**

Testing Concepts

Once a concept statement has been refined and polished to the point where it communicates the prospective new product or service effectively and accurately, it should be tested among consumers. Concept testing should provide a quantitative assessment of sales potential and should include a measure of purchase interest. Hence, it is important that price be part of the statement since, without knowing the price, consumers cannot provide a valid indicator of purchase intent. In fact, the issue of price sensitivity might be explored by testing several versions of the concept statement, each having a different price.

Multiple Concepts

If a large number of new product ideas have been developed into concept statements, consumer input would be valuable to separate the most promising candidates from the duds based on their consumer appeal. However, attempting to obtain an extensive in-depth consumer evaluation of each concept would be very expensive. A screening mechanism, such as the one described in the example below, is an appropriate method for quickly and inexpensively evaluating a multitude of concepts.

Applying Marketing Research 10.6

A sample of 400 consumers are recruited via mall intercept, and each is asked to examine ten new product concepts. Participants are asked to divide the ten concepts into two groups--appealing *vs.* unappealing. Next, they are asked to express their purchase interest in the concepts they found appealing using the typical purchase intent category rating scale (see Exhibit 10.5).

Each participant is also asked to identify the concept most appealing to him or her and to describe why the concept is so appealing. Participants are also asked to note briefly what they do not like about the concepts they find unappealing.

DEFINITELY WOULD BUY
PROBABLY WOULD BUY
MIGHT OR MIGHT NOT BUY
PROBABLY WOULD NOT BUY
DEFINITELY WOULD NOT BUY

Exhibit 10.5
Typical 5-point purchase intent scale.

An approach such as the one described in Applying Marketing Research 10.6 provides an inexpensive method for establishing a hierarchy of tested concepts based on consumer appeal. The concepts are first separated on the basis of the percentage of times each was classified as appealing. Those concepts scoring relatively high on appeal are further separated based on the purchase intention results and the percentage of times each was voted most appealing. The reasons participants found some concepts relatively unappealing can serve as diagnostic information by which to modify these concepts, if such modifications are possible. By integrating these findings with financial data, such as potential return on investment, corporate management can determine which options are most attractive and hence worthy of further, more quantitative, testing.

In-Depth Concept Evaluation

For an in-depth concept evaluation, a sample of potential users of the new product or service concept are recruited, exposed to the concept, and interviewed. In-depth concept evaluations require a sample size that is large enough to permit investigation and description of the segment of the sample to whom the concept most appeals. Therefore, the number of people exposed to the concept should be large enough to provide at least fifty potential purchasers, *i.e.*, respondents favorably inclined toward the concept. Previous experience with such tests can provide some guidelines regarding the total sample size required to achieve this objective. For example, if previous experience suggests that 20 percent to 40 percent of a sample are typically found to be potential buyers of new concepts, then a sample size of 250 should provide at least fifty potential buyers.

Table 10.2 shows the flow of an interview that might be used to research the consumer appeal of a concept. The interview includes questions pertaining to: purchase intent and associated reasons, general likes/dislikes about the concept, key attribute ratings, perceived uniqueness, current brands used in the category (if applicable), amount of category usage (if applicable), perceptions regarding which products or services would be displaced, and demographics.

Exposure to concept including price
Purchase interest rating on category scale
Reasons for purchase interest or lack of purchase interest
Likes and dislikes regarding concept
Rating of concept on key attributes
Perceptions of uniqueness/brands or products perceived similar to
Consumption rate for product category and brands or products used
Demographics (age, income, marital status, etc.)

Table 10.2
Concept-test interview format

The research approach just described uses only a simple category rating scale to measure purchase intent. Companies frequently use the "top box" percentage (the percentage of participants saying they definitely would buy) or the "top two box" percentage (the percentage of participants saying they definitely or probably would buy) to measure purchase interest. However, purchase-intent rating-scale data tend to overstate actual behaviors, because respondents often say that they would buy the product when in fact they would not. Therefore, the purchase interest measure is difficult to interpret by itself. Without any other information, management has no idea what sales to expect if 10 percent of the respondents say they "definitely would buy" and another 15 percent say they "probably would buy." Unless they have a benchmark or a point of reference, managers cannot adequately interpret the measure of overall purchase intent and are forced to rely on gut feel to determine the viability of a concept.

Fortunately, results for previously tested concepts that progressed further through the product development process can provide benchmarks or points of reference. For example, concept test results for those concepts that were actually developed but that failed at the product-testing stage and results corresponding to successful new-product entries can provide points of reference for current research. Concept test results comparable to the latter are encouraging, while results comparable to the former might be cause to abandon a project. Sometimes, a norm (*e.g.*, average score) developed from the history of concept tests serves as a benchmark. As a rule of thumb, managers frequently require concept-test results to be above the norm before continuing a project.

In an attempt to obtain better predictors of actual marketplace results than purchase-intent ratings, behavioral measures are often obtained. Participants in a concept test may be offered their choice of a discount coupon toward the purchase of the new product or the comparable amount of cash to measure purchase commitment. Those choosing the coupon are arguably more committed to purchasing the new product. The percentage choosing the coupon is therefore a more valid[26] indicator of market potential than the percentage merely saying they definitely or probably would buy the product, but is still far from an accurate predictor of actual behavior. Benchmarks, or norms, are still required to interpret these measures.

The demographic and behavioral characteristics of potential buyers should be examined when concepts are tested since these data shed light on to whom the product appeals and help determine the appropriate media strategies. Questions regarding brands currently used within the product category and category usage rates are also vital for uncovering potential problems with the concept. A concept that appeals primarily to light users of the category of good or cannibalizes an existing brand's business is not an attractive proposition. For instance, General Foods' Maxwell House Coffee Division would be hesitant to develop a new coffee product if they found that the concept appeals primarily to non-coffee drinkers who buy coffee only to serve to guests. Similarly, Procter & Gamble would not develop a new deodorant bar soap if the concept appealed primarily to users of their Safeguard brand.

The decision to begin the actual development of a new product or service and its subsequent introduction into the marketplace involves a tremendous commitment of corporate resources. Equipment, space, and personnel must be allocated to continue with the project. To make an intelligent choice to proceed or to discontinue the development of a concept, management must have information about the volume of sales that can be expected so that the potential profit or return on investment can be estimated. Purchase interest or the data collected in an in-depth concept evaluation do not adequately address the question of sales volume or return on investment. There are, however, research systems, such as BASES and ASSESSOR, that do.

BASES I

BASES, a service offered by BBI Marketing Services, Inc., is a system designed to provide sales-volume estimates at various stages in the new product introduction process. **BASES I**, described in Exhibit 10.5, is the first component in this system and provides year one and trial sales volume estimates for new product concepts. To estimate sales volume, BASES I uses managerial input regarding the introductory marketing strategy that will be used, product category information, and consumer data to estimate purchase intention.

How does BASES work at each succeeding stage?

BASES I—THE CONCEPT TEST STAGE

BASES I provides you with an accurate estimate of Year I trial sales, plus the opportunity to simulate Year I sales volume potential.

BASES I requires no finished product or packaging, just a simple concept board. The product doesn't even need a finalized brand name.

Methodology: Using 3 or more geographically dispersed shopping malls, BASES exposes a concept board to 240 to 300 shoppers. Because BASES estimates volume, not share, the shoppers are not usually screened for prior category useage. But in some cases—denture users for denture products, or pet ownership for pet foods, for example—certain pre-conditions must be met. In these cases screening is obviously necessary.

The concept board used in BASES I shows a rough or finished package, a product description, unit price and size information.

BASES I gives you the kind of information you've come to expect from a traditional concept test.

BASES' extra dimension is that we apply empirically derived learning to adjust each point of the 5-point purchase intent scale for over and under-statement in estimating trial potential.

Next BASES marries this initial estimate to the client's assumptions of distribution build, media plans (or assumed awareness level) and trade and consumer promotion plans. This "marriage" of BASES learning, consumer behavior data and client's marketing plan assumptions produces an accurate estimate of Year I trial rate potential.

Finally, BASES uses its own considerable experience and client inputs to develop assumptions for reasonable levels of repeat purchasing, purchase cycle and average repeat purchase units. These assumptions, the trial rate estimate and appropriate seasonal and category sales development indices are entered into the BASES model. In some cases brand development indices will be entered, too.

The output provides a simulation of Year I sales volume potential.

Result: BASES I translates concept test data into an accurate estimate of Year I trial rate potential and a simulation of Year I sales volume. So you can identify potentially profitable ideas—or obvious losers—right at the concept test stage.

Exhibit 10.6
Description of the BASES 1 System. (Source: The BASES Group.)

Required managerial input includes the distribution level that the concept will achieve during the first year, the planned advertising budget, and the spending pattern for these advertising expenditures. These three factors have an impact upon availability and consumer awareness for the new product, important factors in estimating the rate at which consumer trial of the product is obtained. A product that is widely distributed will generate higher trial and year one sales than one that is distributed in only limited areas. Consumer awareness, a prerequisite for trial, depends heavily not only on the size of the new product's advertising budget but also on how these dollars are spent. A campaign in which a large amount of the advertising budget is spent early in the introductory period will result in consumer trial building more rapidly than will a campaign in which promotional dollars are spread out over the introduction. Hence, post-trial year one sales would be higher in the former case than in the latter.

Information about product category purchasing is also needed to develop estimates of year one sales volume. The company sponsoring the research will likely have data regarding the frequency at which the product category is typically purchased by individuals or households as well as any seasonality effects. However, consumers are also questioned directly about purchase frequency to provide a point of comparison for managerial input on this issue.

In a **BASES** I study, a primary survey of 300 consumers is conducted to provide information on the likelihood that consumers will purchase the product. To estimate this purchase intent, participants in the consumer survey are shown a concept board, containing the concept description, like the one shown in Exhibit 10.7. The concept description contains information on both the product price and quantity offered. Respondents indicate their purchase intent, using the traditional five-point purchase intent scale, and also answer questions regarding frequency of use of existing brands in the category, brands currently used, and other diagnostic questions about the concept.

Introducing the sore throat gargle that blocks the nerve that carries sore throat pain

The ninth cranial nerve. That's what doctors call the telegraph line that carries sore throat pain to your brain. You need it to tell you something's wrong. Once. But you don't need a constant reminder.

That's why there's Product R Sore Throat Gargle. Product R acts as an anesthetic, so it actually helps block the pain impulses. while you get fast pain relief, you also get antiseptic action. Remember, Product R gets to the nerve of sore throat pain, fast.

PRODUCT
R
SORE THROAT GARGLE
• ANESTHETIC
• ANTISEPTIC
FOR RAPID RELIEF OF MINOR
THROAT AND MOUTH SORENESS
8 FL. OZ.

UNIT PRICE = $1.89
AVERAGE DOSES PER BOTTLE = 16

PRODUCT R BLOCKS THE NERVE THAT CARRIES SORE THROAT PAIN.

Exhibit 10.7
An example of a hypothetical BASES 1 concept board. (Source: The BASES Group.)

As has already been mentioned, five-point purchase intention measures do not accurately reflect true purchase levels. The key to the BASES system is the conversion of these purchase intent ratings into more realistic purchase rates. BASES uses a large data base of previous concept test results to estimate the actual purchase levels that are likely to occur given the observed purchase intent ratings.

M/A/R/C Macro Market Modeling System Phase I

M/A/R/C, Inc., offers the Macro Marketing Modeling System, which is similar to BASES in that it is designed to evaluate new products from the concept stage through the market introduction. Phase I of the system is designed to provide concept guidance and is particularly useful when considering several concepts for further development. Consumers provide data regarding their purchase behavior in the general category as well as their brand preferences and then are exposed to one of the concepts under consideration. After evaluating this single concept, several concepts are evaluated relative to one another, including the one just evaluated by itself.

For each concept, Phase I of M/A/R/C's system provides information on: trial potential, strength of concept appeal relative to the individuals' relevant sets of brands, demographic and behavioral profiles of consumers expressing interest, general estimates of sales potential, and how the concept ranks against the others with respect to intensity of appeal. The ranking of each concept helps establish development priorities.

Summary

Companies are constantly seeking ideas for new products and services because they are crucial to sustaining corporate growth. These ideas come from many sources, including consumers themselves. A number of programmed approaches focus on identifying ideas for new products or services. These can be organized into five basic categories: attribute analysis, need assessment, relationships analysis, scenario analysis, and group creativity.

New ideas must pass an internal screening process. Management may dismiss ideas at this point for numerous reasons, including incompatibility with existing offerings, excessive capital investment requirements, or distribution channels that are foreign to the company. Ideas that receive approval for further consideration are molded into concepts to be tested among consumers. Concepts describe ideas for new products or services using both attributes and benefits. Concept optimization, in the form of qualitative marketing research, is frequently used to refine a concept statement. The goal is to develop a concept statement that effectively communicates the idea.

Optimized concepts are subjected to quantitative marketing research to assess consumer appeal. The concept statement tested should include the price so consumers can somewhat realistically decide how interested they would be in purchasing the new product or service. It is very important that concept tests have benchmarks or points of reference. Norms--historical average results -- often serve this purpose. Some commercially-available concept testing systems, such as BASES I, use historical data, marketing management input, and current test results in a mathematical model to predict financial results. Such systems are particularly attractive because they provide managers with a financial basis for evaluating a new product concept.

In some situations quantitative concept tests are inappropriate because formal consumer assessment is impossible. Consumers are reacting only to the description of a product or service, and verbally conveying some benefits is impossible. For example, how can consumers be made to appreciate the clarity of sound produced from a compact disc player or the crispness of the picture obtained with a high resolution television without actually experiencing it? Clearly, the decision to embark on developing these new technologies could not have been based solely on the results of consumer concept tests. Similarly, how can one adequately assess a screenplay, play, or symphony using a concept test? The emotions and feelings stirred by these forms of entertainment would have to be experienced to be evaluated.

In situations where it is totally unrealistic to assess consumer demand or appeal for a new concept quantitatively, concept testing can still be very valuable. Concept optimization is still appropriate, but subsequent concept testing should focus on exploring the concept with consumers rather than seeking to quantify its appeal. The objectives of the concept tests should be to identify consumer concerns, potential barriers to purchase, price expectations, particular likes and dislikes about the idea, perceived uniqueness, and alternatives. These results can be used to guide the design and development of the product or service rather than to make a go/no go decision.

Key Terms

analogy

attribute analysis

BASES I

benefit structure analysis

brainstorming

checklist

concept

concept optimization

dimensional analysis

gap analysis

internal screening

Kelly repertory grid

need-assessment techniques

problem analysis

problem inventory analysis

relationships analysis

scenario analysis

synectics

Concept Testing at Nimslo

The Nimslo three-dimensional photography system is an example of a product for which using concept testing to quantify consumer appeal is very tenuous at best. On the surface, it seems easy to describe the concept--an easy-to-operate, lightweight, look-and-shoot 35 mm camera that uses ordinary 35 mm color film and produces negatives that can be used to print photographs that appear three-dimensional to the naked eye. However, people's experiences with 3D include movies requiring special glasses, pictures that when moved give the impression of three dimensions, holograms (3D images produced by special laser/lighting technology), and the like. What would the phrase "3D to the naked eye" conjure in consumers' minds? Could the 3D pictures produced by the Nimslo system really be communicated without actually showing sample prints?

Consequently, concept testing of the Nimslo system was qualitative in nature. Focus groups were conducted, and participants were questioned regarding concerns about the system. Participants

Participants were also asked what they would expect such pictures to cost and what they would be willing to pay. They were also questioned regarding current picture-taking practices and how the Nimslo camera might fit into these activities.

The research revealed consumer doubt over the ability of the system to produce high-quality three-dimensional photos and concern over the price of the pictures. Nimslo management became acutely aware of the need to include thorough instructional materials with each camera sold to make the first picture-taking experiences positive ones and thus quickly alleviate critical consumer concerns.

Review Questions

10.1 Give examples of four new products or services and describe the trends that your feel led to them.

10.2 What are two attribute analysis techniques for generating new product ideas? How might the Kelly repertory grid be of value in this context?

10.3 Describe the four types of need assessment idea generation techniques.

10.4 Give an example of how relationships analysis could be used to generate new-product ideas. Give an example for new services.

10.5 Describe how marketing research input aids in scenario analysis.

10.6 What are the fundamental principles of brainstorming?

10.7 What makes synectics different from brainstorming?

10.8 What is meant by internal screening of new-product ideas? Give an example.

10.9 What is a concept? Give an example.

10.10 Why is it so important to test concepts?

10.11 What is meant by concept optimization? What types of marketing research are useful in this context?

10.12 What is meant by a behavioral, as opposed to an attitudinal, approach to measuring purchase intent? Which is more valid? Why?

10.13 Describe BASES I. What are the advantages of systems like the BASES I approach to concept testing? What is a disadvantage?

Discussion Questions

10.1 Why is it sometimes basically impossible to quantify the consumer appeal of a product or service concept? Give examples of such services and products, and discuss the value of concept testing in such situations.

10.2 Discuss the following statement:

Given that concept test purchase intention measures, behavioral or otherwise, have very little value as predictors of actual marketplace behavior, why bother with concept testing at all?

Include in your discussion the use of reference points or benchmarks to which concept test purchase intention measures can be compared.

10.3 Discuss the role of the corporate market research group in the process of identifying and screening new-product ideas.

Chapter 10 Endnotes

Endnotes

1. See "AMA to Honor Top New-Product Marketers," *Marketing News*, January 30, 1989, p. 5.

2. Judann Dagnoli, "Nabisco Entries Get $100M Blitz," *Advertising Age*, September 11, 1989, p. 3.

3. 1995 Edison Best New Products Awards Winners, supplement to the May 6, 1996 issue of *Marketing News*.

4. See "A Bill to Sweeten Cyclamate Losses," *Business Week*, March 25, 1972, p. 66, and "Cyclamates' Sour Aftertaste," *Time*, October 31, 1969, p. 79.

5. See Gene Bylinsky, "The Battle for America's Sweet Tooth," *Fortune*, July 26, 1982, pp. 28-32.

6. See "Whatever Happened to....Grain to Fuel Cars," *U.S. News & World Report*, April 12, 1976, p. 86.

7. See C. Merle Crawford, *New Products Management*, 3rd ed. Homewood, IL: Richard D. Irwin, Inc., 1991, pp. 94-145, for a thorough discussion of these categories of techniques.

8. See B.B. Goldner, *The Strategy of Creative Thinking*, Englewood Cliffs, NJ: Prentice-Hall, 1962; or J.H. McPherson and D.A. Guidici, *Advances in Innovative Management*, Palo Alto, CA: Stanford Research Institute, 1978, for discussions and examples.

9. See, for example, Marvin Small, *How to Make More Money*,

New York: Pocket Books, 1959; Alex F. Osborn, *Applied Imagination*, 3rd ed., New York: Charles Scribner's Sons, 1963; George J. Abrams, *How I Made a Million Dollars with Ideas*, Chicago: Playboy Press, 1972; and D.W. Karger and R.G. Murdick, *Managing Engineering and Research*, New York: Industrial Press, 1963.

10. See, for example, Paul E. Green, Donald S. Tull, and Gerald Albaum, *Research for Marketing Decisions*, 5th ed., Englewood Cliffs, NJ: Prentice-Hall, 1988, pp. 712-713.

11. See C. Merle Crawford, *New Products Development*, 3rd ed., Homewood, IL: Richard D. Irwin, Inc., 1991, p. 97.

12. See Claes Fornell and Robert D. Menko, "Problem Analysis--A Consumer-Based Methodology for the Discovery of New Product Ideas," *European Journal of Marketing* 15, 5 (1981), pp. 61-72.

13. C. Merle Crawford, *New Products Development*, Homewood, IL: Richard D. Irwin, Inc., 1983, p. 248.

14. Edward M. Tauber, "Discovering New Product Opportunities with Problem Inventory Analysis," *Journal of Marketing* 39 (January 1975), pp. 67-70.

15. James H. Myers, "Benefit Structure Analysis: A New Tool for Product Planning," *Journal of Marketing* 40 (October 1976), pp. 23-32.

16. Susan Caminiti, A Star Is Born, Fortune, November 29, 1993, pp. 44-47

17. See C.L. Alford and J.B. Mason, "Generating New Product Ideas," *Journal of Advertising Research*, (December 1975), pp. 27-32, for a discussion of new household cleaning product ideas using six dimensions.

18. C. Merle Crawford, *New Products Development*, 3rd ed., Homewood, IL: Richard D. Irwin, Inc., 1991, p. 140.

19. See Seiichi Kanise, "Japan's Underground Frontier," *Time*, February 6, 1989, p. 74.

20 See Dan Frost, "How to Think About the Future," *American Demographics*, February, 1998, pp. 6-11, for a discussion of the use and value of scenario forecasting.

21. See Alex F. Osborn, *Applied Imagination: Principles and Procedures of Creative Thinking*, New York: Charles Scribners'

Sons, 1953.

22. See Morris I. Stein, *Stimulating Creativity*, Vol. 2. New York: Academic Press, Harcourt Brace Jovanovich, 1975, for a good summary of how brainstorming has worked, when it has not worked, and what techniques have been developed for increasing effectiveness of the approach.

23. See W.J.J. Gordon, *Synectics, the Development of Creative Capacity*. New York: Harper and Row, 1961, for a thorough treatment of synectics.

24. See Peter Sampson, "Can Consumers Create New Products?" *Journal of the Market Research Society* 12, 1 (1975), pp. 40-53, for a brief discussion of synectics.

25. See, for example, G. M. Prince, *The Practice of Creativity*, New York: Harper & Row, 1970, for an in-depth discussion of synectics.

26. See Neil Bruce Holbert, Robert J. Golden and Mark M. Chudnoff, *Marketing Research for the Marketing and Advertising Executive*. New York: American Marketing Association, 1981, pp. 120-121, for a discussion of this issue.

Chapter 11

Product Testing

Learning Objectives:

After reading this chapter you should be able to:

- explain the importance of testing products and services before attempting to market them.
- describe the relative advantages and disadvantages of central-location *vs.* home-use testing.
- compare and contrast the various types of home-use product tests.
- present and discuss critical issues associated with designing home-use tests.
- discuss multiple-product tests.

The redesigned Ford F-150 pickup truck has been a tremendous success for the company. When they redesigned the F-150, they not only altered dramatically changed its appearance, they the new car development process. Instead of carefully examining rivals' successful cars to determine features critical to success, Ford relied primarily on consumer research to redesign the F-150 pickup.[1]

Ford identified six distinct generations in the U.S. population. These groups differed in their values because of their experiences growing up, as well as those of their parents which had an indirect effect. One of these generations was the "Baby Boomers" (born between 1946 and 1964). Baby Boomers comprise the first television generation and seek immediate gratification. Ford targeted this generation with the F-150 because of its large size and the fact that a relatively high percentage of Baby Boomers purchased minivans and sport-utility vehicles.

Research among Baby Boomers indicated that any attempt to communicate power by designing the F-150 to look like a big rig would be unsuccessful. The group was very fitness conscious and equated power

with sleekness. Consequently, Ford narrowed the cab by two inches, lengthened it by five inches, and gave the exterior a more rounded look than before (see Exhibit 11.1).

Product tests, involving target consumers examining the cabs and simulating driving, helped provide insight regarding the interior design and instrumentation. Test drives by target consumers led to increases in wheel size and a new tire tread design to improve the ride. Also, research among target consumers led to a six-seater version of the F-150.

Exhibit 11.1
Ford F-150 Pick-up.

Brands have tangible and intangible properties. The tangible properties refer to the product itself and what function it is designed to perform. The intangible side has to do with communications regarding the brand and the image it portrays. Sometimes an uninteresting, poorly performing brand can be given new life by only changing the communication about the brand and thus altering its image. Altoids (Exhibit 11.2), the "curiously strong" peppermint, had a small following primarily in the Seattle area of the United States. Shortly after the brand was acquired by Kraft Foods, a division of the Philip Morris Company, it was assigned to the Leo Burnett advertising agency. Research indicated that users of Altoids were young, active and on-the-go, and therefore difficult to reach with conventional media.[2] Leo Burnett devised zany and creative outdoor advertising to reach the target audience and to promote the brands' mystique. One billboard showed a figure in a space suit with only the word Altoids as accompanying text. Another outdoor ad showed a well-developed male body builder flexing and holding a package of Altoids in his hands accompanied by the phrase "Nice Altoids." The text further referred to Altoids as extra strength mints. The advertising and promotional efforts gave the brand a huge lift and its share has grown dramatically.[3] Hence, it is important not to underestimate the power of the intangible side of a brand.

Exhibit 11.2
Altoids.

In this chapter, however, we will focus attention on the tangible side of a product and marketing research methods for developing the product itself, devoid of its imagery created primarily by marketing communications including advertising. Image and related research are discussed in Chapter 12 (Segmentation and Positioning), Chapter 13 (The Name, the Package, and the Price), Chapter 15 (Advertising Research) and Chapter 18 (Market Monitoring). This tangible or functional side of a product is just as important as its intangible side. A product which does not perform up to consumer expectations, that is, does not do what it is supposed to do or has unappealing physical characteristics, will have a short life span. As noted in the introductory example, Ford made extensive use of physical product testing to successfully redesign the F-150 pickup.

The Product-Testing Process

Product prototypes are developed from ideas that pass the internal screening process and show promise in the concept-testing stage. The prototypes are typically subjected to an iterative consumer-testing process where, at each stage in the process, refinements are made in the product based on the previous research findings and these changes are evaluated in subsequent consumer research. Proposed changes in existing brands usually follow this same procedure.

In this chapter, we will discuss product testing. Do not be misled by the use of the term *product* in product testing. Although the bulk of such testing is conducted with consumer packaged goods, many of these research techniques are equally applicable to consumer durables or services. As indicated in Applying Marketing Research 11.1, product testing is even used to test alternative versions of movies.[4]

Applying Marketing Research 11.1

In one version of the movie "Fatal Attraction," the jilted lover, Alex (Glenn Close), commits suicide, but makes it appear as though the cheating husband (Michael Douglas) murdered her. However, audiences who previewed this version did not like the ending, so the movie ultimately released to the public ends differently. Alex's deranged behavior toward her ex-lover and his family ends when she is killed by her one-time lover's wife.

Similarly, test screenings of the baseball movie "Major League" revealed that the intended ending was not believable to audiences, so changes were made. The "confession" scene, in which the ruthless owner, who had done everything in her power to disrupt the team throughout the movie, claims that her ulterior motive was to unify and motivate them, was removed and replaced with one more consistent with her character.

Product testing provides a critical measure of a new product's consumer acceptance. Also, before making changes in existing brands, proposed changes are tested among consumers to assess acceptance using the same techniques applied to new products.

Many a marketing manager has been disappointed when product improvements noticeable in highly controlled laboratory tests are not appreciated by consumers in the marketplace. Product testing can prevent this from happening. The following list demonstrates the variety of questions that can be addressed by product testing:

- Can Nutrasweet in diet Coke be replaced by a new, less expensive artificial sweetener without consumers tasting the difference?

- Are the technical improvements in Wisk liquid laundry detergent suggested by product development engineers noticeable to consumers?
- Should Procter & Gamble invest in an improved adhesive for the fastening tape on its Pampers brand of disposable diapers?
- Which of two new loan application forms is preferred by Citibank customers?
- How many people can tell the difference between a store-brand orange juice and Minute Maid?
- Which of two perfumes should be used in a new antiperspirant product being developed by Gillette?
- Can McDonald's find a cholesterol-free cooking oil that does not change the taste of their french fries?

There is no question that product testing can be lengthy and expensive. Testing may keep a company's product out of the marketplace for months, or even years, while expenses accumulate for production of prototype products tested by consumers and for the research conducted to evaluate the performance of these prototypes. A company developing an innovative disposable diaper may have to make products by hand during the testing phase, but these costs are far lower than the costs of introducing a new-product failure. Before a company commits to developing even a pilot manufacturing facility for a new product, the product must show enough promise to warrant the investment.

The typical scenario for product testing is that product prototypes are evaluated by consumers, refined on the basis of these evaluations, and then evaluated by consumers again. This iterative process continues until either a product prototype is developed that meets the project requirements with respect to consumer acceptance, or no further refinements are possible. Throughout the process **blind testing** of products is conducted in which only generic packaging, involving no brand name, graphics, or promotional material, is typically used. Blind testing forces consumers to evaluate the product itself, divorced from the other elements of the marketing mix.[5] Exhibit 11.3 shows examples of blind test products.

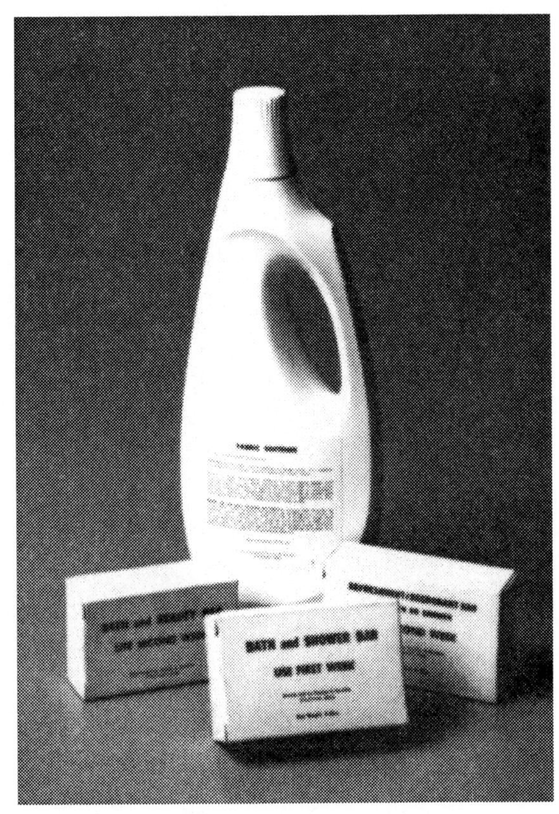

Exhibit 11.3

The use of blind testing format ensures that consumers do not use packaging or branding cues to evaluate test products.

Product tests are most commonly conducted in either a central location, such as a mall, or a home-use environment, such as the home. We will examine the pros and cons of central-location and home-use product tests and discuss specific applications of each in the following sections.

Central-Location Product Testing

As described in Chapter 6, **central-location tests**, sometimes referred to as spot tests, are conducted among consumers at a designated facility such as a shopping mall. Participants typically are recruited while in a mall to take part in a product test, such as a taste test of a new soft drink. Alternatively, consumers can be recruited, usually by telephone, to come to a central location to participate in a research project.

While not as realistic as tests conducted in a home-use environment, central-location tests can be very useful for determining whether consumers can discriminate (notice the difference) between alternative products. In this context, these tests might be used to assess whether a proposed product change will go unnoticed by current users. Central location tests also provide an economical vehicle for reducing a large number of alternatives, for example, potential flavors for a new salty snack item, down to a few generally preferred options to be tested in the more realistic home-use format. In addition, central-location tests can also provide a measure of consumer preference used to support an advertising claim. Applying Marketing Research 11.2 contains examples of central location tests used in an advertising claim dispute.

Applying Marketing Research 11.2

The Coca-Cola Company aired comparative advertising that claimed people preferred the taste of Sprite over the taste of 7Up. To support the claim for network clearance, paired comparison taste tests between Sprite and 7Up were conducted in ten cities. In each market 100 regular sugar soft drink users participated. Mall intercepts were used to select respondents.

Each respondent first drank one product and was questioned about the product, then drank the second product and was asked the same questions. Next, the respondent tasted both products again and stated his or her overall preference between the two brands. The results indicated that 49% of the respondents preferred Sprite, 41% preferred 7Up, and 10% had no preference. The difference between the two percentages was statistically significant at the 1% risk level.

The 7Up Company commissioned research to challenge the accuracy of the Sprite advertising claim. Twelve hundred mall-intercept interviews were conducted across twelve geographically dispersed markets. Respondents were persons six years of age or older who routinely consumed at least one carbonated soft drink in a two-week period. A standard discrimination test (triangle difference) was administered to each respondent to determine what percentage of consumers could discriminate between the taste of 7Up and Sprite. Each respondent who was able to discriminate was then asked which of the unmarked samples was preferred. The results of these tests are shown in Table 11.1.

	Lemon-Lime Users	Total Soft Drink Users	Age	
			Children 6-17	Adults 18+
No Discrimination	53%	54%	52%	54%
Preference - Sprite	24.5%	24.5%	28.5%	23.5%
Preference - 7Up	22.5%	21.5%	19.5%	22.5%
Base size	1089	1200	240	960

Table 11.1

Results of 7-Up research

Based upon their findings, the 7Up Company argued before the National Advertising Division (NAD) of the Better Business Bureau that the majority of respondents in any selected group could not discriminate between Sprite and 7Up. Furthermore, among those carbonated soft drink users (as well as lemon-lime users) who could discriminate, there was no significant preference. Therefore, the 7Up Company claimed that the Sprite advertising claim should not be allowed.

Adjusting for correct guessing among discriminators in the 7Up study presents a different picture as we will show later in this chapter. The adjusted results agree with the Coca-Cola preference test results. The NAD rejected the 7Up argument and allowed the Sprite advertising to continue.

Discrimination Testing

Discrimination tests are conducted to determine the percentage of consumers who can detect a difference between product alternatives.[6] Central-location testing is particularly appropriate for this type of research. The most common discrimination tests involve tasting foods and beverages, although discrimination testing of scents, textures, or colors is also possible.

Applying Marketing Research 11.3

In selecting carpet, consumers usually rely on swatches of carpet viewed at the retail store. However, slight variations in color can be produced from one production run to another, depending upon how long the carpet remains in the dyeing vat, minute differences in the absorption rate of different fibers, temperature, and a host of other factors. Although sophisticated spectrometers can be used to detect even the slightest color variations, consumer research is used to determine the degree of color difference required to be "consumer noticeable." The results of discrimination tests focused on this issue are used to determine quality-control standards for manufacturing.

Discrimination research is often conducted for product reformulation decisions that arise when a company is considering changing one or more of the ingredients of a product, or changing how a product is made. Sometimes product reformulation becomes necessary because safety concerns about an ingredient, such as the banned artificial sweetener saccharin, mandate that its use be discontinued, or because the availability of a particular ingredient becomes limited making it prohibitively expensive. At other times, changes may be initiated by the manufacturer to reduce cost and hence increase profit. In such situations, a company wishes to make the change without any fanfare, and the main question is whether current users can detect the change, and if so, what percentage of the consumer franchise is at risk. The first part of this question can be addressed by discrimination testing among users of the brand; the second by assessing how discriminating users feel about the ingredient change.

Another application of discrimination testing is to assess product parity. For example, a company might be interested in introducing a low-priced entry in a product category. Store brands found in supermarkets are examples of this strategy. One question to be addressed is simply what percentage of category users can tell the difference between the proposed entry and market leaders. Generally speaking, the lower the discrimination, the better the chances for the new product to capture business from the market leaders.

Methods of Testing Discrimination

Numerous test techniques exist for determining the percentage of respondents who can notice the difference between two distinct product alternatives. The key to analyzing such test results is to reduce the number of correct respondents by a factor that accounts for those who guessed correctly. We next demonstrate these calculations in the context of two commonly used types of discrimination tests, the duo-trio and the triangle difference test.

Duo-Trio Tests. In the **duo-trio test**, participants are asked to identify which of the first two stimuli received (*e.g.*, soft drinks to taste) is identical to a third. The research design is balanced so that each of the two stimuli being tested is presented as the "odd," or third, stimulus half of the time. Further, the order of presentation of the first two stimuli is rotated (alternated) across participants. Balancing and rotating the order of presentation help prevent biasing the results in any way.

When analyzing the data obtained in a duo-trio test, those participants who are incorrect in identifying which of the two initial stimuli is the same as the third are obviously nondiscriminators. However, an adjustment must be made to the number of participants who are correct to account for guessing. Since only two initial stimuli are presented, a nondiscriminator has a 50-50 chance of being correct simply by guessing. Therefore, for every nondiscriminator who guessed incorrectly, one guessed correctly. Applying Marketing Research 11.4 illustrates how adjustments for guessing are made in a duo-trio test.

Applying Marketing Research 11.4

Suppose that a duo-trio test of diet Coke *vs*. Diet Pepsi is conducted among 500 adult users of diet colas. Of the 500 participants, suppose that 400, or 80 percent, correctly identify the third product sample, and 100, or 20 percent, are incorrect. Since the number of nondiscriminators who guess correctly is about the same as the number who guess incorrectly, about 100 of the 400 participants who are correct are actually nondiscriminators. The adjusted estimate of the percentage of true discriminators is:

$$\frac{(400 - 100)}{500} = \frac{300}{500} = .60\ (60\%).$$

Triangle Difference Tests. In the **triangle difference test**, participants are asked to identify which of three successively experienced stimuli is different from the other two. Again, the research design is balanced, and the order of presentation of the stimuli is rotated. As in the duo-trio test, adjustments must be made for guessing as demonstrated in Applying Marketing Research 11.5.

Applying Marketing Research 11.5

Suppose that a triangle difference test of Jif *vs.* Skippy creamy peanut butter is conducted among 400 children aged six to twelve who eat creamy peanut butter regularly. Of the 400 participants, suppose that 300, or 75 percent, correctly identify the odd sample, and 100, or 25 percent, are incorrect. Because they are choosing among three samples, nondiscriminators have a one-in-three chance of guessing correctly. Thus, the 100 incorrect participants represent about two-thirds of the guessers, or nondiscriminators. Another approximately 50 guessers are included among the 300 correct participants. Therefore, the fraction of participants who are true discriminators is estimated to be:

$$\frac{(300 - 50)}{400} = \frac{250}{400} = .625\ (62.5\%).$$

General Remarks about Discrimination Tests

The more difficult the task, the lower the observed discrimination rate. For example, the discrimination rate between Jif and Skippy peanut butter would likely be higher in a triangle difference test than in a test requiring the participant to identify the one odd sample from among five. Hence, the rate of discrimination between two products is not an absolute value, but rather is a variable that can change depending on the discrimination task used.

Because the form of the discrimination test influences the results obtained, it is important to be able to calibrate the test results with reality. For instance, when using a triangle difference test to determine the ability of consumers to discriminate between two stimuli, it is useful to have available the triangle difference test discrimination rates for pairs of existing brands in the category as points of reference. In other words, benchmark results are needed to interpret the results of a discrimination test. Further, the particular discrimination test to use really depends on what works best in a given context in terms of costs and how the test results reflect the differences among known entities (*e.g.*, existing brands).

Screening Alternatives

In the early stages of product development, management may be considering many alternative prototypes. For example, a large number of new possible bar soaps having various colors, perfumes, and shapes could be produced. A central location **round robin test** is often used to reduce the product prototypes to a manageable number prior to evaluations in a realistic home-use environment.

In sports, a round robin tournament is one in which every team plays every other team an equal number of times and the winner is the team with the best overall record. In a round robin product test, each option is tested against all others an equal number of times in a paired comparison format. In a **paired comparison**, respondents evaluate a pair of options and then state a preference or rate each option according to some criterion, such as acceptability.[7] Typically, the same number of participants evaluates each pair. A score is computed for each option by calculating the percentage of times the option was preferred across all pairs involving that particular option, or by calculating an average rating scale score. The options are ranked on the basis of these scores.

Screening does not have to be based on preference or consumer acceptance. Alternatives might also be screened according to the extent to which consumers perceive them to be consistent with the product's theme or positioning strategy. In Applying Marketing Research 11.6, both consumer acceptance and consistency with the product theme are used to screen alternative perfumes using a round robin procedure.

Applying Marketing Research 11.6

Suppose that a central-location round robin test design was used to screen eight potential perfumes for a new hand and body lotion. There were twenty-eight pairs of products [8!/2!6! = (8 X 7)/2], and each of the eight products was included in seven of the twenty-eight pairs (once with each of the other perfumes). A total of 420 participants were recruited at a central location, so that fifteen participants could evaluate and compare each pair of perfumes on overall acceptability. Thus, each perfume competed in 105 (7 X 15) separate judgments. The variation in the percentage of times each of the eight perfumes was preferred, as shown in the first column of Table 11.2, reveals that some of the perfumes had much higher overall acceptance than others.

Candidate	Acceptability Percentage of preference votes	Positioning support Percentage of preference votes
A	58	44
B	36	70
C	56	47
D	42	39
E	65	58
F	45	42
G	60	60
H	38	40

Table 11.2
Round robin test results for eight perfume candidates.

Management was also concerned about the appropriateness of each scent to the moisturizing theme that had been proposed for the new product. Because consumers might rank the appropriateness of the scents differently for consistency with this theme than they rank them for preference, the same participants were requested to take part in a second round robin study in which each participant evaluated another pair of perfumes, different from the first pair evaluated. In this second paired comparison, participants indicated which perfume was most appropriate for the product described in a statement, which stressed moisturizing benefits, read to each respondent. The second column of percentages in Table 11.2 shows the percentage of times each perfume was chosen in this context. As you can see, the most preferred perfumes that were not always seen as most appropriate for the product theme.

Exhibit 11.4 contains a plot for visually demonstrating the results of the two round robin experiments shown in Table 11.2. The *x*-axis represents acceptability, and the *y*-axis represents consistency with the product theme. Perfumes H, D, and F in the third quadrant do not support the product theme, and consumers rate them as unacceptable, while the perfumes in the fourth quadrant, A and C, are acceptable, but do not support the product theme. Perfumes G and E, plotted in the first quadrant, support the theme, are highly acceptable, and are logically the best candidates.

However, management might be wise also to continue to explore candidate B because of its very high score for support of the product theme. Sometimes shortcomings in the acceptability of an alternative that strongly supports the product theme can be exploited, as was done when Listerine mouthwash capitalized on a poor taste ("the taste you love to hate") to successfully promote the germ-killing effectiveness of the brand.

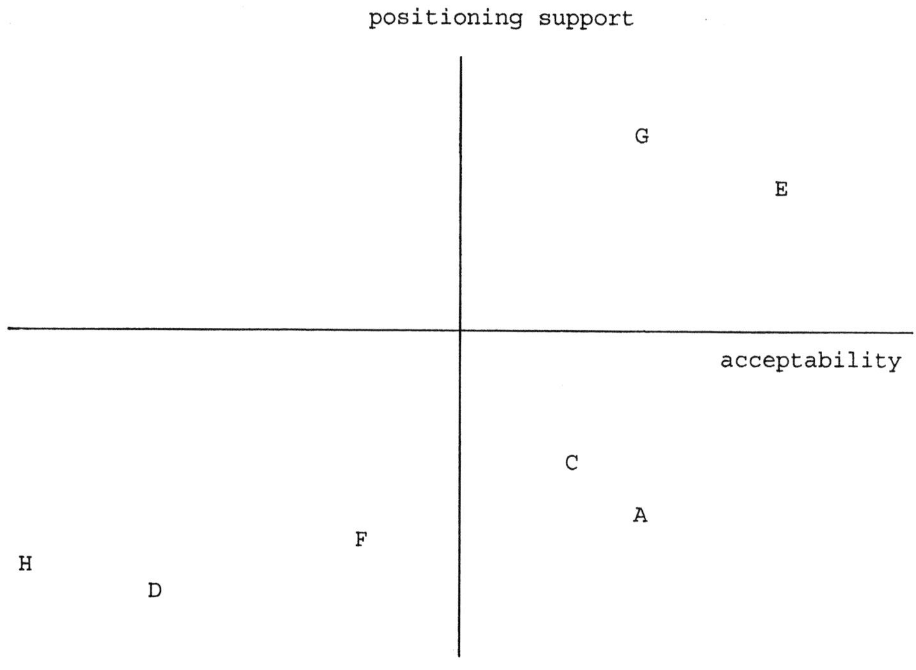

Exhibit 11.4
Display of round robin test results for screening perfume candidates.

The round robin design provides an efficient way to reduce a large number of alternatives to a manageable few. By pooling information across all the paired comparisons involving a specific product alternative, and doing this for each option in the test, enough information is obtained to make judgments about the relative merits of all of the alternatives tested in an affordable manner.

Round robin designs are not without their drawbacks, however. These designs do not produce nearly enough data for an in-depth evaluation of one alternative directly against another, since only a few people evaluate any single

pair of alternatives. For example, only fifteen participants evaluated each pair of perfumes in Applying Marketing Research 11.6.

As-filmed Photo-Script
Date FEBRUARY/1970
Producer

Client WARNER-LAMBERT
Product LISTERINE ANTISEPTIC

Film No. 69-01327-45
Film Title "HOCKEY LADY"
Film Length 45 SECONDS COLOR TV

1. CAROLINE: Play to win, girls. (BLOWS WHISTLE)

2. ANNCR: (VO) We asked Caroline Diehl what she thought of the taste of Listerine.

3. CAROLINE: Oh, I hate it.

4. ANNCR: (VO) Ah, then we asked her if she used it .....

5. CAROLINE: Oh! I certainly do. I'm not fond of the taste, . . .

6. but my dear, I am LESS fond of bad breath!

7. Ha! Listerine's strong -- it kills germs that can cause bad breath . . .

8. well, I figure that's what a mouthwash is all about!

9. So I don't worry about the taste of Listerine . . .

10. I just use it. Twice a day!!

11. ANNCR: (VO) Listerine Antiseptic.

The taste
people hate.
Twice a day.

12. It's got the taste people hate ... twice a day.

Exhibit 11.5
Sometimes a product deficiency can be used in a brand's favor
(Courtesy of Warner-Lambert Company)

Preference Testing

As indicated earlier, central-location product tests are sometimes used to generate a measure of consumer preference between two alternatives. The preference measure is usually obtained directly using a paired comparison format in which respondents evaluate two alternatives and then state their preferences. The order of presentation of the two alternatives is rotated to avoid order bias. Brands are typically not identified in these tests so preference is based on the products themselves. However, occasionally products may be labeled as in the development of diet coke

(see opening vignette for Chapter 1.) Pepsi-Cola's famous "Pepsi Challenge" campaign used commercials in which Coca-Cola drinkers were "challenged" to compare Pepsi-Cola and Coca-Cola (unlabeled) in a paired comparison preference taste test.

A paired comparison test involving the same two products is sometimes added to the basic duo-trio or triangle difference discrimination test to assess preference as well as discrimination using the same participants.[8]

Conducting the discrimination and preference tests with the same participants adds information that would not be obtained if the tests were conducted using different consumers. In the context of product reformulation, for example, data pertinent to discrimination as well as relative acceptability of the two products among discriminators are provided. The percentage of the current brand users who can tell the difference and who also prefer the original formulation is an indication of the size of the franchise at risk if the change is made in an existing brand.

In the next sections we will describe how preference among discriminators is assessed in conjunction with a duo-trio test or a triangle difference test. We will also describe a third technique that is often used to assess discrimination and preference among discriminators, the pair repeat test.[a]

---

[a]In the discussion that follows, it is assumed that respondents are forced to state a preference, *i.e.*, "no preference" votes are not allowed. When "no preference" votes are allowed in these procedures, the analysis is somewhat more complicated.

Preference in Conjunction with the Duo-Trio Test

As discussed earlier, in the duo-trio discrimination test, participants are asked to identify which of two previously evaluated (*e.g.*, tasted) product samples is the same as a third sample. The example below shows how to obtain a preference rate among discriminators when a paired comparison preference test is added to the task.

Applying Marketing Research 11.7

In the duo-trio test described in Applying Marketing Research 11.3, 400 participants out of 500 correctly identified the third sample. Assume that after the discrimination test the participants were also asked to taste and compare the two products (unidentified) and to state which of the two products they prefer.

Suppose that 250 of the 400 correct respondents preferred diet Coke and 150 preferred diet Pepsi. We estimated in Applying Marketing Research 11.3 that there were 100 guessers among these 400 respondents, so only 300 respondents were true discriminators. It is reasonable to assume that the preference of the 100 guessers is split evenly between the two brands. The number of true discriminators who prefer diet Coke is then:

$$250 - 50 = 200.$$

Hence, based on these hypothetical results, about two-thirds (200 out of 300) of adult diet cola drinkers who can tell the difference between the two diet colas in a duo-trio test prefer diet Coke to diet Pepsi.

Preference in Conjunction with the Triangle Difference Test

As shown in Applying Marketing Research 11.8, the estimation of preference among discriminators when using the triangle difference test follows the same logic just described for the duo-trio test.

Applying Marketing Research 11.8

Returning to Applying Marketing Research 11.2, recall that the 7Up objection was based on the results of a triangle difference test shown in Table 11.1. For the total sample, there were 648 respondents who incorrectly identified the odd sample. Hence, the total number of guessers, i.e., non-discriminators, is estimated to be 972, the 648 who were incorrect plus 648/2 = 324 who are projected to have guessed correctly. Only 288 respondents are projected to have actually discriminated between the two tastes.

Among the 552 respondents who correctly identified the odd sample in the triangle difference test, 294 (.245 * 1200) preferred Sprite and 258 (.215 * 1200) preferred 7Up. Assuming the 324 correct guessers,, i.e., non-discriminators, among these 552 respondents split equally between Sprite and 7Up on the preference question, 132 (294-162) actual discriminators preferred Sprite and 96 (258-162) preferred 7Up. The projected rate of preference for Sprite among discriminators is then 132/(132 + 96) or 132/228 = .58. Hence, a closer look at the 7Up results indicates that among discriminators, 58% prefer Sprite and 42% prefer 7Up. These figures are much more consistent with the Coca-Cola Company findings of 49% prefer Sprite, 41% prefer 7Up and 10% no preference obtained in paired comparison taste tests mentioned in the example.

Pair Repeat Test

Another type of test providing both discrimination and preference rate data is the **pair repeat test.** The pair repeat test consists of two paired comparison preference tests involving the same two stimuli, administered back-to-back. As opposed to the duo-trio or triangle difference test with a paired comparison test appended, the pair repeat test focuses on preference first and then discrimination. For a pair repeat test of stimulus A against stimulus B, participants would be categorized into four groups — people who prefer A twice, people who prefer B twice, people who prefer A the first time and B the second time, and people who prefer B the first time and A the second time. Nondiscriminators guess when stating a preference and hence can fall into any one of the four groups with equal probability. Therefore, the inconsistent respondents — those respondents who prefer one product and then the other — represent only half of the guessers or non-discriminators. The other half of the nondiscriminators are consistent in their preferences and are about equally divided between preferring A twice and preferring B twice. Applying Marketing Research 11.9 demonstrates the calculations for estimating discrimination rate and preference among discriminators in the pair repeat test format.

Applying Marketing Research 11.9

Suppose that 400 male beer drinkers participate in a pair repeat test of Budweiser *vs.* Coors. The hypothetical results are shown below:

		Second pair	
		Prefer Budweiser	Prefer Coors
First pair	Prefer Budweiser	140	80
	Prefer Coors	70	110

Of the 400 participants, 150 (70 + 80) switched preference and are therefore nondiscriminators. Accordingly, another 150 nondiscriminators are assumed to have guessed consistently when stating their preference and are included in the 250 (140 + 110) consistent responses. The estimated number of true discriminators, then, is: 250 - 150 = 100, or 25 percent of the sample.

The correct guessers are assumed to be equally split in preference between the two brands. Therefore, 65 (140 - 75) discriminators prefer Budweiser, and the 35 (110 - 75) remaining discriminators prefer Coors. The conclusion is that the vast majority of beer drinkers cannot consistently notice the difference between Budweiser and Coors. However, among those who can, 65 percent prefer Budweiser.

Home-Use Tests

As the name implies, a **home-use test** entails consumers evaluating test products in their homes, or more generally, in a natural usage environment. Home-use testing tends to be considerably more expensive than central-location testing but is also far more realistic. In other words, as experimentation on a new or an existing brand moves from a central location into the home, costs increase but the external validity of the results also increases.

It is extremely important to obtain consumers' assessment of potential new products in a natural setting because these assessments may be different from what is found in central-location tests. For example, the aroma of an air freshener designed for use in an automobile might have high consumer acceptance in a central-location test but not test well when used in an automobile because the scent is too strong for the small enclosed area. Similarly, consumers might prefer the taste of a new chip flavor when subjected to a central- location test, but not like the taste when it is eaten with a drink or with other food. Hence, promising product alternatives that emerge from central-location testing are usually evaluated in a natural setting next.

Most home-use testing is conducted using one of two formats — either respondents compare a pair of products or they evaluate one product. A third, but infrequently used design, is the protomonadic design, which is a hybrid of the paired comparison and single-product designs. Exhibit 11.6 contrasts the formats of these three home-use test designs.

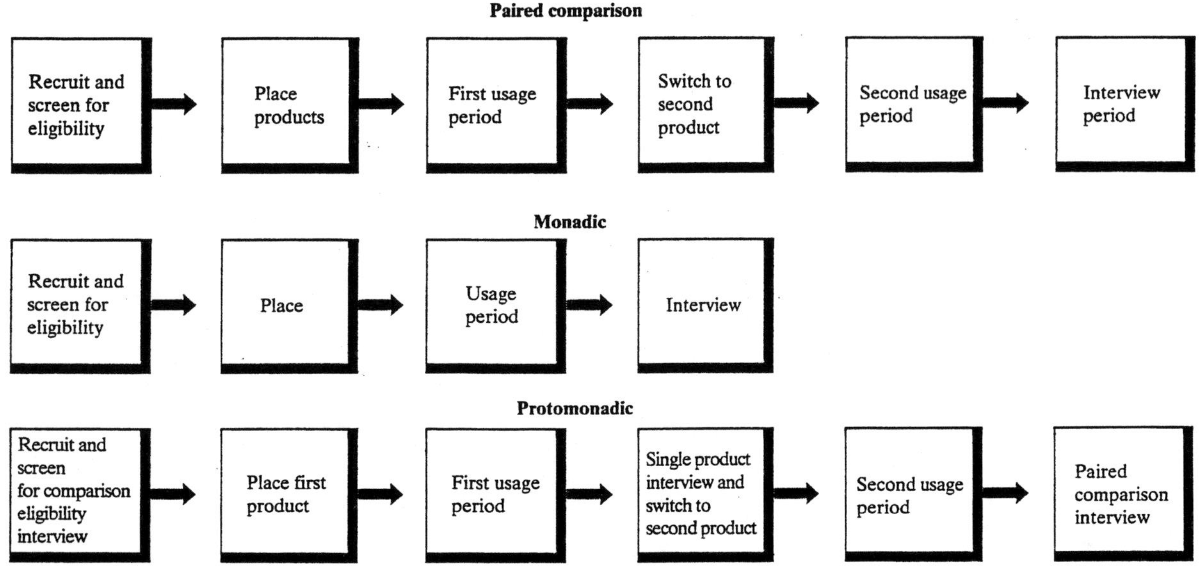

Exhibit 11.6
Flowchart of home-use tests.

Paired Comparison Home-Use Tests

In a paired comparison home-use test, participants evaluate two products in normal usage situations and provide information regarding their preference and corresponding reasons for preference. One product is used for a designated period of time, perhaps one or two weeks, and then the second product is used for an equal period of time. The specific length of time each product is used is chosen to allow the consumer ample time to gain experience with each product. Exhibit 11.7 contains typical participant instructions for a paired comparison home-use test.

Dear Participant:

Enclosed are two different laundry additives with all-fabric bleach which I'd like you, yourself, to use during the next four weeks in place of any other additives.

These products are to be used in the washer along with your regular detergent for any laundry done at home. They may also be used to pre-soak heavily stained or soiled clothes.

One product is labeled "Use First Two Weeks", the other "Use Second Two Weeks". Please be sure to use them in that order.

1) Use the product marked "Use First Two Weeks" for the entire first two weeks after you receive these products. DO NOT USE ANY OTHER LAUNDRY ADDITIVES OR PRE-SOAK PRODUCTS while using this product. IMPORTANTLY, DO NOT USE CHLORINE BLEACH WHICH INACTIVATES THIS PRODUCT. If you should happen to use all of the product marked "Use First Two Weeks" before the end of the first two weeks, please begin using the product marked "Use Second Two Weeks" right away. This is so you don't use any other product in-between.

2) At the end of two weeks, set aside any of the product marked "Use First Two Weeks" which you may have remaining and begin using only the product marked "Use Second Two Weeks" for the entire second two weeks. DO NOT USE ANY OTHER LAUNDRY ADDITIVES OR PRE-SOAK PRODUCTS while using this product. IMPORTANTLY, DO NOT USE CHLORINE BLEACH WHICH INACTIVATES THIS PRODUCT.

At the end of four weeks I will be sending you a questionnaire, so that you can tell me which, if either, of these products you like better. It is important that you have a chance to use both products before you receive my questionnaire.

Thanks so much for your help and cooperation.

Exhibit 11.7

Example of placement instructions for paired comparison test.

A blind test format is typically used, and the home-use test design is balanced so that one-half of the participants use the products in one order, while the remainder use the products in the reverse order. It is quite common to give both products, labeled "use first" and "use second," to participants, along with instructions regarding when to switch, at the beginning of the test. Sometimes participants are reminded, either by postcard or by telephone, to switch over to the second product at the designated time. Alternatively, participants can be provided with only one product at a time in the proper sequence. While more costly, placing only one product in the home at a time does ensure that the products will be used one at a time and in the proper order.

Reasons for Using Paired Comparison Home-Use Tests

The paired comparison home-use test provides useful information about the relative merits of one product *vs.* another. Hence, this design can be used to assess how a potential new product entry is perceived relative to an existing brand solely on the basis of the products themselves. For example, the goal for a new product project could be to be preferred to the market leader in a paired comparison home-use test. Funds for the development of other elements of the marketing mix might be withheld until this objective is achieved.

By its nature, a paired comparison home-use test forces consumers to look for differences between products rather than evaluate each on its own merits.[9] As such, the test is somewhat artificial, but the examination of differences is the desired effect. In designing a product, decisions must be made regarding some product attributes or characteristics that are not nearly as salient as others. The shape and color of a bar of soap are not nearly as important to consumers as the fragrance; the taste of toothpaste tends to dominate texture or color considerations; and the fragrance and consistency of a hand and body lotion overshadow subtle changes in the packaging. Consumers tend to pay less attention to these less salient characteristics when evaluating products and make their choices based primarily on the more salient ones.

However, if the two products tested in a paired comparison test format are made to differ only with respect to a single characteristic, then the comparison is based solely on that characteristic. Hence, participants can be forced to evaluate the pair of products on a relatively nonsalient characteristic using this approach. For example, to test which shade of beige is preferred for Safeguard hand soap, a paired comparison test, holding all other product attributes equal except color, would be ideal. The researcher may even go as far as to instruct participants to pay particular attention to the product characteristic being investigated, which is called a directed-interest test.

To force even a more direct comparison, the paired comparison format described above can be changed to a format which is, or approaches, a simultaneous paired comparison.[10] For example, participants might be asked to use one fingernail polish on the left hand and another on the right, or to use one toothpaste in the morning and another at night. Simultaneous paired comparison studies are balanced with respect to usage in a manner analogous to that of the typical paired comparison to avoid any bias due to how the products are used.

Data Collected

Regardless of whether products are used sequentially, simultaneously, or on an alternating basis, participants are interviewed at the end of the test period. Table 11.3 provides examples of the types of questions asked during a paired comparison interview. Usually, the first question addresses which of the two products is preferred. Participants are then asked, in an open-ended format, for their reasons for preference.

To measure:	Participants are asked:
Product preference	Which of the two products did you like best, the one you used first or the one you used second?
Reasons for preference	What did you like better about the product used first (second)?
Product ratings	On a scale of Excellent, Very Good, Good, Fair, or Poor, how would you rate the product you used first overall? What is your overall opinion of the product you used second using the same scale?
Comparisons on specific product attributes	Did you notice any difference between the two products with respect to ________ ?
Respondent behavior	Frequency of use, where purchased, etc.
Demographics	Age, income, education, etc.

Table 11.3
Examples of questions asked during a paired comparison interview

Participants also are often asked to rate the overall acceptability of both products on a category rating scale, such as the one described in Table 11.3. These overall ratings provide insight into how strongly one product is preferred over the other. Also, situations can arise where one product is preferred to another, but both products are rated an average relatively high or relatively low. In the latter case, the preferred product is actually a winner by default. Therefore, the average overall rating each product receives should be examined to determine the general acceptability levels of the respective products.

Following the overall product ratings, participants are often asked to compare the two products with respect to specific product attributes. Participants testing two bar soaps might be asked if they noticed any difference in the amount of lather produced by each. Those noting a difference would then be asked which soap produced more lather. Demographic questions, and questions pertaining to purchase frequency and brands usually purchased typically comprise the last sections of the questionnaire.

Examining the Intensity of Preference Data

Intensity of preference refers to how strongly one product is preferred over the other. This information greatly enhances the understanding gained in a paired comparison test. Intensity of preference can be measured by the difference in the overall acceptability scores for the two products given by a participant or directly by asking a separate question. For instance, participants might be asked to indicate how much more they liked the preferred

product using a category scale such as: "only slightly" (they were almost the same), "somewhat more," or "a whole lot more."

Three scenarios, representing very different situations and having different marketing implications, are possible when examining the intensity of preference measures. First, consumers might perceive the products as very similar. This could occur with two products that are the same except for a minor difference that consumers ignore or do not notice. Replacing one laundry detergent ingredient with a similar one could produce such a result. In this case, approximately equal numbers of participants prefer each of the two test products, and the intensity of preference for each product is low.

Second, consumers might be polarized with regard to preference for the two products so that two distinct segments of consumers exist. One segment strongly prefers one product and the other segment strongly prefers the other product. The size of the segments might also differ considerably. Testing a very spicy versus a moderately spicy nacho cheese dip could produce such results. Two distinct groups might emerge — one small group strongly in favor of the very spicy dip and one large group averse to very spicy foods.

In the third and final scenario, one group of respondents only marginally prefers one of the products, while the other group strongly prefers the other product. Again, the two groups could differ greatly in size. If the strong preference group is considerably larger than the group exhibiting weak intensity of preference, in all likelihood the preferred product is actually much better than the other. Testing a premium ice cream against one of the low-calorie, artificial substitutes among users of regular ice cream would be likely to produce these results. The vast majority of participants would prefer the premium ice cream, and their intensity of preference would be much stronger than the minority stating a preference for the artificial product.

It is also possible in this third scenario for the group who prefer the losing product in the pair test to express a strong intensity of preference, while the group who prefer the winning product expresses low intensity of preference. Imagine testing a paper towel with no design against a paper towel with a floral design. Two groups of respondents could exist — a small group who really like the idea of a decorated paper towel and a large group who are almost indifferent but slightly prefer the plain product. In this situation, it is conceivable that the less frequently preferred product is in fact the more attractive market opportunity because it has strong appeal to a reasonably sized segment of consumers.

In summary, when analyzing the results of a paired comparison test, one must look beyond the basic preference percentages to gain a full understanding of how the products were perceived. Reasons for preference for the respective products and intensity of preference data should also be examined.

Limitations of Paired Comparison Home-Use Tests

At times, the artificial nature of the paired comparison procedure and its focus on product differences makes the paired comparison test totally inappropriate. When testing a liquid detergent whose cap also serves as a measuring cup against the same product with an ordinary cap, the former would obviously be preferred in a paired comparison test. Similarly, evaluating a resealable potato chip bag versus an ordinary bag that is not resealable, but is otherwise the same, would yield a large win for the resealable bag.

Also, some products have carry-over effects that alter the testing environment for a substantial period of time, making paired comparison testing infeasible.[11] Products such as hair colorings, skin conditioning agents, weight-loss products, and natural tanning products change the physical appearance or condition of the user if they are effective. Hair changes from gray to black; dry skin becomes moist and smooth; extra pounds melt away. Even if consumers were willing to return to their "normal" condition to test other products, the process would be far too slow to be practical.

Finally, the preference observed in a paired comparison might not translate to market preference. Applying Marketing Research 11.9 points this out.

Applying Marketing Research 11.9

Procter & Gamble introduced the beauty bar soap Monchel to compete with Lever Brothers Company's Dove. The bar had a very pleasing fragrance and a scallop shell shape, which made it unique and attractive. The fragrance and unique shape were the most noticeable differences between Monchel and Dove in blind paired comparison home-use tests. Monchel's attractive shape propelled it to wins over Dove in these tests.

However, the paired comparison home-use test preference for Monchel over Dove was deceiving. In the beauty bar category, by far the most important consideration is the product's effect on the skin. Monchel had no advantage relative to Dove in this context.[12]

The paired comparison home-use test win did not translate to a market preference. Monchel was quickly withdrawn from the market shortly after its introduction.

In summary, the paired comparison research design, although artificial, offers the researcher the opportunity to focus consumer attention on a single product dimension and to determine which of two alternatives is preferred more often. It also provides a means of assessing how a new product is perceived relative to a currently marketed product in a head-to-head comparison. However, there are situations for which the paired comparison design is inappropriate and for which the single-product design, which we discuss next, should be used.

Single Product Home-Use Tests

In a **single-product test**, respondents are asked to use and evaluate one product for a specified period of time. A single-product test, often called a **monadic test**, addresses the fundamental question: How will consumers react to this product? Exhibit 11.8 shows typical placement instructions for a single-product test.

Dear Participant:

Enclosed in this package is a BLEACH product which I'd very much like you to use for your machine laundry during the NEXT FOUR WEEKS. The product in both packages is the same. This product is to be added to the wash water of your family's laundry.

Please put away any other bleach products you now have on hand and use ONLY THIS PRODUCT I'M GIVING YOU. Start using the product right away, the next time any machine laundry is done, and use it for the entire four weeks.

Instructions on how to use this product are printed on the box. PLEASE BE SURE TO READ THE INSTRUCTIONS THOROUGHLY.

I hope you'll be able to start using this bleach right away. At the end of four weeks, I'll be sending you a questionnaire to ask what you thought of this product.

Thank you so much for your help and cooperation.

Exhibit 11.8
Example of placement instructions for single-product test.

As with home-use testing in general, the length of the usage period in a single product test is dependent on how frequently the product is used. Less frequently used products, such as household cleansers, require longer test periods for participants to gain adequate experience to make a judgment than do more frequently used products, such as toothpaste. Occasionally, extended-use product tests, in which participants may use the product for months, are conducted to measure long-term effects, such as wear-out or novelty, or to determine how well the product stays fresh or maintains its effectiveness over time.[13]

Reasons for Using Single-Product Tests

The single-product test design provides a more realistic assessment than does the paired comparison because participants evaluate the test product just as they do when trying any new offering in the marketplace. Also, single product tests are particularly appropriate for situations where a paired comparison test would yield meaningless results. Thus, if one product is obviously better than another or if the differences are so great that a paired comparison would be like comparing apples and oranges, a single-product test should be used. A single-product test is also useful when a substantial carry-over effect exists.

Although the name implies that only one product is being tested, it is quite common for more than one product to be included in the single-product research design. Participants are randomly assigned to groups or cells, and each cell receives a different test product. To demonstrate such a design, consider the situations mentioned earlier of testing a resealable bag of potato chips and of testing a

liquid detergent cap that also serves as a measuring cup for

dispensing the product. As noted, these product improvements are too obvious for a paired comparison test to be meaningful. However, a single-product design with two cells could be used. One cell would use the product of interest (the resealable bag or the detergent with the measuring cup cap) and the other cell would use the reference product (the ordinary bag or detergent package). In each case, comparing results between the two cells provides insight regarding how much additional overall consumer appeal the added benefit generates. Parity between the overall ratings for the two cells indicates that the product enhancement has little impact on consumer acceptance.

Data Collected

The line of questioning at the end of the product-evaluation period typically includes open-ended questions pertaining to likes and dislikes of the test product, an overall evaluation of the product on a category rating scale, scale ratings of the product on specific product attributes, questions pertaining to participant purchasing behavior in the product category, and demographics. Typical questions for a single product test are listed in Table 11.4.

To Measure:	Participants are asked:
Likes and dislikes	What in particular, if anything, did you like about the product? What in particular, if anything, did you not like about the product?
Overall product evaluation	Overall, how would you rate the product on the following scale: Excellent, Very Good, Good, Fair, Poor?
Rating of specific attributes	Using the same scale (excellent, very good, good, fair, poor), how would you rate the product for ________?
Respondent behavior	Frequency of use, where purchased, etc.
Demographics	Age, income, education, etc.

Table 11.4
Examples of questions asked during a single-product interview.

Single-product test results can be difficult to interpret. What does it mean, for example, if 25 percent of the participants rate the product "excellent," and another 30 percent rate it "very good"? Without some point of reference, such numbers are of very little value. As in concept testing, norms based on past single-product tests are often developed to serve as benchmarks to which single-product test results can be compared.[14] Single-product ratings of any other products included in the research design provide another basis of comparison. A currently marketed product (blind packaged) is often included as a separate cell to serve as such a benchmark or point of reference.

Protomonadic Home-Use Tests

A **protomonadic test** is a hybrid design in that the test includes both a single product and a paired comparison evaluation. Participants use one product for a specified period of time, after which a single-product interview is administered. They then use a second product for an equal period of time, after which a paired comparison interview is administered. The protomonadic test design thus provides a paired comparison as well as monadic information about both products.[b]

There are limits to the effectiveness of a protomonadic test, however. One shortcoming is that very limited single- product data are provided because the single-product interview is restricted to likes and dislikes regarding the product and an overall assessment. No questions pertaining to specific product attributes are included in the single-product interview to avoid biasing participants' evaluations of the second product. For instance, in a protomonadic toothpaste test, if questions pertaining to aftertaste were asked at the single product stage, participants would be likely to pay particular attention to aftertaste when evaluating the second product.

Sample size is also an issue when using a protomandic design. Since a single-product evaluation is only obtained for the first product used, the number of participants providing a monadic product evaluation is only one-half the number providing the paired comparison evaluation. Thus, a test involving 300 respondents has only 150 respondents for each single-product evaluation, because half of the respondents would use one product first and the other half would use the other product first. Therefore, to obtain a sufficient sample size for each monadic evaluation, a greater number of paired comparisons are obtained than would be necessary if only a paired comparison design was used.

Critical Issues in Designing Home-Use Tests

The relative advantages and disadvantages of paired comparison and single product formats are summarized in Table 11.5. As already discussed, some of the relative pluses and minuses of each method are inherent in the design. Others, which we discuss next, are factors that may create a problem when using one or the other of the two test formats and must be considered when designing the particular product test.

---

[b]A variation of the protomonadic design is the sequential monadic design in which single-product interviews are administered after each product is used. The objection to the sequential monadic design is that the second product is not truly evaluated in a monadic fashion, but rather is evaluated relative to the first.

	Paired Comparison	Monadic
Advantages	Makes subtle differences obvious Answers "which is preferred" question Reduces concern over sample composition Efficient in sense of number of participants required	Realistic Versatile with respect to types of products that can be compared Requires half the test time of paired comparison for equivalent usage
Disadvantages	Artificial Preferences subject to order effect and external factors	Can lack sensitivity when used to compare products Comparability of samples important issue when used to compare products Requires more participants when used to compare products

Table 11.5
Advantages and disadvantages of paired comparison and monadic home-use tests

Sample Composition

When designing a product test, consideration must be given to the composition of the sample of participants selected for the test. Deciding what eligibility requirements to set for participants depends on the research objectives. For instance, when researching possible changes in an existing brand, it is important to include a large base of users of the brand in the sample. Likewise, when developing a product specifically for attacking a competitive brand's business, it is desirable to include a large base of users of the competitive brand. Products targeted for specific demographic subgroups (*e.g.*, housewives, teenagers, or sports enthusiasts) require testing among these subgroups.

Potential bias due to differences in the composition of the groups comprising the test cells must be avoided. Paired comparison testing avoids this issue because each participant evaluates both products. In a single-product test involving more than one cell, however, different groups of people evaluate different products, so biased results can be obtained if the compositions of the groups differ. Suppose several quite different cable TV programming packages are being evaluated in a single-product design. Some program packages might have a rock-music video channel while others do not, and some might have a medical information channel while others do not, some a weather channel while others do not. Clearly, differences among the age compositions of the households comprising the cells could dramatically affect the overall ratings of the various programming packages. In fact, the observed differences in the acceptability of the programming options might be entirely due to these demographic differences. In a situation such as this, care must be exercised to ensure comparability of the cells with respect to factors known to affect programming preferences. Random allocation of participants to cells, the use of large sample sizes, and demographically matching the composition of each cell are among the steps researchers can take to obtain comparable sample compositions (see Chapter 3 "Experimental Research").

Impact of External Factors

External, or environmental, factors that randomly occur during the testing of a product influence a participant's reaction to a product. Such external factors can make it very difficult to detect the superiority of one product over another in a paired comparison home-use test.

If two headache remedies, one of which is actually superior to the other, were tested on two consecutive headaches using the paired comparison format, parity would be the likely result. Preference would be dictated to a large degree by the severity of the headache to which each remedy was applied, and the product preferred would depend basically on the luck of the draw. In extreme cases like this, the paired comparison test may be doomed to parity, making this design inappropriate.[15]

On the other hand, a single-product test of two headache remedies would involve each respondent using one of the remedies on his or her next headache. The overall severity pattern of headaches is likely to be similar for the two groups. Thus, a truly superior remedy has a better chance to display overall superiority in the single-product design.

The degree to which external factors are operating must be considered in order to determine whether a paired comparison test or a single product test is appropriate. It can be particularly frustrating to product development engineers when a product demonstrates superiority in laboratory testing but fails subsequently to demonstrate the expected degree of superiority in a consumer paired comparison home-use test. If external factors are believed to be operating at a reasonably low level, different rates of preference can be detected in a paired comparison home-use test design. Otherwise, a single-product test should be considered.

Order Effect

Order effect in a paired comparison test, refers to the tendency to prefer the first (or second) product used.[16] When both product variations are better than what consumers typically use, or both are extremely innovative, the first product tends to make a greater impression than the second simply because it is experienced first. Consequently, there can be a tendency to favor the first product. In other situations, however, the product used second might have an advantage. Participants in a paired comparison home-use test of two cake mixes might change the recipe slightly for the second cake mix based on their experiences with the first one used. Hence, the second product used may tend to be preferred.

Even though the test is balanced with regard to which product is used first, a large order effect, just like external factors, drives the paired test result toward parity and makes it difficult to observe a difference in preference. In the cake mix example, if everyone in the test doctors the recipe for the second cake and thus prefers the second mix, then an equal number of participants will prefer each product because order of use is rotated across participants. Therefore, a potentially large order effect forces the researcher to consider the single-product test design.

Multiple Product Tests

Occasionally, a company wants each consumer to evaluate more than two products. Consumer evaluation of more than two products in a home-use context is rare because of the general belief among marketing researchers that including more than two products in a home-use test would result in confusion among respondents regarding perceptions about the test products. However, research in which consumers evaluate more than two products is occasionally conducted in a central location format. In this context, several products are tested and evaluated in a short period of time, and the participants report their assessments immediately. Respondents might be asked to look at several alternate designs for decorating a paper towel and to choose a favorite or rank them in order of preference. Similarly, respondents could be asked to dispense liquid detergent for dishes using several alternate dispensers and to comment on each.

Summary

In this chapter, we have discussed how product testing, which is typically an iterative process, is an integral part of bringing a new product or service to the market. Product tests can be conducted in central locations such as shopping malls or can entail consumers using and evaluating test product(s) in their homes. Sensory tests such as discrimination tests conducted to determine how many consumers can detect a difference between two products, preference tests such as taste tests comparing two products, and screening tests involving multiple options normally use a central-location format.

Home-use tests are typically single-product (monadic) or paired comparison. Both have relative advantages and disadvantages. The single-product design is more realistic than the paired comparison and provides an absolute evaluation of a product. However, the paired comparison attracts attention to the difference(s) between two products.

A number of critical issues must be considered when designing a home-use test. Sample composition is generally more critical in single-product tests involving comparisons across groups (cells) than in paired comparison tests. External factors, not related to the products themselves, can dictate preference in a paired comparison test and must therefore be carefully considered. These occur to varying degrees across product categories. Finally, order effect — the tendency to prefer the first (or second) product used — can occur in a paired comparison test. Order effect drives preference toward parity.

Multiple-product tests entail participants evaluating more than two alternatives. Such designs are used occasionally in central-location tests.

The product testing material has been presented primarily in the context of consumer packaged goods. However, as noted in the opening vignette to this chapter and in the following material regarding Nimslo, product testing is used in the development of durables. The same is true for services. Naturally, modifications often must be made to accommodate peculiarities encountered in these contexts. A new service would not be "placed" in the home, but instead would be made available to respondents for a limited period of time. Also, relatively long test periods might be required because the service is infrequently used. A large-based paired comparison home-use test of alternative new car designs is not practical because of the tremendous expense involved in auto manufacturing. Rather, alternative prototypes might be made for consumers to examine and drive, perhaps on a private track.

Key Terms:

blind testing

central-location tests

discrimination tests

duo-trio test

home-use test

intensity of preference
monadic test
order effect
pair repeat test
paired comparison
protomonadic test
round robin test
single-product test
triangle difference test

Product-Testing the Nimslo Camera

Nimslo conducted a product test of its 3D camera prior to the test-market introduction. Eighty households were recruited in each of two cities to use the camera for several months. Special provisions were made for the participants to submit film for developing and printing. Participants purchased their own 35 mm color film wherever they chose and paid for developing and printing according to a photo finishing price schedule provided to them.

Each participant's photo finishing orders were monitored to provide data on the number of rolls of film used, exposure length of the rolls used, potential decline in the usage rate of the camera, and types of pictures taken. The first three issues were crucial in anticipating the demand on the initially limited photo finishing capacity that each newly sold camera would generate. The fourth issue, comparing the types of pictures taken by test participants with industry data regarding typical picture-taking behavior by 35 mm camera owners, provided insights into peculiarities regarding the use of the Nimslo camera were obtained.

The table below contains some of the data on the amount of film used with the Nimslo camera and the usage of other cameras during the test period:

Usage of Nimslo vs. "Other" Camera (Base = 137[*])

	Nimslo	Other
	percentage	percentage
Used camera	97	67
Less than 1 roll	12	8
1 roll	20	18
2 rolls	27	14
3 rolls	18	7
4 rolls	10	6
5 or more rolls	10	14
Mean	2.6[**]	3.3[**]

*23 dropped out of study during the test period

**Mean based only on those using the camera

These data painted a bleak picture. For one thing, the mean of 2.6 rolls used by the 137 participants during the test period translates to about 10 rolls per year, far less than originally projected based on typical 35 mm film usage. Further, it seemed that the Nimslo camera was not replacing the family's existing camera since about two-thirds of the participants continued to use other cameras during the test period. In fact, these participants used their other cameras more on average than the Nimslo camera. This was very disturbing in light of the camera's novelty and the encouragement to use it provided by the test environment. All in all, the home-use test pointed to a difficult uphill struggle for Nimslo.

Review Questions

11.1 Define a paired comparison home-use test.

11.2 Define a single-product home-use test.

11.3 What is meant by intensity of preference? How can this measurement be useful?

11.4 Describe the protomonadic test design, and discuss its strengths and weaknesses.

11.5 What is meant by order effect in a paired comparison test?

11.6 What is a central-location test?

11.7 A random sample of 500 regular instant-coffee drinkers participated in a duo-trio taste test of Maxwell House *vs.* Taster's Choice regular instant coffees. Of these, 400 participants were correct and 100 were incorrect. Estimate the rate of discrimination.

11.8 Suppose a paired comparison preference taste test was also conducted after the discrimination test in the example of question 11.7 and that 300 of the 400 correct respondents prefer Maxwell House. Estimate the preference rate for Maxwell House among discriminators.

11.9 A random sample of 300 beer drinkers participated in a triangle difference taste test comparing Michelob and Lowenbrau. Of the participants, 200 correctly identified the odd sample. Estimate the discrimination rate.

11.10 Suppose that a paired comparison taste test was conducted after the triangle difference test described in question 11.7. Estimate the preference for Michelob among discriminators if 125 of the 200 correct respondents prefer Lowenbrau.

11.11 A pair repeat test of Hershey *vs.* Nestle powdered chocolate mixes was conducted among 600 children, ten to fourteen years of age, who drink chocolate milk. The results are shown below:

11.12

		Second pair	
		Prefer Hershey	Prefer Nestle
First Pair	Prefer Hershey	310	55
	Prefer Nestle	45	190

Estimate the discrimination rate and the preference for Hershey among discriminators.

11.12 Give an example of a round robin market research design. What are the advantages and disadvantages of this test design?

Discussion Questions

11.1 Discuss the importance of home-use testing in the development of new products. Why can't product development engineers rely solely on laboratory tests?

11.2 Contrast the relative advantages and disadvantages of paired comparison *vs.* single-product testing. Give examples where each design is clearly preferred and explain why.

11.3 Discuss the impact of external factors and order effect on the ability to detect differences in preference in a home-use test.

11.4 Discuss the pros and cons of central-location testing. Give examples where such tests are useful and examples where such testing would be inappropriate.

Chapter 11 Endnotes

1. See Keith Naughton, "How Ford's F-150 Lapped the Competition," *Business Week*, July 29, 1996, pp. 74-76.

2. See "Altoids, Chick-Fil-A," *Advertising Age*, August 5, 1996, p. A4.

3. Pat Wechsler, "A Curiously Strong Campaign," *Business Week*, April 21, 1997, p. 134.

4. See Susan Spillman, "The Importance of Parting Shots," *USA_Today*, May 7, 1992, p. 40.

5. For discussions of blind *vs.* branded product testing, see Glen L. Urban and John R. Hauser, *Design and Marketing of New Products*. Englewood Cliffs, NJ: Prentice-Hall, 1980, p. 376; and Richard R. Batsell and Yoram Wind, "Product Testing: Current Methods and Needed Developments," *Journal of the Market Research Society* 22, 2 (1980), pp. 115-139.

6. See, for example, Maynard A. Amerine, Rose Marie Pangborn, and Edward B. Roessler, *Principles of Sensory Evaluation of Food*, New York: Academic Press, 1965, for a thorough treatment of sensory testing.

7. See, for example, Neil Bruce Holbert, Robert J. Golden, and Mark M. Chudnoff, *Marketing Research for the Marketing and Advertising Executive*. New York: American Marketing Association, 1981, p. 139, for a discussion of round robin testing.

8. See Maynard A. Amerine, Rose Marie Pangborn, and Edward B. Roessler, *Principles of Sensory Evaluation of Food*. New York: Academic Press, 1965, p. 444, for a discussion of the advantages of conducting a separate paired-comparison test as opposed to simply asking respondents in a duo-trio or triangle difference test to state a preference after the discrimination task.

9. See Neil Bruce Holbert, Robert J. Golden, and Mark M. Chudnoff, *Marketing Research for the Marketing and Advertising Executive*. New York: American Marketing Association, 1981, pp. 136 – 137.

10. *Ibid.*, pp. 135 – 136.

11. *Ibid.*, p. 137.

12. Zachary Schiller, "Ready, Aim, Market: Combat Training at P&G College," *Business Week*, February 3, 1992, p. 56.

13. William R. Dillon, Thomas J. Madden, and Neil H. Firtle, *Marketing Research in a Marketing Environment*. St. Louis, MO: Times Mirror/Mosby College Publishing, 1987, p. 626.

14. *Ibid.*, p. 138.

15. Neil Bruce Holbert, Robert J. Golden, and Mark M. Chudnoff, *Marketing Research for the Marketing and Advertising Executive* New York: American Marketing Association, 1981, p. 137.

16. See, for example, Richard R. Batsell and Yoram Wind, "Product Testing: Current Methods and Needed Developments," *Journal of the Market Research Society* 22, 3 (1980), pp. 115 - 139; and Peter Daniels and John Lawford, "The Effect of Order in the Presentation of Samples in Paired Comparison Product Tests," *Journal of the Market Research Society* 16, 2 (1974), pp. 127 - 133.

CHAPTER 12

Segmentation and Positioning

Learning Objectives:

After reading this chapter, you should be able to:

- define segmentation and discuss the various bases for segmenting markets.
- demonstrate how various sophisticated analytical methods are applied in the context of segmentation.
- define positioning and discuss the various ways to position or reposition a brand.
- describe different approaches to perceptual mapping, which is an analytical method particularly useful in the context of positioning.

The Gillette Company has grown over the years both from acquisitions and from new product introductions. In the past 10 years, Gillette has acquired the Waterman, and subsequently, the Parker Pen writing instrument companies, both known globally as marketers of pens priced over $5. Parker is the top-seller in this category followed by Cross, Mont Blanc and Waterman.

After the acquisition of Parker Pen, Gillette conducted an extensive consumer research study among current Parker and Waterman users to: 1) better understand the consumer profile for key high quality writing instrument brands; and 2) form the basis for advertising development. Through the results of the research, Gillette was able to develop two unique brand identities.

Based on the consumer research findings, Gillette launched a global advertising campaign to give the two brands separate identities so that they would appeal to different segments. The new Parker ads highlight craftsmanship and performance. The new Waterman ads stress self-expression and a wide variety of styles. Hence, Parker is designed to appeal to those who seek functional benefits, while Waterman's appeal is designed to be the pen's aesthetic qualities, as well as its reputation for performance. Gillette is hopeful that this campaign will create separate identities for the two brands.

Exhibits 12.1 and 12.2 show print ads from this campaign for each of the two brands.

Attitude statements	Factor* 1	2
I always look for shoe sales.		+
I don't like shopping at discount shoe stores.	+	
I'm willing to pay more to get quality.	+	
I look at prices in the window before entering a shoe store.		+
I usually buy shoes on sale.		+
Shoes are not an important part of my wardrobe.		
I typically shop at fine stores.	+	
I hate shopping for shoes.		
I prefer self-service stores.		
I'm willing to pay extra for well-known brands.	+	
I usually buy inexpensive shoes.		+
Shoes wear out quickly, so it doesn't pay to spend a lot of money on them.		+
I like to window-shop to keep up with shoe styles.		
Buying well-known brands is the best way to get quality shoes.	+	
I avoid low-priced shoe stores because I'm concerned about quality.	+	

*+ (−) indicates that the statement was positively (negatively) correlated to the factor.

Exhibit 12.1
Gillette positioned Parker pens to stress their craftsmanship and performance.

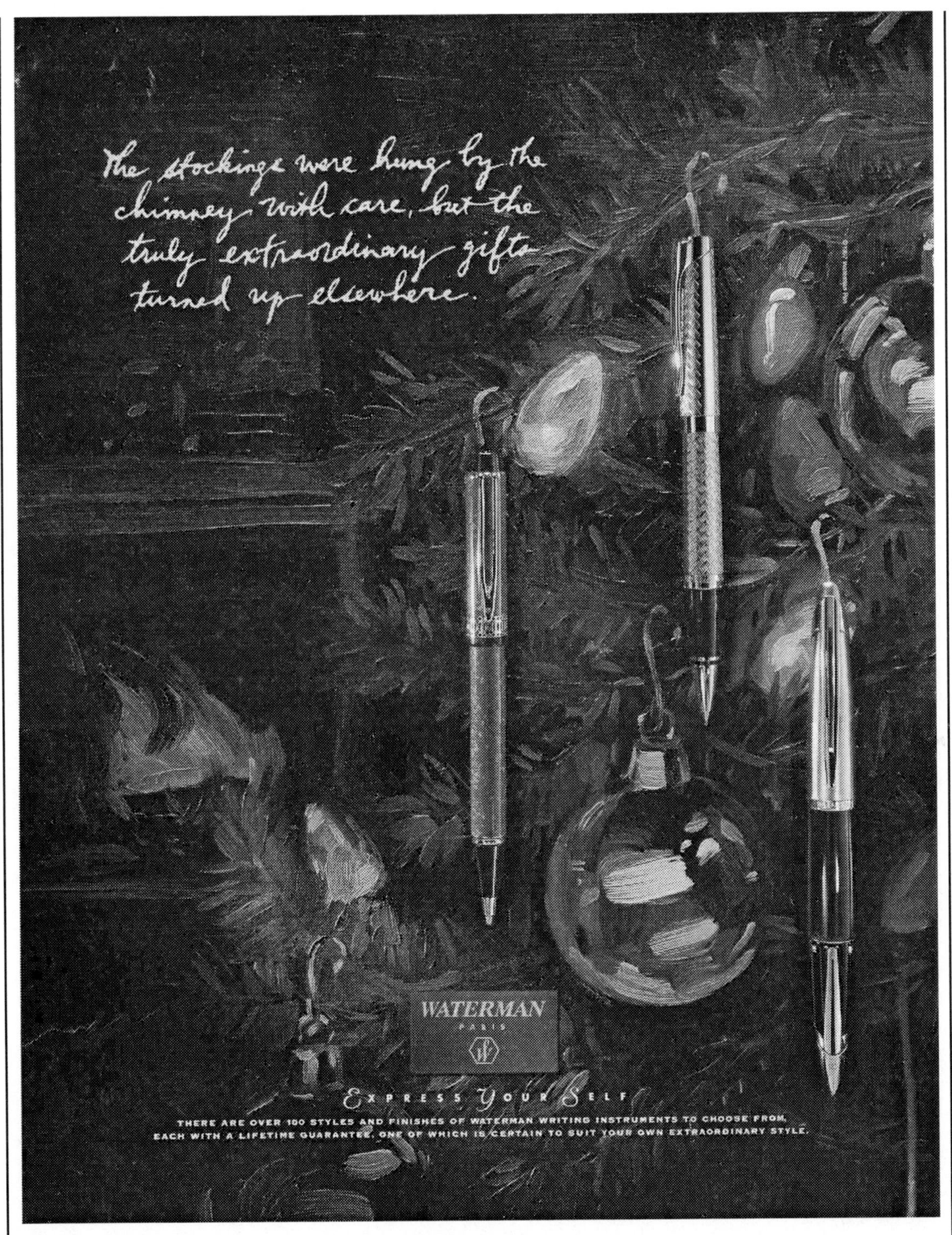

The stockings were hung by the chimney with care, but the truly extraordinary gifts turned up elsewhere.
WATERMAN
PARIS
EXPRESS YOUR SELF
THERE ARE OVER 100 STYLES AND FINISHES OF WATERMAN WRITING INSTRUMENTS TO CHOOSE FROM,
EACH WITH A LIFETIME GUARANTEE, ONE OF WHICH IS CERTAIN TO SUIT YOUR OWN EXTRAORDINARY STYLE.

Exhibit 12.2

Gillette positioned Waterman pens based on their aesthetic qualities.

In recent years, marketers have moved away from marketing products and services designed to appeal to all consumers in favor of products and services that appeal to specific niches within the market. Consequently, the number of brands available to U.S. consumers has skyrocketed. Even in a mundane category like toothpaste, brands come in gel, paste, and powder forms, packaged in tubes and pump dispensers, and promoting benefits ranging from "kissing-sweet" breath to antiplaque formulations. Similar situations can be found in many product categories, so that even the largest stores carry only a fraction of all available products. Defining niches, or segments, and designing offerings to match consumer needs involves both market segmentation and product positioning. The principles of segmentation and positioning have become the cornerstone for the development of a marketing plan.

Identifying target segments and developing positioning strategies are complementary activities. Positioning strategies are designed to make a particular brand especially appealing to one or more segments of the market. In other words, the positioning strategy for the brand implies the existence of a target consumer segment.[1] For example, Haagen-Dasz Ice Cream is positioned as "premium ice cream at a premium price," and the high quality of the ice cream is the focal point of the brand's advertising. At the same time, the obvious target consumers for the brand are ice-cream lovers willing and able to pay for the very best. The task that faces today's marketers is to identify well-defined market segments, select one or more segments as the target market, design brands specifically for the target market, and develop strategies to position their offerings in a way that makes them appealing to the target market. In this chapter we will first describe ways in which segments can be identified and the role of marketing research in this process. Then we will turn our attention to research activities that facilitate the development of positioning strategies.

Bases for Segmentation

Segmentation is the process of partitioning a market into groups of potential customers who are similar in designated ways and who are likely to exhibit similar purchasing behavior.[2] Although there is similarity within each group, or segment, there should be differences across the segments that suggest different marketing strategies for satisfying different segments. The key to a successful segmentation strategy is the ability to capitalize on similarities within a segment that are important from a marketing point of view. Gillette's advertising for Parker and Waterman is designed so that each brand appeals to the interests of a different segment. Various criteria, ranging from where people live to what they like and dislike, can be used to identify consumer segments.[3] Likewise, various sources of marketing research information can be used to provide information on these segments.

Geographic Segmentation

Segmentation based on geography is the simplest and easiest to implement. Any geographic areas, such as those defined by census regions, state lines, or county lines, can be used to organize consumers into groups based on where the consumers live. Anheuser-Busch markets Pacific Ridge Pale Ale (Exhibit 12.3) exclusively to northern Californians using a "think globally and drink locally slogan."

Exhibit 12.3
A brand that uses geographic segmentation.

Peculiarities in product preferences or purchase behavior often exist between geographic areas. For example, chicory-flavored coffee is popular in some regions of the United States but not at all popular in other regions. A wealth of secondary data sources exist that provide information on the characteristics of individuals or households in geographic areas.

Applying Marketing Research 12.1

Usage of sunscreen or sunblock products varies geographically and is especially high along coastal beaches of the United States. Yet, as recently as the 1980s, no sunscreen or sunblock products existed that would continue to protect during and after exposure to water. Recognizing the opportunity, Oceanside Laboratories of California developed BULLFROG, a waterproof sunscreen, and used geographic segmentation initially to launch the product.

BULLFROG was positioned as an amphibious formula -- good for six hours in and out of the water — and was targeted to California surfers. Surfers are exposed to the sun for extended periods of time, and they obviously spend a lot of time in the water. Exhibit 12.4 is a store display poster announcing that BULLFROG was available at the location, and Exhibit 12.5 illustrates a clever product sample, labeled a "tadpole," that was used to encourage trial of the product. BULLFROG was so successful that the rights to the product were purchased by Chattem, Inc. of Chattanooga, Tennessee, which now broadly markets the brand to all individuals in need of a waterproof sunscreen product.

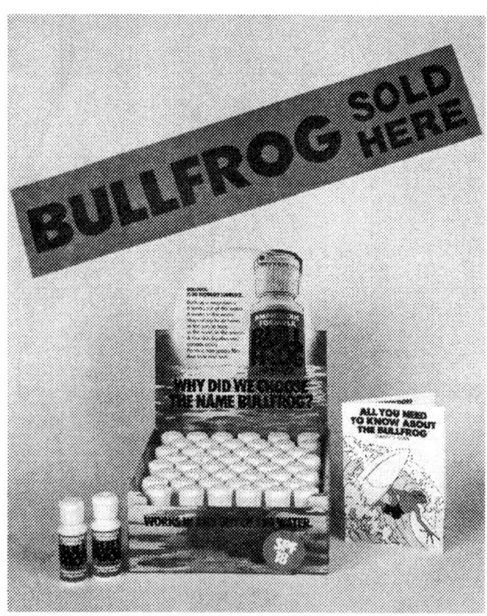

Exhibit 12.4
A product that used geographic segmentation when entering the market. (Courtesy of Peachtree Creek Business Group, Atlanta, Georgia.)

Exhibit 12.5
BULLFROG sunscreen used this clever tadpole product sample to encourage trial of the brand. (Courtesy of Peachtree Creek Business Group, Atlanta, Georgia).

Demographic Segmentation

Demographic variables, such as age, income, household size, or sex, provide another common base for organizing consumers into groups. Secondary sources such as the Census of the Population and syndicated sources such as Simmons data provide useful information on the size of such segments. Jergens positions its Biore line of skin care products (see Exhibit 12.6) to "20 somethings." Advertising focuses on the target audience of women aged 18 to early 30s. Promotional efforts include visiting college campuses and giving product samples to coeds.

Exhibit 12.6
Biore skin care products are positioned to "20-something segment."

Some products, such as baby foods or retirement properties, obviously are designed to appeal to specific demographic segments. Many other products, however, including movies, television shows, and magazines, are also developed to appeal to selected demographic segments.

Geodemographic Segmentation

Geodemographic segmentation systems organize small, well-defined geographic units into groups that are similar with respect to the demographic, housing, and socioeconomic characteristics of the households comprising the units. U.S. Census information is used in concert with statistical models to organize census blocks, tracts, or ZIP-code areas into such segments.

Geodemographic segmentation systems are based on the principle that birds of a feather flock together. That is, people with similar cultural backgrounds and chosen lifestyles tend to live near each other within communities. Hence, small geographically defined groups of similar people can be identified and combined with similar groups in other geographic areas to create segments having unique socioeconomic characteristics or lifestyle perspectives.

A geodemographic segmentation system creates efficiencies for direct marketing campaigns by focusing the mailing on segments having high percentages of households in the target market instead of relying on a mass mailing. Similarly, indices of sales potential for a product or service can be calculated for each segment based on its characteristics. A weighted average of household characteristics associated with ownership of a particular product, or usage of a particular product or service, might be used to develop the index of potential. For example, the index of potential for a domestic luxury car was reported to range from a low of 19 (average = 100) for the segment of low-income blue-collar workers living in the rural fringes of manufacturing areas to a high of 271 for the segment of highly affluent professionals who are homeowners in prime suburban neighborhoods.[4] Obviously, a dealer of domestic luxury cars could use this information to target advertising and promotional materials to households in the high-potential segments.

Another potential application of geodemographic segmentations is to profile a company's customer base, using customers' addresses to assign them to segments. For instance, O.M. Scott & Co., an Ohio-based lawn-care products company, gathered thousands of customers' names and addresses by offering a $5 rebate on the purchase of selected Scott products.[5] Purchasers submitted proofs-of-purchase and their addresses to receive their rebates through the mail. The addresses were then used to assign customers to geodemographic segments and to establish a profile of segment membership for Scott's customers. This profile, compared to the general population of the area and to the target audience, provides insight into the types of consumers attracted to the company's products and how well the company is doing at attracting business from its target audience.

Classifying customers into geodemographic segments based on their addresses can also be useful to determine the subset of customers to whom selected products and services are marketed. When Perpetual Savings Bank in Virginia sent promotional materials for a new service designed for affluent, older individuals to customers classified as members of geodemographic segments known to contain high concentrations of such individuals, not only did the campaign generate seven times the normal response rate, it generated $15.5 million in new deposits within six weeks.[6]

Several geodemographic segmentation systems are commercially available. All of the systems make extensive use of census data and create the geodemographic segments in a similar manner, but the systems do vary in terms of the number of segments generated. Donnelley Marketing Information Services' ClusterPlus consists of forty-seven segments, CACI's ACORN system contains forty-four segments and PRIZM, a product of Claritas, Inc., consists of forty basic segments, which are further organized into twelve social groups. The forty PRIZM segment have been given clever nicknames such as "Blue Blood Estates," "Pools and Patios," "Shotguns and Pickups," and "Leathertown USA." Table 12.1 lists several of the

PRIZM social groups and the segments comprising them.

	Factor*		
Attitude statements	1	2	3
I always look for shoe sales.		+	
I don't like shopping at discount shoe stores.	+		
I'm willing to pay more to get quality.	+		
I look at prices in the window before entering a shoe store.		+	
I usually buy shoes on sale.		+	
Shoes are not an important part of my wardrobe.			+
I typically shop at fine stores.	+		
I hate shopping for shoes.			+
I prefer self-service stores.			+
I'm willing to pay extra for well-known brands.	+		
I usually buy inexpensive shoes.		+	
Shoes wear out quickly, so it doesn't pay to spend a lot of money on them.		+	
I like to window-shop to keep up with shoe styles.			−
Buying well-known brands is the best way to get quality shoes.	+		
I avoid low-priced shoe stores because I'm concerned about quality.	+		

*+ (−) indicates that the statement was positively (negatively) correlated to the factor.

Table 12.1
PRIZM Segmentation Scheme

Neighborhoods which at first glance seem very similar, may differ greatly in potential for specific products and services. PRIZM's Young Suburbia and Young Influential segments live in similar appearing neighborhoods and on the surface are virtually identical yuppie communities. Both groups play golf and tennis, and both groups tend to belong to health clubs. However, the Young Suburbia households generally have children living at home, while the Young Influential households do not. This makes a big difference when it comes to taking cruises and buying pregnancy tests and Irish whiskey.[7] Applying Marketing Research 12.2 provides another example of how distinguishing between these two groups can be crucial from a marketing perspective.

Applying Marketing Research 12.2

Mountain Bell Telephone Company in Denver targets Young Suburbia for its call-waiting and call-forwarding services. The company's internal analyses had convinced them that households with children would be the best customers for these services. However, a tabulation of subscribers by PRIZM segment showed that the childless Young Influentials were the primary customers for these services.[8] Young Influentials are ambitious and active, and do not like missing phone calls. The company had missed the biggest target market for the new services. Marketing tactics were changed to focus on these consumers.

Most geodemographic systems are linked to various syndicated data sources so that media and product preferences can be examined across the geodemographic segments. For example, linking Simmons data to a geodemographic segmentation system would reveal which segments tend to read a magazine such as *Bon Appetit*. The publisher might attempt to increase subscriptions by running a direct-mail campaign aimed only at these geodemographic segments.

Psychographic Segmentation

Psychographics refers to segmentation based on values and lifestyles. Many products and services are positioned to groups that are defined psychographically. Some food products are specifically designed for individuals who are extremely health-conscious and concerned about physical fitness. Many automobiles are also positioned to appeal to specific lifestyle groups. For instance, the Mazda Miata (Exhibit 12.7) appeals to middle-aged "sporty" individuals with traditional values who remember and appreciate the classic design of the roadster sports cars of the 1950s and 1960s.

Exhibit 12.7
A brand using psychographic segmentation.

The most prominent psychographic segmentation system is **VALS** (Values and Lifestyle) offered by the Stanford Research Institute (SRI). The VALS2 system, the second generation of the VALS segmentation, is based on the premise that a person's lifestyle is dictated by the individual's self-orientation and the resources (psychological, physical, demographic, material means, and capacities) available to the individual. Self-orientation refers to the patterns of attitudes and activities that people use to reinforce, sustain, or even modify their social self-image. VALS2 specifies three self-orientation patterns: principle-oriented (behavior is consistent with how the world is or should be), status-oriented (seek a secure place in a valued social setting) and action-oriented (attempt to affect the environment in tangible ways), which, when combined with level of resources, yield the eight VALS2 segments shown in Exhibit 12.8. Individuals are classified into these eight groups based on their answers to a brief battery of thirty questions pertaining to social, economic, and demographic issues. A six-point agree — disagree scale is used for the majority of the questions.

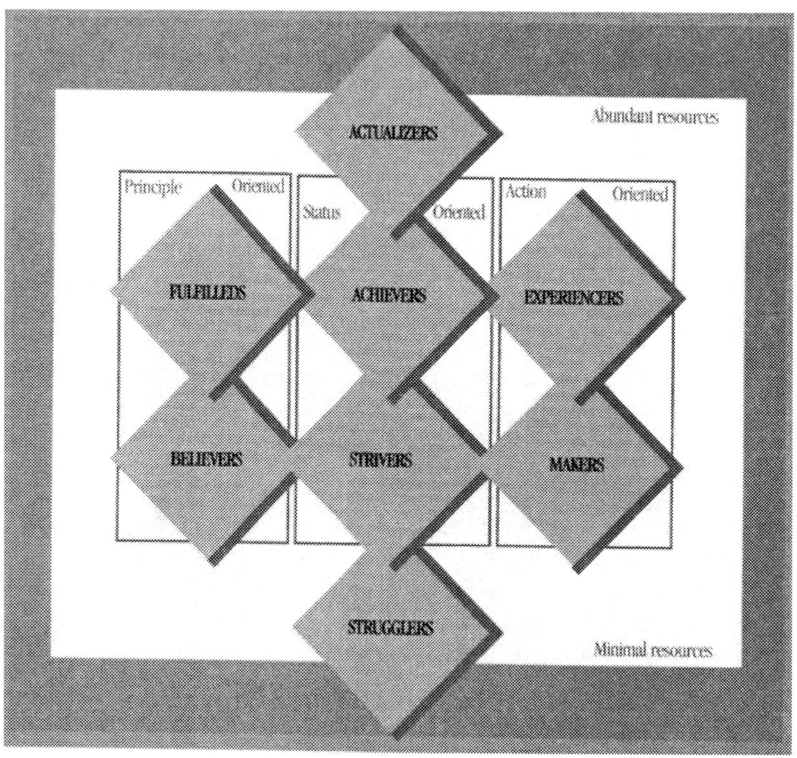

Exhibit 12.8

VALS2 segmentation scheme. Using these two dimensions—self-orientation and resources—VALS defined eight segments of adult consumers who have different attitudes and exhibit distinctive behavior and decision-making patterns. The segments are balanced in size so that each truly represents a viable target. VALS2 is a network of interconnected segments. Neighboring types have similar charactcs and can be combined in varying ways to suit particular marketing purposes. (Courtesy of SRI International,

formerly Stanford Research Institute.)

The VALS2 segmentation system has been linked to most geodemographic segmentation systems. By determining which geodemographic segments have the highest concentrations of particular VALS2 lifestyle groups, particular lifestyle groups can be reached very efficiently. VALS2 is also linked with the Simmons *Survey of Media and Markets*, so vast amounts of information are available pertaining to the media consumption, shopping habits, and product category usage of the VALS2 lifestyle groups.

The VALS2 system provides insight regarding lifestyle trends by monitoring the relative sizes of the eight segments. This information is vital for anticipating changes that could deeply effect a company's business. A company might also use VALS2 data to improve the effectiveness of its advertising and promotion activities as Applying Marketing Research 12.3 illustrates.

Applying Marketing Research 12.3

Merrill Lynch used the "bullish on America" slogan in its advertising for many years. This slogan and the corresponding advertising appealed to people with a "herd instinct" rather than the entrepreneurial, upwardly mobile and self-motivated investors the firm was trying to reach.[9] These entrepreneurial self-made investors, primarily found in the VALS2 Achiever segment, seek an investment firm that would

focus on the individual investor's needs and goals.

To position the firm to the independent Achiever segment, Merrill Lynch changed its advertising. TV commercials in the new campaigns showed a single bull wandering through the canyons of Wall Street or seeking shelter in a cave. A print ad showed a lone bull silhouetted on a mountaintop in the sunset. The campaign used the slogan " a breed apart." The new strategy, which stressed imagination, versatility and instinct, was designed to emotionally appeal to the Achiever target.

The concept of psychographic segmentation has gone international. SRI has initiated research to develop a psychographic segmentation system for Japan.[10] Also, the economic union of Europe has produced a market both larger and more complex than the United States, and marketers are using psychographic segmentation systems as a framework for exploring the wants and needs of "Euro-Consumers."

Another international psychographic segmentation program, called Global Scan, is aimed at developing a global psychographic segmentation scheme. Global Scan has identified five global psychographic types: Strivers, Achievers, Pressureds, Adapters, and Traditionals.[11] However, developers of Global Scan are quick to point out that marketers must be sensitive to cultural differences within the same basic segment across nations. For example, U.S. Strivers are under financial pressure, but not restricted in the sense of living space, while the opposite is true of Japanese Strivers. As a result, U.S. Strivers want cars that are fun, stylish, and a good value. Their Japanese counterparts want much the same in their cars, but also view their automobiles as added living space. Hence, Japanese Strivers are quite willing to pay extra for frills such as expensive stereo systems, which U.S. Strivers tend to avoid. Obviously, a car manufacturer, while able to capitalize on the commonalities among Strivers to market basically the same automobile to both groups, must still vary the finishing touches in developing the final appeals for the two groups.

Behavioral Segmentation

Consumers can be segmented based on their hobbies, shopping location preferences, product or service usage, or other behaviors. Since the heavy users of a product account for the vast majority of the total product category sales, households are often classified as light, moderate, or heavy users. Identifying the demographic and lifestyle peculiarities of the heavy users enables a company to develop a promotion and advertising strategy to concentrate effectively on these most valuable customers. A survey of category users, information from diary panels, or data from syndicated sources such as Simmons *Study of Media and Markets* would provide the key data for this segmentation.

Benefit Segmentation

Consumers in any product or service category can also be segmented based on the relative importance they place on key benefits of the product or service. This process, called **benefit segmentation**, has received increasing attention because "experience with this approach has shown that benefits sought by consumers determine their behavior much more accurately than do demographic characteristics or volume of consumption."[12]

A common research approach to implementing benefit

segmentation is to survey a sample of consumers and ask them to rate the importance of various benefits and features of a product or service, or to express their level of agreement with statements relating to benefit importance. Statistical techniques, described in more detail later in this chapter, are used to reduce the list of benefits or statements to a manageable number and to group similar consumers into distinct segments. Other information collected as part of the survey, such as demographics and brand preferences, can be used to differentiate the segments from each other further. Applying Marketing Research 12.4 illustrates this approach to benefit segmentation.

Applying Marketing Research 12.4

As the world's largest manufacturer of chewing gum, the Wm. Wrigley Jr. Company constantly examines the gum market seeking opportunities for growth through new brands positioned to satisfy specific segments in the market. Sometimes, as was the case with their Big Red brand of cinnamon chewing gum, this market vigilance pays off in a big way.

From previous research the Wrigley Company knew that the gum market was segmented according to type of gum (chewing gum *vs.* bubble gum) and gum flavor. The company did not have a strong competitive brand in the cinnamon flavor segment. Research was undertaken to learn more about the cinnamon chewing-

gum segment and about how best to position a gum to be successful against the segment leader, Dentyne.

The research finds revealed that the cinnamon chewing-gum segment was comprised primarily of teens and young adults and that the main benefit sought from a cinnamon gum was breath freshening. Furthermore, the company learned that some cinnamon gum users were dissatisfied with existing cinnamon gum brands because these gums did not keep breath fresh long enough, and the sticks of gum offered by some brands were too small.

Armed with this information, Wrigley began a project to develop a cinnamon chewing gum that provided the benefits of larger size and longer-lasting flavor. The brand Big Red (see Exhibit 12.9) was the result of this product development effort. Product testing showed that Big Red was superior to Dentyne for duration of breath freshening. In addition, Big Red sticks were manufactured to be 30 percent larger than the Dentyne sticks. Wrigley aggressively began advertising these facts in an attempt to position Big Red as the superior cinnamon chewing gum. Big Red's sales began to grow by double-digit amounts, and within ten years the brand had become the market leader.

Exhibit 12.9
A successful application of benefit segmentation. (Reprinting courtesyof the Wm. Wrigley Jr. Company.)

Occasions-of-Use Segmentation

The segmentation schemes discussed so far have all concentrated on organizing *consumers* into groups. An alternative is to group *usage occasions* according to their similarity. The premise of occasions-of-use segmentation is that different usage situations dictate different criteria for brand choice. Thus, usage occasions can be organized into segments having similar brand selection criteria. For example, wine can be purchased as a gift or consumed on a number of different types of occasions, including a social gathering, a formal dinner, or a picnic. If differing brand selection criteria are operating in the various usage situations, marketing strategies can be developed to enhance a wine's image in terms of its appropriateness for a particular usage occasion or set of occasions.

Exploratory research, in the form of focus groups or in-depth interviews conducted with category users, can be useful for generating a list of usage occasions. Surveys or diary panel studies then can provide information as to the relative frequency of occurrence of the various usage occasions. A survey of users can also be used to develop the importance assigned to benefits or product characteristics in each usage occasion. In some cases, it may be advantageous to take the process one step further and identify segments of consumers who differ with respect to the importance attached to various attributes or benefits in a given usage situation. Thus, a brand might be positioned for a particular occasion of use to a segment of consumers desiring a particular set of product attributes or benefits on such an occasion.

An example of the usage occasion segmentation strategy is the General Foods' "celebrate the moments of your life" advertising campaign for its line of International Coffees. In one TV commercial (see Exhibit 12.10), a mother is shown enjoying one of these coffee varieties by herself in the evening. The baby is asleep, and it is "her time." The brand is advertised as perfect for such times.

YOUNG & RUBICAM NEW YORK

CLIENT: GENERAL FOODS CORP.
PRODUCT: INTERNATIONAL COFFEES
TITLE: "DREAMS REV."

LENGTH: 30 SECONDS
COMM. NO. GFMI 6849CC
DATE: 5/16/86

1. (MUSIC UNDER) MOTHER: (VO) I still can't believe how amazing you are.

2. So sweet dreams, little Katy.

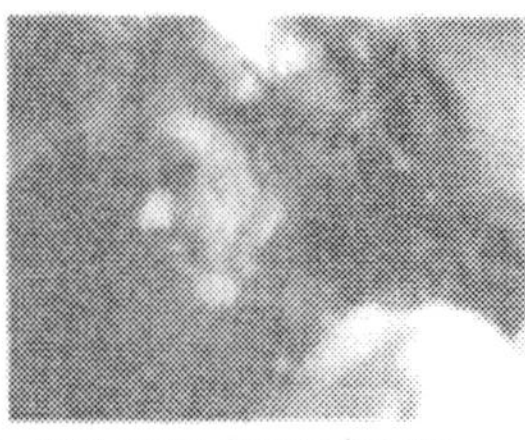

3. And sweet dreams for me, too.

4. Because I'm about to have something so rich, so creamy...

5. ANNCR: (VO) General Foods International Coffees Cafe Vienna...

6. with the spicy sweetness

7. of cinnamon.

8. (MUSIC)

9. Unlike anything else...turning quiet time into a quiet celebration.

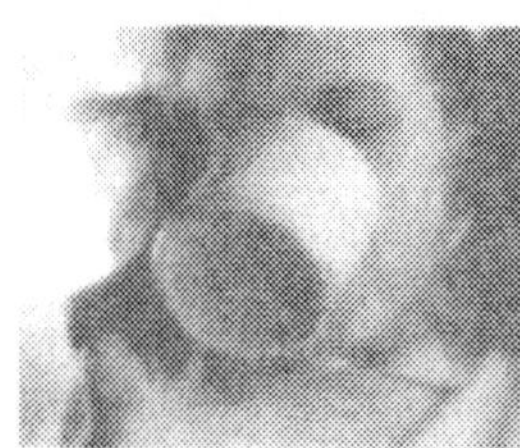

10. SINGER: Celebrate the moments

11. of your life...

12. ANNCR: (VO) With General Foods International Coffees.

Exhibit 12.10
An example of occasion-of-use segmentation. (General Foods is a registered trademark of the General Foods Corporation.)

Analytical Methods Used in Segmentation

As noted in the previous section, marketing research plays an important role in defining consumer segments and in developing strategies for appealing to those segments. Three statistical techniques are particularly useful in the context of segmentation: factor analysis, conjoint analysis, and cluster analysis.

Factor Analysis

As discussed in Chapter 8, rating scales are often used in conjunction with survey research to collect consumer attitude or opinion data. Scale ratings to measure the relative importance individuals attach to various characteristics of fast-food restaurants might include such things as: play area for children, special meals for children, wide variety in types of food, a salad bar, polite employees, and special low-fat meals. In many cases, the list of characteristics being rated is quite long but only a few underlying attitudinal dimensions are really being measured. Factor analysis can be used to reduce the total list of statements to a few dimensions, called factors, that capture the essence of what is being measured.

It is important to point out that the list of items to be rated should also be based on marketing research, not simply created by marketing or marketing research managers. Qualitative research using focus groups or depth interviews might be used to determine a list of characteristics (such as the one just given) that consumers consider when selecting a fast-food restaurant.

Factor analysis identifies patterns of ratings, based on how each statement rating correlates with the others, and groups related statements together to form factors. Names are assigned to factors by examining the statements comprising each factor. Individuals are then assigned scores for each factor according to their ratings for the corresponding statements. Therefore, not only can a large set of statements be reduced to a smaller number of dimensions, but also individuals can be assigned scores on these fewer dimensions and segmented based upon these scores.

The actual analysis and scoring is quite complex but is easily performed using any one of a number of available computer programs. Applying Marketing Research 12.5 clarifies how factor analysis can be used in segmentation studies.

Applying Marketing Research 12.5

A survey of 800 female heads-of-household

was conducted to examine female attitudes toward shopping for shoes. As part of the survey, participants were shown fifteen phrases

regarding shopping for shoes and were asked to indicate their level of agreement with each statement using a nine-point scale ("1" = Strongly Disagree and "9" = Strongly Agree). The fifteen statements were then factor-analyzed to determine underlying dimensions, and factor scores were assigned accordingly to each respondent.

Factor analysis revealed that the fifteen statements were measuring three dimensions, or factors. Table 12.2 shows which phrases correspond to each of the factors. Note the minus sign for the last item, "I like to window-shop to keep up with shoe styles," associated with Factor 3. This means that, although the item is related to the factor, the correlation is negative. In other words, there was a tendency to disagree with this statement when agreeing with the other phrases comprising Factor 3, and vice versa.

	Factor*		
Attitude statements	1	2	3
I always look for shoe sales.		+	
I don't like shopping at discount shoe stores.	+		
I'm willing to pay more to get quality.	+		
I look at prices in the window before entering a shoe store.		+	
I usually buy shoes on sale.		+	
Shoes are not an important part of my wardrobe.			+
I typically shop at fine stores.	+		
I hate shopping for shoes.			+
I prefer self-service stores.			+
I'm willing to pay extra for well-known brands.	+		
I usually buy inexpensive shoes.		+	
Shoes wear out quickly, so it doesn't pay to spend a lot of money on them.		+	
I like to window-shop to keep up with shoe styles.			–
Buying well-known brands is the best way to get quality shoes.	+		
I avoid low-priced shoe stores because I'm concerned about quality.	+		

*+ (–) indicates that the statement was positively (negatively) correlated to the factor.

Table 12.2
Factor analysis of shoe attitude data.

Examining the items comprising the three factors, Factor 1 appears to measure a concern over quality of the shoes purchased with little or no worry about price since respondents having high (low) scores on Factor 1 attach high (low) importance to quality and brand name. Factor 2 represents price consciousness, with respondents receiving low scores not being concerned about price. Factor 3 represents interest in shoes as apparel. Respondents having high scores on Factor 3 view shoes from a functional point of view and are not very style-conscious, while those scoring low on this factor view shoes as an important element of dress and very style-conscious.

Cluster Analysis

Cluster analysis is a technique that organizes items or individuals into groups, called clusters, so that there is similarity with respect to the clustering criteria within each cluster but dissimilarity across the clusters. By its very nature, cluster analysis is extremely useful for segmentation applications, with the clusters being treated as segments. For example, food stores might be clustered based on annual sales, number of employees, and number of items carried. Individuals might be clustered based on factor scores derived from their responses to rating scale questions measuring what they consider important and not important in choosing a product or services.

Cluster analysis typically involves the use of sophisticated mathematical algorithms and, like factor analysis, is performed using one of a number of available computer programs. A number of solutions are generated, and the determination of the proper number of clusters is as much an art as a science.

Applying Marketing Research 12.6 illustrates how cluster analysis can be used in a segmentation context.

Applying Marketing Research 12.6

In Applying Marketing Research 12.5, factor analysis was used to identify three factors or dimensions from consumer agreement/disagreement ratings for a series of statements pertaining to shopping for shoes. The first factor appeared to be measuring a concern for quality, the second factor was a price-consciousness dimension, and the third factor indicated level of interest in shoes as apparel. Individual scores on each factor were computed by using the respondent's rating on each of the statements comprising the factor. These individual factor scores were then used as the basis for a cluster analysis to identify groups of similar individuals.

Four clusters emerged from the cluster analysis of the factor scores. Table 12.3 shows the average factor scores for the four clusters and the number of participants assigned to each. The unique characteristics of each cluster were determined by examining the average factor scores.

Factor	**Clusters***			
	1	2	3	4
1	−1.2	.8	.9	−1.0
2	.9	−1.1	.1	1.0
3	.1	1.2	−1.3	−1.8
Cluster size	120	150	80	50

*Numbers in the table are mean factor scores of each cluster.

Table 12.3
Four segments of shoe shoppers based on cluster analysis of factor scores

Based upon their average factor scores Cluster 1 and Cluster 4 both consist of price-conscious shoppers who are willing to sacrifice quality or brand name to get lower prices. What makes these two clusters different from one another is that Cluster 4 shoppers like to shop for shoes more than Cluster 1 shoppers (remember that a negative score on factor three implies a high level of interest in shoes as apparel). Unlike Cluster 1 and Cluster 4 shoppers, Cluster 2 and Cluster 3 shoppers are concerned about shoe quality. However, Cluster 2 shoppers seem completely unconcerned about price and do not have much interest in shoes as apparel, while Cluster 3 shoppers are very interested in shoes as apparel and are somewhat sensitive to the price that must be paid.

Once the clusters have been identified, cross-tabulation of other information obtained in the survey, such as demographic data, serves to reinforce the segment descriptions and identify the segment members. For example, lower household incomes would be expected in Clusters 1 and 4 than in Cluster 2. Differences in behavioral characteristics, such as when, how, and where people shop; how they pay; and media habits across the segments, also help to describe the respective cluster compositions and point out ways to market to the different groups.

Conjoint Analysis

Conjoint analysis is a useful statistical technique for measuring the relative importance individuals attach to product or service benefits and features.[13] In a typical conjoint study, various levels of several key features or benefits are selected for study, and product or service profiles are constructed using a level of each benefit or feature. A survey is conducted, and respondents are asked to rank the product or service profiles according to their preference. These rankings are then used to determine the relative impact of each feature on the individual's overall preference.

The objective of conjoint analysis is to assign a weight, called a part-worth, to each level of each feature, so that the ranking of the profiles based upon the summation of the corresponding part-worths reproduces the participant's original overall preference ranking. A computer algorithm is used to find the particular part-worths that most closely reproduce the overall preference ranking. Since, in many cases, the overall preference ranking cannot be perfectly reproduced by any set of part-worths, conjoint analysis algorithms also provide measures of how well the ranking based on the best part-worth weights fits the original input ranking.

The ranges of the best part-worth values for the features are used to determine relative importance scores for the features. The resultant individual importance scores in turn can become the basis of a cluster analysis to develop a segmentation of the market based on the relative importance of the specific benefits. Applying Marketing Research 12.7 demonstrates the use of conjoint analysis in a segmentation context.

Applying Marketing Research 12.7

A financial institution conducted a survey of 500

checking account customers to investigate the relative importance of three checking account features: minimum balance to avoid service charges, monthly service charge, and overdraft policy. Three levels of each feature, as described in Table 12.4, were used to design the profiles. Twenty-seven profile descriptions were created by combining each feature level with all levels of the other features. Each survey participant ranked all twenty-seven profiles in order of preference.

	Features		
Level	Minimum balance to avoid monthly service charge	Monthly service charge	Overdraft policy
1	$1500	$6	No overdraft provision; bad checks returned
2	$2000	$8	Overdrafts covered up to $100 at 10% interest
3	$2500	$10	Overdrafts covered up to $500 at 10% interest

Table 12.4
Attribute levels for checking account survey

Each respondent's ranking of the twenty-seven profiles was submitted to a conjoint analysis computer algorithm, and each individual's importance scores for the three features were calculated using the ranges of the resulting part-worths. For example, if the respective ranges of part-worth for one individual are: 72 for minimum balance requirement, 100 for monthly service charge, and 28 for overdraft policy, the most important feature to this participant is the monthly service charge, and its relative importance score is 100/(72 + 100 + 28) = .50. The importance scores for the other two features are .36 and .14 respectively.

A cluster analysis of the individual importance scores yielded three segments of the 500 survey scores yielded three segments of the 500 survey

participants. Table 12.5 shows the mean importance scores and sizes for these three groups. The largest segment (segment 1 in Table 12.6) comprised half of the participants and contained individuals who were almost exclusively concerned with the monthly service charge. The second largest segment (Segment 3), containing 30 percent of the respondents, consisted

of individuals who were equally concerned about the minimum balance and service charge and were relatively unconcerned about the overdraft policy. Finally, the smallest segment (Segment 2) was the most concerned about overdraft policy and placed little concern on monthly service charge and minimum balance requirements. This segment presented a market opportunity since the bank currently did not offer a checking account with liberal overdraft protection.

		Mean importance scores		
Segment	Size	Minimum balance	Service charge	Overdraft policy
1	250	.1	.8	.1
2	100	.15	.15	.7
3	150	.45	.45	.1

Table 12.5
Checking account attitude segment obtained via conjoint analysis

Positioning

Once a market has been segmented, a company must develop a strategy for positioning a product or service so that it appeals to one or more of the segments. Positioning exists in the minds of customers; that is, it is based on how consumers perceive the brand relative to competition. A brand's **positioning**, then, can be thought of as the niche a brand occupies in the target segment's overall perception of the relevant brands in the category. The goal of a positioning strategy is to differentiate the brand from its competitors on attributes and/or benefits considered important by the target segment in such a way as to make the brand most appealing to this target segment.

Clearly, segmentation and positioning must be considered jointly. For example, as noted earlier in Applying Marketing Research 12.4. Wrigley positioned Big Red chewing gum to appeal to those users of cinnamon-flavored chewing gum who wanted larger sticks of gum and longer breath-freshening. Wrigley markets many other brands of gum, designed to appeal to different segments of users. For example, Wrigley's Freedent is positioned to denture wearers as a gum which will not stick to dental work.

Positioning Approaches

Marketers can attempt to position, or differentiate, a brand from its competitors in a variety of ways.[14] Table 12.6 lists common positioning strategies and provides examples of brands using each. The choice of positioning approach depends on the strengths and weaknesses of the brand relative to competitive brands and the peculiarities of the target segment(s).

Positioning strategy	Illustrative brands
Specific product features	Listerine mouthwash, Jolt Cola
Product benefits	diet Coke, Ensure
Specific use	General Foods International Coffees, Gatorade
Type of user	Centrum Silver Vitamins, Biore Skin Care Products
Against another product	Avis car rental, Visa Credit Card
Product class dissociation	7-Up, USA Today
Price	Tiffany's jewelers, Heineken beer, Lady Godiva Chocolates
Hybrid	Coast soap, Tums antacid

Table 12.6
Alternative positioning strategies

Specific Features

Characteristics of the brand can be used to differentiate it from competitors. If a particular feature of the brand implies a benefit that is important to the target segment, it can become a basis for positioning. For instance, Listerine mouthwash's unpleasant taste was used in the brand's positioning as evidence of germ-killing power. Sprite touts the fact that it is a caffeine-free soft drink. Perhaps the best example of positioning by specific features is Jolt Cola, which is advertised as being made with "real sugar and twice the caffeine," implying that the brand does not cheat on taste.

Benefits

Brands can be positioned to specific user segments on the basis of the benefits provided. While the benefits may be created by the brand's attributes, the emphasis of the positioning is on the benefit to the user as opposed to the attribute. Diet Coke is positioned as providing good taste while still being a low-calorie soft drink. Shout Wipes, a line extension of the original Shout spray stain treatment, are sheets individually packaged in pouches, so you can "wipe out stains wherever you go!" The benefits of portability and convenience are emphasized in the advertising.

The French company Generale Ultrafrais uses an unusual benefit to position its Mamie Nova line of dairy products.[15] The products, which contain lime blossom extracts that are said to help people to relax, are being marketed as natural recipes for a good night's sleep. The target market is the 25% of the French population who are said to have difficulty falling asleep.

There is growing interest in neutraceuticals, food products which naturally contain, or are fortified with ingredients providing health benefits. Mars, Inc. introduced a calcium-fortified rice as a line extension of the Uncle Ben's brand.[16] Kellogg Company has created a Functional Foods Division which will market nutraceuticals. Ensure and Resource are adult drinks designed to be nutritional supplements which help aging adults to maintain an active lifestyle. Power bars are positioned as healthy alternatives to candy bars.

Specific Use

Positioning by specific usage is used in conjunction with an occasion-of-use segmentation strategy as the company attempts to show that the brand is best suited for particular use situations. Gatorade is positioned for those occasions when athletic activity has generated a huge thirst and a bodily need for fluid and minerals. Another good example is General Foods International Coffee campaign mentioned earlier.

Type of User

Some brands are positioned to appeal to specific user categories, defined by such factors as demographics, lifestyle, or frequency of use. For example, Avia athletic shoes are positioned for the serious athlete (see Exhibit 12.11). McDonald's developed its Arch Deluxe line of sandwiches to appeal to adult tastes (see Exhibit 12.12). Various clothing retailers position themselves specifically to selected segments such as tall men, petite women, or teenage girls. Finally, Campbell Soup Company developed Intelligent Cuisine, a series of low-fat and low-sodium meals for heart and hypertension patients.

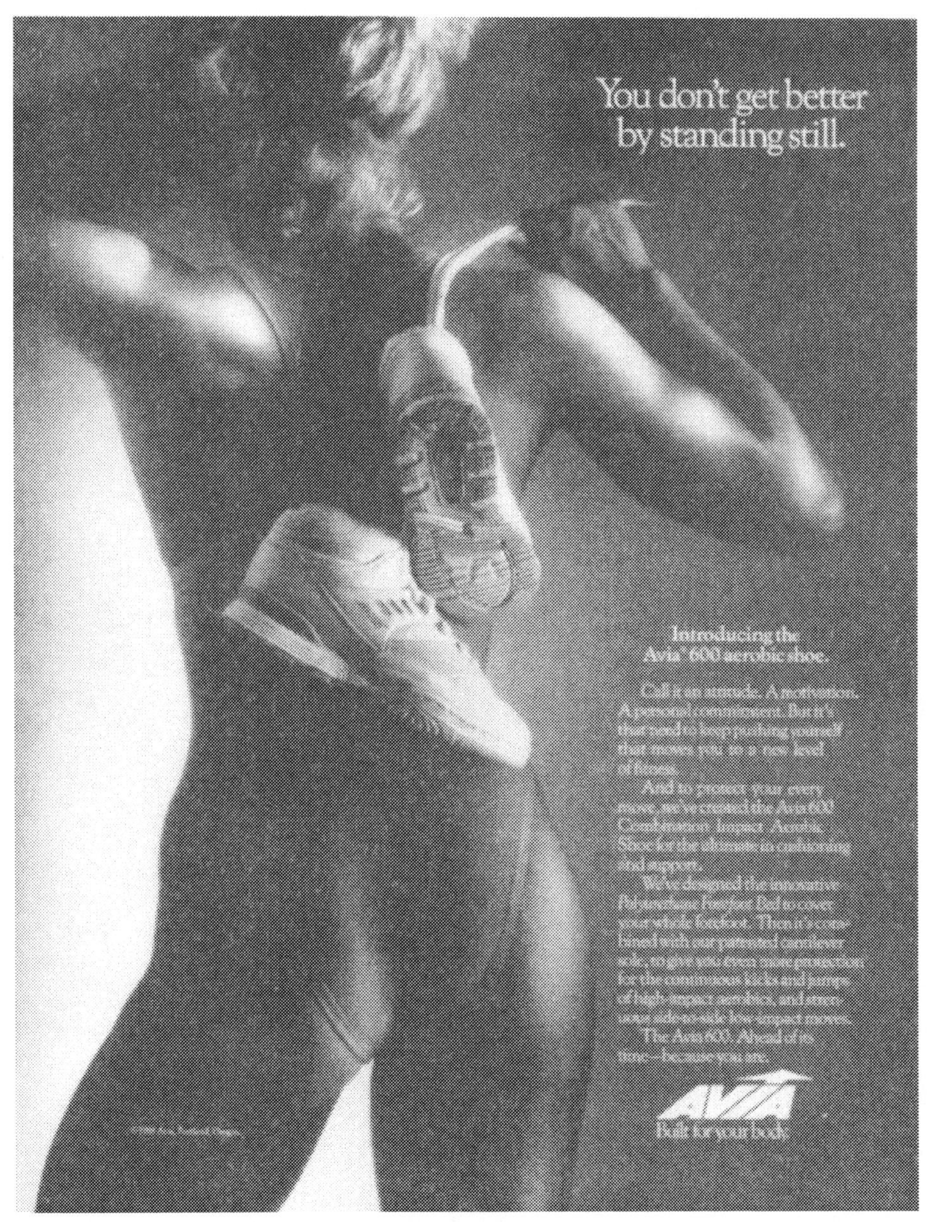

Exhibit 12.11
Positioning based on type of user. (Courtesy of Avia Group International, Inc.)

TAKE YOUR KID
TO McDONALD'S.

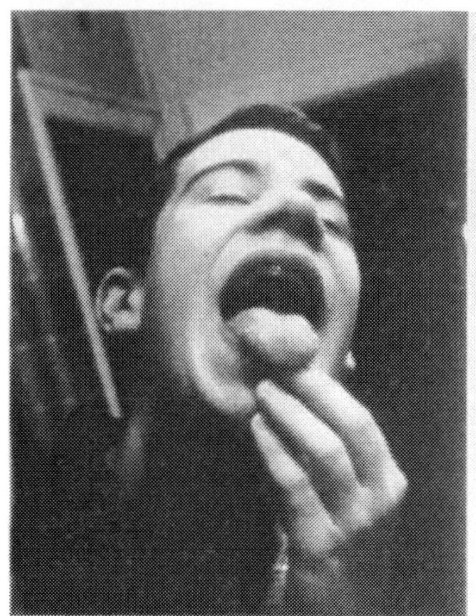

A LITTLE KNOWN FACT
ABOUT BECOMING A MAN: YOUR
TASTE BUDS CHANGE TOO.

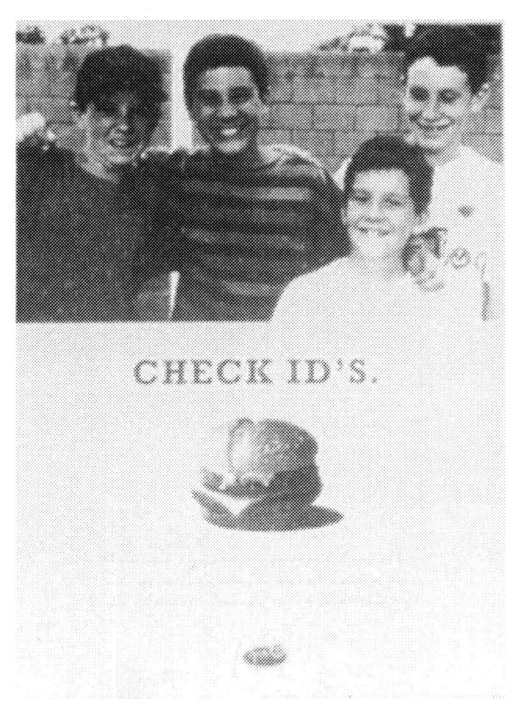
CHECK ID'S.

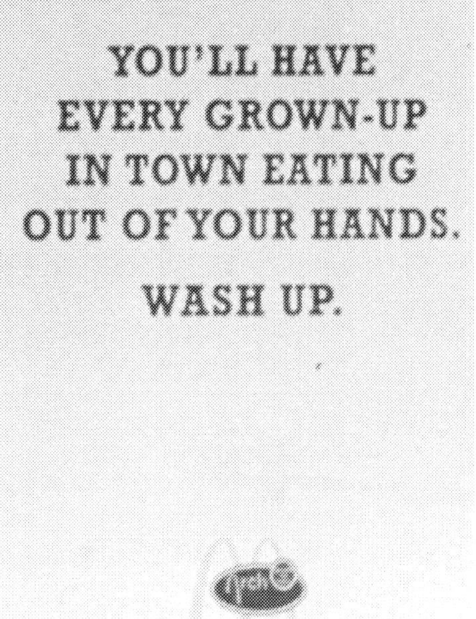
YOU'LL HAVE
EVERY GROWN-UP
IN TOWN EATING
OUT OF YOUR HANDS.
WASH UP.

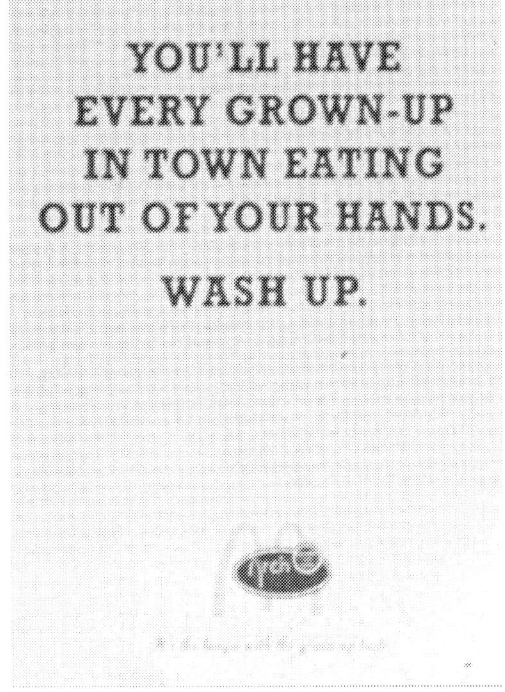
YOU'LL HAVE
EVERY GROWN-UP
IN TOWN EATING
OUT OF YOUR HANDS.
WASH UP.

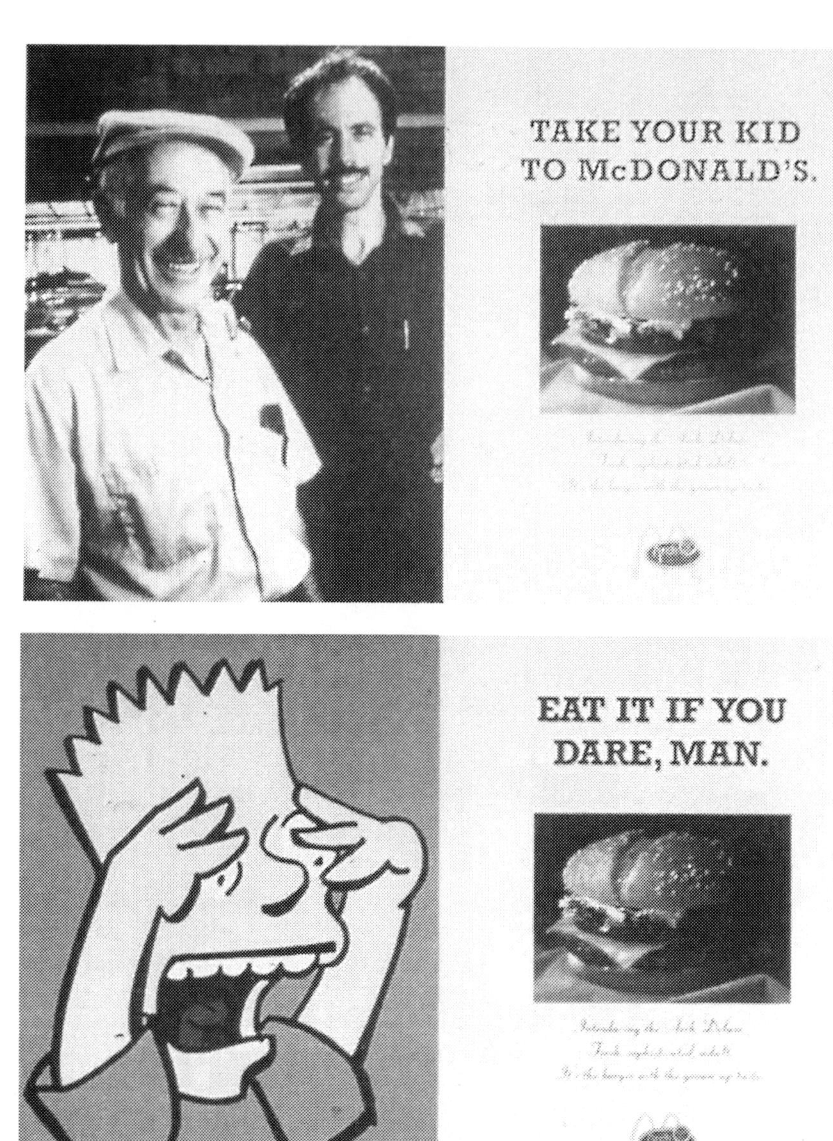

Exhibit 12.12
McDonald's Arch Deluxe line of sandwiches are positioned to adults.

Against Another Brand

Occasionally a firm will use a competitive brand to position its own brand. A company typically attempts to position its product or service as better than a well-known competitive brand. Visa USA has positioned its credit card by pointing out places in its advertising where its card is accepted, but the American Express card is not. The Visa campaign used the tagline "it's everywhere you want to be." The classic example of this strategy is perhaps the Avis "We try harder" campaign. The advertising stated that Avis was the second largest car rental company at the time and, as a consequence, was more concerned about pleasing its customers than was the largest car rental company, Hertz.

Class Disassociation

The class disassociation positioning strategy involves communicating what the advertised brand is not. The 7-UP brand was positioned as the "uncola" and hence the major alternative to cola brands (see Exhibit 12.13). Similarly, the USA Today newspaper is positioned not as a local newspaper but as one that focuses on national and international news instead.

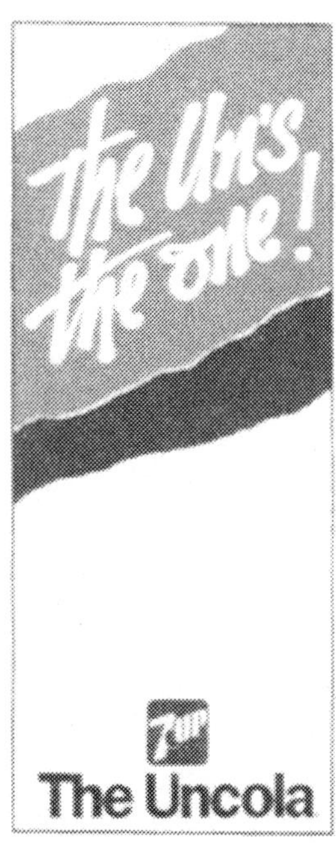

Exhibit 12.13
An example of class disassociation positioning. (Reproduced courtesy of The Seven-Up Company.)

Price

Price is a brand feature and, as such, positioning by price can be argued to be a special case of positioning by features. Further, a positioning strategy emphasizing relatively low price can appropriately be viewed as positioning by a specific benefit, namely cost savings. However, the use of price to position a brand is so common that we have listed it as a separate positioning approach. The Wal-Mart chain of stores is an example of a brand positioned as providing generally lower prices. On the other hand, a brand can be purposely positioned as being high-priced. As opposed to a low-price strategy that provides a cost-savings benefit to the consumer, the high-price strategy attempts to communicate high quality through high price. Lady Godiva chocolates are positioned this way.

Hybrid

Some brands are positioned using a combination of the approaches given above. Procter & Gamble uses a heavy perfume feature and a refreshment benefit to position Coast bar soap. Tums is advertised as containing calcium (product feature) as well as providing the soothing relief of an antacid (benefit). One danger of using a hybrid strategy is that the target segment will not have a clear perception of the brand.

Repositioning

Companies sometimes attempt to change the way consumers perceive an existing brand, that is, a **repositioning** of a brand is undertaken in order to stimulate sales. Camay bar soap was packaged for many years with a rich-looking wrapper bearing a cameo logo. The brand was positioned to women as a beauty bar designed to keep skin feeling soft and smooth. Over time the Camay franchise aged, and sales of the product dropped due to the brand's limited appeal among young females. In an effort to reposition the brand to young females, the packaging was dramatically changed (see Exhibit 12.14)and young women were used frequently in the advertising.

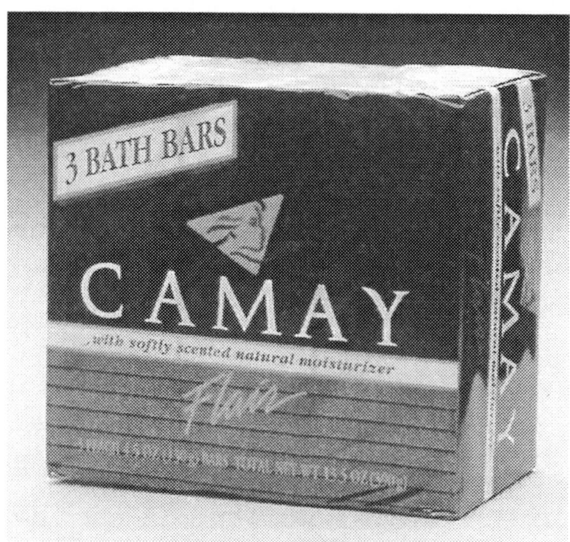

Exhibit 12.14
Camay was repositioned to appeal young females.

Sometimes brands are repositioned to increase sales by using advertising to promote the brand to new users or to encourage usage of the brand in another context other than previously intended. Johnson & Johnson originally used the tagline "no more tears" to position its shampoo as mild and gentle enough for use on babies. They later used the same mild and gentle appeal to position the brand to adult frequent shampooers, particularly males, who might be concerned about possible damage to the hair and scalp from frequent shampooing. They used "macho" male characters, including football players, in the advertising associated with the repositioning. Arm and Hammer's baking soda was repositioned as a freshening agent as well as a baking ingredient. The goal was to increase consumption of the brand by encouraging this additional use for the product. Exhibit 12.15 is a print ad promoting the use of baking soda to freshen laundry as well as to enhance the cleaning power of laundry detergent.

TRY ADDING ME FOR A CLEANER, FRESHER WASH.

I'LL HELP MAKE YOUR LIQUID DETERGENT CLEAN AND FRESHEN BETTER.
ARM & HAMMER
Pure Baking Soda
Washed with liquid detergent plus ½ cup of ARM & HAMMER Baking Soda.
Washed with liquid detergent alone.

Here's how to get your whole wash looking cleaner and smelling fresher. For just pennies a load. Add half a cup of ARM & HAMMER® Baking Soda to your favorite liquid detergent. Colors and whites look so different, you won't believe your eyes. Or your nose.

43,428,000 coupons for **40¢ off**
any 2 or 4 lb. size box of
ARM & HAMMER® Baking Soda
will appear in **QUAD MARKETING**
on Sunday, **July 12, 1992.**

MARKETS	NEWSPAPERS	ABC CIRC (000)
NEW ENGLAND		
Boston, MA	Globe	799
Worcester, MA	Telegram	138
Springfield, MA	Republican	157
Pittsfield, MA	Berkshire Eagle	34
Hartford, CT	Courant	321
New Haven, CT	Register	134
Waterbury, CT	Republican	77
New London, CT	Day	43
Bridgeport, CT	Post	88
Danbury, CT	News-Times	47
Stamford/Greenwich, CT	Advocate/Time	57
Norwalk, CT	Hour	22
Providence, RI	Journal	265
Portland, ME	Telegram	140
Bangor, ME	News	93
	Region Total	2,415
NEW YORK METRO		
New York, NY	Times	1,132
Long Island, NY	Newsday	961
Newark, NJ	Star-Ledger	708
	Region Total	2,801
MIDDLE ATLANTIC		
Poughkeepsie, NY	Journal	62
Middletown, NY	Record	100
Albany, NY	Times Union	164
Schenectady, NY	Gazette	62
Troy, NY	Record	42
Buffalo, NY	News	384
Binghamton, NY	Press & Sun-Bulletin	93
Elmira, NY	Star-Gazette	51
Ithaca, NY	Journal	20
Utica, NY	Observer-Dispatch	68
Rochester, NY	Democrat & Chronicle	260
Syracuse, NY	Herald-American	223
Watertown, NY	Times	43
Philadelphia, PA	Inquirer	988
Camden, NJ	Courier-Post	105
Trenton, NJ	Times	95
Atlantic City, NJ	Press	98
Wilmington, DE	News-Journal	140
Harrisburg, PA	Patriot-News	176
Sunbury, PA	Item	27
Scranton, PA	Times	81
Wilkes-Barre, PA	Independent	59
Wilkes-Barre, PA	Times Leader	62
Williamsport, PA	Sun Gazette	40
Baltimore, MD	Sun	492
Washington, DC	Post	1,130
Hagerstown, MD	Herald/Mail	39
	Region Total	5,104
EAST CENTRAL		
Akron, OH	Beacon Journal	226
Canton, OH	Repository	79
Cincinnati, OH	Enquirer	352
Hamilton, OH	Journal-News	30
Cleveland, OH	Plain Dealer	562
Columbus, OH	Dispatch	400
Dayton, OH	News	234
Springfield, OH	News-Sun	46
Toledo, OH	Blade	216
Lima, OH	News	51
Youngstown, OH	Vindicator	132
Warren, OH	Tribune-Chronicle	47
Detroit, MI	News And Free Press	1,216
Pontiac, MI	Oakland Press	83
Flint, MI	Journal	125
Saginaw, MI	News	66
Bay City, MI	Times	51
Grand Rapids, MI	Press	192
South Bend, IN	Tribune	130
Elkhart, IN	Truth	32
Indianapolis, IN	Star	417
Evansville, IN	Courier & Press	119
Lexington, KY	Herald Leader	162
Louisville, KY	Courier Journal	329
Pittsburgh, PA	Press	557
Johnstown, PA	Tribune-Democrat	54
Altoona, PA	Mirror	40
Greensburg, PA	Tribune-Review	85
Roanoke, VA	Times & World News	129
Lynchburg, VA	News & Advance	45
Charleston, WV	Gazette Mail	105
Beckley, WV	Register Herald	35
Huntington, WV	Herald-Dispatch	50
	Region Total	6,397
SOUTHEAST		
Norfolk, VA	Virginian Pilot	238
Newport News, VA	Press	123
Richmond, VA	Times Dispatch	255
Knoxville, TN	News-Sentinel	173
Memphis, TN	Commercial Appeal	290
Jackson, TN	Sun	42
Nashville, TN	Tennessean	269
Chattanooga, TN	News-Free Press	112
Birmingham, AL	News	213
Montgomery, AL	Journal-Advertiser	80
Huntsville, AL	Times	81
Charlotte, NC	Observer	300
Gastonia, NC	Gazette	46
Salisbury, NC	Post	26
Raleigh, NC	News & Observer	182
Durham, NC	Herald	64
Fayetteville, NC	Observer & Times	78
Wilmington, NC	Star-News	60
Greensboro, NC	News & Record	135
Winston-Salem, NC	Journal	106
Columbia, SC	State	174
Charleston, SC	News & Courier Post	127
Greenville, SC	News-Piedmont	138
Spartanburg, SC	Herald-Journal	67
Anderson, SC	Independent-Mail	46
Asheville, NC	Citizen-Times	73
Atlanta, GA	Journal Constitution	701
Gwinnett, GA	News	45
Savannah, GA	News	82
Augusta, GA	Chronicle-Herald	99
Athens, GA	Banner-Herald/News	35
Mobile, AL	Press Register	115
Pascagoula, MS	Mississippi Press Register	24
Biloxi-Gulfport, MS	Sun Herald	54
Tallahassee, FL	Democrat	78
Panama City, FL	News-Herald	42
Jacksonville, FL	Times-Union	251
Orlando, FL	Sentinel	389
Leesburg, FL	Commercial	35
St. Petersburg, FL	Times	501
Tampa, FL	Tribune	409
Lakeland, FL	Ledger	105
Fort Lauderdale, FL	News & Sun Sentinel	350
West Palm Beach, FL	Post	246
Miami, FL	Herald	554
	Region Total	7,613
METRO CHICAGO		
Chicago, IL	Tribune	1,132
Aurora, IL	Beacon-News	42
Elgin, IL	Courier News	33
Joliet, IL	Herald-News	50
Waukegan, IL	News-Sun	44
Wheaton, IL	Journal	9
Rockford, IL	Register Star	88
	Region Total	1,398
WEST CENTRAL		
Milwaukee, WI	Journal	491
Racine, WI	Journal Times	39
Kenosha, WI	News	31
Madison, WI	State Journal	158
Green Bay, WI	Press Gazette	86
Appleton, WI	Post-Crescent	71
Sheboygan, WI	Press	28
Minneapolis, MN	Star Tribune	674
St. Paul, MN	Pioneer Press	268
Des Moines, IA	Register	345
Cedar Rapids, IA	Gazette	84
Davenport, IA	Quad City Times	83
Moline, IL	Dispatch	37
Rock Island, IL	Argus	18
Springfield, IL	State Journal-Register	78
Decatur, IL	Herald & Review	57
Champaign, IL	News-Gazette	53
Bloomington-Normal, IL	Pantagraph	57
Omaha, NE	World-Herald	289
Lincoln, NE	Journal & Star	84
Denver, CO	Post	414
Boulder, CO	Camera	44
Kansas City, MO	Star	424
St. Louis, MO	Post-Dispatch	586
Alton, IL	Telegraph	37
Belleville, IL	News Democrat	59
Carbondale, IL	Southern Illinoisan	36
Springfield, MO	News & Leader	99
Joplin, MO	Globe	47
Wichita, KS	Eagle-Beacon	199
Hutchinson, KS	News	42
Salina, KS	Journal	31
	Region Total	5,049
SOUTHWEST		
New Orleans, LA	Times-Picayune	325
Baton Rouge, LA	Advocate	141
Shreveport, LA	Times	104
Monroe, LA	News-Star-World	48
Dallas, TX	News	818
Fort Worth, TX	Star-Telegram	353
Tyler, TX	Courier-Times-Telegraph	51
Longview, TX	Journal	44
Texarkana, TX	Gazette	37
Austin, TX	American Statesman	228
Waco, TX	Tribune-Herald	64
Bryan-College, TX	Eagle	28
Houston, TX	Chronicle	623
Beaumont, TX	Enterprise	87
San Antonio, TX	Express News	281
Albuquerque, NM	Journal	163
Oklahoma City, OK	Oklahoman	336
Tulsa, OK	World	242
Little Rock, AR	Arkansas Democrat-Gazette	370
	Region Total	4,343
PACIFIC		
Seattle, WA	Times/Post Intelligencer	516
Tacoma, WA	News-Tribune	140
Everett, WA	Herald	65
Spokane, WA	Spokesman-Review	147
Portland, OR	Oregonian	441
Boise, ID	Statesman	81
Idaho Falls, ID	Post-Register	28
Pocatello, ID	Journal	20
Twin Falls, ID	Times-News	23
Salt Lake City, UT	Tribune-Deseret News	215
Ogden, UT	Standard-Examiner	58
Provo, UT	Herald	31
Las Vegas, NV	Review Journal & Sun	213
San Francisco, CA	Examiner & Chronicle	705
Oakland, CA	The Tribune	116
San Mateo, CA	Times & News Leader	45
Hayward, CA	Review	52
Fremont, CA	The Argus	34
Livermore, CA	Herald	36
Marin County, CA	Independent Journal	43
Palo Alto, CA	Peninsula Times Tribune	44
Santa Rosa, CA	Press-Democrat	102
Napa, CA	Register	22
Walnut Creek, CA	Contra Costa Times	100
Pinole, CA	West County Times	36
Pleasanton, CA	Valley Times	37
Antioch, CA	Ledger/Post Dispatch	23
Sacramento, CA	Bee	339
Modesto, CA	Bee	95
Stockton, CA	Record	60
Phoenix, AZ	Republic	596
Mesa, AZ	Tribune	52
Tempe, AZ	News Tribune	12
Chandler, AZ	Arizonan Tribune	8
Gilbert, AZ	Tribune	4
Tucson, AZ	Star	175
Fresno, CA	Bee	188
Visalia, CA	Times Delta	31
	Region Total	4,933
METRO LOS ANGELES		
Los Angeles, CA	Times	1,577
Anaheim, CA	Bulletin	7
La Habra-Brea, CA	Star-Progress	5
Santa Ana, CA	Register	430
Torrance, CA	Daily Breeze	124
Long Beach, CA	Press-Telegram	152
Ventura, CA	Star Free-Press	57
Thousand Oaks, CA	News Chronicle	24
Santa Barbara, CA	News-Press	59
Oxnard, CA	Press-Courier	19
Simi Valley, CA	Enterprise	18
Camarillo, CA	Daily News	11
Riverside, CA	Press-Enterprise	171
San Bernardino, CA	Sun	105
Palm Springs, CA	Desert Sun	62
San Diego, CA	Union	457
Escondido, CA	Times Advocate	44
Oceanside, CA	Blade-Citizen	41
Temecula, CA	Californian	12
	Region Total	3,375
	TOTAL CIRCULATION	**43,428**

Exhibit 12.15
Arm & Hammer Baking Soda Positioned as a Laundry Alternative.

Repositioning can follow any of the same strategies used

originally to position a brand. However, the company must overcome the perceptions that consumers have already formed about the brand based on the earlier positioning strategy. This often makes repositioning a brand much more difficult than the initial positioning.

Analytical Methods Used in Positioning

Positioning deals with molding consumer perceptions and, as such, requires communication to the consumer.[17] All components of the marketing mix must work in concert to enhance the desired positioning. Hence, one purpose of positioning research is to determine whether the proposed elements of the marketing mix effectively communicate the desired positioning strategy.

Exploratory research is often used to screen alternative marketing mix elements being considered. This exploratory research is usually followed by survey research to investigate formally those alternatives that appear most promising. For example, consumers in the target group might be asked to react to print ads, packaging alternatives, television commercials in storyboard form, or concept statements to evaluate how well each option communicates the desired image.

A second purpose of positioning research is to determine how various segments of the market perceive alternative brands. **Perceptual mapping** is a marketing research tool specifically designed to provide such insight by exploring how consumers view a new concept or brand relative to alternatives. Perceptual mapping can also be used to investigate how consumers view existing brands for the purpose of developing possible repositioning strategies.

Perceptual mapping can be accomplished using a number of sophisticated mathematical techniques for graphically portraying relationships among entities such as brands or companies. These techniques typically produce a graph, or map, in which entities (*e.g.*, brands) perceived by consumers to be similar are located close together, while those perceived as dissimilar are located far apart. We next discuss some commonly used approaches for constructing perceptual maps.

Nonmetric Multidimensional Scaling

Nonmetric multidimensional scaling is a perceptual mapping technique that uses a rank ordering of the pairs of entities, according to similarity, to generate a perceptual map.[18] The ordinal nature of the data is the reason for the term nonmetric in the name of the technique.

Various forms of consumer input can be used to generate the rank order data. Consumers might be asked to rank all pairs of items being mapped according to similarity, and the average results could be used to determine input rankings.[19] The pair of items perceived as most similar would be ranked first, the pair seen as next most similar would be ranked second, and so on. Alternatively, consumers could be asked to rate the perceived similarity of each pair using a five-point category rating scale ranging from "not at all similar" to "almost the same." The mean ratings are then used to determine the similarity ranking of all the pairs.

Nonmetric multidimensional scaling computer algorithms attempt to position each item spatially in such a way that the ranking of the pairs of items according to distances between them in the space, or map, is exactly the same as the input ranking based on perceived similarities. One-dimensional (a straight line), two-dimensional (similar to a graph with *x*-and *y*-coordinates), and higher-dimensional solutions are provided by the algorithm. While the solution provided for each dimensional space is the best in terms of its ability to reproduce the original similarity rankings in that number of dimensions, it is typically impossible to reproduce perfectly the input ranking in a few dimensions. Therefore, a measure of how well each solution fits the input ranking is provided as part of the output of the computer algorithm. The objective is to obtain an adequate solution with as few dimensions as possible.

The resulting map provides insight into how the brands are perceived by the particular segment or segments being investigated. Positioning opportunities, attractive positioning strategies not currently being used by any brands, can also be discovered. It is possible to label the axes of the map by observing which brands serve as "anchors." For this reason, it is particularly useful when collecting the similarity ratings or rankings to ask participants why pairs of brands that are indicated to be quite different are perceived to be so different. Applying Marketing Research 12.8 demonstrates the use of nonmetric multidimensional scaling.

Applying Marketing Research 12.8

A sample of one hundred consumers who own microwave ovens and buy microwave breakfast products were randomly intercepted in a mall, screened for eligibility, and exposed to a new breakfast-food product concept. The concept was designed to position the product as an alternative to fresh donuts or pastries. The description of the concept stated that the product was simply warmed in the microwave, resulting in a fresh, "store-bought" flavor.

As part of the survey questions, participants were asked to rate all possible pairs of ten breakfast food products (including the concept) on a five-point similarity scale ranging from "almost the same" to "not at all similar." The resultant 45 average ratings were used to rank the pairs according to similarity. Applying a nonmetric multidimensional scaling (MDS) algorithm to this ranking yielded the two-dimensional map, shown in Exhibit 12.6, which fit the data very well.

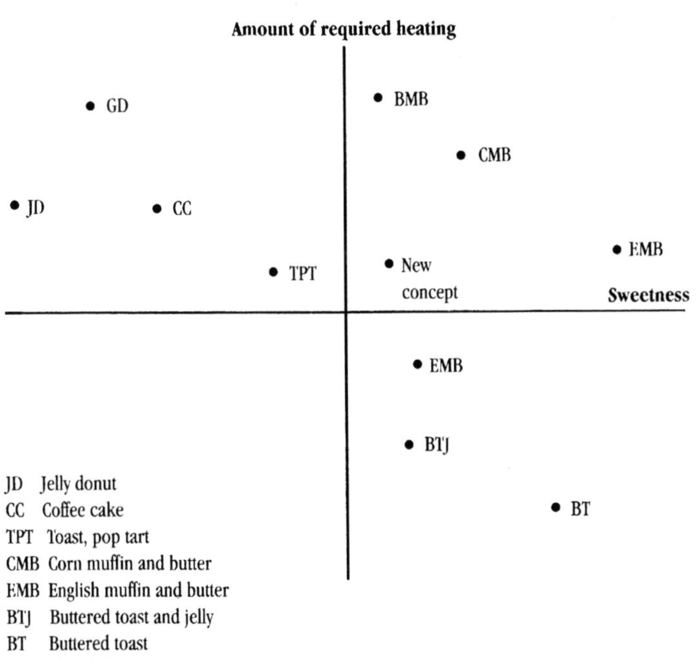

Exhibit 12.16
Perceptual map of breakfast foods using nonmetric multidimensional scaling. (Adapted from Paul E. Green, Donald S. Tull, and Gerald Albaum, *Research for Marketing Decisions*, 5th ed. Englewood Cliffs, NJ: Prentice Hall, 1988, p. 607.)

Examining the map in Exhibit 12.16, we see that the *x*-axis seems to be sweetness; the sweeter the product, the further left it is situated on the *x*-axis. The *y*-axis appears to represent the amount of warming or heating required prior to serving; the more heating required, the lower the product is situated on the *y*-axis. Furthermore, the new product concept's location in the map indicates that the participants perceived the product to be more of a pop tart than a donut with respect to sweetness and to require almost the same amount of heating as pop tarts. These results seem to indicate that the concept, as currently communicated, does not produce the desired positioning.

Factor Analysis

Factor analysis can also be used to produce perceptual maps.[20] The typical input information would be ratings of brands on attributes. A factor analysis would be performed on the ratings data accumulated for all brands being rated, and the underlying dimensions, or factors, on which the brands are really being evaluated, would be determined. The average factor scores for each brand define the respective mapping coordinates. Applying Marketing Research 12.9 illustrates this use of factor analysis.

Applying Marketing Research 12.9

As part of the study described in Applying Marketing Research 12.5 and 12.6, respondents were also asked to rate each of six retail shoe chains on ten attributes, using a 5-point scale ranging from 1 = "Does Not Apply At All" to 5= "Completely Applies." A factor analysis of these ratings yielded two factors relating to price and amount of sales assistance, respectively. Each chain received a score on each of the two factors for each respondent based on how the person rated the chain on the attributes comprising the respective factors. A respondent giving a high (low) score on the price factor for a specific chain felt the shoes sold by the chain were expensive (inexpensive). Similarly, a respondent giving a high (low) score on the sales assistance factor for a particular chain felt that the store employees were (were not) helpful and courteous.

Average factor scores across respondents were calculated for each chain. These factor scores provided mapping coordinates for plotting the six chains in a 2-dimensional perceptual map, where one dimension is perceived price and the other is in-store sales assistance. The resultant map is shown in Exhibit 12.17. Chain B is seen as very inexpensive, and having little staff available in the store to help customers (a Payless store for example), while Chain D is perceived as the opposite (a Florsheim store for example). Chain E is perceived to have high prices, but not having in-store sales assistance. Chains A, F and C are all seen as having moderate prices, but A differs from C and F in the level of in-store sales assistance. Knowledge of how target consumers perceive a chain and its competition allows management to assess whether their advertising and merchandising strategies are creating the desired image, and to develop a strategic plan for the future.

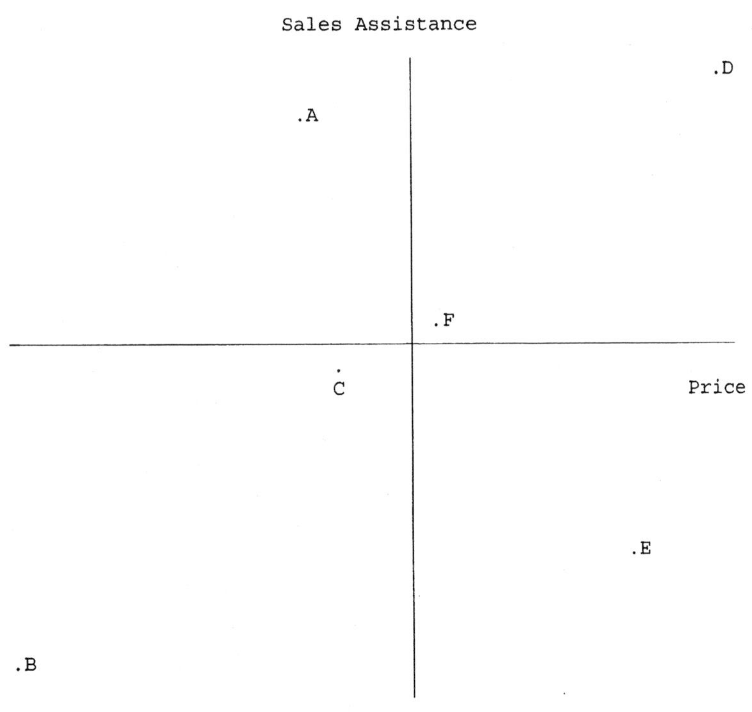

Exhibit 12.17
Map of retail shoe chains based on factor analysis.

Correspondence Analysis

The perceptual mapping techniques discussed so far require consumers either to rate or rank pairs of brands according to similarity or to rate a set of brands on a list of attributes. When a large number of ratings or rankings are involved, the task becomes tedious and time-consuming, and it becomes difficult for survey participants to maintain their concentration and provide accurate and reliable ratings.[21] In cases where a large number of brand-attribute evaluations are required, correspondence analysis is a particularly attractive perceptual mapping alternative.

Correspondence analysis only requires participants to indicate which attributes particularly apply to each brand.[22] For example, participants could be given an array consisting of rows and columns, where each row denotes an attribute, and the brands of interest appear as entries (perhaps randomly ordered) within each row. Participants simply circle the brands to which each attribute particularly applies. The resulting frequency table, based on the number of people indicating that an attribute applies to a brand, is the basis for the correspondence analysis. The correspondence analysis produces mapping coordinates for the brands and attributes and also provides an indicator of how many dimensions are required to reproduce the input information adequately. Quite often, a two- or three-dimensional solution is adequate, and a map that depicts relationships among the brands and attributes can be constructed accordingly, as illustrated in Applying Marketing Research 12.10.

Applying Marketing Research 12.10

A sample of over 1000 wine drinkers were asked to indicate which of twenty-four attributes they particularly associated with each of five brands of wine. The resulting data were analyzed using correspondence analysis and yielded the map shown in Exhibit 12.18. Only those attributes having a reasonably large association or disassociation with any of the five brands are included in the map.

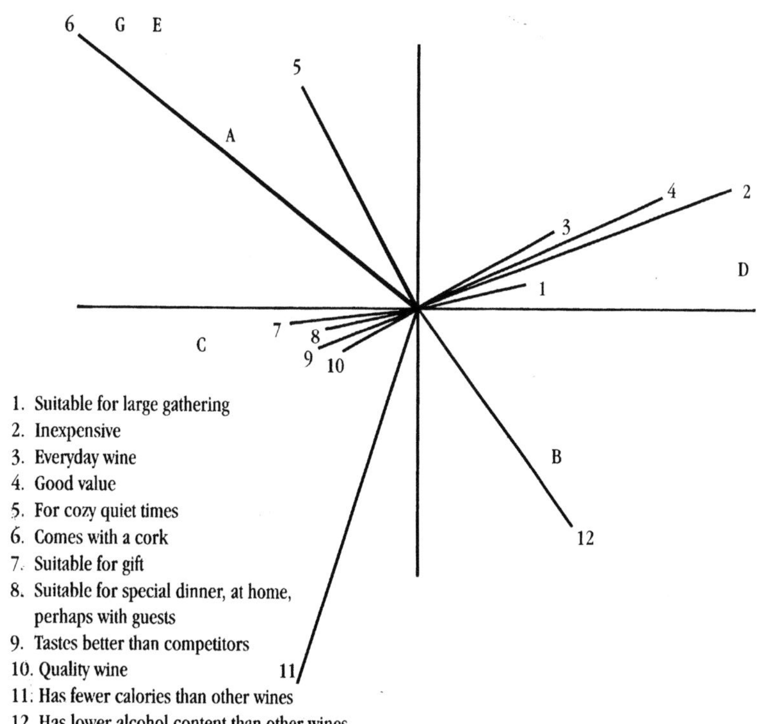

Exhibit 12.18
Perceptual Map of Wine Brands.

The makers of Brand B had hoped to position it close to Brands E and A, but the results indicate that the strategy had failed. Brand B seemed to have a unique association with fewer calories and lower alcohol, possibly the result of the company's earlier attempt to launch a line of "light" wines under the same brand name.

Summary

Segmentation involves partitioning the market into dissimilar groups within which consumers are similar in some sense. Segmentation can be based on geography, demographics, geodemographics, psychographics, behavioral issues, or desired product or service benefits. Factor analysis allows the researcher to reduce a long list of attributes and/or benefits to several underlying factors. Scores are produced for each of these factors and for each respondent based on his or her corresponding ratings. These scores become the criteria for grouping respondents into segments. Cluster analysis is frequently used mathematically to develop the segments.

Conjoint analysis entails deducing the relative importance of key characteristics of a product or service from an individual's stated preferences. Cluster analysis can be applied to these individual importance scores to develop segments.

A brand's positioning is its perception among consumers relative to competition. A positioning strategy is a plan to differentiate a brand from its competitors to make the brand particularly appealing to the target segment(s) of consumers. Positioning and segmentation go hand-in-hand, because marketing efforts to position a brand imply the existence of a target segment. Brands can be positioned (or repositioned in the case of established brands) on the basis of specific features, specific benefits, specific uses, type of user, comparison with another brand, product class disassociation, price, or some combination of these (hybrid).

Positioning involves understanding how consumers perceive brands. Perceptual mapping, which produces graphical displays of how brands are perceived relative to one another, is particularly useful in this context. Several analytical methods, including factor analysis, nonmetric multidimensional scaling, and correspondence analysis, each requiring different types of data, can be used to produce a perceptual map.

Key Terms:

benefit segmentation

cluster analysis

conjoint analysis

correspondence analysis

factor analysis

geodemographic segmentation

nonmetric multidimensional scaling

perceptual mapping

positioning

psychographics

repositioning

segmentation

VALS2

Nimslo's Segmentation and Positioning Strategies

The Nimslo Company developed a two-stage strategy for their 3D camera. In the introductory stage, the camera was positioned as a major technological advance in amateur photography that produced more realistic pictures than did conventional cameras. The market segment targeted at this stage was the small percentage of individuals willing to pay a high price for innovative photographic technology.

Limited photofinishing and camera production capacity at the time of introduction was a driving force behind the choice of this strategy. Nimslo did not want demand for the camera and photofinishing to outstrip their limited capacity. Consistent with this strategy, the camera was introduced at a relatively high price (about $250 list price). While not prohibitive for 35 mm SLR camera users (35 mm SLR cameras retailed for about $225 to $400), this price would serve to reduce introductory demand while meeting the company's need for a high profit margin per unit.

The second stage of the strategy, as camera production and photofinishing capacity came on line, called for a repositioning of the camera to appeal to a larger target segment. As part of this repositioning, the price of the camera was to be lowered substantially and advertising, publicity, and point-of-purchase materials would communicate the ease of use (the fixed focus and autoexposure features), convenience (due to its light weight, compact size and the fact that it used standard 35 mm film), and quality (the 35 mm film format and realistic pictures).

The target market sought for this second stage was demographically defined to be upscale households with children living at home. This target market had several attractive characteristics. First, it was much larger than the segment targeted in the introductory strategy. Second, families with children tend to be "memory recorders" (collectors of items that capture special moments in their lives), so they are inclined to be heavy users of camera equipment and photofinishing services. Finally, upscale households could easily afford the Nimslo system.

Review Questions

12.1 Why should segmentation and positioning strategies be considered simultaneously?

12.2 What is meant by geodemographic segmentation? Discuss the PRIZM geodemographic segmentation system, and give an example of a marketing application of the system.

12.3 What is meant by the term psychographics? Discuss the VALS2 segmentation system, and give an example of a marketing application.

12.4 Give a hypothetical benefit segmentation of the toothpaste market, including a likely demographic description of the segments and the brands positioned to the segments. What product opportunities can be derived from your segmentation?

12.5 Describe how conjoint analysis might be used to segment the market for automobile tires based on benefits.

12.6 What is cluster analysis? Give an example of its use in benefit segmentation.

12.7 Develop a hypothetical occasion-of-use segmentation for potato chips. Give a positioning strategy for marketing to one of your segments.

12.8 Define positioning, and give examples of differing positioning strategies used by restaurants.

12.9 What is meant by repositioning? Give two examples, other than those given in the text, of brands that have been repositioned.

12.10 Describe five ways to position a product or service, and give examples for each.

12.11 What is meant by the term *perceptual mapping*? Of what value are such maps in developing positioning or repositioning strategies?

12.12 On what basis does nonmetric multidimensional scaling develop a perpetual map?

12.13 What kinds of information are required to construct a factor analysis perpetual map? Give an example.

12.14 What is correspondence analysis? What are the benefits of the correspondence analysis approach to perceptual mapping as opposed to the factor analysis approach?

Discussion Questions

12.1 Compare the various perceptual-mapping techniques. What are the relative advantages/disadvantages of each?

12.2 Why might different companies, each competing within the same product category, each use a different basis for segmenting the market?

12.3 Pick several brands of breakfast cereals, and describe what you believe to be the target segments, associated segmentation schemes, and positioning strategies for each brand. How might marketing research have been involved in developing these brand strategies?

12.4 Discuss occasion-of-use segmentation as it might be applied to the soft drink market. Describe various occasions of use. What brands, if any, have positioned themselves for specific uses, and what particular occasions have they targeted?

12.5 Discuss how nonmetric multidimensional scaling might be used to develop a perceptual map of major airlines. Describe the data-collection process.

Chapter 12 Endnotes

1. Yoram Wind, "Going to Market: New Twists for Some Old Tricks," *The Wharton Magazine* 4,3 (1980), pp. 34-39.

2. Art Weinstein, *Marketing Segmentation*, (Chicago, IL: Probus Publishing Company, 1987), p. 4.

3. See, for example, Subhash C. Jain, *Marketing Planning and Strategy*, 2nd ed. Cincinnati: South-Western Publishing Co., 1985, pp. 222-225.

4. Art Weinstein, *Market Segmentation*. Chicago: Probus Publishing Company, 1987, p. 81.

5. Edmondson, Brad, "Green Lawns and Rebates for Scott," *American Demographics*, October 1986, p.20.

6. See Len Strazewski, "Welcome to 'Blue Blood Estates,'" *Advertising Age*, August 22, 1988, p. 5-18 for an example of an application of geodemographic segmentation in financial marketing.

7. See Betsy Morris, "Placing Products, Marketing Firms Slice U.S. Into 240,00 Parts to Spur Clients' Sales," *Wall Street Journal*, November 3,1986 for a discussion of Claritas' PRIZM system.

8. *Ibid.*

9. James Atlas, "Beyond Demographics," *The Atlantic Monthly*, October, 1994, pp. 49-58.

10. See Rebecca Pürto, "Global Psychographics," *American Demographics*, December 1990, p. 8.

11. *Ibid.*

12. See Russell I. Haley, "Benefit Segmentation: A Decision-Oriented Research Tool," *Journal of Marketing* 32 (July 1968), pp. 30-35.

13. See Paul E. Green and Yoram Wind, "New Way to Measure Consumers' Judgments," *Harvard Business Review*, July-August 1975, pp. 107-117, for an easy-to-understand discussion of conjoint analysis.

14. See, for example, Yoram Wind, "Going to Market: New Twists for Some Old Tricks," *The Wharton Magazine* 4,3 (1980), pp. 34-39, and David J. Reibstein, Marketing *Concepts, Strategies, and Decisions*. Englewood Cliffs, NJ: Prentice Hall, 1985, pp. 253-255.

15. Anika Michalowska, "French Yogurt Sends Consumers to Sleep," *Advertising Age International*, April, 1997, p. I18.

16. Judann Pollock,"Mars Acquiring Organic Food Marketer Seeds of Change," *Advertising Age*, October 13, 1997, pp. 3,53.

17. Al Ries and Jack Trout, *Positioning: The Battle for Your Mind*. New York: McGraw-Hill, 1981, p. 1.

18. See, for example, S. James Press, *Applied Multivariate Analysis*. New York: Holt, Rinehart, and Winston, Inc., 1972, pp. 400-408; Glen L. Urban and John R. Hauser, *Design and Marketing of New Products*. Englewood Cliffs, NJ: Prentice-Hall, 1980, pp. 212-220; or Joseph F. Hair, Jr., Ralph E. Anderson, and Ronald L. Tatham, *Multivariate Data Analysis*, 2nd ed. New York: Macmillan Publishing Company, 1987, pp. 349-370, for a discussion of nonmetric multidimensional scaling.

19. Caution is urged in aggregating data across subjects to produce a single map. Aggregation is justified when there is general agreement across subjects. See, for example, Barbara Bund Jackson, *Multivariate Data Analysis: An Introduction*. Homewood, IL: Richard D. Irwin, Inc., 1983, pp. 216-218.

20. See, for example, Barbara Bund Jackson, *Multivariate Data Analysis: An Introduction*. Homewood, IL: Richard D. Irwin, Inc., 1983, pp. 131-152; or Glen L. Urban and John R. Hauser, *Design and Marketing of New Products*, Englewood Cliffs, NJ: Prentice-Hall, 1980, pp. 187-212.

21. See M.B. Holbrook, W.L. Moore, and R.S. Winer, "Constructing Joint Spaces from Pick-Any Data: A New Tool for Consumer Analysis," *Journal of Consumer Research* 9 (1982), pp. 99-105.

22. See, for example, Donna L. Hoffman and George R. Franke, "Correspondence Analysis: Graphical Representation of Categorical Data in Marketing Research," *Journal of Marketing Research 23* (August 1986), pp. 213-227, for a discussion of correspondence analysis.

Chapter 13

The Name, the Package, and the Price

Learning Objectives:

This chapter covers the major issues involved in naming, packaging, and pricing a brand and describes how marketing research can aid the manager faced with these crucial decisions. Specifically, after reading this chapter, you should be able to:

- describe the criteria used in selecting a name.
- explain how research can aid name selection.
- describe the umbrella brand name strategy.
- explain why companies change their names and the names of their brands.
- describe the criteria used in selecting a package.
- explain how research can aid in packaging decisions.
- discuss the issues involved in setting a price.
- describe research techniques used in price selection.

Campbell's Soup adopted its familiar red-and-white can almost 100 years ago. Previously, cans were colorfully illustrated with different brand names for each product. Campbell's switched to the red-and-white can design to unify and simplify its line of soups.

The original Campbell's red-and-white can with the gold medal signified warmth, stability, nourishment and home. Eventually, the can no longer meant food. Research indicated that almost every household had at least one can of Campbell's Soup in the cupboard. However, according to one former company executive, "the problem was to get them to eat the soup."[1] It was suggested that the package be redesigned to include a picture of the can's contents at the bottom of the label. The idea was to remind people that the can contained food.

Needless to say, Campbell's management was leery of any change to the familiar package which had remained the same for nearly a century. However, marketing research eased their concerns. Research showed that consumers associated a red and white can with Campbell's Soup, but little else. They were even confused about whether the red was at the top or the bottom. (It's at the top.) Hence, management concluded that the label could be modified as long as the red and white remained. The label was then changed to include a picture of the soup (Exhibit 13.1).

Exhibit 13.1
Campbell's changed their soup packaging based on research findings.

What's in a name? A great deal, when you consider the amount of money companies spend establishing or changing the names of their brands or companies. A rose by any other name might smell as sweet, but would Downey fabric softener or Healthy Choice frozen entrees fare as well with a different name? What about the package? Would you, unlike Dr. Seuss's poor Sam-I-Am, be willing to try green eggs and ham? And how much would you be willing to pay? The name, the package, and the price all play important roles in molding consumer perceptions regarding a brand. As a result, managers must make name, package, and price decisions carefully and should base their decisions on good marketing research information.

Selecting a Name

Choosing a name for a company or brand is serious business. The name itself can be a big help in communicating the image the company hopes to project. For instance, from the very beginning, the name Apple Computer helped Steven Job's new company communicate simple and user-friendly computers. The choice of the name America On-Line for a service providing consumers access to the Internet and worldwide web is another good example of a name which communicates essence of the company.

K-III Communications, which publishes numerous magazines including Seventeen and Modern Bride, wishes it had spent more time and research effort before choosing its name. When the company was formed, the name K-III was chosen to reflect the company owners. Since then, the company chairman has been introduced as the head of "Kill Communications" and jokes have been made about a sinister link to the Ku Klux Klan.[2] The company has also had to explain to kids that its kids' newspaper *Weekly Reader* is not designed only for kindergarten through third grade children. For these reasons, the company will soon endure the expense of changing its name to Primedia. Needless to say, the new name has been thoroughly researched to make sure there are no negatives associated with the word.

Idea generation techniques, such as focus groups and brainstorming, are useful tools for developing alternative names. Participants are provided with a description of the attributes and benefits of the proposed product, service, or company and attempt to generate appropriate names. Sometimes, companies use specially designed computer software to create a list of name alternatives. Names that the company has previously tested but not used can provide other possible candidates.

A company must also make sure that the rights to a potential brand name are not owned by another company. In 1997, Coca-Cola introduced a new soft drink called Surge using TV commercials during the 1997 Super Bowl to launch the new drink. The firm Bio-Tech Pharmacal, Inc., based in Arkansas, began marketing a fruit-flavored drink called Surge in 1994.[3] A letter of protest against Coca-Cola was filed with the Assistant Commissioner for trademarks shortly before the 1997 Super Bowl creating an "11th hour" crisis for Coca-Cola. Earlier Coca-Cola had settled out-of-court with an Illinois-based company which claimed that sales of its automatic milking machine, also called Surge, would be hurt. Needless to say, legal clearance issues must be carefully examined prior to usage of a new brand name.

Qualities of a Good Name

The more clearly a brand name communicates the features and benefits of the product, the more successful the product is likely to be. However, demanding that the chosen name exactly communicate the desired meaning can eliminate many exciting, and potentially rewarding, alternatives. For example, "Zap Mail" (Federal Express's fast delivery service) is far more exciting than "Fast Mail." Keeping the following criteria in mind can help marketers choose good names for their companies and brands.

Memorability

Is the name easy to remember? Obviously, recall of the brand name is important at the time of purchase. Companies burdened with antiquated names based on long-departed founders or on technology that has been superseded often resort to crunching the cumbersome name down to an acronym or simply to initials.[4] For example, Ling Tempko Vought became LTV, and National Cash Register became NCR. This is a simple solution, but may create a name that is not very memorable.

Memorability is often assessed by how well consumers recall, or remember, alternative brand names. A commonly used procedure is to recruit consumers in the target audience using a mall-intercept interview format. Early in the interview, these consumers are shown a list containing the potential brand names and other fictitious or existing brand names. Later in the interview, these consumers are asked to recall each name they remember. The ranking of the prospective brand names, based on the percentage of participants who remember each, would be a measure of relative memorability.

One approach when presenting the list of names is to vary, or rotate, the position of each name on the list to minimize any effect caused by the name's position on the list. A second approach is to expose each participant to only one of the prospective names within a constant list of other names. A separate group of consumers would view each prospective name, and the name would always appear in the same place on the list. Because neither the position of the prospective name nor the list of other names varies, any possible position effect is eliminated. However, this approach is much more expensive due to the larger number of total participants required.

Uniqueness

The brand name should be distinctive and not easily confused with other brands in the category. A distinctive name is an important aspect of the positioning strategy because it helps to communicate a unique brand image. For example, the choice of the name "Bits 'n' Pieces" for a new dry dog food would not be very wise in light of the fact that a well-established brand, Kibbles 'n' Bits, already exists.

The uniqueness of the brand name can be measured by word association. Participants are shown a proposed name and are asked to respond with the first existing brand name that comes to mind. If one or more existing brand names are mentioned frequently, the proposed brand may be discarded for fear of consumer confusion or trademark infringement suits.

Pronounceability

For products and services that the consumer must ask for when purchasing, pronounceability is particularly important. People do not want to look foolish trying to pronounce the name of the brand. The manufacturer of Poulan chain saws (pronounced like the country Poland without the "d") had to resort to an expensive advertising campaign to teach the public to pronounce their brand name (see Exhibit 13.2). The campaign was clever, entertaining, and probably increased brand awareness. Nevertheless, the choice of the brand name remains questionable based upon the difficulty consumers have pronouncing the name.

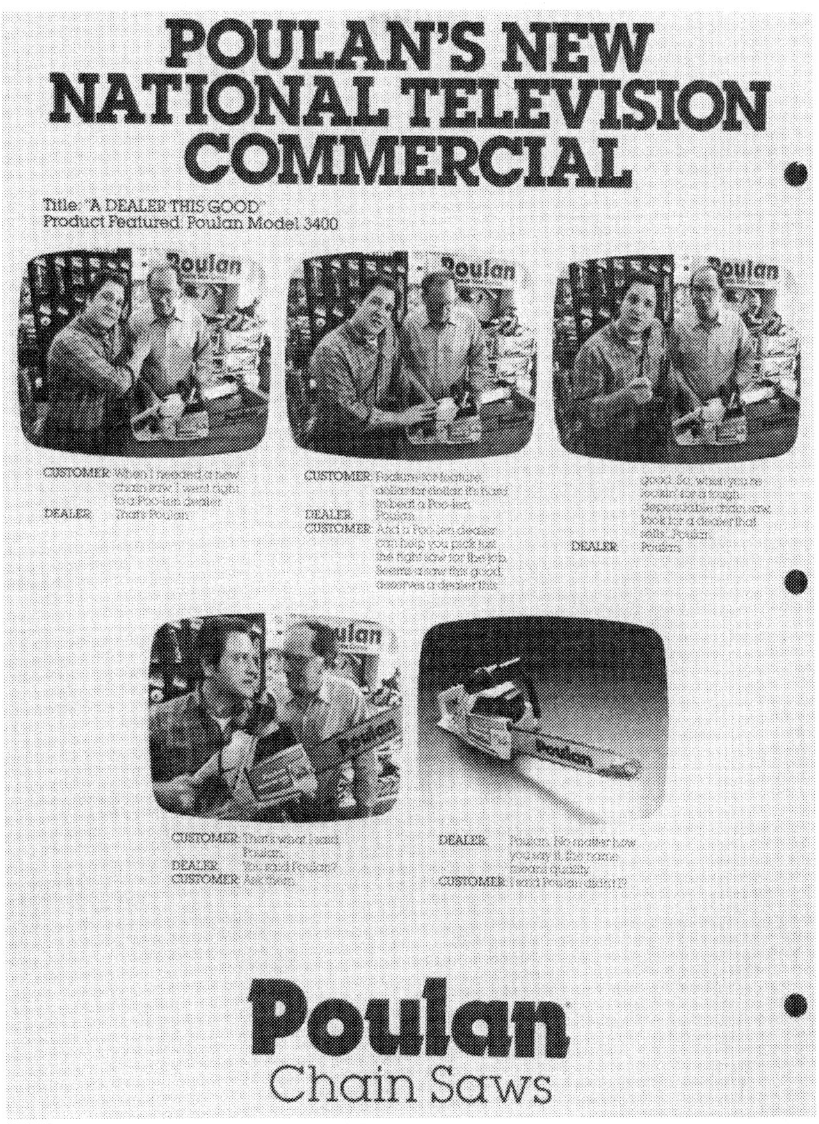

Exhibit 13.2
A name that is difficult to pronounce can be hard to overcome.
(Courtesy of Poulton Weed Eater.)

The problem of pronounceability is exacerbated when brands are sold in several countries. For example, the Hershey Company successfully markets a candy bar in the United States named Whatchamacallit. However, when the product was introduced into Canada, Hershey was forced to change the name to Special Crisp because French Canadians found the original name difficult to pronounce.[5]

Image

An important consideration in choosing a name is image — the perceptions created in consumers' minds by the name. Consumers should readily associate the brand name with the product category, and the name should reflect the brand's benefits. Liquid Plumber drain cleaner and Cling Free fabric softener are good examples of brand names that create the right perceptions. Both names clearly classify the respective brands into their product categories and denote what the brands are supposed to do. On the other hand, the Liggett Group's choice of Pyramid as the brand name for a new cigarette is subject to second guessing since, in reality, pyramids are elaborate tombs. Likewise, one wonders about the choice of the name Fisherman's Friend for a cough drop.

The image created by a name can go beyond its linkage to a product category or the attributes of the brand. It can also help create a personality for the brand that is greater than the brand's physical attributes. For instance, Samuel Adams beer communicates a New England heritage and tradition, which are cornerstones of the overall strategy for the brand. On the other hand, some names, especially acronyms, do little to communicate a personality to consumers. What is the name Unisys supposed to communicate, for example? According to one Unisys corporate executive, the name reflects three concepts: unity, information, and systems.[6] Although this meaning may be clear to Unisys employees, how many other people understand it? Such contrived names require much more explanation through advertising or other communication to create a personality than do simple names like Book-of-the-Month Club. Imagine the time and money RCA, IBM, and AT&T needed to establish images and personalities for their brand names.

Word association is an excellent technique for examining the image connotation and communication value of various name alternatives. When using this technique, consumers are asked to respond immediately to a potential brand name with another word that has been triggered by that name. As Applying Marketing Research 13.1 points out, tabulating the responses for a sample of participants provides insight into the connotations and associations consumers attribute to the names.

Applying Marketing Research 13.1

When the Ford Motor Company introduced a new model car named Edsel, in honor of Henry Ford's only son, word association tests were conducted to determine the general impact of the name. When the responses were tabulated, the results revealed that, instead of generating positive connotations among consumers, the name "Edsel" was most often associated with like-sounding words such as "pretzel," "diesel," and "hard sell." Management, unfortunately, ignored these findings and chose this name anyway.[7] While other features of the car and the state of the U.S. economy when the car was introduced had much to do with its ultimate failure, the name contributed to the problem.

New brand names can also be evaluated with completion techniques. The appropriateness of a brand to a product category can be assessed by using sentence completion. Participants might be asked to complete a sentence such as: "Bliss is a brand of . . . ," where "Bliss" is the proposed brand name. Story completion works well for evaluating the image conveyed by a proposed name, because the task allows the respondent to elaborate on the connotations of the name. Participants might be presented the proposed name, told that it represents a new brand within a particular category, and be asked to describe the characteristics of the brand or the type of person who would buy it.

Consistency with Overall Corporate Branding Strategy

Different companies often select strikingly different branding strategies for their products or services. Some firms elect to name each brand independently so that any brand that fares poorly in the market does not tarnish the image of the firm's other brands. Most of the dozens of products sold by Procter & Gamble, for example, have unique brand names.

Other companies give all of their products or services a related name, called a **family branding strategy**. Avon uses its corporate name for all its products and McDonalds, which starts the names of many of its sandwiches with "Mc," are firms using a family branding strategy. Family branding constrains the choice of brand name for a new offering, but has the advantage of associating the new product or service with the others sold by the firm.

The Umbrella Brand Name Strategy

A popular branding strategy in today's business environment is the umbrella branding strategy. With the **umbrella branding strategy** an existing brand name is used to name a new brand, called a brand extension, in a different product category. In some cases, the new brand is a companion product to the parent brand, and the connection to the parent brand is rather obvious. Log Cabin pancake mix is a companion product to the well-known Log Cabin syrup brand, and the Crest toothbrush is a companion to the parent brand Crest toothpaste.

Sometimes a company uses an umbrella branding strategy even when the connection between the new entry and the parent brand is not clear. Sometimes the connection is a unique benefit or characteristic of the parent brand used to position the new brand. The positioning of Ivory shampoo stresses the mildness that is associated with Ivory soap, and Jell-O Pudding Pops are frozen versions of the familiar Jell-O pudding.

Nearly half of all new packaged goods use existing brand names, so umbrella branding is a very popular strategy.[8] The difficulty associated with building an image for an unknown new brand causes umbrella branding to be so attractive. A large number of brands compete for every consumer's attention, and a tremendous advertising expense is required to build the desired image for an unknown new brand.[9] Leveraging an existing brand name gives the new product or service "instant credibility" by allowing the new brand to draw upon the existing brand's image and past advertising.

Before embarking on an umbrella branding strategy, however, a company must make sure that the image of the new brand is consistent with that of the parent brand. For instance, when Kraft introduced Bull's Eye brand barbecue sauce, no reference was made to the Kraft name because the brand was positioned as a premium brand and did not fit with the Kraft image.[10] On the other hand, the Clorox Company attempted unsuccessfully to market a detergent with bleach under the Clorox brand name. One reason for the brand's poor performance was that consumers thought of Clorox as a laundry additive product, not a detergent.[11]

Investing in marketing research to understand the image component of an existing brand name is extremely important when using an umbrella strategy for naming new products or services. The hard-earned image of a flagship brand name must not be tarnished by dissonance resulting from an inappropriate use. Academic research has indicated the possibility of negative effects on the parent brand when such an extension is launched. A marketer must assess how broadly a brand's franchise can be stretched to new categories without damaging the parent brand.[12] For example, what is the connection between Dannon Natural Spring Water and the parent brand Dannon yogurt? Likewise, one questions the decision to launch a line of pasta sauces using the brand name Sutter Home, long associated with moderately priced quality wine. Projective techniques again play an important role in making such assessments.

Changing a Name

Establishing a good name for a company, product, or service takes a great deal of time and money. Changing a name can take even more. In fact, reintroducing a product under a new name is often easier than leaving the product on the market while attempting to change its name. However, reintroduction is not an option when considering a change in the name of a company, making most corporate name changes extremely expensive. UAL, Inc., spent about $7.5 million to kick off an ultimately abandoned campaign to change its name to Allegis, and BP Oil Company (the new name for British Petroleum) was expected to spend nearly $40 million in advertising to unify the Gulf, Mobil, Boron, and Sohio gasoline brands under the BP brand name.[13]

Companies change their names for various reasons. As noted earlier, K-III Communication changed its name to Primedia because of negative connotations associated with the original name. Sometimes a company simply outgrows its name. International Harvester Company sought a new identity after divesting itself of much of its farm equipment business and changed its name to Navistar. Similarly, Allegheny Airlines changed its name to USAir to project the image of a national, rather than a local carrier. Dow Chemical dropped chemical from its name to underscore the fact that the company's business has expanded far beyond industrial chemicals. ValuJet acquired AirTran Airways and changed the company name to AirTran shortly after a ValuJet airplane crashed in the Everglades killing all aboard.

A company may change its name to influence the price of its stock. That was the reason Consolidated Foods changed its name to Sara Lee Corp. By adopting the name of its best-known brand, the company hoped to enhance the perceived value of its stock to investors. The United Fruit Company changed its name to Chiquita Brands for the same reason. The immediate evidence suggested that Consolidated Foods was right, as the stock price rose about 22 percent in the three months after the name change to Sara Lee Corporation.[14] Furthermore, the name change was accomplished for a total marketing cost of less than $1 million, a feat that made many renamed companies envious.[15]

Finally, a company sometimes changes its name to project a different image. When Sperry Corp. and Burroughs Corp. merged, the new company was named Unisys Corporation as part of an effort to distinguish it from either parent corporation. Novartis is the new name for the company formed by the merger of Swiss pharmaceutical companies, Sandaz and Ciba Energy. The new company's public relations firm developed a campaign to position the new pharmaceutical company as "innovative, revolutionary, and a major world player."[16] The name Novartis comes from Latin and means new skills, which is consistent with the image the firm wants to project. However, how many people know the meaning of this Latin word? Word association research would be very valuable in this situation to assess the image communicated by Novartis, as well as possible alternatives. Sentence completion research would also be quite useful. Respondents could be asked to complete the sentence: "The new company Novartis specializes in producing . . . ." It may be that the connotations of the word Novartis make achieving the desired image for the new firm an uphill struggle. Again, properly designed and conducted research can address this issue.

The globalization of markets and the associated expansion of brands into new countries sometimes creates the need for a name change. Words which are fine in one language may have negative connotations in another. Research is necessary to ensure that this is not the case. Although "nova" literally means star in Spanish, General Motors ran into problems when it introduced the Chevy Nova into South America. The company apparently was unaware that "no va" means "it won't go" in Spanish. They renamed the car Caribe in Spanish markets. Likewise, the Stroh Brewing Company changed the name of its Augsberger Rot ("rot" is German for red) to Augsberger Red when it introduced the beer into the red beer segment in the United States (see Exhibit 13.3). No company would want the word rot in a brand name of a food or beverage product sold in the U.S.

Exhibit 13.3
Augsberger Red Beer

Coca Cola was first pronounced in China as "ke-kou-ke-la." The company soon found out that this phrase translated into "bite the wax tadpole" or "female horse stuffed with wax" depending in the dialect. After much research, Coke found the close phonetic equivalent, "ko-kou-ko-le" which loosely means "happiness in the mouth."

Selecting a Package

Louis Cheskin, a marketing psychologist who began his research in the 1930s, is acknowledged as the pioneer in studying peoples emotional response to packages.[17] His most famous experiment involved asking subjects to evaluate two identical products placed in different packages, one identified by circles on the outside, the other with triangles. Eighty percent (80%) of the subjects preferred the product in the box with the circles. The most frequently given reason for preferring this product was that it was a higher quality product than the one in the box with the triangles even though the contents were identical. Cheskin repeated the experiment for a wide variety of types of products and found that the appearance of the package consistently had a dramatic impact on how the contents were perceived. He named this phenomenon "sensation transference," which became the foundation of his career as a consultant to many corporate giants. In fact, the familiar design of concentric circles found on Tide detergent was the result of Cheskin's work.

An interesting variation of Cheskin's experiment involved consumers using and evaluating three underarm deodorant products. The products were identical except for the color combinations used on the package. Subjects were told that the deodorants were different formulations under consideration. One color scheme was the overwhelming winner in the test because of its pleasant fragrance and its ability to stop wetness and odor for up to twelve hours. One of the other products was found to be ineffective and to have a strong fragrance; the remaining product was found to be irritating to the skin.

The work of Cheskin and subsequent research have proved that the package, including the graphics and colors used, is a crucial element of the marketing mix. For products where only minor real differences exist among brands, packaging can create a strong point of difference among brands. Likewise, for product categories where little brand loyalty exists, packaging can become an extremely important in-store selling feature. The image conveyed by a brand's packaging also influences the consumer's purchase decision for products heavily influenced by self-image or socioeconomic status. A novel package can also contribute to the perceived value and innovativeness of a new product, and thus can contribute substantially to its success. Borden's Classico® pasta sauce, discussed at the start of Chapter 5, is packaged in a glass mason jar (see Exhibit 13.4) which gives the product a homemade appearance. The package supports the brand's premium positioning and helps to clearly differentiate the brand from its competition.

Exhibit 13.4
The packaging for Borden's Classico pasta sauce helps to convey a homemade image. (Courtesy of Borden's Food Corporation.)

Sometimes the package, rather than what it contains, is the essence of a new product. Plastic two-and three-liter containers revolutionized the take-home soft drink category. Likewise, aseptic packaging technology made selling fruit juice and milk in non-refrigerated single-serve cartons possible. Duracell's inclusion of a tester as part of the packaging for its batteries added extra value to the brand in the consumer's mind (see Exhibit 13.5). Recognizing that vinegar was used as a household cleaner, H. J. Heinz Company introduced a concentrated version of its regular vinegar in a pump spray bottle and called the product Heinz Cleaning Vinegar.[18] Coffee Singles, similar to teabags, allow users to "brew" individual cups of coffee. The product is possible because of the development of a pouch which seals in the coffee aroma and flavor. Coffee does not behave like tea, and a package, other than a simple tea bag, was needed.

Exhibit 13.5
Duracell's Copper Top tester package

The importance of package design cannot be overstated, and hence changes to existing packages should be carefully considered and researched. Applying Marketing Research 13.2 shows how one company avoided a packaging disaster by conducting marketing research before making a package change.

Applying Marketing Research 13.2

A toy manufacturer developed new packaging graphics for a line of products. Marketing management was uneasy about the change and insisted that marketing research be conducted to obtain a full consumer evaluation.

Test quantities of the new packaging were produced from 15 products in the line.[19] A store test was conducted in which 18 stores stocked the new package and a comparable group of 18 stores, the control panel, stocked the existing package. During the six-week test period, the control panel sold 63% more units than the test panel. More units were sold in the test stores than in the control stores for only one of the 15 products.

Needless to say, the new package was abandoned and the company continued to use its existing package design. A potentially huge loss was averted by conducting basic marketing research.

Developing a Company/Brand Logo

An important package component is the company or brand logo. A **logo** is a sign or symbol, often containing the brand or company name displayed in a distinctive way, that is used visually to represent a brand or company. Logos are powerful communication devices and must be carefully chosen to be consistent with the desired image of a product or service.[20] When properly designed, logos can help reinforce the perceptions and image the marketer is attempting to instill. Apple Computer used a distinct apple-shaped logo to help position its computers as simple and user-friendly, and as such, very unlike existing computers. As noted earlier, different shapes can have different connotations. The same is true for colors. Hence, it is important to research options among consumers.

Criteria for Selecting a Package

As with brand names, the manager must consider several specific selection criteria when making packaging decisions.[21]

Distinctiveness

Distinctiveness refers to whether the package stands out on the shelf and whether the brand name can easily be seen and recognized. Obviously, a brand must be seen to be purchased. The distinctive red script "K" on a white background make Kellogg's® Special K® cereal highly visible on the supermarket shelf (Exhibit 13.6).

Exhibit 13.6
Kellogg's Special K is highly visible on the supermarket shelf. (Courtesy of Kellogg Company.)

Package distinctiveness is often researched using a tachistoscope, or T-scope. A **tachistoscope** is a device that allows the researcher to vary the length of time a picture or image can be viewed. Tachistoscopic research helps measure the recognizability of a brand logo or other key visual aspects on the package. This research is conducted in the following manner.

Consumers view a picture of one of the alternative package designs for a fraction of a second and are then asked what they saw. The process is repeated, using increased exposure time, until key aspects of the package are noticed and recognized. The results for each package are then tabulated and compared. The package design requiring the lowest exposure time before key package aspects are recognized is considered the most noticeable.

Eye-tracking cameras are also used to evaluate packaging appearance. As the name suggests, an **eye-tracking camera** allows the researcher to track the movement of the consumer's eyes as an object is scanned. Consumers fitted with eye-tracking cameras are shown mock displays containing one of the proposed packages as well as the packages of competing brands. Alternatively, they could be shown photographs of such product displays. The visual impact of each proposed package is measured by how quickly the person's eyes move to that package.

Eye cameras also allow the researcher to evaluate the graphic aspects of the package itself. Having a consumer examine a package alternative while wearing an eye camera provides a wealth of information. Researchers can measure what package aspects the consumer examines and how long each aspect is viewed. The speed with which various graphic components, such as the logo, are noticed and whether the consumer goes back for a second or third look at any package element can also be measured.

Communication

A new product's points of distinction or "reason for being" should be clearly communicated by its packaging. For example, as can be seen in Exhibit 13.7, the package for Clorox 2 clearly states that the laundry product helps brighten colors.

Exhibit 13.7
A package should communicate key brand attributes.

Image

The package should reinforce the desired brand image in the consumer's mind. The choices of packaging materials, colors, graphics, and shape all play very important roles in how the product is perceived. The use of distinctive packaging by Starbucks Coffee (see Exhibit 13.8) helps portray the desired gourmet image, for instance. As the following example illustrates, a packaging change can even become a cornerstone for repositioning an entire company.

Exhibit 13.8
Packaging can help project a particular brand image. (Starbucks Coffee Company's packaging courtesy of Starbucks Coffee.)

Applying Marketing Research 13.3

Despite the fact that sales in the fruit-products industry was growing by 2 percent per year, the Welch's Company was experiencing declining sales volume. The company's CEO commissioned research to uncover the reasons. Results revealed that consumers rated the quality of Welch's products very highly, but the only products strongly associated with the company were grape juice and jelly. Fortunately, even though consumers did not think of Welch's as a diversified fruit-products marketer, the research indicated that consumers had no trouble positioning Welch's as a fruit-products marketer.

Based on these results, management embarked on a repositioning strategy for the company designed to communicate a more diversified fruit product selection. Central to this strategy was the complete changeover of all corporate logos, symbols, and packages. The new package design, shown in Exhibit 13.9, communicates the company's heritage while also downplaying the grape juice and jelly connection.[22]

Exhibit 13.9
Welch designed its new package to downplay its connection with grapes. (Courtesy of Welch Foods.)

The experience of Crayola, described in Applying Marketing Research 13.4, provides another illustration of the importance of packaging in the perception of a brand.

Applying Marketing Research 13.4

Binney & Smith has used its familiar green and yellow colors, used in Crayola crayon packages for many years, to package numerous line extensions. The unique color scheme is synonymous with the Crayola brand (see Exhibit 13.10). However, research indicated that the similarity of the packaging across products confused consumers. Some complained about purchasing magic markers when they really wanted crayons.[23]

Additional research indicated that a green and yellow box of Crayola crayons had been a part of the lives of three generations -- baby boomers, their parents, and their own children.[24] The brand was a symbol for fun and an old friend to all. A new design was introduced which allowed the company to separate the products in the line, but the traditional green and yellow color scheme was retained for all products.

In fact, these colors and the nostalgia they communicated to adults were the basis for a collection tin of 64 crayons offered during the Christmas holidays.

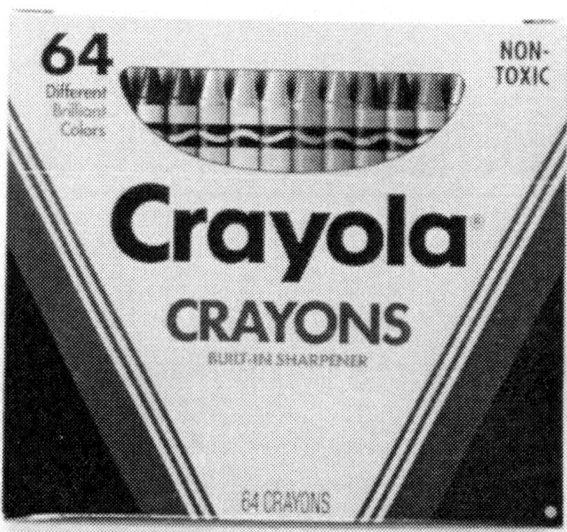

Exhibit 13.10
Crayola's green and yellow packaging are familiar to people of all ages. (Courtesy of Binney & Smith.)

Appeal

Is the package pleasant to look at? Does it encourage the consumer to buy the product? These are obviously important questions. Furthermore, studies have shown that people with different personalities and different lifestyles have different color preferences.[25] Therefore, choosing package colors that are consistent with the desired image of the brand and that are attractive to the target audience increases the likelihood of success.

Preliminary information about the image and appeal conveyed by a package or logo is usually obtained by qualitative research. Focus groups or depth interviews can help separate promising options from poor ones and provide insights about potential problems or necessary improvements. Those packaging or logo options that appear promising based on the qualitative research are next subjected to quantitative research. To determine what image is conveyed by various packages or logos being considered, a sample of consumers might be briefly shown a package or logo and then questioned about the characteristics of the company, brand, or brand consumer. Likewise, to find out what information is communicated by a logo or package, consumers who had been shown the package or logo could be questioned regarding what they remember. Typical questions might include: Who makes the product? What kind of product is it? What picture is on the package? What color/shape is the package? What is the name of the product? What special ingredients are listed? Finally, to assess relative appeal, consumers could be asked to rank or rate their overall preference of the package alternatives and state what they particularly like or dislike about each.

When using an umbrella branding strategy, packaging alternatives should be tested without the brand name. Doing so provides information on what image the packaging alone conveys and whether this image is consistent with the image associated with the brand name. If the packages are tested with the brand name or logo, the well-established imagery associated with the existing brand name may force greater similarity in the images conveyed by the package alternatives than actually exists. The following example illustrates this situation.

Applying Marketing Research 13.5

The Ivory brand name is practically synonymous with Procter & Gamble. Ivory soap was the company's first major brand, and the brand name has been extended to a dishwashing detergent and a shampoo. All products share a mild and gentle positioning strategy.

Suppose that Procter & Gamble tested two package alternatives for a new hand and body moisturizing lotion that was to carry the Ivory brand name. One package was a conventionally shaped blue and white, the Ivory soap colors, bottle. The other was a blue and white tear-shaped bottle. Tested without a brand name, these packages would likely show dramatically different images. However, if the Ivory brand name was included on both packages when conducting the test, a much smaller difference would be noted. The image conveyed by the Ivory name would probably overshadow the image differences created by the packages.

Functionality

The functionality of a package — its ability to perform the intended purpose — must be examined from the point of view of both the consumer and the trade. The package must meet the needs of the consumer when the product is used as intended. For example, some breakfast cereal brands include resealable inner bags to keep the cereal fresher and crisper. The package must also be designed with distributors in mind, so that storage, stacking, or display problems are prevented. Procter & Gamble's Pringle's potato chips, for instance, are packed in a canister, which benefits both the trade and consumers. The canister offers stacking and display benefits to the trade and provides the consumer with a resealable package and less chip breakage.

Package functionality is typically examined by questioning consumers and the trade. Focus groups or depth interviews are often used to discover problems that have been experienced with existing packages. These techniques can also be used to elicit ideas for package improvements or to discuss the pros and cons of new packaging alternatives. Qualitative research, such as role playing, is sometimes used as well. For instance, to uncover problems that consumers would associate with a plastic beer can, a small group of individuals might be asked to imagine themselves as plastic beer cans and to write down the problems they encounter as such.

Before a final decision is made on a new package design, the package is usually subjected to quantitative research. For instance, home-use tests are often conducted to assess the functionality of the package and to reveal any unexpected problems. Sometimes these tests lead to packaging improvements before the product is launched nationally. For example, when conducting home-use tests of liquid laundry detergents, manufacturers found that consumers disliked the mess created when measuring the detergent. This finding led to improved packages having built-in measuring caps that eliminated the need for cleaning a measuring cup.

Companies can also benefit by questioning whether selected packaging features designed to perform a function are really necessary. Applying Marketing Research 13.6 describes how one company achieved a cost savings by challenging the packaging status quo. The company received the additional benefit of reduced packaging waste which is the criterion discussed next.

Applying Marketing Research 13.6

The manufacturer of a carpet freshening and deodorizing product, which came in several scents, included an overwrap to doubly seal the container. The overwrap was designed to prevent shoppers from opening the canister containing the powder product to determine what fragrance option to buy. The degree to which this might happen had not been investigated.

An in-store research project was conducted in which unwrapped canisters were placed on the shelves in a sample of stores. The number of opened packages on the store shelves was monitored for a period of time. The incidence of this phenomenon was negligible. The decision was made to remove the overwrap from the package, thus reducing waste as well as saving the company hundreds of thousands of dollars annually.

Packaging Waste Created

Growing consumer concerns over solid waste disposal have created another factor that companies must consider when making packaging decisions. Consumers are becoming sensitive to the amount of waste generated by a company's packaging and are voicing their disapproval of some packaging forms. For example, pressure from environmentalists was instrumental in McDonald's decision to replace the Styrofoam packaging for its sandwiches with paper-based packaging.[26] Similarly, aseptic packages, such as the popular palm-sized juice box, were once praised by food technologists as the greatest achievement of the past fifty years. Now these packages have been banned in some states because of waste concerns.[27]

In response to these concerns, many companies have designed environmentally friendly packages for existing brands. These packages often contain less material, frequently are designed to be recyclable, and may even use recycled materials in their construction. For instance, Procter & Gamble spent three years redesigning the package of its Sure brand of deodorant so that the cardboard shadowbox outer package could be eliminated. The new package was anticipated to save about 3.4 million pounds of packaging waste per year.[28] Likewise, detergent manufacturers decided to offer superconcentrated, or "ultra," versions of their brands to reduce packaging wastes (see Exhibit 13.11).[29]

Exhibit 13.11
Concerns about solid waste have cause companies to offer superconcentrated versions of some brands to reduce packaging waste.

Environmental consequences will continue to be a major consideration in packaging decisions. However, companies must still ensure that packages meet the storage, stacking, and durability requirements needed during the distribution process. Otherwise, as the following example illustrates, new packages may meet with trade resistance.

Applying Marketing Research 13.7

Compact discs, or CDS, were initially sold in 5-inch-by-11-inch cardboard packages. From the outset, consumers criticized record companies for the nearly 23 million pounds of garbage created each year by the CD packaging. Packages were designed to help reduce shoplifting at the retail store. The long cardboard package, which enclosed the 5-inch "jewel box" containing the CD, also allowed retailers to use existing racks previously used for record albums.

Retailers vehemently opposed the distribution of CDS packaged in a jewel box only. Faced with such strong, but opposing, views from the trade and from consumers, record companies began testing alternative package designs. They sought a package that would maintain the original dimensions but would reduce packaging waste. Based on the results of the mall interviews conducted, executives soon adopted a new package design the following year.[30]

Setting a Price

When consumers evaluate alternative brands, price is often a key feature examined. A brand priced above competitive offerings may be attributed higher quality or merely be viewed as overpriced. A brand priced below others might be seen as a bargain or merely as being of cheap quality. Therefore, the initial pricing decision and any changes to this initial price have major ramifications on both the sales of the brand and its image.

Price plays a pivotal role in a brand's potential profitability to the firm. Therefore, the attractiveness of a new brand depends a great deal on the price that can be charged. Not only does price have an impact on the total sales attained by the new brand, it also influences the amount of profit achieved on each item sold. One of the first steps in determining the price for a new brand, then, is to estimate the range of feasible prices given the constraints of the product's cost structure, the firm's pricing strategy, and the price charged for other existing brands in the category.

The brand's variable costs, such as manufacturing and marketing costs, determine the absolute minimum price that could be charged. At any price lower than this, the firm would lose money on each item sold. However, companies also require that the sales of a brand cover its fixed costs and generate a profit. The relationship of profit, volume, variable costs, and fixed costs is:

profit = (price x volume) - (volume x unit variable costs) - fixed costs.

Different pricing strategies, and corresponding sales volumes, can produce the same profit. One strategy is penetration pricing. With a penetration strategy a low price is charged to achieve a high sales volume. Because of the low price, each item sold covers only a small amount of fixed costs, so profits depend on a large volume being sold. A penetration strategy is often used to discourage competitors from entering the market or to produce economies of scale in production.

At the other extreme, a firm might opt for a skimming strategy. With a skimming strategy, a high price is charged for each item so that a low sales volume is required to achieve the desired profit. Limited manufacturing capacity that can support only a low demand for the product is one possible motivation for adopting a skimming strategy. A skimming strategy might also be used if patent protection exists for the brand, making it harder for competitors to enter the market.

By rearranging the terms in the above profit equation, the sales volume necessary to cover fixed costs and generate desired profit can easily be computed for any price:

volume = (fixed costs + profit)/(unit price - unit variable costs).

Obviously, as the difference grows between the price charged for the brand and its variable costs, the sales volume necessary to meet given fixed costs and provide the desired profit decreases. However, prior to setting the price, a manager needs information as to the likelihood of achieving the required sales volume at different price levels. That is, insight into the price-demand relationship is needed. The manager can obtain this information through marketing research.

Researching Price

Actual market tests provide a realistic estimate of the impact of price on volume. If several markets are entered initially and a different price is set in each market, the brand's performance can be compared across markets to assess the impact of price on volume and profit. Firms often manipulate price as part of market tests, but market tests are an expensive way to gauge the profitability of a new brand. The firm must also commit manufacturing and distribution resources to the brand. Therefore, firms try to address pricing issues well in advance of market tests.

Pretest market systems provide a vehicle for assessing the sensitivity of potential sales volume or market share to price. While such tests are less expensive than test marketing, they do require that the firm be very far along in the process of developing the new offering. Firms would much prefer gathering pricing information even earlier in the development process so the viability of the new brand can be assessed with as little investment as possible.

Unfortunately, an accurate measurement of a new brand's sales potential at a given price is very difficult early in the product development process. Even so, marketers begin estimating price sensitivity as early as the concept stage in hopes of making more informed pricing decisions later on in the process. Such early research also prevents further testing of concepts that are obviously unprofitable.

As discussed in Chapter 10, concept tests usually include a measure of purchase interest, either attitudinal or behavioral. To investigate purchase intent accurately, consumers must be told the price that would be charged for the concept. Therefore, the price of the concept can be varied across respondent groups to assess price sensitivity. The following example illustrates this approach using a monadic, or single-product, approach.

Applying Marketing Research 13.8

A manufacturer of canned cat food is considering the development of a new line of specialty cat foods. Information is needed on the sensitivity of consumer purchase intent to price in order to determine the price to charge for the new product. A series of concept descriptions, identical except for the price, are developed. The price varies in the concept descriptions from 39¢ to 89¢ in ten-cent increments.

A concept test is conducted using a mall-intercept format. Participants in the study are shown one of the concept descriptions and asked to indicate their purchase interest on the typical five-point purchase intent scale. For each concept, the total percentage of respondents saying either that they "definitely would buy" or that they "probably would buy" the concept is calculated. Comparing the percentages across concept descriptions helps the company determine how rapidly purchase intent declines as the price increases.

Exhibit 13.12 shows the different types of results that could be obtained. Each has a different implication for the pricing strategy. For result A, purchase intent is basically unaffected by price in the range explored in the concept test. Since the same sales volume would be expected at any price between 39¢ and 89¢, a price of 89¢ would maximize profit.

The second result, B, shows a steady, steep

decline in purchase interest as price increases. Hence, sales volume appears very sensitive to price. A careful analysis of the equation for profit would be required to determine the price that maximizes profit in this case.

Finally, in case C, purchase intent is fairly constant up to a threshold price of 59¢. At that price, purchase intent drops rapidly, suggesting that the product should be priced at 59¢ to maximize profit.

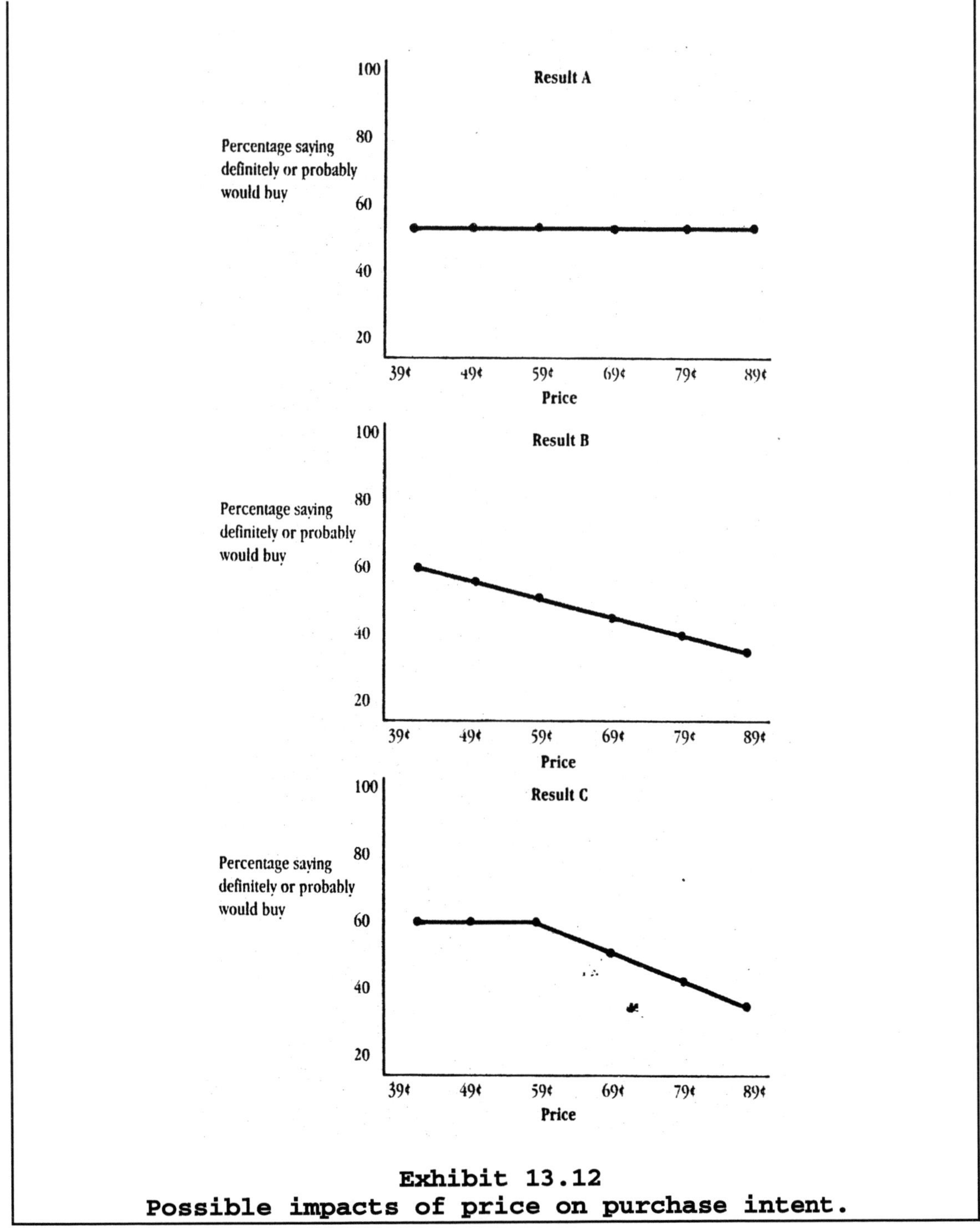

Exhibit 13.12
Possible impacts of price on purchase intent.

Conjoint analysis is also useful for investigating price sensitivity issues. As discussed in Chapter 12, conjoint analysis is the technique that uses the respondent's overall preference ranking of a series of concept statements, or product profiles, to infer the relative importance of the attributes under study and to describe how perceived value

changes across the levels of each attribute. To examine price sensitivity, price can be included as one of the attributes being studied.[31] The range of part-worth values assigned to the price levels, relative to the ranges of part-worths for the other attributes, provides information on the relative importance of price in determining preference. Differences in the part-worths assigned to particular price levels measure the sensitivity of consumer preference to various price changes. The following example illustrates the use of conjoint analysis to investigate price sensitivity.

Applying Marketing Research 13.9

Suppose that Amtrak, a U.S. passenger rail service, was considering a rail pass that would entitle the purchaser to unlimited travel on Amtrak for a specified period of time. Amtrak management feels that the price of the pass, the period of time for which the pass would be valid, and whether or not restrictions would be imposed on departure days all would influence consumer acceptance of the pass. Three different prices ($500, $700, and $900) and three different time periods over which the pass would be valid (two, three, and four months) were being considered. They were also considering not allowing Friday departures instead of allowing departures on any day (restrictions *vs.* no restrictions).

To explore these issues, suppose that a conjoint study was conducted among a sample of 300 past users of Amtrak. Participants in the study ranked the eighteen alternative travel pass descriptions, or profiles (3 price levels x 3 duration levels x 2 restriction levels), in terms of overall preference. Assume that the results were fairly consistent across respondents so averaging was appropriate. Table 13.1 contains the average part-worth values obtained for the attribute levels. Table 13.2 contains the importance scores for the three attributes based on these average part-worth values.

	Level		
	I	II	III
Price (I=$500, II=$700 III=$900)	42.0	16.0	-58.0
Duration (I=2 mo., II=3 mo., III=4 mo.)	-15.0	1.0	14.0
Restrictions (I=none, II=no Friday travel)	13.0	-13.0	

Note: LINMAP, the program used to perform the analysis, scales the values for each respondent so that they sum to zero for each attribute and the largest range is 100.

Table 13.1
Average Part-Worth Values.

Attribute	Relative Importance
Price	64.5
Duration	18.7
Restrictions	16.8
	100.0

Note: The relative importance score for each attribute is the range of the attribute's values divided by the sum of the corresponding ranges for the three attributes.

Table 13.2
Attribute Importance Scores

As would be expected, the part-worths for price decline as price increases, while the part-worths for duration increase as the duration increases. Also as expected, a smaller part-worth is assigned to the restricted departure than to the unrestricted departure. Therefore, the most attractive offering (the profile with the highest total score, or utility) is the unrestricted travel pass costing

$500, which would be valid for four months. The least attractive offering is the two-month, restricted pass costing $900.

Based on the relative importance scores, price is the most important attribute. Duration and restrictions appear about equal in importance.

Not only do the results show that price has the dominant impact on consumer acceptance of the travel pass, the $900 price also appears to be prohibitively expensive in the current context. Looking at the average part-worth values for each price level, you can see that increasing the price from $700 to $900 has a large negative impact on acceptance that no other attribute can offset.

The unrestricted, three-month, $700 pass was of particular interest to Amtrak, because such a pass had been offered in the past with favorable response. Thus, it served as a benchmark for assessing consumer acceptance of the profiles.

For any specific duration, consumer acceptance of a restricted $500 pass is the same as that of a $700 unrestricted pass. Therefore, offering a three-month pass at $500 that excludes Friday travel should generate the same level of customer enthusiasm as the previously used three-month, unrestricted, $700 pass promotion. Similarly, dropping the price from $700 to $500 would more than compensate for a reduction in the duration of the pass from three months to two.

Armed with this information, Amtrak management would have a better understanding of customer attitudes toward price, duration, and travel restrictions. They can explore alternative travel pass promotions with more confidence as to what the customer response is likely to be.

Summary

Companies use several criteria to evaluate potential brand names. The name should be easily remembered by consumers and it should be unique. It must be easily pronounceable and must convey the correct image. Finally, the name must be consistent with the firm's overall corporate branding strategy.

Idea generation techniques are useful when a company is searching for a new brand name. When evaluating potential names, projective techniques are commonly employed to assess image. Direct questioning techniques are often used to determine the memorability and pronounceability of alternative names.

More and more companies are opting for an umbrella brand name strategy. With this strategy, an existing brand name is chosen for a new brand in a completely different category. By extending, or leveraging, an existing brand name, companies reduce the expense necessary to generate an image for the new brand. If successful, the equity in the existing brand name can be transferred to the new brand.

A company sometimes changes its name because the old name no longer describes what the company does. At other times, a company will change its name to change the company image. Firms even change their names to try to influence the price of their common stock.

For many products, a brand's package plays a major selling role. Therefore, the package selected must be distinctive, communicate the brand's points of distinction, and catch the consumer's eye. The package must also perform the storage, stacking, and other functional tasks required. In today's world, a firm must also be concerned about the amount of packaging waste that is created.

Qualitative research is commonly employed to determine what a brand's package communicates to consumers. The visibility and distinctiveness of a package are often researched using tachistoscope tests and eye-tracking cameras. Problems with a package's functionality are usually uncovered by questioning the trade and consumers and through home-use tests.

In setting the price of a new product, a firm must first determine whether a penetration or a skimming price strategy is appropriate. Then, the firm must determine what range of prices the consumer views as feasible and how demand for the brand varies across this price range. Companies research price from the concept stage all the way through to the market test stage, refining the price estimates at each level.

Key Terms:

eye-tracking camera

family branding strategy

logo

tachistoscope

umbrella branding strategy

Researching the Price for Nimslo Photofinishing

The Nimslo Company anticipated that photo processing would be a major source of the revenue generated by the sales of the 3D camera. Unlike conventional photos, which can be processed by numerous photofinishers, the 3D process could only be done by the Nimslo Company. Therefore, all pictures shot with 3D cameras would generate photo processing income for the company. For customer convenience, the company planned to have a nationwide network of distributors where consumers could drop off their film and pick up their pictures.

The company estimated that each roll of film would have a fixed developing cost of about $2.00, regardless of the number of exposures on the roll. To generate the desired return, the company felt that it would be necessary to charge from 65¢ to 85¢ per picture printed plus the $2.00 developing fee. Because it took two frames for each 3D picture, a twelve-exposure roll of film would yield only six pictures and cost between $5.90 and $7.10 to process, or about 98¢ to $1.18 per processed picture. Larger-exposure rolls would have a smaller per picture cost because the $2.00 fixed cost would be spread over more pictures.

To research consumer reaction to these processing charges, the Nimslo Company recruited a panel of consumers matching the target market profile. Each consumer was given a 3D camera to use and was instructed to mail the film to Nimslo for processing. Nimslo paid for the cost of mailing and charged half of the panel $2.00/roll plus 65¢ per picture for processing and the other half of the panel 85¢ per picture plus the fixed charge. Nimslo monitored film usage of the two groups and, after the trial period was over, questioned the panelists about the camera and film processing.

The results were not encouraging. Although very little difference in the level of film usage was noted between the two groups, both groups took far fewer pictures in the allotted time than the average 35 mm camera owner would have taken. When questioned, both groups felt that the cost of processing was much too high compared to normal 35 mm processing of about 35¢ per picture. Neither group felt that the 3D feature offset the higher price.

Review Questions

13.1 Describe some of the reasons why corporations are willing to bear the expense of changing names.

13.2 List and describe the criteria for choosing a brand name.

13.3 How might projective techniques be used to generate a list of potential names? Give an example.

13.4 How might projective techniques be used to evaluate alternative potential brand names? Give an example.

13.5 What is meant by an umbrella strategy for naming new brands? What are the advantages of this approach? What are the disadvantages?

13.6 Why is packaging an important component of the marketing mix for many products? Describe the criteria for evaluating a new package.

13.7 Describe three new products, other than those discussed in the chapter, whose differential advantages are based primarily on packaging.

13.8 What is a tachistoscope? How is a tachistoscope used in researching alternative packaging designs?

13.9 How does home-use testing play a role in researching packaging designs?

13.10 What is meant by a logo? Give an example. What issues regarding the selection of a logo lend themselves to marketing research?

13.11 What are the advantages and disadvantages of using test markets to estimate price sensitivity?

13.12 How can price sensitivity be assessed in a concept test?

13.13 Describe how conjoint analysis can be used to estimate the impact of price on consumer acceptance.

Discussion Questions

13.1 Set up a research plan to select the name for a new sunscreen product. Briefly describe the nature of the research you would commission both for generating and for screening alternative names, and state the purpose of each research study you would conduct.

13.2 Procter & Gamble is considering selling bulk detergent refills for some of their liquid laundry detergents to reduce the amount of packaging waste that accumulates in landfills. How might the company research the consumer acceptance of these bulk refills? What issues do you think they would wish to examine? Why?

13.3 Design a marketing research experiment to investigate the shelf visibility of several alternative new package designs.

13.4 Design a marketing research project to investigate the relative recognizability of several alternative new logos for an existing brand.

13.5 Suppose that the RCA record company commissioned a conjoint study to examine how membership price, number of required purchases, and the number of free selections offered for joining influenced consumer preference for mail-order music clubs. The following levels of each of the three attributes were examined:

	Levels			
	I	II	III	IV
Membership price	\$5.95	\$12.95	\$19.95	\$24.95
Number of required purchases	1	3	5	10
Number of free selections when joining	2	4	6	

RCA had previously offered a club having a \$5.95 membership fee with two free selections for joining and requiring five additional purchases. This offer had been very successful.

The average part-worths obtained for each attribute level were (assume results were consistent across consumers so averaging is appropriate):

	Average Ratings			
	I	II	III	IV
Membership price	25.0	-5.0	-8.0	-12.0
Number of required purchases	40.0	10.0	-5.0	-45.0
Number of free selections when joining	-15.0	2.0	13.0	

What attribute combination would be the most preferred? the least preferred? What is the most important attribute? The least important? How sensitive is consumer preference to the various price levels? Is it possible that the company can market a record club with a \$24.95 membership fee that would be accepted by consumers almost as much as previous club charging the \$5.95 membership fee? How?

13.6 A company considering the introduction of a new brand estimates that each item will cost them about 30¢ to produce and distribute. They plan on an introductory marketing campaign that will cost $1,000,000 for the first twelve months. In addition, the company desires a profit of at least $500,000 the first year. Graph the first-year sales volumes necessary to meet these objectives for selling prices of 40¢, 50¢, 60¢, 70¢, 80¢, 90¢, and $1.00. What types of marketing research might the company undertake to determine the feasibility of any of these price levels?

Chapter 13 Endnotes

1. Thomas Hine, "Why We Buy," *Worth*, May 1995, pp. 80-83.

2. "Look Who's Name-Dropping," *Business Week*, November 17, 1997, p. 8.

3. See Melanie Wells, "Coke's Surge Faces Third Challenge," *USA Today*, January 23, 1997, p. 4B and Dow Jones News, "Coke Ordered to Appear for Surge Trial," *The Arizona Republic*, September 14, 1997, p. D7.

4. Henri Charmasson, *The Name is the Game: How to Name a Company or Product*. Homewood, IL: Dow Jones-Irwin, 1988, p. 29-30.

5. William F. Schoell and Joseph P. Guiltinan, *Marketing: Contemporary Concepts and Practices*, 5th ed. Boston: Allyn & Bacon, 1992, p. 297.

6. See "Unisys Explained" in "Viewpoint: Letters," *Advertising Age*, September 22, 1987, p. 20.

7. Robert F. Hartley, *Marketing Mistakes*, 3rd ed. New York: John Wiley & Sons, 1986, pp. 189-203.

8. See Edward M. Tauber, "Expanding Your Brand," *Advertising Age*, December 7, 1987, p. 18.

9. Ronald Alsop and Bill Abrams, *The Wall Street Journal of Marketing*. Homewood, IL: Dow Jones-Irwin, 1986, pp. 42-44.

10. "Kraft Hits the Bull's Eye with Barbecue Sauce," *Marketing Communications*, February 1988, p. 47.

11. Bradley Johnson, "Wash-day Washout: Clorox Miscalculated with Failed Detergent," *Advertising Age*, June 3, 1991, p. 54.

12. See Barbara Loken and Deborah Roedder John (1993), "Diluting Brand Beliefs: When do Brand Extensions Have a Negative Impact," *Journal of Marketing*, 57 (3), 71-84; and Kevin Lane Keller and David A. Aaker (1992), "The Effects of Sequential Introduction of Brand Extensions," *Journal of Marketing Research*, 29 (February), 35-50 for discussions of the potential for the reciprocal effects of brand extensions on parent brands.

13. L. Eric Elie, "The Corporate Name Game," *The Atlanta*

Constitution, March 12, 1987, pp. 1C, 3C; and Patricia Strand, "BP Pumps Up Change," *Advertising Age*, November 27, 1989, p. 20.

14. "Dow Chemical Ponders Change in Corporate Identity," *Marketing News*, December 5, 1988, p.1.

15. L. Eric Elie, "The Corporate Name Game," *The Atlanta Constitution*, March 12, 1987, pp. 1C, 3C.

16. Mark Gleason, "Why Sandaz-Ciba Ads Went to PR Agency," *Advertising Age*, July 22, 1996, p. 41.

17. See Thomas Hine, "The Total Package," Boston, MA: Little, Brown and Company, 1995, pp. 210-215 for a discussion of Cheskin's work on the impact of the package on perception of the product.

18. Julie Liesse, "Everything Old Can Be New Again," *Advertising Age*, October 5, 1992, p. 12.

19. Frank Tobolski, "Package Design Requires Research," *Marketing News*, June 6, 1994, p. 4.

20. See Davis L. Masten, "Logo's Power Depends on How Well It Communicates with Target Market," *Marketing News*, December 5, 1988, p. 20, for a discussion of the communication value of logos and the role of market research.

21. See Kenneth A. Fox, "Packaging Research: An Overview," *Journal of Data Collection* 27, 1 (Spring 1987), pp. 20-24, for a discussion of the criteria for evaluating packaging and a general review of packaging research.

22. The information in this example is based on information provided in John S. Blyth, "Designers Becoming Enlightened about the Value of Research," *Marketing News*, May 10, 1990, pp. 33, 39.

23. Cynee Miller, "Right Package Sets Mood for Image-Driven Brands," *Marketing News*, August 5, 1991, p. 2.

24. See Kate Kitzgerald, "Family Values Shade Crayola's First Image Ad," *Advertising Age*, November 30, 1992, p. 15 and Mercedes M. Cardona, "Crayola Breaks Ad Effort to Target Parents' Nostalgia," *Advertising Age*, July 21, 1997, p. 35.

25. Fred Feucht, "Which Hue Is Best? Test Your Color I.Q.," *Advertising Age*, September 14, 1987, p. 18.

26. Matthew Grimm, "McDonald's `Flip-Flops' Again and Ditches Its Clamshell," *Adweek's Marketing Week*, November 5, 1990, pp. 4-5.

27. Gary McWillimans, "The Big Brouhaha Over the Little Juice Box," *Business Week*, September 17, 1990, p. 36.

28. Jennifer Lawrence and Pat Sloan, "Toiletries to Strip Excess Packaging," *Advertising Age*, May 13, 1991, pp. 3, 50.

29. See Bradley Johnson and Laurie Freeman, "Clorox Joins Ultras," *Advertising Age*, November 12, 1990, p. 73.

30. Meg Cox, "Music Firms Try Out 'Green' CD Boxes," *Wall Street Journal*, July 25, 1991, p. B1.

31. Richard J. Fox and Ellen Day, "Enhancing the Appeal of Service Contracts: An Empirical Investigation of Alternative Offerings," *Journal of Retailing* 64, 3 (1988): 335-351, uses conjoint analysis to investigate the impact of price and other variables on consumer acceptance of novel service contract formats.

Chapter 14

Simulated Test Markets and Test Marketing

Learning Objectives:

After reading Chapter 14 you should be able to:

- provide an overview of simulated test market systems.
- compare and contrast the various simulated test market systems.
- discuss the predictive power of simulated test markets.
- present the pros and cons of test markets.
- explain how test market cities are chosen.
- discuss the use of marketing research in a test market.
- show how to project test market results to a national level.

Nestle's Alpine white milk chocolate and white milk chocolate with almonds are the only popularly priced and widely distributed white chocolate candy bars.[1] Shortly after Nestle introduced these candy bars, a competitor considered challenging Nestle's dominant position in the category. The competitor launched a project to develop its own white chocolate bar, and the resulting candy exceeded project objectives. Marketing research indicated that it was very appealing to consumers and performed favorably when product-tested against Alpine.

The competitor's marketing management required specific information regarding the market potential of a new white milk chocolate bar before continuing the project. They understood that, although the product was very favorably received by consumers, it might not be an especially attractive business opportunity. To assess market potential, they conducted a simulated test market. Results indicated that their new candy would only slightly increase the size of the white chocolate candy market.

Furthermore, although the new white milk chocolate bar would be likely to capture a significant portion of Alpine's market share, the projected sales volume would not be enough to justify the business venture. The company decided to suspend work on the white chocolate bar, at least for the time being, and to pursue other business options that had far more potential.

The example just discussed demonstrates how simulated test markets can be of great value to marketing managers. The example points out that, although a new product might have great consumer appeal, the important issue from a corporate perspective is the business potential. Is the expected revenue enough to justify the investment of resources and capital? In this case, it became clear from the marketing research that, despite the product's excellence, the investment was not justified at the time. The simulated test market saved the company the substantial expense of a test market that would have been the next step in bringing the brand to the market.

A critical factor in the decision to market a new brand is its projected volume. Test markets provide accurate assessments of new brand potential, but it is estimated that about two-thirds of the brands introduced in test markets fail to meet their volume objectives.[2] Unfortunately, forecasting a new brand's potential volume, short of test marketing, is difficult to say the least.

For many years, marketers were restricted either to introducing a new product or service broadly and hoping for the best or to conducting a test market where the new product or service was distributed in a limited area and the sales results were used to project to the national level. Test market research is extremely expensive, costing millions of dollars to conduct.[3] Test markets also tend to require from twelve to eighteen months to complete. This allows competitors time to plan and prepare countermeasures before the new product is introduced nationally. These shortcomings of test market research led several marketing research firms to develop simulated test market systems that are designed to provide relatively inexpensive sales volume estimates prior to test market.

A **simulated test market** is designed to produce an estimate of sales potential by making a new brand available to a sample of target consumers. A simulated test market takes a short period of time, typically less than two months, and is very inexpensive relative to a test market (roughly $100M, depending on specific requirements). Simulated test markets provide marketing management with a prediction of the sales that could be expected in a test market and with diagnostic information as to why that prediction is made. Marketing managers use these predictions to decide whether to stop further development, to make changes to the product and/or the marketing plan before proceeding to a test market, or to proceed directly to a test market.

Overview of Simulated Test Markets

In the typical simulated test market scenario, a sample of several hundred target market consumers are recruited, in many cases in a shopping mall, and exposed to the product, its advertising, and competitive advertising. Test participants are then given an opportunity to shop in a simulated store environment in which the test product or competitive products can be purchased. Participants who do not purchase the test product in the store are given a sample of the test product to try. Follow-up interviews are conducted after a suitable time period to determine reaction to the product. Participants are also given the opportunity to repurchase the new product at the follow-up interview to yield estimates of repurchase rates.

Test results and particulars regarding the marketing plan, such as the anticipated advertising spending level, serve as inputs to marketing models used to develop projections regarding product volume and/or market share. These volume projections are used to decide whether to proceed to a test market (or perhaps regional introduction). Hence, a simulated test market serves as a powerful screening tool to identify potential problems associated with a new product entry quickly and relatively inexpensively *before* conducting an expensive and time-consuming test market.

Benefits of Simulated Test Markets[4]

Product Screening

As discussed above, the primary objective of a simulated test market is to provide an estimate of market potential, thus acting as a screening device for uncovering losers without incurring the costs of an actual test market. If the simulated test market projection of potential sales volume or market share is well below what is required, and no way can be found to improve the situation, the product may have to be abandoned.

Evaluation of Alternate Marketing Plans

The projections of volume and/or market share provided by simulated test markets typically require input such as the level of promotional support planned for the new product and the expected distribution of the product. Thus, managers can use these models to play "what if" games. Promotional support or expected distribution can be altered to represent different introductory scenarios, and the impact of these changes can be assessed by recalculating the estimate of volume potential. For example, heavier free sampling of the new brand than originally planned might more than pay for itself with the increased business it generates.

Diagnostic Information

Simulated test markets provide diagnostic information that can be useful for modifying the offering to improve the expected sales volume. For example, simulated test market results might signal a problem such as low repurchase interest stemming from a price-value concern among consumers. The manufacturer may be able to lower the price and change the positioning slightly to correct the problem. Diagnostic information can also be used to enhance the probability of a success. Refining the target audience based on observing who reacts most positively to the product in the simulated test market and revising the advertising strategy accordingly is another example of how diagnostic information can be used.

Limitations of Simulated Test Markets

A simulated test market is not a replacement for a test market. Simulated test markets have distinct limitations in terms of the information they supply and the situations in which they can be used.

Accuracy of volume and share estimates

While simulated test markets provide a reasonably good picture of business potential, the estimates are based on mathematical models that only approximate the real world. The data are obtained in an artificial environment. How the trade will react and, more importantly, how one's competition will respond are still unknown. Further, although advertising copy is often included in a simulated test market, the total advertising strategy, consisting of the spending levels, spending patterns, and media plan, is not evaluated.

Narrow range of applications

Simulated test markets are best suited for frequently purchased, inexpensive consumer packaged goods. Hence, the focus of the models tends to be on consumer awareness, trial, and repeat purchasing of the new brand in a typical supermarket environment. Although attempts are being made to extend the same procedures to durables, services, and industrial products, little data are available on the results of such efforts. Further, many available systems are best suited for introductions to existing product categories either because the new product is evaluated directly against a competitive set of similar products or because experience with similar products is used to generate the prediction of business potential. Hence, new products, such as TreeTop Apple Chips (see Exhibit 14.1), which are not easily classified into existing product categories, present problems to some simulated test market systems.

Exhibit 14.1
Some simulated test market systems would have a difficult time estimating market potential for an apple chip because the product does not fit into existing product category.

Types of Simulated Test Market Systems

There are a number of simulated test marketing systems available, all having much in common.[5] The choice of a system to use in a particular application may simply come down to the one with which the marketing and marketing research managers are most comfortable or the one with which the firm has had good experience. However, there are considerations that eliminate some systems from specific applications. For example, a new product may not belong to a well-defined product category. Thus, those systems requiring a competitive set of brands would be eliminated from consideration.

There are generally two basic approaches to estimating new product potential: using consumer attitude data or using observed consumer purchase behavior. The different simulated test market systems generally involve variations of these approaches to develop volume or share estimates for a new product. One of the more well-known systems, **ASSESSOR**[6], uses both an attitudinal and a behavioral model to forecast business potential for a new brand. These models are typical of the logic associated with the two distinct approaches. In addition, specific information pertaining to the research design and the mathematical models used in the

ASSESSOR system has been made public in the marketing literature while comparable information on other systems is often classified as proprietary. For these reasons, we next review the ASSESSOR system in detail, and only briefly discuss some of the other well-known systems.

ASSESSOR

ASSESSOR was originally developed by Marketing Decision System (MDS), which was later acquired by Information Resources, Inc. (IRI). Subsequently, M/A/R/C, Inc. of Dallas, Texas, purchased the ASSESSOR system from IRI, and merged it with their own simulated test market system, ENTRO.[7] Since then, M/A/R/C has developed the Macro Market Modeling System, designed to provide marketing research guidance from the concept stage to in-market evaluation. The ASSESSOR models are an integral part of this system.

A detailed discussion of the ASSESSOR models can be found in the Appendix to this chapter. What follows is an overview.

The Basic Approach

ASSESSOR relies on managerial input as well as the study results to construct two separate estimates of market share for a new product. As noted above, one of the estimates is based on attitudinal data, while the other relies on actual purchase behavior. The system is geared to a new product introduction in a well-defined category of consumer packaged goods.

Respondents are intercepted in a shopping mall and screened for eligibility and willingness to participate. Eligibility is based primarily on being a member of the target market for the new brand, *e.g.*, users of artificial sweeteners or dog owners who purchase canned dog food. It is an obvious waste of time to test the new brand with individuals who have no interest in the product category, and such individuals are excluded in the recruiting process. This step is vital to the integrity of the results and care must be taken to define the target market and associated eligibility requirements properly.

Each participant completes a self-administered questionnaire that, among other things, establishes a relevant set of brands with which he or she is familiar and brand preferences within the relevant set. Rating scale data, used for diagnostic purposes, are also obtained to establish the relative importance of key attributes and perceptions of the brands on these attributes.

Next, respondents are exposed to advertising for existing brands in the category and for the test brand. They then shop in a simulated store where the test brand and competitive brands are available for sale. In appreciation for participating in the study, they are provided with seed money, which they do not have to spend in the store. Those not purchasing the test brand in the store are given a free sample to try at home to simulate product trials obtained by product sampling.

After a reasonable period of time in which to use the test product, respondents are contacted by telephone. They are given another opportunity to buy the test product and brand preferences are again obtained with the test brand included in each participant's relevant set. Exhibit 14.2 is a schematic of the ASSESSOR approach.

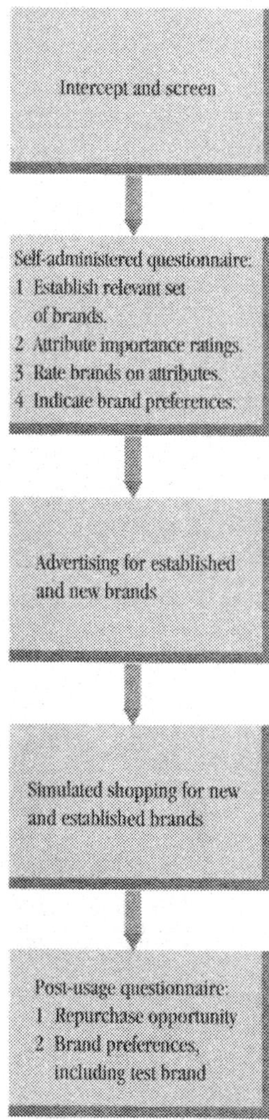

Exhibit 14.2
ASSESSOR schematic

Preference Model

The ASSESSOR **preference model** is based on attitudinal data. Measures of preferences for the brands are obtained by having respondents evaluate each possible pair of brands in their respective relevant sets. For each pair, respondents are asked to divide eleven points between the brands based on how much they prefer one to the other. For each brand in each respondent's relevant set, a value is obtained based on the total number of points awarded to the brand across the comparisons. The respective probabilities of purchase are assumed to be proportional to these values.

A telephone interview is conducted after participants have used the test product in their homes. The pairwise constant sum eleven-point allocation is repeated for all possible pairs of brands in the relevant set and all additional paired comparisons involving the test brand. These data are used to calculate a new set of postexposure purchase probabilities for the brands which reflect the impact of the test brand.

The preference market share model is based on the following equation:

$$M(t) = E(t) * L(t),$$

where $M(t)$ represents the market share for the test brand, $E(t)$ represents the proportion of consumers who will include the new brand in their relevant sets, and $L(t)$ represents the average probability that consumers will purchase the test brand (based on postexposure preference data). In other words, the estimate of market share is the product of two components. The first component represents the percentage of consumers who will adopt the brand, and the second component represents the average probability of purchase among these consumers. The value of $E(t)$ is calculated taking into account the level of marketing support to be given to the new brand. The average probability of purchase is obtained by averaging the individual probabilities of purchase obtained after exposure to the test brand across the entire panel.

The impact of the introduction of the new brand on existing brands is important and can be estimated from the preference model. In other words, the amount of business taken from competitors as well as the level of **cannibalization** — the amount of business taken from existing company brands — can be calculated. The following equation represents the estimate of market share for an existing brand, say k, after the new brand has been introduced:

$$M(k) = E(t) * L(k) + (1-E(t)) * P(k)$$

where $P(k)$ and $L(k)$ are respectively the average pre- and post-probability that brand k is purchased. Naturally, if brand k is not an element of a particular respondent's relevant set, then L(k) and P(k) are both zero for that particular respondent. Thus, the projected share for an existing brand after the test brand is introduced is the sum of two terms. The first term is the product of the proportion of consumers who include the test brand in their respective relevant sets and the average probability of purchasing the existing brand after exposure to the test brand. The second term is the product of an estimate of the fraction of households that will not adopt the test brand and the average probability of purchasing the existing brand in question before exposure to the test brand.

Using the calculations just described, a set of pre-shares for existing brands and a set of post-shares for existing brands and the test brand are obtained. The pre-shares can be used to check the credibility of the estimates by calibrating them to known shares in the marketplace. The post-shares are used to measure the source of business for the new brand. If the new brand's primary source of business is an existing brand manufactured by the same company, then the cannibalization rate is high, and it may be unwise to introduce the new brand. Obviously, this information is critical in the assessment of the potential for the new brand.

Applying Marketing Research 14.1

How to. . .

Estimate Source of Business

in the ASSESSOR Preference Model

Suppose that Procter & Gamble is considering introducing a new deodorant bar soap. Further, suppose that product tests have indicated a high degree of consumer acceptance, a preferred name and package design have emerged from consumer testing, copy has been developed and tested, and the price has at least initially been determined. The company decides to conduct an ASSESSOR study to evaluate the entire offering.

The study is conducted among 350 heads of households in which deodorant bar soaps are used. The average preference scores before and after exposure to the test brand are given below:

Brand	Pre (P(k))	Post (L(k))
Safeguard	.26	.22
Dial	.40	.30
Coast	.14	.11
Irish Spring	.10	.06
Lever 2000	.04	.04
Shield	.06	.05
Test Brand	___	.22

It is estimated that about 25 percent of the households will include the test brand in their relevant sets, *i.e.*, $E(t) = .25$. Hence, the estimate of share for the test brand, $M(t)$, is given by:

$$M(t) = E(t) * L(t)$$

$$= .25 * .22 = .055.$$

To estimate source of business, new shares are calculated for all the existing brands assuming that the test brand was introduced. Recall that for any existing brand, k, its share after the introduction of the test brand is estimated by:

$$M(k) = E(t)*L(k) + (1-E(t))*P(k)$$

For example, the revised share for Dial is calculated as (.25)(.30) + (.75)(.40)

= .375. The revised shares are given below:

Brand	Share Percentage
Safeguard	25.0
Dial	37.5
Coast	13.2
Irish Spring	9.0
Lever 2000	4.0
Shield	5.8
Test Brand	5.5

Comparing these shares with the average preferences given earlier, we see that the primary source of business for the new brand is Dial, which is estimated to lose 2.5 share points.

Trial-Repeat Model

The ASSESSOR **trial-repeat model** is based primarily on observed purchase behavior toward the test product. Market share for the test brand, again denoted by $M(t)$, is also estimated by the product of two components. The first component, T, stands for trial, and the second component, S, stands for the new brand's share of subsequent purchases in the product category among triers of the new brand. The trial-repeat model is given by the equation:

$$M(t) = T * S.$$

The trial component, T, relies heavily on managerial input regarding the introductory plan for the new brand, as well as the observed rate of purchasing of the new brand in the simulated store. The retention factor, S, is derived from a probabilistic brand-switching model and incorporates the observed repurchase rate as well as the post-usage purchase probability for the test brand based on the preference model. A detailed explanation is provided in the Appendix to this chapter.

Applying Marketing Research 14.2

How to . . .

Estimate Market Share for the Test Brand in the ASSESSOR Trial-Repeat Model

Suppose that of the 350 heads of households who participated in the ASSESSOR study for the new Procter & Gamble deodorant bar soap brand just discussed, seventy (or 20 percent) purchased the new brand in the simulated store. Combining this result with key aspects of the introductory marketing plan yields an estimated trial rate, T, of .144.

Suppose further that observed repurchase

rates and probabilities of purchasing the new brand are such that S = .30. The ASSESSOR trial-repeat model estimate of share would then be:

$$M\ (t) = T * S = .144 * .30 = .043.$$

The ASSESSOR trial-repeat model estimate of share would then be:

M (t) = T * S = .144 * .30 = .043.

Reconciling the two models

Exhibit 14.3 shows the logic involved in the two separate estimates produced by the ASSESSOR system. If the two approaches to estimating the share for the new brand yield radically different answers, then the difference must be reconciled, as indicated in Exhibit 14.3. By examining the components of the estimates derived from the two models, the source of the difference between the estimates can be identified. A detailed analysis of the basic attitudinal and behavioral data can perhaps explain the difference and provide insight into which of the two estimates, if either, has merit. On the other hand, consistency between the two estimates, as is the case of the deodorant soap research just discussed, reinforces the basic conclusion.

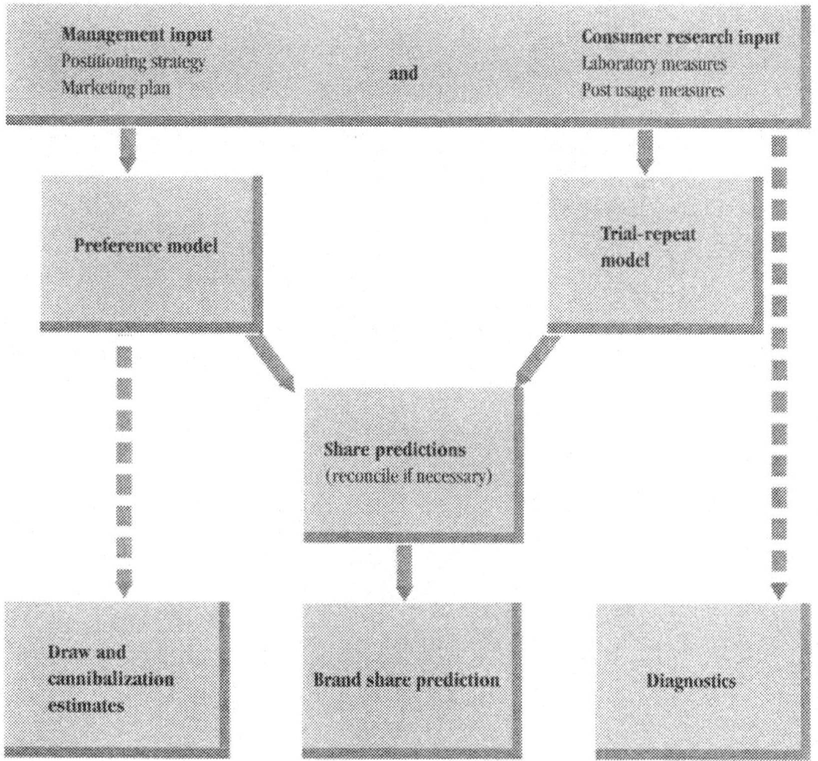

Exhibit 14.3
Structure of the ASSESSOR system.

Laboratory Test Market (LTM)

The **Laboratory Test Market (LTM)** system, developed by Yankelovich, Skelly and White, Inc., was the first simulated test market system.[8] The basic LTM approach is outlined in Exhibit 14.4. Participants are first exposed to advertising for the new and competitive brands. They are given seed money, typically 20 to 30 percent of the average price of the products available for purchase and are allowed to shop in a simulated store where they have the opportunity to purchase the new brand or competitive products. A normal in-home usage period follows. At the end of this period, a telephone follow-up interview is conducted to assess reaction to the test brand, usage patterns, and repurchase intentions. Respondents are also given the opportunity actually to repurchase the product at the follow-up interview, as well as during any subsequent interviews.

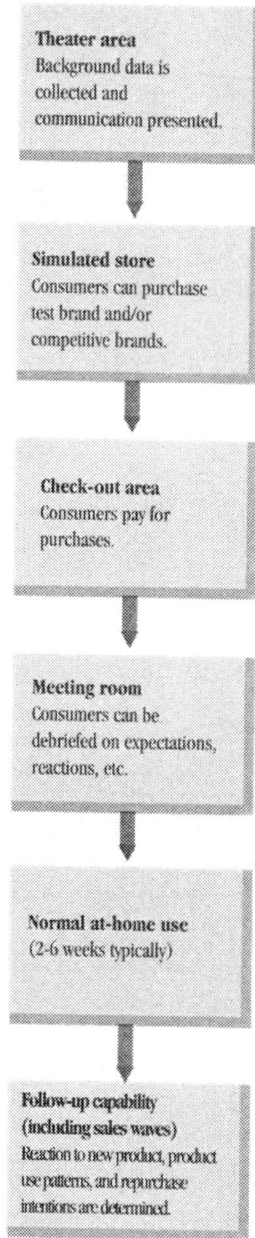

Exhibit 14.4
The Laboratory Test Market (LTM) approach.

The LTM estimate of market share is based on observed purchase behavior and is similar in nature to the ASSESSOR trial-repeat estimate. In the fundamental estimation model shown in Exhibit 14.5, the share estimate is the product of three components: LTM purchase rate, LTM repurchase rate, and a frequency factor. The market share estimate can easily be translated into a unit volume estimate.

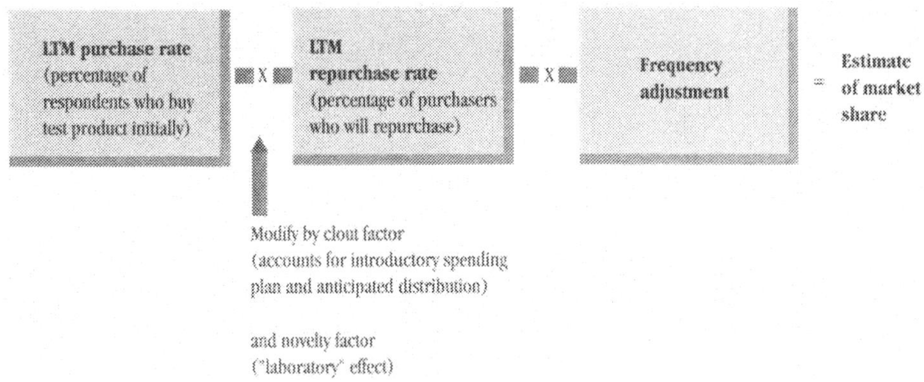

Exhibit 14.5
The LTM estimation model.

As in the ASSESSOR system, the LTM approach also requires managerial input regarding the marketing plan for the brand. This input is incorporated into a "clout factor" used to modify the observed LTM purchase rate. In other words, the 100 percent awareness of the new brand achieved in the artificial research environment is obviously inflated, and a correction, based on managerial input, must be applied in the estimation procedure.

Likewise, LTM purchase rates have been found to be inflated due to the artificial laboratory environment, so the LTM purchase incidence is further adjusted by a novelty factor to obtain a real-world trial rate. The novelty adjustment factor is based on cumulative results for products tested in the LTM system and subsequently introduced in the market.

Applying Marketing Research 14.3

How to...

Estimate Share Using the LTM Model

General Mills' Benefit, an adult cold cereal, contained the grain psyllium, rich in soluble fiber, and was thus positioned as providing the health benefit of cholesterol reduction without sacrificing taste. Suppose Benefit was tested in the LTM system among 300 heads of households who purchased adult health-oriented cold cereals, and that the following results were obtained. Of the 300 participants, 150 (50 percent) purchased the product in the simulated store and 100 (67 percent) expressed repurchase interest in the follow-up interview. Also, suppose that the company's marketing plan called for a relatively low level of supportive spending. Incorporating these facts and using LTM actual experience as a reference lead to a clout factor of .40. Further, the novelty factor for this category was estimated to be .75. The adjusted market share estimate was therefore .10 = .40 * .75 * .50 * .67, or 10 percent of the adult health-oriented cold cereal category. Volume was easily computed by multiplying this estimate by the annual category volume.

The Benefit share estimate of 10 percent obtained above does not involve any frequency-of-use adjustment. The implicit assumption is that brands in the category are used at about the same frequency and that the new brand will be used similarly. However, this need not be the case. For example, a highly concentrated laundry detergent requiring the use of a smaller quantity per wash would be purchased less frequently than the typical laundry detergent. The appropriate adjustment to make in such cases must be provided by the manufacturer.

If the new entry being tested does not clearly fit into an existing product category, the LTM market share estimate is not meaningful, because there is no reference category volume against which to apply the share. For example, if the new product is an oat bran food supplement designed to be added to a cold cereal, then no category volume reference would be available. In such cases, participants are asked how many times per year they would purchase the product, and this average figure, adjusted downward to account for overstatement based on LTM experience, is multiplied by the LTM share figure described earlier and by the number of households comprising the target market to provide an estimate of annual volume.

As just indicated, unlike ASSESSOR, LTM does not depend on the existence of a reference category and can be applied to new products that cross several categories or have no well-defined category of competition. On the other hand, the LTM system does not produce an estimate of source of business/cannibalization as ASSESSOR does. Such information is vital when introducing a new brand in an existing category where the company already has brands.

BASES

BASES, a service offered by BBI Marketing Services, Inc., is another research system designed to reduce the large expense and high risk associated with the development and introduction of a new product. There are several phases of the BASES system, each designed to provide assistance at the progressive stages of a new product introduction. Pre-Bases provides a technique for screening new product ideas on the basis of market potential. Promising ideas can be developed into concept statements which can be evaluated using BASES I, which was discussed at length in Chapter 10. A BASES II test is really not a simulated test market because the product, which is typically packaged like "blind" test product, is not sold the participants. BASES II combines a concept test with a home-use test and provides an estimate of volume potential. However, BASES II is often included in discussions of STMs because of its volume forecasting potential.

BASES III falls into the general category of a simulated test market system. However, BASES III is rarely used probably because the far less expensive BASES II is about as accurate.[9] In a BASES III test, six to twelve actual retail outlets in three or four geographically dispersed markets are used. The new brand is placed in these stores, and anywhere from 1200 to 3000 shoppers are shown TV commercials or print ads for the test product and two other noncompetitive products. Each participant is then given a book of six coupons worth 20 percent off retail price, which are redeemable in the test stores. One of the coupons is for the test brand. Purchases of the test brand are used to estimate trial, and postusage data is obtained via telephone follow-up interviews conducted among a minimum of 240 test brand buyers.

A major selling point for the BASES system in general is the vast company in-market experience with new product introductions. This extensive experience and the corresponding research results are used to adjust attitudinal information, or behavioral results observed in an artificial research setting, to behavior in the actual market. Adjustments of this type are used extensively in BASES I and II, as well as in BASES III. The coupon-induced trial of BASES III described above is converted to an actual trial rate estimate in this manner. Input regarding advertising plans, trade and consumer promotion plans, and distribution strategy are obtained from marketing management. Under these assumptions regarding the marketing plan, BASES III applies historical experience and forecasting models to the observed trial rates and after-usage data to estimate trial, first repeat rates, average time between purchases, average number of units purchased at trial, average repeat units and, finally, retail sales volume.

BASES III has the advantage of using actual retail outlets instead of "laboratory" stores as used in other simulated test market systems. However, the approach does not lend itself to estimating source of business, which may be critical in a project, as noted earlier.

RealTest™

RealTest™, developed by Elrick and Lavidge, Inc. is similar to BASES III in that consumers purchase the test brand in real supermarkets. Several supermarkets are enlisted to cooperate in the test by stocking the test brand. Heads-of-households who shop at these selected stores are identified and sent an announcement regarding the new brand which includes a discount coupon for the brand. Purchases of these households are monitored over time to identify trial, repeat and second repeat rates. A forecasting model using company management input as well as the results of the research is used to predict volume potential. Again, no source of business results are obtained.

Summary of Simulated Test Market Systems

As you can see, a variety of simulated test market systems are commercially available. Table 14.1 provides a brief comparison of the systems discussed in this section.

System	Type of Forecasting Model (Attitudinal *vs.* Behavioral)	Focus of Model[1] (Volume *vs.* Share)	Competitive Set Required	Source of Business Estimate Provided	Follow-up Interview(s) (Telephone *vs.* Personal)	Store Environment (Simulated *vs.* Real)
ASSESSOR	Both	Share[2]	Yes[2]	Yes	Telephone	Simulated
Laboratory Test Market (LTM)	Behavioral	Share	No	No	Telephone	Simulated
LITMUS	Behavioral	Share	No[3]	Yes	Telephone	Simulated
BASES III	Behavioral	Volume	No	No	Telephone	Real
COMP	Both	Share	Yes	Yes	Personal	Simulated

[1]Knowing category volume, share can of course be converted to volume. If category volume is unknown, or the category is unclear, systems that focus on estimating share may not be easily adapted to focus on volume.

[2]M/A/R/C's Macro ASSESSOR includes a model whose focus is volume and does not require a competitive set.

[3]Competitive set not formally required for model, but some information regarding competitive brands needed to estimate source of business.

Table 14.1
Comparison of simulated test market systems

Validity of Predictions

Simulated test marketing has become an integral part of the marketing research business as the number of available systems and their use has increased over recent years. Sponsoring firms speak highly of the accuracy of the estimates of market potential derived from their respective simulated test marketing systems, and the data in Table 14.2 support their claims. However, one such system received much negative publicity in the late 1980s because of an inaccurate prediction that so angered the client firm that they sued the marketing research firm for malpractice. We discuss this case in Applying Marketing Research 14.4, which follows, to point out the importance of not blindly accepting model projections.

	Overall (n = 44)	Health and beauty aids (n = 13)	Household items (n = 11)	Food products (n = 20)
Average test market share	7.16	7.35	10.14	5.40
Average simulated test market share	7.77	7.78	10.75	6.13
Mean difference	.61	.43	.61	.73
Mean absolute difference	1.54	1.66	1.37	1.56
Standard deviation difference	1.99	2.08	1.71	2.06

Adapted from Glen L. Urban and Gerald M. Katz, "Pre-Test-Market Models: Validation and Managerial Implications," *Journal of Marketing Research, 20* (August 1983), pp. 221–234.

Table 14.2
Comparison of simulated test market and actual test market shares

Applying Marketing Research 14.4

Delicare, a cold-water wash product for laundering delicate fabrics, was designed to compete with American Home Products' Woolite, which had captured almost the entire market at the time. Beecham, Inc. had invested several years of product development effort in the Delicare project, and the company was optimistic about the brand's potential. Much of this optimism was fueled by a simulated test market of Delicare conducted for Beecham by Yankelovich, Clancy and Schulman, Inc.

The marketing research, which cost $75,000,

resulted in a prediction that Delicare would surpass the well-entrenched market leader, Woolite, and obtain a market share of 45 to 52 percent.[10] The brand was launched with an $18 million media budget[11] for the introductory year, a figure recommended on the basis of the research. Delicare's market share never exceeded 25 percent, and hovered far below the lofty levels predicted.

Beecham sued Yankelovich for $24 million, charging malpractice. Adding to Beecham's case was the fact that in 1986 Yankelovich revised its initial estimate of Delicare's market share to 24 percent. The research firm cited "errors" due to "management malaise" associated with the 1984 Saatchi & Saatchi takeover of Yankelovich.[12] It was conjectured that instead of using 30 percent as the percentage of U.S. homes that use fine-fabric detergents, carelessness by Yankelovich management led to the use of the highly inflated figure of 75 percent in their volume forecasting model.[13]

The most obvious way to evaluate the predictive power of simulated test markets is to compare the predictions with the actual results observed in the market. However, as in Table 14.2, the point of comparison is typically the test market results because many brands do not make it beyond the test market stage; and test market results are closer in time, and hence more relevant from a validation perspective, than the national or regional results associated with brands expanded beyond the test market.

There are inherent problems with evaluating the accuracy of simulated test market systems that should be pointed out.[14] For one thing, the marketing mix, media plan, and so forth, used for the simulated test market projection are often not what is actually used in the test market. Although simulated test market models typically allow the manager to vary different elements of the introductory strategy, such as the product sampling plan and advertising support dollars, and to develop revised forecasts accordingly, some changes are impossible to accommodate. For example, the product and/or the package itself may actually be changed from the time of the simulated test market to the actual test market, the copy may be altered, and the positioning strategy may be fine-tuned. The actual marketing environment can also change fairly dramatically from the time of the simulated test market to the test market. New brands are continually being introduced, existing brands are being physically changed or repositioned, and consumer attitudes are continually in a state of flux. Hence, there are typically many differences that could be cited as causing an observed difference between a test market result and a corresponding simulated test market result.

There is also the issue of the accuracy of the test market result itself. Competitive reaction, for instance, may result in a distorted picture emerging from the test market. The fact that the test market result itself may not accurately reflect true potential must be kept in mind.

Products that are abandoned as a consequence of poor simulated test market results present another validation problem. In comparing results, a natural bias exists, because comparisons can only be made for those brands taken to test market. How many products tested poorly in a simulated test market, but actually would have been market successes? This side of the coin should also be considered when evaluating the validity of the predictions obtained from simulated test marketing systems.

Finally, there is the issue that test market forecasts tend to become goals. In other words, the marketing team becomes committed to a sales forecast and does everything in its power to achieve it with the allocated corporate resources. Obviously, this ends to drive the actual test market results toward the forecast, a prediction often derived from a simulated test market.

Test Marketing

Test markets provide a real world, in-market evaluation of a new brand. The typical controlled environment of marketing research is eliminated and an assessment is made "where the rubber meets the road." Test marketing is necessary because even the most sophisticated simulated test market system cannot predict with certainty what will happen in the actual marketplace. Marketers are sometimes very surprised by consumer, trade, or competitive reaction to a new product.

The consumer backlash to the introduction of New Coke was unprecedented. The original formula was quickly returned as Coca-Cola Classic. Coca-Cola did not test market New Coke, but rather introduced the new formula nationally with great fanfare. Afterwards, they were criticized for not test marketing the change. Coca-Cola was very careful not to make the same mistake when the company reformulated Cherry Coke. Consumer research had indicated that users of the brand preferred a stronger cherry flavor. The reformulated Cherry Coke was test marketed in five cities before the company felt secure enough to proceed with a national rollout.[15]

In a **test market**, a new brand, be it a product or service, is introduced in one or more limited geographical areas (typically cities). During the test market period, the marketing plan is followed and competitive reactions, consumer responses, and sales results are carefully monitored. Hence, real in-market experience is obtained. After sufficient test market experience, typically twelve to eighteen months, a decision is made either to expand the test market to other areas or to withdraw the brand from the market. The decision to expand or withdraw is based primarily on whether prescribed sales objectives are achieved.

We tend to think of test markets as being associated with totally new brand introductions. However, test markets are also used to evaluate alternative positioning strategies or pricing changes for existing brands or to experiment with alternative marketing strategies such as changes in advertising and/or promotion. Procter & Gamble conducted test markets to determine whether to reposition BIZ as a detergent booster instead of a laundry presoak.

Test marketing can be used in an experimental research mode where each of several test markets receives one of a set of alternatives under consideration, and the results are compared across markets. Naturally, these comparisons are valid only if the markets are comparable to begin with and no unusual events occur that could bias the results one way or another. For example, Igloo Corp. determined the level of advertising spending to use to support its coolers by test marketing the impact of different levels of advertising expenditures on sales.[16]

The Value of a Test Market

The primary objective of a test market is to obtain in-market information on the feasibility of a new brand without the expense associated with a broad geographic introduction. Not only does test marketing reduce the marketing and distribution costs, but also a pilot plant (as opposed to a full-scale manufacturing facility) might provide the manufacturing capacity required to supply a test market.

Test markets provide information on a number of important issues, including:

- market share and volume estimates;
- who is buying the new brand, how frequently they are buying it, and for what purposes;

- where purchases are being made and at what price;
- competitive strategic reactions; and
- effects on established brands, including source of business, imagery, and cannibalization.

Test markets can even uncover unexpected problems as demonstrated in Applying Marketing Research 14.5 and 14.6.

Applying Marketing Research 14.5

Sensormatic Corp., makers of electronic theft-protection devices, developed a product to help supermarkets reduce their losses resulting from stolen goods.[17] Magnetically sensitized labels were attached to merchandise. Electronic exit gates at the ends of checkout aisles set off an alarm when a sensitized item passed thru which had not been rung up at the checkout counter. The electronic system worked fine in the lab, and was subsequently test marketed in a group of supermarkets where a fatal flaw was discovered.

Supermarket checkout aisles vary in width, and some were much narrower than Sensormatic had anticipated. The exit gates were too wide for these stores. The company moved quickly, and designed a single gate system as an alternative to the original double gate system. Sensormatic introduced its new product broadly when it was able to fit both wide and narrow checkout aisles.

Applying Marketing Research 14.6

Anheuser-Busch test marketed Chelsea,[18] a "not-so-soft drink" containing a trace of alcohol. They positioned the brand as an adult alternative to soft drinks. Religious and local community groups objected to the brand on the basis that it was encouraging children to drink beer. It was claimed that the brand looked like beer because of its foam and, as a consequence, children were pretending it was beer. Even though other similar brands already existed, Anheuser-Busch received considerable negative publicity and eventually withdrew the brand.

Unilever wishes that it would have test marketed Power detergent before introducing the brand in Europe.[19] The brand was positioned as a stain-annihilating detergent based on its patented manganese-based catalyst, the Accelerator. Unilever was so enthusiastic about the new brand and its potential that the company decided to skip a test market in favor of a full blown introduction. The result was a disaster. The Accelerator damaged clothes under certain conditions. Unilever placed revised washing instructions on the package, which recommended laundering clothes in cold water to prevent damage when using Power detergent. However, it was too late to save the brand.

Problems Associated with Conducting a Test Market

Test markets are very expensive. A great deal of money may be required to obtain distribution, to measure retail sales in a limited geographic area, and to manufacture the brand. The average test market costs in excess of $3 million.[20] There are also significant indirect costs, including the corporate personnel allocated to the project.

Test markets also take considerable time. At least twelve months may be required to obtain stable test market estimates of trial and frequency of repeat purchasing.

Competitive activity compounds the problems found in the test market. Competition commonly runs huge consumer promotions for their brands in test markets, thus making it difficult for a company to assess potential sales of a new brand accurately. Ralston-Purina Co. has handed out thousands of coupons for free five- or ten-pound bags of its Purina Dog Chow in markets where competitors were testing new dog foods.[21] Of course, many shoppers took advantage of the offer and stocked up, keeping them out of the market for dog food for some time. Due to competitive reactions, it may take a long time for things to settle down in a test market so that realistic sales data can be obtained. Procter & Gamble had to be patient when it introduced Wondra hand and body lotion into test market. The company had to wait several months before beginning to collect realistic sales data because of the huge discount coupons Chesebrough-Ponds, Inc., distributed for its Vaseline Intensive Care hand and body lotion when Wondra was introduced.[22]

Test markets also provide competitors the opportunity to examine a new offering and develop a plan to react to it. A competitor may even preempt the firm conducting the test market by developing a similar offering and introducing it nationally ahead of the original firm. The loss of secrecy associated with test marketing is a minor issue if the new offering is extremely difficult to imitate or requires a very large capital investment to produce. However, in the case of easily imitated products or services, loss of secrecy may be the paramount consideration.

Are Test Markets Always Necessary?

Clearly, the test market *vs.* no test market decision must be handled on a case-by-case basis. Management must carefully assess the risks of each option and act accordingly. Although test marketing is generally an important phase in the introduction process, there are situations when test marketing is inappropriate.

Reaction to a Successful Competitive Entry

If a brand is being introduced in reaction to a successful competitive entry, the new brand is really a defensive maneuver, and time is of the essence. Test marketing will often be by-passed in such a situation as is the case in Applying Marketing Research 14.7.

Applying Marketing Research 14.7

When Colgate-Palmolive introduced Irish Spring, it opened up the new category of "refreshment" bar soaps. Irish Spring was characterized by its high-impact perfume and its unusual green and white striated (striped) appearance. To prevent Colgate-Palmolive from making further inroads with Irish Spring, Procter & Gamble, the leader in the bar soap category, quickly developed its own similar refreshment bar called Coast. A blue and white striated bar and a perfume with a citruslike fragrance were used to distinguish Coast. More than the usual amount of perfume was used to make Coast, and the advertising positioned the brand as the one that "wakes you up." Coast was rolled out nationally without a test market and quickly captured a meaningful share of the market, thus allowing P & G to defend its position. Other imitators, including Spirit Armour-Dial) and Shield (Lever Bros.), soon followed.

The New Product Is Easily Imitated

For an easily imitated product, secrecy is of primary importance. As noted earlier, a test market tips a competitor to the idea, and there is a risk that a competitor might preempt the company that originally developed the product. In fact, concern over competitors seizing the idea and immediately taking it national led Sara Lee to bypass test marketing and introduce Hearty Fruit Muffins nationally.[23] The product was a high fiber, no cholesterol, freezer-stored, microwavable breakfast and snack food and would have been easily imitated by competitors.

Scientific Advances

In order to capitalize on an opportunity resulting from a scientific discovery or invention available to all, a company must act fast and, consequently, cannot afford the delay of a test market. For example, medical studies linked oat bran with cholesterol reduction. High cholesterol had been associated with heart disease, so oat bran offered a potential medical benefit to consumers. Major manufacturers of cold cereals quickly introduced brands with oat bran, or touted its presence in existing brands, in an attempt to capitalize on this medical finding (see Exhibit 14.6).

Exhibit 14.6
When medical studies found a link between oat bran and cholesterol reduction, many companies quickly touted the fact that their brands contained oat bran. Such decisions are seldom test marketed. (Courtesy of General Mills.)

Simple Line Extensions to Existing Brands

For many line extensions to existing brands, only minor modifications, such as a new flavor, scent, or color, are involved. Exhibit 14.7 shows Lever 2000 deodorant bar soap, (center of figure) positioned as "best for your skin" because it is milder than other deodorant bar soaps, along with two line extensions. Lever 2000 Pure Rain is positioned as refreshment deodorant bar soap. The other extension, AntiBacterial Lever 2000, contains a bacteria killing agent. Line extensions such as these are relatively "safe," and often are not test marketed, but rather introduced nationally right away. Other examples include: Unscented Sure Antiperspirant, Folger's Decaffeinated Instant Coffee, Lender's Blueberry Frozen Bagels, and Ocean Spray's Cran-Strawberry Drink. For line extensions, the issue of cannibalization of existing business is paramount and should be researched prior to the introduction. However, a full test market may not be required to investigate this issue.

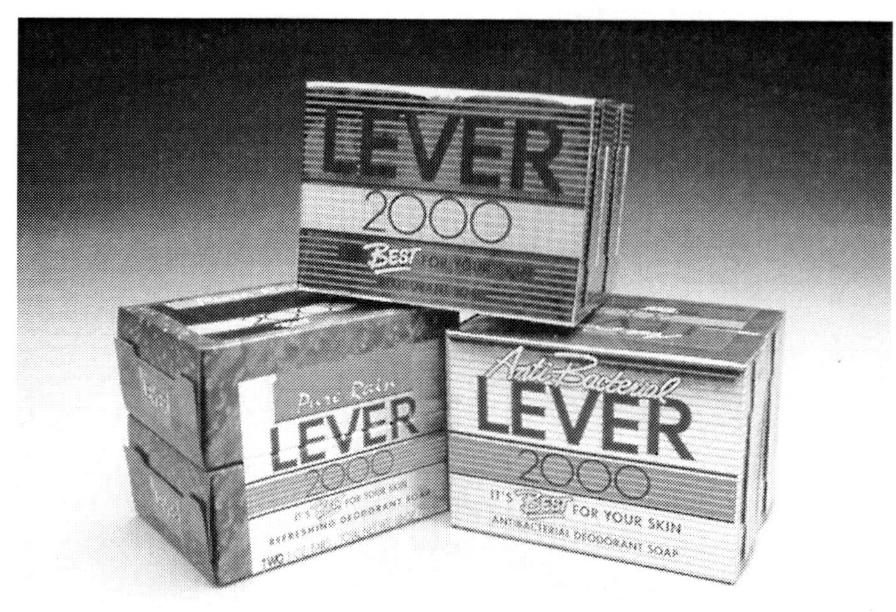

Exhibit 14.7
Lever 2000 and line extension.

Types of Test Markets

There are two basic approaches to conducting a test market. In a **standard test market** scenario, the firm obtains distribution in the test market(s) using its own sales force. Hence, all things are basically as they would be in a national introduction, making the standard test market approach very realistic, particularly with respect to the interface between the manufacturer and the trade. The result is a high degree of generalizability to other markets. The term test market typically refers to a standard test market.

In a **controlled test market**, small cities or "minimarkets" are used, and a market research firm is contracted to serve as a middleman. The research firm secures distribution, handles the shelving and warehousing, and audits stores to monitor sales and to prevent out-of-stocks. The research company pays retailers for shelf space so that high distribution levels can be guaranteed.

One advantage of the controlled test market approach over the standard test market approach is that costs are lower because of the smaller markets used. Second, sales results are obtained quicker because of the speed at which distribution is obtained. Also, secrecy is enhanced because of the lower visibility of the markets and the fact that sales results are not automatically monitored by syndicated retail audit services such as A.C. Nielsen or Information Resources, Inc. In fact, sales results are known only to the company introducing the brand through the auditing efforts of the research firm serving on the project.

On the other hand, a controlled test market is not as valid an indicator of potential as the standard test market. The atypically high distribution and lack of a normal trade and manufacturer interface, plus the difficulty of executing the intended national media plan in the test because of the small size of the market, make controlled test markets artificial.

For existing brands, controlled test markets offer a way to experiment in the market with specific changes to the marketing mix. For example, different pricing strategies might be evaluated in a series of controlled test markets more effectively and efficiently than in an experiment involving standard test markets, because monitoring and controlling the test conditions is far more difficult in the latter. Thus, factors that can affect sales, such as out-of-stocks, number of shelf facings obtained, and shelf position, can be held constant across markets more easily in the controlled than in the standard test market approach. Further, the research is far less expensive using the controlled as opposed to the standard test market approach. While actual sales levels observed for the different strategies in the controlled test market scenario may not be completely accurate predictors of what to expect under normal conditions, comparisons across the markets are likely to be valid because the same artificiality is operating in each.

Choosing a Test Market

Since the primary objective of a test market is to obtain a realistic assessment of a new offering's potential, it is imperative that no unusual lifestyle or demographic factors that can distort the picture be present in the market. Put simply, good test markets are typical with respect to the factors relating to success. For example, using Palo Alto, California, as a test market for a new fast-food restaurant chain specializing in country cooking would be likely to result in disappointingly low sales, while an atypically enthusiastic consumer response might be obtained in Nashville, Tennessee. Neither test's results would provide understanding of how the chain is likely to fare nationally.

Peoria, IL and Boise, ID have been used extensively as test market cities because they score well in the factors discussed next which make a city desirable as a test market.[24] Other cities that have been found to be desirable as test markets are shown in Table 14.3.

Metropolitan Area
Detroit, MI
St. Louis, MO - IL
Charlotte/Gastonia/Rock Hill, NC - SC
Fort Worth/Arlington, TX
Kansas City, MO - KS
Indianapolis, IN
Philadelphia, PA - NJ
Wilmington, NC
Cincinnati, OH - IN
Nashville, TN

Talbe 14.3
Attractive test market cities

Size of Market

The larger the city, the more expensive the test market. A large market requires a relatively large amount of test product, and media buys cost more for large markets than for small markets. On the other hand, concerns over projectability and reliability are associated with very small cities. Hence, the ideal market is large enough to make the results meaningful but not so large that costs become excessive.

Demographics

Generally speaking, the more the demographic profile of a market is a representative cross-section of the country's population, the better. In other words, the good test markets are microcosms of the United States. Miami, Florida, and San Antonio, Texas, are not good test market cities because the Hispanic populations are atypically large in these cities. Similarly, St. Petersburg, Florida, has a higher-than-average number of elderly residents and consequently is not a good test market city.

Isolation

A test market should be somewhat isolated from a media point of view. If there is **spill-in**, outside media coming into a market, it may be necessary to buy advertising time in these outside media to cover the test market adequately. Spill-in becomes a problem because the new product is advertised in an area where it is not available. Likewise, **spill-out**, media reaching areas outside the test market, also creates problems because it results in publicity in areas where the product is not available. Boise, ID remains among a diminishing number of markets which are relatively isolated media markets.[25]

Out-Purchasing

Are sales in the test market attributable to that city's population? If not, then problems are created when projecting sales volume. If substantial sales of a test market brand are to residents of neighboring communities, then a manufacturer, not aware of this phenomenon, might considerably overestimate sales potential. General Foods encountered such a situation in their Albany test market results for Maxim freeze-dried instant coffee. Store owners from the New York City area commuted up the Hudson regularly to purchase the product and make it available in their stores, making Maxim raw shipment data misleading.[26] Similarly, if residents of the test market do a considerable amount of shopping in a neighboring community, then sales volume in the test market might appear disappointingly low on a per-capita basis, when in fact the results should be interpreted as encouraging. Hence, it is desirable that a test market be a self-contained trading area.

Competitive Environment

The competitive environment, just like the demographics, should also be representative. For example, it would be foolish for a company to use Cincinnati, Ohio, home of Procter & Gamble, to test market a new disposable diaper. For one thing, Procter & Gamble has a huge presence in the community, and, consequently, an unusually loyal consumer following. Procter & Gamble's Pampers disposable diapers brand is likely to have a very strong hold on the Cincinnati market. Further, testing in a competitor's backyard invites strong reaction and makes surveillance by the competitor a lot easier. A similar argument could be made against testing a new soft drink in Atlanta, Georgia, home of The Coca-Cola Company.

Research in the Test Market

Monitoring Sales

Obviously, sales are closely monitored in a test market. In the case of a controlled test market, the research firm involved uses store audits to monitor sales of the test product and competitors. In the case of a standard test market of a typical consumer packaged good, retail sales estimates such as those provided by A.C. Nielsen and Information Resources, Inc. (see Chapter 5) are purchased. Special supplemental sampling of retail outlets may be required depending on the particular market(s).

Diagnostic Research

Learning from the test market does not stop with sales estimates. Sales may be disappointingly low or unexpectedly high for a number of reasons, so diagnostic information is also required to understand what is behind the overall sales results. Surveys among consumers in the test market are conducted to estimate awareness levels, brand image, reaction to the product, purchase interest, and reasons for buying or not buying. Although sales of a Lifesaver lollipop that contained cough syrup were excellent in a test market, the company abandoned the idea because of consumer concern over children confusing candy with medicine.[27] U.S. West learned in test market that a consumer resistance to a new customer service stemmed in many cases to reluctance to buy a special required component. The company offered a lease option which is used by about 50% of the new subscribers to the now broadly offered service.[28]

Surveys can also be used to estimate trial and repurchase rates for the new brand. As demonstrated in Applying Marketing Research 5.3 of Chapter 5, scanner panels in a test market are particularly useful in this context because trial, repurchase rates, and purchase cycles can be monitored directly among participating households. Further, surveys of one-time triers or of repurchasers can be conducted among panelists far more efficiently than by random telephone interviewing. Both A.C. Nielsen and Information Resources, Inc. (IRI), continue to use scanner technology to expand their monitoring of household purchase behavior.

Survey research such as that just described provides detailed information about why sales are not as expected. Based on this knowledge, a company can react to any problem. For example, if awareness of the new brand is very low, increased advertising expenditure might solve the problem. If trial is low, increased promotional activity, *e.g.*, coupons, might be the answer. If repurchase rate is the problem, but no problems exist with the product, simply placing coupons on the product package might help to stimulate repurchase. If the problem is simply a lack of availability, greater sales effort or promotional activity could be directed toward the trade to obtain more distribution.

On the other hand, diagnostic marketing research may uncover problems that are far more serious and not so easily corrected. For example, if the lack of sales is primarily due to the price, then obviously a price reduction may be needed, which changes the entire financial structure of the project.

Usage Over Time

It would be very unusual for a brand to fail in test market because the target market did not find it appealing since, in most cases, considerable marketing research has already established its appeal. However, the brand may not be consumed at the expected rate, usage may erode with time as the novelty wears off, or the brand simply may not reach the required volume objectives. For example, Procter & Gamble introduced a disposable dish cloth called Fling into a test market after product testing had indicated a very high level of consumer appeal. However, test market results indicated that the new brand never really displaced the dish cloth. Consumers put Fling away and reserved the brand for special occasions such as a camping trip or having dinner with guests. Consumers liked the product but just didn't use enough of it. Monitoring interpurchase times or purchase frequencies among customers using scanner or diary panel data helps identify such a problem.

Some new offerings enjoy initial success because of their novelty but do not have staying power and sales erode over time. Egg Beaters, a cholesterol-free substitute for eggs, fluorescent-colored golf and tennis balls; an alcoholic beverage made with beer and Gatorade called Hop 'n' Gator; and D'Lite's, a fast-food restaurant chain specializing in "health" foods, are but a few examples of this phenomenon. Again, monitoring individual household purchasing over time, perhaps with scanner or diary data, would reveal the ominous decline in repurchase rates.

Projecting Test Market Results

The real value of test markets depends on how well sales volume results can be projected to a national level. Three basic approaches are used to estimate national performance from test market results.

Projections Based on Population

To project test market volume to a national basis using population only, the test market volume is simply divided by the decimal representing the portion of the total nation that the test market comprises. The formula is:

$$\text{National volume estimate} = \frac{\text{Test market annual sales}}{\text{Population factor}}$$

For example, suppose Pittsburgh, Pennsylvania, was used as a test market for a new brand, and annual sales of 500,000 cases was achieved. Since Pittsburgh represents 1.08 percent of U.S. households, a simple estimate of annual sales for the total United States would be 46.3 million cases (500,000 ÷ .0108).

Projection Based on Population and Category Development

A **category development index (CDI)** compares an area's per-capita consumption of a product category to the national consumption rate. Atypically high or low consumption of a product category in an area is captured by its CDI. For example, CDIs of 80 and 120 for two test markets indicate consumption in the category to be 80 percent and 120 percent of the national average, respectively. If sales per capita in the test market differs from the national average, this discrepancy must be accounted for when estimating national sales from test market results. The following equation shows the appropriate calculation for estimating national sales volume for the test product:

$$\text{National volume estimate} = \frac{\text{Test market annual sales}}{(\text{CDI}/100)(\text{Population factor})}$$

Again, suppose Pittsburgh is the test market and that its CDI is 110, making consumption in Pittsburgh for the new product's category 10 percent higher than the national average. Hence, sales of 500,000 cases annually in the test market would first be modified to 454,545, the national equivalent, before dividing by the population factor (.0108). The final national sales estimate would be about 42.1 million cases annually.

Projection Based on Test Market Share

The observed market share in the test market can be used to project national volume if national sales in the category is known. The national category volume is simply multiplied by the share for the new brand obtained in the test market:

National volume estimate = Market share in test market * National category volume.

No adjustment for test market CDI is necessary when estimating based on test market share, because category development in the test market should not affect the share obtained by the test brand.

Using test market brand share to estimate volume assumes that the category for the new brand is well-defined, that total national category sales are accurately measured, and that the new brand will not increase total consumption in the category. These assumptions are probably justified for some product categories, such as toothpaste, paper napkins, deodorants/antiperspirants, and hand soaps. Other new brands, such as Lean Cuisine frozen prepared meals, may increase category consumption. Some new brands may not even have a reference category. TreeTop Apple Chips, mentioned earlier, is a prime example. The brand is clearly a snack food item, but has no obvious direct competitors on which a share calculation can be made. Projection based on population as described above would be likely to be the most appropriate technique for a new brand such as this.

Summary

Simulated test markets provide a useful final screening device before launching a test market. Simulated test markets can uncover fatal flaws inherent in the brand or its marketing strategy, and thus prevent a costly test market failure. Further, the results of a simulated test market may identify weaknesses that, if corrected, enhance the likelihood of a successful test market.

A variety of simulated test market systems exist. Typically, respondents are exposed to advertising for the new and competitors' brands, are given the opportunity to purchase the new brand and/or a competitive brand in a store environment, and are later given an opportunity to repurchase the brand. The mathematical models used to predict share and/or volume for the new brand tend to be similar across systems and the two models comprising the ASSESSOR system are quite representative.

It is difficult to evaluate the predictive validity of simulated test market systems because so much can change from the time a simulated test market is conducted to the actual test market. Further, there is no way of assessing the accuracy for those new brands that are projected to fail and hence never reach test market.

Test marketing is typically associated with a new brand introduction. However, test marketing applies equally to testing alternative marketing strategies for existing brands. Test marketing in either context is expensive and time-consuming, but the benefits can far outweigh the cost. The test market is the only real-world test where all of the market forces are at work in a natural environment. Thus, test markets play the critical role of providing a basis for projecting potential annual sales volume.

However, there are occasions when the negatives outweigh the positives, and thus the test market stage is bypassed. For example, a company may not want to expose a new product in test market because they are afraid that a competitor may copy the idea. The imitator may then introduce its version nationally, thus preempting the original developer.

Test market cities are not chosen arbitrarily. A number of criteria are considered when selecting test market sites. Market size, demographics, degree of media isolation, amount of out-purchasing, and the competitive environment are all important considerations.

There is often a need to conduct supplemental marketing research in the test market area. This research provides diagnostic information including awareness, reasons for buying and, more importantly, not buying, the source of the sales, and trial and repurchase rates.

Test market sales results are projected to a national level. The projection can be based on the market population alone or in conjunction with a category development index. Market share in the test market can also be used to project national sales volume.

Key Terms:

ASSESSOR

BASES

cannibalization

category development index (CDI)

controlled test market

Laboratory Test Market (LTM)

preference model

simulated test market

spill-in

spill-out

standard test market

test market

trial-repeat model

Nimslo's Test Market

Nimslo used the state of Florida as a test market for its new 3D photography system. Nimslo chose Florida because of its proximity to the Atlanta home office and because Florida's population was more of a blend of people from different parts of the country than any of the other neighboring southern states.

However, the choice of Florida presented problems. For one thing, the population contains a disproportionate share of retirees and senior citizens, a group who use cameras relatively infrequently. Hence, there was a risk that the test market's reaction to the Nimslo camera might not represent the general population very well.

The major problem that resulted from the use of Florida as a test market was out-purchasing. Several years of publicity preceded the introduction of the Nimslo camera, and interested consumers had been anxiously awaiting its arrival, which had been postponed several times. As a consequence, many of the initial purchases of the Nimslo camera were made through the mail or telephone by individuals from all over the United States and even the world. The problem was compounded by the fact that Florida has a huge tourism industry. Hence, many visitors to Florida made a point to purchase a Nimslo camera either for themselves or a friend during their visits.

The scope of the problem was made clear by the large percentage of registration/warranty cards returned to Nimslo headquarters by non-Florida residents. Further, the percentage of camera purchasers who typically return a product registration card was unknown, so there was no way to estimate the total number of Nimslo cameras sold to Florida residents from the number of product registration cards received from these purchasers.

The problems encountered by using Florida as a test market meant that the number of cameras sold in the test market could not easily be translated into a national volume figure. Nimslo had planned to project national sales volume by making use of the fact that Florida accounted for about 4.5 percent of all sales of photographic equipment in the United States. Nimslo ultimately made the decision to reduce the observed Florida sales by an amount based on the percentage of returned registration cards received from non-Florida residents, and used the reduced sales volume as the basis for a projection for the total United States. (Of course, this approach required the tenuous assumption that Florida and non-Florida purchasers returned registration cards at the same rate.)

Review Questions

14.1 What is meant by source of business and cannibalization? Why are these important issues to marketing managers when evaluating a new product or service introduction?

14.2 What is meant by a simulated test market? Describe how such systems operate.

14.3 Why are simulated test markets useful to marketing managers?

14.4 What particular problems do new products, which have no real reference categories, present to simulated test market models such as the preference model in ASSESSOR?

14.5 Suppose in an ASSESSOR application that an existing brand, denoted by ***k***, had an average purchase probability in the premeasure of .30 ($L(k) = .3$); and in the postmeasure, the average purchase probability for this existing brand was .20 ($P(k) = .2$). Also it is estimated that 30 percent of households will make the test brand part of their relevant set. That is, $E(t)$ is estimated to be .30. Estimate the share for the existing brand after the new brand is introduced.

14.6 Describe the fundamental estimation procedure of the LTM approach.

14.7 A new antiperspirant product is tested in the LTM system. Of the 300 study participants (users of antiperspirant products), 100 purchase the product in the simulated store, and 60 of these 100 express repurchase interest in the follow-up interview. The company is a major force in the category and has a clout factor of .80. Further, the salience factor is .60. Assuming no frequency of use adjustment, estimate the share for this new antiperspirant product.

14.8 What is a test market?

14.9 What is the difference between a standard and a controlled test market? What are the relative advantages of each?

14.10 What are the desirable characteristics of a test market city?

14.11 Describe how test market volume can be projected to a national basis based on population alone.

14.12 Define category development index (CDI). Would you expect a high or low CDI for grits in Albany, Georgia? How about automotive oil in Los Angeles, California?

14.13 A new consumer packaged good is test marketed in Columbus, Ohio, which accounts for .74 percent of U.S. households. Annual unit sales in the test market are estimated to be 10,000 cases. Columbus, Ohio has a category development index (CDI) of .90. Estimate annual national sales.

NOTE: Problems 14.14 and 14.15 are based on the ASSESSOR material included in the Appendix of this chapter.

14.14 Suppose that in an ASSESSOR study, a respondent had three brands, labeled A, B, and C, in her relevant set. Suppose that an exponent of 2.0 is used in the purchase probability calculations, and that the constant sum scale results for this respondent after using the test product are as follows:

A	7	A	6	B	6	A	6	B	4	C	3
B	4	C	5	C	5	Test	5	Test	7	Test	8

Calculate the estimated probability of buying the test brand for this respondent.

14.15 Given the following information, use the ASSESSOR logic to construct an estimate of market share for a new product:

- Awareness and distribution/availability are estimated to be 70 percent and 60 percent respectively by marketing management.
- Ten percent of all category users are to be sampled with new product according to the current marketing plan.
- Management estimates that half of the consumers sampled with test product will actually use it.
- Forty percent of respondents in the ASSESSOR study purchased the product in the simulated store.
- At callback, 60 percent of those respondents who purchased the product in the simulated store repurchased it. The average probability of purchase, $L(t)$, for the test product among the remaining 40 percent who bought the product in the simulated store is 30 percent.
- Thirty percent of the respondents who did not buy the test product in the simulated store, but were given it, bought the test product at callback. The average probability of purchasing the test product among the remaining 70 percent of the respondents who did not buy in the store is 15 percent.

Discussion Questions

14.1 Discuss the pros and cons of test marketing from a managerial perspective. Give several examples of situations where test marketing would be inappropriate.

14.2 Discuss the importance of conducting traditional marketing research such as consumer surveys, trade surveys, and so forth, in a test market.

14.3 Discuss the difficulties associated with evaluating the predictive power of simulated test market systems.

14.4 As manager of a new product that has reached the test market stage, what value would a simulated test market be to you?

14.5 Discuss the statement: "The simulated test market results were quite favorable for our new product, so we can skip the test market we had planned."

Appendix to Chapter 14

ASSESSOR Preference and Trial-Repeat Models

Preference Model

Preexposure Probabilities of Purchase

The sums of the scores awarded to the brands in the pairwise eleven-point constant sum ratings are used to produce values for each brand in the individual respondent's relevant set. In developing the ASSESSOR preference model, it was found that making the respective probabilities of purchase proportional to these raw values raised to a positive power, instead of simply proportional to the values themselves, improved the results. The exact value to use for this positive power is determined separately for each study and is based on applying the statistical procedure of maximum likelihood estimation using the last brand purchased by each participant. The individual purchase probability calculations are demonstrated in the following example.

Applying Marketing Research 14.A1

How to . . .

Calculate Preexposure Preference Scores

Suppose that for an individual respondent, the relevant set contains three brands, say A, B, and C. Further, suppose that the pairwise eleven-point constant sum results are as follows:

- A *vs*. B: 7 for A and 4 for B;
- A vs. C: 3 for A and 8 for C;
- B vs. C: 9 for C and 2 for B.

The total points awarded to the three brands, A, B, and C, are respectively 10, 6, and 17.

Assume that the positive power to which each value is raised before calculating purchase probabilities is estimated to be 2 for this study. This means that the brand point totals obtained from the constant sum scale pairwise ratings are each squared before calculating the purchase probabilities. According to the preference model, the probabilities of purchasing the three brands for this individual participant are then:

A: $10^2/10^2 + 6^2 + 17^2 = .235$; B: $6^2/10^2 + 6^2 + 17^2 = .085$; C: $17^2/10^2 + 6^2 + 17^2 = .680$.

Postexposure Probabilities of Purchase

The postexposure probabilities of purchase are calculated for all brands in the respondent's relevant set and for the test brand in exactly the same manner as the preexposure purchase probabilities are calculated.

Applying Marketing Research 14.A2

How to . . . .

Calculate Postexposure Preference Scores

Continuing with the same respondent used in the previous example to demonstrate preexposure purchase probability calculations, the postexposure interview includes six pairwise eleven-point constant sum evaluations. Assume these six eleven-point constant sum results are as follows:

- A *vs.* B: 7 for A and 4 for B;
- A *vs.* C: 3 for A and 8 for C;
- B *vs.* C: 2 for B and 9 for C;
- A *vs.* test: 4 for A and 7 for test;
- B *vs.* test: 3 for B and 8 for test;
- C *vs.* test: 6 for C and 5 for test.

The total points awarded to the four brands, A, B, C, and test, are respectively 14, 9, 12, and 20. The respective purchase probabilities are then:

A: 14_/14_+9_+23_+20_ = .163;

B: 9_/14_+9_+23_+20_ = .067;

C: 23_/14_+9_+23_+20_ = .439;

Test: 20_/14_+9_+23_+20_ = .331.

Trial-Repeat Model

Trial

The equation for trial, T, is:

$$T = KDF + (1 - KDF) * CU,$$

where K represents awareness; D represents availability or distribution rate; F represents the probability of a first purchase; C represents the probability that an individual will receive a free sample of the new brand, *i.e.*, the sampling rate; and U represents the probability the individual receiving a sample will use it. D and K are managerial input and depend on the distribution strategy and the planned amount of marketing support, respectively. F is estimated by the percentage of respondents who actually buy the test brand in the simulated store. The values C and U are also derived from managerial input.

The equation for T assumes that trial comes about in two ways. First, a respondent can become aware of the product, have the product available, and decide to purchase the product for the first time. Alternatively, a consumer can receive a free sample of the product (if this promotional activity is part of the introductory plan) and actually use the sample. However, this form of trial comes about only among that fraction of the target audience who do not initiate trial on their own. That is, sampling trial is obtained among that fraction of consumers who do not try the product on their own, *i.e.*, $1 - KDF$.

Repeat

A probability model is used to estimate the long-term share of purchases of the test brand among triers. Based on this model, the long-run share of purchases of the test brand among triers, denoted by S, is given by:

$$S = a/(1 + a - b).$$

where a and b are parameters estimated with the data obtained in the follow-up interview. Respondents who agree to repurchase the test brand in the follow-up interview provide an estimate of b. The average postusage probability of purchase of the test brand, based on the preference data, among respondents who do not choose to repurchase the test brand at the follow-up is used to estimate a. Finally, the projected share for the test product, $M(t)$, is then obtained by multiplying T and S.

A refinement of this technique is to apply the logic used to obtain S separately to the respondents who try the product on their own and to those who are given the product at the simulated store. That is, long-term share of purchases might be viewed to be different among those who voluntarily try the product as opposed to those who are induced to try the product by being given a free sample. Under this scenario, the two components of trial are separately multiplied by their respective estimates of *S*, and the results of these two multiplications are added to estimate share. That is, the following equation is used to estimate share for the test brand:

$$M(t) = (KDF)(S_1) + (1\text{-}KDF)CU(S_2),$$

where S_1 represents long-term share for the test product among voluntary triers, and S_2 represents the analogous figure for those who try the product as a result of receiving a free sample.

Applying Marketing Research 14.A3

How to...

Estimate Share in the Trial-Repeat ASSESSOR Model

Returning to the deodorant soap research used to demonstrate the use of the preference model, suppose that of the 350 participants, 70 (20 percent) buy the product in the simulated store. The remaining 280 participants are given a free sample of the product to try. At the telephone interview conducted three weeks later, 35 of the 70 original purchasers repurchase, and the average preference value for the test product among the remaining 35 participants is .20. Among the 280 who received free samples, 70 (25 percent) purchased the test product at the follow-up interview, and the average preference value for the test product among the other 210 participants is .10.

Management estimates that awareness will be 80 percent and the distribution factor will be 90 percent. Further, the introductory marketing plan calls for delivering free samples to about 30 percent of the households. It is estimated that 75 percent of the households receiving a free sample will actually use it.

The trial-repeat estimate of share is obtained by analyzing triers who actually purchase the product and triers who use a free sample separately. Trial by purchase is estimated by $K*D*F$, where K is the awareness factor (.8), D is the distribution factor (.9), and F is the first purchase factor estimated to be .20 from the simulated store data. Trial obtained by sampling is estimated by $(1-KDF)*C*U$, where C = .30, and U = .75. Hence, the two trial rates are estimated to be .144 and .193 respectively.

The long-run share of purchases for the voluntary triers, say S_1, is given by:

$$S_1 = \frac{a_1}{1 + a_1 - b_1}$$

where a is estimated to be .20 based on preference data for the test brand among participants who buy in the store, but not at the telephone interview, and b is estimated to be .50 based on the fact that one-half of the original purchasers in the simulated store repurchase. Hence, S_1 is estimated to be .286 (.2/(1 + .2 - .5)). Analogously, S_2, the long range share for the test brand among those for whom trial is induced by free sampling, is given by:

$$S_2 = \frac{a_2}{1 + a_2 - b_2}.$$

The estimates of a_2 and b_2 are .10 and .25, based on the telephone interview data, so that the estimate of S_2 is .118 (.10/(1 + .10 -.25)).

Finally, the estimate of share based on the trial-repeat model is given by:

$$M(t) = (KDF)(S_1) + (1-KDF)(C)(U)S_2$$

or

$$M(t) = (.144)(.286) + (.193)(.118) = .064.$$

Hence, it is estimated that the new brand will capture a 6.4 percent share of the deodorant bar soap market.

Chapter 14 Endnotes

---

1. See Gay Jervey, "Candy Makers Sweet on Adults" *Advertising Age*, February 7, 1985, p. 45.

2. See, for example, A.C. Nielsen Company, "New Product Success Ratios 1977," *The Nielsen Researcher*, 1979.

3. See, for example, Glen L. Urban and John K. Hauser, *Design and Marketing of New Products*. Englewood Cliffs, NJ: Prentice-Hall, Inc., 1980, p. 386.

4. See Allan D. Shocker and William G. Hall, "Pretest Market Models: A Critical Evaluation," *Journal of Product Innovation Management*, Vol. 3, 1986, pp. 86-107, for a thorough discussion of the strengths and weaknesses of simulated test markets.

5. See Yoram Wind, Vijay Mahajan and Richard N. Cardozo, *New Product Forecasting*. Lexington, MA: Lexington Books, 1981, pp. 181-204, for a comparison of various simulated test market systems.

6. See Alvin J. Silk and Glen R. Urban, "Pre-Test-Market Evaluation of New Packaged Goods: A Model and Measurement Methodology," *Journal of Marketing Research* 15 (May 1978), pp. 171-191, for a thorough discussion of ASSESSOR.

7. See *ENTRO*[SM] *From M/A/R/C. The New Business Development and Evaluation System* and *Introducing ENTRO from M/A/R/C*, sales brochures, M/A/R/C, Inc., Dallas, TX, for discussions of the ENTRO approach; and Howard Schlossberg, "Merger of STM Systems Possible Prelude to 'Titanic' Operation," *Marketing News*, October 23, 1989, p. 2, regarding the merger of ASSESSOR and ENTRO.

8. See Yoram Wind, Vijay Mahajan and Richard N. Cardozo, *New Product Forecasting*. Lexington, MA: Lexington Books, 1981, pp. 249-267, for a thorough discussion of the LTM approach.

9. See Allan D. Shocker and William G. Hall, "Pretest Market Models: A Critical Evaluation," *Journal of Product Innovation Management*, Vol. 3, 1986, pp. 86-107.

10. See Annetta Miller and Dody Tsiantar, "A Test Market for Research," *Newsweek*, December 28, 1987, pp. 32-33.

11. Ellen Neuborne, "Researchers See 'Chill' from Suit," *Advertising*

Age, July 20, 1987, pp. 3, 50.

12. Stewart Alter, "Beecham vs. Saatchi," *Advertising Age*, July 13, 1987, pp. 1, 86.

13. See Matt Rothman, "A Case of Malpractice — In Market Research?" *Business Week*, August 10, 1987, pp. 28-29.

14. See Glen L. Urban and Gerald M. Katz, "Pre-Test-Market Models: Validation and Managerial Implications," *Journal of Marketing Research* 20 (August 1983), pp. 221-234, for a good discussion of the validity of simulated test marketing systems.

15. Melissa Turner, "Coca-Cola Charges Up the Flavor in Cherry Soda," *The Atlanta Constitution*, July 23, 1991, p. C-1.

16. T. Bayer, "Igloo is Taking Its Case to Consumers in Ad Drive," *Advertising Age*, June 21, 1982, p. 4.

17. See "Test Marketing a New Product: When It's a Good Idea and How to Do It," *Profit - Building Strategies for Business Owners*, 23-3 (March, 1993, pp. 14-15.

18. See "Nurses Foaming Over Chelsea," *Advertising Age*, October 23, 1978, p. 8; and Christy Marshall, "A-B withdraws Chelsea Ads but Says Product to Stay in Test," *Advertising Age*, October 30, 1978, pp. 2, 140.

19. Laurel Wentz, "Unilever's Power Failure a Wasteful Use of Haste," *Advertising Age*, March 6, 1995, p. 421.

20. Madhav N. Segal and J. S. Johar, "On Improving the Effectiveness of Test Market Decisions," *European Journal of Marketing*, 26-4, 1992, pp. 21-33.

21. See Niles Howard with Marjorie Siegel, "Fighting It Out In Test Market," *Dun's Review*, June (1979), pp. 69-71.

22. *Ibid.*

23. See William F. Schoell and Joseph P. Guiltinan, *Marketing*, Fourth Edition, (Boston: Allyn and Bacon, 1990),

p. 363.

24. See "If It Plays in Peoria, Will They Buy It in Boise?," *Marketing News*, February 17, 1992, pp. 7, 21.

25. *Ibid.*

---

26. See "Why Four Years to Test Maxim," *Sales Management Magazine*, March 1, 1969, pp. 48-51.

27. If It Plays in Peoria, Will They Buy It in Boise?," *Marketing News*, February 17, 1992, pp. 7, 21.

28. *Ibid.*

Case III.1

People's National Bank

Suppose that the name of the bank discussed in the opening vignette of this chapter is People's National. As mentioned, the bank used focus groups conducted among its customers to explore and refine the concept of renting retail space in bank lobbies. The findings from the focus groupss were used to help define the concept. For example, the services/stores under consideration were determined from these results. A telephone survey was conducted among a random sample of 400 of the bank's current customers to test the concept formally. The following is the concept read to the survey participants over the telephone.

> Your bank, People's National, is considering making selected services available to its customers for their convenience. The services would be open only during banking hours, and would be located in the bank lobby. Four services would be provided--a florist, post office, barber shop/salon and a travel agent. Each would occupy a small boutique-type shop, and the only access to the stores would be through the bank lobby. Prices would be comparable to other such services. The U.S. Government would operate the post office, but the other shops would be owned and operated by small independent companies.

Survey participants were first asked to rate the idea overall using the following scale: excellent, very good, good, fair, and poor, and to give reasons for their ratings. For each service/store included in the retail configuration, participants were asked to indicate how likely they would be to use the store or service on the following scale: very likely, somewhat likely, not at all likely. Those answering very likely or somewhat likely were asked to describe any concerns they might have, and those not at all likely to use the service/store were asked why they would not. Respondents were also questioned about their frequency of visiting a People's National branch office, their use of ATMs (automatic teller machines), and the types of financial accounts owned. Participants were also classified as rural, semiurban, or urban customers based on the branch they visited most often. Demographic questions, such as age, household income, and household size, were also asked.

Tables III.1.1 through III.1.7 contain results from some of the key questions. Discuss these results and their implications.

Table III.1.1

Overall Rating of Concept

	Base = 400
	percentage
Excellent	37
Very good	18
Good	10
Fair	20
Poor	10
No answer	5

Table III.1.2

Reasons for Overall Rating

Excellent/Very Good/Good Responses (Base = 260)	percentage	Fair/Poor Responses (Base = 120)	percentage
Save Time	60	"Banks should stick to banking"	55
Make going to bank more pleasant	35	Lobby crowded	40
Make certain services more convenient to use	20	Security	25
Miscellaneous	15	Miscellaneous	10

(Note: Some respondents gave more than one answer.)

Table III.1.3

Use of Specific Services/Shops

	Travel agent percentage	Florist percentage	Barber/salon percentage	Post office percentage
Very likely	52	15	10	80
Somewhat likely	33	20	35	11
Not at all likely	10	62	50	5
No answer	5	3	5	4

Table III.1.4

Reasons for Likelihood of Use Rating

Travel Agent

Very/Somewhat Likely (Base = 340)	(%)	Not At All Likely (Base = 40)	(%)
Get vacation ideas	80	Don't travel much	50
Get best prices for travel	40	Have agent	45
Miscellaneous	15	Rarely visit bank	20
		Usually rushed when visit bank	15
		Miscellaneous	20

Florist

Very/Somewhat Likely (Base = 140)	(%)	Not At All Likely (Base = 248)	(%)
Like idea	60	Don't/rarely buy flowers	80
Buy flowers often anyway	45	Rarely visit bank	40
Would buy flowers if			

convenient	22	Have a florist	25
Miscellaneous	15	Miscellaneous	20

Table III.1.4 (continued)

Barber/Salon

Very/Somewhat Likely (Base = 180)	(%)	Not At All Likely (Base = 200)	(%)
Would be convenient/ time saving	85	Have barber/hairdresser	90
Miscellaneous	20	Rarely visit bank	40
		Miscellaneous	15

Post Office

Very/Somewhat Likely (Base = 364)	(%)	Not At All Likely (Base = 20)	(%)
Need to go to post office often	60	Live/work near post office	90
Would save time	58	Rarely visit bank	25
Great convenience	44	Miscellaneous	15
Miscellaneous	22		

Table III.1.5

Frequency of Branch Visit by Very/Somewhat Likely to Use Service

	Total (400) percentage	Travel agent (340) percentage	Florist (140) percentage	Barber/salon (180) percentage	Post office (364) Percentage
More than once per week	10	9	10	20	11
About once per week	15	16	10	30	13
Two or three times per month	45	43	20	30	47
About once per month	20	21	35	15	18
Less than once per month	10	11	25	5	11

Table III.1.6

Type of Customer by Very/Somewhat Likely to Use Service

Type of Customer percen-	Total (400) percen- tage	Travel agent (340) percen- tage	Florist (140) percen- tage	Barber/ salon (180) percen- tage	Post office (364) tage
Rural	15	10	5	25	15
Semiurban	25	20	10	35	20
Urban	60	70	85	40	65

Table III.1.7

Household Income by Very/Somewhat Likely to Use Service

Type of <u>Customer</u> percen-	Total (400) percen- tage	Travel agent (340) percen- tage	Florist (140) percen- tage	Barber/ salon (180) percen- tage	Post office (364) tage
Under $25K	20	10	5	30	18
Between $25K and 40K	40	46	20	45	43
Between $40K and $75K	30	34	50	20	
Over $75K	10	10	25	5	10

Case III.2

Tasty Snacks' Flavorfills

Tasty Snacks introduced a new salty snack food called Flavorfills. This new snack product consisted of a cracker shell and a cheese-flavored filling. The manufacturing process involved extruding the filling into the shell. Some of the unused filling was recycled into the process, and the remainder was scrapped. Tasty Snacks' management was very much interested in increasing the amount of recycled filling used in the manufacturing process to decrease waste and hence reduce cost. The marketing research department was asked to determine whether there was a difference in consumer preference between standard Flavorfills and Flavorfills made with an increased amount of recycled filling.

A total of 400 adults between the ages of 18 and 54, 100 in each of four cities, were recruited to take part in the mall-intercept study. Potential respondents were screened to ensure that each participant in the product test had eaten at least one of a list of salty snacks within the past month. This list included peanuts, potato chips, corn chips, pretzels, and taco or tortilla chips.

Participants tasted the two Flavorfill versions (standard *vs.* test) and were asked for their preference and reasons for preference. The order of presentation was rotated so that half of the sample tasted the standard product first and the other half tasted the test product with increased recycled filling first. Participants also rated how different they felt the two products were using a four-point scale (Extremely different = 4, ..., Not at all different = 1). Then the products were compared on a list of attributes including:

- Overall taste
- Overall texture
- Overall appearance
- Taste of cheese filling
- Crunchiness of cracker shell

Demographic information on marital status, number and age of children, and income level was also obtained from each participant.

Tables III.2.1 through III.2.4 contain the key results of the research. Interpret these research results. What would be your recommendation to management? Discuss the research design. What alternative questions, if any, would you recommend? What other information, if any, would you like to have to facilitate interpretation of these results?

Table III.2.1

Preference Data

Among the total sample (base = 400)

	Percentage
Prefer test	49*
Prefer standard	39
No preference	12

*Significantly larger than the preference for the standard at the 5% risk level (95% confidence level)

Among Those Stating a Preference (base = 351)

	Percentage
Prefer test	56*
Prefer standard	44

*Significant at the 5% risk level (95% confidence level)

Table III.2.2

Reasons for Preference. The following data reveal the frequency with which various preference reasons were mentioned by persons preferring either the standard or the test product.

	Prefer test (base = 197) percentage mentioning	Prefer standard (base = 154) percentage mentioning
Cheesier/more cheese	31	28
More spicy/tangy	20	26
Better cheese taste	18	19
Not too salty	15	11
Better flavor/taste	13	12
Not as spicy	11	14
Not as much cheese	11	7
Could taste salt more	9	11
Mild cheese	6	11
Crunchier	10	10

Table III.2.3

Attribute Comparisons and Preferences. The following data show the preference for each alternative for specific product attributes.

Percentage of total respondents (base = 400)

	No Difference (percentage)	Prefer test (percentage)	Prefer standard (percentage)	No preference (percentage)
Do you prefer the test or standard for...				
Overall taste	16	46 ---*---	36	2
Overall texture	58	20	18	3
Taste of cheese filling	15	48 ---*---	36	2
Crunchiness of cracker shell	54	26 ---*---	18	3
Aftertaste	36	33	28	3
Spiciness of cheese filling	14	47	38	1
Strength of cheese filling	18	46 ---*---	36	1
Overall saltiness	44	30	24	3

*Statistically significant at 5% risk level

Table III.2.4

Magnitude of Perceived Difference Between Products

	Percentage of total respondents (Base = 400)
Extremely different	10.5
Quite different	19.8
Slightly different	61.5
Not at all different	8.2
	100.0

Case III.3

Segmenting the Hispanic Market

Companies conducting business in the United States have recognized the growing importance of the Hispanic portion of the U.S. population. As shown in Exhibit III.3.1, the portion of the U.S. population of Hispanic descent is expected to grow to 30 million, almost 12 percent of the projected entire population, by the turn of the century.[a] Furthermore, by the year 2020, Hispanics are projected to outnumber African Americans in the United States. (See Exhibit III.3.2).

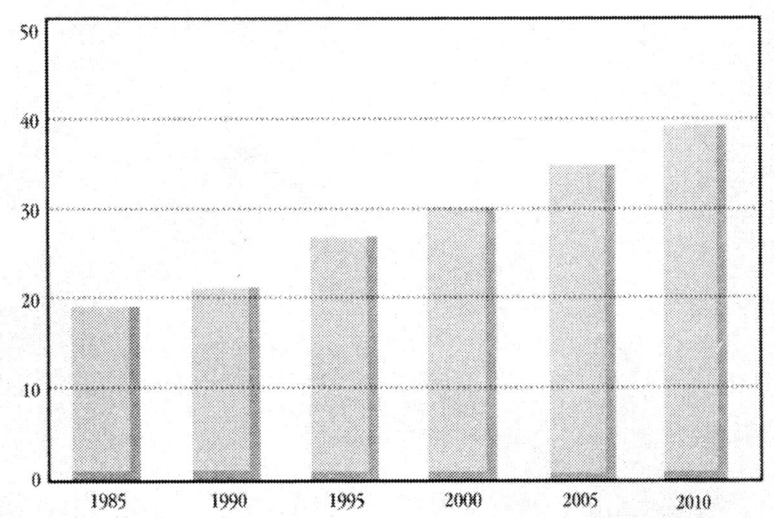

Exhibit III.3.1
Hispanic population growth (millions of people). (Source: Thomas Exter, "How Many Hispanics?" *American Demographics*, May 1987, pp. 36-38, 67.)

---

[a] See "Hispanic Americans: An Emerging Group - Part I. Magnitude, Ethnicity and Geographical Location," *Statistical Bulletin*, Oct.-Dec. 1988, pp. 2-7, for a discussion of the growth of the Hispanic population in the U.S., the factors behind the growth, and the problems associated with estimating the size of the group.

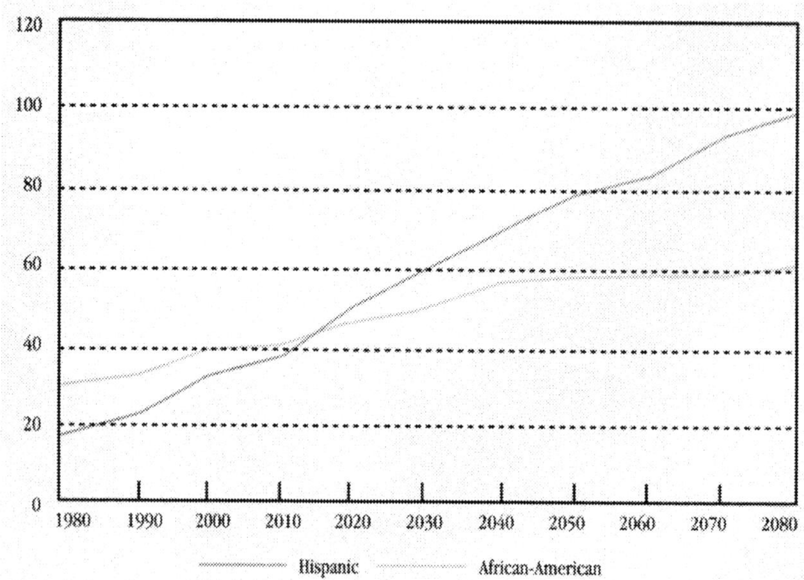

Exhibit III.3.2
Hispanic vs. African-American population (millions of people). (Source: Thomas Exter, "How Many Hispanics?" *American Demographics*, May 1987, pp. 36-38, 67.)

A major manufacturer of consumer packaged goods conducted a survey to gain insight into the attitudinal segments that exist within the U.S. Hispanic community. A battery of questions was administered to a random sample of 2000 Hispanics residing in ten geographically dispersed cities (200 per city). Telephone interviews were conducted within telephone exchanges serving areas having high percentages of Hispanic households. Included in the survey was the list of statements shown in Table III.3.1. Each respondent rated his or her level of agreement with each statement using the following five-point scale.

5 = Strongly agree

4 = Agree

3 = Neutral

2 = Disagree

1 = Strongly disagree

Statement	Factor 1	Factor 2
I consider myself Hispanic first and American second.	.42	.66
I have about an equal number of American and Hispanic friends.	−.58	.01
It is important to preserve my Hispanic heritage and culture.	.08	.72
I do not want to be thought of as an American.	.65	.06
I still celebrate Hispanic holidays with my family.	.61	.57
I have special respect for Hispanics who have become successful in America.	−.02	.52
Many Hispanics have contributed to the growth of America.	−.71	.03
I am interested in American history.	−.07	.63
I find many American customs silly.	.57	.04

Table III.3.1

Factor analysis was used to reduce the list of statements. The resulting two factors related to the level of assimilation into the American "scene" (Factor 1) and the degree of pride in Hispanic heritage and interest in maintaining Hispanic traditions and culture (Factor 2). A high score on Factor 1 indicates a low degree of assimilation; a high score on Factor 2 indicates a high degree of pride in Hispanic heritage. Table III.3.1 contains factor loadings (*i.e.*, correlations between the items and the factors) for each of the statements on each of the factors. High loadings indicate a high degree of association between a factor and an item.

Individual respondent scores were calculated for each of the two factors, and a cluster analysis was performed to determine whether attitudinal segments could be constructed based on these factors. The cluster analysis suggested a three-cluster solution. The average factor scores for each of the three clusters, as well as the respective sizes, are shown in Table III.2.

	Cluster 1	Cluster 2	Cluster 3
	(900)	(650)	(450)
Factor 1	.66	−.40	−.74
Factor 2	.45	.30	−1.33

Table III.3.2
Mean factor scores by cluster

Next, responses to various other questions included in the questionnaire were tabulated for each cluster. Table III.3.3 shows the results for key questions by cluster.

	Cluster 1	Cluster 2	Cluster 3
	(n = 900)	(n = 650)	(n = 450)
Mean hours per week spent watching Spanish TV network	8.8	1.7	.4
Mean annual household income in $M	$12.7	$17.7	$18.8
Mean rating for frequency of shopping for household goods at Hispanic-owned store (1 = often, 2 = sometimes, 3 = rarely, 4 = never)	1.6	2.8	3.6

Table III.3.3
Key results by cluster

Based on the factor score means for the three clusters, describe in your own words what these three segments represent in an attitudinal sense. Also, what kinds of differences, with respect to the key issues pursued in the questionnaire, exist across the segments? What other information regarding the Hispanic growth rate would be important to obtain and why? Finally, what are the marketing implications of these findings?

Case III.4

Hallmark Photo Albums[1]

For most consumers the name Hallmark immediately brings to mind greeting cards. However, Hallmark Cards, Inc., sells numerous other products, including photo albums, through their specialty card shops. Hallmark's photo albums range in price from $12 to $25 and typically have some form of artwork on the cover. Most of the albums offered by Hallmark have magnetic pages.

The marketing management of Hallmark decided to take a close look at the photo album market. In particular, they wanted to identify the segments that comprise the market based on photo album preferences and purchase motivation. In addition, they sought information related to shopping habits, purchase behavior, and perceptions of the various channels of distribution for photo albums. The marketing research team assigned to the photo album business worked closely with their counterparts in marketing management to develop a study to address these issues.

A nationally representative telephone survey was conducted with 400 randomly selected consumers who had purchased photo albums within the past twelve months. Participants in the survey were questioned regarding their general purchasing habits with respect to photo albums, their perceptions of the various retail outlets where photo albums could be purchased, circumstances surrounding their last purchase, information regarding Hallmark purchases if applicable, attitudes regarding photo albums, and finally, demographics.

Key results of the study, including where photo albums are purchased (Exhibit III.4.1), occasions for purchase (Exhibit III.4.2), reasons for purchasing the last photo album (Table III.4.1), and purchase behavior (Table III.4.2) are contained in the accompanying exhibits and tables. Table III.4.3 contains the results of a segmentation analysis performed by applying cluster analysis to a series of agree/disagree ratings pertaining to the relative importance of various photo album attributes. Responses to shopping behavior and demographic questions were cross-tabulated by segment, and resulting key points of differentiation are noted in Tables III.4.4 through III.4.6.

---

[1]Statistical data have been altered and printed with the permission of Hallmark Cards, Inc.

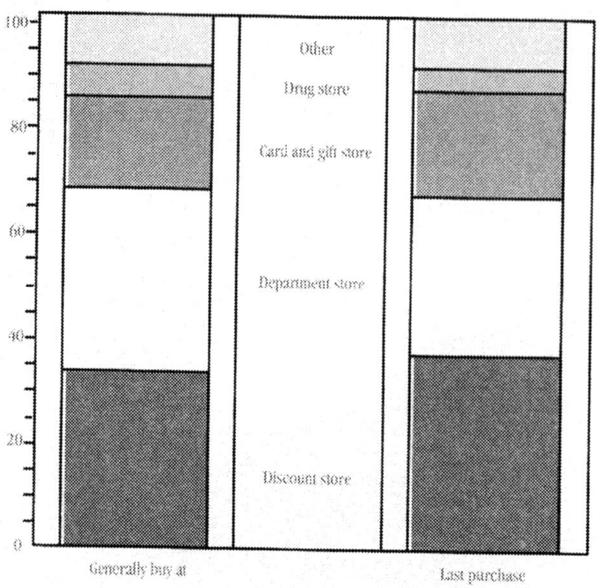

Exhibit III.4.1.
Where are photo albums bought?

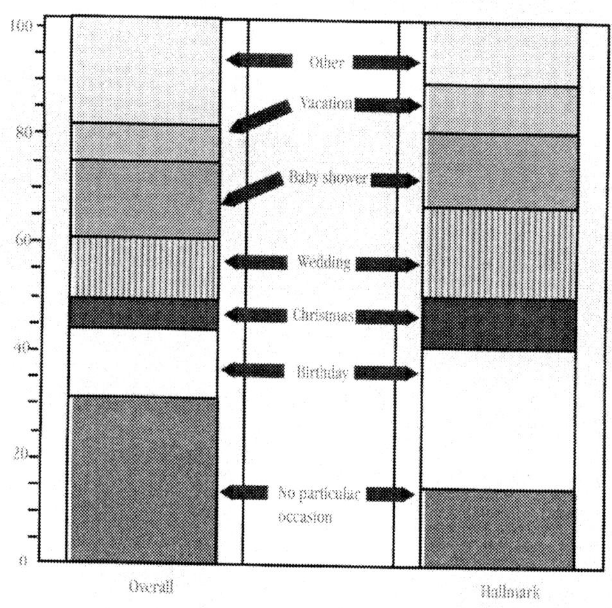

Exhibit III.4.2
Occasions for purchasing

Reason	Total	
Capacity	45	
Lots of pages		22
Big/hold lots		23
Cover (like it)	36	
Size	30	
Right size		15
Like small		15
Quality	27	
Quality		24
Strong binder		1
Three-ring		2
Price/value	15	
Good value		6
Low price		8
Sale		1
Impulse	2	
Location	2	

Table III.4.1
Reasons for last album purchase

	Percentage	
Paid over $20 on last purchase	35	
Ever paid over $10	74	
Ever paid over $20	50	
Purchased last album at Hallmark Store	5	
Ever purchased album at Hallmark Store	24	
Last purchase was gift	20	
Artwork cover		24
Plain cover		76
Last purchase was for self	80	
Artwork cover		9
Plain cover		91
Last purchase planned	91	
Last purchase impulse	9	
Page type of last purchase		
Pocket		41
Magnetic		37
Flip		20
Other		2

Table III.4.2
Purchase behavior

		Percentage
Group 1:	**Affluents**	20
	Children at home Will spend over $20 for self or gift Very value-sensitive Age 30–50 Income 40K+ Prefer plain covers Shop card shops	
Group 2:	**Singles**	15
	Singles Young (<30) or old (>60) No children Prefer magnetic pages Will spend over $10 for self or gift Value-sensitive Under $20,000	
Group 3:	**Young Couples**	18
	Young children Age under 30 Married Prefer magnetic pages Prefer artwork Middle income (20–40K) Never spend over $10	
Group 4:	**Retired**	22
	No children Age over 50 Prefer plain covers Never spend over $10 No opinion on pages Shop card shops	
Group 5:	**Fringe**	25
	Shop supermarkets Not value-sensitive No opinion on cover Never spend over $10 Age 30–50	

Table III.4.3
Segment descriptions and size

	Total	Affluent	Singles	Young couples	Retired	Fringe
n =	400	80	60	72	88	100
Average albums purchased	2.5	1.8	1.5	3.5	3.5	2.0
Self	1.8	1.0	0.5	3.0	3.2	1.2
Gift	0.7	0.8	1.0	0.5	0.3	0.8
Average price paid	$15.11	$20.03	$9.95	$14.35	$16.03	$15.20
Total spent	$37.64	$36.54	$14.93	$50.22	$56.10	$30.40
Percentage spent over $10	74.	89.	55.	72.	79.	74.
Segment size	100.%	20.%	15.%	18.%	22.%	25.%
Percentage of all annual units purchased		15.	9.	25.	31.	20.
Percentage of all annual $ spent		19.	4.	24.	33.	20.

Table III.4.4
Purchases by segment

Occasion for purchase	Total	Affluent	Singles	Young couples	Retired	Fringe
Everyday	60	57	61	58	64	60
No particular occasion	30	25	36	35	26	28
Vacation	6	11	5	5	6	3
Other	24	21	20	18	32	29
Special	40	43	39	42	36	40
Christmas	5	10	2	5	4	4
Birthday	15	12	18	18	15	12
Wedding	10	10	12	7	10	11
Baby shower	10	11	7	12	7	13

Table III.4.5
Occasion by segment

	Total	Affluent	Singles	Young couples	Retired	Fringe
Generally buy photo albums at						
Discount	30	24	36	32	30	28
Department Store	40	44	42	40	38	36
Card/Gift	20	25	18	20	22	15
Drug/Store	5	3	3	4	5	10
Other	5	4	1	4	5	11
Last photo album bought at						
Discount	33	30	40	30	30	35
Department Store	32	38	35	33	30	24
Card/Gift	25	30	15	28	25	27
Drug/Store	3	1	6	2	4	2
Other	7	1	4	7	11	12

Table III.4.6
General Channel by segment

What are the implications of these research findings to Hallmark? As a marketing manager, what specific actions or strategy would you recommend to enhance the company's photo album business?

Case III.5

Nature's Way Products

Homeopathic Medicines are based on the principle of "like cures like."[a] Treatment consists of administering minute quantities of "remedies" that in large doses would produce symptoms of the disease the treatment is designed to cure. For example, a cold formula might use the natural ingredients found in onions to produce tears and a running nose, which of course are the symptoms of someone suffering from a cold. A remedy made from coffee is prescribed to calm nerves and induce sleep and a substance that usually causes vomiting is prescribed for nausea.

Homeopathy has been around since the 1700s and has remained somewhat popular in Europe. Pressure from the American Medical Association forced homeopathy into oblivion in the United States. However, consumers' increasing skepticism of the medical community and growing wariness of the side effects of synthetic drugs have rekindled interest in the use of homeopathic remedies in the U.S. Homeopathic drugs are sold primarily through health- and natural-food stores. Sales are growing at a rate of 25 percent per year and are estimated to double to $572 million by the year 2000. The major obstacle to general acceptance of the remedies is that no one can explain how they work.

Nature's Way Products, Inc., has introduced a line of homeopathic medicines called Medicines From Nature.[b] The line is designed to appeal to consumers' current desire for alternative health care. Exhibit III.5.1 is an advertisement for this line of products featuring three of the remedies. Notice how the products are named for the symptoms they treat. The packages are also color-coded to designate different formulas for women, children, or the entire family.

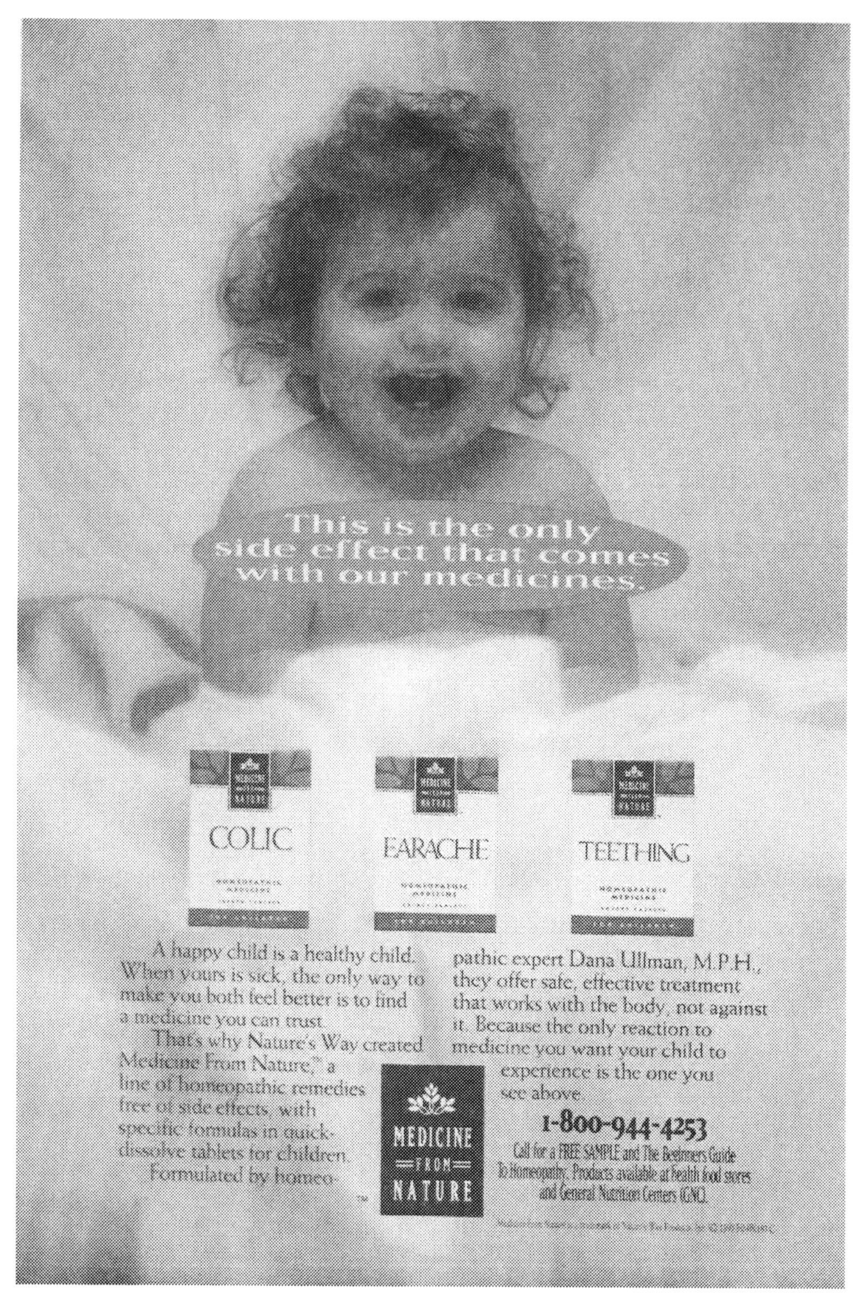

Exhibit III.5.1

Nature's Way Products' medicines from nature. (Courtesy of Nature's Way Products, Inc.)

Nature's Way Products faced a number of problems related to packaging and naming this new line of health remedies. Discuss specific criteria that you feel were particularly important to the choice of name and package for this line of products. Also, discuss the decisions to use the symptoms or sicknesses as names for the products in the line and to use a single packaging design, across the various product line color-coded to identify the target malady. What particular research projects would you recommend to evaluate alternative names and to investigate the packaging issues for this product line? Include a description of respondent qualifications in any survey research recommendations.

---

[a] See Lineil Smith, "Homeopath Growing Despite Lack of Explanation," *Athens Daily News/Athens Banner-Herald*, April 10, 1995, p. 10A.; and "Homeopathic Products Will Do," *Marketing News*, September 23, 1998, p. 2.

[b] Cyndee Miller, "Homeopathy Opes to Meet Consumers' Desires for Alternative to Traditional Drugs," *Marketing News*, April 12, 1993, pp. 1-2.

Case III.6

Test Market of the Discover Card

Sears introduced the Discover Card in Atlanta as a test market prior to the national introduction. Wanting to capitalize on increasing profitability in the credit card industry as well as to expand its existing financial services, Sears, the world's largest retail merchandiser, entered the credit card market. At the start of the test, Sears kicked off an aggressive advertising campaign aimed at retailers and consumers. Their advertising mix initially consisted of print advertising for retailers, and television as well as print for consumers. Retail advertising began two months before the consumer campaign.

Sears tried to differentiate the card by providing services that other credit card companies did not (Table III.6.1). The Discover Card was issued with no annual fee, a refund of up to one percent on every purchase, and no interest if the balance was paid in full at the end of each month. Sears also set up an ATM system that allowed customers to use the cards to receive instant cash at convenient locations.

	Discover Card	Your card
No membership fee; no annual fee	✓	
Real dollar dividends; up to 1.0 percent back on all charge purchases. The more you charge, the more you get back.	✓	
Discover savers' account; high money market rates, FDIC insured. Tiered rates let you earn more as your savings grow.	✓	
Accepted at Sears stores.	✓	
Wide usage; retail stores, restaurants, travel agencies, hotels, gas stations, specialty shops, etc., nationwide.	✓	
Cash access; instant cash twenty-four hours a day from hundreds of ATMs.	✓	
Additional Discover Cards; free for members of your household.	✓	
Travel accident insurance; at no charge to you.	✓	
Preapproved status; no long forms to complete, no waiting for approvals.	✓	
Convenient monthly payments option.	✓	

Table III.6.1
Benefits of the Discover Card

Sears tapped its existing credit customer data base and offered the card to choice customers. Because of this strategy, Sears was also able to issue $35 billion in credit lines immediately. Due to its national presence, Sears was able to gain acceptance for its Discover card with many nationally known firms, such as Denny's and American Airlines; however, Rich's and Macy's, Atlanta's largest department stores, refused to accept the card.

Interest in the Discover Card was not confined to Sears. Major banks that issued credit cards also had a vested interest in the impact of the new card. Brittain Associates, Inc., a market research firm in Atlanta, conducted a study to monitor the performance of the Discover Card in the Atlanta test market. The study was syndicated, that is, the results of the research were made available to all interested parties at a fixed subscriber rate. Naturally, Sears became one of the subscribers.

The success of the Discover Card depended on both consumer usage and merchant acceptance. Hence, Brittain Associates periodically monitored the number of owners of the card, their usage of the card, and the number of merchants who accepted the card. The research method used in each wave of the merchant survey is described below. Five waves of merchant acceptance data are shown in Table III.6.2, indicating for example that Sears' claimed rate of merchant acceptance of 40 percent was considerably inflated.

	Percentage of Total					**Percentage of those who Accept Credit Cards**				
	Wave 1 (185)	Wave 2 (185)	Wave 3 (185)	Wave 4 (185)	Wave 5 (185)	Wave 1 (147)	Wave 2 (142)	Wave 3 (145)	Wave 4 (142)	Wave 5 (149)
MasterCard	75	73	74	76	79	95	95	98	99	99
VISA	74	73	74	75	79	93	95	98	98	98
American Express	37	41	31	41	43	47	53	41	54	54
Discover	2	15	13	19	22	2	19	18	25	27
Diners Club	8	10	8	8	9	10	13	10	11	11
Carte Blanche	6	5	3	5	3	7	7	4	7	4
Stores's own card	5	6	3	2	5	7	8	4	3	7
Other	1	2	5	1	1	2	2	6	1	3
Do not accept credit cards	21	23	24	23	19	NA	NA	NA	NA	NA

[a]Data for this case are provided courtesy of Brittain Associates, Inc.

Table III.6.2
Merchant credit card acceptance

Merchant penetration tracking study method. The sampling frame for this study included merchants in thirty-seven categories identified as frequent acceptors of credit and Travel and Entertainment (T&E) cards. From each category, five metro Atlanta merchants were randomly selected for a total of 185 interviews. Interviews were conducted via telephone. Care was taken to exclude from the sampling process those merchants who had been sampled in earlier waves.

The interview was conducted with anyone in the merchant location who would have knowledge of the types of credit and T&E cards accepted at that location. Although respondents were asked whether the merchant had any immediate plans to accept Discover, not all respondents would be knowledgeable about such future plans.

The first wave of merchant data was collected while the card was initially being promoted to merchants and before the card was made available to consumers. Hence, there are only four corresponding waves of consumer data. The research method for the waves of consumer study was as follows:

Consumer penetration tracking study method (Wave 4). Data were collected via telephone interviews. The universe included metro Atlanta adults living in households owning telephones who claimed to have at least one of the following: nationally accepted bank credit card, travel and entertainment card, or a credit card for a national retail chain. Appropriate security screening was conducted to eliminate consumers employed in financial services, advertising, marketing research, retail department stores, or national credit card firms.

Random-digit telephone number generation was used to provide the sampling frame, using the three-digit prefixes that appear in the Atlanta telephone director (in correct proportion), thus ensuring a representative calling pattern that included listed and unlisted numbers in the metro area.

In total, 1848 contacts were made with adults who passed the security screener. Of these, 739 did not have, or had not applied for, the Discover Card, and 200 of these consumers were interviewed. Also, 200 customers who had possession of the card were interviewed.

Consumer survey results are reported in Tables III.6.3 through III.6.14.

Total contacts (excluding security screening)	1.848	
Eligible nonowners (including 200 interviewed)	739	(40%)
Ineligible (credit)	871	(47%)
Owners interviewed	200	(11%)
Owners who refused interview	12	(1%)
Have applied, not received	26	(1%)

Table III.6.3
Disposition of interviewing (Wave 4)

Total households in metro Atlanta	747,000
Households without telephone (6 percent)	44,820
Study universe	702,180
Penetration factor: all owners contacted plus 80 percent of those who have applied	12.5%
Households with Discover (estimate)	87,772
Cards per household factor (assume 1.68 cards/household)*	
Total estimated cards in metro Atlanta*	147,458

*Based on cards per household measured in National Study.

Table III.6.4
Households and consumers projected to have Discover in Atlanta metro area (Wave 4)

	Nonowners Wave 1 (207)	**Nonowners Wave 2 (201)**	**Nonowners Wave 3 (208)**	**Nonowners Wave 4 (200)**
	percentage	percentage	percentage	percentage
Definitely will	2	2	1	3
Probably will	6	6	3	9
Undecided	14	13	12	16
Probably won't	31	32	39	32
Definitely won't	38	43	42	34
Don't know	8	2	2	7

Table III.6.5
Likelihood of Discover application in the next three months

	Discover Card owners			
	Wave 1 (150) percentage	Wave 2 (162) percentage	Wave 3 (200) percentage	Wave 4 (200) percentage
Because it is Sears	31	23	23	22
No annual fee	29	20	49	44
Use at more places	28	38	38	42
Discounts and rebates	18	16	38	37
Spouse wanted it	18	9	6	3
Lower interest rate	8	13	6	10
ATM access	8	7	8	8
Access to Sears financial network	6	1	2	1
Tied to savings account	3	4	1	—
Line of credit	3	1	8	1

Table III.6.6
Reasons for Discover application (multiple responses allowed)

	Through 12/85 Discover Card owners (Wave 1, 150)		Through 3/8 Discover Card owners (Wave 2, 162)		Through 9/86 Discover Card owners (Wave 3, 200)		Through 3/87 Discover Card owners (Wave 4, 200)	
	number	percentage	number	percentage	number	percentage	number	percentage
Have not used	(106)	71	(81)	50	(100)	50	(94)	47
Used once	(20)	13	(21)	13	(44)	22	(29)	14
Used twice	(16)	11	(24)	15	(25)	12	(33)	16
Used three times	(3)	2	(10)	6	(11)	6	(17)	8
Used four times	(3)	2	(8)	5	(4)	2	(8)	4
Used five or more times	—	—	(15)	9	(14)	7	(17)	8
Don't know	(2)	1	(3)	2	(3)	2	(2)	1

Table III.6.7
Monthly card usage through March 1987

	42 who have used Discover Card (Wave 1)	78 who have used Discover Card (Wave 2)	98 who have used Discover Card (Wave 3)		104 who have used Discover Card (Wave 4)
	percentage	percentage	percentage		percentage
Sears retail store	66	73	85		86
Clothing store	7	29	18	⟶	58
ATM cash advance	7	12	23		19
Restaurant	14	9	17		21
Hotel/motel	—	3	10	⟶	26
Rental car	—	3	8		13
Gasoline	5	1	12	⟶	20
Lawn/garden supplies	2	1	5		10
Drug prescription	—	—	8		9
Airline ticket	—	—	8		10
Doctor or other medical	—	—	5		4
Concert tickets	—	—	1		4

Note: Arrow denotes significant difference at .05 level.

Table III.6.8
Card usage specifics

	Discover Card owners					Nonowners				
	Wave 1 (150) (percentage)	Wave 2 (162) (percentage)	Wave 3 (200) (percentage)		Wave 4 (200) (percentage)	Wave 1 (207) (percentage)	Wave 2 (201) (percentage)	Wave 3 (208) (percentage)		Wave 4 (200) (percentage)
VISA	53	38	51	←	38	44	34	45		40
MasterCard	21	26	26		27	28	31	22		28
American Express	13	20	10	→	20	14	14	14	→	24
Sears (regular card)	6	8	4		3	7	12	10		3
Discover Card	2	4	4		8	—	—	1		*
Diners Club	1	1	*		1	*	*	—		2
Carte Blanche	1	*	—		*	*	*	—		*

*.5% or less

Table III.6.9
Top-of-mind awareness (first mention, unaided)

	Discover Card owners				Nonowners			
	Wave 1 (150) (percentage)	Wave 2 (162) (percentage)	Wave 3 (200) (percentage)	Wave 4 (200) (percentage)	Wave 1 (207) (percentage)	Wave 2 (201) (percentage)	Wave 3 (208) (percentage)	Wave 4 (200) (percentage)
VISA	92	86	90	87	86	72	80 →	90
MasterCard	86	85	81	82	84	74	77 →	88
American Express	67	57	46 →	58	56	46	47 →	65
Discover Card	59	51	79 ←	64	8	7	14 →	22
Sears (regular card)	51	55	37 →	48	26	38	33 ←	26
Diners Club	23	10	10	15	19	10	10 →	18
Carte Blanche	16	4	4	4	10	3	5	6

Table III.6.10
Total unaided awareness

	Discover Card owners			
	Wave 1 (150) (percentage)	Wave 2 (162) (percentage)	Wave 3 (200) (percentage)	Wave 4 (200) (percentage)
Addition to current credit base	73	85	78	74
Replace one or more other credit cards	19	8	18	21
Don't know	8	7	4	5

Table III.6.11
Discover as addition or replacement for other cards

Discover to replace	Wave 1 (29)	Wave 2 (13)	Wave 3 (36)	Wave 4 (42)
Sears (regular card)	(10)	(12)	(11)	(22)
MasterCard	(10)	(1)	(13)	(11)
VISA	(8)	0	(10)	(10)
American Express	(1)	0	(2)	0
Diners Club	—	—	(1)	(1)
Gasoline card	—	—	(1)	(1)

Table III.6.12
Credit cards Discover to replace among those consumers who will use it as replacement card

	Discover Card Owners			
	Wave 1 (150) (percentage)	Wave 2 (162) (percentage)	Wave 3 (200) (percentage)	Wave 4 (200) (percentage)
Familiar with saver's account	NA	50	47	46
Households with saver's account	NA	*	2	**

*.5% or less
**one household

Table III.6.13
Familiarity and usage of Discover saver's account

	Discover Card Owners			
	Wave 1 (150) (percentage)	Wave 2 (162) (percentage)	Wave 3 (200) (percentage)	Wave 4 (200) (percentage)
"More than expected"	14	12	24 →	32
"About what expected"	22	36	34	38
"Fewer than expected"	21	26	18	15
No opinion	43	24	24	15

Table III.6.14
Perceived number of merchants accepting Discover

Despite setbacks, Sears said it was pleased with the response to its new card and launched its national campaign budgeted at $115 million, or 16 percent of Sears' earnings at the time. Discuss the research results and their implications. What actions would you recommend regarding the Discover Card based on the Atlanta test market results?

PART IV

Using Research to Market a Brand

Research plays an important role in guiding the many marketing decisions that must be made for an existing brand. New advertising is continually being developed and tested. A brand's advertising strategy, including the amount of money spent, the media used, and the allocation of advertising dollars across various media, is constantly being assessed and revised based on research information. Decisions regarding how to promote the brand to consumers and the trade must be made, and marketing research also provides valuable insights to aid these decisions. Annual sales forecasts are crucial to the development of the marketing plan for the year, and the marketing environment must continually be monitored to provide management with current information regarding trends or competitive activity.

In Part IV of the text, we discuss the use of marketing research to support decision making in the contexts just described. In Chapter 15 we explore how research assists management in the development of the advertising strategy and specific copy executions for a brand. We also discuss the use of research to investigate legal issues associated with advertising claim support. Chapter 16 discusses how promotional activities for the brand are better planned and evaluated using research information. Various techniques used to develop short- and long-range sales forecasts for the brand are introduced in Chapter 17. In Chapter 18 we discuss the use of research to monitor the performance of the brand on an ongoing basis.

Chapter 15

Advertising Research

Learning Objectives:

Chapter 15 is designed to acquaint you with the role played by marketing research in the advertising process. After reading this chapter, you should be able to:

- explain how research aids in the selection of the proper advertising media and determining advertising spending levels.
- discuss research techniques used in the development of advertising copy.
- describe how research assists in the evaluation of advertising effectiveness.
- explain how advertising claims are substantiated.
- describe what is meant by deceptive advertising.

Peak usage of long distance services naturally occurs on weekdays during regular business hours. During off-peak periods, i.e., evenings, nights, and weekends, long-distance facilities are underutilized. AT&T conducted a large customer segmentation study among residential users as a first step to increasing off-peak usage of long distance. One segment, residential light users of long distance, was particularly interesting. This large group of customers closely resembled the heavy user segment in demographics, psychographics and size of their "communities of long distance friends." In other words, based on outward appearances, this group seemingly should use long distance services as much as their heavy user counterparts.

The segmentation study also pointed to a perceived price barrier to further use of long distance, particularly among the light user group.

Another research study indicated widespread misperception of long distance costs. About 98% of AT&T customers were unaware of long distance costs and overestimated these costs by about 50%.

AT&T set the large light user group as its target to increase residential usage of long distance, particularly during off-peak periods. Based on research conducted within this segment, several advertising strategies were developed which focused on different benefits to the caller. These included feeling good after calling a friend or relative and establishing a "life line" with others. The strategy which evolved from this research was "Cost of Visit," which focused primarily on how inexpensive long distance calling was, particularly during weekends and nights. The TV commercials employing this strategy communicated that a 20 minute visit costs no more than $4.50 during the deep discount period, and typically costs considerably less than this amount. Further, the commercials pointed out that the next 20 minutes cost less than the first 20 minutes of a call, and that there were "no hidden extras."

AT&T tested the Cost of Visit campaign using a split-cable system which allowed them to show different TV commercials to two separate groups of households within the same market. In effect, 20,000 customer households were randomly divided into two groups. One group, the control group in the experiment, continued to see the classic "Reach Out and Touch Someone" campaign. These commercials were heart-warming spots which showed friends and relatives keeping in touch by long distance telephone. The second group, the test group, saw the Cost of Visit campaign. A pre-assessment period of about 5 months was used to establish the usage segment, e. g., light long distance user, to which each household belonged. The assessment period lasted 15 months. At the end of this period, the test group's long distance calling was 2.5% higher than the control group's long distance calling during the deep discount periods of late nights and weekends. The light user group was primarily responsible for this difference as this segment's usage during these deep discount times was 9% higher in the test group than in the control group. Overall, AT&T's long distance revenues were 1% higher from the test group during deep discount periods than from the control group. Again, this difference was primarily due to the light user segment, where the test group's revenue was 14% higher than the control group's revenue.

The difference in long distance usage between the test and control groups projected to a $22 million net increase nationally. Just as important, this incremental revenue was attributable to net increased long distance usage during off-peak periods, thus "smoothing" demand.

Basic Advertising Decisions

Choosing the Media

Advertisements, like the products and services they represent, are designed to appeal to a specific group of target consumers. An advertising strategy and specific executional style must be determined for communicating to the target. Cost of Visit, with its direct message about how inexpensive long distance calling could be, was the strategy chosen by AT&T in the introductory example for this chapter.

Certain forms of media may be more effective than others for reaching target consumers. Billboards placed on main highway arteries and radio commercials aired during rush hours would be more efficient than television and magazine ads for promoting car pooling. Particular vehicles (for example, specific magazines and television shows) also have a greater chance than others of reaching the desired audience. As with media types, the choice of vehicles depends on the composition of the respective audiences. Television advertising for golfing equipment is likely to be most effective when shown during a major golf tournament. Similarly, print advertisements for softball equipment would be most effective when appearing in sports periodicals like Sports Illustrated.

The size of the audience is an important consideration, not only because it indicates the number of individuals or households potentially exposed to an ad but also because it plays a primary role in determining advertising costs. Advertising costs tend to be directly proportional to audience size, so network television advertising is more expensive than radio or print. Further, production costs for television commercials can be enormous when compared to those associated with radio and print. However, absolute costs are misleading; the cost per person reached is the more meaningful point of comparison. Television reaches mass audiences and thus can be less expensive than radio or print on a cost-per-person-reached basis.

Measuring Audience Size and Composition

Marketing managers want to communicate efficiently to their target audiences. Choosing the forms of media and specific vehicles in which to advertise depends on having a clear understanding of the composition and size of the audience. Thus, accurate measures of audience sizes and compositions are crucial to the marketing planning process. Adding to the importance of such measures is the fact that they are the keys to determining advertising rates as mentioned earlier.

Television

Television uses rating points as a measure of audience size. A **rating point** represents one percent of the TV households in the United States.[1]. Thus, a prime time network TV show with a rating of 10 is watched by about 10 percent of the households in the United States that have a TV. One rating point represents close to one million households. The **gross rating points** (GRPs) for a campaign refer to the total advertising for the measured period (*e.g.*, week or month). Applying Marketing Research 15.1 illustrates how GRPs are calculated.

Applying Marketing Research 15.1

Suppose that Procter & Gamble decides to run a network television advertising campaign for its laundry detergent Oxydol to stimulate interest in the brand. Oxydol normally does not receive television advertising support, and the company is interested in the impact such support might have on brand sales.

Procter & Gamble schedules ten ads per month on TV during the daily "Good Morning America" show, which has a rating of 4. (This means that 4 percent of all TV households watch the program.) The company also schedules the ad to run four times per month, once each week, during "Home Improvement," which has a rating of 12. (Again, this figure means that 12 percent of the TV households watch the program.) The total GRPs per month are: (10 x 4) + (4 x 12) = 88

A.C. Nielsen is the dominant supplier of television audience size information. The **Nielsen Television Index**, launched in 1950, provides information regarding network television audiences at the national level. Nielsen originally used a national sample of 1700 households and data from a national sample of 865 diary respondents to assess the size and composition of audiences.[2] Audimeters, devices attached to panel members' televisions, electronically recorded what TV stations were being watched, and diaries were used to provide information regarding who was watching what. The use of diaries raised concerns regarding the accuracy of the data. The proliferation of viewing alternatives resulting from the development of cable, satellite, and video recording technologies made it difficult to complete the diary accurately, particularly if one reports from memory.

Beginning in 1987, Nielsen switched to "people meters" instead of audimeters and diaries to keep track of what is being watched and who in the household is watching on a national basis.[3] A **people meter** (see Exhibit 15.1) is a device connected to a television set that monitors both the station being watched and who is watching. Individual household members punch a keypad when starting and ending a viewing session. The information is relayed to a central computer, which accumulates and tabulates data overnight. Exhibit 15.2 describes the Nielsen system for measuring audience size and composition.

Exhibit 15.1 Nielsen People Meter

How A.C. Nielsen surveys the television audience
Nielsen counts the overall television audience by two methods:

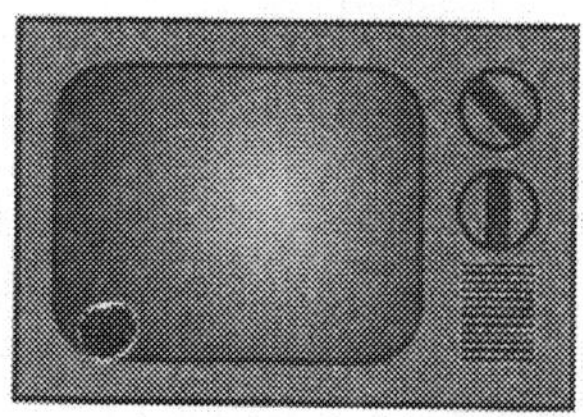

• The national sample is gathered through 4000 families with in-home "people meters." Viewers punch buttons on a remote control box to indicate their viewing habits and demographic details such as age and gender.

• Local samples are taken with diaries, which viewers fill out by hand. The weekly diaries are supposed to supply the same information as the "people meters."

• A single national rating point represents 921,000 television households; a local rating point represents 31,000 households. Out-of-home audiences such as bars and motels are not registered.

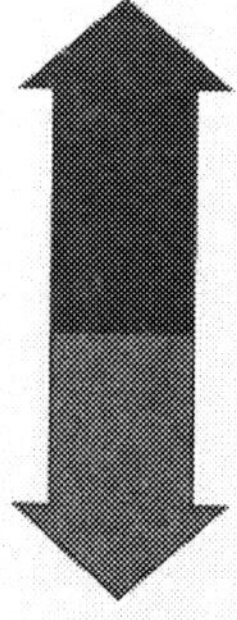

• The loss of a single rating point takes $8000 off the price of a prime-time, thirty-second commercial. The revenue difference is $112,000 per hour or $5.8 million annually.

Exhibit 15.2
How A.C. Nielson surveys the television audience

Table 15.1 is a sample of the summary data regarding television viewing provided by Nielsen. Ratings such as these are used to determine prices for advertising time on the various shows. Table 15.2 demonstrates how expensive television advertising is, as well as how much prices vary. Note how relatively inexpensive it is to advertise on "Diagnosis Murder." This show aired opposite "Seinfeld," and hence had a small audience.

		Rank Program	Network	Number of Viewers (millions)
The Top Ten	1	NFL Monday Night Football	ABC	23.42
	2	Touched by an Angel	CBS	23.18
	3	Seinfeld	NBC	22.45
	4	Frazier	NBC	19.60
	5	60 Minutes	CBS	19.12
	6	ER	NBC	18.72
	7	All the Winter . . .	CBS	18.61
	8	The Simpsons	FOX	17.44
	9	Dateline NBC (Tuesday)	NBC	17.36
	10	King of the Hill	FOX	17.39

* Source: The Atlanta Journal/The Atlanta Constitution, September 24, 1997, p. D4.

Table 15.1 Nielsen weekly TV ratings summary

Program	Cost per thirty-second Commercial
Seinfeld (NBC)	$575,000
ER (NBC)	$560,000
Friends (NBC)	$410,000
The Nanny (CBS)	$200,000
Monday Night Football (ABC)	$360,000
Diagnosis Murder (CBS)	$ 75,000

Table 15.2 TV advertising rate data

Nielsen's adoption of people meters to measure national audience size and composition has created controversy. In particular, the major networks, whose audience share has been eroded dramatically by the number of options made available by cable TV and satellite, have complained that the ratings are not accurate. Also, Music Television (MTV) has complained that the ratings underestimate MTV's 12 to 17-year old audience by 34 percent.[4] The reason cited is this age group's relatively high tendency to forget to punch in and out on the people meter. As noted, there are huge amounts of money at stake in the ratings game, and as a consequence, any change is going to make someone unhappy. The controversy continues, and the major networks have begun development of an alternative ratings system which they believe will be more accurate than the current one.

Television viewing is also monitored at the local level. The **Nielsen Station Index** provides TV audience data at the local level (see Exhibit 15.2). Except in the largest markets, where audimeters, now called set meters, supplemented by diary data are used, Nielsen relies on diary data to provide local audience size and composition estimates.

Television markets are mutually exclusive geographical areas to which individual counties are assigned on the basis of share of viewing of particular television stations. Nielsen refers to television markets as **Designated Marketing Areas (DMAs)**. Nielsen monitors each of the over 200 local markets four times per year, referred to as "sweeps," to provide data on the size and composition of television audiences at the local level.

Radio

Radio advertising is experiencing a rebirth[5] due to the increasing cost of television time. Like television, radio advertising is done at both the network and the local (spot) level. In the network situation, a group of local affiliates broadcast common programming originating from one of the national networks (*e.g.*, ABC or the Mutual Network). At the local level, a single market is reached. Naturally, network time is more expensive than local time due to the size of the audience reached. The most expensive and popular radio time is "drive time," when people are commuting to and from work.[6]

The most basic radio audience measure is coverage, which refers to the geographical region (number of households) that can clearly receive the signal. Unfortunately, this does not give a very accurate measure of the actual radio audience. A preferred measure is circulation, which refers to the number of listeners of a particular station.[7]

A number of research services measure radio audiences. Arbitron measures individual station audiences quarterly in nearly 200 markets, relying on seven-day diaries administered to samples of consumers in each of the markets. The total sample involves about 375,000 mail-in diaries.[8] Another service, Birch Radio, a division of Birch/Scarborough Research Corporation, uses telephone interviews to measure audiences for local radio stations. Interviewers question respondents about the radio station they listened to the day before. This procedure is referred to as yesterday radio listening[9], and special efforts are made to ensure that respondents correctly identify the stations to which they listened.

Statistical Research Inc. (SRI) measures network station listenership by interviewing a sample of about 12,000 listeners for its biennial RADAR® (Radio's All Dimension Audience Research) reports.[10] These reports contain estimates of audiences for network programming and rely on reports listing local stations that carry specific network programming. Interviews are conducted with sample respondents by telephone on a daily basis for seven consecutive days.

Arbitron is developing a Portable People Meter sound measurement device.[11] Arbitron envisions a hand-held device which records inaudible signals encoded in radio (and television) sound transmissions. If perfected, the device could replace the mail-in diaries presently used to measure radio audiences. For instance, it might be possible to place these meters in selected locations near major highways in a market during drive time, and measure station share for the cars which pass the meters. Such a totally passive observation system has clear advantages.

Magazines and Newspapers

Advertising rates in magazines and newspapers are based on circulation, *i.e.*, number of copies sold. The **Audit Bureau of Circulation**, an independent auditing group representing both advertisers and publishers, audits subscription and newsstand sales to ensure that the promised circulation is in fact obtained.[12]

The Simmons Market Research Bureau's *Annual Survey of Media and Markets* provides data on the socioeconomic characteristics and purchasing behavior of the readerships of major magazines. Such information is vital for determining magazines in which to advertise. For example, the Pillsbury marketing managers responsible for baking products need to be aware that an atypically high percentage of the readers of Southern Living magazine and an atypically low percentage of the readers of Psychology Today purchase packaged pie crusts. Likewise, Borden's marketing managers responsible for dairy products should be aware that atypically high percentages of the readerships of Bon Appetit, Organic Gardening, and Prevention, and an atypically low percentage of the readership of Soap Opera Digest buy cottage cheese regularly.

MediaMark semiannually provides psychographic, demographic, and product usage information regarding magazine readerships in their MRI service. The Magazine Publishers Association (MPA), an organization of more than 230 publishers who represent over 1200 magazines, also provides demographic data pertaining to magazine readership in an effort to promote the use of magazines for advertising.

The Newspaper Advertising Bureau of the American Newspaper Publishers Association provides its members with market information on newspaper readership by conducting primary research and conducting case histories.

Comparing Campaigns

The term *advertising campaign* refers to the scheduled exposures of specific advertising to communicate a message. Campaigns can differ with respect to the advertising itself, total spending, media mix, and/or resource allocation across the media mix. We next discuss marketing research techniques for evaluating advertising campaigns.

Test Markets

Test markets, discussed in detail in Chapter 14, can be used to evaluate two or more alternative advertising campaigns. Each is used in one or more selected markets that are comparable with respect to factors such as the market shares of the major brands in the category. Comparing the results, including sales and/or brand image, provides insight as to which campaign is more effective. When evaluating a single campaign this same approach can be used. The new campaign is run in selected markets, and a comparable set of markets, in which the current campaign is running, serves as a control or point of comparison.

The research approach just described provides a means of investigating strategic advertising issues. For example, using the same message, spending could be skewed toward television in one market and toward radio and print in another market. Comparing results between markets after a sufficient period of time has elapsed provides insight into which allocation of resources is more effective.

Split-Cable Systems

Split-cable systems provide a vehicle for controlling the television advertising copy and/or the advertising weight to which groups of households in a single city are exposed. If alternative advertising campaigns differ only with respect to television advertising spending levels and/or the mix of TV commercials used, then a split-cable system can be employed to evaluate the campaigns. Otherwise, test markets must be used. The advantage of using a split-cable system to experiment with television advertising copy and/or advertising weight as opposed to the test market approach is that split-cable systems eliminate the possibility that observed differences are due to market-to-market variations instead of the advertising copy or weight.

The advertising message received by a household can be controlled in split-cable markets so that different groups of homes see different commercials. In the introductory example for this chapter, AT&T showed two different sets of TV commercials, Cost of Visit and Reach Out and Touch Someone, to two separate sets of long distance customers. Split-cable markets also allow the experimenter to control the number of times commercials are shown to households. A commercial may be shown in all the time slots purchased for a brand to one group of households and only in 50 percent of the time slots for another comparable group of households. Commercials for brands in other product or service categories or public service announcements would be inserted in the remaining time slots for the second group.

In addition, store purchases by samples of consumers from each group in the split-cable market can be monitored using scanner checkout technology. (In their experiment, AT&T measured long distance sales directly using their own information systems). Participating consumers agree to identify themselves at supermarket checkouts, and their purchases are automatically recorded in a database. Hence, a company can determine whether showing a particular commercial twice as often to one group than to another results in a meaningful increase in sales of the advertised brand. Whether one copy alternative or commercial mix sells more of the advertised brand than another can also be determined in the same way. In fact, the technology of split-cable systems has advanced to the point where markets can be divided into several panels as opposed to just two, allowing for the simultaneous evaluation of several alternatives.

Split-cable studies are expensive and time-consuming, but, in light of the amount of money spent on television advertising, these studies are often well worth the expense. Further, these systems are extremely useful for the validation of copy testing techniques, as will be discussed later in this chapter. Information Resources' BehaviorScan, available in seven geographically dispersed markets, is the sole remaining split-cable research service.

Media Models

Today's managers can get help in making decisions regarding spending levels and allocation of resources across media from sophisticated mathematical models that have been developed to assist managers in this task. These models are more appropriately covered in a course on media management, however, and will not be discussed further in this text.

Developing Advertising Copy

Producing television advertising can be very expensive. For example, one fifteen-second television spot for cherry-flavored Rolaids, an inexpensive simple product, took six months to develop at a cost of close to half a million dollars.[13] It is important, therefore, to obtain consumer feedback as early in the process as possible. Even for print and radio ads, where production costs are not such a critical issue, it still makes good sense to use consumer information to guide copy development.

As discussed in Chapter 12, marketing research provides information to help guide product positioning and market segmentation. The particular market segments chosen and the positioning strategy adopted to appeal to the target segment(s) obviously have a great impact on advertising strategy. Research is also valuable in determining the communication strategy for the brand, *e.g.*, a serious as opposed to tongue-in-cheek approach, and in providing guidance regarding personalities, settings, and language to use in the advertising. As described in the introductory example of this chapter, AT&T conducted extensive research before finally deciding on the Cost of Visit strategy to appeal to the light long distance user segment. Also, research revealed that the target audience for cherry-flavored Rolaids, mentioned above, was family-oriented middle-American females, thirty-five and over, who watch a lot of television. This information was used in selecting the actress to appear in the ad as well as the clothing and makeup she wore.

In addition to decisions regarding physical characteristics of the actors, settings, and so forth, marketing research is frequently used to assess the communication value of copy early in the development process. A sample of target market consumers is often

exposed to rough versions of alternative copy. The rough versions may be storyboards in the case of TV commercials, such as the one for General Foods International Coffee shown in Exhibit 12.10 of Chapter 12, or mockups to represent print ads. Respondents are questioned regarding what they remember after being exposed to the ad and what is being communicated about the brand advertised. Qualitative techniques, such as focus groups, are often used to reduce a large number of possibilities down to a manageable few to be further evaluated in quantitative research. Also, promising versions can be modified based on the research feedback and then can be subjected to further testing to enhance the effectiveness of the copy.

A finished ineffective commercial or advertisement can be a headache for everyone involved. So much money may have already been invested that there is a temptation to run the ad anyway. However, considering the high cost of advertising, especially TV time, this just compounds the waste. Using marketing research during the development process will not totally eliminate ineffective finished copy but will reduce the frequency of such an occurrence.

Applying Marketing Research 15.2 demonstrates how research can be used to guide advertising development.

Applying Marketing Research 15.2

The Ford Motor Company's Lincoln-Mercury Division has been trying for decades to define an image for its Mercury cars. Part of the problem is the fact that over the years Mercury cars have tended to be more expensive versions of Ford vehicles. The Mercury Sable is a spiffier version of the Ford Taurus, the Mercury Mountaineer is an upscaled Explorer, and so forth. Extensive marketing research indicated that Mercury buyers were individualistic and wanted imaginative vehicles.[14] Further, Mercury owners were relatively old, in their late fifties, so it was imperative that the brand attract young buyers.

A television advertising campaign which focused on the word "imagine" was developed for Mercury. The tagline "imagine yourself in a Mercury" was retained, but a series of new commercials was produced. The new commercials all opened with an unseen viewer watching a fictitious "Imagine TV" network. The spots included spoofs of courtroom dramas, kung fu movies and the film classic "Casablanca." The Lincoln-Mercury Division had hopes that this campaign, based on marketing research findings, would help resolve the ambiguity between the Ford and Mercury brands.

Evaluating Advertising Copy

Given the amount of money companies typically spend on advertising and what is at stake, particularly in a situation such as the Mercury campaign described in Applying Marketing Research 15.2, it seems imperative that copy executions be thoroughly researched to ensure that they increase sales. However, it is very difficult to evaluate the direct impact of advertising on sales because external factors such as competitive activity and trade behavior also influence the sales of a company's brand in the market.

Split-cable systems experiments are ideal for directly evaluating the ability of advertising copy to increase sales. Panelists in a split-cable market are divided into two groups so that one group sees one execution of a TV commercial and the other group sees another execution or no commercial at all for the brand. Sales to panelists are monitored using supermarket checkout scanners over a sufficient period of time (*e.g.*, six months). Sales of the brand are compared between the two groups to determine whether there is an effect attributable to the advertising copy. However, such experiments are both very expensive and time-consuming, and hence, are not used routinely.

Because of the difficulties associated with directly measuring the effect of advertising on sales, surrogate measures are often used to evaluate advertising copy. These **copy testing** techniques are designed to evaluate the effectiveness of specific advertisements. To be effective, advertising must be remembered and must favorably affect viewers' impressions. We next discuss these two dimensions of advertising and how effectiveness is measured in each context.

Intrusiveness

Intrusiveness pertains to an advertisement's ability to cut through the clutter and be remembered. Intrusiveness can be measured relatively easily. A variety of services specialize in providing marketers with this information. Obviously, the memorability of an ad depends on the context in which it is seen/heard. The memorability of an ad shown to an audience recruited to a central location to preview television programming (including commercials) is generally higher than the memorability of the same ad to an audience watching TV in the natural setting of their own homes. The time delay between viewing and being questioned about what was seen also has an impact on memorability measurements. Hence, norms, or other points of reference, play a vital role in the interpretation of intrusiveness research.

TV Copy

For many years, TV commercials were evaluated solely on intrusiveness. The **Day After Recall (DAR)** system developed by Burke Marketing Research was adopted by many companies as the standard measure of TV commercial intrusiveness. The DAR measure is obtained in a straightforward way. Test commercials are spliced into network television programming. One day later, a sample of viewers of the program in which the test commercial appeared is contacted by telephone, and the percentage of viewers who recall seeing the commercial is obtained. This recall score is compared to norms established over time and television commercials scoring above average, *i.e.*, above the given norm, are considered effective, while those scoring below the norm are considered ineffective. In many companies, these scores became key determinants as to whether or not a commercial was actually run.

The communication effectiveness of a commercial is also measured as a somewhat secondary objective of systems such as DAR through the use of information given by respondents regarding what they specifically remember about the ad. This measure of communication effectiveness provides an understanding of what the commercial conveys to consumers when seen in a natural environment. A very intrusive ad may fail to communicate the intended message to consumers.

Recall Plus is a service of ASI Market Research designed to measure the intrusiveness and communication of TV commercials. Respondents, recruited from cable TV households in at least two cities, are invited to preview a proposed new television program that will be shown on an unused local cable channel at a prescribed time. The test program is an unaired thirty-minute situation comedy containing test and filler commercials as they would appear on normal TV programming. The following day, respondents are recontacted by telephone, and those who viewed the program are questioned about the show itself and the commercials which appeared in the show. Recall scores for test commercials are compared to historical norms. Also, information regarding what those individuals recall seeing concerning the commercial is provided.

Another way of assessing intrusiveness is through **clutter reels** which are simply videotapes containing a variety of TV commercials including the one(s) being tested. Respondents in the target audience are shown the clutter reels and then asked which commercials they remember seeing. The percentage of participants recalling a specific ad is a measure of the ad's effectiveness. Once again, norms to which recall scores can be compared are necessary to determine whether an ad is "good" or "bad." Such norms are obtained by averaging the results of repeated applications of the clutter reel test over time.

If more than one copy execution is to be tested, a comparison of the intrusiveness measures across groups can be made. Each group views a clutter reel that differs only in the execution shown for the test brand. Applying Marketing Research 15.3 demonstrates how a clutter reel could be used this way. In this situation, a norm is not necessary to determine which of the test ads is better, but still provides a valuable point of reference for understanding the relative effectiveness of the better option(s).

Applying Marketing Research 15.3

Sun Bank of Florida was interested in improving its image as a place where "everyday people" are welcome. To this end, two thirty-second commercials were developed by the bank's advertising agency. Each commercial was designed to communicate to its audience that Sun Bank could help them achieve their retirement objectives. In one commercial, "Fishin'," a grandfatherly man was shown fishing with his grandson in a boat on a peaceful lake at sunrise. The voice-over pointed out that the commercial was not for a vacation resort, fishing equipment, or boats, but rather for a bank, namely Sun Bank, and that Sun Bank could help you "get to the lake" by careful financial planning and investing.

The second commercial, "Vacation," showed a senior-citizen couple enjoying themselves on a cruise.

The voice-over pointed out that careful planning and investing now were important to enjoying retirement, and that Sun Bank could help people to be financially able to live the retirement life they would like.

Marketing research was conducted to compare the two ads. A random sample of 100 adults, half male and half female, between the ages of 35 and 60, were recruited in each of four shopping malls. At each location, respondents were randomly divided into two groups, balanced by sex. Each participant was shown a clutter reel of eight ads including one of the two ads — "Fishin'" for one group, and "Vacation" for the other group. After viewing the commercials, respondents were asked which ads they remembered, thus producing recall scores (Table 15.3) for each of the two test ads. Those who remembered the test ad were asked to describe what they perceived to be the ad's main message (Table 15.4).

The two commercials scored comparably on recall (Table 15.3). However, Fishin' clearly communicated the "ordinary people" image that the bank wanted to project better than Vacation based on the perceived main message data (Table 15.4). Fishin' became an integral part of the bank's campaign.

	Recall of Test Commercials	
	Fishin' (200)	Vacation (200)
	%	%
Remember name of bank	58	62
Remember some portion of ad only	4	5
No recall	38	33

Table 15.3 Recall of test Commercials

	Perceived Main Message of Test Commercials	
	Fishin'(116)	Vacation (124)
	%	%
Important to plan/save for retirement	24	27
Possible for ordinary people to enjoy retirement	31	3
Would be nice to be able to travel during retirement	—	35
Retirement will be fun	18	22
Miscellaneous	27	13

Table 15.4 Perceived main message of test commercials

The clutter reel test design tends to be relatively expensive, since it requires face-to-face interviewing, typically using mall intercepts. Hence, additional questions are usually asked to take advantage of the captive audience. For example, after obtaining the intrusiveness measure using the clutter reel, the same respondents might be shown only the test commercial, *i.e.*, subjected to a "forced exposure," and then questioned regarding what the commercial communicates. Results could be compared between groups seeing different copy executions to assess relative communication value.

Radio

Radio commercials can be evaluated for intrusiveness in a manner similar to television commercials. Test commercials can be aired normally on a selected station (or stations) at a given time, and, after a prescribed amount of time has elapsed, listeners to the particular programming can be contacted and questioned about commercials they recall hearing. Those recalling the test commercial would be questioned regarding the message content. Comparisons against norms developed over time would provide information on the intrusiveness of the ad. Analogously, two commercials might be aired at the same time on separate stations having similar programming and audience characteristics. Recall and communication results would be obtained separately, and these results would be used to compare the ads on the basis of intrusiveness.

Also, the clutter reel concept, discussed in the context of TV ads, could easily be adapted for testing radio commercials for intrusiveness. As with TV ads, norms would be required for evaluating a single radio commercial.

Radio Recall Research of Holmdel, NJ uses a technique that is designed to provide a more realistic assessment of intrusiveness than the clutter reel approach. Consumers are recruited in a shopping mall to answer a brief (about ten minutes) questionnaire regarding entertainment interests.[15] While the respondents are completing the questionnaire, a "radio" (actually a disguised tape recorder) is playing in the room. Three radio commercials (the test and two filler commercials) are included in the musical program that is "aired." Respondents are contacted the next day by telephone and asked if they recall hearing any commercials while they were completing the questionnaire at the mall.

Another interesting variation is a technique called Radio Test, which was developed by Barnes/Hollander, Inc., of Atlanta for testing radio commercials for pharmaceuticals. Listeners to PRN (Physicians' Radio Network) are recruited to listen to a thirty-minute audio cassette of normal PRN programming that includes the test commercial. Telephone interviews are conducted twenty-four hours after respondents listen to the cassette, and a recall score is obtained for the test commercial. Information pertaining to the main message of the ad is also obtained. The approach can be used to test the intrusiveness of a single ad, or, by using a separate group for each test ad, to compare ads in terms of effectiveness.

Print Ads

A number of techniques have been successfully used to assess the intrusiveness of print ads. One method is an analog of the clutter reel approach for TV commercials. Participants in the target audience are asked to review a portfolio of print ads and are then questioned regarding which ads they remember and what they recall about these ads. Recall scores and information regarding copy communication are thus generated. Different executions of an ad could be tested among different groups of participants and the results compared; scores could also be compared to norms developed over time. As with clutter reels, a forced exposure evaluation of the ad might follow.

Another approach, commonly called the "tip-in" approach, is to insert a test ad manually into copies of a current issue of a magazine, give the magazine to a sample of people in the target audience, and interview them at a later date. Participants are asked which ads they recall and what they remember about them. Again, two ads could be compared using two groups of participants, or recall results from a single ad could be compared to existing norms.

Perhaps the most widely known commercially available system for evaluating the intrusiveness of print advertising is the one provided by Starch INRA Hooper, Inc. A sample of at least 100 adult respondents of each gender who have read a specific recent issue of a magazine are interviewed in person. Special samples are used when appropriate such as in the case of a magazine designed for teenage girls. The interviewer shows ads from the magazine issue to each reader and asks whether he or she has read each ad. Some 75,000 advertisements in 1000 issues of consumer magazines, business publications, and newspapers are assessed each year using over 100,000 personal interviews. Three measures related to intrusiveness, called **Starch scores**, are provided for each and evaluated:

- Noted — the percentage who remember seeing the ad in the issue.
- Associated — the percentage who associate the ad with the brand or the advertiser.

- Read Most — the percentage who read half or more of the copy.

These measures can be compared to norms obtained by averaging scores for all tested comparable ads in a given product or service category that appeared in the particular magazine over a period of time.

Table 15.5 contains excerpts from a Starch Readership Report for ads appearing in *Sports Illustrated*. Table 15.6 is a guide to interpreting the indices and rank data provided in a Starch report. The entire issue of the magazine, with scores on all evaluated ads, is included with each report.

Advertiser	Rank in issue	Percentages: Noted	Percentages: Associated	Percentages: Read most	Readership indexes: Noted	Readership indexes: Associated	Readership indexes: Read most
Beer							
Heineken & Amstel Light beer	2	67	65	10	129	133	125
Sharp's beer/Miller	4	62	61	5	119	124	63
Bud Light beer	10	56	52	15	108	106	188
Communications/public utilities							
GTE Corp.	28	43	39	7	83	80	88
AT&T Cordless telephones & answering machines/Sears	18	51	48	15	98	98	188
Computers/data processing equipment							
Smith Corona word processors/laptop	19	53	47	6	102	96	75
Financial							
Franklin Distributors Inc. funds	32	40	33	6	77	67	75
Footwear							
Timberland shoes	19	58	47	7	112	96	88
Freight							
UPS/Next Day Air Letter	19	50	47	6	96	96	75
Golf equipment							
Spalding golf balls/ Top-Flite XL	23	49	46	7	94	94	88

Table 15.5
Excerpts from Starch Readership Report for an issue of *Sports Illustrated*, total of thirty-three half-page or larger ads; men readers.

Readership Indexes	Rank in Issue
Readership indexes compare each ad's readership performance against the issue average. Median readership percentages for largest advertisements are assigned indexes of 100, other percentages proportionally higher or lower indexes. A "Noted" readership index of 150 indicates an ad that is 50 percent above the issue average in attracting attention. In addition to showing relative performance within an issue, readership indexes make possible more meaningful comparisons among ads from different issues and different publications. . .because they automatically adjust for the differences in average score levels that occur between issues and among publications.	Rank shows the relative standing of each ad in terms of its associated percent. The ad with rank 1 obtained the highest associated percent in the issue.

Table 15.6
How the Starch advertisement readership indexes are computed.

A similar service, Starch Ballot Readership Study, is available for business magazines. A sample of subscribers is surveyed by mail and questioned regarding the extent of their readership of ads in a particular issue of the magazine. Similar measures, i.e., "looked at," "read partially," etc., are provided for the ads appearing in the issue.

The information provided by Starch scores is obviously very useful to advertisers and publishers. Advertisers can assess how well their ads score relative to those of their competitors. Publishers can assess the strengths and weaknesses of their magazines as advertising vehicles and use this information when selling advertising space. However, Starch measurements are after the fact; the ad has already run! Learning that an ad is poor at this point prevents wasting more money by not using it again, but much money may have already been wasted. Recognizing this problem, Starch has introduced a monthly newsletter, Tested Copy. The newsletter provides customers with insights into developing good print copy by tapping the company's huge database of test results.

Persuasion

The marketing community has long recognized that copy effectiveness depends on more than intrusiveness. **Persuasion**, the ability of the message to affect consumers' impression of the brand favorably, is also a key determinant of advertising effectiveness. That is, advertising must persuade the consumer to buy the brand. Slowing population growth and low inflation rates have changed the competitive environment in American consumer markets. Annual sales are no longer guaranteed to grow just because of a rapidly increasing population and rising prices. Growth now, to a large extent, comes at the expense of one's competition, contributing to the expanding interest in measuring the persuasive dimension of advertising.[16] However, persuasion is much more difficult to define and measure operationally than is intrusiveness.

TV Copy

It took considerable time to develop measures of persuasion (other than sales) that were acceptable to marketers and marketing researchers. Even today, many advertising agency creatives continue to object to attempts at quantifying persuasion. They view this aspect of copy as intangible and artistic, not something that lends itself to scientific measurement. In fact, they argue that such measurements stifle creativity and encourage agencies to develop "safe" commercials, *i.e.*, commercials that will score high on a test, which in the long run will promote mediocrity.[17]

The debate between "rationalists," who view advertising as more science than art, and "emotionalists," who view advertising as a creative effort which is difficult, at best, to evaluate in any testing system, continues today.[18] Rationalists tend to accept copy testing systems, while emotionalists tend to reject them. Rationalists point to lists of award-winning creative commercials that did not sell. Emotionalists counter that sales volume is not the only criteria on which advertising should be evaluated, and that the rationalist approach leads to bland "ring around the collar" commercials which give the industry a bad name. The art versus science debate is likely to never be resolved. However, there is mounting evidence that measures of persuasion, although imperfect, are valid indicators of a commercial's ability to sell.

Systems that measure the persuasion dimension of television copy often focus on directly measuring changes in consumer attitudes produced by the ad. The Brand Advertising Test (BAT)[19], for example, is based on the premise that the brand has a positioning strategy that consists of several key communication points. If these key points are effectively communicated, then the perception of the brand will be favorably shifted. Further, if perceptions of the brand change, attitudes toward the brand are affected and, presumably, behavior toward the brand will also be affected. The goal of BAT is thus to measure how well the copy communicates the key points.

BAT uses a pre-post experimental design and mall intercept interviewing. Respondents are first screened for eligibility, *e.g.*, product category usage, which varies with the brand for which copy is being tested. Basically, BAT participants rate the brand of interest on a list of characteristics, including those relating to the key points of communication, before (pre) and after (post) viewing the television commercial being tested. The differences between the "before" and "after" brand attribute ratings related to the key points of communication are then calculated. The final BAT score is a composite of changes in perceptions regarding key communication points produced by the ad. A test commercial can conceivably generate a negative score,

meaning that the test commercial has a detrimental effect in the context of the communication objectives.

The precursor to BAT was QCT (Quantitative Communication Test), which utilized a test group (view ad) *vs.* control group (not view ad) design as opposed to a pre *vs.* post design. QCT used differences in brand perceptions between the test and control groups to produce a score for the ad. BAT does not require a control group and is therefore less expensive than QCT. However, research had to be conducted to establish that the pre *vs.* post design was as effective in the sense of measuring communication of key copy points as the test *vs.* control design before implementing BAT. One of the all-time high-scoring commercials in the QCT system was Coca-Cola's "Mean Joe Greene" ad. The commercial featured an encounter between a young boy and the Pittsburgh Steelers' all-time great defensive tackle, Joe Greene, in a tunnel leading from the field after a game. At first, Joe, who is battered and exhausted, wants nothing to do with the boy, who offers Joe his bottle of Coca-Cola. After drinking the Coke, Joe's mood changes, and he offers the boy his game jersey. The poignant ad had a certain magic that attracted people and captured their hearts. QCT results showed that the ad touched people, leaving them with a warm feeling toward Coca-Cola.

ASI Market Research offers a service called Persuasion Plus, which is designed to measure a TV commercial's ability to persuade. The procedure for Persuasion Plus is the same as the one for Recall Plus, discussed earlier, with a few modifications. The recruitment interview in Persuasion Plus includes questions on brand preferences in categories including those containing brands for which commercials will be tested. The post-viewing interview contains similar questions, and shifts in preference are used to calibrate the commercial's effectiveness.

Radio and Print

The two techniques just discussed for evaluating the persuasiveness of TV copy could easily be adapted to evaluate radio and print ads. However, the issue of copy effectiveness is generally far more salient for television copy than for other forms of media because both production costs and the costs of buying advertising time are generally much higher for TV copy than other media forms. The cost of research, as a percentage of advertising cost, is therefore much lower for TV commercials than for radio or print commercials. Consequently, less testing is conducted for radio and print, and the bulk of what is done focuses on intrusiveness. Occasionally, however, the persuasion of print copy is tested, often using split-run advertising.

Split-run advertising entails placing two or more versions of a newspaper or magazine ad in alternating copies of the same issue. The resulting alternative issues are distributed equally in a geographic region or in comparable separate regions. The ads typically contain a discount coupon, which can be traced to the source ad, and the rates of redemption of the coupons are compared to evaluate the relative effectiveness of the ads. A mail or telephone offer of promotional material, such as a T-shirt containing a product logo or name, could be used as part of the ads instead of a coupon. In this case, the telephone number or mailing address is varied to identify the ad source.

Measuring Persuasion and Intrusiveness Simultaneously

TV Copy

Not only is there generally much more at stake financially when making decisions regarding TV copy than other media, but also the stakes continue to grow at a rapid pace. The most popular network prime time television shows charge well in excess of one-half million dollars for a thirty-second spot.[20] These ever-rising costs have increased concerns among advertisers regarding the return to the company from money invested in television advertising. Consequently, a number of research firms have developed and promoted systems for simultaneously evaluating TV copy in the context of persuasion and intrusiveness.

In these systems, several noncompeting commercials are usually evaluated at the same time among the same respondents to reduce cost. The different systems have their peculiarities but also have much in common. The following sections cover several of these commercially available testing systems. The discussion does not exhaust the list of such systems but is designed to introduce the various alternative approaches and point out common elements.

Advertising Research System (ARS[b]) ARS, a service of rsc (research systems corporation), uses the central-location theater setting pioneered in the 1950s by Horace Schwerin and Paul Lazarsfeld[21] and typical television programming to evaluate TV copy. Respondents are recruited randomly to come to a central location to preview and evaluate potential new television programming. Participants are included at geographically dispersed locations, so the total base of participants for a particular television commercial is well over 500.

Before any programming is shown, participants are asked to indicate from sets of competitive brands which brands they would like to receive if they were among the winners of market-basket door prizes. These preferences are used to establish preexposure shares for the brands whose respective commercials are to be tested.

Commercials, including those being tested, are embedded in half-hour television programs. Commercial time is scheduled in the programs in a way that is typical of television shows. After viewing the television programming, participants evaluate the shows and are asked again to indicate their brand preferences from sets of competitive brands for additional market-basket door prizes to be awarded. Choices made at this time are used to establish postexposure shares. The shift in preexposure to postexposure brand share is the ARS PERSUASION[c] score for a commercial.

About three days after the viewing session, participants are telephoned and asked what commercials they remember seeing during the pilot television shows and are also questioned about what they specifically remember about these commercials. The percentage remembering a test commercial is the related recall score, and the percentage remembering the major message of a test commercial is the key message comprehension score. All three scores for a test commercial, ARS PERSUASION and the two intrusiveness measures related to recall and key message comprehension, are compared to norms (historical averages) to assess the commercial's effectiveness.

Exhibit 15.3 shows the ARS test results for a commercial for Colgate's Stand-Up Toothpaste (Exhibit 15.4). All three ARS measures, including ARS PERSUASION, were considerably above what is considered average for a commercial of this type in the ARS system.

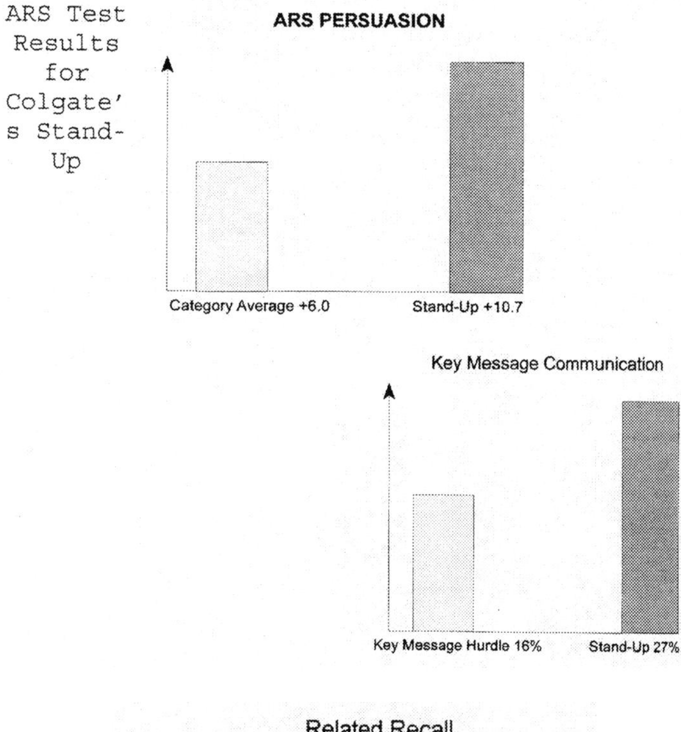

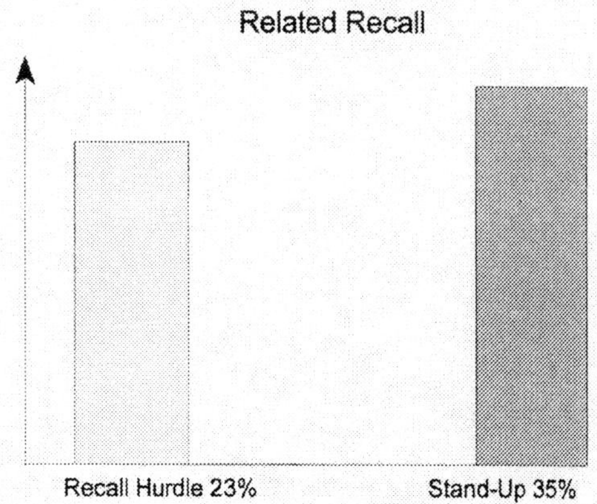

Exhibit 15.3 ARS test results for Colgate stand-up

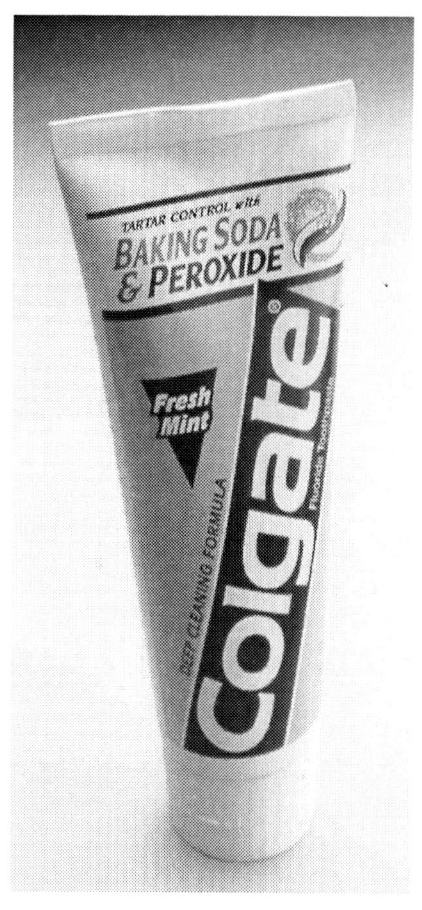

Exhibit 15.4 Colgate stand-up toothpaste

The ARS system has been used primarily for evaluating copy for frequently purchased consumer packaged goods. However, the system has been shown to also work in the context of automotive products, specifically tires.[22] In any event, adjustments are needed in the context of durables or services. For example, the car one would like to receive would likely be the most expensive, not necessarily the car one would buy. Also, it is generally very expensive and impractical to try to include durables in gift baskets. Analogous problems exist with evaluating many services. ARS has developed some alternatives for handling these special problems.

McCollum/Spielman The McCollum/Spielman & Company system, like ARS, uses a central-location theater setting. A sample of about 450 people in four geographically dispersed locations is recruited to preview television programming. The participants, in groups of twenty-five each, first view a half-hour variety program; seven commercials, four of which are being tested, are shown at the midpoint. Respondents are next questioned regarding the program and are then asked to recall what brands they remember seeing advertised. The recall responses form the basis of the intrusiveness measure.

Respondents are next shown additional TV programming in which the four test commercials have been interspersed. An attitude shift measure is obtained by comparing the brand designated as purchased most often in a preexposure interview with postexposure brand preference as determined by a gift-basket scenario analogous to that used by ARS. Preexposure and postexposure information regarding favorite brand, next preferred alternative, brands not considered, and brands to which the respondent is indifferent are used to measure attitude shifts in the case of durables and services.

A major difference between McCollum/Spielman and ARS is the use of two commercial exposures as part of the process for measuring persuasion. ARS findings suggest that one exposure is sufficient for evaluating a commercial's effectiveness.[23] However, McCollum/Spielman argues that using fewer than two exposures represent an invalid test of a commercial's effectiveness.[24]

Gallup & Robinson, Inc. In-View, a service offered by Gallup and Robinson, Inc., provides information regarding the effectiveness of a TV commercial in the context of on-air viewing by a recruited audience. Test commercials are inserted into prime time television programs aired by independent stations. Participants are recruited by telephone on the day of the test to watch the program. Participants are recontacted the next day by telephone, and those who watched the programs are questioned regarding commercials they remember seeing. Questions about what in particular is remembered are also asked. Norms are available for comparative purposes.

Questions pertaining to attitudes toward brands, including those advertised with test commercials in the program, are asked before and after viewing. Changes in attitudes toward brands for which commercials were tested are attributed to exposure to the commercial. Hence, the system provides information regarding the commercial's ability to cut through clutter, communicate the message and change opinion.

ASI Apex System Clients can purchase a combination of Recall Plus and Persuasion Plus, called ASI Apex, and thus obtain information regarding the effectiveness of a TV commercial in terms of its intrusiveness, including what the commercial communicates, and its ability to convince viewers to buy.

Comparing Services The primary difference between either the ARS or the McCollum/Spielman approach and the ASI and Gallup & Robinson approach is that, in the latter, the participants view programming in their own homes (as opposed to a central-location theater setting). In the case of Gallup & Robinson, viewers also watch an ordinary TV program. Proponents of in-home viewing argue that the natural setting enhances the validity of the measures. On the other hand, proponents of the ARS and McCollum/Spielman approach argue that the control over the process provided by the central location format is well worth the small sacrifice of realism.

The general audiences recruited in the ARS and McCollum/Spielman systems make them particularly suited for products having mass appeal, *e.g.*, laundry detergents, cooking oils, toothpaste, and soft drinks. The individual telephone recruiting approach used by ASI and Gallup & Robinson allows for a custom-tailored audience. Hence, commercials for products that do not have broad appeal, *e.g.*, Grecian Formula 44 for graying hair, Similac infant formula, and Clearasil for problem skin blemishes, can be tested among their respective target audiences. Potential test participants are screened on the basis of eligibility requirements at the telephone recruiting stage before being invited to participate. Naturally, the cost increases as the number of eligibility requirements increase.

Clearly, when it comes to evaluating the effectiveness of television commercials, there are many alternatives. These various approaches, which differ in focus, cost, and degree of artificiality, are organized and summarized in Exhibit 15.5.

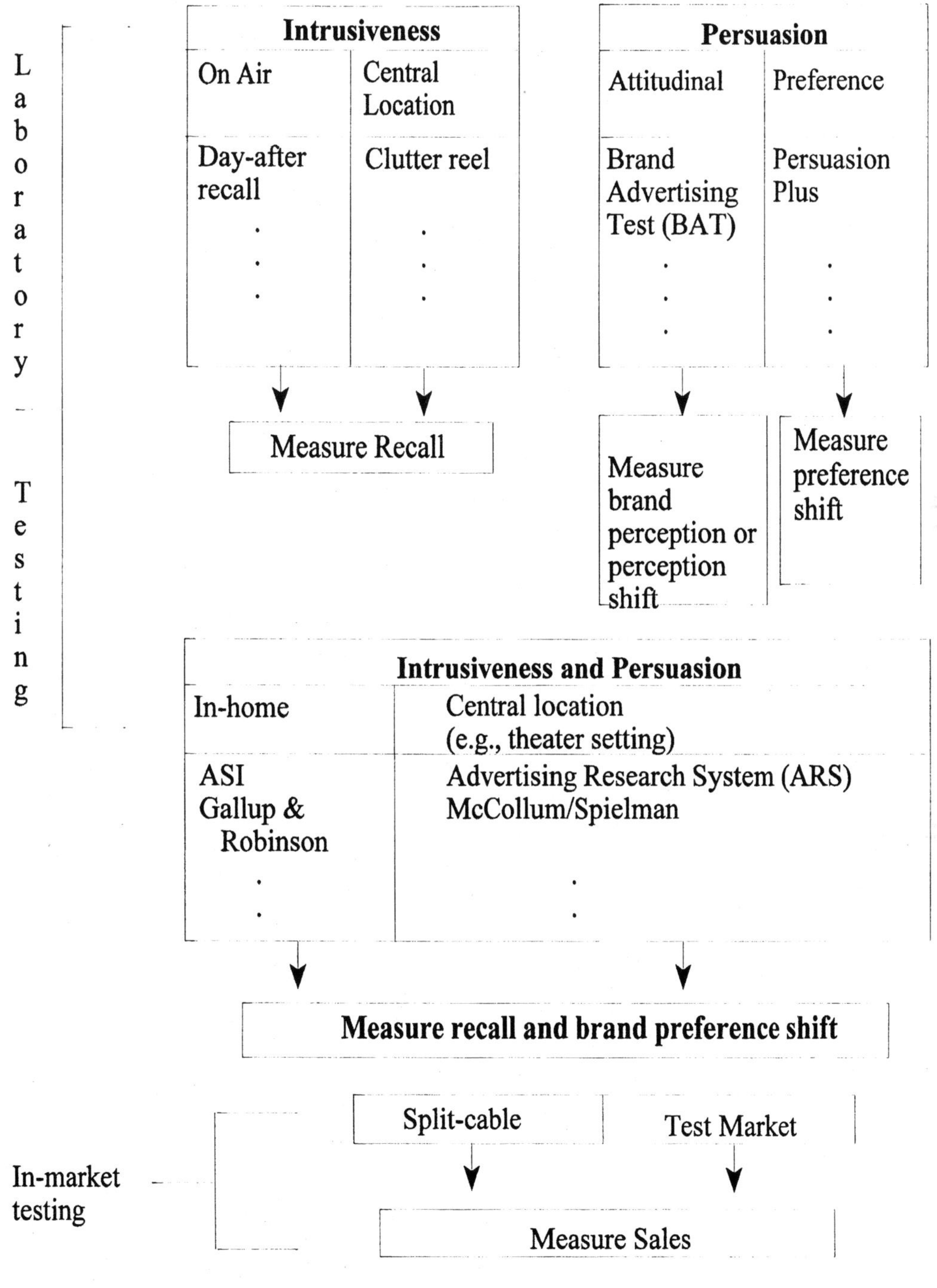

Exhibit 15.5 Testing television commercials paradigm

Print

The "tip-in" method described earlier is used in Print Plus, a service of ASI Market Research, to evaluate print advertisements in current editions of popular magazines. Test advertisements are glued into copies of a particular edition of the magazine, which are then placed in the homes of qualified participants. At recruitment, qualified respondents are asked to participate in a study of attitudes toward the magazine. They are asked to read the magazine and agree to be interviewed afterward.

Recall of test ads is obtained in the interview by measuring the percent of respondents who can describe the ad from memory when prompted with the brand name. Changes between preexposure and postexposure preference and interest toward the advertised brand are measured as indicators of the ad's persuasiveness.

MIRS (Magazine Impact Research Service), offered by Gallup & Robinson, Inc., provides tracking of client and competitor print advertising appearing in popular magazines. Ads under development can be pretested in the system using a tip-in approach. Measures of recall, communication of key copy points and persuasiveness are provided.

Reliability and Validity

How does one determine whether a copy testing system is good or bad? Two accepted criteria for assessing the value of copy testing systems are the reliability and validity of the measurements provided.

Reliability

The **reliability** of copy test measurements refers to the consistency of test scores over different comparable samples of respondents. Reliability can be readily investigated, and several copy testing services have conducted studies to show that their commercial test scores are reproducible on subsequent independent tests. For example, one company obtained test-retest correlations ranging from .81 to .88 for their persuasion scores across fifteen product categories.[25] A rsc report showed consistency in ARS PERSUASION scores across a base of 325 commercials with a test-retest correlation of +.92.[26] Consistency in recall scores has also been demonstrated.[27]

Validity

The **validity** of copy test measurements refers to whether results obtained in a test environment can be projected to the actual market. This concept was referred to as external validity when discussed in Chapter 3, which was devoted to experimental research. To establish the validity of a measure of persuasiveness, for example, one might show that a commercial found more persuasive than another in the test environment results in higher sales in the actual market. Validity is more difficult to assess than is reliability because both market results as well as test results must be obtained for the same commercials. Nevertheless, validation of copy test measurements has been attempted.

Research Systems (rsc) has examined the validity of their ARS PERSUASION score using split-cable advertising weight experiments, which typically ran from nine to twelve months. Experimental results, such as those shown in Exhibit 15.6, demonstrated that increased exposure to commercials having relatively high ARS PERSUASION scores increased sales, while increased exposure to TV commercials with low ARS PERSUASION scores did not appear to increase brand sales regardless of the increased advertising weight given to the commercial.[28] As can be seen in Exhibit 15.6, all five cases for which the ARS PERSUASION score was at least +7.0 produced a sales effect large enough to be measurable at the end of the split-cable test. On the other hand, only one of the twenty-nine cases for which the ARS PERSUASION measure was +5.0 or less produced a measurable sales effect by the end of the split-cable test, while about half of the cases for which the ARS PERSUASION measure was between +5.0 and +7.0 resulted in a noticeable sales effect. In other words, the results suggest that advertising weight is far more influential in determining sales when the copy is persuasive in the sense of the ARS measure than it is when the copy is not persuasive in the same sense.

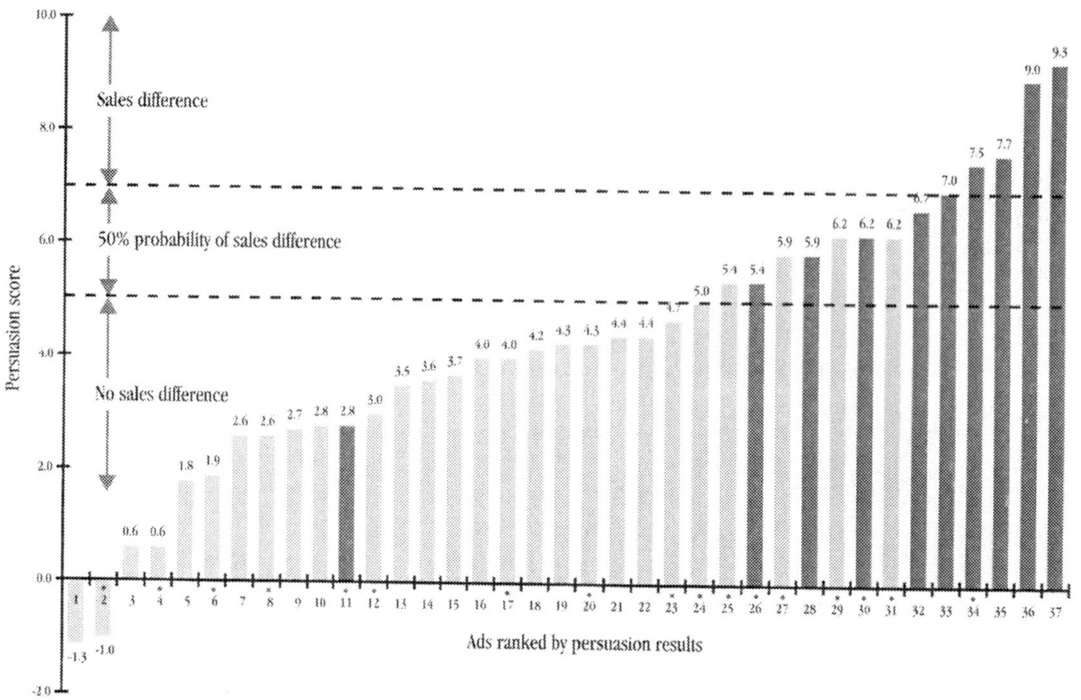

Exhibit 15.6
Split-cable advertising weight test results.

Note: A shaded bar indicates that there was a measurable sales difference during the split-cable test.

ARS has also used split-cable experiments involving two different commercials for the same existing brand to validate their measure of persuasion. Brand sales data from two panels (each exposed to a different commercial for the same brand, but at the same advertising weight) were monitored over time. Table 15.7 shows that the commercial having the significantly higher ARS PERSUASION score produced significantly higher sales than the other commercial. Also, commercials having comparable ARS PERSUASION scores produced comparable sales results. Hence, results of these experiments also support the validity of the ARS PERSUASION measure.

We wanted to compare our Savin 7065 to a Xerox 1065. But we couldn't afford one.

The Savin 7065. $17,290.

The Xerox 1065. $24,895.

We were curious. We heard the Xerox 1065 could turn out 62 copies a minute. Just like the Savin 7065.

And that it would hand you your first copy in 7.6 seconds. Which isn't *that* much slower than the 4.0 clocking of our 7065.

Of course, the Xerox copier *is* rumored to have only two modes of reduction, and one mode of enlargement. Which doesn't really compare to Savin's four and three.

And we did read that their copier can't copy from two-sided originals, the way our 7065 can.

But Xerox is a nice company. So we thought we'd give them the benefit of the doubt, put the two copiers side by side, and compare them ourselves.

Then we learned that the Xerox 1065 costs almost $8,000 more than the Savin 7065.

So we called the whole thing off.

It's nothing personal against Xerox.

It's just that if we start buying copiers at those prices, before long, we'd have to start charging more for our own.

savin

Follow the leaders.

Exhibit 15.7
An example of superiority claim

McCollum/Spielman also has investigated the validity of its test measures. Selected TV copy tested by McCollum/ Spielman was organized into 412 campaigns, some of which consisted of several commercials, and the 412 campaigns were classified into two groups (high and low) for both attitude shift (*i.e.*, persuasion) and intrusiveness. The same campaigns were evaluated by the respective advertisers according to whether the brand had exceeded marketing objectives over the time the campaign was used. Table 15.8 shows the percentage of campaigns exceeding marketing objectives for each of the four categories defined by the McCollum/Spielman test results. Clearly, far more of those campaigns using copy that scored high for attitude shift were perceived by their respective advertisers as effective than were those scoring low for attitude shift. Not surprisingly, campaign success based on this long-term assessment did not exhibit a relationship with the intrusiveness measure.

		Attitude shift	
		Low (percentage)	High (percentage)
Intrusiveness	Low	13	79
	High	24	71

Source: Adapted from Peter R. Klein and Melvin Tainter, "Copy Research Validation: The Advertiser's Perspective," *Journal of Advertising Research* 23 (October-November 1983), pp. 9-18.

Table 15.8 An example of a parity claim

Substantiating Advertising Claims

Most advertising copy makes one or more claims. An **advertising claim** is a specific assertion or implication made about the brand. Such claims must be truthful and are scrutinized by many groups. The federal Trade Commission evaluates advertising to ensure that claims are not deceptive, misleading, or unfair. The National Advertising Division (NAD) of the Better Business Bureau and the National Advertising Review Board (NARB) both act as self-regulatory agencies of the advertising industry, arbitrating complaints about untrue or unsubstantiated claims. In addition, consumer groups, such as Action for Children's Television, and companies selling competing products review commercials looking for unsubstantiated or deceptive statements. Furthermore, the television networks require substantiation of claims made in a commercial before agreeing to air the commercial and each of the networks has a commercial clearance department that reviews evidence used to substantiate claims. Thus, companies spend tremendous amounts of money on marketing research to substantiate their advertising claims.

Types of Advertising Claims

There are three general types of advertising claims: 1) comparative performance claims, 2) noncomparative performance claims, and 3) market performance claims. Each may require different types of research to substantiate the claim made.

Comparative Performance Claims

A **comparative performance claim** is one that states or implies that the brand provides a value or consumer benefit relative to one or more other brands. The other brands might be explicitly named ("OcuClear eye drops relieve three times longer than Visine") or might be implied ("better than the leading brand").

A comparative performance claim can take two forms. One form, a **superiority claim**, states that the advertised brand is preferred over, or is better than, another brand or brands. In Exhibit 15.7 you can see that Savin claims superiority for one of its copiers relative to a specific Xerox model on several dimensions, including price. The other form, a **parity claim**, states that the advertised brand is preferred as often as another brand, has the same attribute(s) as another brand, provides the same benefit(s) as another brand, or that consumers cannot distinguish it from another brand. For example, in the television commercial illustrated in the storyboard in Exhibit 15.8, it is claimed that the Bic razor provides as close a shave as the move expensive Trac II razor. A **product improvement claim** for a brand is a superiority claim relative to the previous version of the same brand. For instance, Estee Lauder made the product improvement claim that its "Advanced Night Repair has been shown to be three times more effective than original Night Repair in helping skin recover from the effects of daily environmental exposure."

ARS PERSUASION			Sales difference	
Commercial A		Commercial B	Cable A	Cable B
5.0	=	4.4	=	
2.8	=	2.0	=	
4.6	>	1.1	>	
3.8	>	2.0	>	
9.0	>	2.6	>	
7.0	>	2.8	>	
15.9	>	11.1	>	

Table 15.7 Split-Cable experiments; ARS PERSUASION

		Attitude shift	
		Low (percentage)	High (percentage)
Intrusiveness	Low	13	79
	High	24	71

Source: Adapted from Peter R. Klein and Melvin Tainter, "Copy Research Validation: The Advertiser's Perspective," *Journal of Advertising Research* 23 (October-November 1983), pp. 9-18.

Table 15.8 Validity of McCollum/Spielman test measures

Comparative performance advertising claims create the greatest risk of suit or challenge because competitors almost feel compelled to dispute the claim. If the claim deals with technical aspects of the product, such as the number of calories, amount of vitamins, or cleaning ability, scientific evidence is required. However, if the claim deals with consumer preference or perceptions, consumer research is required.

The appropriate form of consumer research to substantiate a comparative performance claim is typically one of the comparative product tests described in Chapter 11. For example, to support a superiority claim for preference, the research must show that a statistically greater number of consumers prefer the advertised brand than prefer the other brand(s). Further support is garnered if only a small percentage of the consumers expressed "no preference" and if the advertised brand demonstrates superiority on important product attributes as well.

To support parity preference claims, the research must show that at least as many people preferred the advertised brands as the reference brands. A parity claim of no difference between the brands would require some form of product discrimination test as discussed in Chapter 11, perhaps a triangle difference test. Results must indicate a very low level of discrimination between the brands.

It is possible to research a comparative claim using a noncomparative product test. For example, the claim "orange juice that tastes as good as fresh-squeezed" could be tested using a monadic test. Consumers could be asked to taste the orange juice, and the percentage of those consumers who agreed with the statement "tastes as good as fresh-squeezed" would provide the claim substantiation data. However, the use of a single-product test to provide evidence for a comparative claim will provide weaker evidence than if the claim is tested using a comparative test. For the above claim, stronger evidence would be provided if the juice is tested against fresh-squeezed juice, and no taste preference for the fresh-squeezed alternative is found.

NonComparative Performance Claims

A **noncomparative performance claim** specifies or implies a consumer benefit or product value for the brand with no reference to another product. These claims might be preparation benefits ("cooks in five minutes"), benefits to users ("fresher breath"), or literal product descriptions ("long-lasting taste"). Again, scientific evidence may suffice to support the claim, but if consumer perceptions are involved, then consumer data are necessary.

A single-product test, in which consumers experience the brand advertised, can be appropriate to test a noncomparative performance claim. After usage, most consumers should agree with the claim. However, a noncomparative performance claim is difficult to support in this way, because there will always be some proportion who do not agree with the claim. If the claim is subsequently challenged, the company may have to qualify the claim somewhat to indicate that the claim applies to "the majority," or a certain percentage, of people.

Market Performance Claims

A **market performance claim** relates to popularity, usage, or competitive position. Data used to support these claims must be market performance data, such as sales, market share, usage, or preference. Market performance claims are often challenged by competitors because of the type of data used to support the claim. That is, the ability of a particular brand of pain reliever to say that it is the most preferred brand in Chicago might depend upon whether brand usage (obtained from survey data), or market share (obtained from product movement data) was used to support the claim. Furthermore, different usage levels, preference levels, or market shares can be calculated depending upon whether the results apply to all consumers in Chicago or to only a subsegment of the population. If challenged, a company may have to modify the claim to reflect the nature of the data used to collect it or the fact that it only applies to a portion of the population.

What is Deceptive Advertising?

A second aspect of advertising claims that comes under scrutiny is whether the advertisement is deceptive. **Deceptive advertising** is advertising that contains a material representation, omission, or practice that is likely to mislead reasonable consumers. You might think that the existence of evidence to support a claim indicate that there is no deception, but that is not necessarily so. A substantiated claim can still be ruled to be deceptive and a grossly false claim may not.

Obviously, an advertisement can be deceptive if the claim made is not true. For instance, an ad is deceptive if it claims that the advertised brand has an ingredient or provides a benefit that it does not, as was the charge levied by the FTC against Solar Gold Tanner, which claimed that its tanning beds were safer than tanning under the sun because they did not emit ultraviolet radiation.[29] An advertisement is also deceptive if it exaggerates the benefits of an ingredient that the brand has, such as the claim made for the Fuel Magnetizer that it would yield a 25 percent increase in gas mileage, a claim which the FTC ruled was an overstatement of the truth.[30] However, the presence of a false claim does not **always** mean that the advertisement will be deceptive. False claims are only illegal if they might deceive consumers. Thus, blatantly false statements or claims which no one would believe, such as "this car flies," are not deceptive.

A false claim is not the only reason an advertisement may be ruled to be deceptive. Even if every word or claim is true, an advertisement may be determined to be deceptive if the ad does not disclose something else about the product that offsets the claim or if the perception caused by the claim is false. For example, American Home Products' slogan that hospitals recommend "acetaminophen, the aspirin-free pain reliever in Anacin-3, more than any other pain reliever" was ruled to be misleading because, even though the statement is true, the court felt that consumers might not know that the brand of acetaminophen pain reliever that hospitals recommend most often is Tylenol, not Anacin-3.[31]

Finally, an advertisement can be deceptive due to the way in which a claim is presented or depicted, even if the claim is true. For example, in producing a commercial for Campbell's Soup, clear marbles were placed in the soup bowl to cause the vegetables to be more visible. The commercial was ruled to be deceptive. Similarly, Volvo Cars of America attempted to demonstrate the strength of the Volvo car body by creating a commercial where it alone withstood being crushed by a 10,000 pound "monster truck." In producing the commercial, however, the Volvo was reinforced while the other cars were altered to make them crush more easily.[32] The commercial was ruled to be deceptive. Neither Campbell's nor Volvo intended to deceive the consumer. Campbell's merely wished to make the ingredients in the soup bowl more visible in the commercial. The Volvo car body actually will withstand 10,000 pounds, but was reinforced because of the multiple "takes" necessary during the production of the commercial. However, intent to deceive is not a necessary condition for deception. An advertisement is deceptive if reasonable consumers will be misled.

The Consequences of Deceptive Advertising

The potential costs of deceptive advertising are high. Besides having the power to require a company to "cease and desist," i.e., quit running advertising that is found to be false and misleading, the FTC is empowered to levy severe financial penalties. In one case, U-Haul was awarded a $40 million settlement when it was ruled that the advertising claim by Jartran that their moving rats were lower was false. The size of the settlement sent Jartran into bankruptcy.[33]

FTC-imposed penalties are not the only consequence of deceptive advertising. The adverse publicity surrounding a negative judgement can result in substantial sales losses or a drop in stock prices. Problems might also be created among suppliers or the trade. For all of these reasons, advertising is subjected to a great deal of testing.

Summary

Audience size and composition are basic but crucial considerations when deciding where to advertise. Various marketing research syndicated services provide information of this nature for magazines, newspapers, radio, and television. The Nielsen Television Index is the most well-known service of this type. These Nielsen ratings, supplemented with audience composition data, are not only vital to marketing managers, they are also the basis for setting television advertising rates for the various shows.

Split-cable systems are particularly useful for evaluating alternative television spending levels and/or different television commercials. Test markets, discussed in Chapter 14, are used to assess alternative advertising campaigns. However, both of these forms of marketing research are expensive and time-consuming and thus not appropriate for evaluating the relative effectiveness of individual television commercials.

The increasing cost of advertising, particularly television advertising, makes it imperative that copy be effective. This underscores the important role of marketing research, not only in assessing the effectiveness of copy, but also throughout the development process. Obviously, uncovering copy problems early in the process saves both time and money. Various copy testing systems are used to evaluate individual copy executions.

Besides testing the effectiveness of advertising copy, companies must be able to demonstrate that claims made in the copy are truthful and can be substantiated by evidence. Sometimes scientific evidence is required, but many times the evidence comes from marketing research. The most appropriate type of research to conduct depends upon the nature of the claim made. In addition to substantiating claims, companies must work to ensure that the final advertising is not viewed to present the claim in a deceptive fashion.

In recent years, technological developments have changed the television industry, raising concerns among advertisers. Cable television has dramatically increased the number options, including some that do not contain any advertising, and fragmented once-large network audiences. Even more of a premium has been placed on advertising time on highly popular network shows that still deliver large audiences.

Add to this the growing use of VCRs, which provide viewers the ability to "zap" commercials when viewing prerecorded material, and you begin to appreciate the concern among marketing managers over the value of television advertising. The Internet has added a new ingredient to the media mix. As discussed in Chapter 5, new terms are emerging to refer to advertising on the Internet, and methods for determining advertising costs for this medium are still under development and discussion. One thing seems certain - advertising on the Internet will grow rapidly. The future promises an even more challenging advertising environment for both the marketing manager and the marketing researcher.

Key Terms:

Advertising claim
Audit Bureau of Circulation
clutter reels
comparative performance claim
copy testing
Day-After Recall (DAR)
deceptive advertising
Designated Marketing Areas (DMAs)
gross rating points (GRPs)
intrusiveness
market performance claim
Nielsen Station Index
Nielsen Television Index
noncomparative performance claim
parity claim
persuasion
product improvement claim
rating point
reliability
split-cable systems
Starch scores
superiority claim
validity

Testing Nimslo's Introductory Television Commercial

The unique challenge to Nimslo in developing TV copy was to communicate three-dimensionality in a two-dimensional medium. The advertising had to communicate that the system produced photographs that appeared 3D to the naked eye. Could a television commercial produce the illusion of 3D?

The same special-effects expert who worked on the film "Star Wars" was consulted to develop the illusion of 3D within an ordinary television commercial. The result was a unique special effect, referred to at Nimslo as the "emerge," which was used in the television commercial.

Marketing research conducted by Nimslo to evaluate its TV copy indicated that the emerge was effective and memorable. This research is the basis for Case IV.1.

Review Questions

15.1 Define a gross rating point (GRP). What do GRPs basically measure?

15.2 What is meant by a "people meter"? How have people meters changed the process of measuring TV audience size and composition?

15.3 Give an example of a product and a service that would be most effectively advertised by each of the following media: radio, television, and magazine. Give a rationale for each of your choices.

15.4 What is meant by a split-cable market? Why are they useful in marketing research?

15.5 What is the difference between circulation and coverage as measurements of radio audience size?

15.6 Define intrusiveness and persuasion.

15.7 Why was intrusiveness the dominant issue in copy evaluation for so long?

15.8 What is a DAR test? How does it work, and what does it measure?

15.9 What is a clutter reel and how is it used in marketing research?

15.10 Describe the BAT approach to evaluating the persuasiveness of TV commercials.

15.11 What are the three types of Starch scores, and what does each measure?

15.12 What is meant by the reliability of a copy test measurement? How is reliability established?

15.13 What is meant by the validity of a copy test measurement?

15.14 What is meant by a comparative performance claim? What are the requirements for research used to substantiate comparative performance claims?

15.15 What is meant by a noncomparative performance claim? What are the requirements for research used to substantiate noncomparative performance claims?

15.16 What is meant by a market performance claim? What are the requirements for research used to substantiate a market performance claim?

15.17 What is meant by deceptive advertising? What conditions lead to an ad being deceptive? What are the consequences of deceptive advertising?

Discussion Questions

15.1 What do Nielsen ratings measure? Discuss the importance of these ratings to the television industry and advertisers.

15.2 Discuss factors that must be considered when making advertising media decisions. What particular information sources are useful in this context?

15.3 Discuss the role of norms in evaluating copy test results. Why are norms so important?

15.4 Discuss the ARS process for measuring the intrusiveness and the persuasiveness of a TV commercial.

15.5 Describe how companies have addressed the issue of the validity of measures of copy persuasiveness.

15.6 Describe the ASI and Gallup & Robinson approaches to measuring the effectiveness of TV commercials. What are the pros and cons of these two services relative to those offered by McCollum/Spielman and ARS?

15.7 Discuss the measurement of radio audiences. What services are available and how do they differ from each other?

15.8 Discuss the issue of advertising effectiveness in general. What criteria exist? What conflicts exist? What are the measurement problems?

15.9 For each of the following advertising claims, indicate the type of claim being made, what type of research evidence would be appropriate to substantiate the claim, and what research procedure you would use.

a) "The plumper hot dog."

b) "Cleans better than the leading brand."

c) "The taste more people prefer."

d) "The bread with the homemade taste."

e) "The chip with the zesty taste."

f) "The number-one hot dog in the South."

15.10 At one time Pizza Hut ran an advertising campaign that poked fun at Domino's Pizza. The commercials included scenes showing Domino's employees ordering pizza for delivery and the Pizza Hut delivery number replacing Domino's number on people's phonebooks, refrigerators, and so on. The jingle for the commercial urged consumers to "change for the better change for the best." The claim was based on mall-intercept taste tests comparing Pizza Hut pepperoni pan pizza and Domino's regular pepperoni pizza. Domino's Pizza challenged the claim. Discuss the aspects of the research that Domino's might challenge and what research they might undertake to strengthen their position.

Chapter 15

Endnotes

1. See, for example, J. Thomas Russell, Glenn Verrill, and W. Ronald Lane, *Kleppner's Advertising Procedure*, 10th ed. Englewood Cliffs, NJ: Prentice-Hall, 1988, p. 666.
2. See Robert M. Ogles and Herbert H. Howard, "Keeping Up w
3. See, for example, William Wells, John Burnett and Sandra Moriarity, *Advertising Principles and Practices*. Englewood Cliffs, NJ: Prentice-Hall, 1989, p. 255.
4. Wayne Walley, "MTV Network vs. the People Meter," *Advertising Age*, June 26, 1989, p. 59.
5. Harold W. Berkman and Christopher Gilson, *Advertising*, 2nd ed. New York: Random House, 1987, p. 283.
6. *Ibid*, p. 286.
7. William Wells, John Burnett and Sandra Moriarity, *Advertising Principles and Practices*. Englewood Cliffs, NJ: Prentice-Hall, 1989, pp. 264-5.
8. Donna Petrozello, "Arbitron, SRI Drop Joint Ratings Plan," *Broadcasting & Cable*, August 19, 1996, p. 42
9. See Alan D. Fletcher and Thomas A. Bowers, "Fundamentals of Advertising Research," Balmont, CA: Wadsworth Publishing Co., 1991, pp. 245-268 for a thorough discussion of media audience size and message effectiveness research services.

10. *Ibid*, p. 277.

11. Donna Petrozello, "Arbitron Moves to Offer Audio Measuring," *Broadcasting & Cable*, August 26, 1996, p. 38.

12. See William F. Arens and Courtland L. Bovée, "Contemporary Advertising," 5th ed., Burr Ridge, IL: Richard D. Irvin, 1994, p. 423 for a discussion of services measuring print audiences.

13. See John Pfeiffer, "Six Months and Half a Million Dollars, All for 15 Seconds," *Smithsonian* 18 (October 1987), pp. 134-139.

14. Jean Halliday, "Imagine That: Mercury Clarifies Its Muddy Image," *Advertising Age*, October 6, 1997, p. 4.

15. See Murphy A. Sewall and Dan Sarel, "Characteristics of Radio Commercials and Their Recall Effectiveness," *Journal of Marketing* 50 (January 1986), pp. 52-60, for a study of the impact of various characteristics of a radio commercial on recall.

16. See Margaret Henderson Blair, Allan R. Kuse, David H. Furse, and David W. Stewart, "Advertising in a New Competitive Environment: Persuading Customers to Buy," *Business Horizons*, (November-December 1987), pp. 20-26.

17. See Marcy Magiera, "Admen Question Carnation Plan,"

Advertising Age, March 13, 1989, p. 4.

18. See Anthony Vagnoni, "Creative Differences," *Advertising Age*, November 17, 1997, p. 1 and Eric Marder, "Ads As Pieces of Art, Not Tools for Selling," *Advertising Age*, November 17, 1997, p. 46 for discussion of the art versus science debate regarding advertising.

19. BAT (Brand Advertising Test) is a research service offered by Kenneth Hollander Associates, Inc., a custom market research firm located in Atlanta, Georgia.

20. Joe Mandese, "Seinfeld Nears Price Ceiling as Sophomore Shows Soar," *Advertising Age*, September 15, 1997, pp. 1, 18.

21. See Benjamin Lipstein, "An Historical Perspective of Copy Research," *Journal of Advertising Research* 24 (December 1984), pp. 11-15.

22. Ronald Conlin, "Goodyear Advertising Research: Past, Present and Future," *Journal of Advertising Research*, May/June 1994, pp. RC7-10.

23. See "Single Versus Double Exposure In Copy Testing...An Experiment," Research Systems Corporation, Evansville, IN, technical report, March, 1983.

24. See David A. Aaker and John G. Myers, *Advertising Management*, 3rd ed. Englewood Cliffs, NJ: Prentice-Hall, 1987, p. 410.

25. *Ibid.*, p. 412.

26. "Global ARS Reliability of ARS PERSUASION and Diagnostics," Evansville, IN: research systems corporation, 1995.

27. See Kevin J. Clancy and Lyman E. Ostlund, "Commercial Effectiveness Measures," *Journal of Advertising Research* 16 (February 1976), pp. 29-34.

28. See Anthony J. Adams and Margaret Henderson Blair, "Persuasive Advertising And Sales Accountability: Past Experience and Forward Validation," *Journal of Advertising Research* 32-2 (March/April 1992), pp. 20-25, for a discussion of the validity of the ARS PERSUASION measure.

29. Laurie Freeman and Janet Myers, "FTC Gets Tough on Catalog Claims," *Advertising Age*, November 12, 1990, p. 73.

30. *Ibid.*

31. *Wall Street Journal*, May 13, 1987, p. 33.

32. Raymond Serafin and Gary Levin, "Ad Industry Suffers Crushing Blow: Volvo Faces FTC Inquiry Over Rigged Cars in 'Monster Truck' Ads," *Advertising Age*, November 12, 1990, pp. 1 & 76.

33. Cyndee Miller, "Ads Must Back Up Their Claims – Or Pay the Legal Price," *Marketing News*, February 1, 1988, p. 22.

Chapter 16

Sales Promotions

Learning Objectives:

After reading this chapter, you should be able to:

- o define the available types of consumer promotions.
- o explain how consumer promotions can be pretested and evaluated with marketing research.
- o describe how marketing research assists in the pretesting and evaluation of trade promotions.

Product sampling, giving free trial quantities of a brand to consumers, has long been one of the most successful, but most expensive, promotional tools. In spite of its high costs, more and more companies are using sampling. These newer efforts are a far cry from the old days when a person gave out tastes of a food product inside a supermarket, as the following examples illustrate.

Edy's sent young people dressed in leafy Adam and Eve costumes to roam the streets of various cities to distribute samples of a new lowfat yogurt while Pace picante sauce was similarly distributed by cowboys and cowgirls from the back of chuckwagons. Gatorade even ran two sampling campaigns simultaneously. Samples of their Frost flavor line were distributed in cities by employees dressed as backpackers traveling in specially-designed vans while 500,000 packets of their Stix instant drink mix were given out to construction workers, road crews, and others by blue-jean-wearing men traveling in sports utility vehicles and trucks.

Other, even more expensive, sampling programs were undertaken by Nabisco, Pepsi, and Coca-Cola. Nabisco handed out samples of their Triscuits, Ritz, and Wheat Thins brands at more than 40 events in 20 cities and gave aways over 1.6 million sample bags of their Air Crisp brand at concerts, beaches, and summer festivals in 21 markets. Pepsi sponsored an All City Hip Hop Van Tour from a fleet of customized vans having giant see-through plexi-coolers, a 50,000 watt stereo system, and 27-inch video monitors. To promote their Fruitopia brand, the Coca-Cola Company sponsored a 60-city tour in their own customized fleet of vans. The tour included mimes on roller blades, musicians (including one who sang rap music in Japanese), and improvisational comedians and was estimated to cost nearly $30 million.

These are but a few of the examples of sampling efforts recently undertaken by U.S. companies. As these efforts grow in complexity and size, the total amount spent by U.S.

companies on product sampling approaches one billion dollars annually. Therefore, more attention is being given to researching the impact and cost/benefit of these and other promotions.[1]

A **sales promotion** is any direct inducement to distributors or consumers with the primary objective of creating an immediate sale. Sales promotions can be divided into two categories, depending on the specific audience targeted. Promotions such as coupons, rebates, games, and contests that are directed at the ultimate user of the brand are classified as **consumer promotions.** Promotions, such as case allowances and co-op advertising, that are directed at distributors of the brand are called **trade promotions.**

The percentage of the advertising and promotional budget that companies allocate to sales promotions has steadily increased in recent years. Currently, as shown in Exhibit 16.1, consumer and trade promotions together comprise nearly three-fourths of the total budget.[2] This emphasis on consumer and trade promotions is projected to continue over the next several years.

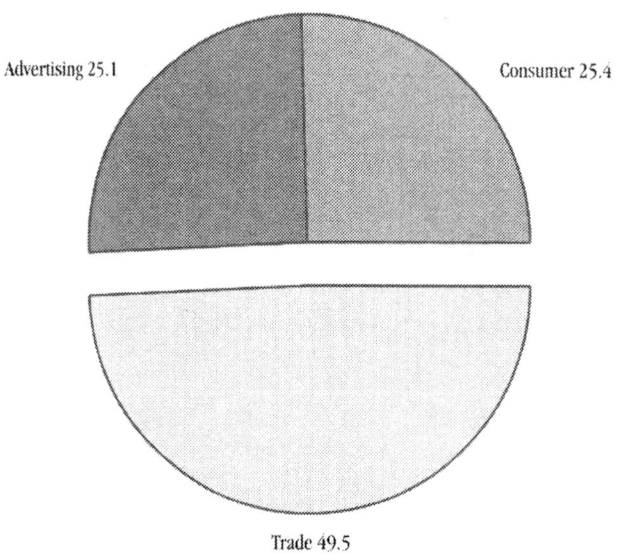

Exhibit 16.1
The promotional pie, 1991. (Source: Donnelley 14th Annual Survey of Promotional Practices).

Several factors have contributed to the shift from advertising to sales promotions. First, media costs have skyrocketed. Promotions, which typically cost only a fraction of this amount, have thus become a very economical alternative to advertising.

Second, managers who are concerned with short-run brand performance can manipulate a brand's sales or short-term market share easier with promotions than with advertising. Advertising tends to be more effective for enhancing or establishing the image of a brand than for producing immediate sales. Conversely, most promotions are designed to stimulate immediate sales.

Third, many of the new brands being introduced into the marketplace are parity products — products that are identical, or very similar to, existing competitive brands. Parity brands usually require a great deal of promotional effort, because their sales tend to be extremely price- sensitive.

Finally, manufacturers are finding that they have less influence over the trade than in the past, so that more inducements are necessary to get their brands distributed. The dominance of high-volume national chains and more sophisticated buying practices have increased the economic power of the trade. Chain stores buy in larger quantities, giving them more bargaining leverage. The information provided by electronic scanning helps stores determine the profitability of various brands that are carried. Manufacturers are finding that trade promotions are a necessary incentive to gain distribution and that the trade expects adequate levels of consumer promotion to guarantee sufficient sales volume.

As the amount of money being spent on sales promotions has increased, so has the manager's need for information about sales promotions. Not every promotion is effective. As Applying Marketing Research 16.1, 16.2, and 16.3 demonstrate, unsuccessful promotions can cost the company a great deal of money and possibly a loss of consumer goodwill.

Applying Marketing Research 16.1

In conjunction with the 1988 Summer Olympics, McDonald's reran a promotion that had proven to be highly successful during the 1984 games. Customers received a game card with each purchase that, when rubbed, revealed one of the Olympic events. If the U.S. athlete entered in that event won a medal, customers could redeem the game card for a food item that varied depending upon the medal won. The 1988 contest was not nearly as successful as anticipated.

The difference in time zones between Seoul, Korea, the site of the 1988 Olympic games, and the United States made live television coverage of many of the premier Olympic events difficult during prime time. Much of the air time was devoted to covering the less glamorous events, and television audiences were much smaller than had been hoped. The effect was that the American public was not as aware of the outcomes as they had been in 1984 when the Olympics were held in Los Angeles, creating less interest in McDonald's game.

Applying Marketing Research 16.2

When Kraft ran a sweepstakes for one of its cheeses, a printing foul-up caused 500 thousand winning cards to be issued. Instead of costing the approximately $36,000 that had been budgeted for the winning prizes, Kraft spent several million dollars recovering the promotion packages, canceling the promotion, and reaching a settlement with the many people who thought they had won.[3]

Applying Marketing Research 16.3

Burger King offered a premium for children that was tied in with "Ghostbusters," a popular movie at the time about a company that exorcized, or "busted" ghosts. The premium was a small toy that made noise, gave off light, and was designed to allow children to "bust" ghosts like in the movie. During the course of the promotion, it was discovered that children could easily remove the toy's battery. Although the promotion was very successful in attracting customers, Burger King withdrew it and offered to buy back premiums that had been sold due to their concern that small children might swallow the battery.

As the opening vignette to this chapter mentioned, the growing importance of sales promotions in marketing strategy and the increased monies spent on them has caused companies to become more concerned with evaluating sales promotions. These companies have turned to marketing research to provide the answers. Research techniques used for consumer and trade promotions often differ because the objectives and information needs vary between these promotion types. Therefore, we will examine these two promotion types separately.

Types of Consumer Promotions

A wide variety of consumer sales promotion options are at the manufacturer's disposal. The most common forms are displayed in Figure 16.1. These are:

- **value packs** — additional amounts of the brand provided free on purchase of the regular amount;
- **samples** — free quantities of the brand given to consumers, often through the mail;
- **premiums** — gifts that brands offer consumers, either free or for a reduced price;
- **point-of-purchase (POP) promotions** — displays, demonstrations, or special signs that are placed in stores;
- **price-offs** — direct price reductions or rebates offered to purchasers;
- **coupons** — certificates, typically distributed by mail or newspaper, that offer the consumer a reduced price on the brand;
- **prizes** — competitions in which entrants can win cash or merchandise;
- **tie-in promotions** — promotional offer for one brand typically contingent on the purchase of a complementary brand.

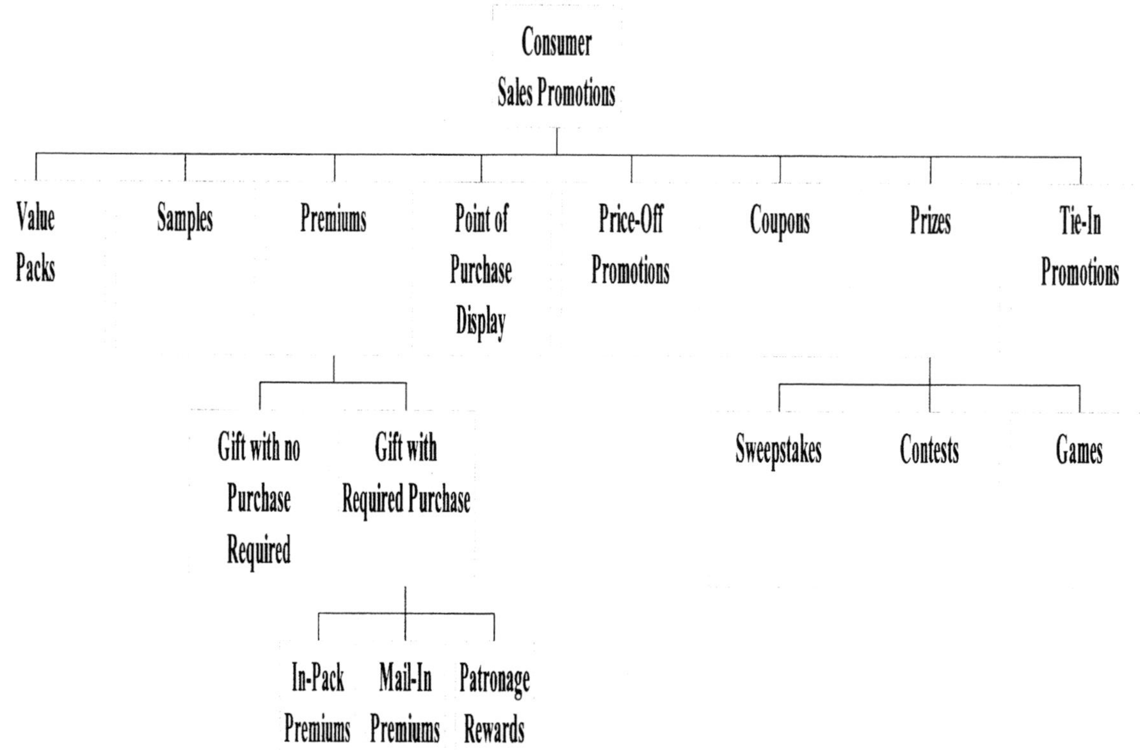

Figure 16.1
Typology of Consumer Sales Promotion

As Table 16.1 illustrates, the type of consumer promotion best suited to a given situation depends on the specific objective the company sets for the promotion. Most of the objectives listed in Table 16.1 are designed to increase short-run sales by getting nonusers to try the brand, getting users to buy larger amounts, or stimulating unplanned purchases. Promotions used in such situations are designed either to clear the distribution pipeline of excess inventory or to defend against the marketing efforts of a competing brand. For example, one common strategy to discourage purchasing of a competitor's new brand is to promote an existing brand heavily, hoping that consumers will stock up on the promoted brand and be less likely to try the new one.

Objective	Types of consumer promotions						
	POP	Coupons	Samples	Price-offs	Contests	Premiums	Bonus packs
To generate product trial	*	*	*	*	*		
To convert triers to users	*			*			*
To encourage larger purchases		*		*		*	*
To stimulate unplanned purchases	*	*	*		*		*
To increase acceptance of trade deal				*	*		
To improve advertising effectiveness					*		
To enhance brand image					*	*	

Table 16.1
Consumer promotion types best suited for various objectives

Two of the objectives listed in Table 16.1, increasing the effectiveness of an advertising campaign and enhancing the image of the brand, tend to be longer-term in nature. A promotion might create excitement among target market consumers and, as a result, increase the effectiveness of the advertising campaign used in conjunction with the promotion. Similarly, a promotion might be used to enhance the perceived value of the brand to the consumer, thereby increasing brand loyalty or improving the image that consumers have of the brand.

The long-term impact of a promotion is not easy to measure. A shift in brand loyalty or brand image or an increase in sales during the advertising campaign may be hard to attribute directly to the promotion. Because these promotions are designed to reinforce or strengthen the positioning of the brand to the target audience, the impact on sales is less apparent than for promotions having a short-term sales objective.

Consumer Promotions for Increasing Short-Run Sales

As you can see in Exhibit 16.2, a brand's sales volume in any time period is the product of three components: the number of different people who buy the brand during the time period, the average number of times each person buys the brand during the time period, and the average amount each person buys at each purchase occasion. Therefore, a company can increase short-run brand sales by increasing any of these three components. That is, sales will increase if more people buy the brand, if users purchase the brand more frequently, if consumers buy larger amounts of the brand each time, or because of some combination of all of these factors. The best type of consumer promotion to use depends to some extent on which components are targeted.

Sales = (number of purchasers) x (average number of purchase occasions) x (average amount purchased each occasion)

Exhibit 16.2
The components of sales volume.

Several promotion types work especially well if the objective is to increase the number of users of the brand, that is, to get nonusers of the product category to try the brand or to get users of competitive brands to switch. A point-of-purchase (POP) promotion, such as the special brand display shown in Exhibit 16.3, is a good choice, as are coupons, like the one shown in Exhibit 16.4, samples, price-off promotions, contests, or tie-in promotions.

Exhibit 16.3
Point-of-purchase promotions can be extremely effective in generating brand sales.

Exhibit 16.4
Manufacturers distribute billions of coupons annually.

To be successful, brands in frequently purchased product categories must obtain a high level of repeat purchase. Because of the cost savings to the consumer, coupons, price-off promotions, and value packs are very effective at converting triers to repeat purchasers or for increasing the frequency of purchase of the brand. These three promotions, as well as the use of premiums, also are effective at encouraging current buyers to purchase larger quantities of the brand, which often results in increased consumption of the brand.

Consumers often select a particular brand within a product category once they get to the store. Such in-store decision making makes POP promotions effective at increasing the sales of a brand because attention is drawn to the brand. POP promotions, coupons, price promotions, premiums, or tie-in promotions can also stimulate unplanned purchases within product categories by causing the consumer to buy sooner than had been planned in order to take advantage of the premium offer, the price savings, or the complementarity of the brand with another product purchased.

Manufacturers continually try to obtain better in-store locations or local advertising support from retailers. Consumer price promotions or contests are often used to solicit such trade support. These consumer promotions increase retailers' willingness to agree to a trade requirement, such as installing a special display, because they have more confidence that consumer sales will increase sufficiently to offset any costs associated.

Consumer Promotions for Longer-Term Objectives

Contests or premiums are especially effective for long-term, image, or advertising enhancement objectives. Applying Marketing Research 16.4 and 16.5 demonstrate how contests can enhance the image of a brand or improve the effectiveness of an advertising campaign.

Applying Marketing Research 16.4

One successful long-running contest was Canadian Club's "Hide-a-Case" promotion, shown in Exhibit 16.5. Hiram Walker began this promotion in 1967 when a case of Canadian Club was dropped by parachute onto Mt. Kilimanjaro. Magazine advertising provided clues to the whereabouts of the case, and the person discovering the case got to keep it. The promotion continued for many years, with cases being hidden in both exotic and common locations. In addition, in 1979, a "C.C. Hawaii Sweepstakes" was combined with the contest, and twenty-five winners of the sweepstakes won a trip to Hawaii to hunt for a hidden case of Canadian Club. The "Hide-a-Case" promotion has helped position Canadian Club as a unique imported whiskey that appeals to adventurous spirits.[4]

Exhibit 16.5
This example will show the magazine advertisement for the Canadian Club whiskey which describes how to win the contest by finding the hidden case of whiskey. This long-running promotion helped give Canadian Club a distinctive image. (Courtesy of Hiram Walker and Sons, Limited.)

Applying Marketing Research 16.5

In West Germany, television commercials run in blocks lasting about seven minutes instead of being interspersed throughout the programming as is done in the United States. Procter & Gamble, concerned about the recall of its advertising in Germany due to this advertising difference, felt that something needed to be done to make consumers pay more attention to its commercials. Thus, they initiated a contest.

Procter & Gamble bought an entire seven-minute block, during which seemingly familiar P&G commercials were aired. However, five of the commercials were altered. For example, an Ariel brand detergent commercial was changed so that a woman soils her clothing while riding an elephant instead of while jogging. Viewers mailing in the correct list of altered commercials were entered into a contest drawing. The large number of entrants Procter & Gamble received for the contest provided evidence that consumers were paying attention to the commercials.[5]

Premiums come in a variety of forms, from giveaways of items containing a brand's logo to free merchandise upon purchase of the brand. Not all premiums generate long-term loyalty or increase brand image, but one form, patronage loyalty, or patronage reward, programs do. **Patronage reward programs** encourage regular use of the brand by providing points or credits that can be redeemed for premiums such as merchandise, discounts, or cash. These programs have become extremely popular in recent years and much of their growth can be attributed to the success of the airline industry's frequent flier programs. Another very successful program, the American Express Membership Rewards program, is described in Applying Marketing Research 16.6.

Applying Marketing Research 16.6

Like many such programs, the American Express Membership Reward program gives customers one point of credit for every dollar spent with any of the various American Express cards. The points do not expire and there is no limit on the number of points that can be accrued. In operation since 1991, the American Express Membership Rewards program has been expanded to cover a wide range of premium offers.

Members receive a 30-page catalog offering premiums from over 50 different retail partners. Members can receive frequent flyer or frequent guest points from any of twelve participating airlines or six hotels, free car rentals, gift certificates for any of 20 major retailers, sports-related merchandise, gourmet food, or even free vacations.

Extremely successful, this program now has over 6 million members. Research has also revealed that members' spending increases 25 percent or more in the first year of enrollment. The program has been found to appeal to a wide audience and strengthens American Express's relationships with both their customers and retail partners.[6]

A secondary advantage of patronage reward programs is the wealth of data that companies can accumulate about the members and their purchasing patterns. Thirdly, such programs can assist independent retailers in competing with larger chains. For instance, one local grocer in a small Southern market saw an erosion of sales when Wal-Mart opened. Examination of its frequent-shopper data revealed that it had lost 50 percent of its customers to Wal-Mart. Instituting a continuity offer for a few weeks helped gain back most of the defecting customers.[7] Such quick actions are difficult for larger chains to implement.

Researching Consumer Promotions

U.S. companies spend over $70 billion each year on consumer promotions, and, as some of the examples in this chapter have illustrated, not all of these promotions are successful. Historically, little research was conducted on promotions either to investigate how effective a promotion was likely to be prior to implementing it or to evaluate the performance of promotions after they were concluded. As one author bemoaned, "It seems that sales promotion is one of the few areas of marketing in which evaluation is done on a 'seat of the pants' basis, if at all."[8] However, as expenditures have increased and promotions have become more complex, companies today are turning to research to pretest proposed promotions and to evaluate the effectiveness of promotions that have been run.

Pretesting Consumer Promotions

Promotion pretesting involves research prior to running a promotion to assess the likely results. The major reason for pretesting consumer promotions is to determine if the promotion will achieve its objectives. While a manager might argue that pretesting is not necessary because similar promotions run in the past were successful, past success does not guarantee future success, as Applying Marketing Research 16.1 illustrated. Therefore, promotions that involve a major allocation of funds or, if unsuccessful, might have a negative impact on how consumers view the brand should be pretested.

Focus Groups and Mall-Intercept Interviews

Quick and inexpensive pretests of promotional ideas can be conducted using focus groups or mall-intercept interviews. Focus groups are useful for developing promotional ideas. Then, mall-intercept interviewing might be used to assess consumer interest in various promotion ideas quantitatively to screen the proposed promotions down to those that have the highest appeal. However, as in product testing, the best indicator of a proposed promotion's effectiveness is actually to test consumer reaction to the promotion in the marketplace.

Market Tests

Market testing of promotions is done using experimental formats like those described in Chapter 3. The impact of the promotion may be estimated by comparing the behavior of a group of people after they have been exposed to the promotion to their behavior prior to the promotion (known as a pre-post design). At other times the change in the behavior of the group exposed to the promotion is compared to any change in behavior occurring in a group not exposed to the promotion (known as a pre-post with control group design). Market testing of promotions takes place in two settings.

Store promotions, such as displays or price reductions, are

tested using a controlled-store test. In a **controlled store test**, an in-store experiment is conducted using some stores as test stores and some as control stores. The promotion is run in the test stores, and an equal number of other stores, where the promotion is not run, are chosen as control stores. Sales volumes of the brand are monitored in the test and control stores during the test period, and any difference between the average test and control group sales is attributed to the promotion. The test of the end-of-aisle display for Pringles potato chips that was discussed in Applying Marketing Research 3.3 in Chapter 3 is an example of a controlled-store test. Control stores can be selected to match the test stores on characteristics such as normal brand and category sales volume, demographic composition of shoppers, and store sales volume because such characteristics obviously influence the sales of the product category or brand.

Consumer promotions that take place outside the store environment, such as mail coupons or product samples, are normally pretested using a test market approach. Evaluation of a promotion using a test market format proceeds in a similar fashion to a controlled-store test. That is, the average sales volume to consumers in the market exposed to the promotion is compared to the average sales volume to consumers in the market serving as the control. Test markets are chosen to be similar with respect to characteristics that influence brand sales.

Promotions can also be test marketed within a single market or city. For example, pretesting the impact of coupons offering different amounts off the regular price can be tested by using a split-run approach. In a **split-run**, coupons of varying values are inserted in a newspaper (or magazine) in the usual way, and differences in the redemption rates across the different coupon values are used to estimate the impact of coupon face value.

The ability to alter the marketing efforts across households within a scanner panel makes these panels ideal for consumer promotion experiments. The promotion can be offered to some panel members and not to others. For example, a sample of the brand might be sent to some panel members and not to others. Any difference in the subsequent trial rate of the brand between the two groups of panel members would be attributed to the promotion.

One advantage of using scanner panels for pretesting promotions is that it is also possible to determine who is sensitive to the promotion. That is, the source of the extra sales volume can be traced. For example, management can determine if consumers who responded to the promotion were already loyal to the brand, had switched from another brand, or had not purchased the category previously. This information is obviously crucial in assessing the ability of the promotion to achieve the specific objectives set for it.

Estimating Promotion Synergy

Not only do promotional experiments allow management to isolate the impact of an individual promotion, they also can be used to estimate any synergy, or interaction, created when promotions are used in combination. **Promotion synergy** is a greater total sales effect when using multiple promotions than would be expected from the sum of the individual impacts of each promotion run in isolation. Exhibit 16.6 illustrates the promotion synergy created by an in-store display and a price reduction for Hi-C Fruit Drink used simultaneously.

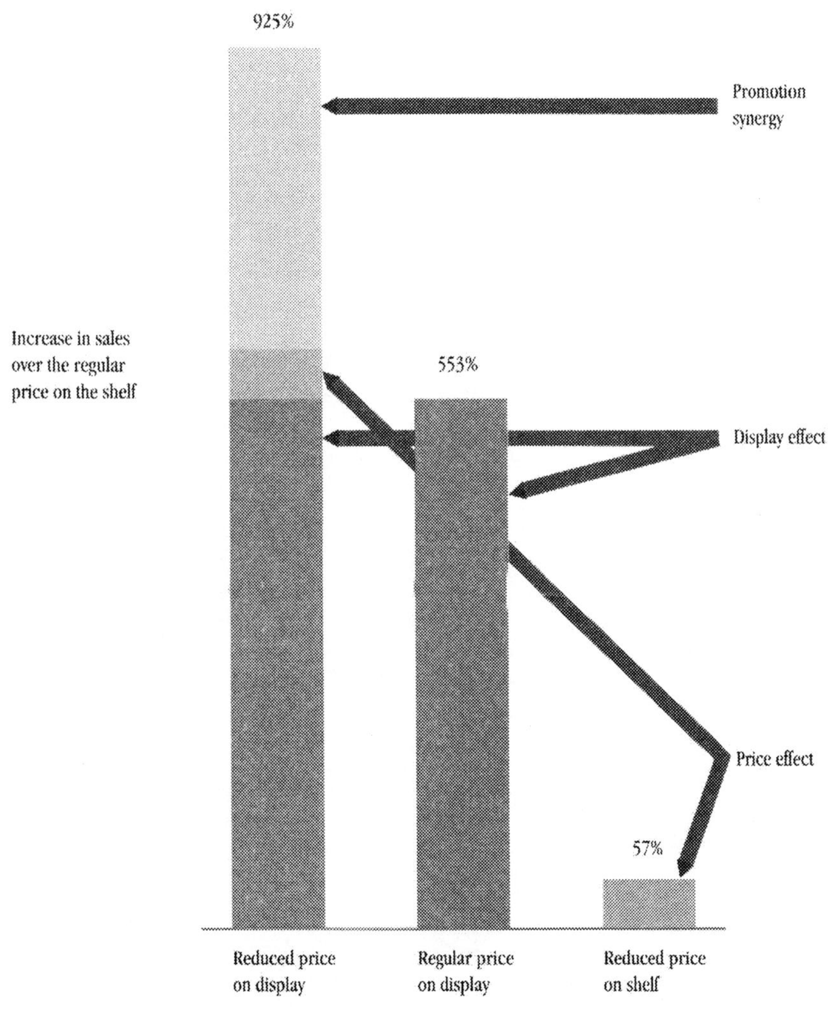

Exhibit 16.6
Example of promotional synergy for Hi-C fruit drink (hypothetical data.)

In stores where Hi-C was reduced in price (but displayed in its on-shelf location), sales increased by 57 percent, and in stores where it was placed on a special end-of-aisle display (but the price was not changed), sales increased by 553 percent. However, in stores where the brand was reduced in price and placed on the end-of-aisle display, sales increased by 925 percent.

If the two promotions created no synergy, the expected sales increase of both a reduced price and an end-of-aisle display would be 610 percent (57% + 553%). The 315 percent additional sales increase (925% - 610%) was caused by the interaction, or synergy, created when the two promotions were used in combination. That is, the two promotions together caused greater sales than the sum of their separate sales effects.

Consumer Promotion Evaluation

Promotion evaluation involves assessing the results of a promotional campaign after the promotion has been completed. Promotion evaluation is the only way to learn whether the promotion reached its stated objectives and whether it was worth the money spent for it. Promotion evaluation can also aid in the development of future promotions by identifying those that have tended to work, or not work, particularly well in the past.

Many times, promotions are evaluated based on the level of consumer response to them. Typical measures are the number of coupons redeemed, premiums liquidated, or contest entries. However, most consumer promotions are designed to have impact on short-run sales, so, when possible, incremental sales should be the measure of effectiveness. Only in those cases where a change in short-run sales is hard to determine or where the impact is expected to be longer-term should other measures be used.

Measuring the Sales Impact

Ideally, a brand manager would like to see the promotion results shown in the first panel of Exhibit 16.7, where sales increased during the promotion and stayed above the prepromotion level long after the conclusion of the promotion. However, this pattern of sales response is rare. The more typical sales changes caused by a promotion are depicted in the second, third, and fourth panels of Exhibit 16.7. In these cases, at least some of the increase in sales is merely a cannibalization of future sales.

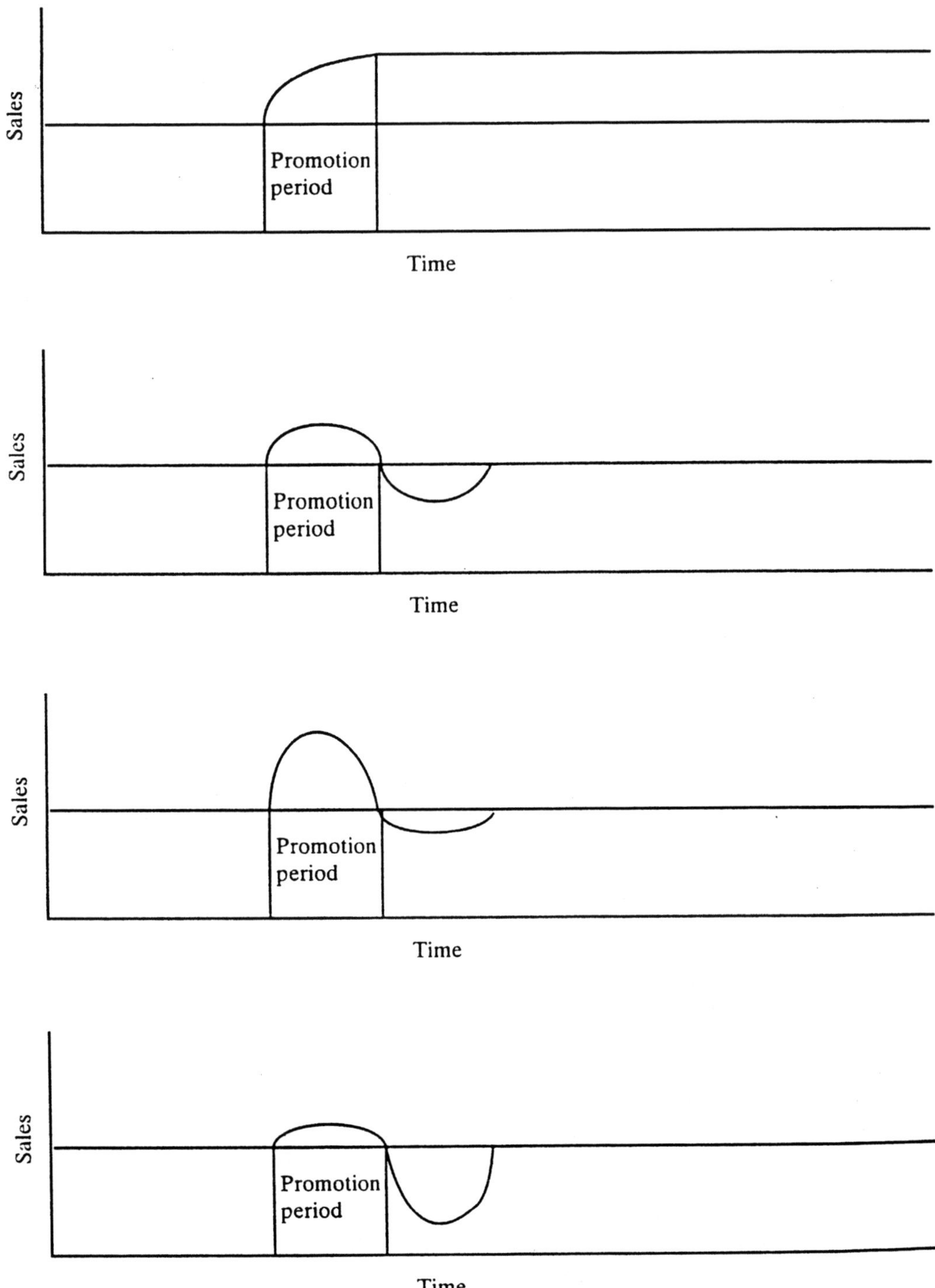

Exhibit 16.7
Short-term promotional impacts.

In the second panel, the sales increase during the promotion is completely offset by a decrease in sales at the conclusion of the promotion. Such an impact might be caused by consumers not increasing consumption of the brand but merely changing the timing of their purchases. Thus, the sales increase during the promotion, caused by consumers stocking up on the brand, is completely offset by the reduction in sales after the promotion, as consumers used up their inventory of the brand. Running a promotion on laundry detergent, for instance, might simply cause consumers who were planning to buy the brand in the near future anyway to purchase during the promotion period. Since it is unlikely that the amount of detergent used by these consumers would increase, sales after the promotion period would go down.

In the third panel of Exhibit 16.7, the sales increase achieved during the promotional period is not completely offset afterwards. This sales pattern is common for many brands and is frequently caused by consumers switching to the promoted brand or using more of the brand than is typical. For example, for products such as snack foods, soft drinks, beer, or ice cream, people may buy more of the product during a promotion and also increase their consumption of the product at the same time. If consumers are not very brand loyal, many may also switch to the promoted brand.

The worst situation is depicted in the fourth panel of Exhibit 16.7, where the sales decline after the promotion is greater than the increase noted during the promotion. Such a situation might occur if consumers buy and consume more of the product during the promotion and become tired of the product, so they do not purchase it again for a relatively long time. A fast-food restaurant that runs a promotion might find a substantial sales decline when the promotion is over, because people stop eating out for some time or go to alternative restaurants for a change of pace.

Sales evaluations of promotions are usually conducted by simply comparing the sales figures for the brand prior to, during, and after the promotion. Internal shipment data might be used in such an evaluation, but store sales data are most commonly used because they more accurately track consumer sales caused by the promotion. Scanner-equipped stores facilitate sales measurement, but syndicated services are also available for measuring sales in many types of stores that are not scanner-equipped. However, depending on the particular mix of stores in which the brand is marketed, custom audits may be required to obtain sales estimates.

Table 16.2 demonstrates how store sales data can be used to estimate the effectiveness of a promotion. As you can see, several sales periods have been included prior to and after the promotional period. Averaging the sales of several periods before and after the promotion eliminates the chance that something unusual occurred in the sales period immediately before or after the promotion that caused sales in those periods to be atypical.

	Sales Periods						
	P-3	P-2	P-1	Promotion	P+1	P+2	P+3
Sales	1003	1028	945	2306	805	911	942

Average sales prior to promotion = (1003 + 1028 +945)/3

= 992

Average sales after promotion = (805 + 911 + 942)/3

= 886

Cannibalization per period = 992 - 886 = 106

Net sales gain due to promotion = 2306 - 992 - (106 x 3) = 996

Net percent gain in sales = 996/992 = 1.0 or 100%

Table 16.2
Example of computing short-term promotional impacts

The difference between the average sales prior to the promotion and the sales achieved each period after the promotion provides an estimate of sales each period that have been cannibalized by the promotion. That is, if the sales levels for several months after the promotion are less than the average sales level prior to the promotion, the promotion has caused some consumers to buy during the promotion and not repurchase as quickly as normal. As the calculations in Table 16.2 show, this promotion did cannibalize future sales by about 268 units, since sales for two of the periods after the promotion were less than the average pre-promotion sales. However, the 2306 units sold during the promotion were 1314 units above the sales volume achieved going into the promotion. Thus, in spite of the slight cannibalization of later sales, the promotion increased sales by a net amount of 1046 units, a 105-percent increase in sales volume.

Estimating Promotional Profits

Promotions are almost never cost-free, so they usually reduce the profit margin of items sold during the promotion. An obvious example would be one in which the promotion involved a reduction in the selling price of the brand. Even those promotions that do not directly change the selling price normally have a cost associated with them that must be covered by additional sales of the brand. Therefore, one critical question that needs to be answered in evaluating a promotion is: How much additional sales volume will be required before the promotion pays for itself?

The answer to the question is fairly straightforward. For example, when the profit margin is cut in half, then sales must double for the promotion to pay for itself. For any reduction in profit margin, promotion profitability can be easily estimated, as Applying Marketing Research 16.7 demonstrates.

Applying Marketing Research 16.7

Suppose that the profit margin per case of Head & Shoulders shampoo is normally $5.00 and that sales typically average 1000 cases per day. If a promotion is being considered that will cost $2.75 per case, how much will sales volume have to increase to cover the cost of the promotion?

By simple subtraction, net profit per case during the promotion would be $2.25. The following formula can be used to figure the sales volume necessary to break even on the promotion:

volume required × promotional margin = normal volume × normal margin or

volume required = normal volume × normal margin/promotional margin

= 1000 cases X ($5.00/$2.25)

= 2223 cases.

Therefore, the promotion would have to generate a 122 percent sales increase [(2223 - 1000)/1000] to break even.

Calculating the incremental sales required to make a promotion cost-effective can keep a company from spending more on a promotion than it is worth. For instance, Pepsi tested two alternative sampling programs in the U.K. In one, consumers were given a free four-pack of Pepsi and, in the other, they were given a free single can. Results revealed that consumers who received the single cans later purchased Pepsi at the same rate as those who received the larger amount. Thus, the company instituted the single-can sampling program, saving substantial amounts of money.[9]

Measuring Long-Term Impact

At present, marketing research information is able to provide only crude estimates of the long-term impact of promotions. Periodic surveys measuring any shifts in consumers' attitudes toward the brand on such factors as perceived value for the money or brand image are often conducted to estimate any changes that might be attributable to past promotional activities. However, scanner panels seem to hold the promise of better evaluation of the long-term impact of promotions.

The ability to monitor individual household purchase and media behavior using scanner panel data and the ability to alter the brand's marketing effort across households allow for detailed tracking of purchase behavior at the household level. As single-source data evolves into a reality, and as marketing researchers become more adept at using this data source, much greater testing of the long-term impact of promotions will occur. Research that alters the value or type of promotion to which a household is exposed to determine the sensitivity of different consumer segments to various promotions will become commonplace.[10] Research will also be able to determine which potential promotions are most effective at switching various types of consumers to a particular brand and to determine how best to make these switchers brand loyal.

The ability to track consumer reactions to promotions over time is a major advantages of the use of patronage programs. Not only do such programs increase loyalty, they also provide a wealth of data about member behavior. These data can provide answers about the long-term value of such programs based on cost and incremental sales over time.

Trade Promotions Research

Trade promotions are designed to increase orders by retailers or other members of the distribution channel or to obtain special short-term merchandising support in exchange for some form of purchase allowance or advertising effort.[11] **Merchandising support** typically takes the form of increased shelf space, display space, a price reduction to consumers, or local advertising. As was shown in Exhibit 16.1, packaged-goods manufacturers spend more money promoting to the trade than on either media advertising or consumer promotions.

Several factors are responsible for this high level of spending on trade promotions. Trade deals became commonplace in the early 1970s when manufacturers artificially inflated list prices due to the threat of government price controls and then rolled back prices to retailers through trade deals.[12] The high inflation rates of the mid- and late-1970s also contributed to an increase in the use of trade deals, as manufacturers frequently raised prices to artificially high levels and dealt against these high levels to remain competitive. Even as inflation rates cooled and the threat of price controls waned, trade deals had become so ingrained in the business relationships between the trade and manufacturers that discounts to the trade had become more a rule than an exception. Furthermore, the shift in the balance of power toward the retailer and away from the manufacturer, which we will discuss later in more detail in Chapter 18, compounded the problem and made it increasingly difficult for companies to reduce their levels of trade promotions.

Applying Marketing Research 16.8

While the use of trade promotions has increased in recent years, their origin is not new. Trade deals were used to increase distribution more than one hundred years ago. In fact, the practice of breweries and distilleries providing trade promotional material to bars such as signs, calendars, and clocks, known as "saloon art," had its origin in a trade promotion run by Anheuser-Busch in 1896.

Adolphus Busch had acquired a 16-foot-by-9-foot canvas painting entitled "Custer's Last Fight" from a bankrupt saloon that owed him money. A smaller 49_-inch-by-39_-inch lithograph was created and an initial run of 15,000 copies was made. These lithographs were given to saloons who agreed to distribute the Budweiser brand.

Although the painting was completely inaccurate in its presentation of the battle, saloons quickly grabbed up the offered lithographs and the Budweiser brand spread across the country. The success of the initial campaign led to its being repeated nearly 20 times in the next eighty years. The last time the campaign was used was in the mid 1970s. At last count, over one million copies of the lithograph had been given away.[13]

The success of a trade promotion depends in part on **deal acceptance**, *i.e.*, the number of distributors who participate in the deal. Success is also a function of how well the trade adheres to any performance requirements of the deal. **Performance requirements** are conditions under which the trade can take advantage of the deal and may involve reducing the price to the consumer, providing

in-store display space, running local advertising, or providing other merchandise support. Pretesting of trade promotions can aid in identifying what factors are necessary to give a trade promotion high acceptance.

Pretesting Trade Promotions

A trade promotion's acceptance rate can easily be measured at the end of a deal period and can be used as one measure of the effectiveness of the promotion. Unfortunately, by that time it is too late to do anything about it — either the promotion was successful or it was not. Of greater importance to management is an understanding of how to tailor a deal that will appeal to the trade and will achieve a high acceptance rate. Not only does such knowledge improve the acceptance rate, it can also improve the overall success of the promotion because the trade is likely to execute merchandising support requirements fully for promotions that they find appealing. Marketing research can be very valuable in pretesting trade promotions to assess promotion appeal.

Trade surveys, as well as focus groups or depth interviews with retailers, can provide insight into what makes a promotion appealing, what the trade likes and doesn't like with respect to trade deals, and how a company's promotions are perceived relative to those of competitors. Armed with this information, the manufacturer can tailor promotions to increase the likelihood of trade acceptance and perhaps the rate of compliance with performance requirements.

Sophisticated research approaches like conjoint analysis, which was described in Chapter 12, can also be used to understand how to make trade promotions appealing. For instance, a manufacturer might study the impact of brand attributes (such as market share, inventory turnover, and retailer margin) and deal attributes (such as the size of the price allowance and the type of performance requirements mandated) on deal acceptance. Using the conjoint results, the manufacturer could determine the tradeoffs necessary to make a deal attractive to the trade and to identify any segments of the trade that differ in the importance attached to various attributes. For example, the manufacturer might find that a brand that is not the market leader and sells slowly, but has a high margin, needs a trade deal offering a high price allowance and very few performance requirements to make the deal attractive to the trade.

Deal acceptance can be enhanced if the benefit of any deal requirements can be demonstrated to retailers. That is, if retailers can be shown that any local advertising they are required to do or any required in-store promotional efforts will increase sales enough to offset the cost, then distributors will be more likely to accept the trade requirements. For this reason, manufacturers often use controlled-store tests or test markets of proposed merchandising efforts to gather data that can be used to substantiate the effectiveness of any deal requirements.

Measuring Effectiveness

As mentioned above, deal acceptance can be used as one measure of the effectiveness of a trade promotion. However, determining whether retailers provided the required merchandising support and consumer promotional efforts can be difficult. The extent to which in-store promotional requirements have been provided can be obtained from the company's sales force, but assessing local advertising support is very difficult unless this information is aggregated by the sales staff as well.

Summary

Companies have a wide range of consumer promotions at their disposal. Sometimes a consumer promotion has a short-run sales objective. At other times, a longer-term image or customer loyalty objective is involved. The more commonly used promotions and the marketing objectives to which they are best suited are shown in Table 16.1.

Two aspects of consumer promotions are researched, consumer interest and promotion effectiveness. Promotion ideas are pretested using focus groups, mall-intercept interviews, or market tests to determine the level of interest in the promotion. At the conclusion of a promotion period, sales data are analyzed to evaluate its effectiveness in terms of incremental sales, cannibalization, and cost-effectiveness.

Trade promotions are researched in much the same fashion as consumer promotions. Trade surveys, focus groups, or depth interviews are used to determine the level of dealer acceptance of a trade promotion. Syndicated services are commonly used to determine the effectiveness of any trade promotion actually used.

Key Terms:

consumer promotions

controlled store test

coupons

deal acceptance

merchandising support

patronage reward programs

performance requirements

point-of-purchase (POP) promotions

premiums

price-offs

prizes

promotion evaluation

promotion pretesting

promotion synergy

sales promotion

samples

split-run

tie-in promotions

trade promotions

value packs

Promoting the Nimslo Camera to the Consumer

In preparing the marketing plan for the introduction of the Nimslo 3D camera, Nimslo management considered the use of discount coupons to speed the introductory sales. To determine the effectiveness of this proposed promotion and to estimate the price sensitivity of the market, a test market was conducted in Florida.

A free-standing insert was placed in the Sunday newspapers of two thousand subscribers who were randomly selected from the various carrier routes in the test market city. In one-half of the inserts, consumers were offered a $25 discount coupon that could be applied toward the purchase of a Nimslo camera and a free 3D print if they called Nimslo's toll-free number. The other half of the inserts were identical except that a $35 coupon was offered. The toll-free numbers in the two ads were different so that the response rates to the two promotions could be compared.

Results were discouraging. Very few calls were received for either offer, and almost no difference in response was noted between the two price offers. Management concluded that a promotion of this nature would not be effective in promotion of this nature would not be effective in generating purchases.

Review Questions

16.1 What factors have contributed to the shift in promotional dollars away from advertising?

16.2 What are the major short-run objectives of consumer promotions? Which types of promotions are best suited for these various objectives?

16.3 What are the major long-run objectives of consumer promotions? Which types of promotions are best suited for these various objectives?

16.4 In an ideal situation, what would be the sales effect from a consumer promotion? What are the more common sales effects? Why?

16.5 Why should consumer promotions be pretested? How can pretesting be conducted?

16.6 What aspects of consumer promotions need to be evaluated? What forms of research are commonly-used to conduct such evaluations?

16.7 What is meant by promotion synergy? How can synergy be estimated?

16.8 What is a controlled-store test? Give an example.

16.9 What is a split-run test? Give an example.

16.10 Suppose that the normal profit margin for a brand is $10.00, and typically 500 cases are sold per day. A promotion costing $2.00 per case is being considered. Is the promotion profitable if it increases sales by 10 percent? What is the minimum percentage increase in case sales required to make the promotion generate comparable profits to those obtained without the promotion?

16.11 What are trade promotions? What factors have led to their proliferation?

16.12 What factors impact the success of a trade promotion?

16.13 Describe how marketing research might be used to pretest the acceptability of a trade promotion.

Discussion Questions

16.1 Based on what you have learned so far, describe how household scanner panels could be used to evaluate the long-term impact of consumer promotions. What factors are impeding this assessment at present?

16.2 Manufacturers are often concerned that continual price dealings on a brand erode its price/value relationship. How might a company assess the impact of price deals on the price/value relationship?

16.3 A promotion was run during the month of August, and the following sales data were obtained. Compute the short-term impact of the promotion on sales volume. Was the promotion successful? Why or why not? Assuming that the promotion reduced the profit margin per case from $3.00 to $2.00, was the promotion profitable? Explain.

Month	Sales (in cases)
April	1123
May	998
June	1054
July	1176
August	3543
September	544
October	611
November	601
December	865

16.4 The brand manager for Kool-Aid commissioned a test market to assess the sales impact of a specially designed end-of-aisle display. In addition, the test examined the impact of a trade deal that required the manufacturer to provide local advertising for the brand. The test market was constructed so that; in some cities, only the end-of-aisle display was used; in another set of cities both the end-of-aisle display and local advertising was used; in a third set of cities only local advertising was used; and in a final set of cities, no promotional activities were undertaken. The following results were obtained:

	Average sales
No promotional activities	2879
End-of-aisle only	3021
Local advertising only	3766
Both end-of-aisle and local advertising	4491

What was the impact of each promotional activity? Was

there any synergy created when the two promotions were used simultaneously?

16.5 Discuss the difficulties that might be encountered in evaluating the impact of a trade promotion.

Notes

1. This example is based on information provided in "Fruitopia Tour Blends Performances with Sampling," *Promo: The International Magazine for Promotion Marketing*, August 1994, pp. 39 and Dan Hanover, "Being There," *Promo: The International Magazine for Promotion Marketing*,September 1997, pp. 35-44, 124-126.

2. See Scott Hume, "Trade Promos Devour Half Of All Marketing $," *Advertising Age*, April 13, 1992, pp. 3, 53.

3. Julie Liesse Erickson and Ira Teinowitz, "Not Really 'Ready to Roll': Kraft Puzzles Over Who Crashed Its Minivan Promo," *Advertising Age*, June 19, 1989, pp. 1, 74.

4. Information for this example came from William A. Robinson, *Best Sales Promotions*, Volume 5, Chicago: Crain Books, 1982, pp. 79-83.

5. Facts for this example were obtained from Dagmar Mussey, "P&G: Remember Our Ads," *Advertising Age*, March 6, 1989, p. 48.

6. Information for this example came from Dan Hanover, "Hitting the Jackpot," *Promo: The International Magazine for Promotion Marketing*, May 1997, pp. 40-1.

7. Betsy Spethmann, "Loyalty's Next Level," *Promo: The International Magazine for Promotion Marketing*, November 1997, pp. 49-50, 146-147.

8. Don E. Schultz and William A. Robinson, *Sales Promotion Management*. Chicago: Crain Books, 1982, p. 428.

9. "Getting Your Money's Worth", *Promo: The International_Magazine of Promotion Marketing*, May 1997, pp. 11-17.

10. Kapil Bawa and Robert W. Shoemaker, "Analyzing Incremental Sales from a Direct Mail Coupon Promotion," *Journal of Marketing* 53 (July 1989), pp. 66-78, found, for example, that coupon redeemers differed demographically from nonredeemers, and that redeemers had ten times the purchase rate of nonredeemers in the test that the authors examined

11. Don E. Schultz and William A. Robinson, *Sales Promotion Management*. Chicago: Crain Books, 1982, pp. 89-95.

12. See Richard Edel, "Trade Wars Threaten Future Peace of Marketers," *Advertising Age*, August 15, 1985, p. 18.

13. The example is based on Rod Taylor, "A Little Big Promotion" *Promo: The International Magazine of Promotion Marketing*, March 1996, pp. 35.

Chapter 17

Sales Analysis and Sales Forecasting

Learning Objectives:

This chapter reviews the roles of sales analysis and sales forecasting in the marketing decision-making process. After reading this chapter, you should be able to:

- o explain the purpose of a sales analysis.
- o describe the sources of data for a sales analysis.
- o discuss the sources of sales variation that must be captured in a sales forecast.
- o differentiate the various methods of creating sales forecasts.
- o describe the criteria for selecting a sales forecasting technique.

In industries where companies have stable market shares, forecasting sales can be

relatively easy. Since market shares vary little from year to year, a firm only to multiply its market share by the forecasted industry sales. Unfortunately, the total expected sales of the industry is sometimes extremely difficult to forecast. Forecasting citrus production in Florida is a vivid example of such a situation and illustrates one method of generating an industry forecast.

Most of the citrus produced by Florida growers is purchased by companies that process the fruit into juice or juice concentrate to be sold through retail stores. The amount of citrus available for purchase can be quite variable from year to year, depending in large part on weather conditions during the growing season. Also, as citrus production changes, so does the price that must be paid for the fruit or juice. Therefore, companies purchasing oranges from the growers need an accurate estimate of what the annual citrus production will be so they can better estimate both the cost of their finished products as well as their sales.

The citrus crop begins in the spring of the year, when the trees set their blooms. Some

varieties matter in late fall while other varieties do not mature until early summer of the following year. As a consequence, the harvest season lasts for several months and forecasts must be periodically reevaluated over the entire season.

The U.S. government publishes the first estimate of the season's crop in October, with additional estimates published each month thereafter until the crop is totally harvested, usually in June of the following year. Traditionally, these forecasts were based on trends from earlier years but fluctuating weather conditions often created grossly inaccurate forecasts. In the late 1950's, the Florida citrus growers passed a resolution to pay a fee per box of harvested fruit to cover the costs of getting better forecast data. The forecasting system, created in cooperation with the U.S. Department of Agriculture, is still in place today and generates very accurate forecasts of the size of the citrus crop.

The citrus production forecasting model uses data on four factors that, when multiplied together, yield a forecast of the total size of the citrus crop. These four factors are: 1) the number of citrus trees in production, 2) the amount of fruit per tree at the time of the survey, 3) the percentage of fruit remaining on the tree at harvest, and 4) the size of the fruit at harvest. The estimate of the size of the fruit is necessary since citrus is sold in 90-pound crates. More smaller citrus are required to yield a full crate.

Elaborate procedures are followed to estimate each of these four factors. For example, the number of citrus trees in production are determined by aerial photographs and sophisticated sampling plans are followed to calculate the amount of fruit on selected trees so the amount of fruit on all trees at the time of the survey can be estimated. Based on the fruit size at the initial survey, the size of the fruit at harvested is estimated using growth curves developed from previous harvests. These size estimates are periodically updated during the season, as harvest gets nearer. Estimates of droppage are calculated by monitoring a random sample of trees during the growing season and their droppage rates are applied to the population.

Unless the growing season is extremely unusual, such as the 1989-90 season where a hard freeze reduced the size of the crop by about 25 percent, the forecasts are generally within a few percentage points of the actual harvest. Such accuracy is even more impressive when considering that Florida citrus production is over 200 million 90-pound boxes. Armed with forecasts that close to actual production, citrus-processing companies find forecasting their sales much easier.

In this chapter, we will examine two different, but related, marketing research applications: sales analysis and sales forecasting. A **sales forecast** is a prediction of the amount of sales that will occur for a brand. A **sales analysis** is concerned with identifying the source of a brand's sales volume.

A sales analysis provides information on such things as the types of consumers buying the brand, how frequently consumers make purchases within the product category, and what competing brands are bought by those consumers. The information gained in a sales analysis has a variety of applications. A sales analysis can help management determine the characteristics of the market segments buying the brand, can reveal the brands consumers see as most easily substituted, and can indicate weaknesses in the marketing effort for particular market areas. One of the most important uses of sales analysis information, however, is to help generate the sales forecast.

Sales forecasting is a vital element of the planning process for a brand's marketing strategy. Obtaining a sales forecast or refining its accuracy is the reason much of the marketing research is conducted throughout the new product introduction process. For an existing brand, sales forecasting remains a critical element in the annual marketing plan because the amount of resources the company will be willing to allocate to a brand is dependent on the level of sales expected for it. We will examine both sales analysis and sales forecasting more closely in the following sections.

Sales Analysis

As illustrated in Exhibit 17.1, the volume of sales a brand achieves during any period of time is comprised of three components:

1. the number of purchasers of the brand,

2. the amount of the brand bought at each sales occasion (the average transaction size), and

3. the number of times each purchaser buys the brand during the time period (the purchase frequency).

Purchasers may be further classified as those buying the brand for the first time (triers) or those having bought it before (repeat purchasers). Obviously, the same total sales volume can be achieved with various combinations of these components.

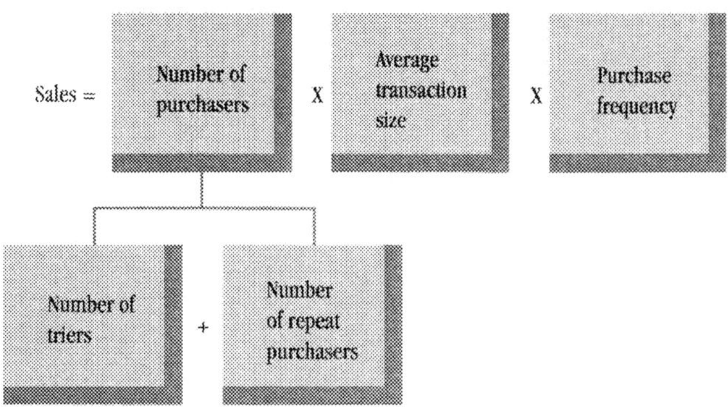

Exhibit 17.1
Components of sales volume.

The marketing manager needs to know what combination of purchasers, transaction sizes, and purchase frequencies yielded the brand's sales volume. Different combinations may require different marketing strategies or may indicate a potential weakness in the brand's current marketing strategy. Sales comprised mainly of a large number of triers and a small average transaction size signals something different to management than the same sales volume comprised of a large percentage of repeat buyers. An ongoing activity of marketing research, therefore, is to provide sales analysis information to management.

Various sources of information pertaining to brand sales can be used when conducting a sales analysis. To identify the distributors who contribute most to overall sales or to determine how brand sales are geographically dispersed, company shipment data may prove useful. Other information, however, will require data not found within the internal records of the company. External sales analysis data typically comes from two sources: consumer panels and product movement data.

Using Consumer Panel Data

As you learned in Chapter 5, a consumer diary panel consists of a sample of several thousand households. These households are chosen to be reflective of all of the types of households found in the United States. Mail panelists maintain a weekly, biweekly, or monthly diary providing information about the items purchased by the household during that time period. Electronic scanner panelists present their identification cards at checkout and their purchases are electronically stored and later retrieved. Combining the purchase information in the diary with the demographic characteristics of the individual panel member provides a wealth of information. A company can learn about the users of specific brands, about differences in the purchase frequency of brands, and about transaction size. Since members also provide information about coupon usage and special price deals, the promotion sensitivity of a brand can be evaluated as well.

One key piece of information provided by panel data is brand-switching behavior. Because the same panel members complete diaries each period, switches between brands from one purchase occasion to another are easy to calculate. This information is used to create brand switching tables like the one illustrated in Table 17.1.

First Purchase	Second purchase occasion				
	Mighty Clean	Potent Clean	Solid Clean	Dynamo Clean	Super Clean
Mighty Clean	67[1]	10	2	5	16
Potent Clean	5	75	3	2	15
Solid Clean	8	6	66	4	16
Dynamo Clean	10	5	2	71	12
Super Clean	3	4	3	2	88

[1]These numbers are the percentage of the row brand's customers who bought each brand the second time the product category was purchased.

Table 17.1 Example of a brand-switchig table.

The numbers in each row of Table 17.1 represent the percentage of each row brand's customers who bought the various brands the second time a purchase was made in the category. For example, the first row illustrates what brands those people who purchased Mighty Clean the first time bought the second time a purchase was made in the product category. As you can see, 67 percent purchased Mighty Clean again; the remaining 33 percent switched to one of the other brands.

For most product categories, a certain amount of brand switching is to be expected. However, a large increase in the percentage of people who switch away from a brand can be symptomatic of a problem that needs correcting. For instance, in Table 17.1, all brands lost significantly to the Super Clean brand. Further research would thus be warranted by the companies selling the other brands to determine why Super Clean was so successful and to identify alternative courses of action to reduce further switching.

Concerns about the accuracy of mail-based diary panel data have led to an increased reliance on scanner panels. Not only do scanner panels provide the same information as diary panels, scanner panel data can also easily be augmented to determine the competitive environment the consumer faced when making a brand choice. By including competitive factors such as the selling price of each available brand and any special promotional deals being offered by each, any sudden gains or losses in a brand's sales within a geographic area can be more easily explained.

Product Movement Data

Product movement data, also discussed previously in Chapter 5, are the second key source of sales analysis information. Product movement data provide information on a brand's sales and share of market. In addition, differences in the performance of a brand across types of outlets or geographic areas can be spotted by calculating sales and market share separately by outlet type or geographic region.

Distribution is a key element in the successful marketing of a brand. The way distribution is calculated is critical. Computing distribution as the percentage of stores in which the brand is stocked would provide a biased estimate since all stores, large and small, would be counted equally. Because of this problem, distribution levels are frequently computed as percentages of **all commodity volume**, or **ACV**, which can be thought of as the total sales volume of all products sold through a particular type of store. Thus, for a product sold in supermarkets, a distribution level of 40 means that the brand is sold in supermarkets accounting for 40 percent of ACV, not that the brand is distributed in 40 percent of all supermarkets. Computing distribution as a percentage of ACV adds valuable information since it incorporates the importance of the stores, in terms of sales potential, in which the firm's brand is sold.

Sales Forecasting

Sales forecasting has been compared to driving a car blindfolded while following directions given by a person who is looking out of the back window. This analogy is most appropriate, not only because the future is hidden, but also because most forecasting techniques rely on past data for guidance. Whether past data help predict the future depends on how closely the future resembles the past. If no changes occur in any of the factors that have an influence on brand sales, sales volume in the coming year will be equal to last year's volume. Unfortunately, this is rarely the case.

Marketing research helps determine what variables influence brand sales and assesses how future changes in these variables will influence sales. Very simply put, the sales volume a brand achieves is a function of two factors: the size of the market for the product category (the **market potential**) and the percentage of those sales captured by the brand (the market share). Thus, to develop a good sales forecast, accurately estimating changes in market potential and in market share is essential.

Factors Influencing Market Potential

As can be seen in Exhibit 17.2, five general factors can influence the market environment and thus an impact on market potential. Within each of these five broad categories, it is first necessary to predict what specific changes will occur within the forecast period. Next the possible impact of each change on market potential must be estimated. While some changes are easy to predict, others are not. Likewise, some impacts are direct; some are not.

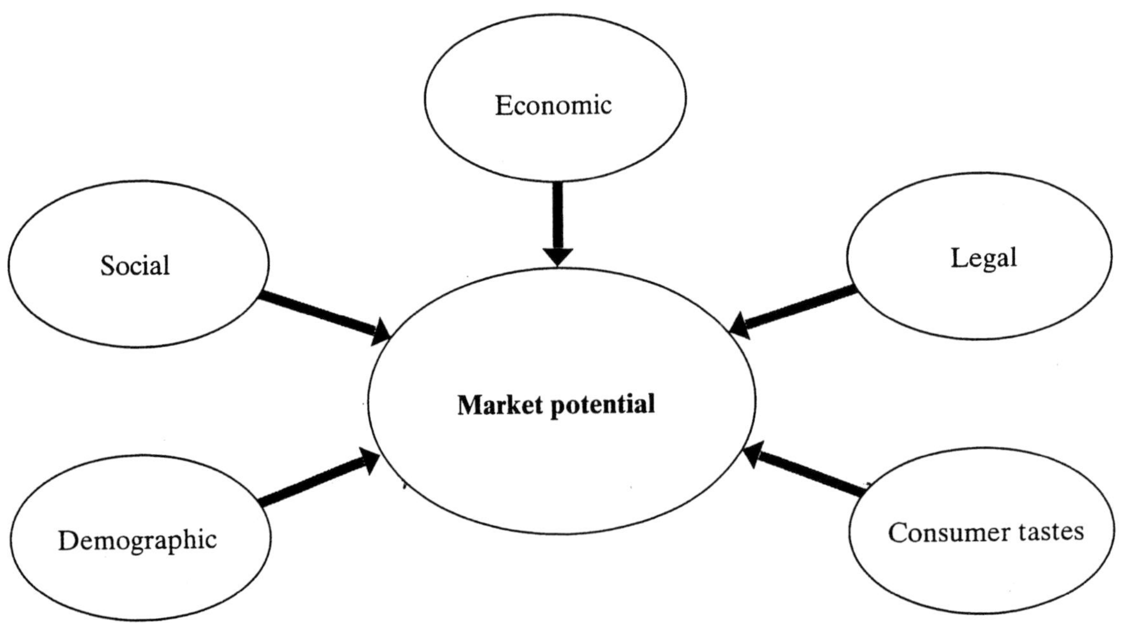

Exhibit 17.2
Factors influencing market potential.

Economic Changes

Changes in the economic environment in which the brand is sold may affect market potential. Rising costs for labor or materials used to make the brand are likely to alter the price that must be charged. Changes in unemployment or inflation rates influence the amount of money consumers have to spend and can have a dramatic impact on expensive or nonessential products such as furs, automobiles, and major appliances. A substantial increase in the price of even an inexpensive product can have a drastic impact on market potential if the demand for the product is highly elastic. For example, noticeable swings in the demand for coffee occur as the price of coffee beans changes due to variations in the size of the coffee crop.

Demographic Changes

Changes in the demographic composition of the market can alter market potential by changing the size of the target market. "Baby booms," such as the one following World War II, substantially alter the demand for some products. Baby booms are often likened to a "pig in a python" since the size of each age group progressively swells and contracts as the large number of persons born in the baby boom period enter and depart the age category. Conversely, the lower U.S. birth rates noted in the 1960s and 1970s caused companies marketing primarily to infants to scramble for new market opportunities.

Fortunately, short-run changes in population demographics can be predicted with reasonable accuracy. The number of persons who will be of a certain age next year is simply the number of persons one year younger this year, adjusted for mortality rates and immigration gains or losses. Thus, for products or services that are very closely tied to demographic segments, the impact of demographic changes on product category demand can be easily assessed using demographic forecasts.

Consumer Tastes

Changes in consumer tastes have an impact on the size of a market. Unfortunately, predicting a change in consumer tastes is far more difficult than predicting changes in demography. Often changes in taste occur with little warning. One merely needs to look at how quickly night clubs and restaurants that were once the "in" places to go lose their popularity to appreciate how quickly tastes can change.

Social and Legal Changes

Various social and legal changes influence market potential. Many times the impact of such a change on the sales of a product or service is obvious, such as the impact on alcoholic beverage sales when the legal drinking age in the United States was raised to twenty-one or when social pressures to stop drinking and driving increased. At other times the influence of a change, such as the increased participation of women in the labor force, is more subtle, and the possible impact on brand sales is much harder to estimate.

Quantifying the Impact

Quantifying the total impact of all potential economic, social, demographic, legal, and consumer taste changes is extremely difficult. The researcher must estimate not only the probability that each change will occur but also the size of the impact on market potential if any or all of the changes do occur. Sometimes firms generate several market potential estimates based on various assumptions about which changes will occur and what their total impacts will be. Exhibit 17.3 illustrates how such a procedure might be used to generate future market potential estimates for a product category.

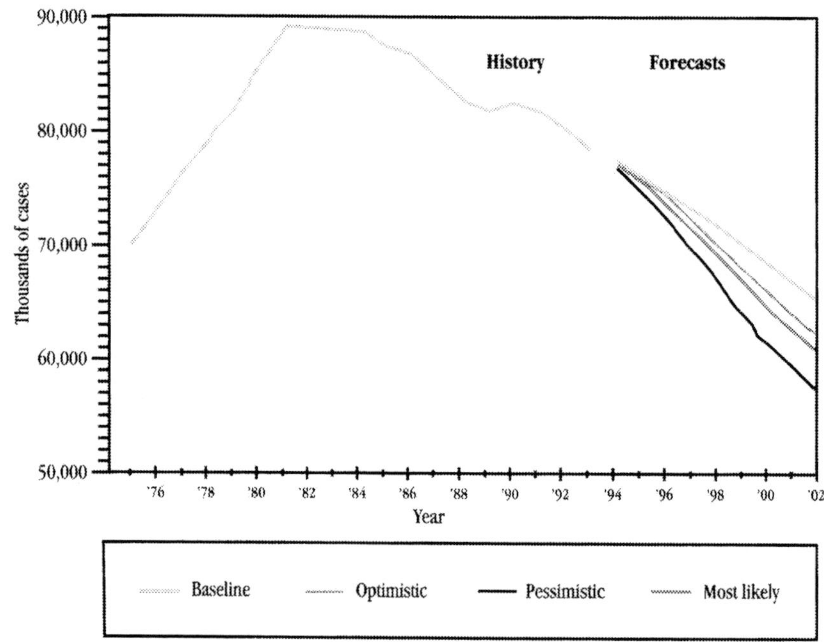

Exhibit 17.3
Market potential estimates under various assumptions.

In Exhibit 17.3, a pessimistic forecast and an optimistic forecast have been generated for the product category. The pessimistic forecast assumes that all possible changes having a negative impact on sales volume will occur. Conversely, the optimistic forecast assumes that only the changes having a positive impact on sales volume occur. A most-likely forecast, the average of a large number of forecasts that assume that some negative and some positive changes occur, has also been generated. These three forecasts are then compared to the baseline forecast, a forecast that assumes that none of the changes, either positive or negative, occur. That is, the baseline forecast assumes that future conditions will be exactly the same as present conditions. As you can see in Exhibit 17.3, under no expected set of conditions is future demand for this product category expected to be as large as the baseline forecast would predict, boding trouble ahead for the industry.

Factors Influencing Market Share

Even with a reasonably accurate estimate of the market potential of a product category, forecasting the sales of an individual brand may not be easy. What market share the brand will obtain is still uncertain. Changes in the number of brands competing within the category as well as changes in the level or effectiveness of competitors' marketing efforts can certainly influence the market share of the forecasted brand. In addition, the amount and quality of the marketing effort the company puts behind the brand will have an impact on its projected sales.

One method of forecasting sales that uses estimates of market potential and market share is the chain ratio forecasting method. The **chain ratio forecasting method** begins with the total population of interest and multiplies by a succession of factors to arrive at a more realistic estimate, similar to what is done to determine incidence levels for a study. The factors, which might be percentages, probabilities, or dollars, reduce the total population to an estimate of market potential or, if also multiplied by an assumed market share, to a sales forecast. The citrus production forecasting model described in the opening vignette to this chapter is an example of the chain ratio forecasting method.

The logic of the chain ratio method can be illustrated further by imagining that we wanted to estimate the market potential for custom-made golf clubs for left-handed golfers in the United States. Besides living in the United States and being left-handed, a potential buyer would also have to be a golfer and have sufficient income and motivation to afford and desire such clubs. The chain ratio approach to estimate market potential might look like: Total population in the United States X percentage who are left-handed X percentage who play golf X percentage with incomes over $50,000 X percentage of golfers who have custom-made clubs. Our sales forecast could be obtained by multiplying this market potential estimate by our estimated market share.

Sometimes forecasting a brand's sales becomes even more complicated, if the total marketing effort expended for all of the brands in the product category increases the overall market potential. For example, in the 1970s when the R.J. Reynolds Tobacco Company introduced Winchester cigars, which were shaped and packaged like cigarettes, not only were some sales of Winchester cigars obtained at the expense of competing cigar brands but also the total size of the market for cigars expanded dramatically. A similar phenomenon occurred in the wine industry during the 1980s when The Coca-Cola Company purchased Taylor wines and marketed them aggressively. In such cases, forecasting a brand's sales requires determining not only the effect of the company's marketing efforts on brand share but also its effect on the factors that influence total sales in the product category.

Sales Forecasting Methods

Now that you are aware of the types of factors that influence market potential and brand sales, we will examine various methods that can be used to forecast sales.[1] These methods can be categorized into three broad groups:

1. judgmental methods,
2. extrapolation methods, and
3. causal models.

As you will see, some of them take into account the factors we have discussed more explicitly than do others.

Judgmental Methods

Judgmental forecasting methods rely heavily on subjective sales estimates provided by individuals to forecast sales. One consideration in evaluating these forecasts, then, is the accuracy of these judgments. We will discuss four common types of judgmental forecasting methods in this section.

Sales Force Composite Approach

Because of their knowledge of the market and of competitive conditions, the company's sales personnel should be able to provide reasonable estimates of expected sales for the forecasted period. The sales estimate for each salesperson's territory can be aggregated to generate a total sales forecast, a procedure known as the **sales force composite approach**. Many companies use this forecasting approach.[2]

The accuracy of the sales estimates provided by the sales force can be a major concern when using a sales force composite forecast. Unless a reward for providing an accurate estimate or a penalty for providing an inaccurate one exists, the sales staff will not be very concerned about the accuracy of their estimates. Salespeople may even perceive that it is in their best interest to provide inaccurate estimates purposely if performance is evaluated relative to their sales forecasts. In such cases, a salesperson can make his or her performance look better by providing a sales estimate that is very likely to be less than the sales expected. On the other hand, one study noted that estimates provided by sales personnel tend to be overly optimistic in companies where the sales personnel were compensated under commission plans.[3]

Customer Demand Estimate Approach

If a brand's sales are highly concentrated in a few key sales accounts, estimating the change in the sales to these key accounts can be used to predict how total sales will change. The key accounts might be surveyed, or the sales staff can be asked for estimates of how the sales to these key accounts are likely to vary. Either a simple or weighted average of the percentage change forecast for these key accounts can then be applied to the total sales achieved for the previous year to estimate the total sales change for the forecasted period. When using such an approach, one must be concerned not only about the accuracy of the key account sales estimates, but also about how accurately the key accounts reflect the sales changes of other customers.

Using Published Estimates

Sometimes a firm will forecast its sales using estimates of the industry market potential found in published sources. Market potential estimates for many industries are generated and published by trade associations, by the government, or by private companies. Simply estimating the share of the market that the firm anticipates getting during the period and multiplying this share by the market potential estimate gives the sales forecast for the brand.

One of the dangers when using published estimates is that more credence will be given to them than is deserved. That is, the assumption may be made that the estimates are somehow better than ones the company might generate because they have been published. The accuracy of any published estimate should not be assumed but should be assessed by examining the credibility and expertise of the individual or group making the estimate.

Jury of Expert Opinion Approach

With a **jury of expert opinion approach**, a group of knowledgeable individuals is polled to generate sales estimates.

When using this approach, some way must be found to resolve the differences in the sales forecasts generated. A Delphi approach is often used to aid in this process.

The **Delphi approach** attempts to bring convergence to the forecasts generated by a group of individuals by providing information about the initial sales forecasts given by the others in the group, such as the high and low forecast of the group and the average forecast and asking each person for a revised estimate based on this information.[4] After two or three such iterations, the Delphi approach tends to yield a consensus of opinion that then can be used as the best estimate of sales.

One thing to keep in mind when developing the jury of experts is that individuals who have greater expertise or knowledge about the brand or the product category are likely to generate more accurate estimates of sales.[5] Another point to remember is that jury members are not likely to be able to provide accurate sales estimates for situations that are outside their normal range of experiences.[6]

Extrapolation Methods

Extrapolation forecasting methods are so named because they use past sales data to predict future sales. Because extrapolation methods rely only on historical sales data, these methods must assume that the past sales pattern will continue in the future. Any changes that occur in the sales pattern because of changing environmental conditions usually will not be detected until it is too late.[7] In spite of this serious drawback, extrapolation techniques are widely used because of their simplicity.[8] Five extrapolation methods will be discussed here:

1. history-repeats-itself,

2. percentage change,

3. moving average,

4. exponential smoothing, and

5. time series analysis.

History-Repeats-Itself Approach

The **history-repeats-itself approach** assumes that the sales for the next period will be equal to this period's sales. It provides a simple way to forecast sales by believing that history will repeat itself. In a stable market environment, such a forecast may be reasonable. If sales of the industry are flat and if no significant changes are expected in market shares, next year's sales should be nearly equal to current sales.

Even in industries that are not stable, a history-repeats-itself forecast may be generated for use in a "devil's advocate" role. Thus, sales forecasters are required to explain why they feel that future sales will not be the same as current sales. Used in this manner, a history-repeats-itself forecast helps identify environmental factors whose impacts need to be incorporated into the actual sales forecast.

Percentage-Change Approach

The **percentage-change approach** uses logic similar to the history-repeats-itself approach, but, instead of assuming that sales will be identical next year, the percentage-change approach assumes that the percentage change in sales in the future will be identical to the percentage change observed in the past. Table 17.2 shows the application of this approach.

Year	Actual Sales	Percent Change	Sales Forecast[1]	Percent Error
1	1,234,912	—	—	—
2	2,346,333	90	—	—
3	4,340,716	85	4,458,033	2.7
4	7,813,289	80	8,030,325	2.8
5	13,673,256	75	14,063,920	2.9
6	23,244,534	70	23,928,198	3.0

[1]Based on the percentage of change in the previous two year's sales volumes.

Table 17.2
Use of percentage-change method to forecast sales

The first column in Table 17.2 gives the actual sales figures for a six-year period. As can be seen by examining the percentage change in the annual sales volumes, sales have been growing rapidly, though at a slightly declining rate. The forecasted sales shown in column 3, predicted using the percentage change between the two preceding years, reveal only a slight error between the actual sales and the forecasted sales for any year. Small errors would be expected because the difference between the actual percentage growth in sales in any year and the percentage growth used for each prediction is small. For example, the 90-percent growth rate experienced between Year 1 and Year 2 is used to forecast Year 3 sales. The actual growth in sales between Years 2 and 3 is 85 percent, very close to the predicted growth rate, resulting in a forecast that is fairly close to the actual sales.

On the other hand, if the actual growth rates experienced are significantly different from those used to predict, substantial errors will occur in the forecast. Obviously, if Year 3 sales had been predicted using a 90 percent growth and the actual growth turned out to be 40 percent, the forecast would have grossly overestimated actual sales. Discrepancies between forecasted and actual growth rates tend to become magnified when current growth rates are used to project sales for periods in the relatively distant future. To illustrate this point, consider the problem of forecasting sales for Years 3 through 6 at the end of Year 2. The forecasted sales for each of these years using a 90-percent growth rate, the growth rate noted between Year 1 and Year 2, and the actual sales for Years 3 through 6 that were provided in Table 17.2 have been graphed in Exhibit 17.4. As can be seen, the forecast quickly diverges from the actual sales, because the actual growth in sales declined steadily over this period from 90 percent to 70 percent.

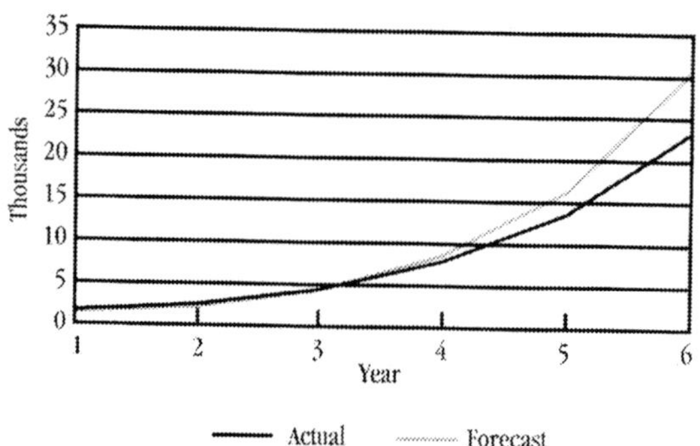

Exhibit 17.4
Actual *vs.* forecasted sales using the same percentage change over time.

Moving-Average Approach

A **moving-average approach** forecasts future sales by averaging a set number of past sales periods. The forecast is a moving average because earlier sales periods are dropped from the calculation of the average as more recent sales periods become available. When using a moving-average approach, one consideration is the number of periods of sales that will be averaged. A three-year moving average would forecast sales using the three most recent years of data; a five-year moving average would use the five most recent years. In fact, the history-repeats-itself method may be thought of as a one-year moving average.

Forecasting sales using an average of several past sales

periods makes the sales forecast less sensitive to any sales aberrations occurring in a single year. At the same time, however, averaging across periods makes this method less sensitive to sales trends. When sales have been increasing over time, moving-average forecasts underestimate future sales; and when sales have been decreasing over time, moving-average forecasts will overestimate actual sales. Furthermore, the greater the number of periods used to calculate the average, the larger the overestimation or underestimation will be when a sales trend exists.

Table 17.3 contains monthly sales figures for a hypothetical brand for a five-year period. Exhibit 17.5 contains both three-year and four-year moving-average estimates of the monthly sales for Year 5. For example, the three-year moving average forecast for January sales in Year 5 is (10,560 + 13,200 + 15,840) ÷ 3 = 13,200 (the average of the January sales figures for the most recent three years — Years 2 through 4). You can readily see that monthly sales have been increasing for each of the past five years. Therefore, both the three-year and the four-year moving-average forecasts underestimate the actual fifth year's monthly sales. Furthermore, the four-year moving average underestimates by a greater amount than does the three-year moving average.

	Year 1	Year 2	Year 3	Year 4	Year 5
January	9,600	10,560	13,200	15,840	20,640
February	4,800	5,280	6,600	7,920	10,320
March	3,600	3,960	4,950	5,940	7,740
April	3,600	3,960	4,950	5,940	7,740
May	8,400	9,240	11,550	13,860	18,060
June	10,800	11,880	14,850	17,820	23,220
July	19,200	21,120	26,400	31,680	41,280
August	19,200	21,120	26,400	31,680	41,280
September	15,600	17,160	21,450	25,740	33,540
October	10,800	11,880	14,850	17,820	23,220
November	8,400	9,240	11,550	13,860	18,060
December	6,000	6,600	8,250	9,900	12,900
TOTAL SALES	120,000	132,000	165,000	198,000	258,000

Table 17.3
Five years of monthly sales data for a hypothetical brand

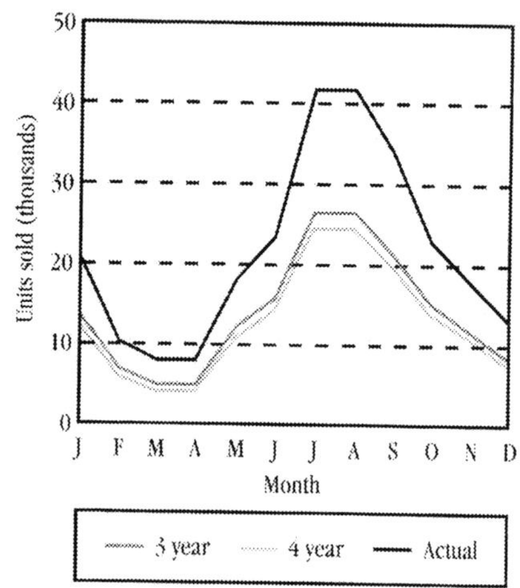

Exhibit 17.5
Use of three-year and four-year moving averages to forecast sales.

Exponential-Smoothing Approach

Exponential smoothing is a moving-average approach that allows the forecaster to weight the most recent sales period differently from earlier sales periods. When a sales trend exists, a forecast generated using exponential smoothing will be more accurate than a simple moving average forecast. However, exponential smoothing will not totally eliminate the overestimation and underestimation problem created by a sales trend.

Symbolically, the exponential-smoothing sales forecast is calculated as:

$$F_{t+1} = aS_t + (1 - a)F_t$$

where: F_{t+1} is the sales forecast for next period; a is the smoothing constant, and $0 \leq a \leq 1$; F_t is the forecasted sales for this period; and S_t is the actual sales for this period.

The **smoothing constant** is the weight between zero and one that is to be given to the most recent sales period when using exponential smoothing. The remainder of the emphasis, $(1 - a)$, is placed on previous sales periods. The actual sales for the period, S_t, is used as the estimate of the sales for the most recent sales period. The forecasted sales for the most recent period, F_t, is used as an estimate of the sales of previous sales periods since it is based entirely on those past sales periods.

Determining how much weight to give to the most recent period is a matter of trial and error. Various sales forecasts are generated for past periods using different values for the smoothing constant, and the forecasts are compared to actual sales. The smoothing constant that best predicts these past sales levels is used to make the forecast for the coming period. Exhibit 17.6 displays three exponential-smoothing forecasts based on using .1, .5, and .9 as the smoothing constant, for the fifth year of sales data found in Table 17.3. In each case, the forecast for a particular month in Year 2 was the actual sales for the corresponding month in Year 1, and subsequently monthly forecasts were generated using the exponential-smoothing formula given earlier and the specified smoothing constant. For example, the following are the estimates of sales for January in Years 2 through 5 using _ = .9:

Year	Forecast
2	9,600
3	10,464
4	12,926
5	15,549

As you can see, the smoothing constant of .9 provides the closest forecast to actual sales data. In general, the more that sales exhibit an upward or downward trend, the larger will be the value of the smoothing constant providing the most accurate results.

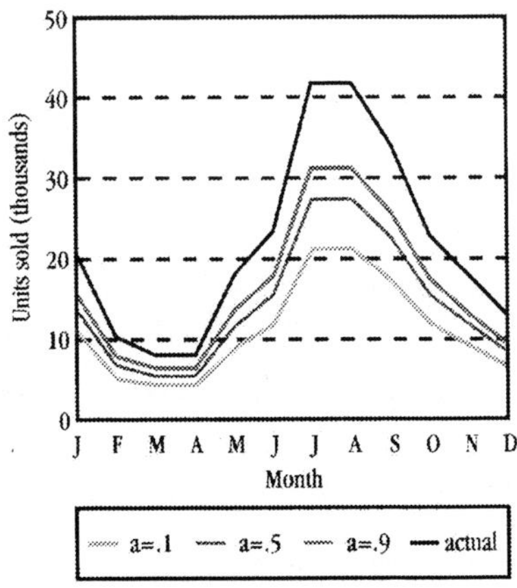

Exhibit 17.6
Use of exponential smoothing to forecast sales.

Time-Series Forecasting

Time-series forecasting is an extrapolation approach that breaks the historical pattern of sales into four components: trend, seasonal, cyclical, and error. The **sales trend** is the long-term upward or downward movement of sales. A **seasonal variation** is a swing in sales that occurs regularly at a certain time of the year. A **cyclical variation** is a regular swing in sales that occurs at an interval greater than twelve months. Any variations in sales that cannot be explained by these three factors are assumed to be random fluctuations, or error.

To better understand these components, consider the sales data given in Table 17.3 and graphically displayed in Exhibit 17.7. The general upward trend in sales across the five years is apparent; the sales achieved in any month are always higher than for the same month the previous year. Furthermore, a regular pattern of higher-than-average and lower-than-average sales are noted for various months within each year. Peaks in sales are noted each January, July, and August, and troughs occur each March, April, and December.

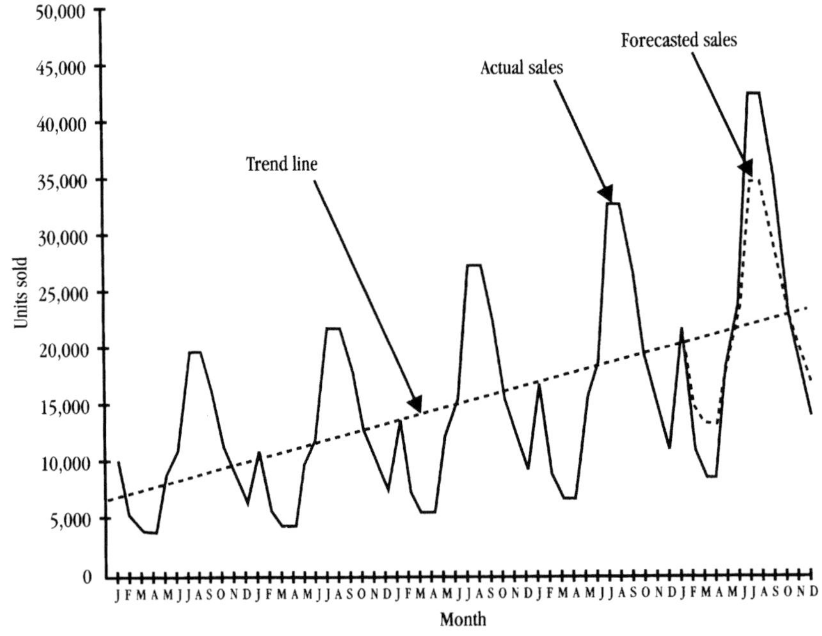

Exhibit 17.7
Times-series forecast with seasonal adjustments.

Time series forecasting first removes the trend from the sales data using linear regression, a technique that determines the straight line that best fits the data (see Chapter 9). This straight line is known as the **trend line**. The trend line computed for the data of Table 17.3 using simple regression is also shown in Exhibit 17.7.

Forecasting the sales of each month using only the trend line will overestimate the sales of some months and underestimate others in our example. Therefore, time-series forecasting next attempts to remove any seasonal variations from the data by adjusting the sales predicted from the trend line using the average amount that the trend line is in error for each period. For example, the trend line in Exhibit 17.7 always underestimates July sales. By averaging the amount of the underestimation noted for all July sales periods and adding this average amount to the forecasted trend value for the next July, the forecasted sales level comes much closer to the actual sales value. Doing the same for each month produces the forecasted sales indicated by the dotted line in Exhibit 17.7. If sufficient past data are available, a similar procedure could be used to remove any cyclical variations remaining.

Time-series forecasting works reasonably well as long as the seasonal or cyclical swings in sales are of approximately the same magnitude each year and occur with regularity. However, if the swings in sales are increasing or decreasing over time, like the data shown in Exhibit 17.7, the sales forecasts will become further and further in error unless the prediction equation is continually updated as more recent data become available.[9] Furthermore, if the pattern of the sales swings changes, the sales forecast will be in error until enough historical data are obtained to recognize the new pattern.

The existence of several time-series forecasting programs that decompose the data into trend, seasonal, and cyclical components greatly simplifies the process of using a time series approach. Two of these programs are Census Method II and FORAN II, both developed for use by the Bureau of the Census.[10] In addition, several programs are available that apply the Box-Jenkins procedure. The **Box-Jenkins procedure** combines a simple extrapolation approach with a sophisticated form of time-series regression to forecast sales. While the methodology of the technique is too complicated to be discussed here, the overall approach is easy to understand.[11]

The Box-Jenkins procedure first attempts to determine the existence of trend or seasonal components in the data. Then a tentative forecasting model is developed to see if the actual sales pattern is reproduced accurately. Revisions are made in the model, if necessary, until the best forecasting model that can be created with the procedure is developed.

Causal Models

The biggest shortcoming of extrapolation forecasting methods is that, because they merely use past sales patterns to predict the future, they cannot predict changes in sales that are not evident in past sales data. Thus, extrapolation methods are subject to severely erroneous estimates if environmental factors cause the pattern of sales to change from what has been observed in the past. Forecasts using causal models do not suffer from this limitation. **Causal models** attempt to determine what factors have caused sales to vary in the past and then use this knowledge to predict how sales will vary in the future. That is, if the forecaster can discover a few variables that adequately predict past brand sales, then future sales can be predicted by knowing the future values of those few variables.

Various forms of regression analysis are often used to develop causal forecasting models. The intent is to find a variable, or set of variables, whose values change systematically with changes in the variable to be forecasted. The complexity of the model needed to develop the forecast depends upon the number of factors that have an impact on the forecasted variable. Some models, such as those used to forecast rates of growth in the economy, are extremely complicated. On the other hand, many universities predict the freshman grade-point average of an applicant fairly closely using only the applicant's score on the Scholastic Aptitude Test and high school grade-point average. The following example should help illustrate how a causal model is used to forecast sales.

Applying Marketing Research 17.1

Benson's, a furniture store located in a mid-sized Southern city, developed a model to forecast the annual sales of furniture in the city. The model used the change in the size of the population of the metropolitan area and the number of new housing starts to predict furniture sales. Predicted values of these two variables for the forecast period are readily available from the state economic forecasting center.

The regression equation Benson's used to forecast furniture sales was:

$$\text{Sales} = 6{,}923 + .0402X_1 + .312X_2$$

where: sales were measured in thousands of dollars, X_1 is the change in the size of the population, and X_2 is the number of new housing starts in the area.

The equation yielded a coefficient of determination, R^2, of .848, indicating that 84.8 percent of the variation in furniture sales could be predicted using this equation. By substituting the predicted values of population change and housing starts for the coming year into the equation, Benson's is able to develop a fairly accurate estimate of next year's furniture sales. For example, if it was estimated that the population of the metropolitan area would grow by 5000 in the next year and that 15,000 new housing starts would occur, the estimate of furniture sales in the area would be:

$$\text{Sales} = 6{,}923 + .0402 * (5000) + .312 * (15{,}000)$$

$$= 11{,}804.$$

Since sales were measured in thousands of dollars, this means that the forecasted furniture sales for the area would be $11,804,000.00.

Sometimes, future levels of some or all of the variables used in the regression equation to forecast sales must also be forecast. Each variable might be forecast with its own equation, leading to a series of forecasting equations. Such a procedure is called **econometric modeling**. Applying Marketing Research 17.2 illustrates an econometric modeling procedure.

Applying Marketing Research 17.2

When managers at Mary Kay Cosmetics first began to develop a forecasting system to estimate the monthly sales of the company, they assumed that sales could be forecast simply as the number of sales force members multiplied by the sales per member. However, on closer examination of the situation, they found that average sales differed between new and existing sales force members, so each group's sales had to be forecast separately. In turn, they found that the sales forecast for each of the two groups required a series of equations.

For instance, estimates of the number of new sales members recruited each month were required. In addition, estimates of the percent of new sales members ordering and the average size of their orders were required. For existing sales members, the number of terminations had to be estimated as well as order rates and order sizes. In all, they found they needed an econometric model containing from 10 to 15 equations to estimate their monthly sales.[12]

Regardless of the complexity of the causal model developed to forecast sales, two considerations should guide the selection of variables to be included. First, each predictor variable should make sense. That is, the variable should be expected to vary consistently with variations in the sales of the brand. Sometimes a spurious correlation can be found. A **spurious correlation** exists when one variable predicts the value of another variable very well for no apparent reason. Spurious correlations do not make good predictors because one is never sure if the relationship will continue to hold in the future.

When forecasting sales, a plausible reason should exist to explain why sales should vary consistently with changes in the variables used to predict sales. Economic, demographic, and competitive variables, therefore, should make good predictor variables, since these variables would be expected to relate to sales changes. On the other hand, predicting future sales of the brand based on changes in the barometric pressure in Chicago would not be sensible, even if these barometric changes somehow tracked past sales changes, since no reason exists to expect sales to be related to this variable.

The second consideration for variables used in the prediction equation is that their values be known or be easily predicted. Otherwise, forecasts can easily be very inaccurate due to errors in the estimates used for the values of predictor variables. This consideration often leads to the use of leading indicators. **Leading indicators** are variables that change before a change in sales, and thus have predictive value. A leading indicator of retail sales, for example, is wholesale sales, because changes in wholesale sales tend to occur before corresponding changes occur in retail sales.

Even if the predictor variable does not lead sales, its value sometimes can be easily predicted. Many economic variables, such as GNP and disposable personal income, fall into this category. Because of their importance to so many different segments of the economy, forecasts of these economic variables abound and can easily be used in developing a causal model.[13]

Selecting a Forecasting Technique

Choosing the best sales-forecasting technique for any situation is not a simple task. None of the forecasting methods presented above is perfect. Each technique has advantages and disadvantages that may make it more or less appropriate for any given situation. Table 17.4 lists several factors that should be considered in selecting any sales-forecasting technique.

1. Potential for accuracy
2. Length of time period to be forecast
3. Needed precision
4. Ease of use
5. Pattern of past sales

Table 17.4
Factors to consider in selecting a sales-forecasting technique

One factor to consider in selecting a forecasting technique is its potential for generating an accurate forecast. A large number of studies have examined the relative accuracy of various forecasting techniques. While some inconsistencies exist in the findings of these studies, in general it appears that, as might be expected, judgmental forecasting methods do not provide as much accuracy as other methods.[14] Furthermore, exponential-smoothing and moving- average methods seem to generate forecasts that are at least as accurate as the more complicated Box-Jenkins or causal-models approaches.

The time horizon that is to be forecast is another factor that needs to be considered when selecting a forecasting procedure, since some methods are likely to work better for short time horizons while others work better as the time horizon increases. For example, the relative accuracy of the time-series and causal-models approaches improves as the time horizon to be forecast increases, because the influence of a sales trend is likely to be greater in longer time horizons. For very short time horizons, such as monthly sales forecasts, fluctuations around the trend are likely to dominate the sales changes that occur, and these short-term changes are much easier to capture in moving average and exponential smoothing procedures than in time-series approaches.

A third factor that must be considered is the precision required in the forecast. In many cases, precision can only be gained at increased cost since better data and more complicated forecasting procedures will be required. The value or need for this increased precision must offset the additional cost.

The ease with which the forecasting procedure can be used is another factor to consider. Some forecasting procedures either require data that are not normally collected by the firm or require data in a form different from the one in which the data are usually gathered. Furthermore, some procedures are complicated to use and to understand unless one is a trained forecaster.

Finally, the pattern of past sales should be examined before deciding on a particular sales-forecasting procedure. Such an examination can help determine the amount of expected variation that must be explained and can aid in deciding if the strengths of a particular method will prove useful in explaining that variation. If past sales do not show much trend or seasonality, for example, time series methods are not likely to prove useful.

Summary

The purpose of a sales analysis is to provide information about the nature of a brand's sales volume. In particular, a sales analysis yields insights into the types of people who bought the brand, how frequently they bought it, and in what quantities. A sales analysis typically relies on consumer panel data or product movement data.

A brand's sales are influenced by changes in the market potential for the product category and by changes in its market share. Market potential can be affected by changes in the economic environment, in the demographic composition of the market, in consumer tastes, in social values, or in laws. A brand's market share can vary if there is a change in the number of brands competing, a change in the amount or effectiveness of the marketing effort expended for each competing brand, or a change in the amount or effectiveness of the brand's marketing effort.

Three general methods exist for forecasting sales. Judgmental forecasting methods use subjective estimates provided by individuals to forecast sales. Commonly used judgmental forecasting methods are the jury of expert opinion approach and the sales force composite approach. Extrapolation forecasting methods use past history to forecast sales. History-repeats-itself, percentage change, exponential smoothing, moving average, time series forecasting, and Box-Jenkins are all extrapolation methods. Causal models attempt to find a historical relationship between a brand's sales and other variables and use that relationship to predict future sales.

Alternative sales-forecasting techniques should be examined to determine their appropriateness to the situation faced. Some techniques forecast better for short time horizons, others are better for longer time horizons. Some are likely to be able to generate more accurate forecasts given historical data than are others. Some are more difficult to use, while others provide more precise estimates.

Key Terms:

all commodity volume

Box-Jenkins procedure

causal models

chain ratio forecasting method

cyclical variation

Delphi approach

econometric modeling

exponential smoothing

extrapolation forecasting methods

history-repeats-itself approach

judgmental forecasting methods

jury of expert opinion approach

leading indicators

market potential

moving-average approach

percentage-change approach

sales analysis

sales force composite approach

sales forecast

sales trend

seasonal variation

smoothing constant

spurious correlation

time-series forecasting

trend line

Sales Forecasting at Nimslo

The Nimslo Company anticipated revenues from two sources: income from the sale of 3D cameras and accessories and money earned from photofinishing. The interrelated nature of these two revenue sources meant that the accuracy of the sales forecast for photofinishing revenue was dependent in large part on the accuracy of the sales forecast for camera sales.

Nimslo used a very simple forecasting method for estimating 3D camera sales. Based upon consumer research, Nimslo estimated that sales of 3D cameras would account for about 2 percent of total camera sales volume. Applying this percentage to published estimates of the future sales volume of cameras yielded an estimate of Nimslo camera sales volume for the introductory year. Also, using trade information on the seasonality of camera sales (almost half of all camera sales take place in October, November, and December, for example), Nimslo divided the annual sales forecast into monthly sales estimates for the introductory year. These estimates were then adjusted downward to reflect the percentage of the U.S. market that Nimslo anticipated serving at that particular point in time.

Nimslo used a spreadsheet model to forecast photofinishing revenues. The months of the year defined the rows and columns of the spreadsheet. Each row designated the particular month in which a camera was sold. Photofinishing revenue was generated in that month and in subsequent months (columns). Table 17.5 demonstrates how the spreadsheet was organized.

Month of Camera Sale	Month in which Photofinishing Orders Are Generated									
	Mar.	Apr.	May	June	July	Aug.	Sep.	Oct.	Nov.	Dec.
March	XX	XX	XX	XX	XX	XX	XX	XX	XX	XX
April		XX	XX	XX	XX	XX	XX	XX	XX	XX
May			XX	XX	XX	XX	XX	XX	XX	XX
June				XX	XX	XX	XX	XX	XX	XX
July					XX	XX	XX	XX	XX	XX
August						XX	XX	XX	XX	XX
September							XX	XX	XX	XX
October								XX	XX	XX
November									XX	XX
December										XX
TOTAL	XXX[1]	XXX	XXX	XXX	XXX	XXX	XXX	XXX	XXX	XXX

[1]Column totals represent the total rolls of film to be photofinished each month based on sales of cameras in that month or earlier.

Table 17.5
The Nimslo photofinishing forecast system

Using trade information regarding film usage and its seasonality among 35 mm owners as well as information gathered from consumer product tests of the camera, Nimslo generated a monthly forecast of the number of rolls of film that would be submitted to Nimslo photofinishing by consumers buying the camera in each individual month of the introductory year. To estimate the monthly total number of photofinishing orders (row entries) generated by cameras sold in a particular month, the average number of rolls assumed to be shot in each respective month was multiplied by the corresponding number of cameras sold. Therefore, summing across a row of the table generates the total photofinishing orders generated by cameras sold during the corresponding month. More importantly, the column totals are the monthly photofinishing forecasts. For instance, the first column of Table 17.5 contains only one entry, the estimate of photofinishing volume for the month of March — the introductory month for the Florida test market. The second column, April photofinishing volume, contains two entries, the photofinishing volumes generated by cameras sold in March and in April, which, when added, yield the total photofinishing volume estimate for April.

Revenue for each month was easily computed from the estimated total number of photofinishing orders for the month. First, the number of orders was multiplied by the development charge per roll, which was fixed regardless of the exposure length (number of possible 35 mm pictures on a roll). Next, the average number of prints delivered per order was multiplied by the number of orders and by the price per print. Total revenue was the sum of the development charge and the print charge. The average number of prints delivered per order was based on industry data regarding the mean exposure length of purchased 35 mm film. The mean exposure length was halved (since each 3D print took two film exposures) and then multiplied by a fraction called the yield factor to obtain an estimated average number of Nimslo prints delivered per order. The yield factor reflected the fact that not all pictures taken produced good 3-dimensional prints that could be sold. Internal monitoring of photofinishing orders over time led to precise estimates of the yield factor and the appropriate average exposure length for Nimslo orders.

Review Questions

17.1. What is a sales analysis? Why would a sales analysis be conducted? What kinds of information would be gathered during a sales analysis?

17.2. The sales volume achieved by a brand is a function of what components?

17.3. Suppose you were the brand manager for Brand D shown in the following brand-switching table. What information could you obtain about your brand from the data presented in the table?

First Purchase	Second Purchase Occasion			
	Brand A	Brand B	Brand C	Brand D
Brand A	72	17	5	6
Brand B	5	86	4 5	
Brand C	8	13	68	11
Brand D	10	15	11 64	

17.4. What makes sales forecasting a difficult task? What factors are likely to cause future brand sales to be different from past sales?

17.5. What is meant by judgmental forecasting methods? Briefly describe various ways to conduct a judgmental forecast.

17.6 What might cause a sales force composite forecast to be in error? What could be done to adjust for such error?

17.7 What is a Delphi approach? Why is it used?

17.8. What is meant by a history-repeats-itself forecast? Why might such a forecast be used?

17.9. What is the purpose of using a moving-average forecasting method? What impact does a change in the number of past periods used have on the resulting forecast?

17.10 How is an exponential smoothing forecast made? How does such a forecast differ from a moving average?

17.11. What components are assumed to comprise the sales data when using a time-series forecasting method? How does time-series forecasting account for each component?

17.1217.12 What makes econometric modeling different from other types of causal model forecasts?

17.13. What two requirements are necessary to create an appropriate causal sales model?

17.14. What factors should be considered in selecting the appropriate sales-forecasting technique?

Discussion Questions

17.1. The increased availability of data that allow more sophisticated sales analyses has led to more frequent requests for such analyses by marketing managers. To reduce the amount of time that the marketing research staff spends on such requests, some companies have begun to ask the marketing staff to conduct their own sales analyses via personal computer. What do you see as the pros and cons of such an approach?

17.2. The sales-forecasting methods described in this chapter assume that historical sales data exist for the brand or the product category to be forecasted. For completely new products, *e.g.*, microwave ovens or VCRs when first introduced, no historical data is available. How might a sales forecast be generated for a product category that has no historical sales data?

17.3. If you were trying to develop a causal model to predict next year's total automobile sales for the city in which your university is located, what are some of the variables that you might consider as predictors? Why?

Chapter 17 Endnotes

---

1. For a concise description of a host of forecasting techniques, see George C. Michael, *Sales Forecasting*, Monograph 10. Chicago: American Marketing Association, 1979.

2. T. R. Wotruba and M. L. Thurbow, "Sales Force Participation in Quota Setting and Sales Forecasting," *Journal of Marketing* **40** (April 1976), pp. 11-16.

3. *Ibid.*

4. See Norman Dalkey, *The Delphi Method: An Experimental Study of Group Opinion*. Santa Monica: The Rand Corporation, RM-5888-PR, for a more complete description of the Delphi technique. For a discussion of how this technique may be applied in marketing, see Marvin A. Jolson and Gerald L. Rossow, "The Delphi Process in Marketing Decision Making," *Journal of Marketing Research* **8** (November 1971), pp. 443-48.

5. See Roger J. Best, "An Experiment in Delphi Estimation in Marketing Decision Making, *Journal of Marketing Research*, **11** (November 1974), pp. 448-52, as well as Jean-Claude Larreche and Reza Moinpour, "Managerial Judgement in Marketing: The Concept of Expertise," *Journal of Marketing Research*, **20** (May 1983), pp. 110-21, for a discussion of this issue.

6. Dipankar Chakravarti, Andrew Mitchell, and Richard Staelin, "Judgement Based Marketing Decision Models: An Experimental Investigation of the Decision Calculus Approach," *Management Science* **25** (March 1979), pp. 251-63; and Dipankar Chakravarti, Andrew Mitchell, and Richard Staelin, "Judgement Based Marketing Decision Models: Problems and Possible Solutions," *Journal of Marketing* **45** (Fall 1979), pp. 13-23, discuss the issue of prior sales affecting the accuracy of the estimate. For a description of approaches that can be taken to adjust for errors in judgement, see Mark M. Moriarty, "Design Features of Forecasting Systems Involving Management Judgements," *Journal of Marketing Research* **22** (November 1985), pp. 353-64, as well as Richard Staelin and Ronald E. Turner, "Error in Judgement Sales Forecasts: Theory and Results," *Journal of Marketing Research* **10** (February 1973), pp. 10-16.

7. See John M. McCann and David J. Reibstein, "Forecasting the Impact of Socioeconomic and Demographic Change of Product Demand," *Journal of Marketing Research* **22** (November 1985), pp. 415-23, for

a discussion of how environmental factors might be incorporated into extrapolation techniques.

8. Douglas J. Dalrymple, "Sales Forecasting Methods and Accuracy," *Business Horizons* **18** (December 1975), pp. 69-73; John T. Mentzer and James E. Cox, Jr., "Familiarity, Application, and Performance of Sales Forecasting Techniques," *Journal of Forecasting* **3** (January-March 1984), pp. 27-36; and James T. Rothe, "Effectiveness of Sales Forecasting Methods," *Industrial Marketing Management* **20** (February 1978), pp. 114-18.

9. See Hoy F. Carman, "Improving Sales Forecasts for Appliances," *Journal of Marketing Research* **9** (May 1972), pp. 214-18, for a description of how additional information can be incorporated into a time-series forecast to improve the accuracy.

10. See Robert L. McLaughlin, *Time Series Forecasting*, Market Research Technique Series No. 6 Chicago: American Marketing Association, 1962; and Robert L. McLaughlin and James J. Boyle, *Short-term Forecasting*, Market Research Technique Series No. 13. Chicago: American Marketing Association, 1968, for a complete description of the Census Method II and FORAN II.

11. For a complete description of the Box-Jenkins procedure, see G. E. P. Box and G. M. Jenkins, *Time Series Analysis, Forecasting, and Control*. San Francisco: Holden-Day, 1974. A more simplified description can also be found in Thomas W. Ferratt and Vincent A. Mabert, "A Description and Application of the Box-Jenkins Methodology," *Decision Sciences* **3** (October 1972), pp. 83-104.

12. Richard C. Wiser, "Sales Forecasting Systems at Mary Kay Cosmetics," *The Journal of Business Forecasting Methods & Systems*, 14 (3), Fall 1995, pp. 26-7.

13. See Philip A. Klein and Geoffrey H. Moore, "The Leading Indicator Approach to Economic Forecasting — Retrospect and Prospect," *Journal of Forecasting* **2** (April — June 1983), pp. 119-35.

14. See, for example, J. Scott Armstrong and M. C. Grohman, "A Comparative Study of Methods for Long-Range Market Forecasting," *Management Science* **19** (October 1972), pp. 211-21; M. D. Geurts and I. B. Ibrahim, "Comparing the Box-Jenkins Approach with the Exponentially Smoothed Forecasting Model with an Application to Hawaii Tourists," *Journal of Marketing Research* **12** (May 1975), pp. 182-7; Gene K. Groff, "Empirical Comparison of Models for Short-Range Forecasting," *Management Science* **20** (September 1973), pp. 22-31; R. M. Kirby, "A Comparison of Short and Medium Range Statistical Forecasting Methods," *Management Science* **13** (December 1966), pp. B202-10; E. Mahmoud, "Accuracy in Forecasting: A

Survey," *Journal of Forecasting* **3** (July – September 1984), pp. 141-52; Spyros Makridakis, A. Anderson, R. Carbone, R. Fildes, M. Hibon, R. Lewandowski, J. Newton, E. Parzen, and R. Winkler, "The Accuracy of Extrapolation (Time Series) Methods: Results of a Forecasting Competition," *Journal of Forecasting* **1** (April – June 1982), pp. 111-53; and Steven P. Schnaars, "Situational Factors Affecting Forecast Accuracy," *Journal of Marketing Research* **21** (August 1984), pp. 290-7.

Chapter 18

Market Monitoring

Learning Objectives:

Firms must monitor factors that might influence future performance of their brands in order to identify potential opportunities and problems. In Chapter 18, you will learn how companies monitor:

- competitors.
- consumers.
- the trade.
- environmental factors that influence the market for a brand.

Days Inns of America, Inc., is a motel chain that began in the Southeastern portion of the United States to meet the in-transit lodging needs of the economy segment of the market. When Day's Inn management began working on plans to market to other segments, however, they realized that they were out of touch with the lodging market they now faced. For example, they did not know the types of travelers who currently patronized Days Inns, how Days Inns were now perceived relative to competitors, or what amenities the traveling public now desired.

Days Inns commissioned two telephone surveys to learn more about the lodging market. One survey randomly sampled recent Days Inns guests and was designed to provide information about the market segment currently being served. The second survey was conducted among a random sample of individuals who had recently traveled but had stayed at motels other than Days Inns. This second survey was designed to explore how Days Inns was perceived relative to competitive chains and to gain insight regarding important lodging amenities for these travelers.

Results of the surveys indicated that Days Inns was still successful at attracting in-transit, nonbusiness travelers who desired economy lodging. However, the results also indicated that a growing segment of economy-minded business travelers now existed that was not being served by Days Inns. These travelers felt that Days Inns' predominantly suburban locations were inconvenient and lacked certain necessary amenities. Subsequently, Days Inns began opening downtown locations and adding amenities such as meeting facilities to adapt to the changing market and to attract the business traveler.

The marketplace a brand faces is not static — competitors come and go, consumer wants and needs change, distributor requirements change, and environmental conditions are constantly in a state of flux. Thus, even though a marketing strategy has been successful, marketplace forces can require revising a brand's strategy over time. A firm must periodically conduct research, like the Days Inns study just described, to determine whether adaptations in the marketing mix for the brand are required. The firm may find, like Days Inns, that a change is required in the product or service offered or that some other component of the marketing mix, such as the advertising or promotional strategy, needs to be changed.

Market monitoring is interrelated with the new-product introduction process in that market monitoring may uncover new product opportunities. For example, researching the current competitive structure of a market may lead to the decision to introduce a new brand to counter a competitive offering. Likewise, identifying new environmental forces at work in the marketplace can lead to new brands. For instance, growing consumer concern over excess packaging and the environmental problems associated with solid waste disposal led Procter & Gamble to introduce Downy Refill (see Exhibit 18.1), a concentrate sold in containers resembling milk cartons. Consumers mix Downy Refill with water in their original plastic Downy bottles, reducing the amount of packaging waste. Similarly, when the United States federal tax laws were changed eliminate non-mortgage interest as a tax deduction, financial institutions developed new types of consumer loans, secured in part by home equity, to give consumers a tax-deductible loan alternative.

Exhibit 18.1
A new product introduced in response to changing market conditions.

Monitoring Competition

Companies frequently conduct studies to obtain information about their competitors. **Market structure studies** are used to identify the major current or potential competitors in a market, to uncover their strengths and weaknesses, and to project what their future marketing strategies might be. Market structure studies are vital in managing existing brands because a new entry can change the way existing brands are perceived. For instance, the introduction of Miller Lite beer created a new category of beer brands and changed the way existing brands were viewed. A new entry commonly has a dramatic impact on the market performance of existing brands as well. When two new brands of antiperspirants, Degree and Powerstick, were introduced in the United States, they captured a combined 8.5 percent market share of the $1.2 billion dollar antiperspirant market.[1] This market share came at the expense of all of the other major brands and caused a flurry of competitive reactions.

Defining the Competition

Identifying a brand's rivals depends upon how broadly one defines competition. As indicated in Exhibit 18.2, competition can be defined at four different levels.[2]

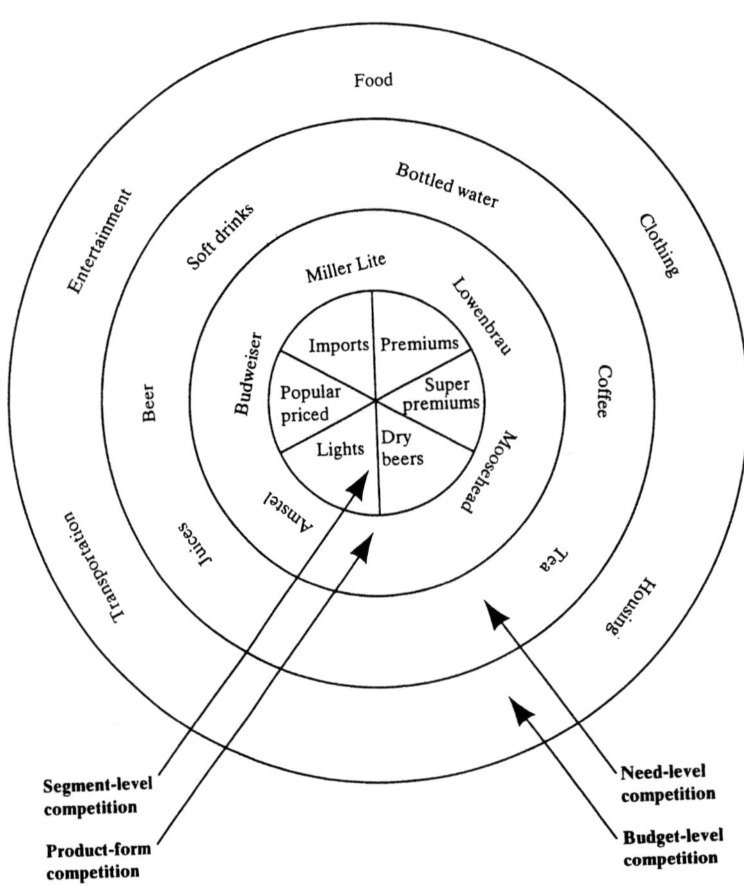

Levels of competition.

Budget-Level Competition

The most general level of competition, **budget-level competition**, is competition among products and services for a share of the total expenditures of the market. All products and services that might be purchased by the individuals in the market would be considered competitors at this level of competition. Obviously, defining a market structure based on budget-level competition is much too broad for typical marketing applications.

Need-Level Competition

Focusing only on those products and services that attempt to satisfy the same basic need would define a second market structure, called **need-level competition**. For the example shown in Exhibit 18.2, need-level competition defines what might be termed the "beverage market." This market would include all products such as soft drinks, bottled water, beer, milk, and coffee.

Defining a market structure at the need level provides an estimate of the total demand for all brands that attempt to satisfy that particular need. In addition, it is useful for identifying *all* potential substitutes for a company's brand(s), not just competitive brands. For example, coffee consumption per capita in the United States has been declining for several years as consumers switch to other beverages.

Understanding market structure at the need level may provide ideas for expanding a brand's business. Sometimes a company will attempt to reposition the brand as a viable alternative to a related product category to take advantage of a larger potential sales volume. This is what Honey Hill Farms did when they initiated an advertising campaign promoting its yogurt as an alternative to ice cream.[3] If successful, this repositioning would have a substantial payoff because the United States ice cream market has a sales volume ten times that of the yogurt market.

Defining a market structure at the need level is not only used to monitor existing brands, but also can serve to generate new product or service ideas that a company might offer. The Coca-Cola Company markets beverages such as Minute Maid orange juice through its Foods Division in addition to the soft drinks for which it is famous. These other beverages are logical offerings given the wealth of knowledge the company possesses about the beverage market.

Product-Form Competition

A third way to define competition is **product-form competition**, which exists among all brands in the same product or service category. In the example shown in Exhibit 18.2, product-form competition defines the "beer market," comprised of all competitive brands of beer.

The set of competitors comprising product-form competition is the market structure most often used when computing performance statistics for brands, such as market share, or when forecasting market sales. However, in today's sophisticated markets, competition is most intense at a narrower level than product form — the segment level.

Segment-Level Competition

For many product categories, such as beer, different variations of the basic product have been introduced to appeal to different consumer segments in the market. Brands are positioned to appeal to particular consumer segments, and those subsets of brands positioned similarly form a competitive set. Organizing the brands into such competitive sets results in the most detailed market structure, known as **segment-level competition.** Competition at this level in the beer market, for example, exists among the various brands that comprise each of the types of beer — the light, import, popular-priced, premium, and super-premium beers. Thus, even though each Anheuser-Busch brand competes with all other brands of beer (including other Anheuser-Busch brands) for a share of the total beer market, each Anheuser-Busch brand is designed to compete within a specific competitive set of similarly positioned brands. Budweiser competes within the premium category, Michelob within the super-premium category, Busch within the popular category, and Bud Light within the light-beer category. The most serious threats to each brand are other brands in the same competitive set.

Segment-level competition is the market structure of most concern to the brand manager because it defines the arena in which the manager's brand competes. Information about other brands comprising the competitive set is vital to the brand manager in developing the marketing strategy for the brand. Defining market structure at the segment level also allows a company to determine what competitive sets exist, thereby generating new product possibilities by identifying attractive segments for which the company currently has no offering.

Using Research to Define Market Structure

A need-level market structure can be obtained by listing all categories of products or services satisfying the same basic need and by enumerating the brands within each category. All brands listed within a category compete at the product form level. However, information about how consumers perceive brands as substitutes for one another is required to develop a segment-level market structure. A segment-level structure can be obtained by examining either actual consumer purchase behavior or consumer perceptions.[4]

Defining Competition by Purchase Behavior

The actual purchases that consumers make within a product category provide information regarding the degree of substitutability existing between brands. The basic premise is that as consumers switch more frequently between two brands, these brands are more easily substituted and compete more strongly against each other. Because of its longitudinal nature, consumer purchase panel data are commonly used to examine consumer brand switching across different purchase occasions.

Several empirical methods have been proposed for using brand-switching data to determine market structure.[5] These methods attempt to determine whether, based on the level of switching that occurs across brands, the total set of brands in the category is actually comprised of distinct groups of brands that compete more closely with each other than with the other brands. These methods also identify the brands comprising each of the groups. Sophisticated mathematical analysis, beyond the scope of this text, forms the basis for these analyses.

Defining Competition by Consumer Perceptions

Instead of using purchase behavior, consumers' perceptions of the similarity among brands can be used to determine market structure. Perceptual mapping techniques, like those discussed in Chapter 12, can be used to portray how consumers perceive the brands available to them. Brands that consumers perceive as similar form a competitive set.

Identifying Competitive Strengths and Weaknesses

Once the competitive set has been defined, the next step in a market structure study is to uncover any strengths or weaknesses of these competitors that could influence the sales potential of the company's brands. Strength or weakness can occur in any aspect of the production or marketing of a brand. Such things as access to raw materials, production capability, quality of management, access to capital, strength of the distribution network, marketing expertise, or extent of consumer loyalty can all provide a strength or weakness.

The majority of the research information used to identify competitive strengths and weaknesses comes from secondary sources. Magazine articles, company reports, trade publications, and newspaper articles comprise the bulk of the sources used. Because of the vast number of potential sources, many companies subscribe to clipping services to reduce the search time required. **Clipping services** scan a wide variety of current periodicals and reproduce any article that might provide information of use to their client companies.

Information on competitive strengths and weaknesses is often provided by a company's sales force as well. Since the company's sales force maintains close contact with the trade, they are often aware of upcoming competitive activities very quickly. For example, the sales staff may become aware of a test market for a competitive brand as soon as the test market begins. For this reason, many firms periodically collect market intelligence information from their sales staffs to keep abreast of developments in the market.

Forecasting Future Competitive Strategies

The final aspect of a market structure study is to predict the future marketing strategies of the competitors. This is extremely difficult at best, since companies very seldom publicize their plans. However, the research information obtained on the strengths and weaknesses of the competitors helps assess what each firm is capable of doing and is most likely to do.

Monitoring Consumers

The sales volume and market share achieved by a brand are the key indicators of a brand's overall performance. However, the firm also needs detailed information regarding consumer attitudes toward the brand and how satisfied they are with it. Most companies also use tracking studies to monitor a brand's performance in this context. A **tracking study** is a form of marketing research that is designed to provide periodic updating of a brand's or company's performance, as well as that of selected competitors, on aspects other than sales. The three non-sales aspects of performance commonly tracked are:

1. brand awareness, attitudes, and usage;

2. brand satisfaction or dissatisfaction; and

3. corporate image.

Tracking Awareness, Attitudes, and Usage

In the last chapter, we discussed the importance of conducting a sales analysis to determine the source of a brand's sales volume (for example, how much of the sales volume comes from first-time buyers as opposed to repeat purchasers). Awareness, attitude, and usage studies, sometimes called **AAU studies**, augment the sales analysis information. AAU studies not only monitor the extent of brand usage by consumers but also track the number of consumers who are aware of the brand and its competitors at any point in time and the attitudes consumers have toward the brand and its competitors.

The Importance of Tracking Awareness, Attitudes, and Usage

Tracking awareness and attitudes toward the brands in the competitive set as well as past brand usage are important because these variables provide diagnostic information related to future sales. Changes in any of these three variables over time may signal problems associated with the marketing efforts being applied to the brand that could lead to a decrease in future sales. Each of these three measures provides different information to management.

Consumers obviously must be aware that a brand exists before they can purchase it. Brand awareness can be achieved by word-of-mouth and can be generated at the point of purchase, either merely by being available or through special displays or other in-store promotions. However, companies rely most heavily on advertising to generate brand awareness, and advertising expenditures are expected to achieve a certain level of consumer awareness of the brand. Tracking the level of brand awareness in the market is one way to ascertain whether this advertising objective has been met.

Brand awareness is a necessary, but not a sufficient, condition for a sale to occur. The attitudes that consumers have toward the brand or the images they have of the brand influence behavior. These attitudes are formed through experience with the brand, through discussions with other consumers, through advertising, or even through attitudes that the consumer holds about the company selling the brand. Sales may be low, even though brand awareness is high due to the attitudes consumers have toward the brand. For example, at one time, Nissan Motor Company conducted an advertising campaign for its Infiniti automobile in which the car was not pictured or described. Instead, nature scenes and beautiful scenery were shown. Tracking studies revealed that general awareness of the Infiniti was extremely high. However, consumer familiarity with the individual models and features was so low that the campaign was abandoned for a more traditional, product-specific advertising format.[6]

Tracking brand attitudes helps detect problems that can affect future sales. Management at the Adolph Coors Brewing Company found that attitudes toward Coors beer as well as the sales of the beer were affected by adverse publicity the company received when accused of unfair labor practices.[7] After settling their differences with the labor unions, the company had to work to undo this damage to its image.

Past usage is also a critical indicator of a brand's health. If consumers are currently buying a brand, it is reasonable to expect them to continue to purchase it, so a drop in recent purchasing signals a problem. Tracking data can help identify which types of consumers have changed their purchase habits and the brands to which they have switched and may suggest ways to recapture sales. For instance, McDonald's might discover from a tracking study that past usage is down among senior citizens due to a promotion being run by Burger King. McDonald's could then devise a strategy to counter this promotion. Applying Marketing Research 18.1 illustrates an elaborate tracking system developed for use in a non-traditional setting.

Applying Marketing Research 18.1

Marketing is vital in the tourism business. Unfortunately, tourist destination areas have never had the ability to track tourists and their spending habits with any efficiency to determine how effective any marketing efforts have been. Now, the state of Florida has begun a massive tracking program of its tourists, thanks in large part to bar-code technology.

Florida distributes hundreds of millions of discount coupon books to various attractions annually. Many of the books are distributed through direct mail, while others are in conjunction with travel agents, airlines, and other merchants. SouthEast Advantage, a discount travel club, developed a proprietary bar code system that provides unique identification of individuals who redeem these coupons.

Recipients of the coupon books must return socioeconomic information about themselves before the coupons become valid. They then receive a set of bar code labels that must be affixed to the coupons prior to redemption. The coupons and bar codes are nontransferable.

When coupons are redeemed, the bar code information can be used to generate a list of redeemer mailing labels as well as statistical tracking of redeemer behavior. The net result has been the creation of the largest tourist profile database in Florida history. Merchants can use this information in a multitude of ways. For instance, the efficiency of their advertising can be examined by reviewing printouts of tourist origins by Zip codes. Similarly, they could determine which travel agents, airlines, auto rental companies, or other retailers have been the best co-promotion partners, based on referrals generated.[18]

Conducting AAU Studies

AAU studies are typically conducted using telephone interviewing and are designed to be repeated at regular time intervals (such as annually). Awareness, attitudes, and usage are often measured in several ways during the course of the interview. For example, three different measures of brand awareness are listed in Table 18.1. (Sometimes, similar measures are also obtained for advertising awareness.) The difference between **unaided awareness** and **aided awareness** is that a brand prompt is included in the question for the latter. Aided brand awareness is not a very meaningful measure for well-established brands in highly familiar product or service categories because virtually all respondents will be aware of such brands when prompted. In other words, **total awareness** is close to 100 percent for such brands. However, aided awareness is useful for a new brand that has yet to attain top-of-mind status among consumers who have heard of the brand. Whatever the measures, they are obtained for each of the brands in a category of goods or competitive set, and changes in the measures from period to period provide signals to marketing managers.

Unaided brand awareness	Consumers are asked to name all of the brands that they can think of in the product category.
Aided brand awareness	Consumers are asked if they are aware of particular brands. This question is typically asked as a follow-up to the unaided awareness question and is only asked for those brands of which the respondent is not aware on an unaided basis.
Total awareness	This is the total number of consumers who are aware of the brand either on an unaided or an aided basis.

Table 18.1
Commonly used measures of awareness

Similarly, a variety of different methods exists for measuring brand attitudes. Consumers might be asked to rate each brand in a competitive set on a series of attributes. The mean ratings of the brands are plotted for each attribute to produce brand profiles that graphically represent consumer perceptions of the brands. Exhibit 18.3 contains an example of using such attribute profiles to monitor consumer perceptions of two brands of snack crackers. If tracking indicates that a change has occurred in how a company's brand is perceived relative to competitors on one or more attributes, corrective marketing action may be required. Another way to measure brand attitudes is to ask consumers to describe the type of person most likely to use the brand or to indicate the usage situation for which the brand would be most appropriate. Finally, consumers might simply be asked what brand is their favorite as an overall measure of attitude.

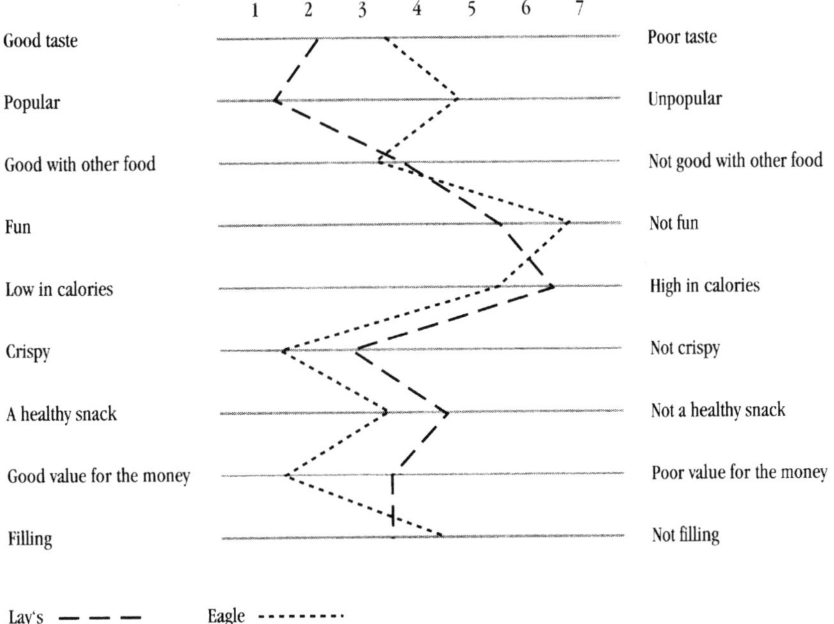

Exhibit 18.3
Example of the use of attribute rating scales to measure attitude toward a brand. (Note: This plot is hypothetical and is not based on actual survey data. The difference between the two brands depicted above is only meant to demonstrate how brands can be profiled in this way.)

To track brand usage, consumers are sometimes asked to list all brands in the competitive set that they have purchased within a particular time frame. Conversely, consumers might simply be asked which brand was purchased most often within that time frame or which brand was purchased last.

Various companies adopt different measures of brand awareness, attitudes, and usage. The specific measures selected are simply a matter of company preference since no evidence exists to suggest that any one measure is best; firms also realize that no measure provides a perfect indicator of any of the three factors. However, it is important that the measures used by a firm remain the same across the tracking studies that it conducts so that comparisons from time period to time period are not influenced by changes in the measure.

Exhibit 18.4 illustrates how the data provided by a tracking study might be presented. As you can see by the top graph of the exhibit, consumer awareness of the Gateway brand of personal computer has dropped in the last two waves of the tracking study. Furthermore, usage of the brand has also dropped in these same periods. On the other hand, both awareness and usage of the Apple personal computer have increased. These two patterns are likely to be related, a conclusion that could be reinforced by other company information. Research data might reveal that Gateway's share of advertising spending, known as share of voice, has declined over the same period relative to Apple's share of voice, suggesting that Gateway should increase advertising spending.

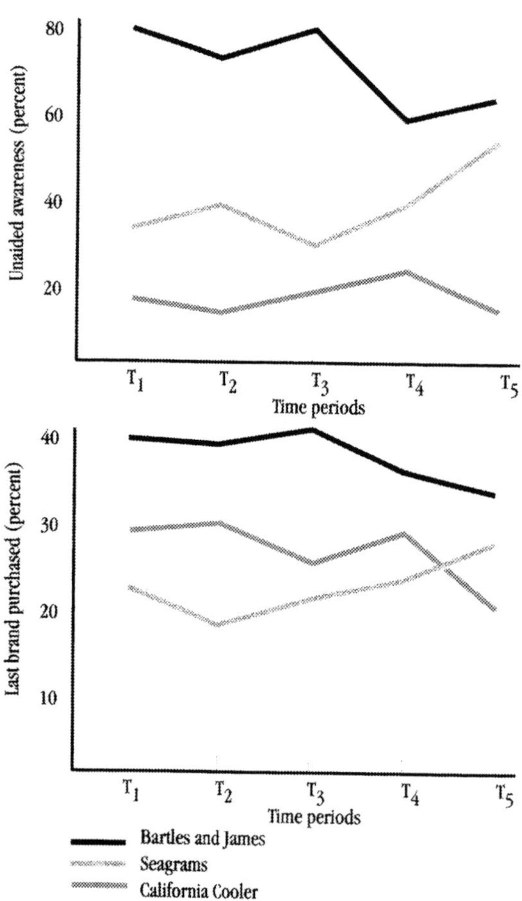

Exhibit 18.4
Five periods of consumer tracking data for three brands of wine coolers.

Tracking Satisfaction/Dissatisfaction Historically, research designed to measure and track consumer satisfaction or dissatisfaction with a company's brands was not a high priority. Consumer comments gathered through informal methods, such as toll-free telephone numbers and patron opinion cards often found in restaurants or hotels, accounted for the bulk of this effort. Many large manufacturers of consumer packaged goods, such as Procter & Gamble and Lever Bros., monitor the number and types of consumer complaints about specific brands using toll-free telephone numbers provided on the product packages. An increase in the total calls received during any period signals a potential problem.

Starting in the 1980s, however, many U.S. firms began to take product quality and customer satisfaction more seriously. Formal and systematic tracking of customer satisfaction was undertaken, and tracking results were given weight in employee performance evaluations and incentive plans. Several factors caused these actions by U.S. businesses.

First of all, two extremely popular management books published during the 1980s, *In Search of Excellence* and its sequel *A Passion for Excellence*, stressed closeness with the customer (*i.e.*, knowing what the customer feels and wants) and pleasing the customer as keys to success. These books cited deteriorating quality and lack of concern for the customer as key factors in the poor performance of many American businesses. Conversely, obsession with quality and customer satisfaction were seen as keys to the huge success of Japanese imports in the United States.

A second reason for the increased concern for quality and customer satisfaction is that, in 1987, the U.S. Congress created the Malcolm Baldridge National Quality Award. This award was the country's first prize recognizing quality in American industry and was developed to underscore the importance of quality.[9] The award has become a coveted and prestigious symbol of success for American companies and has stimulated competition among them (see Exhibit 18.5).

C A D I L L A C  S T Y L E

A victory for the American consumer.

For the first time, an automobile company has won the coveted Malcolm Baldrige National Quality Award for its world-class achievements. The President of the United States has awarded Cadillac this honor on behalf of the U.S. Government.

Cadillac has put the customer first with such programs as a no-deductible warranty* that's among the finest of any luxury car–foreign or domestic, 24-hour Cadillac Roadside Service, and a consumer relations hotline. Plus engineering breakthroughs that include V8 engines that are as responsive as they are responsible–for instance, the 4.9 liter V8-powered Cadillacs have the highest highway mileage of any V8-powered luxury automobiles with an EPA estimated 26 mpg highway.

Cadillac is proud to be honored by this prestigious award. But the real winner is you, the American consumer, who benefits most from Cadillac's commitment to quality and the inherent advantages it fosters.

*See your dealer for terms of this limited warranty.

THE ONLY WAY TO TRAVEL IS  CADILLAC STYLE.

Exhibit 18.5
Cadillac was the first automobile to receive the Malcolm Baldrige National Quality Award. (Courtesy of Cadillac Motor Car Division, General Motors.)

Finally, product quality and customer satisfaction became highly discussed topics in business circles in the 1980s. As mentioned in Chapter 1, a market focus leading to satisfied customers is a key consideration for business decisions in the 1990s. Indeed, one executive declared that the 1990s would be "the decade of customer satisfaction."[10]

Formal tracking of satisfaction/dissatisfaction often proceeds in much the same manner as tracking brand awareness, attitudes, and usage. Telephone interviews are conducted periodically with a random sample of customers, and the level of satisfaction with the product or service is monitored. Overall satisfaction ratings are usually obtained in addition to ratings of the brand on key attribute dimensions.

Service firms in particular find that tracking customer satisfaction/dissatisfaction is crucial. For a tangible product, quality can be monitored, managed, and measured to a large extent at the manufacturing facility through process and quality-control procedures. A service, on the other hand, is not manufactured, packaged, and stored for future sale. Rather, services are typically created and delivered at the point of sale. Furthermore, service quality is subject to more variability because it often depends greatly on the individual performing the service. Therefore, the evaluation of service quality relies almost entirely on the perceptions of the service by the users. Thus, service companies, regardless of whether they are long-distance telephone companies, hotel chains, or airlines, must solicit feedback from their customers regarding their level of satisfaction to assess service quality, as Applying Marketing Research 18.2 illustrates.

Applying Marketing Research 18.2

The University Hospital Consortium is an alliance of 67 academic health centers. The Consortium tracks patient satisfaction to demonstrate to insurance companies and other coverage providers that the health centers are providing quality service. Tracking also helps to identify patient service areas that need improvement.

The survey asks patients what they need, expect, and want, in health care service. In addition, they are asked to rate specific experiences in the hospital. For example, patients are asked to rate how often doctors were available to answer questions or how quickly doctors saw the patient instead of being asked a general question about whether doctors were available. The mail survey generates about a

50% response, using one follow-up mailing, and the University Hospital Consortium plans to continue the tracking indefinitely.[11]

Customer satisfaction is not just an issue for consumer goods and services, either. It is also extremely important for industrial marketers. BellSouth monitors the performance of its corporate telecommunications systems by periodically surveying a random sample of corporate customers. Participants in the survey are questioned regarding their overall satisfaction with the system, as

well as their opinions regarding system specifics such as reliability, versatility, and speed.

Tracking Corporate Image

Like the brands they sell, companies also have images. A company's image is determined in part by the images of its brands but is also influenced by the actions taken by the company. Since the sales of a brand can be influenced by the image of the parent company, corporations are extremely concerned about public relations.

Sometimes a company faces an ongoing public relations battle. Examples are firms manufacturing tobacco products or alcoholic beverages. Citizen groups and government agencies continually attempt to restrict the marketing of these products. The public furor surrounding these debates has a tremendous impact on the image of companies in these industries. At other times, a company must be concerned about the repercussions of a single event, as Applying Marketing Research 18.3 illustrates.

Applying Marketing Research 18.3

Archer-Daniels-Midland is a large, multi-national corporation with sales of over 14 billion dollars. The bulk of the company's profits come primarily from the processing of grains and oil seeds oils and the extraction of various chemicals from these seeds that are used to create both animal-feed additives and food-additives. Because of its position in the industry, the company's stock was highly touted by many stock market analysts. However, this situation quickly changed when news broke that key executives were being indicted for price fixing.

The FBI investigation led to criminal charges being filed against most key executives and fines of over $200 million. In addition, class action civil suits were settled for many additional millions of dollars. During this time, the company's image was severely damaged as stock price plummeted and did not recover for many years thereafter.[12]

A company tracks its corporate image in a fashion similar to the tracking of its brand image. Surveys are conducted periodically, and changes in the image of the company, as measured by the responses to each question, are noted. Sometimes a company will also add additional questions to gauge public awareness of a current issue that might have public relations implications and to determine how serious the issue is in the minds of consumers.

Concern over corporate image is not restricted to companies receiving negative publicity, nor is it restricted to large corporations. Every company, from the largest international corporation to the smallest local business, must be concerned about the image portrayed. However, the amount of corporate-image research conducted does vary greatly. Unlike large companies, a small business may find it hard to justify the expense required to poll its constituency every six months.

Monitoring the Trade

For most brands, the manufacturer must rely on middlemen, commonly referred to as the trade, to do the actual selling of brands to the consumer. However, the trade has been grossly under researched because, historically, large manufacturers were able to gain trade cooperation while making few concessions to these distributors.[13] As noted in Chapter 16, this relationship has changed. The trade has gained much more power and influence, especially at the retail level. This shift in the balance of power has occurred for several reasons.

Reasons for the Increased Power of the Trade

Three factors have caused the trade to become more influential in its dealing with manufacturers:

1. the consolidation of the retail industry,

2. the proliferation of new products, and

3. the advent of scanner technology.

Consolidation of the Retail Industry

Large retail chains now comprise the bulk of the sales for most products. These chains centralize purchasing for all of their stores, producing much larger order sizes than would occur if each store purchased individually. This centralized buying gives these chains a strong negotiating position with the manufacturers. Many small retailers are also able to take advantage of centralized buying by affiliating themselves with wholesale or retail alliances that are able to wield more power with manufacturers.

Proliferation of New Products

A huge number of new products are introduced every year. In a recent year, close to 7000 new packaged-goods products, including both totally new products and different varieties and sizes of established products, were introduced in supermarkets.[14] Each of these new products, as well as all of those already being distributed, competes for shelf space at the retail level. Shelf space has become a more and more valuable commodity, and it is the retailer, not the manufacturer, who has control over it.

Advent of Scanner Technology

The factor most influential in swinging the pendulum of power from the manufacturer to the trade is scanner technology. This technology has had a major impact on the ability of retailers, particularly supermarket chains, to manage their businesses. Computers linked to check-out scanners accumulate sales information by brand in a computer database, that can be readily accessed by retail managers. For the first time, many of these retailers are aware of current sales results for their stores and are able to identify quickly which items are meeting sales expectations and which are not, without relying on information provided to them by the manufacturer. These retailers are able to make more informed decisions than before as to which brands to continue to stock and how much shelf space to allocate to each.

The ability to more accurately assess sales by category has led to an emphasis on category management. **Category management** is the planning of items carried and inventory levels within merchandise categories at the individual store level within retail chains. With category management, a chain can eliminate slow-moving brands and flavors in various stores without reducing profits. Census-level scanner data allows retailers and manufacturers to work together to plan the best inventory mix for the stores.[15]

Evidence of the Supermarket's Power

Slotting allowances, rejection of regional and divisional trade deals, and trade influence on manufacturer couponing practices are examples of the increased power of supermarket chains in the current marketing environment.

Slotting Allowances

Besieged by requests for shelf space for new products, supermarkets have moved to charging slotting allowances for new entries because they know that the vast majority of these products will not be successful.[16] **Slotting allowances** are fees that marketers must pay to retail supermarket chains in order to obtain shelf space for a new product. It is difficult to imagine such a fee being charged to large manufacturers like General Foods a few years ago. However, retailers point out that the number of new items stocked in a typical supermarket is now 26,000, as opposed to only 13,000 two decades ago, and that most new items are neither very original nor successful.[17] Furthermore, supermarket chains argue that slotting allowances compensate for the risk they take when carrying a new item, for the costs associated with stocking a new item and for expenses incurred in introducing it into their system.

However, slotting allowances have come under attack from a number of directions, including scrutiny by the Federal Trade Commission.[18] As a result, manufacturers and supermarkets have begun to search for alternatives acceptable to both parties. One of the most popular of these alternatives is a **failure fee** paid to the supermarket by the manufacturer if a new product fails to sell at a predetermined level.[19] If failure fees become popular, manufacturers will have to be very careful about predictions of new brand sales volume to prevent paying the fee. As Herbert Baum, President of Campbell USA, noted: "It places a greater burden on our people to make sure products are well-tested before rolling out."[20]

Regional and Divisional Trade Deals

Over the last few years, many manufacturers have attempted to regionalize their marketing activities rather than to have one marketing plan for the entire United States. Some supermarkets, however, have resisted such efforts and have made it much more difficult for a manufacturer to engage in regional marketing. The Winn-Dixie supermarket chain threatened to stop carrying products for manufacturers who refused to charge Winn-Dixie a uniform price across all geographic divisions.[21] Winn-Dixie's argument for accepting only national deals was that many supermarket chains order generously to take advantage of regional deals and then simply ship some of the inventory to other regions. Rather than being forced to follow this practice, Winn-Dixie preferred uniform pricing.

Coupons

In an attempt to attract customers, many supermarkets began to double, or even triple, the value of manufacturers' discount coupons. Exhibit 18.6 shows examples of such offers. Like most promotions that are easily copied, these supermarkets found that competitors quickly followed suit. Without the additional volume hoped for, all that these supermarkets were left with were smaller profit margins.

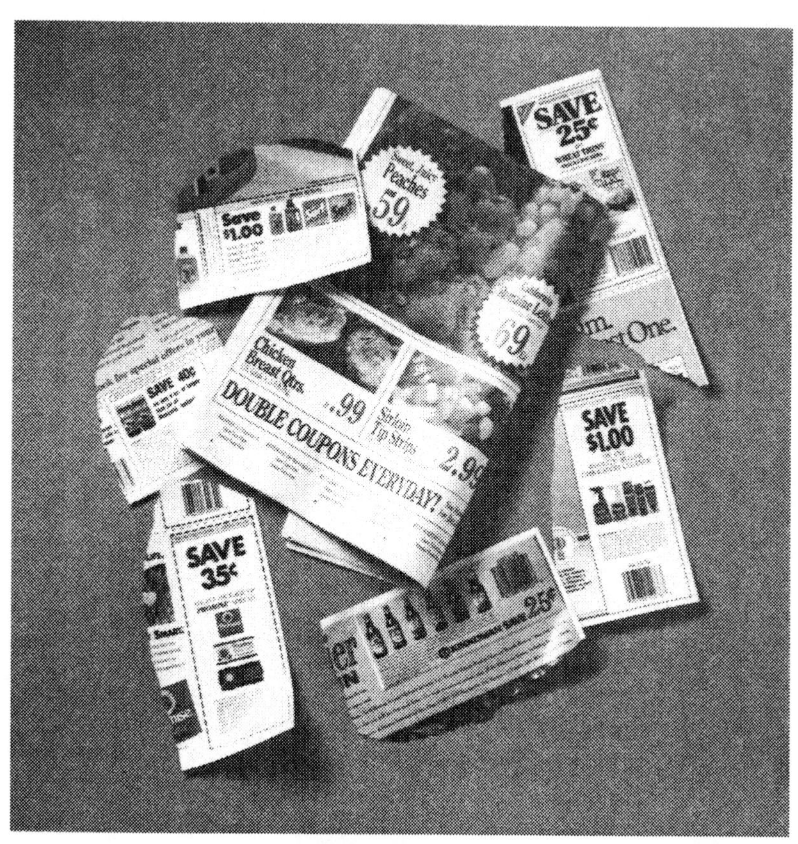

Exhibit 18.6
Many supermarkets increase the value of manufacturers' coupons to try to attract business.

Once most supermarkets begin doubling or tripling coupon values, an individual supermarket cannot unilaterally quit, or it will be at a competitive disadvantage. As a partial remedy for this untenable situation, supermarkets have begun pressuring manufacturers either to reduce coupon values or to increase the values above 50¢, the maximum value that most supermarkets agree to double or triple. As evidence of the power of these supermarket chains, coupons having the unusual value of 55¢, such as the one shown in Exhibit 18.7, are becoming more and more common.

Exhibit 18.7
Supermarket chains put pressure on manufacturers to increase some coupon values above 50 cents, the maximum amount a supermarket normally doubles or triples, to reduce their losses during double or triple coupon value promotions.

Researching the Trade

As mentioned, little attention has been given to researching the trade. The increased importance and influence of the trade, however, demands that companies increase their research efforts toward this group. The following are some of the specific areas in which marketing research information can provide valuable and actionable information for improving a company's relationships with the trade.

Retail Sales

A company must be able to track the retail sales of its own and competitive brands in order to know how its brands are performing. As discussed in Chapter 5, retail sales data are readily available for many categories of goods, from sources such as the A.C. Nielsen Company and Information Resources, Inc. However, in some categories, no such information is commercially available. For example, no syndicated service monitors sales in the home-flooring industry. However, one company in the industry obtains sales data for home-flooring materials on a quarterly basis by interviewing 1800 owners and managers of retail outlets. Information regarding brands, styles, quantities, and prices are obtained each quarter, and selected results are then

shared with the trade to assist them in managing their businesses and to enhance basic trade relationships.[22]

Corporate Image

The trade forms an image of a company just as consumers do. However, a company's image may be different in the two groups, so it is important that a company track its image with the trade as well as with consumers. Routine tracking studies — for example, an annual or semiannual survey of the trade — can help companies measure and assess the current perceptions the trade has of the company and its competitors. As demonstrated in Applying Marketing Research 18.4, such studies can also help identify ways to strengthen or change the corporate image.

Applying Marketing Research 18.4

The name Kodak is associated with photography. At one time, a camera was often referred to as a Kodak, just as facial tissue is frequently called Kleenex today. However, Kodak's dominant position in the film and economically priced camera market has eroded over the years. Consequently, Kodak has diversified (the company acquired Sterling Drug) and expanded into new markets (*e.g.*, video tape) in an effort to sustain growth.

A recent Kodak venture is a high-tech compact disc system for storing photographs and showing them on a television screen. Trade support is of course crucial to success for this new product.

How will the trade react? Will they be dubious about Kodak's ability to deliver the kind of product that they might expect more from Sony or Panasonic than from Kodak? Routine tracking of Kodak's image among the trade would provide this information. It may be that an advertising and public relations campaign directed at the trade is needed to enhance Kodak's corporate image as an innovator and a high-tech company. Routine tracking of Kodak's image with the trade would also allow the company to measure the success of such a campaign.

Sales Force Effectiveness

Companies must sell their brands to the trade. Therefore, marketing research providing an understanding of the sales tactics that work and those that do not work with the trade is vital. Studies conducted among trade buyers that focus on such topics as sales call frequency and display materials can help identify the strengths and weaknesses of the current sales force strategy.

Evaluation of Trade Advertising

Many companies advertise to the trade through trade publications or even through mass media. However, trade advertising is not often subjected to the same rigorous testing and evaluation as consumer advertising. One primary reason for the lack of research on trade advertising is that the amount of money spent on it is typically much less than what is spent on consumer advertising. Nevertheless, many of the techniques for testing consumer advertising that were discussed in Chapter 15 could readily be adapted to measure the intrusiveness and persuasive power of trade advertising.

New Product Feasibility

The introduction of a new product is always risky, and the emergence of slotting allowances and failure fees have raised the costs of introduction even higher. One often- overlooked component in the success of a new product is retailer acceptance. Therefore, the trade's reaction to a new product should be incorporated into any prediction of its performance. As Applying Marketing Research 18.5 and 18.6 illustrate, sometimes trade reactions can lead to modifications in the marketing plan for the brand that improve its chances of success and, at other times, can identify a potential product failure before it is introduced.

Applying Marketing Research 18.5

A U.S. company that had developed a new photofinishing and enhancing device decided to conduct research among the trade prior to marketing the product. In-depth interviews were conducted with executives of companies most likely to purchase the equipment and with retail store owners involved in photofinishing. The research indicated a high degree of interest among the trade but also uncovered isolated concerns regarding the operation and maintenance of the device. Based on these findings, the manufacturer developed communication materials directed to the trade addressing these issues as part of the new-product introduction.[23]

Applying Marketing Research 18.6

Early in the development process, a company conducted research to explore the trade's attitudes toward its proposed new vitamin product. Interviews among twenty representatives of major chains revealed a broad-based negative reaction. None of the people interviewed felt that the product would be successful, and they indicated that they would be very reluctant to place orders for it. Rather than continue the development of a product that would receive little trade enthusiasm, the company abandoned the project.[24]

Point-of-Purchase Materials

Special displays and other point-of-purchase promotional materials, such as posters, brochures, and placards, can be effective sales devices. Many times a company expects the retailer to provide point-of-purchase displays or materials as part of a trade deal. By gathering trade input into the design of such promotional materials, a company can gain greater trade acceptance and cooperation. As Applying Marketing Research 18.7 points out, ignoring the trade when developing such materials can lead to problems.

Applying Marketing Research 18.7

A major U.S. clothing manufacturer designed a special end-of-aisle display for use in major chain stores. Much money was spent to manufacture the displays and to distribute them to the targeted stores. However, most of these displays were never used and were eventually discarded by the stores. The manufacturer was terribly embarrassed to find that the display was too large to be used as intended in the targeted stores.[25]

Resolving Manufacturer/Trade Conflicts

As you learned in Chapter 16, manufacturers are spending larger and larger amounts of money on trade promotions. These increased expenditures are placing a greater strain on the manufacturer/trade relationship. Manufacturers often complain that the trade does not comply with the requirements of the trade deal, such as setting up the required end-of-aisle display, discounting the retail price, or placing the required local advertising.[26] It has been estimated that almost 50 percent of accepted trade deals get no merchandising support at the retail level, and about two-thirds of the cash allowances are not passed on to consumers.[27] Retailers, on the other hand, acknowledge their lack of compliance with deal requirements but cite the failure of manufacturers to pay attention to the trade's objectives as the cause.[28]

In today's environment, the manufacturer cannot ignore the complaints of the trade. The manufacturer must understand the trade's needs, and both parties must develop a spirit of cooperation. Marketing research can play an important role in cultivating this spirit by providing the manufacturer with information to understand the needs of the trade better and to design trade deals that will gain greater acceptance and compliance. Applying Marketing Research 18.8 demonstrates how one company has begun to work with the trade instead of fighting it.

Applying Marketing Research 18.8

Procter & Gamble has formed "key account teams" comprised of several sales executives.[25] Each team is dedicated to serving the needs of a specific major retail account, seeing that the account receives the amount of merchandise required and tailoring promotions to the account and for evaluating its success. The teams often share this information with the retailer as well. For example, information on the overall effectiveness of a trade promotion run by Procter & Gamble, aggregated across several chains, might be provided to an individual chain to serve as a benchmark by which it can assess its own performance.

These key account teams are part of P & G's overall attempt to reduce friction with the trade. The long-term goal of these efforts is to reduce the amount of money the company spends on trade promotions by increasing the attractiveness and effectiveness of the promotions which are run.

Monitoring the Environment

Companies routinely use information gathered from opinion polls to spot changes in consumers' opinions, attitudes, or behavior that might influence the way in which their brands must be marketed in the future. In addition, companies frequently must commission ad hoc, or issue-specific, studies to investigate the repercussions of a specific event that might have an immediate and dramatic impact. These two types of environmental monitoring studies will be examined here.

Opinion Polls

Opinion polls are studies designed to take the pulse of the public with respect to issues of broad interest. Opinion polls are not designed to provide information to solve a particular problem but rather are designed to capture the mood of consumers and to detect changes in their attitudes or behaviors. Table 18.2 shows selected findings from several recent polls. By themselves, these findings may not seem of much interest to a company, but, if these polls were repeated periodically, a company could spot shifts in the responses that may signal an important change.

Reasons why people drink bottled water *vs.* tap water[1]

	1990	1987
Concerned about tap water purity	32%	42%
Bottled water tastes better	44	33
Both	20	19
Other/Don't know	4	6

Percent of pet owners who give their pets Christmas presents[2]

Dog owners	69%
Cat owners	64
Other pet owner	46

Percentage of parents controlling children's television viewing[3]

	1976	1990
For children 6 and under	49	62
For children 7–12	60	69
For children 13–17	37	45

How much attention TV viewers give to commercials compared with attention they give the programs[4]

More	.2%
As much	16
Somewhat less	32
Much less	34
None	16

How people say their lives would be if television were taken out of their homes[5]

Much worse	6%
Somewhat worse	29
Not much different	46
Somewhat better	14
A lot better	5

Do you favor a special tax on sales of disposable diapers?[6]

Oppose	52%
Favor	38
Don't know/refused	10

Do you favor a ban on sales of disposable diapers?[7]

Oppose	47%
Favor	43
Don't know/refused	10

Table 18.2
Selected findings from a few recent opinion polls

Research firms specializing in polling, such as the Gallup Organization and the Roper Organization, conduct many of the opinion polls we encounter. Even if conducted for a single client, the results of these polls are often made public, although the client does have the right to prevent dissemination of the results. An opinion poll gives a snapshot at one point in time. However, the views expressed are often hard to interpret without some point of comparison. For this reason, many polls are periodically repeated to look for changes in the responses obtained. DDB Needham Advertising annually conducts a survey of nearly 2000 females and 2000 males to gather information on consumer attitudes, activities, product usage, and media behavior. Needham uses the results of this survey to spot trends that might influence the way particular brands might best be advertised.

Ad Hoc Opinion Studies

A firm will frequently conduct research to examine the implications of a particular environmental trend or event. Unlike the more general opinion poll, these studies are more issue-specific, and the findings will generally be of little interest to other firms. Such studies typically examine consumer awareness of the event or issue as well as any associated changes in consumer attitudes or behaviors. For instance, American Express commissioned a consumer poll to determine what factors led consumers to select a particular restaurant. Value was nearly a unanimous first reason given by consumers, but only 50 percent of restauranteurs surveyed felt value was an attractant. Similarly, 90 percent of consumers surveyed ranked ambiance as an important factor, compared to only 40 percent of restauranteurs. By sharing such results with restauranteurs, American Express can improve their image with the trade.

Summary

As you can see from what you learned in this chapter, there is much more to market monitoring than keeping track of brand volume, brand share, and category sales. Firms must also remain knowledgeable about competition and their business strategies. Market structure studies are used for this purpose. However, defining competition is not always easy. Competition can be defined at four levels: budget, need, product form, and segment. Competition is typically examined at the product form (*e.g.*, coffee) or segment (*e.g.*, instant coffee) level.

Companies must also monitor consumers. Tracking studies are used to monitor consumers' awareness and perceptions of brands and companies; attitudes, usage, and habits; and satisfaction/dissatisfaction with products and services.

Manufacturers must also pay increasing attention to the trade (typically the retailer), particularly in the case of consumer packaged goods. As noted in the chapter, friction has developed over manufacturers' growing dissatisfaction with the increasing spiral of trade discounts and the ineffectiveness of these promotions. The trade's lack of compliance with deal requirements further frustrates manufacturers. Manufacturers must conduct research to improve their understanding of the trade's wants and needs and to monitor the effectiveness of their efforts to forge a solid working relationship with the trade.

Finally, companies must stay in touch with the world around them. Opinion polls and *ad hoc* opinion studies provide this type of information.

It is important to note again how the process of developing and introducing a new brand and monitoring its performance is often cyclical. The knowledge obtained from monitoring frequently provides ideas for new products or services, and the process is regenerated.

The Nimslo Epilogue

The Nimslo 3D photography system never achieved the goal of being a firmly established alternative to instant and conventional picture taking. Sales were far below expectations during the introductory year. This poor start dealt the company a blow from which it could not recover; the company reorganized as a small business focusing on portrait photography and serving the photofinishing needs of the small group of Nimslo camera owners. Therefore, market monitoring never really became a major issue at Nimslo.

The Nimslo 3D camera appears to be a product "in search of a market." The Nimslo experience suggests that the system is not a viable alternative for "everyday" photography. Indeed, marketing research often played the role of "Cleopatra's messenger" — delivering disconcerting news about Nimslo's potential and, later, its market performance. However, the company should not be judged too harshly since the Nimslo venture was very risky from the outset.

For durable goods and technology-driven products, a huge investment of capital and time is often necessary to reach the development stage, when a prototype product can be made for consumer testing. By the time an actual product is available to test, so much time and money has already been invested that a "go/no go" decision is sometimes not really an option. Instead, marketing research information is used to make refinements in the final product and in its marketing strategy, which will, one hopes, enhance the likelihood of a successful entry. Nevertheless, failure is still a possibility and, if failure occurs, it is quite often much more dramatic than in packaged goods because of the amount of money involved.

Ten years of research and development effort and a large amount of venture capital were spent before Nimslo had a reasonable prototype camera and photofinishing capacity to support a modest number of users. Investors in the project grew impatient over past delays and pressured the company to quicken the pace of the introduction. In fact, when the camera was introduced, postponement was not an option because funding another year of preparation was out of the question. In addition, bad economic conditions existed in the United States at the time of the introduction; unemployment and inflation reached some of the highest levels in the country's history. All of these factors contributed to the camera's failure.

While the marketing research conducted on the 3D camera was not able to prevent its failure, it did provide useful information to management during the introductory process. Research alerted management to consumer concerns over the planned prices for the camera and for photofinishing, as well as concerns over the perceived quality of the pictures produced. Nimslo management reacted to this information in setting prices and photofinishing standards. Instructional materials, that were included with the camera, were designed to help consumers avoid the mistakes in taking pictures that were identified during product tests. These product tests also raised doubt as to the accuracy of anticipated photofinishing revenue and led to revised forecasts revised forecasts. Similarly, information obtained through retail audits indicated that the forecast of camera sales was overly optimistic. Finally, the copy testing research provided an understanding of the relative effectiveness of the thirty-second versus the sixty-second commercial and guided the selection of the commercial mix used during the introductory campaign.

The final chapter of the story of Nimslo's 3-D system cannot yet be written. As mentioned at the end of Chapter 1, Nishika acquired the rights to the 3-D technology in 1988 and recently introduced its own 3-D camera, the Nishika N8000.[29] The camera retails for approximately $200.00 and prints cost about $1.50 each. It appears that Nishika plans to market the camera on a very limited basis, making it available primarily through catalogs. At this point in time, it seems that the company is content to focus on the existing small group interested in "stereo" photography. Only time will tell whether Nishika succeeds in its attempt to market 3-D photography.

Review Questions

18.1 What is meant by market monitoring? What makes market monitoring studies different from other marketing research projects?

18.2. What is meant by a market structure study? What are the primary reasons for conducting a market structure study?

18.3. In what situations do you feel that need-level competition would be the appropriate market structure to examine? What about product-form competition? Segment-level competition?

18.4. Explain how consumer purchase information can be used to determine market structure.

18.5. Explain how consumer perceptions can be used to determine market structure.

18.6. What aspects of brand performance are typically tracked?

18.7. What is a clipping service?

18.8. Why is it important to track awareness, attitudes, and usage? What makes it essential to track all three of these variables? How is a tracking study usually conducted? How is the gathered information used?

18.9. What factors have caused firms to begin a more careful tracking of customer satisfaction and dissatisfaction?

18.10. Why is the tracking of customer satisfaction and dissatisfaction so important for service firms?

18.11 Why is it important to track corporate image? How is corporate image tracked?

18.12. What factors have led to the increased power of the trade?

18.13 How is the power of the trade evidenced?

18.14 In what specific areas can marketing research provide information that could be used to improve a company's relationship with the trade?

18.15 What are opinion polls? ad hoc studies? How do companies use opinion polls and ad hoc studies for monitoring the environment?

Discussion Questions

18.1. For each of the following markets, indicate whether or not you feel that the market exhibits segment- level competition and, if so, suggest the basis for the segments and the major brands in each:

a. soft drinks

b. cookies

c. coffee

d. salty snack foods

e. consumer credit cards

18.2. For each of the markets listed in the preceding question, describe the need that is being satisfied and list some of the other major product categories that attempt to satisfy this same need.

18.3. Briefly outline a study that you might conduct to examine market structure using consumer purchase data. Be sure to include the types of data needed, the source of the data, and how the data would be examined.

18.4. Briefly outline a study that you might conduct to examine market structure using consumer perceptions data. Be sure to include the types of data needed, the source of the data, and how the data would be examined.

18.4. At various points throughout this book we have discussed single-source data. Discuss the ways in which you feel that single-source data would improve a company's ability to monitor the market.

18.5. General Motors has several divisions, *e.g.*, Buick, Pontiac, and Chevrolet, and each division manufactures many different models of automobiles. Does it seem that the product mix of General Motors is based on an examination of segment level competition? Why or why not? Discuss how General Motors might use research to determine the segments that exist in the automotive market and how it might determine in which segments its various divisions and automobiles compete.

18.5.1. In 1990, Volvo was accused of airing a deceptive advertisement. The incident received national attention and the president of Volvo apologized to the public in a full-page advertisement taken out in *USA Today*. Describe the types of market monitoring research that Volvo might have instituted during this period of time and what information they might have sought.

Chapter 18 Endnotes

---

1. Pat Sloan, "Degree Makes Leaders Sweat," *Advertising Age*, December 10, 1990, p. 16.

2. See Tony Lunn, "Segmenting and Constructing Markets," in Robert Worcester and John Downham, eds., *Consumer Market Research Handbook*. Amsterdam, Netherlands: Elsevier Science Publishers, 1986, pp. 387-424, for a discussion of the relationship between levels of competition and market segmentation.

3. Alice Z. Cuneo, "Yogurt Takes on Ice Cream," *Advertising Age*, May 29, 1989, p. 28S.

4. See George S. Day, Allan D. Shocker and Rajendra K. Srivastava, "Customer-Oriented Approaches to Identifying Product-Markets," *Journal of Marketing* **43** (Fall 1979), pp. 8-19, for a good discussion of behavioral or perception based methods of market structure analysis.

5. A number of research studies have examined the use of brand-switching data to estimate market structure. See, for example, Gregory S. Carpenter and Donald R. Lehmann, "A Model of Marketing Mix, Brand Switching, and Competition," *Journal of Marketing Research* **22** (August 1985), pp. 318-29; Steven M. Shugan, "Estimating Brand Positioning Maps Using Supermarket Scanning Data," *Journal of Marketing Research* **24** (February 1987), pp. 1-18; Rajiv Grover and V. Srinivasan, "A Simultaneous Approach to Market Segmentation and Market Structuring," *Journal of Marketing Research* **24** (May 1987), pp. 139-53; and Wagner A. Kamakura and Gary J. Russell, "A Probabilistic Choice Model for Market Segmentation and Elasticity Structure," *Journal of Marketing Research* **26** (November 1989), pp. 379-90.

6. Cleveland Horton, "Infiniti Revises Ads, Snubs Nature Theme," *Advertising Age*, April 9, 1990, p. 2.

7. "A Long-Brewing Boycott Ends at Coors," *Newsweek*, August 31, 1987, p. 46.

8. W. Lynn Seldon, Jr. "Bar Code Technology Helps Track Florida Tourists," *Marketing News*, November 12, 1990, pp. 8-9.

9. See, Christopher W. L. Hart, Christopher Brogan and Dan O'Brien, "When Winning Isn't Everything," *Harvard Business Review*, January-February 1990, pp. 208-209, for a discussion of the

Malcolm Baldridge National Quality Award.

10. Lynn G. Coleman, "Those Were the Days: Satisfaction Was King This Year; Focus Shifted to Service, Employees," *Marketing News*, December 10, 1990, p.2.

11. "Patients Help Consortium Shape Health Improvements," *Marketing News*, August 28, 1995, p.25.

12. "ADM, Shareholders Settlement Approved," *The National Law Journal*, April 28, 1997, p. B2; Nancy Millman, "Europe Investigates ADM; Raid On Firm Mimics U.S. Action in Similar Price-Fixing Probe," *Chicago Tribune*, June 12, 1997, Business section, p.1.

13. Gerald Meyers, "Trade Buyers Are Influential, but Under researched," *Marketing News*, February 1, 1988,

pp. 12-13.

14. Judann Dagnoli, "Product Launches Dip in First Half," *Advertising Age*, September 11, 1989, p. 110.

15. Leah Haran, "Grocery Category Management Made Better By Census Data," *Advertising Age*, May 6, 1996, p. 16.

16. See Laurie Freeman and Janet Myers, "Grocery 'Fee' Hampers New-Product Launches," *Advertising Age*, August 3, 1987, pp. 1, 60.

17. For a discussion of the shelf space controversy, see Lois Therrian, "Want Shelf Space at the Supermarket? Ante Up," *Business Week*, August 7, 1989, pp. 66-71.

18. See "FTC Reviews Slotting Fees," *Advertising Age*, October 3, 1988, p.8.

19. See "One Way Out of 'Slotting' Fees," *Advertising Age*, August 7, 1989, p.19.

20. Lois Therrian, "Want Shelf Space at the Supermarket? Ante Up," *Business Week*, August 7, 1989, pp. 66-71.

21. See Laurie Freeman and Julie Liesse Erickson, "Grocers Join Winn-Dixie," *Advertising Age*, November 7, 1988,

pp. 3, 78.

22. See Gerald Myers, "Trade Buyers Are Influential, but Under

researched," *Marketing News*, February 1, 1988,

pp. 12-13.

23. *Ibid.*

24. *Ibid.*

25. *Ibid.*

26. See, for example, John A. Quelch, "Trade Promotion by Grocery Products Manufacturers: A Managerial Perspective," *Marketing Science Institute Report no. 82-106*, 1982; and Michel Chevalier and Ronald C. Curhan, "Retail Promotions as a Function of Trade Promotions: A Descriptive Analysis," *Sloan Management Review*, (Fall 1976), pp. 19-32.

27. Michel Chevalier and Ronald C. Curhan, "Retail Promotions as a Function of Trade Promotions: A Descriptive Analysis," *Sloan Management Review*, (Fall 1976), pp. 19-32.

28. See, for example, Bert C. McCammon, Jr., "Perspectives for Distribution Programming," in *Vertical Marketing Systems*, Louis P. Bucklin ed. Glenview, IL: Scott, Foresman and Company, 1970, pp. 32-51; and Roger A. Strang, *The Promotional Planning Process*, New York: Praeger Publishers, 1980.

25. See Laurie Freeman, "Procter & Gamble 'Teams' Serve Retailers' Needs," *Advertising Age*, August 14, 1989, p. 21.

29. Peter Kolonia, "A Born Again Nimslo," *Popular Photography*, November 1989, pp. 71-72.

Case IV.1

Nimslo Advertising Testing

Nimslo developed one television commercial employing the "emerge" special effect noted at the end of this Chapter for the introduction of its 3D photography system. There were two versions of the commercial — a thirty-second and a sixty-second version. Nimslo marketing managers needed information regarding the relative effectiveness of the thirty- and sixty-second versions of the introductory commercial. If the two were found to be comparable in effectiveness, twice as many exposures could be purchased for the thirty-second as opposed to the sixty-second version for the same amount of money. Management believed, however, that the sixty-second commercial would have more communication value than the thirty-second version, because key points were repeated in the :60, and the overall pace was slower in the :60 as compared to the :30. A study was conducted using the ARS system to address this issue.

The two commercials were evaluated in separate ARS tests. Because of the nature of the product, the persuasion measure was not obtained. However, a forced exposure option was used to explore communication value. Separate audiences were shown a Nimslo commercial (the :30 or the :60) at the end of a typical ARS session and questioned regarding what the commercial communicated to them. Tables IV.1.1 thru IV.1.4 present the key comparisons between the two commercials based on the ARS research.

Recall Summary (percentage remembering commercial three days later)

	:30[1]		:60[2,3]
	percentage		percentage
Total sample	44	<——[4]	60
Income $25M +	48	<——	69
Age 25 — 54	47	<——	64
Attended/graduate college	50		59
Heavy film user	47	<——	73
35 mm owner	47	<——	68

[1]:30 scored significantly higher than ARS norm for :30s.

[2]:60 scored significantly higher than :30 overall and within key subgroups.

[3]: Recall scores for :60 are particularly high in key subgroups.

[4]<— indicates significant difference at 90 percent confidence level.

What are the implications of the in-market test results?

Table IV.1.1
Recall summary (percentage remembering commercial three days later)

Copy point recall

	:30 (101)[1]		:60 (139)[1]
	percentage		percentage
Sales messages:	93		97
3-dimensional (key message)[2]	77		78
Lifelike pictures[3]	18	<——	30
New/different	52		42
35 mm camera/film[3]	5	<——	15
Other attributes	59		60
Situation visual:	93		92
Reference to "emerge"[4]	75		80
Other (situational/visual)	70	——>	58
Sales messages as percentage of recall	93		97
Key message as percentage of recall	77		78

[1]Base equals participants recalling commercial.

[2]Key message recall (three-dimensionality) is substantially higher for both the :30 and :60 than the ARS norm for :30s.

[3]Significantly more recallers of the :60 than recallers of the :30 mentioned "lifelike pictures" and "35 mm camera/film" when asked about the commercial.

[4]Over three-fourths of the participants remembering the commercial mentioned the emerge.

Table IV.1.2
Copy point recall

Key features of camera

	:30		:60
	percentage		percentage
Takes three-dimensional pictures[1]	67		72
Four/multiple lenses	43		45
Light and compact/easy to handle/carry	23		23
Clear pictures	12		9
Fully automatic/easy-to-use/instamatic[2]	10	<——	19
Uses regular 35 mm color film[2]	4	<——	40
35 mm Camera[2]	7	<——	14

[1]"Takes three-dimensional pictures" was most frequently mentioned camera feature for both the :30 and :60.

[2]"Fully automatic/easy-to-use/instamatic," "Uses regular 35 mm color film," and "35 mm camera" were mentioned significantly more often as key camera features by viewers of the :60 than by viewers of the :30.

Table IV.1.3
Key features of camera

Communication of key camera features[1]

	:30		:60[2,3]
	percentage		percentage
35 mm camera	40	<——	84
Uses regular 35 mm color film	20	<——	68
Fully automatic	40	<——	66
Not an instant camera	60	<——	80
Does not have built-in lash	36		36
About same size and weight as instamatic	26	<——	50

[1]This table exhibits estimates of the percentages of the audiences aware of the various camera features after viewing the commercial in a forced-exposure mode.

[2]:60 far superior to :30 in communicating important aspects of camera/system.

[3]Significantly more viewers of :60 than viewers of the :30 knew the following facts regarding Nimslo camera: 35 mm camera; uses regular 35 mm color film; fully automatic; *not* an instant camera; and about same size and weight as instamatic.

Table IV.1.4
Communication of key camera features[1]

After the ARS test, Nimslo decided to conduct an in-market test to compare two strategies for using the company's two TV commercials as part of the Florida test market. Only the :30 commercial was used as part of the introductory campaign in four Florida cities. In the remainder of the state, a mix of :30s and :60s was used, with the :60 used heavily at the beginning of the introductory campaign and the :30 used heavily at the end.

After six weeks, a survey was conducted in eight markets — the four test markets where only the :30 commercial was used and four other comparable Florida markets — to measure awareness of the Nimslo camera and attitudes toward the camera. A total of 400 interviews, fifty in each of the eight markets, were conducted with respondents aware of the Nimslo camera. Hence, for comparative purposes, there were 200 respondents exposed to only the :30 commercial and 200 respondents exposed to a mix of :30 and :60 commercials.

Table IV.1.5 contains some of the key findings from the survey.

Purchase intent (after forced exposure)[1]

	:30		:60
	percentage		percentage
Definitely buy	6		7
Probably buy	15		20
Might or might not buy	38		38
Probably not buy	31		24
Definitely not buy	11		10
Total positive	20	<——	28

[1]Purchase intent is significantly higher among viewers of the :60 than viewers of the :30.

Table IV.1.5
Purchase intent (after forced exposure)[1]

What conclusions should Nimslo management have drawn from the ARS research? What implications do the ARS results have for the introductory TV advertising strategy? Are the results of the in-market Florida test consistent with the ARS test results? What are the implications of the in-market test results?

Case IV.2

Schweppes Ginger Ale[1]

Bob Brown was nervous as he sat down in front of the computer terminal. He had just graduated from Midwestern State the week before and had hoped to have some time to get adjusted to his new job in the marketing research department at Cadbury-Schweppes before anything major arose. Instead, his boss informed him this morning as the two of them made their way down the hall that he wanted Bob to prepare a presentation for the Schweppes Ginger Ale brand team. The presentation, scheduled for tomorrow, was to summarize promotional activities that had been run on the Ginger Ale brand in the past year and to provide estimates of the sales effects of the various promotions that had been used.

As Bob logged on to the computer system, he was glad that he had spent the last three days learning how to use the in-house database system. Because of the massive amount of data generated by supermarket scanner systems, simply organizing and aggregating the data could be a nightmare. Bob knew that, by punching a few keys in response to the menus provided by the company's program, he could quickly organize the hundreds of soft drink promotions that the company had run across all of the supermarkets included in the scanner database for the past year.

Soon Bob had isolated the data relevant to Schweppes Ginger Ale from the database. To get a better understanding of the data, Bob first generated a frequency count of the various promotions that had been run on the brand. He found that a wide variety of different promotions had been conducted on the brand during the past year and that, quite often, more than one type of promotion was used within a supermarket at the same time. However, many of these promotions or promotion combinations occurred only rarely. Bob decided to eliminate infrequently used promotions from consideration because he was concerned that the sales impact might be too dependent on the individual markets where these promotions had been run. Bob was left with three promotion types that occurred frequently enough to examine individually: price promotions, end-of-aisle displays, and local retailer advertising.

Bob was not sure that the same type of promotion would have the same sales impact for all package sizes, so he wanted to examine the sales effect of each promotion separately for each package size. If he found no differences in the impact across package sizes, he could then generalize results across all packages. Therefore, he next cross-tabulated the three promotion types by package size. Examining the resulting table, Bob noticed that some package/promotion combinations had few if any observations. Rather than risk confounding the sales impact of a promotion type by lumping different package sizes together, Bob decided to focus only on the two package sizes, six-packs of cans and one-liter nonreturnable bottles, for which a sufficient number of observations existed across the three promotion types.

For each promotion type conducted for cans and for one-liter bottles, Bob aggregated the

[1]The accounts in this case are fictional and are not meant to reflect anything actually done by Schweppes management.

data across all stores that had run the same promotion. The average sales of this group of stores was then compared to the average sales during the same time period for those stores not conducting any promotion. The results, shown in Table IV.2.1, were displayed to show the sales increase of each promotion relative to normal, nonpromoted, on-shelf sales. For example, promotion 1, a 120 six-pack display, increased sales 42 percent above the average sales that occurred during the same time period when the brand was on the shelf and not promoted in any way.

As Bob scanned the data he had accumulated on the promotions that had been run, it was obvious that all of the promotions had increased sales above normal levels. However, the amount of sales increase one could expect with each type of promotion was still not obvious. One problem was that both end-of-aisle displays and price reductions contained multiple levels. That is, there were different display sizes and different amounts of price reductions. Thus, Bob knew that he could not simply talk about the impact of a price reduction or display on sales, but would have to talk about the effect of a given level of price reduction or size of display.

Similarly, much of the data were generated from promotion combinations (*e.g.*, a display and a price reduction), and Bob was not sure how to estimate the separate effect of each of the types of promotions. He remembered his marketing instructor talking about the possibility of a synergistic effect when promotions were used in combination. However, at this point, Bob was not sure how he could estimate the separate effect of each type of promotion, much less any synergistic effect! Bob glanced at his watch and saw that it had only taken him a short time to generate the table of data. Unfortunately, he also felt that he still had a lot of work left to do to be ready for the presentation tomorrow.

Given the data in Table IV.2.1, what are the sizes of the effects of the various levels of each promotion on sales? How much synergy, if any, is present between any two or more of the promotions? Based upon your calculations, do you feel that the promotions have a different sales effect on cans than on one-liter bottles? Why or why not? What advantages, if any, would there be to have conducted in-store experiments to estimate the effects of promotions instead of using this observational data? What difficulties would have been encountered in attempting to test these effects experimentally?

Table IV.2.1

Summary of promotion results

Promotion	Package	Display size	Price change	Local advertising	Sales increase
1	Cans	120 six-pack	-10%	Yes	381%
2	Cans	120 six-pack	0%	No	42%
3	Cans	200 six-pack	0%	No	63%
4	Cans	200 six-pack	-10%	Yes	407%
5	One liter	240 bottle	-10%	Yes	404%
6	One liter	400 bottle	-25%	No	904%
7	Cans	on-shelf	-10%	No	143%
8	Cans	120 six-pack	-10%	No	326%
9	Cans	200 six-pack	-10%	No	352%
10	One liter	240 bottle	0%	No	44%
11	One liter	240 bottle	-10%	No	344%
12	One liter	on-shelf	-10%	No	141%
13	One Liter	400 bottle	-10%	No	347%
14	Cans	120 six-pack	-25%	No	874%
15	Cans	on-shelf	-15%	No	248%
16	Cans	on-shelf	-25%	No	463%
17	One liter	400 bottle	-10%	Yes	424%
18	One liter	240 bottle	-15%	No	494%
19	One liter	400 bottle	0%	No	65%
20	One liter	on-shelf	-25%	No	464%
21	One liter	on-shelf	0%	Yes	30%
22	Cans	on-shelf	0%	Yes	1%

Case IV.3

Fairway, Inc.

As he unpacked the Mizuno driver, Greg Kennedy began to reminisce. He could not remember the first time he picked up a golf club; it seemed like he had always played golf. That love of the game had helped pay his way through Southern Carolina University, which he attended on a golf scholarship, and had also helped him win the championship ring on his finger. He was team captain his senior year when Southern won the national championship.

Coming back to reality, Greg could not believe that it had been almost four years since he had graduated. While his love of the game remained, Greg had not been able to play much golf lately. Instead, he was busy trying to run the business that he had persuaded friends and relatives to help him finance soon after graduation. The business, Fairway, Inc., was a golf specialty shop carrying just about anything that a golfer could want, from balls to clubs to shoes to clothes. If he was not able to play golf, Greg could think of nothing he would rather do than sell golf-related equipment to other people who enjoyed the game.

Greg had started Fairway, Inc., in Myrtle Beach, South Carolina. He was convinced that the Myrtle Beach area, famed for its numerous golf courses and white sand beaches, had tremendous potential for a golf shop offering good value for the money and run by people knowledgeable about the game. He also believed that the contacts he had made with golf merchandise representatives while playing college golf would help insure his success.

At the end of the third full year of operation, Greg was pleased with the results to date. Sales had been higher in some months than in others, but, overall, his business strategy appeared to be working. Sales had grown from $196,730 the first year to $585,244 the third year.

As he continued to unpack the new golf clubs that had just arrived, Greg began to think about the coming year. With sales growing at the rate that they had been, Greg never seemed to get ahead enough financially to be able to pay for all of his merchandise needs. Higher sales meant that more inventory and more sales personnel were needed each month in the peak season. Greg knew that he was going to need to negotiate a line of credit with the bank for next year. Greg also knew that the bank would expect him to present them with a cash-flow analysis for the coming year showing expected revenues and expenses each month as part of the justification for the line of credit.

Determining the monthly expenses he would incur for the coming year would not be difficult once Greg knew what sales to expect; it was the expected sales that he was having difficulty forecasting. Greg had already looked at his past sales figures, but they offered little help since sales fluctuated so much from year to year. Greg had gathered some data on the Myrtle Beach economy from the Chamber of Commerce as well as the Chamber's predictions for the next year (See Table IV.3.1). Eyeballing these data, Greg thought that some of these variables seemed to have the same peaks and valleys as his sales, but he was not sure which variables to use or how to use them. Frustrated, Greg wondered how best to forecast his sales.

Using any or all of the data presented in Table IV.3.1, prepare a sales forecast for the coming year (Year 4). How confident do you feel about the accuracy of your forecast? What other information, if any, do you think might help Greg improve the accuracy of the sales forecast?

Table IV.3.1

Fairway, Inc., sales and selected economic and market indicators

Time Period	Fairway Sales	Durable Goods[1]	Retail Sales[2]	Sporting Goods[3]	Average Precipitation[4]	Disposable Personal Income[5]
YEAR 1						
Jan.	5304.	87.7	2060	52.1	4.57	15.185
Feb.	5338.	88.4	2078	53.4	4.37	15.255
Mar.	12446.	89.1	2096	71.4	3.83	15.350
Apr.	15964.	89.8	2114	81.5	3.01	15.458
May	28414.	90.6	2136	112.5	2.35	15.550
Jun.	28530.	90.7	2153	113.9	2.06	15.710
Jul.	23040.	90.3	2171	96.7	1.89	15.860
Aug.	15966.	89.8	2189	78.9	1.44	15.975
Sep.	12418.	90.3	2207	70.4	2.16	16.080
Oct.	8866.	90.5	2225	61.8	2.67	16.175
Nov.	13492.	90.8	2243	61.3	2.23	16.265
Dec.	26952.	91.3	2263	81.2	1.28	16.408
YEAR 2						
Jan.	10122.	90.0	2281	55.7	3.64	16.520
Feb.	10165.	89.1	2299	57.1	3.42	16.633
Mar.	23604.	89.4	2317	76.4	4.02	16.753
Apr.	30350.	89.9	2336	85.5	3.35	16.935
May	53968.	90.4	2355	119.6	2.54	17.090
Jun.	53956.	88.3	2374	115.4	2.20	17.195
Jul.	43848.	87.2	2392	103.8	1.01	17.303
Aug.	30348.	84.9	2410	84.2	1.79	17.405
Sep.	23622.	89.7	2427	75.0	2.10	17.455
Oct.	16976.	92.9	2445	65.5	2.85	17.498
Nov.	25679.	96.1	2463	63.9	2.03	17.538
Dec.	51236.	96.9	2491	85.3	3.36	17.785

[1]Personal consumption expenditures for the Myrtle Beach market on durable goods---seasonally adjusted monthly totals at annual rates in millions of dollars.

[2]Total retail sales in the Myrtle Beach market---monthly totals at annual rates in millions of dollars.

[3]Retail expenditures on sporting goods in the Myrtle Beach market---monthly totals at annual rates in millions of dollars.

[4]Monthly precipitation in the Myrtle Beach area.

[5]Disposable personal income for the Myrtle Beach area---monthly totals at annual rates in billions of dollars.

Table IV.3.1
Fairway, Inc., sales and selected economic and market indicators (cont'd)

YEAR 3						
Jan.	15888.	98.0	2501	58.8	2.88	17.920
Feb.	15772.	99.1	2519	59.3	2.73	18.050
Mar.	36996.	100.2	2536	80.8	3.31	18.188
Apr.	47582.	101.4	2556	91.9	3.55	18.330
May	84584.	102.8	2576	127.6	3.91	18.490
Jun.	84334.	103.2	2596	125.3	4.59	18.570
Jul.	68876.	103.4	2615	111.6	4.43	18.645
Aug.	47406.	103.6	2634	90.0	4.13	18.713
Sep.	36990.	104.9	2652	82.4	3.47	18.790
Oct.	26572.	106.0	2670	69.1	3.04	18.838
Nov.	40213.	107.0	2688	69.9	3.04	18.875
Dec.	80031.	107.4	2698	90.6	3.74	19.053
YEAR 4						
Jan.		108.1	2735	63.0	3.16	18.990
Feb.		108.3	2752	64.1	2.71	19.068
Mar.		109.9	2750	88.9	3.59	19.228
Apr.		111.1	2768	97.8	3.87	19.448
May		112.6	2782	135.2	4.19	19.753
Jun.		112.8	2802	134.7	4.80	19.893
Jul.		112.6	2820	118.3	4.78	19.998
Aug.		112.3	2848	96.7	4.30	19.960
Sep.		112.9	2880	85.3	4.46	20.000
Oct.		113.3	2898	74.1	3.28	20.035
Nov.		113.5	2921	74.9	3.30	20.300
Dec.		114.9	2996	88.1	4.00	20.686

Case IV.4

Gallo & Sons, Inc.

Gallo & Sons, Inc., is the largest wine-maker in the United States, marketing wines for all occasions, ranging from inexpensive table wines to more expensive varietals suitable for formal dinner parties or special occasions. One of the responsibilities of Gallo's marketing research team is to develop annual forecasts of wine consumption for the United States. These forecasts are a vital ingredient in Gallo's annual planning process.

At one time, the marketing research team decided to experiment with a relatively simple forecasting system that was based on the demographics of the population of the United States. The research team conducted a large national survey of the population during which participants were asked to keep individual diary records of beverage consumption. Each diary tracked all beverages consumed by the participant during a one-month period, except for the consumption of milk and water. The study involved 1400 participants, 200 from each of the demographic subgroups shown in Table IV.4.1. Based on the diary results, the research team projected the average annual consumption of wine, in gallons per year, for each of these demographic subgroups. These consumption figures are also shown in Table IV.4.1.

The U.S. Bureau of the Census regularly publishes projections of the future sizes of various demographic subgroups, including the age groups shown in Table IV.4.1. The forecasting system proposed by the Gallo research team amounted to simply multiplying the projected number of individuals belonging to each age group by the estimated annual individual consumption of wine obtained from the survey. Adding the totals obtained for each of the seven age groups produced a total forecast of wine consumption. Table IV.4.2 contains the forecasts generated for the next ten years using this approach.

In order to assess the potential accuracy of this forecasting system, the research team used past U.S. Bureau of the Census estimates of the number of individuals in each of the seven age groups and their survey results to produce estimates of total wine consumption for the ten previous years. Table IV.4.3 contains these estimates as well as the actual consumption of wine reported for the same years.

Evaluate the accuracy of this forecasting technique for the ten previous years. What factors might have caused the magnitude of the differences noted between forecasted and actual consumption? What suggestions would you make for refining the forecasting technique to improve its accuracy?

Table IV.4.1

Average Per Capita Wine Consumption By Age Group Based on Monthly Diaries

Age Group	Mean per capita Consumption (gals.)
20-24	.8
25-34	3.8
35-44	4.2
45-54	4.6
55-64	3.4
65-74	2.7
75+	1.8

Table IV.4.2

Forecasted wine consumption

For Next Ten Years

	Forecast (in millions of gals.)
current year +1	603.1
current year +2	610.8
current year +3	627.1
current year +4	633.2
current year +5	640.6
current year +6	644.7
current year +7	652.9
current year +8	657.5
current year +9	660.3
current year +10	665.3

Table IV.4.3

Estimated *vs.* Actual Wine Consumption

For the Previous Ten Years

Year	Actual (millions of gallons)	Estimated (millions of gallons)
Current -1	570.1	588.9
Current -2	572.2	579.3
Current -3	578.0	571.9
Current -4	588.9	566.4
Current -5	579.6	556.0
Current -6	554.4	548.1
Current -7	528.1	537.0
Current -8	514.0	529.2
Current -9	505.7	523.1
Current -10	479.6	506.6

Case IV.5

Tracking Consumer Reaction to the Sears Discover Card[1]

After being test marketed in Atlanta, a national media launch of the Sears Discover card took place in January 1986. As a direct competitor against several entrenched credit cards, Sears had charted an expensive and risky course. The creation of significant new markets was unlikely. Instead, Sears had to win market share from VISA, MasterCard, and American Express to succeed. Additionally, Sears hoped to use the card to sell other related financial services provided by the Sears Financial Network to card customers.

The primary promotional technique was the same used in its test market— direct-mail solicitation of current Sears customers, offering the Discover card with no annual fee and an average credit line of $1350. Sears tried to win business from established cards by distinguishing the Discover card as a "financial services card." Sears offered several investment, real estate, insurance, and banking services tied to the Discover card as well as the unique benefit of a cash rebate based on a percentage of annual purchases made with the card.

A study started by Brittain Associates, Inc., in the Atlanta test market area (see Case III.6) was expanded to track the national introduction. Brittain Associates had begun tracking the Discover Card in its Atlanta test market in the summer of 1985. As card presence grew nationally, the study expanded. The first wave of the National Tracking Study was conducted in November 1986, with follow-up surveys in March, June, and September of 1987. Annual updates of tracking information began in September 1988.

The research was designed to collect data periodically on the following issues:

- household penetration of the Discover card,
- demographic profiles of card owners *vs.* nonowners,
- appealing features of the card,
- frequency of card use,
- specific usage occasions,
- market share impact on other general-purpose credit cards,
- cross-selling success of other Sears Financial services, and
- advertising awareness and content recall.

The card ownership data were collected via randomly dialed afternoon and evening telephone

---

[1]Data for this case provided courtesy of Brittain Associates, Inc., Atlanta, Georgia.

interviews conducted within the continental United States. Respondents were adults living in telephone households. To reduce age and income biases, a method of an initial call and at least two call-backs was used.

The results displayed in Tables IV.5.1 through IV.5.18 and Exhibits IV.5.1 through IV.5.10 are primarily focused on the sixth wave of the study reported in September 1989, with references to previous waves for comparison purposes. Discover card ownership incidence data were collected over a two-and-a-half week period (June 16 - July 2, 1989). During this time, 4041 qualified consumer contacts were made. From this sample, 758 households who claimed to have a Discover card were contacted. From this group, 200 Discover card owners were randomly selected, re-contacted, and interviewed. Again, an initial call attempt and at least two call-backs were used to suppress age and income biases.

Analyze the research results and produce a summary of how the introduction of the Discover card has progressed. Indicate problem areas, opportunities, and any actions you would recommend based on the tracking results so far.

	Total (200)
	percentage
More than you expected	22
About what you expected	44
Less than you expected	25
Don't know	8

[1]The percentage of card owners who feel that there are about as many merchants (or more) accepting the card as they expected has risen slightly since the September 1988 study. Twenty-two percent of Discover cardholders believe that there are "more merchants" than they expected and 44 percent say that there are "about as many" as they expected. This compares with 21 percent and 40 percent respectively in September 1988. The percentage of those who feel that merchant acceptance is "less than expected" is 25 percent in the current study, compared to 31 percent in September 1988.

Table IV.5.1
Perceived merchant acceptance[1]

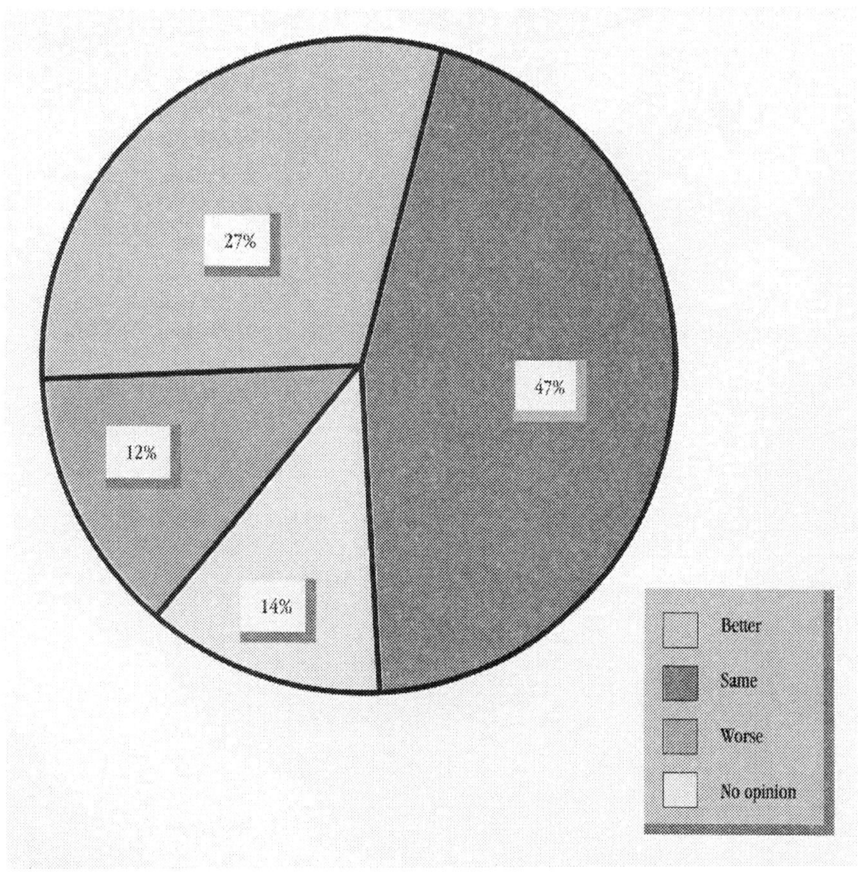

Exhibit IV.5.1

Comparison of Discover to other major credit cards. Those believing Discover to be superior to VISA and MasterCard rose significantly from 18 percent to 27 percent over the past year. Forty-seven percent of Discover cardholders see the card as at least the equivalent of VISA and MasterCard. Fourteen percent think it is a worse product, which is down significantly from 21 percent in 1988. In addition, holders of the Discover card cite its cash rebate feature as its primary advantage over other cards. This factor was mentioned by 17 percent of the respondents *vs.* 12 percent in September 1988.

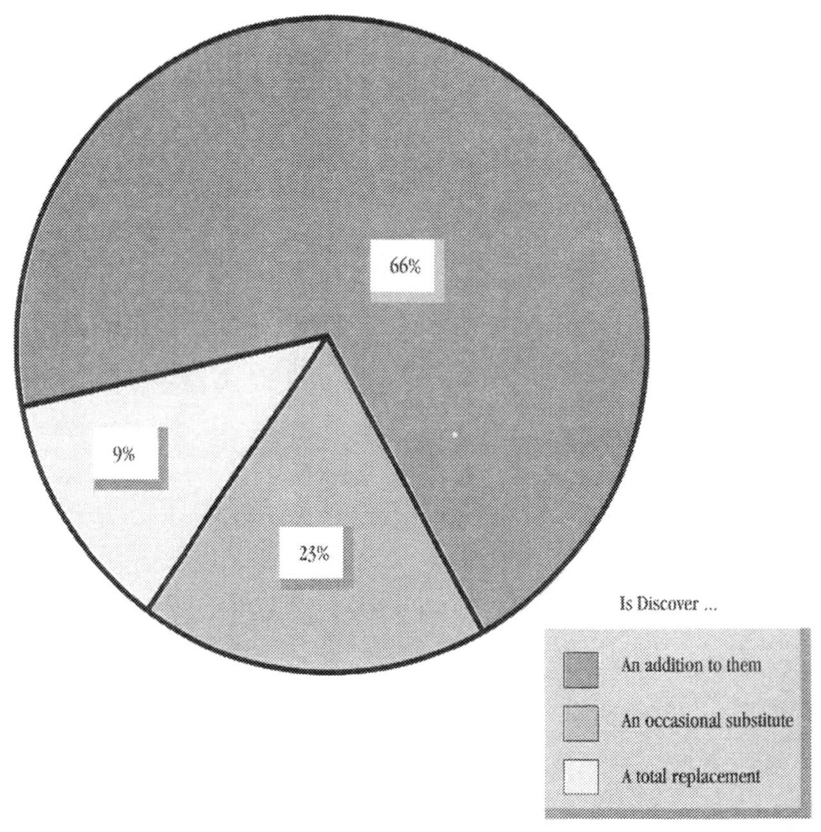

Exhibit IV.5.2
Competitive card cannibalization. In the current tracking study, only 9 percent of Discover card households plan to use Discover as a total replacement for one or more of their current cards, while 23 percent consider it an occasional substitute. These figures are comparable to those experienced in September 1988, when 11 percent planned to use Discover as a total replacement and 22 percent as an occasional substitute. Overall, 66 percent of the sample say that the card will not replace any of their other cards.

	Total (200)
	percentage
Cash rebate	17
No annual fee	5
Low interest rates	4
Use it at more places	3
Believe in/like Sears	2
Easy to get cash; ATM access	1
It was easy to get	1

Table IV.5.2
Perceived advantages of Discover card *vs.* other credit cards

	Total (63)
Cash rebate	(17)
Accepted at more places	(6)
Part of Sears	(5)
To rotate use of cards	(4)
Lower interest rate	(3)
To use just one card	(2)
Can make monthly payments	(2)
For emergencies	(2)
Others	(4)
No answer	(23)

[1]When asked why respondents intended to use Discover in place of other cards, seventeen people stated that the card's cash rebate program was the reason. In the September 1988 study, no one responded with this answer. In addition, six other people stated that they would replace other cards because Discover was accepted at more places. This response was not cited in the last study either. Interestingly, five people responded that Discover's affiliation with Sears was one reason to replace other cards. In September 1988, the primary reason for replacing other cards with Discover were: "to use just one card" and "lower interest rates." Those respondents declaring these factors of primary importance dropped significantly in the 1989 study.

Again, this data further reinforces the notion that consumers have become more definitive in citing the specific features of Discover most touted by Sears in its promotion of the card when declaring reasons for replacing other cards with Discover.

Table IV.5.3
Why will you use your Discover card in place of other cards?

Credit Card	Percent Owning (200)
VISA	74
MasterCard	61
American Express	24
Regular Sears card	87
Carte Blanche	2
Diners Club	6

[1]Virtually all Discover carriers hold at least one other major credit card. Seventy-four percent have a VISA card, 61 percent have a MasterCard and 24 percent have an American Express. Eighty-seven percent of Discover cardholders own a regular Sears card.

Table IV.5.4
Other credit card ownership[1]

	Total (200)
	percentage
Had not used	54
One time	13
Two times	12
Three times	6
Four times	5
Five times	3
Six to eight times	5
Nine or more	2
Average among those who used at least one time	3.3 times

Table IV.5.5
Frequency of Discover card use in past thirty days

	Any Credit Card	Discover Card
	Total (200)	Total (200)
Median times among users	3.12	0.54
Mean times among users	6.67	3.32
Did not use card	10%	54%

[1]Among Discover cardholders, approximately 90 percent used any credit card in the thirty days prior to the study. Forty-six percent of the respondents had used their Discover card during this same period, continuing a slight downward trend in usage since September 1987. Among those who had used a credit card, the average number of uses per month was 6.7. Discover card users presented Discover an average 3.3 times, a somewhat lower frequency than the 3.7 times measured in the September 1988 study.

While at first it may appear that the usage frequency drop from 3.7 times to 3.3 is fairly significant (11 percent), usage of any credit card at all dropped 20 percent (8.4 times in September 1988 *vs.* 6.7 times in September 1989), indicating that while Discover usage may have dropped, some competitors experienced an even more dramatic drop.

Table IV.5.6
Frequency of specific credit card use in the past thirty days[1]

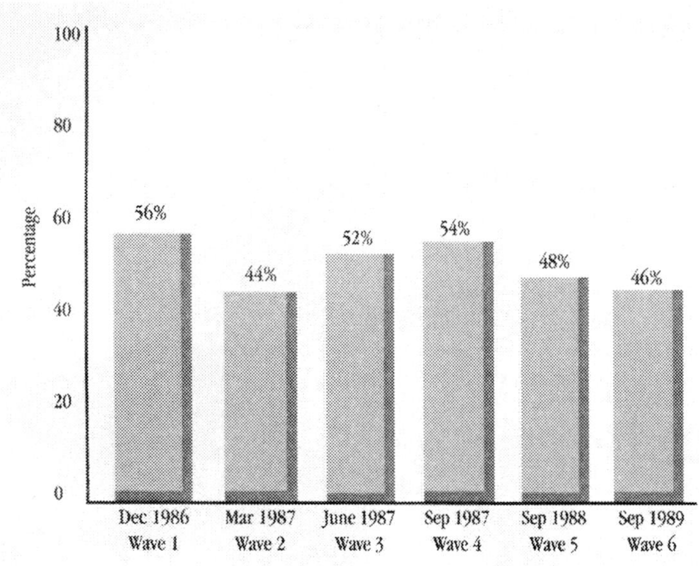

Exhibit IV.5.3
Pattern of use of Discover and competitor cards; among card owners, incidence of using Discover card at least once in the past thirty days.

	Total (180)
	percentage
Clothing	35
Gasoline	18
Lodging	18
Hardware	17
Housewares	15
Shoes	14
Restaurant	12
Electronic equipment	11
Entertainment	4
Cash advance	3
Drug prescription	3
Rental car	2

[1]Among the 90 percent of the respondents who had used a credit card within the previous thirty days, clothing dominated the purchase for which the card was used.

Table IV.5.7
Purpose of card use among users in previous thirty days[1]

	Percentage of potential users
Clothing (non-Sears)	19 (n = 169)
Hardware	16 (n = 96)
Gasoline	14 (n = 113)
Housewares	11 (n = 133)
Lodging	11 (n = 142)
Restaurant	10 (n = 107)
Shoes	10 (n = 137)
Electronic equipment	9 (n = 114)
Drug prescription	7 (n = 43)
Cash advance	6 (n = 53)
Entertainment	5 (n = 89)
Rental car	2 (n = 95)
Medical expense	2 (n = 41)

[1]Among Discover cardholders who claim to ever use a credit card for a purchase in a specific category measured (*i.e.*, among the universe of potential users), our analysis reveals, for example, that 19 percent of those who are likely to use a card for purchasing clothes used Discover for that purpose in the past thirty days. The similar numbers for the various categories are detailed in Table 18.10.

Table IV.5.8
Incidence of card use in past thirty days among potential users[1]

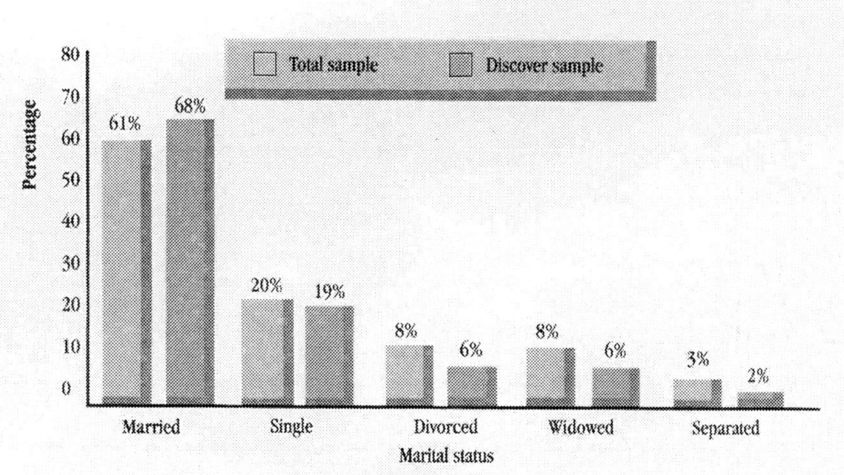

Exhibit IV.5.4
Marital status of card owners.

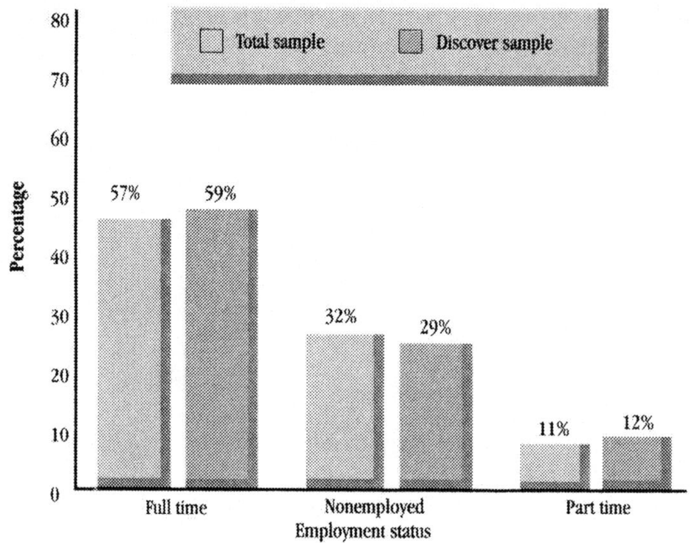

Exhibit IV.5.5
Employment status of Discover card owners.

	First Mention (200)	Total Mention (200)
	percentage	percentage
VISA	45	92
MasterCard	25	82
Discover Card	11	77
American Express	11	59

[1]On an *unaided basis*, approximately 77 percent of Discover card owners mentioned the card when asked to name "all of the major credit cards they could think of." This is a significant increase from the 64 percent who mentioned the Discover card in September 1988, but about the same as the figure of June 1987. By comparison, about 92 percent mentioned VISA, 82 percent MasterCard and 59 percent said American Express. The Discover card, however, is still not strong in "top-of-mind" recall. It was the first credit card mentioned by only 11 percent of card owners.

Table IV.5.9
Unaided awareness of major credit cards[1]

	Unaided Mention (200)	Total Mentions (200)
	percentage	percentage
Discover Card	49	81
MasterCard	40	64
VISA	52	69
American Express	44	83

[1]Advertising awareness of Discover, which jumped significantly in the September 1988 study, increased again in 1989 to 81 percent from 74 percent in "total mentions." While American Express ranked lowest in product awareness, it ranked highest in advertising awareness at 83 percent.

Table IV.5.10
Major credit cards advertising awareness[1]

Have Used Related Sears Financial Service	Total (200)
	percentage
Travel services	6
Discover emergency road service	3
Allstate Term Insurance	2
Discover savers account	2
Discover auto loan	1
Discover home mortgage	—[2]
Dean Witter IRA	—[2]

[1]While the Discover card continues to have only minimal success with regard to cross-selling related Sears financial services, trends since the September 1988 study indicate some slight improvement. Among Discover cardholders, 6 percent had used Sears travel services, which is up from one percent last year. While no one indicated the purchase of each of the following financial services products in September 1988, each has shown at least some usage in the current study: Allstate term insurance, Discover auto loan, Discover home mortgage, Discover savers account, and Discover emergency road service.

[2].5 percent or less

Table IV.5.11
Cross-selling of financial services to Discover card users[1]

	Total Sample (4041)	Discover Sample (758)
	percentage	percentage
Home ownership		
Own	73	83
Rent	26	17
Household members		
One	15	9
Two	32	32
Three or more	53	59
Average (mean)	2.9	3.1

Table IV.5.12
Home ownership and household size of Discover owners

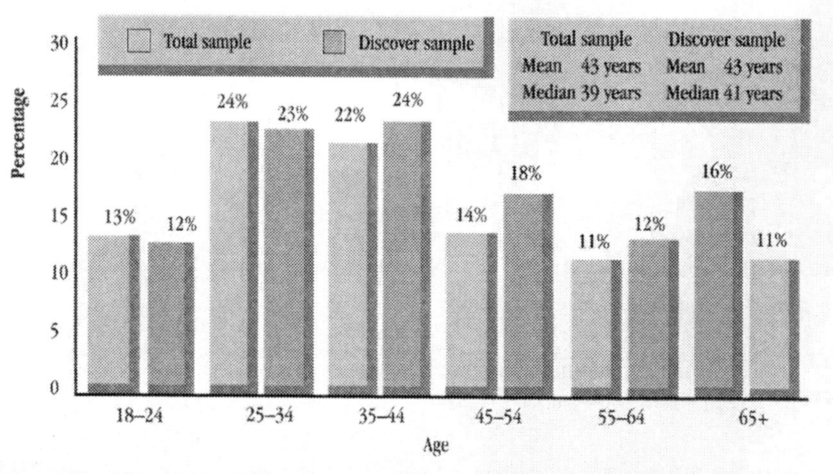

Exhibit IV.5.6
Age of respondent.

	September 1989
Total U.S. households with telephones (FCC industry analysis, September 1989)	87,500,000
Incidence of Discover card ownership based on 4041 randomly placed calls	18.8%
Estimated number of U.S. households currently holding a Discover card (+/−461,000)	16,450,000
Estimated number of Discover cards in circulation based on 1.5 cards per household measured in current study	24,675,000

Table IV.5.13
Estimate of Discover card penetration among U.S. households

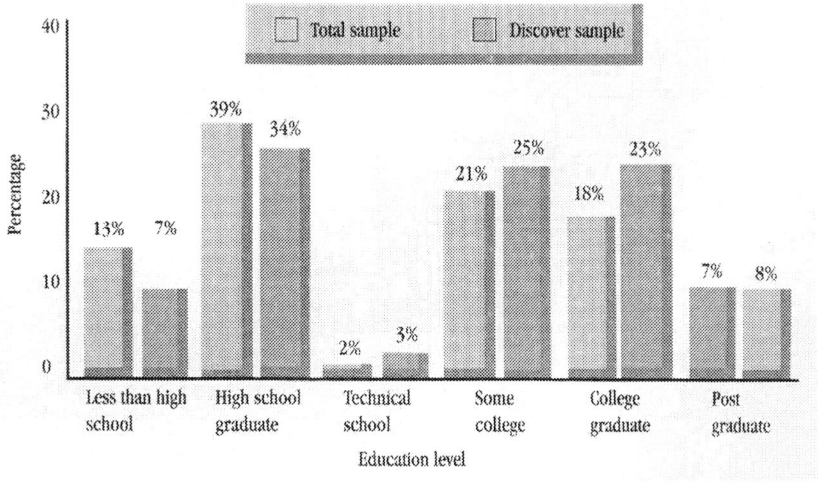

Exhibit IV.5.7
Education level of respondent.

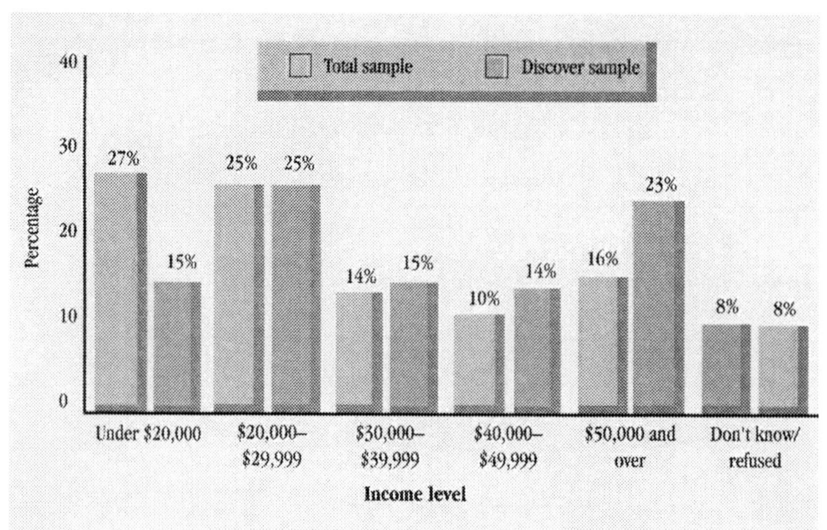

Exhibit IV.5.8
Total annual household income.

	Total (91)
	percentage
$1–$50	18
$51–$100	20
$101–$150	9
$151–$200	6
$201–$250	—
$251–$300	6
$301–$400	4
$401–$500	4
$501–$1000	4
No answer	30
Median	$95
Mean	$183

Table IV.5.14
Thirty-day dollar volume on Discover card

	Total (61)
	percentage
$1–$50	11
$51–$100	5
$101–$150	3
$151–$200	5
$201–$250	—
$251–$300	5
$301–$400	5
$401–$500	7
$501–$1000	18
Over $1000	5
No answer	36
Median	$351
Mean	$498

[1]Based on Discover users' estimates of the actual dollar amount of purchases in the thirty days prior to the interview, plus their estimate of the outstanding unpaid balance from their most recent Discover statement, we have made revenue projections for both interest revenue and merchant discount revenue. The assumptions include: (1) current monthly interest rates of 1.65 percent (19.8 ÷ 12) and (2) merchant discount fee averaging 1.9 percent. Using these assumptions and the data obtained in the study, we estimate Discover monthly revenues at:

Interest revenue estimate	$33 million to $37 million
Merchant discount revenue estimate	$13.3 million to $13.9 million

Forty-six percent of Discover cardholders reported recent activity (last thirty days) in their account, which is down slightly from the 48 percent reported in the September 1988 study.

Although the number of households owning a Discover card grew approximately 14 percent since September 1988, interest revenue dropped substantially as the percentage of people maintaining an unpaid balance dropped from 43 percent to 37 percent, and the median unpaid balance dropped from $426 to $351.

Merchant discount revenues grew approximately 25 percent over the past year, as the median thirty-day dollar volume increased from $83 in September 1988 to $95 in September 1989.

Table IV.5.15
Average unpaid balance on Discover card[1]

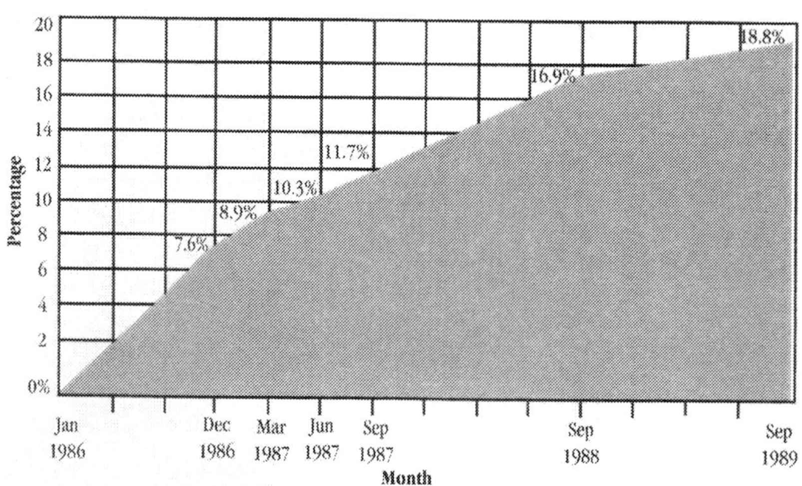

Exhibit IV.5.9
Percent of U.S. telephone-owning households that have the Discover card.

	Dec 1986	March 1987	June 1987	Sep 1987	Sep 1988	Sep 1989
Very likely	57	64	70	65	62	66
Somewhat likely	25	20	12	23	21	18
Somewhat unlikely	6	6	4	2	6	5
Very unlikely	4	4	9	6	6	8
Don't know	7	6	4	4	5	3

[1]Sixty-six percent of Discover card owners believe that they are "very likely to renew" the card when approaching the expiration date. Another 18 percent of the sample say that they are "somewhat likely" to do so and about 3 percent are undecided. Current data suggest that as many as 8% of Discover card owners will not renew.

Last year Discover announced its intention to charge a $15 annual fee on account in two test states, North Carolina and Wisconsin. The extent to which this affects "intent to renew" remains unclear; however, our research suggests that the Discover card may not be sufficiently fixed in the cardholders' payment behavior to support a fee.

Table IV.5.16
Intent to renew card[1]

	Total (200)
	percentage
"I'll keep it as long as there is no annual fee"	1
"Don't use it"	2
"If automatic renewal"	1
No comment	96

[1]There were very few qualifying comments regarding the consumers' intent to renew the Discover card upon expiration.

Table IV.5.17
Comments on renewal[1]

	Total (200)
	percentage
More than you expected	22
About what you expected	44
Less than you expected	25
Don't know	8

[1]The percentage of card owners who feel that there are about as many merchants (or more) accepting the card as they expected has risen slightly since the September 1988 study. Twenty-two percent of Discover cardholders believe that there are "more merchants" than they expected and 44 percent say that there are "about as many" as they expected. This compares with 21 percent and 40 percent respectively in September 1988. The percentage of those who feel that merchant acceptance is "less than expected" is 25 percent in the current study, compared to 31 percent in September 1988.

Table IV.5.18
Perceived merchant acceptance[1]

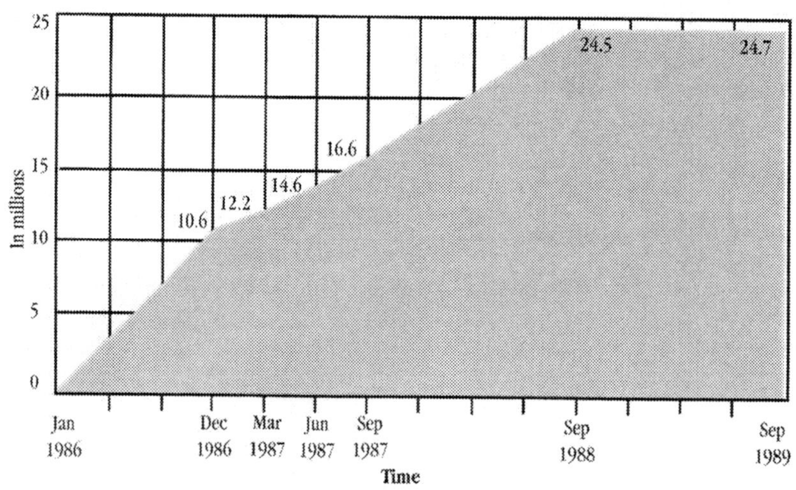

Exhibit IV.5.10
Total Discover cards in circulation in the United States.

Case IV.6

NFL Properties[1]

NFL Properties oversees the merchandising of souvenirs and wearing apparel endorsed by the National Football League, including the NFL's Pro Line brand. During one football season, a study was conducted to assess awareness of, and attitudes toward, NFL-endorsed products and the NFL in general. In addition, the results of the study were to provide a base for future tracking of consumers' attitudes toward NFL-endorsed merchandise and the league.

The study was conducted by telephone, and a nationally representative sample was interviewed. Age quota groups were established to guarantee that the sample would be representative of the U.S. population with regard to age; 380 respondents were over thirty-five years of age, 307 were between the ages of eighteen and thirty-four, and sixty-eight were between the ages of thirteen and seventeen. Within each of the age quota groups, about half of the respondents were male and half were female. Respondents were questioned about their degree of interest in various sports, their favorite NFL team and logo, their awareness and past purchases of NFL merchandise, future purchase interest in NFL merchandise, attitudes toward the National Football League and NFL-endorsed merchandise, and behavior and demographics.

Key results of the study are presented in the following tables. Tables IV.6.1 through IV.6.5 reveal attitudes toward the National Football League. (Respondents were questioned similarly about other sports to provide points of reference to which results for the NFL could be compared.) Table IV.6.6 summarizes results that pertain to perceptions about the NFL, and Tables IV.6.7 and IV.6.8 concern television viewing of NFL games. Finally, Tables IV.6.9 through IV.6.14 contain the results of questions that dealt with purchase behavior and attitudes toward NFL-endorsed merchandise.

What key conclusions should NFL Properties draw from the results of this research? What particular actions and promotions would you recommend to the management of the NFL? What particular measures obtained in this research would be worth tracking in the future? Why?

---

[1]Courtesy of NFL Properties, Inc.

	Fan Incidence (755)	Degree of Interest[1] (755)	Degree of Interest *vs.* Last year[2] (755)
	percentage	percentage	percentage
NFL football	63	40	55
College football	43	19	40
Major league baseball	42	18	37
NBA basketball	32	15	29
Professional tennis	22	9	20
Professional boxing	21	7	18
Professional golf	19	6	17
NHL hockey	14	5	12
Professional bowling	12	4	10

[1]Percent rating degree of interest on a five-point scale ranging from "very" to "not at all" interested.

[2]Percent rating interest "more" or "about the same" relative to last year (three-point scale with third category being "not as much").

Table IV.6.1

NFL football *vs.* other professional sports

	Total (755)	Male (388)	Female (367)
	percentage	percentage	percentage
NFL football fans	63	76	49

Table IV.6.2

NFL fan incidence by sex

	Total NFL Fans
Very interested in NFL football	64
More interested than previous year	26
More/the same interest as previous year	88

Table IV.6.3

Degree of interest in NFL among NFL fans

	Total NFL Fans (473)
	percentage
San Francisco 49ers	12
Chicago Bears	11
Minnesota Vikings	7
New York Giants	7

Table IV.6.4

Favorite NFL team

	Total NFL Fans (473)
	percentage
Cincinnati Bengals	8
Los Angeles Raiders	8
Washington Redskins	7

Table IV.6.5

Favorite NFL team logo

	Percentage Rating Agree Strongly/Somewhat[1]			Percentage Strongly Disagree		
	Total (755) %	NFL Fan (473) %	Non-NFL Fan (282) %	Total (755) %	NFL Fan (473) %	Non-NFL Fan (282) %
NFL football is a sport deeply rooted in tradition.	85	92	73	6	5	8
Although football is a contact sport, the NFL games are mainly played hard and clean.	77	86	62	13	10	18
The NFL represents professional sports at its best.	73	85	51	17	10	28
The NFL management is very tough on players who are caught using drugs or steroids.	68	72	62	23	24	21
The players in the NFL are excellent role models for young people.	65	74	49	25	20	35
Products endorsed by the NFL are high-quality products.	64	74	47	16	12	21
NFL football is the most exciting sport to watch.	63	83	28	31	13	61
NFL players eat a smart, healthy diet.	56	59	51	15	14	16

[1]Five-point scale: strongly agree, agree, neutral, disagree, strongly disagree

Table IV.6.6

Perception of NFL

	Total Fans (473)
	percentage
Weekends	
Once a month or more	95
Every weekend	48
Three out of the past four weekends	20
One or two out of the past four weekends	27
None of the past four weekends	5
Monday Nights	
Once a month or more	83
Every Monday night	32
Three out of four Monday nights	14
One or two out of four Monday nights	37
None of the past four Monday nights	17
Watched the NFL on ESPN this season	
Has watched this season	60
Has not watched this season	40

Table IV.6.7

Frequency of watching NFL games on TV

	Total Fans (473)	Male (294)	Female (179)
	percentage	percentage	percentage
Watched	89	88	90
At a Superbowl party	28	27	30
Did not watch	11	12	10

Table IV.6.8

Whether watched Superbowl

	Total (755) percentage	Sex		Age		
		Male (388) percentage	Female (367) percentage	13–17 (68) percentage	18–34 (307) percentage	35+ (380) percentage
Overall Awareness of Products With NFL Logo						
Is Aware	84	86	82	87	89	79
Is Not Aware	14	12	16	10	10	17
Awareness of NFL Pro Line						
Is Aware	55	62	47	63	58	51
Is Not Aware	42	36	49	35	40	46

Table IV.6.9

Awareness of products with NFL logo/Pro Line™

	Total (755) percentage	Sex		Age		
		Male (388) percentage	Female (367) percentage	13–17 (68) percentage	18–34 (307) percentage	35+ (380) percentage
Have purchased products with NFL logo	51	55	47	66	59	42
Have not purchased products with NFL logo	49	45	53	34	41	58

Table IV.6.10

Incidence of purchasing with the NFL logo

Types of Products	Total (387)
	percentage
Clothing	73
Shirts	56
Sweatshirts	29
T-shirts	19
Shirts (Unspecified)	13
Jerseys	9
Outerwear	34
Hats/Caps	26
Jackets	9
Jogging Outfits/Sweatsuits	8
Pants	5
Football Equipment	4
Mugs	21
Glasses	7
Buttons	3

Table IV.6.11

Products with NFL logo purchased in past year (base = have purchased products)

	Total (387)
	percentage
Sporting Goods Store	39
Department Store	30
Retail Clothing Store	11
At the Stadium	10
Through a Catalogue/Mail Order	4
Airport	2
Grocery/Food Store	2

Table IV.6.12

Purchase location for products with NFL logo (base = have purchased products)

	Total (387)
	percentage
Spur of the Moment Only	43
Planned Only	37
Both Planned and Spur of the Moment Purchases	15

Table IV.6.13

Whether purchase of product with NFL logo was planned (base = have purchased products)

		Sex		Age		
	Total (755) percentage	Male (388) percentage	Female (367) percentage	13–17 (68) percentage	18–34 (307) percentage	35+ (380) percentage
Overall Future Purchase Interest						
Very/Somewhat Interested	53	55	51	87	60	42
Not At All Interested	46	44	48	13	40	57

Table IV.6.14

Future purchase interest of products with NFL logo

TABLES

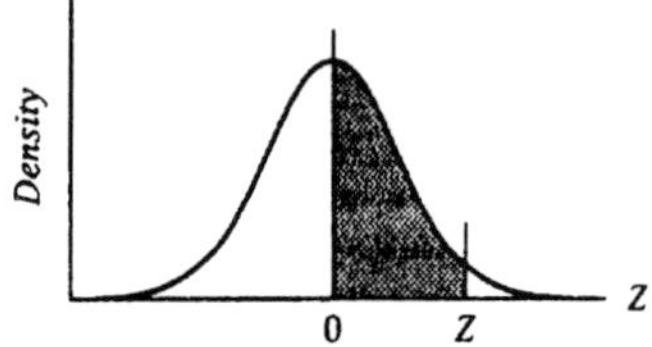

TABLE I
Normal Probabilities: Areas of the Standard Normal Distribution

The values in the body of the table are the areas between the mean and the value of Z.

Z	.00	.01	.02	.03	.04	.05	.06	.07	.08	.09
.00	.0000	.0040	.0080	.0120	.0160	.0199	.0239	.0279	.0319	.0359
.10	.0398	.0438	.0478	.0517	.0557	.0596	.0636	.0675	.0714	.0753
.20	.0793	.0832	.0871	.0910	.0948	.0987	.1026	.1064	.1103	.1141
.30	.1179	.1217	.1255	.1293	.1331	.1368	.1406	.1443	.1480	.1517
.40	.1554	.1591	.1628	.1664	.1700	.1736	.1772	.1808	.1844	.1879
.50	.1915	.1950	.1985	.2019	.2054	.2088	.2123	.2157	.2190	.2224
.60	.2257	.2291	.2324	.2357	.2389	.2422	.2454	.2486	.2517	.2549
.70	.2580	.2611	.2642	.2673	.2703	.2734	.2764	.2793	.2823	.2852
.80	.2881	.2910	.2939	.2967	.2995	.3023	.3051	.3078	.3106	.3133
.90	.3159	.3186	.3212	.3238	.3264	.3289	.3315	.3340	.3365	.3389
1.00	.3413	.3438	.3461	.3485	.3508	.3531	.3554	.3577	.3599	.3621
1.10	.3643	.3665	.3686	.3708	.3729	.3749	.3770	.3790	.3810	.3830
1.20	.3849	.3869	.3888	.3907	.3925	.3944	.3962	.3980	.3997	.4015
1.30	.4032	.4049	.4066	.4082	.4099	.4115	.4131	.4147	.4162	.4177
1.40	.4192	.4207	.4222	.4236	.4251	.4265	.4279	.4292	.4306	.4319
1.50	.4332	.4345	.4357	.4370	.4382	.4394	.4406	.4418	.4429	.4441
1.60	.4452	.4463	.4474	.4484	.4495	.4505	.4515	.4525	.4535	.4545
1.70	.4554	.4564	.4573	.4582	.4591	.4599	.4608	.4616	.4625	.4633
1.80	.4641	.4649	.4656	.4664	.4671	.4678	.4686	.4693	.4699	.4706
1.90	.4713	.4719	.4726	.4732	.4738	.4744	.4750	.4756	.4761	.4767
2.00	.4772	.4778	.4783	.4788	.4793	.4798	.4803	.4808	.4812	.4817
2.10	.4821	.4826	.4830	.4834	.4838	.4842	.4846	.4850	.4854	.4857
2.20	.4861	.4864	.4868	.4871	.4875	.4878	.4881	.4884	.4887	.4890
2.30	.4893	.4896	.4898	.4901	.4904	.4906	.4909	.4911	.4913	.4916
2.40	.4918	.4920	.4922	.4925	.4927	.4929	.4931	.4932	.4934	.4936
2.50	.4938	.4940	.4941	.4943	.4945	.4946	.4948	.4949	.4951	.4952
2.60	.4953	.4955	.4956	.4957	.4959	.4960	.4961	.4962	.4963	.4964
2.70	.4965	.4966	.4967	.4968	.4969	.4970	.4971	.4972	.4973	.4974
2.80	.4974	.4975	.4976	.4977	.4977	.4978	.4979	.4979	.4980	.4981
2.90	.4981	.4982	.4982	.4983	.4984	.4984	.4985	.4985	.4986	.4986
3.00	.4987	.4987	.4987	.4988	.4988	.4989	.4989	.4989	.4990	.4990
3.10	.4990	.4991	.4991	.4991	.4992	.4992	.4992	.4992	.4993	.4993
3.20	.4993	.4993	.4994	.4994	.4994	.4994	.4994	.4995	.4995	.4995
3.30	.4995	.4995	.4995	.4996	.4996	.4996	.4996	.4996	.4996	.4997
3.40	.4997	.4997	.4997	.4997	.4997	.4997	.4997	.4997	.4997	.4998
3.50	.4998	.4998	.4998	.4998	.4998	.4998	.4998	.4998	.4998	.4998
3.60	.4998	.4998	.4999	.4999	.4999	.4999	.4999	.4999	.4999	.4999
3.70	.4999	.4999	.4999	.4999	.4999	.4999	.4999	.4999	.4999	.4999
3.80	.4999	.4999	.4999	.4999	.4999	.4999	.4999	.4999	.4999	.4999

Note: For example, if we want to find the area under the standard normal curve between $Z = 0$ and $Z = 1.96$, we find the $Z = 1.90$ row and .06 column (for $Z = 1.90 + .06 = 1.96$) and read .4750 at the intersection.

TABLE II
t Distribution Values

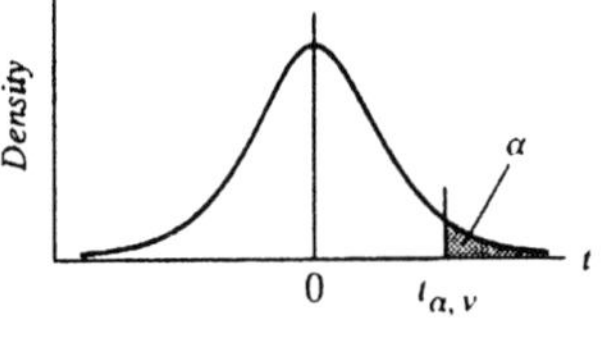

Degrees of Freedom ν	$t_{.10}$	$t_{.05}$	$t_{.025}$	$t_{.01}$	$t_{.005}$
1	3.078	6.314	12.706	31.821	63.657
2	1.886	2.920	4.303	6.965	9.925
3	1.638	2.353	3.182	4.541	5.841
4	1.533	2.132	2.776	3.747	4.604
5	1.476	2.015	2.571	3.365	4.032
6	1.440	1.943	2.447	3.143	3.707
7	1.415	1.895	2.365	2.998	3.499
8	1.397	1.860	2.306	2.896	3.355
9	1.383	1.833	2.262	2.821	3.250
10	1.372	1.812	2.228	2.764	3.169
11	1.363	1.796	2.201	2.718	3.106
12	1.356	1.782	2.179	2.681	3.055
13	1.350	1.771	2.160	2.650	3.012
14	1.345	1.761	2.145	2.624	2.977
15	1.341	1.753	2.131	2.602	2.947
16	1.337	1.746	2.120	2.583	2.921
17	1.333	1.740	2.110	2.567	2.898
18	1.330	1.734	2.101	2.552	2.878
19	1.328	1.729	2.093	2.539	2.861
20	1.325	1.725	2.086	2.528	2.845
21	1.323	1.721	2.080	2.518	2.831
22	1.321	1.717	2.074	2.508	2.819
23	1.319	1.714	2.069	2.500	2.807
24	1.318	1.711	2.064	2.492	2.797
25	1.316	1.708	2.060	2.485	2.787
26	1.315	1.706	2.056	2.479	2.779
27	1.314	1.703	2.052	2.473	2.771
28	1.313	1.701	2.048	2.467	2.763
29	1.311	1.699	2.045	2.462	2.756
30	1.310	1.697	2.042	2.457	2.750
40	1.303	1.684	2.021	2.423	2.704
60	1.296	1.671	2.000	2.390	2.660
120	1.289	1.658	1.980	2.358	2.617
∞	1.282	1.645	1.960	2.326	2.576

Note: For example, if $\alpha = .05$ and $\nu = 15$, then $t_{\alpha,\nu} = t_{.05,15} = 1.753$.

TABLE III

χ^2 Distribution Values

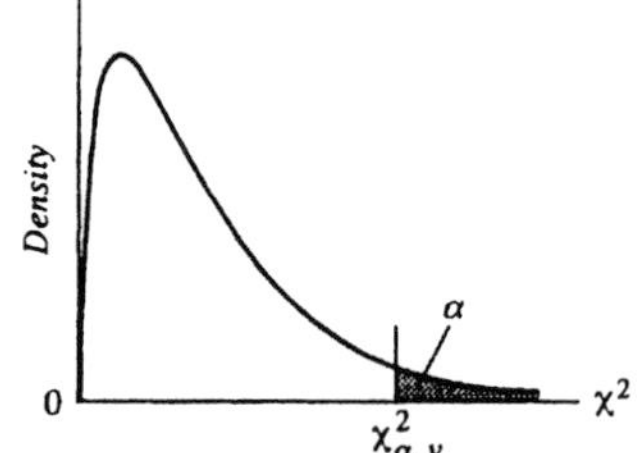

Degrees of Freedom ν	$\chi^2_{.100}$	$\chi^2_{.050}$	$\chi^2_{.025}$	$\chi^2_{.010}$	$\chi^2_{.005}$
1	2.71	3.84	5.02	6.63	7.88
2	4.61	5.99	7.38	9.21	10.60
3	6.25	7.81	9.35	11.34	12.84
4	7.78	9.49	11.14	13.28	14.86
5	9.24	11.07	12.83	15.09	16.75
6	10.64	12.59	14.45	16.81	18.55
7	12.02	14.07	16.01	18.48	20.28
8	13.36	15.51	17.53	20.09	21.96
9	14.68	16.92	19.02	21.67	23.59
10	15.99	18.31	20.48	23.21	25.19
11	17.28	19.68	21.92	24.72	26.76
12	18.55	21.03	23.34	26.22	28.30
13	19.81	22.36	24.74	27.69	29.82
14	21.06	23.68	26.12	29.14	31.32
15	22.31	25.00	27.49	30.58	32.80
16	23.54	26.30	28.85	32.00	34.27
17	24.77	27.59	30.19	33.41	35.72
18	25.99	28.87	31.53	34.81	37.16
19	27.20	30.14	32.85	36.19	38.58
20	28.41	31.41	34.17	37.57	40.00
21	29.62	32.67	35.48	38.93	41.40
22	30.81	33.92	36.78	40.29	42.80
23	32.01	35.17	38.08	41.64	44.18
24	33.20	36.42	39.36	42.98	45.56
25	34.38	37.65	40.65	44.31	46.93
26	35.56	38.89	41.92	45.64	48.29
27	36.74	40.11	43.19	46.96	49.64
28	37.92	41.34	44.46	48.28	50.99
29	39.09	42.56	45.72	49.59	52.34
30	40.26	43.77	46.98	50.89	53.67
40	51.81	55.76	59.34	63.69	66.77
50	63.17	67.50	71.42	76.15	79.49
60	74.40	79.08	83.30	88.38	91.95
70	85.53	90.53	95.02	100.43	104.22
80	96.58	101.88	106.63	112.33	116.32
90	107.60	113.14	118.14	124.12	128.30
100	118.50	124.34	129.56	135.81	140.17

Note: For example, if $\alpha = .05$ and $\nu = 20$, then $\chi^2_{\alpha,\nu} = \chi^2_{.05,20} = 31.41$.

This table is abridged from Thompson, Catherine M.: "Table of Percentage Points of the χ^2 Distribution," *Biometrika,* Vol. 32 (1942), p. 187, by permission of *Biometrika* Trustees.

TABLE IV
F Distribution Values

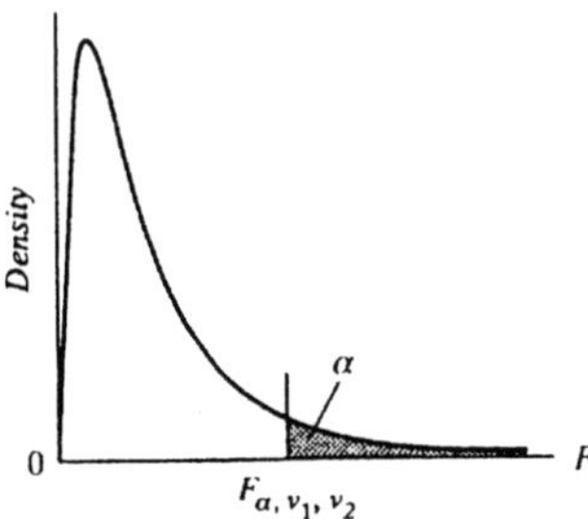

F Values When $\alpha = .05$

ν_2 \ ν_1	1	2	3	4	5	6	7	8	9
1	161.45	199.50	215.71	224.58	230.16	233.99	236.77	238.88	240.54
2	18.513	19.000	19.164	19.247	19.296	19.330	19.353	19.371	19.385
3	10.128	9.5521	9.2766	9.1172	9.0135	8.9406	8.8868	8.8452	8.8123
4	7.7086	6.9443	6.5914	6.3883	6.2560	6.1631	6.0942	6.0410	5.9988
5	6.6079	5.7861	5.4095	5.1922	5.0503	4.9503	4.8759	4.8183	4.7725
6	5.9874	5.1433	4.7571	4.5337	4.3874	4.2839	4.2066	4.1468	4.0990
7	5.5914	4.7374	4.3468	4.1203	3.9715	3.8660	3.7870	3.7257	3.6767
8	5.3177	4.4590	4.0662	3.8378	3.6875	3.5806	3.5005	3.4381	3.3881
9	5.1174	4.2565	3.8626	3.6331	3.4817	3.3738	3.2927	3.2296	3.1789
10	4.9646	4.1028	3.7083	3.4780	3.3258	3.2172	3.1355	3.0717	3.0204
11	4.8443	3.9823	3.5874	3.3567	3.2039	3.0946	3.0123	2.9480	2.8962
12	4.7472	3.8853	3.4903	3.2592	3.1059	2.9961	2.9134	2.8486	2.7964
13	4.6672	3.8056	3.4105	3.1791	3.0254	2.9153	2.8321	2.7669	2.7144
14	4.6001	3.7389	3.3439	3.1122	2.9582	2.8477	2.7642	2.6987	2.6458
15	4.5431	3.6823	3.2874	3.0556	2.9013	2.7905	2.7066	2.6408	2.5876
16	4.4940	3.6337	3.2389	3.0069	2.8524	2.7413	2.6572	2.5911	2.5377
17	4.4513	3.5915	3.1968	2.9647	2.8100	2.6987	2.6143	2.5480	2.4943
18	4.4139	3.5546	3.1599	2.9277	2.7729	2.6613	2.5767	2.5102	2.4563
19	4.3808	3.5219	3.1274	2.8951	2.7401	2.6283	2.5435	2.4768	2.4227
20	4.3513	3.4928	3.0984	2.8661	2.7109	2.5990	2.5140	2.4471	2.3928
21	4.3248	3.4668	3.0725	2.8401	2.6848	2.5757	2.4876	2.4205	2.3661
22	4.3009	3.4434	3.0491	2.8167	2.6613	2.5491	2.4638	2.3965	2.3419
23	4.2793	3.4221	3.0280	2.7955	2.6400	2.5277	2.4422	2.3748	2.3201
24	4.2597	3.4028	3.0088	2.7763	2.6207	2.5082	2.4226	2.3551	2.3002
25	4.2417	3.3852	2.9912	2.7587	2.6030	2.4904	2.4047	2.3371	2.2821
26	4.2252	3.3690	2.9751	2.7426	2.5868	2.4741	2.3883	2.3205	2.2655
27	4.2100	3.3541	2.9604	2.7278	2.5719	2.4591	2.3732	2.3053	2.2501
28	4.1960	3.3404	2.9467	2.7141	2.5581	2.4453	2.3593	2.2913	2.2360
29	4.1830	3.3277	2.9340	2.7014	2.5454	2.4324	2.3463	2.2782	2.2229
30	4.1709	3.3158	2.9223	2.6896	2.5336	2.4205	2.3343	2.2662	2.2107
40	4.0848	3.2317	2.8387	2.6060	2.4495	2.3359	2.2490	2.1802	2.1240
60	4.0012	3.1504	2.7581	2.5252	2.3683	2.2540	2.1665	2.0970	2.0401
120	3.9201	3.0718	2.6802	2.4472	2.2900	2.1750	2.0867	2.0164	1.9588
∞	3.8415	2.9957	2.6049	2.3719	2.2141	2.0986	2.0096	1.9384	1.8799

Note: For example, if $\alpha = .05$, $\nu_1 = 4$, and $\nu_2 = 7$, then $F_{\alpha,\nu_1,\nu_2} = F_{.05,4,7} = 4.1203$, where ν_1 is the numerator degrees of freedom and ν_2 is the denominator degrees of freedom.

TABLE IV (continued)
F Distribution Values

F Values When α = .05

ν_2 \ ν_1	10	12	15	20	24	30	40	60	120	∞
1	241.88	243.91	245.95	248.01	249.05	250.09	251.14	252.20	253.25	254.32
2	19.396	19.413	19.429	19.446	19.454	19.462	19.471	19.479	19.487	19.496
3	8.7855	8.7446	8.7029	8.6602	8.6385	8.6166	8.5944	8.5720	8.5494	8.5265
4	5.9644	5.9117	5.8578	5.8025	5.7744	5.7459	5.7170	5.6878	5.6581	5.6281
5	4.7351	4.6777	4.6188	4.5581	4.5272	4.4957	4.4638	4.4314	4.3984	4.3650
6	4.0600	3.9999	3.9381	3.8742	3.8415	3.8082	3.7743	3.7398	3.7047	3.6688
7	3.6365	3.5747	3.5108	3.4445	3.4105	3.3758	3.3404	3.3043	3.2674	3.2298
8	3.3472	3.2840	3.2184	3.1503	3.1152	3.0794	3.0428	3.0053	2.9669	2.9276
9	3.1373	3.0729	3.0061	2.9365	2.9005	2.8637	2.8259	2.7872	2.7475	2.7067
10	2.9782	2.9130	2.8450	2.7740	2.7372	2.6996	2.6609	2.6211	2.5801	2.5379
11	2.8536	2.7876	2.7186	2.6464	2.6090	2.5705	2.5309	2.4901	2.4480	2.4045
12	2.7534	2.6866	2.6169	2.5436	2.5055	2.4663	2.4259	2.3842	2.3410	2.2962
13	2.6710	2.6037	2.5331	2.4589	2.4202	2.3803	2.3392	2.2966	2.2524	2.2064
14	2.6021	2.5342	2.4630	2.3879	2.3487	2.3082	2.2664	2.2230	2.1778	2.1307
15	2.5437	2.4753	2.4035	2.3275	2.2878	2.2468	2.2043	2.1601	2.1141	2.0658
16	2.4935	2.4247	2.3522	2.2756	2.2354	2.1938	2.1507	2.1058	2.0589	2.0096
17	2.4499	2.3807	2.3077	2.2304	2.1898	2.1477	2.1040	2.0584	2.0107	1.9604
18	2.4117	2.3421	2.2686	2.1906	2.1497	2.1071	2.0629	2.0166	1.9681	1.9168
19	2.3779	2.3080	2.2341	2.1555	2.1141	2.0712	2.0264	1.9796	1.9302	1.8780
20	2.3479	2.2776	2.2033	2.1242	2.0825	2.0391	1.9938	1.9464	1.8963	1.8432
21	2.3210	2.2504	2.1757	2.0960	2.0540	2.0102	1.9645	1.9165	1.8657	1.8117
22	2.2967	2.2258	2.1508	2.0707	2.0283	1.9842	1.9380	1.8895	1.8380	1.7831
23	2.2747	2.2036	2.1282	2.0476	2.0050	1.9605	1.9139	1.8649	1.8128	1.7570
24	2.2547	2.1834	2.1077	2.0267	1.9838	1.9390	1.8920	1.8424	1.7897	1.7331
25	2.2365	2.1649	2.0889	2.0075	1.9643	1.9192	1.8718	1.8217	1.7684	1.7110
26	2.2197	2.1479	2.0716	1.9898	1.9464	1.9010	1.8533	1.8027	1.7488	1.6906
27	2.2043	2.1323	2.0558	1.9736	1.9299	1.8842	1.8361	1.7851	1.7307	1.6717
28	2.1900	2.1179	2.0411	1.9586	1.9147	1.8687	1.8203	1.7689	1.7138	1.6541
29	2.1768	2.1045	2.0275	1.9446	1.9005	1.8543	1.8055	1.7537	1.6981	1.6377
30	2.1646	2.0921	2.0148	1.9317	1.8874	1.8409	1.7918	1.7396	1.6835	1.6223
40	2.0772	2.0035	1.9245	1.8389	1.7929	1.7444	1.6928	1.6373	1.5766	1.5089
60	1.9926	1.9174	1.8364	1.7480	1.7001	1.6491	1.5943	1.5343	1.4673	1.3893
120	1.9105	1.8337	1.7505	1.6587	1.6084	1.5543	1.4952	1.4290	1.3519	1.2539
∞	1.8307	1.7522	1.6664	1.5705	1.5173	1.4591	1.3940	1.3180	1.2214	1.0000

TABLE IV (continued)
F Distribution Values

F Values When α = *.025*

ν_2 \ ν_1	1	2	3	4	5	6	7	8	9
1	647.79	799.50	864.16	899.58	921.85	937.11	948.22	956.66	963.28
2	38.506	39.000	39.165	39.248	29.298	39.331	39.355	39.373	39.387
3	17.443	16.044	15.439	15.101	14.885	14.735	14.624	14.540	14.473
4	12.218	10.649	9.9792	9.6045	9.3645	9.1973	9.0741	8.9796	8.9047
5	10.007	8.4336	7.7636	7.3879	7.1464	6.9777	6.8531	6.7572	6.6810
6	8.8131	7.2598	6.5988	6.2272	5.9876	5.8197	5.6955	5.5996	5.5234
7	8.0727	6.5415	5.8898	5.5226	5.2852	5.1186	4.9949	4.8994	4.8232
8	7.5709	6.0595	5.4160	5.0526	4.8173	4.6517	4.5286	4.4332	4.3572
9	7.2093	5.7147	5.0781	4.7181	4.4844	4.3197	4.1971	4.1020	4.0260
10	6.9367	5.4564	4.8256	4.4683	4.2361	4.0721	3.9498	3.8549	3.7790
11	6.7241	5.2559	4.6300	4.2751	4.0440	3.8807	3.7586	3.6638	3.5879
12	6.5538	5.0959	4.4742	4.1212	3.8911	3.7283	3.6065	3.5118	3.4358
13	6.4143	4.9653	4.3472	3.9959	3.7667	3.6043	3.4827	3.3880	3.3120
14	6.2979	4.8567	4.2417	3.8919	3.6634	3.5014	3.3799	3.2853	3.2093
15	6.1995	4.7650	4.1528	3.8043	3.5764	3.4147	3.2934	3.1987	3.1227
16	6.1151	4.6867	4.0768	3.7294	3.5021	3.3406	3.2194	3.1248	3.0488
17	6.0420	4.6189	4.0112	3.6648	3.4379	3.2767	3.1556	3.0610	2.9849
18	5.9781	4.5597	3.9539	3.6083	3.3820	3.2209	3.0999	3.0053	2.9291
19	5.9216	4.5075	3.9034	3.5587	3.3327	3.1718	3.0509	2.9563	2.8800
20	5.8715	4.4613	3.8587	3.5147	3.2891	3.1283	3.0074	2.9128	2.8365
21	5.8266	4.4199	3.8188	3.4754	3.2501	3.0895	2.9686	2.8740	2.7977
22	5.7863	4.3828	3.7829	3.4401	3.2151	3.0546	2.9338	2.8392	2.7628
23	5.7498	4.3492	3.7505	3.4083	3.1835	3.0232	2.9024	2.8077	2.7313
24	5.7167	4.3187	3.7211	3.3794	3.1548	2.9946	2.8738	2.7791	2.7027
25	5.6864	4.2909	3.6943	3.3530	3.1287	2.9685	2.8478	2.7531	2.6766
26	5.6586	4.2655	3.6697	3.3289	3.1048	2.9447	2.8240	2.7293	2.6528
27	5.6331	4.2421	3.6472	3.3067	3.0828	2.9228	2.8021	2.7074	2.6309
28	5.6096	4.2205	3.6264	3.2863	3.0625	2.9027	2.7820	2.6872	2.6106
29	5.5878	4.2006	3.6072	3.2674	3.0438	2.8840	2.7633	2.6686	2.5919
30	5.5675	4.1821	3.5894	3.2499	3.0265	2.8667	2.7460	2.6513	2.5746
40	5.4239	4.0510	3.4633	3.1261	2.9037	2.7444	2.6238	2.5289	2.4519
60	5.2857	3.9253	3.3425	3.0077	2.7863	2.6274	2.5068	2.4117	2.3344
120	5.1524	3.8046	3.2270	2.8943	2.6740	2.5154	2.3948	2.2994	2.2217
∞	5.0239	3.6889	3.1161	2.7858	2.5665	2.4082	2.2875	2.1918	2.1136

TABLE IV (continued)
F Distribution Values

F Values When $\alpha = .025$

ν_2 \ ν_1	10	12	15	20	24	30	40	60	120	∞
1	968.63	976.71	984.87	993.10	997.25	1001.4	1005.6	1009.8	1014.0	1018.3
2	39.398	39.415	39.431	39.448	39.456	39.465	39.473	39.481	39.490	39.498
3	14.419	14.337	14.253	14.167	14.124	14.081	14.037	13.992	13.947	13.902
4	8.8439	8.7512	8.6565	8.5599	8.5109	8.4613	8.4111	8.3604	8.3092	8.2573
5	6.6192	6.5246	6.4277	6.3285	6.2780	6.2269	6.1751	6.1225	6.0693	6.0153
6	5.4613	5.3662	5.2687	5.1684	5.1172	5.0652	5.0125	4.9589	4.9045	4.8491
7	4.7611	4.6658	4.5678	4.4667	4.4150	4.3624	4.3089	4.2544	4.1989	4.1423
8	4.2951	4.1997	4.1012	3.9995	3.9472	3.8940	3.8398	3.7844	3.7279	3.6702
9	3.9639	3.8682	3.7694	3.6669	3.6142	3.5604	3.5005	3.4493	3.3918	3.3329
10	3.7168	3.6209	3.5217	3.4186	3.3654	3.3110	3.2554	3.1984	3.1399	3.0798
11	3.5257	3.4296	3.3299	3.2261	3.1725	3.1176	3.0613	3.0035	2.9441	2.8828
12	3.3736	3.2773	3.1772	3.0728	3.0187	2.9633	2.9063	2.8478	2.7874	2.7249
13	3.2497	3.1532	3.0527	2.9477	2.8932	2.8373	2.7797	2.7204	2.6590	2.5955
14	3.1469	3.0501	2.9493	2.8437	2.7888	2.7324	2.6742	2.6142	2.5519	2.4872
15	3.0602	2.9633	2.8621	2.7559	2.7006	2.6437	2.5850	2.5242	2.4611	2.3953
16	2.9862	2.8890	2.7875	2.6808	2.6252	2.5678	2.5085	2.4471	2.3831	2.3163
17	2.9222	2.8249	2.7230	2.6158	2.5598	2.5021	2.4422	2.3801	2.3153	2.2474
18	2.8664	2.7689	2.6667	2.5590	2.5027	2.4445	2.3842	2.3214	2.2558	2.1869
19	2.8173	2.7196	2.6171	2.5089	2.4523	2.3937	2.3329	2.2695	2.2032	2.1333
20	2.7737	2.6758	2.5731	2.4645	2.4076	2.3486	2.2873	2.2234	2.1562	2.0853
21	2.7348	2.6368	2.5338	2.4247	2.3675	2.3082	2.2465	2.1819	2.1141	2.0422
22	2.6998	2.6017	2.4984	2.3890	2.3315	2.2718	2.2097	2.1446	2.0760	2.0032
23	2.6682	2.5699	2.4665	2.3567	2.2989	2.2389	2.1763	2.1107	2.0415	1.9677
24	2.6396	2.5412	2.4374	2.3273	2.2693	2.2090	2.1460	2.0799	2.0099	1.9353
25	2.6135	2.5149	2.4110	2.3005	2.2422	2.1816	2.1183	2.0517	1.9811	1.9055
26	2.5895	2.4909	2.3867	2.2759	2.2174	2.1565	2.0928	2.0257	1.9545	1.8781
27	2.5676	2.4688	2.3644	2.2533	2.1946	2.1334	2.0693	2.0018	1.9299	1.8527
28	2.5473	2.4484	2.3438	2.2324	2.1735	2.1121	2.0477	1.9796	1.9072	1.8291
29	2.5286	2.4295	2.3248	2.2131	2.1540	2.0923	2.0276	1.9591	1.8861	1.8072
30	2.5112	2.4120	2.3072	2.1952	2.1359	2.0739	2.0089	1.9400	1.8664	1.7867
40	2.3882	2.2882	2.1819	2.0677	2.0069	1.9429	1.8752	1.8028	1.7242	1.6371
60	2.2702	2.1692	2.0613	1.9445	1.8817	1.8152	1.7440	1.6668	1.5810	1.4822
120	2.1570	2.0548	1.9450	1.8249	1.7597	1.6899	1.6141	1.5299	1.4327	1.3104
∞	2.0483	1.9447	1.8326	1.7085	1.6402	1.5660	1.4835	1.3883	1.2684	1.0000

TABLE IV (continued)
F Distribution Values

F Values When $\alpha = .05$

ν_2 \ ν_1	10	12	15	20	24	30	40	60	120	∞
1	241.88	243.91	245.95	248.01	249.05	250.09	251.14	252.20	253.25	254.32
2	19.396	19.413	19.429	19.446	19.454	19.462	19.471	19.479	19.487	19.496
3	8.7855	8.7446	8.7029	8.6602	8.6385	8.6166	8.5944	8.5720	8.5494	8.5265
4	5.9644	5.9117	5.8578	5.8025	5.7744	5.7459	5.7170	5.6878	5.6581	5.6281
5	4.7351	4.6777	4.6188	4.5581	4.5272	4.4957	4.4638	4.4314	4.3984	4.3650
6	4.0600	3.9999	3.9381	3.8742	3.8415	3.8082	3.7743	3.7398	3.7047	3.6688
7	3.6365	3.5747	3.5108	3.4445	3.4105	3.3758	3.3404	3.3043	3.2674	3.2298
8	3.3472	3.2840	3.2184	3.1503	3.1152	3.0794	3.0428	3.0053	2.9669	2.9276
9	3.1373	3.0729	3.0061	2.9365	2.9005	2.8637	2.8259	2.7872	2.7475	2.7067
10	2.9782	2.9130	2.8450	2.7740	2.7372	2.6996	2.6609	2.6211	2.5801	2.5379
11	2.8536	2.7876	2.7186	2.6464	2.6090	2.5705	2.5309	2.4901	2.4480	2.4045
12	2.7534	2.6866	2.6169	2.5436	2.5055	2.4663	2.4259	2.3842	2.3410	2.2962
13	2.6710	2.6037	2.5331	2.4589	2.4202	2.3803	2.3392	2.2966	2.2524	2.2064
14	2.6021	2.5342	2.4630	2.3879	2.3487	2.3082	2.2664	2.2230	2.1778	2.1307
15	2.5437	2.4753	2.4035	2.3275	2.2878	2.2468	2.2043	2.1601	2.1141	2.0658
16	2.4935	2.4247	2.3522	2.2756	2.2354	2.1938	2.1507	2.1058	2.0589	2.0096
17	2.4499	2.3807	2.3077	2.2304	2.1898	2.1477	2.1040	2.0584	2.0107	1.9604
18	2.4117	2.3421	2.2686	2.1906	2.1497	2.1071	2.0629	2.0166	1.9681	1.9168
19	2.3779	2.3080	2.2341	2.1555	2.1141	2.0712	2.0264	1.9796	1.9302	1.8780
20	2.3479	2.2776	2.2033	2.1242	2.0825	2.0391	1.9938	1.9464	1.8963	1.8432
21	2.3210	2.2504	2.1757	2.0960	2.0540	2.0102	1.9645	1.9165	1.8657	1.8117
22	2.2967	2.2258	2.1508	2.0707	2.0283	1.9842	1.9380	1.8895	1.8380	1.7831
23	2.2747	2.2036	2.1282	2.0476	2.0050	1.9605	1.9139	1.8649	1.8128	1.7570
24	2.2547	2.1834	2.1077	2.0267	1.9838	1.9390	1.8920	1.8424	1.7897	1.7331
25	2.2365	2.1649	2.0889	2.0075	1.9643	1.9192	1.8718	1.8217	1.7684	1.7110
26	2.2197	2.1479	2.0716	1.9898	1.9464	1.9010	1.8533	1.8027	1.7488	1.6906
27	2.2043	2.1323	2.0558	1.9736	1.9299	1.8842	1.8361	1.7851	1.7307	1.6717
28	2.1900	2.1179	2.0411	1.9586	1.9147	1.8687	1.8203	1.7689	1.7138	1.6541
29	2.1768	2.1045	2.0275	1.9446	1.9005	1.8543	1.8055	1.7537	1.6981	1.6377
30	2.1646	2.0921	2.0148	1.9317	1.8874	1.8409	1.7918	1.7396	1.6835	1.6223
40	2.0772	2.0035	1.9245	1.8389	1.7929	1.7444	1.6928	1.6373	1.5766	1.5089
60	1.9926	1.9174	1.8364	1.7480	1.7001	1.6491	1.5943	1.5343	1.4673	1.3893
120	1.9105	1.8337	1.7505	1.6587	1.6084	1.5543	1.4952	1.4290	1.3519	1.2539
∞	1.8307	1.7522	1.6664	1.5705	1.5173	1.4591	1.3940	1.3180	1.2214	1.0000

TABLE IV (continued)
F Distribution Values

F Values When $\alpha = .025$

ν_2 \ ν_1	1	2	3	4	5	6	7	8	9
1	647.79	799.50	864.16	899.58	921.85	937.11	948.22	956.66	963.28
2	38.506	39.000	39.165	39.248	29.298	39.331	39.355	39.373	39.387
3	17.443	16.044	15.439	15.101	14.885	14.735	14.624	14.540	14.473
4	12.218	10.649	9.9792	9.6045	9.3645	9.1973	9.0741	8.9796	8.9047
5	10.007	8.4336	7.7636	7.3879	7.1464	6.9777	6.8531	6.7572	6.6810
6	8.8131	7.2598	6.5988	6.2272	5.9876	5.8197	5.6955	5.5996	5.5234
7	8.0727	6.5415	5.8898	5.5226	5.2852	5.1186	4.9949	4.8994	4.8232
8	7.5709	6.0595	5.4160	5.0526	4.8173	4.6517	4.5286	4.4332	4.3572
9	7.2093	5.7147	5.0781	4.7181	4.4844	4.3197	4.1971	4.1020	4.0260
10	6.9367	5.4564	4.8256	4.4683	4.2361	4.0721	3.9498	3.8549	3.7790
11	6.7241	5.2559	4.6300	4.2751	4.0440	3.8807	3.7586	3.6638	3.5879
12	6.5538	5.0959	4.4742	4.1212	3.8911	3.7283	3.6065	3.5118	3.4358
13	6.4143	4.9653	4.3472	3.9959	3.7667	3.6043	3.4827	3.3880	3.3120
14	6.2979	4.8567	4.2417	3.8919	3.6634	3.5014	3.3799	3.2853	3.2093
15	6.1995	4.7650	4.1528	3.8043	3.5764	3.4147	3.2934	3.1987	3.1227
16	6.1151	4.6867	4.0768	3.7294	3.5021	3.3406	3.2194	3.1248	3.0488
17	6.0420	4.6189	4.0112	3.6648	3.4379	3.2767	3.1556	3.0610	2.9849
18	5.9781	4.5597	3.9539	3.6083	3.3820	3.2209	3.0999	3.0053	2.9291
19	5.9216	4.5075	3.9034	3.5587	3.3327	3.1718	3.0509	2.9563	2.8800
20	5.8715	4.4613	3.8587	3.5147	3.2891	3.1283	3.0074	2.9128	2.8365
21	5.8266	4.4199	3.8188	3.4754	3.2501	3.0895	2.9686	2.8740	2.7977
22	5.7863	4.3828	3.7829	3.4401	3.2151	3.0546	2.9338	2.8392	2.7628
23	5.7498	4.3492	3.7505	3.4083	3.1835	3.0232	2.9024	2.8077	2.7313
24	5.7167	4.3187	3.7211	3.3794	3.1548	2.9946	2.8738	2.7791	2.7027
25	5.6864	4.2909	3.6943	3.3530	3.1287	2.9685	2.8478	2.7531	2.6766
26	5.6586	4.2655	3.6697	3.3289	3.1048	2.9447	2.8240	2.7293	2.6528
27	5.6331	4.2421	3.6472	3.3067	3.0828	2.9228	2.8021	2.7074	2.6309
28	5.6096	4.2205	3.6264	3.2863	3.0625	2.9027	2.7820	2.6872	2.6106
29	5.5878	4.2006	3.6072	3.2674	3.0438	2.8840	2.7633	2.6686	2.5919
30	5.5675	4.1821	3.5894	3.2499	3.0265	2.8667	2.7460	2.6513	2.5746
40	5.4239	4.0510	3.4633	3.1261	2.9037	2.7444	2.6238	2.5289	2.4519
60	5.2857	3.9253	3.3425	3.0077	2.7863	2.6274	2.5068	2.4117	2.3344
120	5.1524	3.8046	3.2270	2.8943	2.6740	2.5154	2.3948	2.2994	2.2217
∞	5.0239	3.6889	3.1161	2.7858	2.5665	2.4082	2.2875	2.1918	2.1136

TABLE IV (continued)
F Distribution Values

F Values When α *= .025*

ν_2 \ ν_1	10	12	15	20	24	30	40	60	120	∞
1	968.63	976.71	984.87	993.10	997.25	1001.4	1005.6	1009.8	1014.0	1018.3
2	39.398	39.415	39.431	39.448	39.456	39.465	39.473	39.481	39.490	39.498
3	14.419	14.337	14.253	14.167	14.124	14.081	14.037	13.992	13.947	13.902
4	8.8439	8.7512	8.6565	8.5599	8.5109	8.4613	8.4111	8.3604	8.3092	8.2573
5	6.6192	6.5246	6.4277	6.3285	6.2780	6.2269	6.1751	6.1225	6.0693	6.0153
6	5.4613	5.3662	5.2687	5.1684	5.1172	5.0652	5.0125	4.9589	4.9045	4.8491
7	4.7611	4.6658	4.5678	4.4667	4.4150	4.3624	4.3089	4.2544	4.1989	4.1423
8	4.2951	4.1997	4.1012	3.9995	3.9472	3.8940	3.8398	3.7844	3.7279	3.6702
9	3.9639	3.8682	3.7694	3.6669	3.6142	3.5604	3.5005	3.4493	3.3918	3.3329
10	3.7168	3.6209	3.5217	3.4186	3.3654	3.3110	3.2554	3.1984	3.1399	3.0798
11	3.5257	3.4296	3.3299	3.2261	3.1725	3.1176	3.0613	3.0035	2.9441	2.8828
12	3.3736	3.2773	3.1772	3.0728	3.0187	2.9633	2.9063	2.8478	2.7874	2.7249
13	3.2497	3.1532	3.0527	2.9477	2.8932	2.8373	2.7797	2.7204	2.6590	2.5955
14	3.1469	3.0501	2.9493	2.8437	2.7888	2.7324	2.6742	2.6142	2.5519	2.4872
15	3.0602	2.9633	2.8621	2.7559	2.7006	2.6437	2.5850	2.5242	2.4611	2.3953
16	2.9862	2.8890	2.7875	2.6808	2.6252	2.5678	2.5085	2.4471	2.3831	2.3163
17	2.9222	2.8249	2.7230	2.6158	2.5598	2.5021	2.4422	2.3801	2.3153	2.2474
18	2.8664	2.7689	2.6667	2.5590	2.5027	2.4445	2.3842	2.3214	2.2558	2.1869
19	2.8173	2.7196	2.6171	2.5089	2.4523	2.3937	2.3329	2.2695	2.2032	2.1333
20	2.7737	2.6758	2.5731	2.4645	2.4076	2.3486	2.2873	2.2234	2.1562	2.0853
21	2.7348	2.6368	2.5338	2.4247	2.3675	2.3082	2.2465	2.1819	2.1141	2.0422
22	2.6998	2.6017	2.4984	2.3890	2.3315	2.2718	2.2097	2.1446	2.0760	2.0032
23	2.6682	2.5699	2.4665	2.3567	2.2989	2.2389	2.1763	2.1107	2.0415	1.9677
24	2.6396	2.5412	2.4374	2.3273	2.2693	2.2090	2.1460	2.0799	2.0099	1.9353
25	2.6135	2.5149	2.4110	2.3005	2.2422	2.1816	2.1183	2.0517	1.9811	1.9055
26	2.5895	2.4909	2.3867	2.2759	2.2174	2.1565	2.0928	2.0257	1.9545	1.8781
27	2.5676	2.4688	2.3644	2.2533	2.1946	2.1334	2.0693	2.0018	1.9299	1.8527
28	2.5473	2.4484	2.3438	2.2324	2.1735	2.1121	2.0477	1.9796	1.9072	1.8291
29	2.5286	2.4295	2.3248	2.2131	2.1540	2.0923	2.0276	1.9591	1.8861	1.8072
30	2.5112	2.4120	2.3072	2.1952	2.1359	2.0739	2.0089	1.9400	1.8664	1.7867
40	2.3882	2.2882	2.1819	2.0677	2.0069	1.9429	1.8752	1.8028	1.7242	1.6371
60	2.2702	2.1692	2.0613	1.9445	1.8817	1.8152	1.7440	1.6668	1.5810	1.4822
120	2.1570	2.0548	1.9450	1.8249	1.7597	1.6899	1.6141	1.5299	1.4327	1.3104
∞	2.0483	1.9447	1.8326	1.7085	1.6402	1.5660	1.4835	1.3883	1.2684	1.0000

GLOSSARY

An **advertising claim** is a specific assertion or implication made about a brand in an advertisement.

Aided awareness is the percentage of respondents who claim awareness of a brand when prompted with the brand name.

All commodity volume, or **ACV,** is the total sales volume of all products sold through a supermarket.

Alternate form reliability compares the results of two versions of the same scale given to the same people at two points in time.

Analogy seeks new-product ideas for one context by examining a different but related phenomenon.

Analysis of variance (ANOVA) is a statistical technique for simultaneously comparing the means of more than two populations.

ASSESSOR is a simulated test market system that uses both an attitudinal and a behavioral model to forecast business potential for a new brand.

ASSESSOR PHASE I is designed to provide concept guidance and is particularly useful when considering several concepts for further development.

Association techniques require respondents to indicate what comes to mind after experiencing a stimulus.

Attribute analysis refers to techniques designed to develop lists of characteristics, uses, or benefits pertaining to a particular product category.

The **Audit Bureau of Circulation** audits subscription and newsstand sales to ensure that the promised circulation is in fact obtained.

Awareness, attitude, and usage studies, sometimes called AAU studies, augment sales analysis information by providing data regarding awareness and usage of a brand and its competitors and attitudes consumers have toward that brand and its competitors.

Backtranslation is a validation process in which the English version of the survey is translated into the foreign language by one group of people and then a second group translates the survey back into English.

In a **banner format,** each question on the survey is tabulated for the entire sample and for each of a set of subgroups selected to comprise the "banner," or column headings.

Each column on the banner is known as a **banner point** and corresponds to a particular respondent subgroup.

BASES is a series of services designed to reduce the large expense and high level of risk associated with the development and introduction of a new product.

BASES I is the first component in the BASES system and provides first-year sales volume estimates for new-product concepts.

Benefit segmentation involves partitioning the market into subgroups according to similarities in the benefits individuals seek.

Benefit structure analysis (BSA) determines what specific benefits and characteristics are desired by consumers within a particular product or service category and identifies perceived deficiencies in what is currently provided.

Blind testing of products is consumer research using generic packaging, devoid of brand name, graphics, or promotional materials.

The **Box-Jenkins procedure** combines a simple extrapolation approach with a sophisticated form of time series regression to forecast sales.

Brainstorming involves assembling a group of knowledgeable participants and soliciting as many ideas as possible about a product or problem.

Budget-level competition is competition among products and services for a share of the total expenditures of the market.

The **Buying Power Index** is [(5 X the effective buying income of the area) + (3 X the retail sales of the area) + (2 X the population of the area)]/10.

Cannibalization refers to the amount of business taken from existing company brands by a new brand.

A **case study** is an attempt to apply what is learned from a detailed, in-depth examination of other situations to the situation at hand.

Computer-Assisted-Self-administered Surveys, or **CASI,** are commonly conducted in central locations such as airports, convention facilities, and malls.

A category development index (CDI) compares an area's per capita consumption of a product category to the national consumption rate.

In a **CATI** system, the logic of the interview and the questions to be asked are programmed into a computer.

Category management is the planning of items carried and inventory levels within merchandise categories at the individual store level within a retail chain.

Causal models attempt to determine what factors have caused sales to vary in the past and then to use this knowledge to predict how sales will vary in the future.

Events or factors have a **cause-and-effect relationship** if one (the effect) is the direct result of the other (the cause).

A **census** entails collecting required information from all members of the sampling frame.

Central location interviewing is conducted face-to-face at one or more specified locations.

Central location tests, sometimes referred to as "spot" tests, are conducted among consumers at a designated facility such as a shopping mall.

The **chain ratio forecasting method** begins with the total population of interest and multiplies by a succession of factors to arrive at a more realistic estimate.

A **checklist** is a list of relevant questions whose answers may provide insight into new product possibilities.

Clipping services scan a wide variety of current periodicals and reproduce any article that might provide Information of use to their client companies.

Closed-ended questions provide respondents with a list of the possible answers.

Cluster analysis is a technique that organizes items or individuals into groups, called clusters, so that there is similarity with respect to the clustering criteria within each cluster but dissimilarity across the clusters.

Cluster sampling is a probability sampling method where the population is divided into mutually exclusive and exhaustive subsets, called clusters, and a sample of clusters is taken.

Clutter reels are videotapes containing a variety of TV commercials including the one(s) being tested and are used to assess a commercial's intrusiveness.

A **code of ethics** is a well-defined set of rights and responsibilities for each party in a relationship.

Organizing responses into categories is the process of **coding.**

R2, known as the **coefficient of determination,** measures the value of the independent variable *x* in the context of predicting the dependent variable *y*.

A **comparative performance claim** is one that states or implies that the brand provides a consumer benefit relative to one or more other brands.

A company must pay increasing attention to its competitors' actions and expected future actions and try to determine how these actions will influence its marketing strategies, a process known as **competitive intelligence.**

Completion techniques require respondents to provide the endings for incomplete situations.

A **concept** is a description of the proposed product or service consisting of attributes and benefits.

Concept optimization is an iterative process aimed at refining the wording of a concept and often involves several "waves" of qualitative research.

The **confidence coefficient** reflects the degree of certainty associated with a confidence interval.

The **Confidence Index** provides a vehicle for tracking consumers' feelings regarding the overall economic environment in the United States.

A **confidence interval** is a range of values, centered at the sample estimate, known to contain the value being estimated with a given degree of certainty.

The two computed endpoints of a confidence interval are called the **confidence limits.**

Conjoint analysis is a statistical technique useful for measuring the relative importance individuals attach to product or service benefits and features.

A **Consolidated Metropolitan Statistical Area** is two or more contiguous MSAs having a total population of one million or more.

Content validity examines whether the measure appears to adequately measure the concept of interest.

Continuous scales present the respondent with some form of continuum, such as an unmarked line, on which to provide a rating.

A **control** is an experimental treatment, typically involving no manipulation of the independent variable, that is often included in an experiment to provide the necessary benchmark or point of comparison.

In a **controlled store test,** an in-store experiment is typically conducted using one set of stores as a test group and another set of stores as a control group.

In a **controlled test market,** small cities or "minimarkets" are used, and a market research firm is contracted to serve as a middleman.

A **convenience sample** is a nonprobability sample in which the sampled members are chosen because they are easily accessible.

Convergent validity examines how well the scale correlates with other scales intended to measure the same concept.

Copy testing techniques are designed to evaluate the effectiveness of specific advertisements.

The **product moment correlation,** or simply the **correlation coefficient,** is a measure of the strength of the relationship between two interval- or ratio-scaled variables.

Correspondence analysis requires participants only to indicate which attributes particularly apply to the brands being studied.

Counterbiasing is an attempt to write a question so that respondents feel that the behavior or attitude being investigated Is more common than may be thought.

Coupons are certificates, typically distributed by mail or newspaper, that offer the consumer a reduced price on a brand.

The most-popular internal consistency measure for scale reliability, **Cronbach's alpha,** is equivalent to the mean reliability for all possible splits of the scale statements.

A **cross-tabulation** is the simultaneous tabulation of responses to two questions.

Custom services are suppliers who conduct projects designed to address a specific client need.

A **cyclical variation** is a regular swing in sales that occurs at an interval greater than twelve months.

Database marketing customizes marketing communications for individuals by using computerized information systems to monitor and record the activities of customers.

The **day-after recall (DAR)** system developed by Burke Marketing Research was adopted by many companies as the standard measure of TV commercial intrusiveness. Deal acceptance refers to the number of distributors who participate in a trade deal.

Deceptive advertising contains a material representation, omission, or practice that is likely to mislead reasonable consumers.

A manager faces a **decision problem** when two or more alternative courses of action exist and the manager is uncertain about which alternative to choose.

The **Delphi approach** attempts to bring convergence to the forecasts generated by a group of individuals by providing each member with information about the initial sales forecasts given by the others in the group and asking each person for a revised estimate based on this information.

The **dependent variable** is potentially affected by the independent variable(s).

Depth interviews, often called "one-on-ones," are lengthy unstructured interviews conducted with one individual at a time.

Descriptive research answers the questions who, what, when, where, how, why, and/or how often.

Television markets are referred to as **Designated Marketing Areas (DMAs)** in the Nielsen rating system.

A **diary panel** typically consists of a sample of several thousand households chosen to be reflective of the country's household composition who record their households' purchase behaviors in selected categories of good or services.

Dimensional analysis lists all the physical characteristics of a product type. Direct questioning techniques entail asking questions of persons who are thought to have the required information.

Discriminant validity looks for low correlations with scales that measure concepts unrelated to one supposedly being measured.

Discrimination tests are conducted to determine the percentage of consumers who can detect a difference between product alternatives.

If some subgroups in the stratified sample are over-represented or under-represented relative to their sampling frame proportions, the procedure is known as **disproportionate stratified sampling.**

Double-barrelled questions ask more than a single question at the same time, making the responses uninterpretable.

In the **duo-trio test,** participants are asked to identify which of the first two stimuli received is identical to a third.

Econometric modeling uses a series of forecasting equations to forecast sales, since some of the variables used to forecast must be forecast themselves.

Editing involves examining each completed questionnaire to determine whether the proper sequence of questions was asked and answers given to closed-ended questions were correctly marked.

An **experience survey** questions people who have encountered a similar situation to or who are knowledgeable about the situation being faced.

Experimental error introduces uncertainty regarding whether observed effects were really caused by the manipulation of the independent variable.

Experimental research identifies cause-and-effect relationships.

In experimental research, different conditions created by varying the independent variable are often referred to as **experimental treatments.**

In an experiment, the objects or people comprising the groups are the **experimental units.**

Exploratory research provides understanding of a problem or situation.

Exponential smoothing is a moving-average approach that allows the forecaster to weight the most recent sales period differently from earlier sales periods.

External secondary data are previously existing data, gathered outside the firm.

External validity concerns the degree to which results can be projected from what may be an artificial or highly controlled setting to a more natural environment.

External variables are factors that are not manipulated in the experiment but that could affect the dependent variable.

Extrapolation forecasting methods are so-named because they use past sales data to predict future sales.

An **eye-tracking camera** allows the researcher to track the movement of the consumer's eyes while viewing an object.

Factor analysis is used to identify patterns of ratings based on how each statement rating correlates with the others and to group related statements together to form factors.

An experiment in which the dependent variable is observed for all possible combinations of levels of all independent variables is called a **factorial experiment.**

A **failure fee** is paid to the supermarket by the manufacturer if a new product fails to sell at a predetermined level.

A company uses a **family branding strategy** when it gives all of its products or services a related name.

The term **field experiment** is used for an experiment conducted in a more natural and less controlled setting than a laboratory.

Field services are limited-service suppliers who specialize in data collection.

A **focus group** consists of eight to twelve persons who are led through an unstructured discussion of a topic by a moderator.

Full-service suppliers are capable of completing an entire research project, from design to analysis.

A **gain score** is the difference between an initial and a post-treatment measurement.

Gap analysis focuses on determining how various brands are perceived relative to each other.

Geodemographic segmentation systems organize small, well-defined geographic units into groups that are similar with respect to the demographic, housing, and socioeconomic characteristics of the households comprising the units.

The **gross rating points (GRPs)** for an advertising campaign refer to the total advertising for the measured period.

History error refers to confusion between effects produced by unexpected events that occur during the experiment and the manipulation of the independent variable.

The **history-repeats-itself approach** assumes that next period's sales will be equal to this period's sales.

A **home-use test** entails consumers evaluating test products in their homes or, more generally, in a natural usage environment.

Hypothesis testing is the statistical procedure used to compare a sample mean to a specified value or to compare a pair of sample means.

Imaginative techniques have people pretend that they, or the products or services being researched, are not what they really are.

An **implied alternative** is one that is not explicitly stated in a question.

The **incidence level** is the rate of occurrence of the target population members in the sampling frame.

Independent variables are deliberately manipulated by the experimenter in attempting to establish cause-and-effect relationships.

InfoScan is a syndicated data service offered by Information Resources, Inc., (IRI) and is the major competitor of A. C. Nielsen's ScanTrack.

Instrumentation error can be introduced if the measurement devices or procedures are changed during the experiment.

Instrument error results from the design of the questionnaire itself.

Intensity of preference refers to how strongly one product is preferred over the other.

Interaction means that the effect of manipulating one variable can vary greatly depending on the level at which the other variables are held constant.

Internal consistency measures split the statements on a multiple- item scale into two groups and correlate the group responses.

Internal secondary data are collected by a company in the normal course of doing business.

Internal screening is used to eliminate some ideas from further consideration without any primary consumer research.

Internal validity of an experiment concerns the degree to which changes observed in the dependent variable can be attributed to the manipulations performed on the independent variables.

Equal differences between scale values correspond to equal differences in the quantity being measured on an **interval scale.**

Interviewer error results from mistakes made by the interviewer.

Intrusiveness pertains to an advertisement's ability to cut through the clutter and be remembered.

Judgmental forecasting methods rely heavily on subjective sales estimates provided by individuals to forecast sales.

Judgment sampling is used when the researcher subjectively chooses sample members who are believed to be representative of the target population or particularly knowledgeable about the topic being studied.

A group of knowledgeable individuals is polled to generate sales estimates when using the **jury-of-expert-opinion approach** to forecasting.

The **Kelly repertory grid** is a useful qualitative consumer research tool for developing a list of relevant product dimensions.

Laboratory experiments are performed in a tightly controlled environment, such as is typical in a scientific laboratory.

The **Laboratory Test Market (LTM)** system, developed by Yankelovich, Skelly and White, Inc., was the first simulated test market system.

Leading indicators are variables that change before a change in sales and thus have predictive value.

A **Likert scale** requires a respondent to express his or her level of agreement with a series of statements related to the attitude being evaluated; an overall measure is obtained by summing the individual responses.

Limited-service suppliers specialize in one or more specific tasks associated with the research project.

In **linear regression** analysis the correlation between two variables is used to develop a predictive equation.

A **literature guide** lists books and periodicals that might contain relevant information by topic.

A **literature index** lists articles and reports appearing in various periodicals that deal with particular topics.

A **logo** is a sign or symbol, often containing the brand or company name displayed in a distinctive way, that is used to represent a brand or company visually.

Mall-intercept interviewing, the most common form of central location interviewing, involves interviewing respondents at a shopping center mall.

The **marketing concept** emphasizes the identification of consumer needs and the development and production of products or services that meet those needs as well as the objectives of the firm.

Marketing research is the function that links the consumer, customer, and public to the marketer through information-information used to: identify and define marketing opportunities and problems; generate, refine, and evaluate marketing actions; monitor marketing performance; and improve understanding of marketing as a process.

Market monitoring is systematically compiling secondary data dealing with environmental forces.

Market orientation is a natural evolution of the marketing concept.

A **market performance claim** relates to popularity, usage, or competitive position. The size of the market for the product category is the market potential.

The American Marketing Association defined **market research** as "the systematic gathering, recording, and analyzing of data about problems relating to the marketing of goods and services."

Market structure studies are used to identify the major current or potential competitors in a market and their strengths and weaknesses and to project what their future marketing strategies might be.

Matching consists of organizing the experimental units into sets in such a way that there is consistency with respect to specified characteristics within each set.

Maturation error occurs in experiments conducted over a period of time when there is gradual development or change in the dependent variable that is not caused by the independent variable.

The **mean** is the arithmetic average.

A **measurement scale** assigns numbers to objects, events, or people according to a set of rules.

Measurement timing refers to when measurements are taken in an experiment.

Measurement timing error occurs if changes in the dependent variable are due to when measurements are taken rather than the manipulation of the independent variable.

The **median** is the value that divides a set of measurements, arranged according to increasing magnitude, into two halves.

Merchandising support typically takes the form of increased shelf space, display space, a price reduction to consumers, or local advertising.

A **Metropolitan Statistical Area** is a population nucleus of 50,000 or more consisting of a city and its immediate suburbs, together with adjacent counties that have a high degree of economic and social integration with that nucleus.

Mini-groups are focus groups held with four to six participants instead of the traditional eight to twelve people.

Mixed mode techniques are more than one direct questioning technique being used in the same study.

The **mode** is the value that occurs most frequently.

A **monadic test** is another name for a single product test.

The Yankelovich ***Monitor*** is a monthly publication containing selected results from a nationally projectable telephone survey of U.S. households.

Mortality error occurs when differences in the compositions of the groups completing the study produce differences in the dependent variable across the experimental groups.

A **moving average approach** forecasts future sales by averaging a set number of past sales periods.

Multiple regression analysis is used to develop a predictive equation involving more than one independent variable.

With **multi-stage cluster sampling,** a random sample of more than one cluster is taken and only a sample of the members of each selected cluster used.

Need-assessment techniques are designed to identify unsatisfied consumer needs or reveal problems that are not solved by existing products or services.

Need-level competition exists among products and services that attempt to satisfy the same basic need.

The **Nielsen Station Index** provides TV audience data at the local level.

The **Nielsen Television Index** provides information regarding network television audiences at the national level.

A **nominal scale** assigns numbers to objects in order to classify the objects according to the characteristic of interest.

A **noncomparative performance claim** specifies or implies a consumer benefit or product value for the brand with no reference to another product.

Nonmetric multidimensional scaling is a perceptual mapping technique that uses a rank ordering of the pairs of entities, according to similarity, to generate a perceptual map.

In a **nonprobability sample,** every member of the sampling frame does not have a nonzero chance of being selected.

Nonresponse error occurs when all members of a chosen sample are not contacted or when contacted members refuse to participate.

A **nonsampling error** is an inaccuracy caused by anything other than sampling error.

Observation involves recording information without relying upon respondent answers or memory.

An **open-ended question** does not provide the possible answers to the respondent.

Opinion polls are studies designed to take the pulse of the public with respect to issues of broad interest.

Order effect in a paired comparison test refers to the tendency to prefer the first (or second) product used.

An **ordinal scale** assigns numbers to specify relative amounts of the characteristic being measured.

In a **paired comparison,** respondents evaluate a pair of options and then state a preference or rate each option according to some criterion such as acceptability.

The **pair-repeat test** consists of two consecutive paired comparisons of the same two alternatives conducted among the same respondents and provides both discrimination and preference information.

A **parity claim** states that the advertised brand is preferred as often as another brand, has the same attribute(s) as another brand, provides the same benefit as another brand, or cannot be distinguished by consumers from another brand.

Patronage reward programs encourage regular use of a brand by providing points or credits that can be redeemed for premiums such as merchandise, discounts, or cash.

A **people meter** is an electronic device attached to a television set that is used to monitor what shows are being watched by whom.

The **percentage change approach** assumes that the percentage change in future sales will be identical to the percentage change observed in the past.

Perceptual mapping is a marketing research tool specifically designed to provide such insight into how consumers view a new concept or brand relative to alternatives.

Performance requirements are conditions under which the trade can take advantage of a deal and may involve reducing the price to the consumer, providing in-store display space, running local advertising, or providing other merchandise support.

Personal interviewing involves conducting interviews in a face-to-face setting.

Personalization techniques require the respondent to create a personality for an inanimate object.

Persuasion is the ability of a commercial favorably to affect consumers' impression of the advertised brand.

The **picture association technique** requires respondents to indicate which of a set of pictures are associated with a stimulus.

Point-of-purchase (POP) promotions are displays, demonstrations, or special signs that are placed in stores.

Improperly defining the target population is known as **population specification error.**

A brand's **positioning** is the niche a brand occupies in the target segment's overall perception of the relevant brands in the category.

Predictive validity hopes to find high correlations with concepts that are theoretically related to the one supposedly being measured.

The ASSESSOR **preference model** provides an estimate of share for a new brand based on attitudinal data.

Premeasurement error refers to confusion between the effect of the treatment and the effect of the premeasurement.

Premiums are gifts that consumers receive for purchasing specific brands.

Price-offs are direct price reductions or rebates offered to purchasers.

Primary data are gathered specifically for the project at hand.

Prizes are competitions in which entrants can win cash or merchandise.

A **probability sample** involves some form of random selection so that every member of the sampling frame has a nonzero chance of being included in the sample.

Problem analysis is a need-assessment technique in which an inventory of consumer problems in a particular product or service category is developed and then used as a basis for new product or service ideas.

Problem inventory analysis techniques approach the question of consumer needs at a general level.

Processing error involves incorrect assignment of values and mistakes in data entry or data analysis.

Product form competition exists among all brands in the same I)roduct or service category.

A **product improvement claim** for a brand is a superiority claim relative to the previous version of the same brand.

The **product moment correlation,** or simply the **correlation coefficient,** is a measure of the strength of the relationship between two interval- or ratio-scaled variables.

Projective techniques are a variety of exploratory procedures that ask the respondent to project his or her feelings, beliefs, or motivations onto another person, object, or situation.

Promotion evaluation involves assessing the results of a promotional campaign after the promotion has been completed.

Promotion pretesting involves research prior to the use of a promotion to assess the likely results.

Promotion synergy means that multiple promotions yield more sales than would be expected from the sum of the individual effects of each promotion run in isolation.

If each subgroup of interest is represented in the stratified sample in the same proportion as in the sampling frame, the procedure is called **proportionate stratified sampling.**

A **protomonadic test** is a hybrid test design including both a single product and a paired comparison evaluation.

Psychodrawing requires respondents to attach abstract notions such as colors, shapes, or symbols to objects.

Psychographics refers to segmentation based upon values and lifestyles.

Qualitative research refers to research in which the results cannot be statistically analyzed because of the limited amount of data or type of data collected.

When using **quota sampling,** the researcher specifies the number of respondents with particular characteristics who will be included in the sample and selects sample members in a nonrandom manner.

Random-digit dialing involves the use of a computer to generate, and perhaps even dial, telephone numbers at random instead of using numbers from a telephone directory or published list.

Randomization uses random chance to assign the individual experimental units to the groups.

The **range** is the difference between the smallest and largest values found in the data.

A **rating point** represents one percent of the TV households in the United States.

A **ratio scale** is an interval scale containing a zero point that represents the absence of the property being measured.

Relationships analysis techniques for stimulating creativity entail examining relationships that are normally not considered.

Relationship marketing is the philosophy that focuses on building long-term relationships with customers to satisfy mutual needs.

The **reliability** of copy test measurements refers to the consistency of test scores over different comparable samples of respondents.

Repositioning attempts to change the way consumers perceive an existing brand.

Research suppliers are marketing research firms that actually conduct research.

Respondent error occurs when a person agrees to complete a survey but provides answers that are unintentionally or intentionally inaccurate.

Role-playing techniques require respondents to play the role of another person and react to a situation as they think the other person would react.

A **round robin test** format is one in which all possible pairs from a set of products are evaluated in a paired-comparison format.

A **sales analysis** is concerned with identifying the source of a brand's sales volume.

The **sales force composite approach** generates a total sales forecast by aggregating the sales estimate for each salesperson's territory.

A **sales forecast** is a prediction of the amount of sales that will occur for a brand.

A **sales promotion** is any direct inducement to distributors or consumers with the primary objective of creating an immediate sale.

The **sales trend** is the long-term upward or downward movement of sales.

A **sample** is a free quantity of the brand given to consumers, often through the mail.

Sample quality error is the inability of the sample to produce accurate estimates of the population values because the sample does not adequately represent the population of interest.

Sample selection error occurs when bias is introduced into an experiment due to the way experimental units are assigned to experimental groups.

Sampling error is the statistical imprecision caused when a sample is used to estimate a target population value.

The **sampling frame** is the list of target population members from which data can actually be collected.

Sampling frame error refers to any discrepancy between the sampling frame and the target population caused by limitations in the sampling frame.

Scale accuracy refers to the degree to which a measurement scale is free of both bias and random error.

Scale reliability refers to the reproducibility of the scale results.

Scale validity assesses whether the scale measures what it is intended to measure.

Instead of requiring individual household members manually to record purchases in diaries, **scanner panels** make use of UPC codes and store scanners to record panelists' purchases.

ScanTrack is a retail sales tracking service provided by the A. C. Nielsen Company.